For more resources, visit the Web site for

Crossroads and Cultures

A HISTORY OF THE WORLD'S PEOPLES

bedfordstmartins.com/smith

FREE ONLINE STUDY GUIDE

Get instant feedback on your progress with

- Chapter self-tests
- Key terms review
- Map quizzes
- Timeline activities
- Note-taking outlines

D0207313

FREE HISTORY RESEARCH AND WRITING HELP

Refine your research skills and find plenty of good sources with

- A database of useful images, maps, documents, and more at *Make History*
- A guide to online sources for history
- Help with writing history papers
- A tool for building a bibliography
- Tips on avoiding plagiarism

Crossroads and Cultures

A History of the World's Peoples

Bonnie G. Smith
Rutgers University

Marc Van De Mieroop
Columbia University

Richard von Glahn
University of California, Los Angeles

Kris Lane
Tulane University

Bedford/St. Martin's
Boston ■ New York

FOR BEDFORD/ST. MARTIN'S

Publisher for History: Mary Dougherty
Executive Editor for History: Elizabeth M. Welch
Director of Development for History: Jane Knetzger
Senior Developmental Editor: Heidi Hood
Senior Production Editor: Anne Noonan
Senior Production Supervisor: Andrew Ensor
Executive Marketing Manager: Jenna Bookin Barry
Associate Editor: Jennifer Jovin
Assistant Production Editor: Laura Deily
Editorial Assistant: Emily DiPietro
Production Assistant: Elise Keller
Copy Editor: Dan Otis
Map Editor: Charlotte Miller
Indexer: Leoni Z. McVey
Cartography: Mapping Specialists, Ltd.
Photo Researcher: Rose Corbett Gordon
Permissions Manager: Kalina K. Ingham
Senior Art Director: Anna Palchik
Text Designer: Jerilyn Bockorick
Cover Designer: Billy Boardman
Cover Art: Night scene of Sihui Bridge, Beijing
© Fotosearch
Composition: Cenveo Publisher Services
Printing and Binding: RR Donnelley and Sons

President: Joan E. Feinberg
Editorial Director: Denise B. Wydra
Director of Marketing: Karen R. Soeltz
Director of Production: Susan W. Brown
Associate Director, Editorial Production: Elise S. Kaiser
Managing Editor: Elizabeth M. Schaaf

Library of Congress Control Number: 2011943843

Copyright © 2012 by Bedford/St. Martin's

All rights reserved. No part of this book may be reproduced, stored in a retrieval system, or transmitted in any form or by any means, electronic, mechanical, photocopying, recording, or otherwise, except as may be expressly permitted by the applicable copyright statutes or in writing by the Publisher.

Manufactured in the United States of America.

7 6 5 4 3 2
f e d c b a

For information, write: Bedford/St. Martin's, 75 Arlington Street, Boston, MA 02116 (617-399-4000)

ISBN: 978-0-312-41017-9 (Combined edition)
ISBN: 978-0-312-57158-0 (Loose leaf)
ISBN: 978-0-312-44213-2 (Volume 1)
ISBN: 978-0-312-57159-7 (Loose leaf)
ISBN: 978-0-312-44214-9 (Volume 2)
ISBN: 978-0-312-57160-3 (Loose leaf)
ISBN: 978-0-312-57161-0 (Volume A)
ISBN: 978-0-312-57167-2 (Volume B)
ISBN: 978-0-312-57168-9 (Volume C)

Acknowledgments: Acknowledgments and copyrights are continued at the back of the book on page C-1, which constitutes an extension of the copyright page. It is a violation of the law to reproduce these selections by any means whatsoever without the written permission of the copyright holder.

A CONVERSATION WITH THE AUTHORS

The Story Behind *Crossroads and Cultures*

Bonnie G. Smith
Rutgers University

Marc Van De Mieroop
Columbia University

Richard von Glahn
University of California, Los Angeles

Kris Lane
Tulane University

Bedford/St. Martin's is proud to publish *Crossroads and Cultures: A History of the World's Peoples,* which incorporates the best current cultural history into a fresh and original narrative that connects global patterns of development with life on the ground. This new synthesis highlights the places and times where people interacted and exchanged goods and ideas and in doing so joined their lives to the broad sweep of global history. Below the authors discuss their goals and approach.

Q. How does the title *Crossroads and Cultures: A History of the World's Peoples* tell the story of your book?

Crossroads

Bonnie: From the beginning we knew that we would be stressing interactions and engagements among the world's peoples. We looked for the places where they would meet—the **crossroads**—whether those were actual places or the intersections reflected in the practices of everyday life. We want students to see how crossroads, interactions, and connections among the world's peoples have changed over time and continue to shape their own lives.

> "We looked for the places where the world's peoples would meet—the crossroads—whether those were actual places or the intersections reflected in the practices of everyday life."

Richard: This focus is a result of our recognition that world history is not simply a matter of covering more areas of the world; it requires rethinking what matters in world history. World history must center on cross-cultural interactions and the ways in which peoples and cultures are influenced and are sometimes transformed by political engagement, cultural contact, economic exchange, and social encounters with other societies.

Cultures

Bonnie: The second half of our title reflects our heartfelt judgment that the past is shaped by **cultures**. Beliefs, ways of living, artistic forms, technology, and intellectual accomplishments are fundamental to historical development and are a part of the foundation of politics and economies. Cultures also produce structures such as caste, class, ethnicity, race, religion, gender, and sexuality—all of which are important themes in our book.

A History of the World's Peoples

Marc: The book's subtitle, ***A History of the World's Peoples***, is crucial. History often focuses on kings and states, but in the end the peoples of the past are the most interesting to study, however difficult that may be considering the nature of the sources for world history. People interact with their immediate and more distant neighbors, and these interactions are, indeed, often a cause of historical change.

Bonnie: *Crossroads and Cultures* focuses on people—individual and collective historical actors—who have lived the history of the world and produced global events. We want to capture their thoughts and deeds, their everyday experiences, their work lives, and their courageous actions—all of which have helped to create the crossroads we travel today.

Q. To follow up on the idea of "crossroads," what are some of the places and interactions that you emphasize in the book, and why?

Marc: In the ancient world, the period that I cover in the book (Part 1, from human origins to 500 C.E.), two regions figured prominently by virtue of their location—the Middle East and Central Asia. From earliest times, the Middle East formed a nexus of interactions among the African, European, and Asian continents, which I try to convey when I discuss the first human migrations out of Africa and when I show how the Roman and Persian empires met—and yes, battled! But I emphasize as well that vast open areas also served as crossroads in antiquity. Indeed, Central Asia, an enormous region, acted as a highway for contacts between the cultures at its fringes: China, South Asia, the Middle East, and Europe. Seas also can play this role, and I include the gigantic Pacific Ocean, which, although a formidable barrier, functioned as a road for migration for centuries.

Richard: Since I also deal with a period remote from the present (Part 2, 500–1450 C.E.), I try to balance my coverage between familiar and recognizable places that remain crossroads today—Rome and Jerusalem, Baghdad and Istanbul, Beijing and Delhi, the Nile Delta and the Valley of Mexico—and places that have faded from view, such as the trading cities of the West African savanna; Melaka, the greatest port of Asia in the fifteenth century; Samarkand, which had a long history as the linchpin of the Central Asian Silk Road; and the Champagne fairs in France, which operated as a "free trade" zone and became the incubator of new business practices that enabled Europeans to surpass the older economic centers of the Mediterranean world.

Kris: Since my section of the book (Part 3, 1450–1750) treats the early modern period, when the entire globe was interconnected for the first time in recorded history, I have almost too many crossroads to choose from. In this period, Seville and Lisbon emerged as hugely rich and important ports and sites of redistribution, but so also did Manila, Nagasaki, and Macao. Most of the obvious crossroads of this seafaring era were ports, but great mining centers like Potosí, deep in the highlands of present-day Bolivia, also became world-class cosmopolitan centers. In other books many of these sites have been treated simply as nodes in an expanding European world, but I try to show how local people and other non-European residents made Manila and Potosí quite different from what the king of Spain might have had in mind. Indeed, I emphasize crossroads as places of personal opportunity rather than imperial hegemony.

Bonnie: The crossroads that we describe are often the obvious ones of war, empire building, and old and new forms of trade, but we also enthusiastically feature the more ordinary paths that people traveled. For example, in my own section of the book (Part 4, 1750 to the present), I trace the route of the young Simon Bolivar, whose travels in Spain, France, and the new United States helped to inspire his own liberation struggles. I also follow the rough road from factory to factory along which a seven-year-old English orphan, Robert Blincoe, traveled. His life occurred at the crossroads of industrial development, where he suffered deliberate torture as the world began industrializing. For me, these personal journeys—filled with interactions—are at the heart of our endeavor to make history vivid and meaningful for students.

"The crossroads that we describe are often the obvious ones of war, empire building, and old and new forms of trade, but we also enthusiastically feature the more ordinary paths that people traveled."

Q. Author teams of world history textbooks typically divide the work based on geographic specialty. Why did you decide to take responsibility for eras instead of regions?

Bonnie: Our goal is to show the interactions of the world's peoples over time and space. Had we divided history by region, our purpose would have been confounded from the start. Many books still take a "civilizational" approach, shifting from one region or nation to another and dividing each author's coverage according to national specialization. We aimed for a more interconnected result by each taking responsibility for narrating developments across the globe during a particular period of time.

Marc: When we look at any period globally, we can see certain parallels between the various parts of the world. There is a huge benefit to weighing what happened in different places at the same time.

Richard: Right. World history fundamentally is about making comparisons and connections. Defining our subject matter by time period rather than by geographic region enabled us to see the connections or parallel developments that make societies part of world history—as well as the distinctive features that make them unique. Our format has the virtue of bringing a coherent perspective to the many stories that each part of the book tells.

Kris: In my chapters, certain themes, such as slavery and the spread of silver money, took on new meaning as I traced them across cultures in ways that regional specialists had not considered. Writing the book this way entailed a huge amount of reading, writing, and reconsideration, but I feel it was a great decision. It allowed each of us to explore a bit before coming back together to hash out differences.

Q. The table of contents for *Crossroads and Cultures* blends both thematic and regional chapters. Why did you organize the book this way?

Bonnie: There is no orthodoxy in today's teaching of world history. Although textbooks often follow either a regional or a thematic structure, we felt that neither of these told the story that a blended approach could tell.

Richard: I particularly relished the opportunity to develop thematic chapters—for example, on cross-cultural trade and business practices, or on educational institutions and the transmission of knowledge—that illustrate both convergence and diversity in history. The thematic chapters were especially suitable for introducing individuals from diverse levels of society, to help students appreciate personal experiences as well as overarching historical trends.

Kris: In my period, the rapid integration of the world due to expanding maritime networks had to be balanced against the persistence of land-based cultures that both borrowed from new technologies and ideas and maintained a regional coherence. The Aztecs, the Incas, the Mughals, and the Ming were all land-based, tributary empires headed by divine kings, but whereas the first two collapsed as a result of European invasion, the latter two were reinforced by contact with Europeans, who introduced powerful new weapons. I felt it was necessary to treat these empires in macroregional terms before grappling with more sweeping themes. I found that in the classroom my students made better connections themselves after having time to get a firm handle on some of these broad regional developments.

"Defining our subject matter by time period rather than by geographic region enabled us to see the connections or parallel developments that make societies part of world history—as well as the distinctive features that make them unique."

Q. Each chapter includes a Counterpoint section as substantial as the main sections of the narrative itself. What purposes do the Counterpoints serve?

Kris: The **Counterpoint** feature helps students and teachers remember that alternative histories—or paths—are not only possible but that they exist alongside "master narratives." In each chapter we have selected a people, a place, or a movement that functions as a Counterpoint to the major global development traced in that chapter. Some Counterpoints highlight different responses to similar circumstances—the successful resistance of the Mapuche of Chile against the European conquistadors, for example, in a chapter that tells the story of the collapse of the Aztec and Incan empires. Other Counterpoints show cultures adapting to a particular environment that either enables persistence or requires adaptation—such as the Aborigines of Australia, gatherer-hunters by choice, in a chapter that treats the rise of agriculture and spread of settled farming. Counterpoint is about human difference and ingenuity.

Richard: The Counterpoint feature is fundamental to our approach. It reminds us that there is much diversity in world history and helps us to think about the causes underlying divergence as well as convergence.

Marc: Right. It helps counter the idea that everyone goes through the same stages of evolution and makes the same choices. There is no uniform history of the world, as nineteenth-century scholars used to think.

Bonnie: One of my favorite Counterpoints centers on the importance of nonindustrialized African women farmers to the world economy during the Industrial Revolution. From a pedagogical standpoint, Counterpoints not only expose basic questions that historians grapple with but also offer material within a single chapter for compare-and-contrast exercises.

Q. Each chapter also offers a special feature devoted to the way that people made their living at different times and at different crossroads in the past. Would you explain how this Lives and Livelihoods feature works?

Richard: The **Lives and Livelihoods** feature helps us provide more in-depth study of one of our key themes, namely how people's lives intersect with larger cross-cultural interactions and global change.

Bonnie: We often spotlight new means of making a living that arose as the result of cross-cultural exchange or that contributed to major global developments. For example, the Lives and Livelihoods feature in Chapter 6 shows students how papermaking originated as a carefully guarded invention in classical China and became a worldwide technology that spawned numerous livelihoods. Similarly, the feature in Chapter 24 on workers on the trans-Siberian railroad exemplifies influence in both directions: the workers built a transportation network that advanced interconnections and fostered global change—change that they and their families experienced in turn.

> "The Lives and Livelihoods feature supports one of our key themes: how people's lives intersect with larger cross-cultural interactions and global change."

Q. *Crossroads and Cultures* has a rich art and map program, and it also includes plentiful primary-source excerpts and clear reading aids. Can you talk about how you had students in mind as you developed these features of the book?

Kris: Throughout the book we chose **images** to match as closely as we could the themes we wanted to stress. We did not conceive of the images as mere illustrations but rather as documents worthy of close historical analysis in their own right, products of the same places and times we try to evoke in the text.

Richard: And our carefully developed **map program** provides sure-footed guidance to where our historical journey is taking us—a crucial necessity, since we travel to so many places not on the usual Grand Tour! Our **Seeing the Past** and **Reading the Past** features, which provide excerpts from visual and written primary sources, give students direct exposure to the ideas and voices of the people we are studying. These features also help students build their analytical skills by modeling how historians interpret visual and written evidence.

Bonnie: Among the many reading aids, one of my favorites is the chapter-opening **Backstory**, which provides a concise overview of previously presented material to situate the current chapter for the student. It is at once a review and an immediate preparation for the chapter to come.

Richard: And we use every opportunity—at the start of chapters and sections, in the features, and at the end of each chapter—to pose **study questions** to help students think about what they are reading and make connections across time and space.

Kris: We wanted to hit as many bases as possible in order to make our book accessible for different kinds of learners. I imagine I'm like most teachers in that I never teach a course in exactly the same way each year. I like to use or emphasize different aspects of a textbook each time I assign it, sometimes hammering on chronology or working through study questions and sometimes paying closer attention to maps, works of art, or material culture. It all needs to be there; I like a complete toolbox.

Q. You have written many well-received and influential works. What response to *Crossroads and Cultures: A History of the World's Peoples* would please you most?

Bonnie: Our hope is that our approach to world history will engage students and help them master material that can otherwise seem so remote, wide-ranging, and seemingly disconnected from people's lives.

Richard: I would like from students who read this book what I want from my own students: a recognition and appreciation of the diversity of human experience that fosters understanding not only of the past and where we have come from but also of our fellow world citizens and the future that we are making together.

Kris: The practical side of me wants simply to hear, "At last, a world history textbook that works." The idealistic side wants to hear, "Wow, a world history textbook that makes both me and my students think differently about the world and about history."

Marc: And I hope that students start to realize not only that the pursuit of answers to such questions is absorbing and satisfying but also that the study of history is fun!

***Crossroads and Cultures: A History of the World's Peoples* makes its new synthesis accessible and memorable for students through a strong pedagogical design, abundant maps and images, and special features that heighten the narrative's attention to the lives and voices of the world's peoples. To learn more about how the book's features keep the essentials of world history in focus for students, see the "How to Use This Book" introduction on the following pages.**

HOW TO USE THIS BOOK

STEP 1

Use the part opener's features to understand the place, time, and topic of the era.

PLACE
Ask yourself what regions are covered.

TIME
Ask yourself what era is under investigation.

TOPIC
Ask yourself what topics or themes are emphasized.

PART 2

TOPIC and TIME

The Formation of Regional Societies

500–1450 C.E.

CH 9

ALTHOUGH NO SINGLE LABEL adequately reflects the history of the world in the period 500–1450, its most distinctive feature was the formation of regional societies based on common forms of livelihoods, cultural values, and social and political institutions. The new age in world history that began in around 500 C.E. marked a decisive break from the "classical" era of antiquity. The passing of classical civilizations in the Mediterranean, China, and India shared a number of causes, but the most notable were invasions by nomads from the Central Asian steppes. Beset by internal unrest and foreign pressures, the empires of Rome, Han China, and Gupta India crumbled. As these once-mighty empires fragmented into a multitude of competing states, cultural revolutions followed. Confidence in the values and institutions of the classical era was shattered, opening the way for fresh ideas. Christianity, Buddhism, Hinduism, and the new creed of Islam spread far beyond their original circles of believers. By 1450 these four religious traditions had supplanted or transformed local religions in virtually all of Eurasia and much of Africa.

The spread of foreign religions and the lifestyles and livelihoods they promoted produced distinctive regional societies. By 1000, Europe had taken shape as a coherent society and culture even as it came to be divided between the Roman and Byzantine Christian churches. The shared cultural values of modern East Asia—rooted in the literary and philosophical traditions of China but also assuming distinctive national forms—also emerged during the first millennium C.E. During this era, too, Indian civilization expanded into Southeast Asia and acquired a new unity expressed through the common language of Sanskrit. The rapid expansion of Islam across Asia, Africa, and

CH 10

266

TOPIC
Read the part overview to learn how the chapters that follow fit into the larger story.

TOPIC, TIME, and PLACE

CHAPTERS IN THIS PART ▼

9 The Worlds of Christianity and Islam, 400–1000
10 Religion and Cross-Cultural Exchange in Asia, 400–1000
11 Societies and Networks in the Americas and the Pacific, 300–1200
12 The Rise of Commerce in Afro-Eurasia, 900–1300
13 Centers of Learning and the Transmission of Culture, 900–1300
14 Crusaders, Mongols, and Eurasian Integration, 1050–1350
15 Collapse and Revival in Afro-Eurasia, 1300–1450

CH 11

even parts of Europe demonstrated the power of a shared reli-

500–1450 C.E.

CH 13

faiths grew ever wider. The rise of steppe empires—above all, the explosive expansion of the Mongol empires—likewise transformed the political and cultural landscape of Asia. Historians today recognize the ways in which the Mongol conquests facilitated the movement of people, goods, and ideas across Eurasia. But contemporaries could see no farther than the ruin sowed by the Mongols wherever they went, toppling cities and laying waste to once-fertile farmlands.

After 1300 the momentum of world history changed. Economic growth slowed, strained by the pressure of rising populations on productive resources and the effects of a cooling climate, and then it stopped altogether. In the late 1340s the Black Death pandemic devastated the central Islamic lands and Europe. It would take centuries before the populations in these parts of the world returned to their pre-1340 levels.

By 1400, however, other signs of recovery were evident. Powerful national states emerged in Europe and China, restoring some measure of stability. Strong Islamic states held sway in Egypt, Anatolia (modern Turkey), Iran, and India. The European Renaissance—the intense outburst of intellectual and artistic creativity envisioned as a "rebirth" of the classical civilization of Greece and Rome—flickered to life, sparked by the economic vigor of the Italian city-states. Similarly, Neo-Confucianism—a "renaissance" of China's classical learning—whetted the intellectual and cultural aspirations of ed

Ma

Bla

Eurasia's major land-based economies struggled to regain their earlier prosperity.

In 1453 Muslim Ottoman armies seized Constantinople and deposed the Byzantine Christian emperor, cutting the last thread of connection to the ancient world. The fall of Constantinople symbolized the end of the era discussed in Part 2. Denied direct access to the rich trade with Asia, European monarchs and merchants began to shift their attention to the Atlantic world. Yet just as Columbus's discovery of the "New World" (in fact, a very ancient one) came as a surprise, the idea of a new world order centered on Europe—the modern world order—was still unimaginable.

CH 15

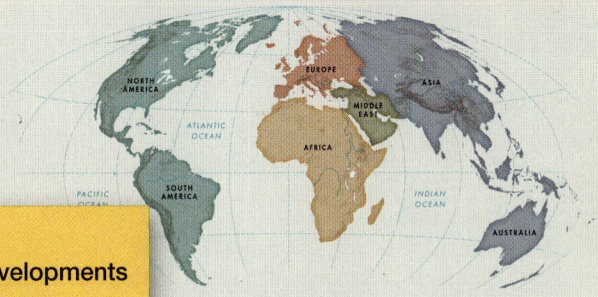

TIME and PLACE

Scan the timeline to see how events and developments in different regions of the world fit together.

500 | 750 | 1000 | 1250 | 1500

Americas

- 500 First permanent settlements in Chaco Canyon
- 500–1000 Andean state of Tiwanaku
- 550–650 Collapse of Teotihuacán
- 700–900 Heyday of Andean state of Wari
- 800–900 Collapse of the Maya city-states
- Rise of Chimu state 900
- 950–1150 Height of Toltec culture
- 1050 Consolidation of Cahokia's dominance
- 1150 Abandonment of pueblos in Chaco Canyon
- 1200 Incas move into Cuzco region
- 1250–1300 Collapse of Cahokia
- 1325 Aztecs found Tenochtitlán
- Columbus reaches the Americas 1492
- 1430–1532 Inca Empire

Europe

- 507 Clovis defeats Visigoths and converts to Christianity
- 590–604 Papacy of Gregory I
- Charles Martel halts Muslim advance into Europe 732
- Charlemagne crowned emperor 800
- 793 Earliest record of Viking raids on Britain
- 988 Rus prince Vladimir converts to Christianity
- 1066 Norman conquest of England
- 1150 Founding of first university at Paris
- 1150–1300 Heyday of the Champagne fairs
- Mongol conquest of Kiev 1240
- 1270–1300 Introduction of overseas navigational aids
- 1347–1350 Outbreak of Black Death
- 1337–1453 Hundred Years' War
- 1400–1550 Italian Renaissance
- Reconquista completed 1492

Middle East

- 527–565 Reign of Byzantine emperor Justinian I
- 570–632 Life of Muhammad
- 661–743 Umayyad caliphate
- 680 Permanent split between Shi'a and Sunni Islam
- 750–850 Abbasid caliphate at its height
- First Crusade ends with Christian capture of Jerusalem 1099
- Saladin recaptures Jerusalem 1187
- 1120 Founding of order of Knights of the Temple
- 1258 Mongols sack Baghdad
- 1291 Mamluks recapture Acre, last Christian stronghold in Palestine
- 1347–1350 Outbreak of Black Death
- 1453 Fall of Constantinople to the Ottomans

Africa

- 500 Spread of camel use; emergence of trans-Saharan trade routes
- 750 Islam starts to spread via trans-Saharan trade routes
- 969 Fatimids capture Egypt
- Fall of kingdom of Ghana 1076
- Reign of Sunjata, founder of Mali Empire 1230–1255
- 1100–1500 Extended dry period in West Africa prompts migrations
- 1250–1517 Mamluk dynasty
- 1250 Kingdom of Benin founded

Asia and Oceania

- 581–618 Sui Empire
- 618–907 Tang Empire
- 600–1000 Polynesian settlement of Pacific Islands
- 668 Unification of Korea under Silla rule
- 755–763 An Lushan rebellion
- 850–1267 Chola kingdom
- 939 Vietnam achieves independence from China
- 960–1279 Song Empire
- 1100–1500 Easter Island's stone monuments
- Formation of first Hawaiian chiefdoms 1200–1400
- 1206–1526 Delhi Sultanate
- 1271–1368 Yuan Empire
- 1336–1573 Ashikaga Shogunate
- 1368–1644 Ming Empire
- 1392–1910 Korean Yi dynasty

STEP 2

Use the chapter's introductory features to understand the place, time, and topic of this chapter.

15

AT A CROSSROADS

The fall of Constantinople to the Ottoman Turks in 1453 marked the end of the Byzantine Empire and heralded the coming age of gunpowder weapons. The Ottoman forces under Sultan Mehmed II breached the massive walls of Constantinople using massive cannons known as *bombards*. The Turkish cannons appear in the center of this book illustration of the siege of Constantinople, published in France in 1455. (The Art Archive/Bibliothèque Nationale Paris.)

PLACE and TOPIC
An important crossroads opens every chapter.

476 PART 2 The Formation of Regional Societies, 500–1450 C.E.

enough cannons to match the heavily armed Ottoman army and navy, which expelled the Venetians from the Black Sea in 1475. Although Venetian merchants still flocked to Constantinople, which Mehmed renamed Istanbul, to obtain spices, silks, and other Asian goods, the Ottomans held the upper hand and could dictate the terms of trade.

The fall of Constantinople to the Ottomans marks a turning point in world history. After perpetuating ancient Rome's heritage and glory for a thousand years, the Byzantine Empire came to an end. Islam continued to advance; in the fourteenth and fifteenth centuries, it expanded most dramatically in Africa and Asia. Italian merchants and bankers lost their dominance in the eastern Mediterranean and turned westward toward the Atlantic Ocean in search of new commercial opportunities. And this shift in commercial power and focus was not the only profound change that followed the Ottoman capture of Constantinople. The bombards cast by the Hungarian engineer for the Ottoman sultan heralded a military revolution that would decisively alter the balance of power among states and transform the nature of the state itself.

The new global patterns that emerged after Constantinople changed hands had their roots in calamities of the fourteenth century. The Ottoman triumph came just as Europe was beginning to recover from the previous century's catastrophic outbreak of plague known as the Black Death. The demographic and psychological shocks of epidemic disease had se-

PLACE and TOPIC
The Mapping the World feature gives a geographical overview of the chapter and highlights important routes and crossroads.

MAPPING THE WORLD

Afro-Eurasia in the Early Fifteenth Century

After the Mongol Empire disintegrated, trans-Eurasian trade shifted from the overland Silk Road to the maritime routes stretching from China to the Mediterranean. Muslim merchants crossed the Sahara Desert and the Indian Ocean in pursuit of African gold, Chinese porcelain, and Asian spices. Although Chinese fleets led by Admiral Zheng He journeyed as far as the coasts of Arabia and Africa, the Ming rulers prohibited private overseas trade.

ROUTES
- Major trade route
- Silk Road
- Voyages of Zheng He

Collapse and Revival in Afro-Eurasia, 1300–1450 CHAPTER 15 477

1315–1317 Great Famine in northern Europe
1325–1354 Travels of Ibn Battuta in Asia and Africa
1336–1573 Ashikaga shogunate in Japan
1337–1453 Hundred Years' War between England and France
• 1378 Ciompi uprising in Florence
• 1381 Peasant Revolt in England
1392–1910 Yi dynasty in Korea
• 1405 Death of Timur; breakup of his empire into regional states in Iran and Central Asia
• 1453 Ottoman conquest of Constantinople marks fall of the Byzantine Empire

1300 | 1325 | 1350 | 1375 | 1400 | 1425 | 1450

1347–1350 Outbreak of the Black Death in Europe and the Islamic Mediterranean
c. 1351–1782 Ayudhya kingdom in Thailand
1368–1644 Ming dynasty in China
1405–1433 Chinese admiral Zheng He's expeditions in Southeast Asia and the Indian Ocean
• 1421 Relocation of Ming capital from Nanjing to Beijing
1428–1788 Le dynasty in Vietnam

TIME and TOPIC
The timeline previews key events and developments discussed in the chapter.

TOPIC

Collapse and Revival in Afro-Eurasia

PLACE

1300–1450

TIME

In [illegible] armies of the Ottoman sultan Mehmed II encircled Constantinople, the Byzantine emperor Constantine XI received a visit from a fellow Christian, a Hungarian engineer named Urban. Urban had applied metallurgical skills acquired at Hungary's rich iron and copper mines to the manufacture of large cannons known as *bombards*. He came to the Byzantine capital to offer his services to repel the Ottoman assault. But although Urban was a Christian, he was a businessman, too. When Constantine could not meet his price, Urban quickly left for the sultan's camp. Facing the famed triple walls of Constantinople, Mehmed promised to quadruple the salary Urban requested and to provide any materials and manpower the engineer needed.

Seven months later, in April 1453, Ottoman soldiers moved Urban's huge bronze bombards—with barrels twenty-six feet long, capable of throwing eight-hundred-pound shot—into place beneath the walls of Constantinople. Although these cumbersome cannons could fire only seven rounds a day, they battered the walls of Constantinople, which had long been considered impenetrable. After six weeks of siege the Turks breached the walls and swarmed into the city. The vastly outnumbered defenders, Emperor Constantine among them, fought to the death.

Urban's willingness to put business before religious loyalty helped tip the balance of power in the Mediterranean. During the siege, the Genoese merchant community at Constantinople—along with their archrivals, the Venetians—maintained strict neutrality. Although the Italian merchants, like Urban, were prepared to do business with Mehmed II, within a decade the Venetians and Ottomans were at war. Venice could not produce bazaar, and this isolation contributed to the birth of Japan's distinctive national culture. For most Afro-Eurasian societies, however, the maritime world increasingly became the principal crossroads of economic and cultural exchange.

Fourteenth-Century Crisis and Renewal in Eurasia

FOCUS How did the Black Death affect society, the economy, and culture in Latin Christendom and the Islamic world?

Islam's New Frontiers

FOCUS Why did Islam expand dramatically in the fourteenth and fifteenth centuries, and how did new Islamic societies differ from established ones?

The Global Bazaar

FOCUS How did the pattern of international trade change during the fourteenth and fifteenth centuries, and how did these changes affect consumption and fashion tastes?

COUNTERPOINT
Age of the Samurai in Japan, 1185–1450

FOCUS How and why did the historical development of Japan in the fourteenth and fifteenth centuries differ from that of mainland Eurasia?

TOPIC
These headings and Focus Questions indicate the main topic and point of each major section of the chapter.

BACKSTORY

In the fourteenth century, a number of developments threatened the connections among the societies of the Afro-Eurasian world. The collapse of the Mongol empires in China and Iran in the mid-1300s disrupted caravan traffic across Central Asia, diverting the flow of trade and travel to maritime routes across the Indian Ocean. Although the two centuries of religious wars known as the Crusades ended in 1291, they had hardened hostility between Christians and Muslims. As the power of the Christian Byzantine Empire contracted, Muslim Turkish sultanates—the Mamluk regime in Egypt and the rising Ottoman dynasty in Anatolia (modern Turkey)—gained control of the eastern Mediterranean region. Yet the Crusades and direct contact with the Mongols had also whetted European appetites for luxury and exotic goods from the Islamic world and Asia. Thus, despite challenges and obstacles, the Mediterranean remained a lively crossroads of commerce and cross-cultural exchange.

TOPIC and PLACE
The Backstory reminds you where you last left off in this part of the world.

TOPICS
The Major Global Development orients you to the large historical change covered in the chapter, and the Overview Questions frame the issues you should consider as you read.

OVERVIEW QUESTIONS

The major global development in this chapter: Crisis and recovery in fourteenth- and fifteenth-century Afro-Eurasia.

As you read, consider:

1. In the century after the devastating outbreak of plague known as the Black Death, how and why did Europe's economic growth begin to surpass that of the Islamic world?
2. Did the economic revival across Eurasia after 1350 benefit the peasant populations of Europe, the Islamic world, and East Asia?
3. How did the process of conversion to Islam differ in Iran, the Ottoman Empire, West Africa, and Southeast Asia during this period?
4. What political and economic changes contributed to the rise of maritime commerce in Asia during the fourteenth and fifteenth centuries?

STEP 3

Use the chapter tools to understand what is important.

Focus questions, which also appear at the start and end of the chapter, tell you what you need to learn from each major section.

Islam's New Frontiers

FOCUS
Why did Islam expand dramatically in the fourteenth and fifteenth centuries, and how did new Islamic societies differ from established ones?

In the fourteenth and fifteenth centuries, Islam continued to spread to new areas, including central and maritime Asia, sub-Saharan Africa, and southeastern Europe. In the past, Muslim rule had often preceded the popular adoption of Islamic religion and culture. Yet the advance of Islam in Africa and Asia came about not through conquest, but through slow diffusion via merchants and missionaries. The universalism and egalitarianism of Islam appealed to rising merchant classes in both West Africa and maritime Asia.

During this period, Islam expanded by adapting to older ruling cultures rather than seeking to eradicate them. Timur, the last of the great nomad conquerors, and his descendants ruled not as Mongol khans but as Islamic sultans. The culture of the Central Asian states, however, remained an eclectic mix of Mongol, Turkish, and Persian traditions, in contrast to the strict adherence to Muslim law and doctrine practiced under the Arab regimes of the Middle East and North Africa. This pattern of cultural adaptation and assimilation was even more evident in West Africa and Southeast Asia.

Islamic Spiritual Ferment in Central Asia 1350–1500

The spread of Sufism in Central Asia between 1350 and 1500 played a significant role in the process of cultural assimilation. **Sufism**—a mystical tradition that stressed self-mastery, practical virtues, and spiritual growth through personal experience of the divine—had already emerged by 1200 as a major expression of Islamic values and social identity. Sufism appeared in many variations and readily assimilated local cultures to its beliefs and practices. Sufi mystics acquired institutional strength through the communal solidarity of their brotherhoods spread across the whole realm of Islam. In contrast to the orthodox scholars and teachers known as *ulama*, who made little effort to convert nonbelievers, Sufi preachers were inspired by missionary zeal and welcomed non-Muslims to their lodges and sermons. This made them ideal instruments for the spread of Islam to new territories.

Topical headings in the margin focus on important topics and are useful for reviewing the chapter.

Timur

One of Sufism's most important royal patrons was Timur (1336–1405), the last of the Mongol emperors. Born near the city of Samarkand (SAM-ar-kand) when the Mongol Ilkhanate in Iran was on the verge of collapse, Timur—himself a Turk—grew up among Mongols who practiced Islam. He rose to power in the 1370s by reuniting quarreling Mongol tribes in common pursuit of conquest. Although Timur lacked the dynastic pedigree enjoyed by Chinggis Khan's descendants, like Chinggis he held his empire together by the force of his personal charisma.

From the early 1380s, Timur's armies relentlessly pursued campaigns of conquest, sweeping westward across Iran into Mesopotamia and Russia and eastward into India. In 1400–1401 Timur seized and razed Aleppo and Damascus, the principal Mamluk cities in Syria. In 1402 he captured the Ottoman sultan in battle. Rather than trying to consolidate his rule in Syria and Anatolia (modern Turkey), however, Timur turned his attention eastward. He was preparing to march on China when he fell ill and died early in 1405. Although Timur's empire quickly fragmented, his triumphs would serve as an inspiration to later empire builders, such as the Mughals in India and the Manchus in China. Moreover, his support of Sufism would have a lasting impact, helping lay the foundation for a number of important Islamic religious movements in Central Asia.

Marginal glossary definitions provide further explanation of key terms boldfaced in the narrative.

Sufism A tradition within Islam that emphasizes mystical knowledge and personal experience of the divine.

The institutions of Timur's empire were largely modeled on the Ilkhan synthesis of Persian civil administration and Turkish-Mongol military organization. Like the Ilkhans and the Ottomans, Timur's policies favored settled farmers and urban populations over pastoral nomads, who were often displaced from their homelands. While Timur allowed local princes a degree of autonomy, he was determined to make Samarkand a grand imperial capital.

Cultural Innovations

Again, as with Islam in West Africa, the intellectual ferment of the Renaissance was nurtured in an urban environment. Humanist scholars shunned the warrior culture of the old nobility while celebrating the civic roles and duties of townsmen, merchants, and clerics. Despite their admiration of classical civilization, the humanists did not reject Christianity. Rather, they sought to reconcile Christian faith and doctrines with classical learning. By making knowledge of Latin and Greek, history, poetry, and philosophy the mark of an educated person, the humanists transformed education and established models of schooling that would endure down to modern times.

Nowhere was the revolutionary impact of the Renaissance felt more deeply than in visual arts such as painting, sculpture, and architecture. Artists of the Renaissance exuded supreme confidence in the ability of human ingenuity to equal or even surpass the works of nature. The new outlook was exemplified by the development of the techniques of perspective, which artists used to convey a realistic, three-dimensional quality to physical forms, most notably the human body. Human invention also was capable of improving on nature by creating order and harmony through architecture and urban planning. Alberti advocated replacing the winding narrow streets and haphazard construction of medieval towns with planned cities organized around straight boulevards, open squares, and monumental buildings whose balanced proportions corresponded to a geometrically unified design.

Above all, the Renaissance transformed the idea of the artist. No longer mere manual tradesmen, artists now were seen as possessing a special kind of genius that enabled them to express a higher understanding of beauty. In the eyes of contemporaries, no one exemplified this quality of genius more than Leonardo da Vinci (1452–1519), who won renown as a painter, architect, sculptor, engineer, mathematician, and inventor. Leonardo's father, a Florentine lawyer, apprenticed him to a local painter at age eighteen. Leonardo spent much of his career as a civil and military engineer in the employ of the Duke of Milan, and developed ideas for flying machines, tanks, robots, and solar power that far exceeded the engineering capabilities of his time. Leonardo sought to apply his knowledge of natural science to painting, which he regarded as the most sublime art (see Seeing the Past: Leonardo da Vinci's *Virgin of the Rocks*).

The flowering of Renaissance humanism in the Renaissance was rooted in the rich soil of Italy's com[illegible] from the Islamic world and Asia. Interna[illegible] production across maritime Asia and gave[illegible] and consumption. In Japan, however, grow[illegible] fostered the emergence of a national cultu[illegible]ated the rest of East Asia.

The final Counterpoint section offers an important exception to the Major Global Development discussed in the chapter.

COUNTERPOINT

Age of the Samurai in Japan 1185–1450

FOCUS

How and why did the historical development of Japan in the fourteenth and fifteenth centuries differ from that of mainland Eurasia?

In Japan as in Europe, the term *Middle Ages* brings to mind an age of warriors, a stratified society governed by bonds of loyalty between lords and vassals. In Japan, however, the militarization of the ruling class intensified during the fourteenth and fifteenth centuries, a time when the warrior nobility of Europe was crumbling. Paradoxically, the rise of the **samurai** (sah-moo-rye) ("those who serve") warriors as masters of their own estates was accompanied by the increasing independence of peasant communities.

Phonetic spellings follow many potentially unfamiliar terms.

[illegible]apter, Japan became more isolated from [illegible]ural exchanges with China reached a pea[illegible] invasion of Japan in 1281, ties with conti[illegible]panese see this era as the period in which Japan's unique national identity—expressed most distinctly in the ethic of *bushidō* (boo-shee-doe), the "Way of the Warrior"—took its definitive form. Samurai warriors became the

samurai Literally, "those who serve"; the hereditary warriors who dominated Japanese society and culture from the twelfth to the nineteenth centuries.

STEP 4

Do historical analysis.

LIVES AND LIVELIHOODS

Lives and Livelihoods features underscore the connections between daily life and global developments.

Urban Weavers in India

Industry and commerce in India, especially in textiles, grew rapidly beginning in the fourteenth century. Specialized craftsmen in towns and regional groups of merchants formed guilds that became the nuclei of new occupational castes, *jati* (JAH-tee). Ultimately these new occupational castes would join with other forces in Indian society to challenge the social inequality rooted in orthodox Hindu religion.

It was growth in market demand and technological innovations such as block printing that drove the rapid expansion of India's textile industries. Luxury fabrics such as fine silks and velvet remained largely the province of royal workshops or private patronage. Mass production of textiles, on the other hand, was oriented toward the manufacture of cheaper cotton fabrics, especially colorful chintz garments. A weaver could make a woman's cotton *sari* in six or seven days, whereas a luxury garment took a month or more. Domestic demand for ordinary cloth grew steadily, and production for export accelerated even more briskly. At the beginning of the sixteenth century, the Portuguese traveler Tomé Pires, impressed by the craftsmanship of Indian muslins and calicoes (named after the port of Calicut), observed that "they make enough of these to furnish the world."[1]

Weaving became an urban industry. It was village women who cleaned most of the cotton and spun it into yarn; they could easily combine this simple if laborious work with other domestic chores. But peasants did not weave the yarn into cloth, except for their own use. Instead, weaving, bleaching, a
professional
living in sep

Like oth
pation that c
Families of w
guilds with b
within their g
not have exc
could include
could becom

Indian Block-Printed Textile, c. 1500

Block-printed textiles with elaborate designs were in great demand both in India and throughout Southeast Asia, Africa, and the Islamic world. Craftsmen carved intricate designs on wooden blocks (a separate block for each color), which were then dipped in dye and repeatedly stamped on bleached fabric until the entire cloth was covered. This cotton fabric with geese, lotus flower, and rosette designs was manufactured in Gujarat in western India. (Ashmolean Museum, University of Oxford)

tions for social recognition. Amid the whirl and congestion of city life, it was far more difficult than in villages to enforce the laws governing caste purity and segregation. As a fourteenth-century poet wrote about the crowded streets of his hometown of Jaunpur in the Ganges Valley, in the city "one person's caste-mark gets stamped on another's forehead, and a brahman's holy thread will be found hanging around an untouchable's neck."[2] Brahmans objected to this erosion of caste boundaries, to little avail. Weaver guilds became influential patrons of temples and often served as trustees and accountants in charge of managing temple endowments and revenues.

In a few cases the growing economic independence of weavers and like-minded artisans prompted complete rejection of the caste hierarchy. Sufi preachers and *bhakti* (BAHK-tee)—devotional movements devoted to patron gods and goddesses—encouraged the disregard of caste distinctions in favor of a universal brotherhood of devout believers. The fifteenth-century bhakti preacher Kabir, who was strongly influenced by Sufi teachings, epitomized the new social radicalism coursing through the urban artisan classes. A weaver himself, Kabir joined the dignity of manual labor to the purity of spiritual devotion, spurning the social pretension and superficial piety of the brahmans ("pandits") and Muslim clerics ("mullahs"):

at ease
mullahs,
come
toil,
asure,
alesced
red on

a trinity of labor, charity, and spiritual devotion. The Sikhs, who gained a following principally among traders and artisans in the northwestern Punjab region, drew an even more explicit connection between commerce and piety. In the words of a hymn included in a sixteenth-century anthology of Sikh sacred writings:

> The true Guru [teacher] is the merchant;
>
> The devotees are his peddlers.
>
> The capital stock is the Lord's Name, and
>
> To enshrine the truth is to keep His account.[4]

Sikh communities spurned the distinction between pure and impure occupations. In their eyes, holiness was to be found in honest toil and personal piety, not ascetic practices, book learning, or religious rituals.

1. Tomé Pires, *The Suma Oriental of Tomé Pires*, ed. and trans. Armando Cortes (London: Hakluyt Society, 1944), 1:53.
2. Vidyapati Thakur, *Kirtilata*, quoted in Eugenia Vanina, *Urban Crafts and Craftsmen in Medieval India (Thirteenth–Eighteenth Centuries)* (New Delhi: Munshiram Manoharlal, 2004), 443.
3. Quoted in Vanina, *Urban Crafts and Craftsmen*, 149.
4. Sri Guru *Granth Sahib*, trans. Gophal Singh (Delhi: Gur Das Kapur & Sons, 1960), 2:427.

QUESTIONS TO CONSIDER

1. **In what ways did the organization of textile production reinforce or challenge the prevailing social norms of Hindu society?**
2. **In what ways did religious ideas and movements reflect the new sense of dignity among prosperous Indian merchants and craftsmen?**

th India. Delhi: Oxford University Press, 1985.
ndia (Thirteenth–Eighteenth Centuries). New Delhi: Munshiram Manoharlal, 2004.

SEEING THE PAST

Reading the Past and Seeing the Past features provide direct exposure to important voices and ideas of the past through written and visual primary sources.

Leonardo da Vinci's *Virgin of the Rocks*

Virgin of the Rocks, c. 1483–1486
(Erich Lessing/Art Resource.)

Leonardo's Botanical Studies with Star-of-Bethlehem, Grasses, Crowfoot, Wood Anemone, and Another Genus,
c. 1500–1506 (The Royal Collection © 2011 Her Majesty Queen Elizabeth II/Bridgeman Art Library.)

the menacing
the cavern; de
there was any
thing within."[1]

Fantastic as the sce
might seem, Leonardo's
meticulous
rocks and p
based on cl
of nature. Th
lehem flowe
left of the pa
izing purity a
also appear
contempora
cal drawing
Geologists h
Leonardo's l
sandstone n
and his prec
of plants wh
most likely t

Master
the *Virgin o*
display Leonardo's careful study of human ar
landscapes, and botany. Although he admire
tion of nature, Leonardo also celebrated the h
rational and aesthetic capacities, declaring th
arts may be called the grandsons of God."[2]

While living in Milan in the early 1480s, Leonardo accepted a commission to paint an altarpiece for the chapel of Milan's Confraternity of the Immaculate Conception, a branch of the Franciscan order. Leonardo's relationship with the friars proved to be stormy. His first version of the painting (now in the Louvre), reproduced here, apparently displeased his patrons and was sold to another party. Only after a fifteen-year-long dispute over the price did Leonardo finally deliver a modified version in 1508.

In portraying the legendary encounter between the child Jesus and the equally young John the Baptist during the flight to Egypt, Leonardo replaced the traditional desert setting with a landscape filled with rocks, plants, and water. Leonardo's dark grotto creates an aura of mystery and foreboding, from which the figures of Mary, Jesus, John, and the angel Uriel emerge as if in a vision. A few years before, Leonardo had written about "coming to the entrance of a great cavern, in front of which I stood for some time, stupefied and uncomprehending. . . . Suddenly two things arose in me, fear and desire: fear of

1. Arundel ms. (British Library), p. 115 recto, cited i
Leonardo da Vinci: The Marvelous Works of Natu
(Oxford: Oxford University Press, 2006), 78.
2. John Paul Richter, ed., *The Notebooks of Leona*
of 1883 ed.; New York: Dover, 1970), Book IX, 32

EXAMINING THE EVIDENCE

1. **How does Leonardo express the conne between John (at left) and Jesus throu gesture, and their relationships with th Mary and the angel Uriel?**
2. **The friars who commissioned the painting sought to celebrate the sanctity and purity of their patron, the Virgin Mary. Does this painting achieve that effect?**

Thus, China influenced patterns of international trade not only as a producer, as with

READING THE PAST

A Spanish Ambassador's Description of Samarkand

In September 1403, an embassy dispatched by King Henry III of Castile arrived at Samarkand in hopes of enlisting the support of Timur for a combined military campaign against the Ottomans. Seventy years old and in failing health, Timur lavishly entertained his visitors, but made no response to Henry's overtures. The leader of the Spanish delegation, Ruy Gonzalez de Clavijo, left Samarkand disappointed, but his report preserves our fullest account of Timur's capital in its heyday.

> The city is rather larger than Seville, but lying outside Samarkand are great numbers of houses that form extensive suburbs. These lay spread on all hands, for indeed the township is surrounded by orchards and vineyards. . . . In between these orchards pass streets with open squares; these are all densely populated, and here all kinds of goods are on sale with breadstuffs and meat. . . .
>
> Samarkand is rich not only in foodstuffs but also in manufactures, such as factories of silk. . . . Thus trade has always been fostered by Timur with the view of making his capital the noblest of cities; and during all his conquests . . . he carried off the best men to people Samarkand, bringing thither the master-craftsmen of all nations. Thus from Damascus he carried away with him all the weavers of that city, those who worked at the silk looms; further the bow-makers who produce those cross-bows which are so famous; likewise armorers; also the craftsmen in glass and porcelain, who are known to be the best in all the world. From Turkey he had brought their gunsmiths who make the arquebus. . . . So great therefore was the population now of all nationalities gathered together in Samarkand that of men with their families the number they said must amount to 150,000 souls . . . [including] Turks, Arabs, and Moors of diverse sects, with Greek, Armenian, Roman, Jacobite [Syrian], and Nestorian Christians, besides those folk who baptize with fire in the forehead [i.e., Hindus]. . . .
>
> The markets of Samarkand further are amply stored with merchandise imported from distant and foreign countries. . . . The goods that are imported to Samarkand from Cathay indeed are of the richest and most precious of all those brought thither from foreign parts, for the craftsmen of Cathay are reputed to be the most skillful by far beyond those of any other nation.

Source: Ruy Gonzalez de Clavijo, *Embassy to Tamerlane, 1403–1406*, trans. Guy Le Strange (London: Routledge, 1928), 285–289.

EXAMINING THE EVIDENCE

1. **What features of Timur's capital most impressed Gonzalez de Clavijo?**
2. **How does this account of Samarkand at its height compare with the chapter's description of Renaissance Florence?**

STEP 5

Review what you have learned.

Remember to visit the Online Study Guide for more review help.

REVIEW

Online Study Guide
bedfordstmartins.com/smith

The major global development in this chapter ▶ Crisis and recovery in fourteenth- and fifteenth-century Afro-Eurasia.

Review the Major Global Development discussed in the chapter.

Review the Important Events from the chapter.

IMPORTANT EVENTS

1315–1317	Great Famine in northern Europe
1325–1354	Travels of Ibn Battuta in Asia and Africa
1336–1573	Ashikaga shogunate in Japan
1337–1453	Hundred Years' War between England and France
1347–1350	Outbreak of the Black Death in Europe and the Islamic Mediterranean
c. 1351–1782	Ayudhya kingdom in Thailand
1368–1644	Ming dynasty in China
1378	Ciompi uprising in Florence
1381	Peasant Revolt in England
1392–1910	Yi dynasty in Korea
1405	Death of Timur; breakup of his empire into regional states in Iran and Central Asia
1405–1433	Chinese admiral Zheng He's expeditions in Southeast Asia and the Indian Ocean
1421	Relocation of Ming capital from Nanjing to Beijing
1428–1788	Le dynasty in Vietnam
1453	Ottoman conquest of Constantinople marks fall of the Byzantine Empire

Review the Key Terms.

KEY TERMS

Black Death (p. 478)
humanism (p. 498)
janissary corps (p. 489)
Little Ice Age (p. 479)
Neo-Confucianism (p. 486)
oligarchy (p. 483)
pandemic (p. 478)
Renaissance (p. 498)
samurai (p. 501)
shogun (p. 503)
Sufism (p. 488)
theocracy (p. 489)
trade diaspora (p. 492)

CHAPTER OVERVIEW QUESTIONS

Answer these big-picture questions posed at the start of the chapter.

1. How and why did Europe's economic growth begin to surpass that of the Islamic world in the after the Black Death?
2. Did the economic revival across Eurasia a benefit the peasant populations of Europe Islamic world, and East Asia?
3. How did the process of conversion to Islam differ in Iran, the Ottoman Empire, West Africa, and Southeast Asia during this period?
4. What political and economic changes contributed to the rise of maritime commerce in Asia during the fourteenth and fifteenth centuries?

SECTION FOCUS QUESTIONS

Explain the main point of each major section of the chapter.

1. How did the Black Death affect society, the omy, and culture in Latin Christendom and Islamic world?
2. Why did Islam expand dramatically in the fourteenth and fifteenth centuries, and how did new Islamic societies differ from established ones?
3. What were the principal sources of growth in international trade during the fourteenth and fifteenth centuries, and how did this trade affect patterns of consumption and fashion tastes?
4. How and why did the historical development of Japan in the fourteenth and fifteenth centuries differ from that of mainland Eurasia?

MAKING CONNECTIONS

Connect ideas and practice your skills of comparison and analysis.

1. What social, economic, and technological c strengthened the power of European mona during the century after the Black Death?
2. How and why did the major routes and con ties of trans-Eurasian trade change after the collapse of the Mongol empires in Central Asia?
3. In what ways did the motives for conversion to Islam differ in Central Asia, sub-Saharan Africa, and the Indian Ocean during this era?
4. In this period, why did the power and status of the samurai warriors in Japan rise while those of the warrior nobility in Europe declined?

VERSIONS AND SUPPLEMENTS

Adopters of *Crossroads and Cultures: A History of the World's Peoples* and their students have access to abundant extra resources, including documents, presentation and testing materials, the acclaimed Bedford Series in History and Culture volumes, and much, much more. See below for more information, visit the book's catalog site at bedfordstmartins.com/smith/catalog, or contact your local Bedford/St. Martin's sales representative.

Get the Right Version for Your Class

To accommodate different course lengths and course budgets, *Crossroads and Cultures: A History of the World's Peoples* is available in several different formats, including three-hole punched loose-leaf Budget Books versions and e-books, which are available at a substantial discount.

- Combined edition (Chapters 1–31)—available in hardcover, loose-leaf, and e-book formats
- Volume 1: To 1450 (Chapters 1–16)—available in paperback, loose-leaf, and e-book formats
- Volume 2: Since 1300 (Chapters 15–31)—available in paperback, loose-leaf, and e-book formats
- Volume A: To 1300 (Chapters 1–14)—available in paperback
- Volume B: 500–1750 (Chapters 9–22)—available in paperback
- Volume C: Since 1750 (Chapters 23–31)—available in paperback

Your students can purchase *Crossroads and Cultures: A History of the World's Peoples* in popular e-book formats for computers, tablets, and e-readers by visiting bedfordstmartins.com/ebooks. The e-book is available at a discount.

Online Extras for Students

The book's companion site at bedfordstmartins.com/smith gives students a way to read, write, and study by providing plentiful quizzes and activities, study aids, and history research and writing help.

FREE **Online Study Guide.** Available at the companion site, this popular resource provides students with quizzes and activities for each chapter, including multiple-choice self-tests that focus on important concepts; flashcards that test students' knowledge of key terms; timeline activities that emphasize causal relationships; and map quizzes intended to strengthen students' geography skills. Instructors can monitor students' progress through an online Quiz Gradebook or receive e-mail updates.

FREE **Research, Writing, and Anti-plagiarism Advice.** Available at the companion site, Bedford's **History Research and Writing Help** includes **History Research and Reference Sources**, with links to history-related databases, indexes, and journals; **More Sources and How to Format a History Paper**, with clear advice on how to integrate primary and secondary sources into research papers and how to cite and format sources correctly; **Build a Bibliography**, a simple Web-based tool known as the Bedford Bibliographer that generates bibliographies in four commonly used documentation styles; and **Tips on Avoiding Plagiarism**, an online tutorial that reviews the consequences of plagiarism and features exercises to help students practice integrating sources and recognize acceptable summaries.

Resources for Instructors

Bedford/St. Martin's has developed a rich array of teaching resources for this book and for this course. They range from lecture and presentation materials and assessment tools to course management options. Most can be downloaded or ordered at bedfordstmartins.com/smith/catalog.

HistoryClass for Crossroads and Cultures. *HistoryClass*, a Bedford/St. Martin's Online Course Space, puts the online resources available with this textbook in one convenient and completely customizable course space. There you and your students can access an interactive e-book and primary source reader; maps, images, documents, and links; chapter review quizzes; interactive multimedia exercises; and research and writing help. In *HistoryClass* you can get all our premium content and tools and assign, rearrange, and mix them with your own resources. For more information, visit yourhistoryclass.com.

Bedford Coursepack for Blackboard, WebCT, Desire2Learn, Angel, Sakai, or Moodle. We have free content to help you integrate our rich materials into your course management system. Registered instructors can download coursepacks easily and with no strings attached. The coursepack for *Crossroads and Cultures: A History of the World's Peoples* includes book-specific content as well as our most popular free resources. Visit bedfordstmartins.com/coursepacks to see a demo, find your version, or download your coursepack.

Instructor's Resource Manual. Written by Rick Warner, an experienced teacher of the world-history survey course, the instructor's manual offers both experienced and first-time instructors tools for preparing lectures and running discussions. It includes chapter review material, teaching strategies, and a guide to chapter-specific supplements available for the text.

Computerized Test Bank. The test bank includes a mix of fresh, carefully crafted multiple-choice, matching, short-answer, and essay questions for each chapter. It also contains the Overview, Focus, Making Connections, Lives and Livelihoods, Reading the Past, and Seeing the Past questions from the textbook and model answers for each. The questions appear in Microsoft Word format and in easy-to-use test bank software that allows instructors to easily add, edit, resequence, and print questions and answers. Instructors can also export questions into a variety of formats, including WebCT and Blackboard.

***The Bedford Lecture Kit:* Maps, Images, Lecture Outlines, and i>clicker Content.** Look good and save time with *The Bedford Lecture Kit*. These presentation materials are downloadable individually from the Instructor Resources tab at bedfordstmartins.com/smith/catalog and are available on *The Bedford Lecture Kit* Instructor's Resource CD-ROM. They provide ready-made and fully customizable PowerPoint multimedia presentations that include lecture outlines with embedded maps, figures, and selected images from the textbook and extra background for instructors. Also available are maps and selected images in JPEG and PowerPoint formats; content for i>clicker, a classroom response system, in Microsoft Word and PowerPoint formats; the Instructor's Resource Manual in Microsoft Word format; and outline maps in PDF format for quizzing or handing out. All files are suitable for copying onto transparency acetates.

***Make History*—Free Documents, Maps, Images, and Web Sites.** *Make History* combines the best Web resources with hundreds of maps and images, to make it simple to find the source material you need. Browse the collection of thousands of resources by course or by topic, date, and type. Each item has been carefully chosen and helpfully annotated to make it easy to find exactly what you need. Available at bedfordstmartins.com/makehistory.

Videos and Multimedia. A wide assortment of videos and multimedia CD-ROMs on various topics in world history is available to qualified adopters through your Bedford/St. Martin's sales representative.

Package and Save Your Students Money

For information on free packages and discounts up to 50%, visit bedfordstmartins.com/smith/catalog, or contact your local Bedford/St. Martin's sales representative.

Sources of Crossroads and Cultures. The authors of *Crossroads and Cultures* have carefully developed this two-volume primary source reader themselves to reflect the textbook's geographic and thematic breadth and the key social, cultural, and political developments discussed in each chapter. *Sources of Crossroads and Cultures* extends the textbook's emphasis on the human dimension of global history through the voices of both notable figures and everyday individuals. With a blend of major works and fresh perspectives, each chapter contains approximately six sources, an introduction, document headnotes, and questions for discussion. Available free when packaged with the print text.

Sources of Crossroads and Cultures e-Book. The reader is also available as an e-book for purchase at a discount.

The Bedford Series in History and Culture. More than one hundred titles in this highly praised series combine first-rate scholarship, historical narrative, and important primary documents for undergraduate courses. Each book is brief, inexpensive, and focused on a specific topic or period. For a complete list of titles, visit bedfordstmartins.com/history/series. Package discounts are available.

Rand McNally Historical Atlas of the World. This collection of almost seventy full-color maps illustrates the eras and civilizations in world history from the emergence of human societies to the present. Available for $3.00 when packaged with the print text.

The Bedford Glossary for World History. This handy supplement for the survey course gives students historically contextualized definitions for hundreds of terms—from *abolitionism* to *Zoroastrianism*—that they will encounter in lectures, reading, and exams. Available free when packaged with the print text.

World History Matters: A Student Guide to World History Online. Based on the popular "World History Matters" Web site produced by the Center for History and New Media, this unique resource, edited by Kristin Lehner (The Johns Hopkins University), Kelly Schrum (George Mason University), and T. Mills Kelly (George Mason University), combines reviews of 150 of the most useful and reliable world history Web sites with an introduction that guides students in locating, evaluating, and correctly citing online sources. Available free when packaged with the print text.

Trade Books. Titles published by sister companies Hill and Wang; Farrar, Straus and Giroux; Henry Holt and Company; St. Martin's Press; Picador; and Palgrave Macmillan are available at a 50% discount when packaged with

Bedford/St. Martin's textbooks. For more information, visit bedfordstmartins.com/tradeup.

A Pocket Guide to Writing in History. This portable and affordable reference tool by Mary Lynn Rampolla provides reading, writing, and research advice useful to students in all history courses. Concise yet comprehensive advice on approaching typical history assignments, developing critical reading skills, writing effective history papers, conducting research, using and documenting sources, and avoiding plagiarism—enhanced with practical tips and examples throughout—have made this slim reference a best-seller. Package discounts are available.

A Student's Guide to History. This complete guide to success in any history course provides the practical help students need to be effective. In addition to introducing students to the nature of the discipline, author Jules Benjamin teaches a wide range of skills from preparing for exams to approaching common writing assignments, and he explains the research and documentation process with plentiful examples. Package discounts are available.

Worlds of History: A Comparative Reader. Compiled by Kevin Reilly, a widely respected world historian and community college teacher, *Worlds of History* fosters historical thinking through thematic comparisons of primary and secondary sources from around the world. Each chapter takes up a major theme—such as patriarchy, love and marriage, or globalization—as experienced by two or more cultures. "Thinking Historically" exercises build students' capacity to analyze and interpret sources one skill at a time. This flexible framework accommodates a variety of approaches to teaching world history. Package discounts are available.

NOTE ON DATES AND USAGE

Where necessary for clarity, we qualify dates as B.C.E. ("Before the Common Era") or C.E. ("Common Era"). The abbreviation B.C.E. refers to the same era as B.C. ("Before Christ"), just as C.E is equivalent to A.D. (*anno Domini,* Latin for "in the year of the Lord"). In keeping with our aim to approach world history from a global, multicultural perspective, we chose these neutral abbreviations as appropriate to our enterprise. Because most readers will be more familiar with English than with metric measures, however, units of measure are given in the English system in the narrative, with metric and English measures provided on the maps.

We translate Chinese names and terms into English according to the *pinyin* system, while noting in parentheses proper names well established in English (e.g., Canton, Chiang Kai-shek). Transliteration of names and terms from the many other languages traced in our book follow the same contemporary scholarly conventions.

BRIEF CONTENTS

PART 4 The World from 1750 to the Present

23 Atlantic Revolutions and the World, 1750–1830 *758*
24 Industry and Everyday Life, 1750–1900 *790*
25 The Rise of Modern Nation-States, 1850–1900 *824*
26 Imperial Order and Disorder, 1850–1914 *856*
27 Wars, Revolutions, and the Birth of Mass Society, 1910–1929 *890*
28 Global Catastrophe: The Great Depression and World War II, 1929–1945 *924*
29 The Emergence of New Nations in a Cold War World, 1945–1970 *958*
30 Technological Transformation and the End of Cold War, 1960–1992 *988*
31 A New Global Age, 1989 to the Present *1022*

CONTENTS

A Conversation with the Authors: The Story Behind *Crossroads* and *Cultures* *v*
How to Use This Book *x*
Versions and Supplements *xviii*
Note on Dates and Usage *xx*
Maps *xxvii*
Special Features *xxix*
Acknowledgments *xxx*

PART 4 The World from 1750 to the Present

23 Atlantic Revolutions and the World, 1750–1830 *758*

Major Global Development ▸ The Atlantic revolutions and their short- and long-term significance.

Backstory *759*

The Promise of Enlightenment *762*
- A New World of Ideas *762*
- Enlightenment and the Old Order *765*
- Popular Revolts in an Age of Enlightenment *767*

Revolution in North America *767*
- The British Empire and the Colonial Crisis, 1764–1775 *768*
- The Birth of the United States, 1775–1789 *768*

The French Revolution and the Napoleonic Empire *771*
- From Monarchy to Republic, 1789–1792 *771*
- War, Terror, and Resistance, 1792–1799 *773*
- Napoleon's Reign, 1799–1815 *774*
- Muhammad Ali and the Revolutionary Spirit in Egypt *774*

Revolution Continued in the Western Hemisphere *777*
- Revolution in Haiti, 1791–1804 *777*
- Revolutions in Latin America, 1810–1830 *778*
- New Ideologies and Revolutionary Legacies *783*

COUNTERPOINT Religious Revival in a Secular Age *784*
- Christianity's Great Awakening *785*
- Government and Religion Allied *785*

Conclusion *786* | ***Notes*** *787*
Resources for Research *788* | ***Review*** *789*

- ▸ **SEEING THE PAST** Portrait of Catherine the Great *766*
- ▸ **LIVES AND LIVELIHOODS** The Cowboy Way of Life *782*
- ▸ **READING THE PAST** Simon Bolivar on Latin American Independence *784*
- ▸ **READING THE PAST** Phillis Wheatley, "On Being Brought from Africa to America" *786*

24 Industry and Everyday Life, 1750–1900 *790*

Major Global Development ▸ The Industrial Revolution and its impact on societies and cultures throughout the world.

Backstory *791*

The Industrial Revolution Begins, 1750–1830 *794*
- The Global Roots of Industrialization *794*
- Great Britain: A Culture of Experimentation *795*
- World Trade and the Rise of Industry *796*
- The Technology of Industry *798*

Industrialization After 1830 *798*
- Industrial Innovation Gathers Speed *799*
- Challenge to British Dominance *802*
- Industrialization in Japan *802*
- Economic Crises and Solutions *804*

The Industrial Revolution and the World *806*
- The Slow Disintegration of Qing China *807*
- Competition in West and South Asia *809*
- A New Course for Africa *810*

Industry and Society *812*
- The Changing Middle Class *812*
- The New Working Class *813*
- The Sexual Division of Labor *815*

The Culture of Industry *815*
- Industry and the Arts *817*

COUNTERPOINT African Women and Slave Agriculture *818*
- Women and Farming in Africa *818*
- Women Slaves in the North American South *819*

Conclusion *820* | ***Notes*** *820*
Resources for Research *821* | ***Review*** *823*

- ▸ **READING THE PAST** Industry Comes to the British Countryside *797*
- ▸ **LIVES AND LIVELIHOODS** Builders of the Trans-Siberian Railroad *800*
- ▸ **SEEING THE PAST** Japan's Industrious Society *803*
- ▸ **READING THE PAST** Mexican Women on Strike *816*

25

The Rise of Modern Nation-States, 1850–1900 *824*

Major Global Development ▶ The causes and consequences of nation building in the nineteenth century.

Backstory *825*

Modernizing Nations *828*
- "What Is a Nation?" *829*
- Latin American Nation Building *829*
- The Russian Empire's New Course *832*
- A Unified Italy and a United Germany *836*

Emerging Powers: The United States and Japan *838*
- Expansion and Consolidation of the United States *838*
- Dramatic Change in Japan *841*

The Culture of Nations *843*
- The Culture of Tradition *843*
- Westernization *845*
- National Institutions *846*

COUNTERPOINT Outsiders Inside the Nation-State *849*
- People of Color *849*
- Women *850*
- The Struggle for Citizens' Rights *851*

Conclusion *852* | *Notes* *853*
Resources for Research *853* | *Review* *855*

- ▶ **READING THE PAST** The Russian People Under Serfdom *835*
- ▶ **SEEING THE PAST** The Korean Flag *844*
- ▶ **LIVES AND LIVELIHOODS** Historians of the Nation-State *846*
- ▶ **READING THE PAST** "Good Wives, Wise Mothers" Build Japan *848*

26

Imperial Order and Disorder, 1850–1914 *856*

Major Global Development ▶ The accelerated competition among nineteenth-century nation-states for empire.

Backstory *857*

Building Empires *860*
- Imperialism: What Is It? *860*
- Takeover in Asia *861*
- Europeans Scramble for Africa *864*
- Japan's Imperial Agenda *868*
- Technology, Environment, and the Imperial Advantage *868*

Imperial Society *869*
- Changing Conditions of Everyday Life *869*
- Medicine, Science, and Well-Being in the Colonies *872*
- Migrants and Diasporas *874*

Culture in an Imperial Age *878*
- The Culture of Everyday Life *878*
- Art and Empire *879*

Imperial Contests at the Dawn of the Twentieth Century *880*
- Clashes for Imperial Control *881*
- Growing Resistance to Foreign Domination *883*

COUNTERPOINT The West Copies from the World *885*
- Changes in the Arts *885*
- Expansion of Ideas *886*
- Lifestyles Transformed *886*

Conclusion *887* | *Notes* *887*
Resources for Research *888* | *Review* *889*

- ▶ **READING THE PAST** Rubber Workers in Congo *871*
- ▶ **SEEING THE PAST** Imperial Architecture in Saigon *872*
- ▶ **LIVES AND LIVELIHOODS** Indentured Laborers *876*
- ▶ **READING THE PAST** The United States Overthrows the Hawaiian Queen *882*

27

Wars, Revolutions, and the Birth of Mass Society, 1910–1929 *890*

Major Global Development ▶ The wars of the decade 1910 to 1920 and their role in the creation of mass culture and society.

Backstory *891*

Revolutions, Local Wars, and World War *894*
- Revolutionaries and Warriors: Mexico, China, and the Balkans *894*
- Fighting World War I *896*
- Civilians at War: The Home Front *900*

Revolution in Russia and the End of World War I *902*
- Revolution in Russia *902*
- Ending the War: 1918 *904*

Postwar Global Politics *905*
- The Paris Peace Conference, 1919–1920 *905*
- Struggles for Reform and Independence *908*
- Postwar Imperial Expansion *912*

An Age of the Masses *913*
- Mass Society *913*
- Culture for the Masses *914*
- Mobilizing the Masses *916*

COUNTERPOINT A Golden Age for Argentineans *919*
- A Flourishing Economy and Society *919*
- Argentina's Cultural Riches *920*

Conclusion *920* | ***Notes*** *921*
Resources for Research *922* | ***Review*** *923*

- ▶ **SEEING THE PAST** Wartime Propaganda *901*
- ▶ **READING THE PAST** Communism Spreads in China *911*
- ▶ **READING THE PAST** Léopold Sédar Senghor, "To the Senegalese Soldiers Who Died for France" *912*
- ▶ **LIVES AND LIVELIHOODS** The Film Industry *916*

28

Global Catastrophe: The Great Depression and World War II, 1929–1945 *924*

Major Global Development ▶ The causes and outcomes of the Great Depression and World War II.

Backstory *925*

1929: The Great Depression Begins *928*
- Economic Disaster Strikes *928*
- Social Effects of the Great Depression *930*
- Protesting Poverty *931*

Militarizing the Masses in the 1930s *932*
- The Rise of Stalinism *933*
- Japanese Expansionism *935*
- Hitler's Rise to Power *936*
- Democracies Mobilize *938*

Global War, 1937–1945 *939*
- Europe's Road to War *940*
- The Early Years of the War, 1937–1943 *940*
- War and the World's Civilians *945*

From Allied Victory to the Cold War, 1943–1945 *950*
- The Axis Defeated *950*
- Postwar Plans and Uncertainties *951*

COUNTERPOINT Nonviolence and Pacifism in an Age of War *953*
- Traditional Tactics: The Example of Nigerian Women *953*
- Gandhi and Civil Disobedience *953*

Conclusion *954* | ***Notes*** *955*
Resources for Research *955* | ***Review*** *957*

- ▶ **READING THE PAST** Promoting Business in the Great Depression *930*
- ▶ **READING THE PAST** "Comfort Women" in World War II *942*
- ▶ **LIVES AND LIVELIHOODS** Soldiers and Soldiering *946*
- ▶ **SEEING THE PAST** Technological Warfare: Civilization or Barbarism? *952*

29

The Emergence of New Nations in a Cold War World, 1945–1970 *958*

Major Global Development ▶ The political transformations of the postwar world and their social and cultural consequences.

Backstory *959*

World Politics and the Cold War *962*
- The New Superpowers *962*
- The Cold War Unfolds, 1945–1962 *963*
- The People's Republic of China, 1949 *965*
- Proxy Wars and Cold War Alliances *965*

Decolonization and the Birth of Nations *969*
- The End of Empire in Asia *970*
- The Struggle for Independence in the Middle East *972*
- New Nations in Africa *973*

World Recovery in the 1950s and 1960s *975*
- Expanding Economic Prosperity *976*
- Building and Rebuilding Communism *978*

Cultural Dynamism amid Cold War *980*
- Confronting the Heritage of World War *980*
- Liberation Culture *981*
- The Culture of Cold War *982*

COUNTERPOINT The Bandung Conference, 1955 *983*
- Shared Goals *984*
- Divisive Issues *985*

Conclusion *985* | *Notes* *985*
Resources for Research *986* | *Review* *987*

- ▶ **LIVES AND LIVELIHOODS** Cosmonauts and Astronauts *966*
- ▶ **SEEING THE PAST** African Liberation on Cloth *975*
- ▶ **READING THE PAST** The Great Leap Forward in China *978*

30

Technological Transformation and the End of Cold War, 1960–1992 *988*

Major Global Development ▶ The technological revolution of the late twentieth century and its impact on societies and political developments around the world.

Backstory *989*

Advances in Technology and Science *992*
- The Information Revolution *992*
- The Space Age *994*
- A New Scientific Revolution *995*

Changes in the World Economy *996*
- The Rising Pacific Economy *996*
- Multinational Corporations *998*
- Global Changes in Work *998*
- The Knowledge Economy *1000*
- Postindustrial Family Life *1002*

Politics and Protest in an Age of Cold War *1003*
- Democracy and Dictatorship in Latin America *1003*
- Domestic Revolution and a Changing International Order *1006*
- Activists Challenge the Superpowers *1009*

The End of the Cold War Order *1012*
- A Shifting Balance of Global Power *1012*
- A Change of Course in the West *1014*
- The Collapse of Communism in the Soviet Bloc *1014*

COUNTERPOINT Agrarian Peoples in a Technological Age *1017*
- Local Farmers Against Multinational Corporations *1018*
- Government Measures to Protect Farmers *1018*

Conclusion *1019* | *Notes* *1019*
Resources for Research *1020* | *Review* *1021*

- ▶ **READING THE PAST** Japan Transforms Business Practices *999*
- ▶ **LIVES AND LIVELIHOODS** Global Tourism *1000*
- ▶ **READING THE PAST** Terror and Resistance in El Salvador *1006*
- ▶ **SEEING THE PAST** The Iranian Revolution as Visual News *1010*

31

A New Global Age, 1989 to the Present *1022*

Major Global Development ▶ The causes and consequences of intensified globalization.

Backstory *1023*

The Impact of Global Events on Regions and Nations *1026*
- North Versus South *1026*
- Advancing Nations in the Global Age *1027*

Global Livelihoods and Institutions *1031*
- Global Networks and Changing Jobs *1032*
- Neoliberalism and the Global Economy *1033*
- Beyond the Nation-State *1033*
- Global Cities *1036*

The Promises and Perils of Globalization *1037*
- Environmental Challenges *1038*
- Population Pressures and Public Health *1040*
- Worldwide Migration *1044*
- Terrorism Confronts the World *1045*
- Global Economic Crisis *1047*

Cultures Without Borders *1048*
- The Quest for Human Rights *1048*
- Religion Worldwide *1048*
- Global Literature and Music *1049*

COUNTERPOINT Who Am I? Local Identity in a Globalizing World *1052*
- Ethnic Strife and New Nations *1052*
- Movements to Protect Tradition *1052*

Conclusion *1053* | ***Notes*** *1054*
Resources for Research *1054* | ***Review*** *1056*

- ▶ **READING THE PAST** Testimony to South Africa's Truth and Reconciliation Commission *1030*
- ▶ **READING THE PAST** Assessing Livelihoods for Women in a Global Economy *1035*
- ▶ **SEEING THE PAST** The Globalization of Urban Space *1037*
- ▶ **LIVES AND LIVELIHOODS** Readers of the Qur'an *1050*

Index *I-1*

MAPS

Chapter 23

Mapping the World Wars and Revolutions in the Atlantic World, 1750–1830 *760*
Spot Map Pugachev Uprising in Russia, 1773 *767*
Map 23.1 Colonial Crisis and Revolution in North America, 1754–1789 *769*
Map 23.2 Napoleonic Europe, 1796–1815 *775*
Map 23.3 Haitian Rebellion and Independence, 1791–1804 *778*
Map 23.4 Revolutions in Latin America, 1810–1830 *780*
Spot Map Arabia, 1802–1807 *786*

Chapter 24

Mapping the World The Spread of Industrialization *792*
Map 24.1 Industrialization in Europe, c. 1900 *795*
Map 24.2 The Spread of Railroads, c. 1900 *799*
Spot Map Industrializing Japan, c. 1870–1900 *804*
Map 24.3 Qing China, 1830–1911 *808*
Spot Map Industrializing India, c. 1857–1900 *810*
Map 24.4 Africa, 1750–1880 *811*

Chapter 25

Mapping the World Nation-States, c. 1880 *826*
Map 25.1 Latin America, c. 1900 *830*
Map 25.2 The Crimean War and Postwar Settlement, 1853–1856 *833*
Spot Map Unification of Italy, 1859–1870 *837*
Spot Map Unification of Germany, 1866–1871 *838*
Map 25.3 U.S. Civil War and Westward Expansion *839*
Map 25.4 Japan, c. 1860–1889 *842*

Chapter 26

Mapping the World The Spread of Imperialism, 1850–1914 *858*
Map 26.1 Imperial Division of Asia, c. 1850–1900 *862*
Spot Map Modernization Projects in Egypt *864*
Map 26.2 Imperial Division of Africa, c. 1880–1914 *866*
Spot Map The Sino-Japanese War, 1894 *868*
Map 26.3 Global Migration, c. 1800–1910 *874–875*
Spot Map The Spanish-American War, 1898 *881*
Map 26.4 Imperialism in the Pacific, c. 1840–1914 *883*

Chapter 27

Mapping the World Wars and Revolutions, 1910–1929 *892*
Spot Map The Mexican Revolution, 1910–1911 *895*
Map 27.1 World War I in Europe and the Middle East, 1914–1918 *898*
Map 27.2 The Peace of Paris in Central and Eastern Europe, 1920 *906*
Map 27.3 The Mandate System in Africa and the Middle East, 1924 *907*
Map 27.4 Turkey Under Mustafa Kemal, 1923 *909*
Spot Map Japanese-occupied Territories in China, 1918–1922 *910*
Spot Map Ireland, 1921 *910*
Spot Map Argentina, c. 1920 *919*

Chapter 28

Mapping the World World War II, 1937–1945 *926*
Map 28.1 Japanese Expansion, 1931–1942 *935*
Spot Map Italian Invasion of Ethiopia, 1935–1936 *940*
Map 28.2 Nazi Expansion, 1933–1939 *941*
Map 28.3 World War II in Europe, North Africa, and the Soviet Union, 1939–1945 *943*
Map 28.4 World War II in the Pacific, 1937–1945 *944*
Spot Map Major Concentration Camps and Extermination Sites in Europe *945*

Chapter 29

Mapping the World Independence Movements and New Nations *960*
Map 29.1 Divided Germany *965*
Map 29.2 Regional Alliances, 1948–1955 *968*
Map 29.3 Partition of India, 1947 *970*
Map 29.4 New States of Southeast Asia, 1945–1999 *971*
Spot Map The Arab-Israeli War of 1948–1949 *972*
Map 29.5 New States in Africa and the Middle East, 1945–2011 *974*

Chapter 30

Mapping the World OPEC, Pacific Tigers, and World Migration *990*
Map 30.1 The Pacific Tigers, c. 1960–1995 *997*
Map 30.2 South and Central America, 1960–1992 *1004*
Spot Map The United States and the Vietnam War, c. 1968–1975 *1008*
Spot Map The Soviet War in Afghanistan, 1979–1989 *1009*
Map 30.3 The Middle East, 1967–1990 *1013*
Spot Map Solidarity Protests in Poland, 1981–1983 *1015*
Map 30.4 Post–Cold War Eastern Europe and Central Asia, c. 1990 *1017*

Chapter 31

Mapping the World A New Global Age *1024*
Spot Map Conflict and Genocide in Sub-Saharan Africa *1027*
Map 31.1 South Africa After Apartheid *1031*
Spot Map Mercosur, 2011 *1036*
Map 31.2 The Global Environment of the Early Twenty-First Century *1039*
Map 31.3 The World's Peoples, c. 2010 *1042–1043*
Map 31.4 Wars in Afghanistan and Iraq, 2001–2011 *1046*
Spot Map Arab Spring, 2010–2011 *1047*

SPECIAL FEATURES

Lives and Livelihoods

The Cowboy Way of Life *782*
Builders of the Trans-Siberian Railroad *800*
Historians of the Nation-State *846*
Indentured Laborers *876*
The Film Industry *916*
Soldiers and Soldiering *946*
Cosmonauts and Astronauts *966*
Global Tourism *1000*
Readers of the Qur'an *1050*

Reading the Past

Simon Bolivar on Latin American Independence *784*
Phillis Wheatley, "On Being Brought from Africa to America" *786*
Industry Comes to the British Countryside *797*
Mexican Women on Strike *816*
The Russian People Under Serfdom *835*
"Good Wives, Wise Mothers" Build Japan *848*
Rubber Workers in Congo *871*
The United States Overthrows the Hawaiian Queen *882*
Communism Spreads in China *911*
Léopold Sédar Senghor, "To the Senegalese Soldiers Who Died for France" *912*
Promoting Business in the Great Depression *930*
"Comfort Women" in World War II *942*
The Great Leap Forward in China *978*
Japan Transforms Business Practices *999*
Terror and Resistance in El Salvador *1006*
Testimony to South Africa's Truth and Reconciliation Commission *1030*
Assessing Livelihoods for Women in a Global Economy *1035*

Seeing the Past

Portrait of Catherine the Great *766*
Japan's Industrious Society *803*
The Korean Flag *844*
Imperial Architecture in Saigon *872*
Wartime Propaganda *901*
Technological Warfare: Civilization or Barbarism? *952*
African Liberation on Cloth *975*
The Iranian Revolution as Visual News *1010*
The Globalization of Urban Space *1037*

ACKNOWLEDGMENTS

Writing *Crossroads and Cultures* has made real to us the theme of this book, which is connections among many far-flung people of diverse livelihoods and talents. From the first draft to the last, the authors have benefited from repeated critical readings by many talented scholars and teachers who represent an array of schools and historical interests. Our sincere thanks go to the following instructors, who helped us keep true to our vision of showing connections among the world's people and whose comments often challenged us to rethink or justify our interpretations. Crucial to the integrity of the book, they always provided a check on accuracy down to the smallest detail.

Alemseged Abbay, *Frostburg State University*
Heather J. Abdelnur, *Augusta State University*
Wayne Ackerson, *Salisbury University*
Kathleen Addison, *California State University, Northridge*
Jeffrey W. Alexander, *University of Wisconsin–Parkside*
Omar H. Ali, *The University of North Carolina at Greensboro*
Monty Armstrong, *Cerritos High School*
Pierre Asselin, *Hawai'i Pacific University*
Eva Baham, *Southern University at Baton Rouge*
William Bakken, *Rochester Community and Technical College*
Thomas William Barker, *The University of Kansas*
Thomas William Barton, *University of San Diego*
Robert Blackey, *California State University, San Bernardino*
Chuck Bolton, *The University of North Carolina at Greensboro*
Robert Bond, *San Diego Mesa College*
James W. Brodman, *University of Central Arkansas*
Gayle K. Brunelle, *California State University, Fullerton*
Samuel Brunk, *The University of Texas at El Paso*
Jurgen Buchenau, *The University of North Carolina at Charlotte*
Clea Bunch, *University of Arkansas at Little Rock*
Kathy Callahan, *Murray State University*
John M. Carroll, *The University of Hong Kong*
Giancarlo Casale, *University of Minnesota*
Mark Chavalas, *University of Wisconsin–La Crosse*
Yinghong Cheng, *Delaware State University*
Mark Choate, *Brigham Young University*
Sharon Cohen, *Springbrook High School*
Christine Colin, *Mercyhurst College*
Eleanor Congdon, *Youngstown State University*
Dale Crandall-Bear, *Solano Community College*
John Curry, *University of Nevada, Las Vegas*
Michelle Danberg-Marshman, *Green River Community College*
Francis Danquah, *Southern University at Baton Rouge*
Sherrie Dux-Ideus, *Central Community College*
Peter Dykema, *Arkansas Tech University*
Tom Ewing, *Virginia Polytechnic Institute and State University*
Angela Feres, *Grossmont College*
Michael Fischbach, *Randolph-Macon College*
Nancy Fitch, *California State University, Fullerton*
Terence Anthony Fleming, *Northern Kentucky University*
Richard Fogarty, *University at Albany, The State University of New York*
Nicola Foote, *Florida Gulf Coast University*
Deanna Forsman, *North Hennepin Community College*
John D. Garrigus, *The University of Texas at Arlington*
Trevor Getz, *San Francisco State University*
David Goldfrank, *Georgetown University*
Charles Didier Gondola, *Indiana University–Purdue University Indianapolis*
Sue Gronewold, *Kean University*
Christopher Guthrie, *Tarleton State University*
Anne Hardgrove, *The University of Texas at San Antonio*
Donald J. Harreld, *Brigham Young University*
Todd Hartch, *Eastern Kentucky University*
Janine Hartman, *University of Cincinnati*
Daniel Heimmermann, *The University of Texas at Brownsville*
Cecily M. Heisser, *University of San Diego*
Timothy Henderson, *Auburn University at Montgomery*
Ted Henken, *Baruch College, The State University of New York*
Marilynn J. Hitchens, *University of Colorado Denver*
Roy W. Hopper, *University of Memphis*
Timothy Howe, *St. Olaf College*
Delridge Hunter, *Medgar Evers College, The City University of New York*
Bruce Ingram, *Itawamba Community College*
Erik N. Jensen, *Miami University*
Steven Sandor John, *Hunter College, The City University of New York*
Deborah Johnston, *Lakeside School*
David M. Kalivas, *Middlesex Community College*
Carol Keller, *San Antonio College*
Ian Stuart Kelly, *Palomar College*
Linda Kerr, *University of Alberta*
Charles King, *University of Nebraska at Omaha*
Melinda Cole Klein, *Saddleback College*
Ane Lintvedt-Dulac, *McDonogh School*
Ann Livschiz, *Indiana University–Purdue University Fort Wayne*
George E. Longenecker, *Vermont Technical College*
Edward Lykens, *Middle Tennessee State University*
Susan Maneck, *Jackson State University*
Chandra Manning, *Georgetown University*
Michael Marino, *The College of New Jersey*

Thomas Massey, *Cape Fear Community College*
Mary Jane Maxwell, *Green Mountain College*
Christine McCann, *Norwich University*
Patrick McDevitt, *University at Buffalo, The State University of New York*
Ian F. McNeely, *University of Oregon*
M. E. Menninger, *Texas State University–San Marcos*
Kathryn E. Meyer, *Washington State University*
Elizabeth Mizrahi, *Santa Barbara City College*
Max Okenfuss, *Washington University in St. Louis*
Kenneth Orosz, *Buffalo State College, The State University of New York*
Annette Palmer, *Morgan State University*
David Perry, *Dominican University*
Jared Poley, *Georgia State University*
Elizabeth Ann Pollard, *San Diego State University*
Dana Rabin, *University of Illinois at Urbana-Champaign*
Norman G. Raiford, *Greenville Technical College*
Stephen Rapp, *Universität Bern*
Michele Reid, *Georgia State University*
Chad Ross, *East Carolina University*
Morris Rossabi, *Queens College, The City University of New York*
Steven C. Rubert, *Oregon State University*
Eli Rubin, *Western Michigan University*
Anthony Santoro, *Christopher Newport University*
Linda B. Scherr, *Mercer County Community College*
Hollie Schillig, *California State University, Long Beach*
Michael Seth, *James Madison University*
Jessica Sheetz-Nguyen, *University of Central Oklahoma*
Rose Mary Sheldon, *Virginia Military Institute*
David R. Smith, *California State Polytechnic University, Pomona*
Ramya Sreenivasan, *University at Buffalo, The State University of New York*
John Stavens, *Bristol Eastern High School*
Catherine Howey Stearn, *Eastern Kentucky University*
Richard Steigmann-Gall, *Kent State University*
Anthony J. Steinhoff, *The University of Tennessee at Chattanooga*
Stephen J. Stillwell, *The University of Arizona*
Heather Streets, *Washington State University*
Jean Stuntz, *West Texas A&M University*
Guy Thompson, *University of Alberta*
Hunt Tooley, *Austin College*
Wendy Turner, *Augusta State University*
Rick Warner, *Wabash College*
Michael Weber, *Gettysburg College*
Theodore Weeks, *Southern Illinois University*
Guy Wells, *Lorain County Community College*
Sherri West, *Brookdale Community College*
Kenneth Wilburn, *East Carolina University*
Pingchao Zhu, *University of Idaho*
Alexander Zukas, *National University*

Many colleagues, friends, and family members have helped us develop this work as well. Bonnie Smith wishes to thank in particular Michal Shapira and Molly Giblin for their research assistance and Patrick Smith, who gave helpful information on contemporary world religions. Her colleagues at Rutgers, many of them pioneers in world history, were especially helpful. Among these, expert historian Donald R. Kelley shaped certain features of the last section of the book and always cheered the author on. Marc Van De Mieroop thanks the friends and colleagues who often unknowingly provided insights and information used in this book, especially Irene Bloom, William Harris, Feng Li, Indira Peterson, Michael Sommer, and Romila Thapar. Richard von Glahn thanks his many colleagues at UCLA who have shaped his thinking about world history, especially Ghislaine Lydon, Jose Moya, Ron Mellor, Sanjay Subrahmanyam, and Bin Wong. He is also grateful for the exposure to pathbreaking scholarship on world history afforded by the University of California's Multi-Campus Research Unit in World History. Kris Lane thanks the many wonderful William & Mary students of History 192, "The World Since 1450," as well as colleagues Abdul-Karim Rafeq, Scott Nelson, Chitralekha Zutshi, Hiroshi Kitamura, Philip Daileader, Chandos Brown, and Ron Schechter. All offered valuable advice on framing the early modern period. He also owes a huge debt to the University of Minnesota for graduate training and teaching assistant experience in this field.

We also wish to acknowledge and thank the publishing team at Bedford/St. Martin's, who are among the most talented people in publishing that we as a group have ever worked with and who did so much to bring this book into being. Among them, our special thanks go to former publisher for history Patricia A. Rossi, who inspired the conceptual design of the book and helped bring us together. The current publisher for history, Mary Dougherty, then picked up the reins from Tisha and advanced the project, using her special combination of professional expertise and personal warmth. It is hard to convey sufficiently our heartfelt appreciation to president Joan E. Feinberg and editorial director Denise Wydra. They always kept us alert to Bedford's special legacy of high-quality textbooks, a legacy based on the benefits a book must have for students and teachers alike. We aimed to be part of that legacy while writing *Crossroads and Cultures.*

President emeritus and founder Charles Christensen was also present at the beginning of this project, and he always cheerfully lent his extraordinary knowledge of publishing to the making and actual production of this book. We know that it would have been less than it is without his wisdom. Alongside all these others, director of development for history Jane Knetzger patiently and skillfully guided the development process, during which each chapter (and sentence) was poked and prodded. We thank Jane for being such a quiet force behind the progress of *Crossroads and*

Cultures. Special thanks go to senior editor and expert facilitator Heidi Hood and the editorial assistants who joined Heidi in providing invaluable help on many essential tasks: Lynn Sternberger, Jennifer Jovin, and Emily DiPietro. All of them moved the project along in myriad ways that we hardly know. We also appreciate the countless schedules, tasks, and layouts juggled so efficiently and well by senior production editor Anne Noonan. On the editorial team were John Reisbord and Daniel Otis, who helped edit and polish our final draft. All along the way Rose Corbett Gordon and Charlotte Miller, our superb photo researcher and talented map editor, respectively, provided us with striking and thought-provoking images and up-to-date, richly informative, and gorgeous maps. No author team could ask for more than to have the book's content laid out in such a clear and attractive design as that provided by Jerilyn Bockorick, with assistance from senior art director Anna Palchik. Jerilyn's special attention to the overall look of our work makes us feel that we and our readers are especially lucky. Senior designer Billy Boardman created our six beautiful covers with help from senior art director Donna Dennison. We are grateful for their craft in building the book's appeal.

Crossroads and Cultures has a wealth of materials for students and teachers to help support the text. Editor Annette Fantasia has guided our creation of the sourcebook that accompanies the main book, and we could hardly have achieved this task without her help; she also edited the instructor's resource manual. The work of associate editor Jack Cashman, who supervised the development of the other elements in our impressive array of supplements, will be appreciated by all teachers and students who use these materials. Jenna Bookin Barry, senior executive marketing manager; Sally Constable, senior market development manager; and Katherine Bates, market development manager, have worked tirelessly at our side to ensure that the book is in the best shape to meet the needs of students and teachers. We are deeply grateful for all the work they have done in the past and all that they will do in so sincerely advocating for the success of *Crossroads and Cultures* in today's classrooms.

Among the authors' greatest *Crossroads* experiences has been our relationship with brilliant executive editor Elizabeth M. Welch and her support team of ace development editors Sylvia Mallory, Margaret Manos, and Jim Strandberg. Beth has guided many a successful book from inception to completion—all to the benefit of tens of thousands of students and their instructors. We thank her for bringing us her historical, conceptual, visual, and publishing talent, all of which she has offered with such generosity of spirit, good humor, and grace. It has been a privilege for all of us to work with Beth and to have spent these *Crossroads* years with the entire Bedford team.

Finally, our students' questions and concerns have shaped much of this work, and we welcome all our readers' suggestions, queries, and criticisms. We know that readers, like our own students, excel in spotting unintended glitches and also in providing much excellent food for thought. Please contact us with your comments at our respective institutions.

Bonnie G. Smith
Marc Van De Mieroop
Richard von Glahn
Kris Lane

PART 4

The World

from 1750 to the Present

CH 23

MANY OF THE TRENDS of the early modern period continued after 1750. Global connections continued to intensify, and science and technology advanced at an ever-faster pace. As part of their growing competition for land, natural resources, and the control of populations, governments armed themselves with more destructive weaponry. As technology developed, the variety of livelihoods expanded across the globe, and many people enjoyed the opportunity to purchase an array of consumer products. The accelerating rate of change in technology, population growth, consumerism, and the introduction of new livelihoods and forms of government marks the shift from early modern times to what historians call the late modern era, the period from about 1750 to the present.

The great empires of the early modern period—the Qing, Mughal, Ottoman, and Spanish—faced challenges as the modern period opened. Many of these challenges arose from the inroads outsiders made on their rule, but these empires also faced problems within their borders, such as the enormous costs of military supremacy. Religious dissent, natural disasters, and the social changes that accompanied modernity also undermined their security. Newly wealthy or ambitious people and those wanting more modern forms of government contested the power of traditional rulers. The Qing, Mughal, Ottoman, and Spanish empires would all disappear in the late modern period.

CH 24

CH 25

Lives and livelihoods were transformed as mechanical power came to substitute for human power in the Industrial Revolution, which began in around 1750 in western Europe and spread throughout the globe. Newly created factory work moved production out of the home to mechanized workplaces, and a variety of other new occupations connected with the rise of industry developed, such as railroad builders, engineers, and conductors, and later, flight

CHAPTERS IN THIS PART ▼

23 Atlantic Revolutions and the World, 1750–1830

24 Industry and Everyday Life, 1750–1900

25 The Rise of Modern Nation-States, 1850–1900

26 Imperial Order and Disorder, 1850–1914

27 Wars, Revolutions, and the Birth of Mass Society, 1910–1929

28 Global Catastrophe: The Great Depression and World War II, 1929–1945

29 The Emergence of New Nations in a Cold War World, 1945–1970

30 Technological Transformation and the End of Cold War, 1960–1992

31 A New Global Age, 1989 to the Present

CH 26

attendants and workers in airplane plants. With the proliferation of science and technology, entirely new service work, in reproductive technology and systems analysis, for example, continued to transform work life. Nonetheless, agriculture remained a primary form of work for the vast majority of people until well into the twentieth century. That livelihood, too, was affected by farm machinery, the development of chemical fertilizers, and ultimately what was called in the late twentieth century a "green revolution" based on seeds and plants designed to flourish in particular parts of the world.

Modern industry did not displace older ways of doing things all at once. Slavery in fact gave a crucial boost to industrial growth by providing raw materials and food for industrial workers. Although a declining labor system, slavery has remained a livelihood down to the present. Women in the workforce often held the worst jobs and were paid less than men even for equivalent tasks.

CH 27

Emboldened by new wealth and industrial technology, a cluster of European states, eventually joined by Japan and the United States, built cohesive, effective governments with modern military capabilities and mass armies. During this period, most of them developed constitutional governments based on the rule of law and the explicit elaboration of the rights of citizens. Constitutional government and legal rights were often gained through revolutions or other dramatic changes in rulership, but these states were backed by unified citizens. As dignified citizens, rather than servile subjects of kings, many felt empowered to join the commercial and industrial innovation that was going on around them. Historians characterize such states as "nation-states." As they became stronger because of their citizen support, the rising nation-states sought to extend their power through what is known as the "new imperialism." Unlike the expansionists of the early modern period, new imperialists had the "tools of empire" to take over the institutions

CH 28

CH 29

and economies of other parts of the world more completely. Late modernity saw the imperial nations try to dominate Africa, Asia, and other parts of the world both economically and politically in the nineteenth century.

Imperial countries justified their rule by celebrating the modern ideas and institutions they would bring to the world's "backward" peoples. Local peoples both resisted and cooperated with the imperialists; some grew incredibly wealthy from trade, manufacturing, and governmental work. However, imperialism also brought devastation and death because of exploitation and outright violence. Imperialism nonetheless developed global networks of unprecedented density, as steamships, telegraphs, and other forms of communications technology circled the earth at a faster pace than ever before.

Competition and conflict among these imperial nations intensified, as did organized resistance to their rule. In the twentieth century the imperial powers waged two horrific wars—World Wars I and II—in the course of which tens of millions of people died. Eventually, colonial people took advantage of the war-weakened imperialists, winning their freedom and setting up independent states after World War II ended in 1945. The rest of the twentieth century down to the present has been a story of these nation-states expanding their capacities and livelihoods and asserting their place in the modern world.

Our most recent modern history is filled with the struggles involved in asserting this independence, first under the conditions of the Cold War between the Soviet Union and United States that followed World War II, and then during the period of U.S. dominance after

CH 30

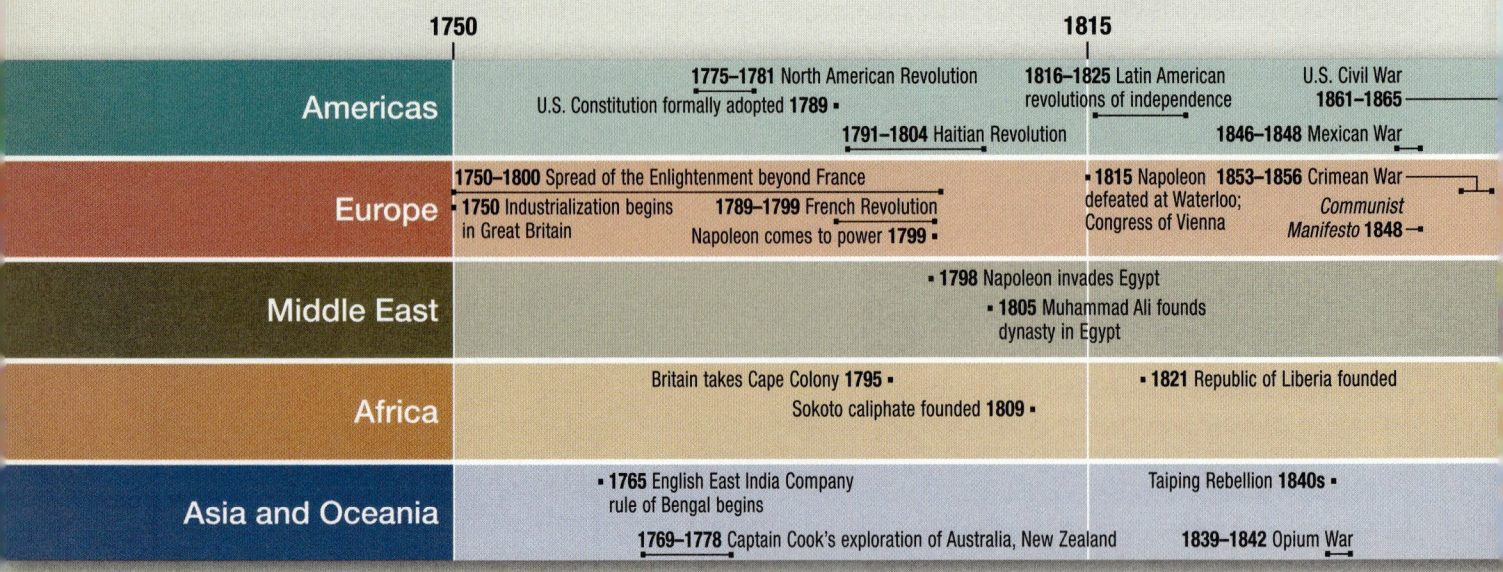

1989. Genocide, civil war, poverty, and an unprecedented migration of peoples globally have characterized human life in the past few decades. Terrorism, the pollution of the earth's atmosphere, and the spread of deadly diseases are also part of our most recent modernity.

Nonetheless, the world's peoples have simultaneously attempted to create new forms of world governance to eliminate the worst abuses of modern life. Writers and artists have innovatively explored modernity's difficulties. Historians and philosophers have also analyzed the consequences of growing military power on the one hand and life-enhancing developments such as medical breakthroughs and the communications revolution on the other. There is no alternative, many of these thinkers believe, to deliberate study of the past as the basis for informed decision-making in our world today.

CH 31

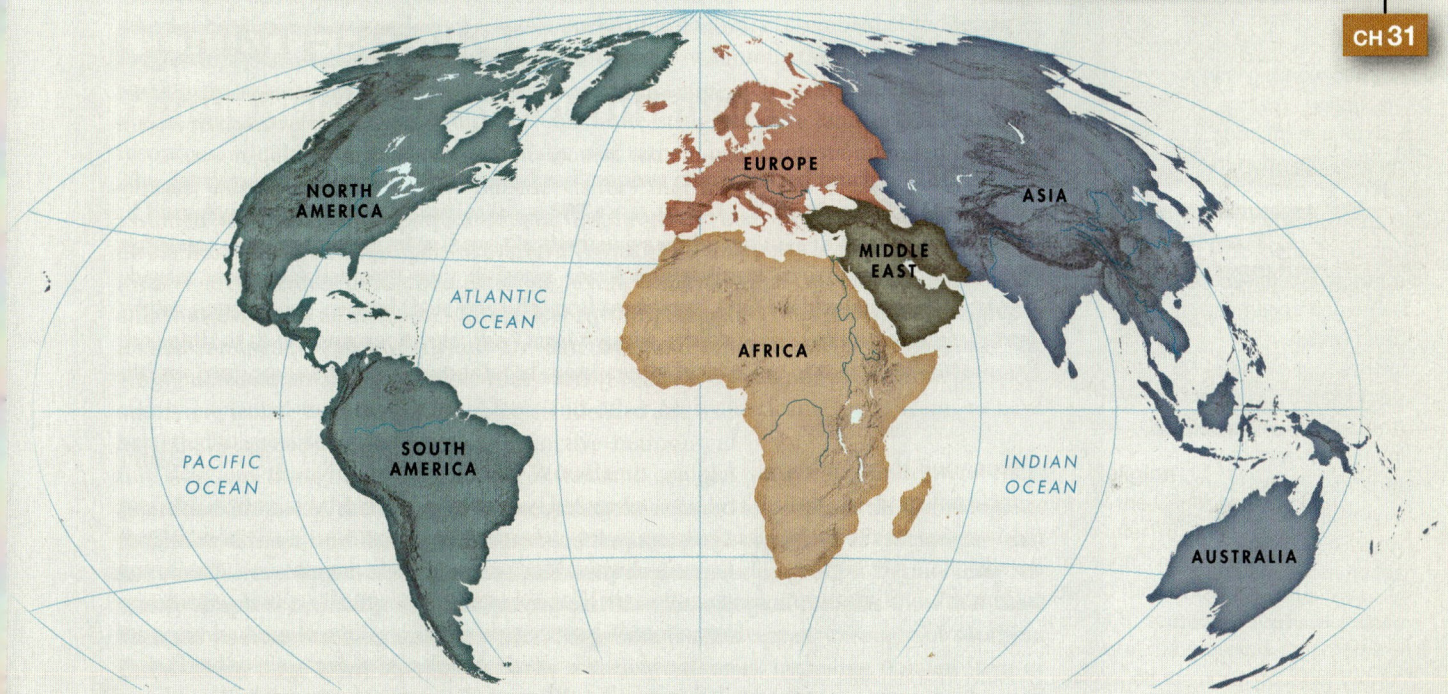

1880 | **1945** | **2010**

1880–1940 Immigration from Europe surges
Spanish-American War **1898** ▪
1910–1920 Mexican Revolution
▪ **1917** United States enters World War I
▪ **1929** U.S. stock market crash sparks the Great Depression
The Feminine Mystique **1963** ▪
▪ **1969** U.S. astronauts land on moon
1945–1989 Cold War
NAFTA enacted **1994** ▪
2007–2008 Global economic crisis unfolds
▪ **2001** Terrorists attack the United States

1861 Emancipation of the serfs in Russia
1880–1900 Impressionism flourishes
1891–1904 Construction of trans-Siberian railroad
1914–1918 World War I
1917–1918 Russian Revolution
▪ **1930s** Welfare state begins in Sweden
1939–1945 World War II in Europe
▪ **1952** Discovery of structure of DNA
▪ **1960** Introduction of birth–control pill
▪ **1967** EEC established
▪ **1990s** New European nations emerge in wake of Soviet collapse

1869 Suez Canal completed
Young Turks' uprising **1908** ▪
▪ **1918** Breakup of Ottoman Empire
1922–1938 Mustafa Kemal modernizes Turkey
▪ **1948** Founding of Israel
Creation of OPEC **1960** ▪
Yom Kippur War **1973** ▪
1980–1988 Iran-Iraq War
1978–1979 Revolution in Iran
Start of Arab Spring uprisings **2010** ▪
▪ **2003** United States invades Iraq

1867 End of Atlantic slave trade
1870–1914 New imperialism in Africa
1884–1885 Berlin Conference on Africa
Ghana gains independence **1959** ▪
▪ **1962** Algeria wins independence
1948–1989 Apartheid in South Africa
Republic of South Sudan founded **2011** ▪

1868 Meiji Restoration
1870–1914 New imperialism in Asia
1894– 1895 Sino-Japanese War
1904–1905 Russo-Japanese War
Gandhi's Salt March **1930** ▪
1937–1945 World War II in the Pacific
▪ **1947** India and Pakistan win independence
1950–1953 Korean War
1954–1975 Vietnam War
1966–1976 Cultural Revolution
▪ **1992** Beginning of socialist market economy in China

23

AT A CROSSROADS

Simon Bolivar traveled the Atlantic world, gaining inspiration from the Enlightenment and revolutionary currents he felt firsthand in Spain, France, the United States, and the Caribbean. On his return to South America, he helped spearhead the movement for independence there. No democrat, Bolivar learned from hard experience that in an independent South America, the rich variety of slaves and other workers would need to be accommodated. (The Art Archive/Museo Historico Nacional Buenos Aires/Gianni Dagli Orti.)

Atlantic Revolutions and the World

1750–1830

Simon Bolivar (1783–1830) began life as the privileged son of a family that in the sixteenth century had settled in Caracas, a city in Spanish-controlled South America (now the capital of Venezuela). His early years were full of personal loss: his father died when he was three, his mother when he was five, and his grandfather, who cared for him after his mother's death, when he was six. Bolivar's extended family sent him to military school and then to Spain to study—typical training for prominent "creoles," as South Americans of European descent were called. Following the death of his young wife, he traveled to Paris to overcome his grief. There Bolivar's life changed: he saw the military hero Napoleon crown himself emperor in 1804 and witnessed crowds of patriotic French fill the streets of the capital with joy. "That moment, I tell you, made me think of the slavery of my country and of the glory that would come to the person who liberated it," he later wrote.[1] After a visit to the newly independent United States, Bolivar returned to his home in 1807, inspired by all he had seen, and determined to reform his homeland by freeing it from the oppressions of Spanish rule. He, too, took up arms, leading military campaigns, which along with popular uprisings eventually ousted Spain's government from much of Latin America. For his revolutionary leadership, contemporaries gave him the title "Liberator."

The creation of independent states in Latin America challenged centuries-old empires and was part of a powerful upheaval in the Atlantic world. North American colonists rebelled against Britain in 1776 and, with the help of the French and Spanish, successfully fought a war of independence, kindling other fires of liberty in the Atlantic world. The French rose up in 1789 against a monarchy that had bankrupted itself, ironically in part by giving military support to the American rebels. In 1791 a massive slave revolt erupted in the prosperous French sugar colony of Saint-Domingue, leading to the creation of the

The Promise of Enlightenment

FOCUS What were the major ideas of the Enlightenment and their impacts?

Revolution in North America

FOCUS What factors lay behind the war between North American colonists and Great Britain?

The French Revolution and the Napoleonic Empire

FOCUS What changes emerged from the French Revolution and Napoleon's reign?

Revolution Continued in the Western Hemisphere

FOCUS What were the motives and methods of revolutionaries in the Caribbean and Latin America?

COUNTERPOINT: Religious Revival in a Secular Age

FOCUS What trends in Enlightenment and revolutionary society did religious revival challenge?

BACKSTORY

Rising global trade and maturing slave systems brought wealth to merchants and landowners in many parts of the world during the seventeenth and eighteenth centuries. Emboldened by this newfound wealth, they joined bureaucrats and aristocrats in the struggle for more influence, not only in the great land-based empires such as the Qing, Mughal, and Ottoman states but also in some of the small states of Europe. These small European states had developed overseas empires, which after several centuries they hoped to exploit more efficiently. They had also built their military capability and gained administrative experience as they fought one another for greater global influence. Maintaining this influence was costly, however. Simultaneously the Scientific Revolution (see Chapter 20) and the beginnings of a movement to think more rationally about government were causing some critics in Europe to question the traditional political and social order.

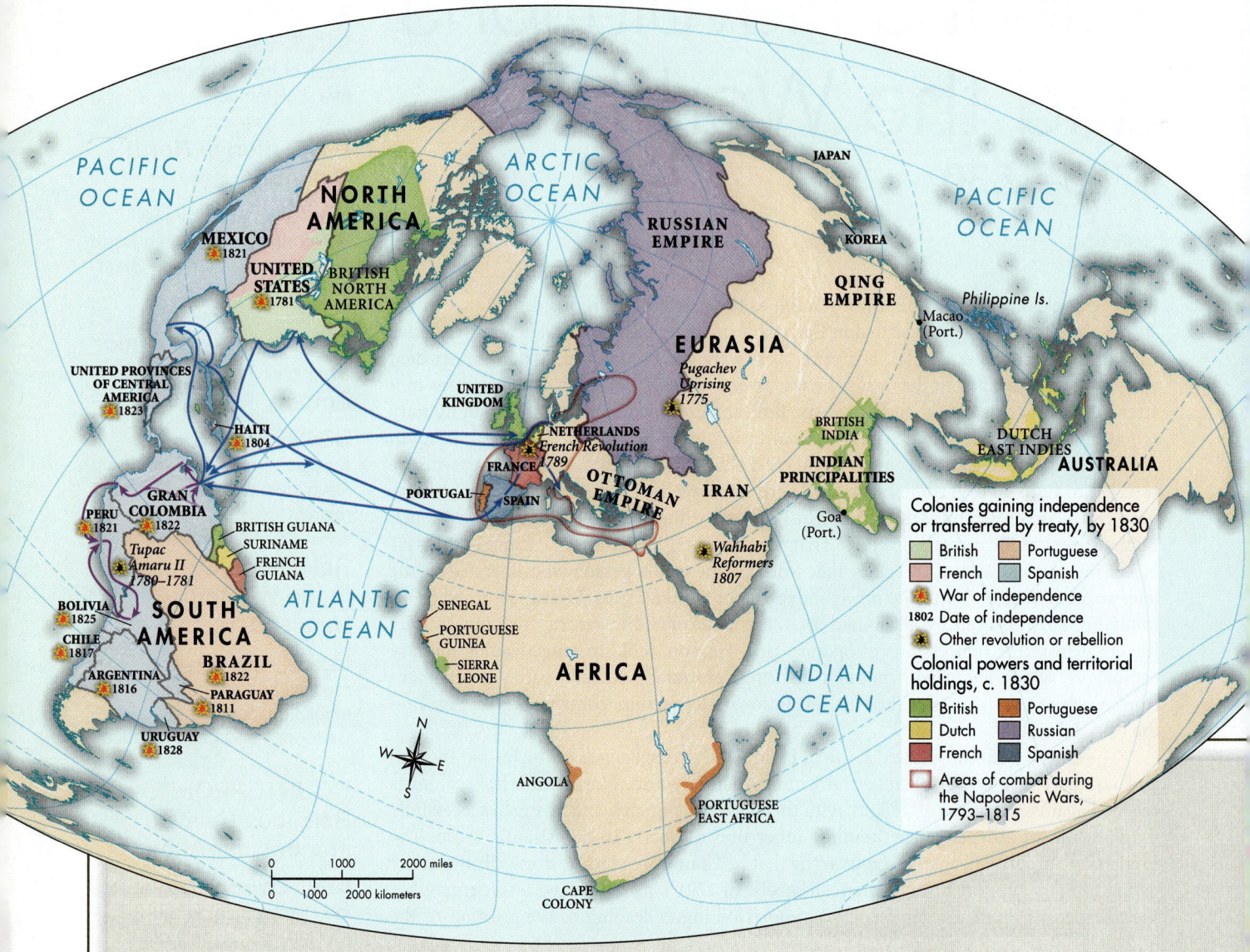

1751–1772 Publication of the *Encyclopedia*

1775–1781 Revolution in North America

Revolution begins in Haiti **1791** ▪

▪ **1776** Adam Smith, *The Wealth of Nations*

France declared a republic; Mary Wollstonecraft writes *A Vindication of the Rights of Woman* **1792** ▪

1750 1765 1780 1795

▪ **1762** Jean-Jacques Rousseau publishes *The Social Contract* and *Emile*

Napoleon comes to power **1799**

▪ **1789** U.S. Constitution formally adopted; revolution begins in France independent state of Haiti. The independence of Latin American states took longer to achieve, but it was globally inspirational. The English poet Lord Byron named his yacht *Bolivar* and in the 1820s went off to liberate Greece from the Ottomans.

These upheavals were connected with a transformation of thought and everyday life in the West called "the Enlightenment." Traders in Asia, Africa, and the Americas had brought ideas and goods to Europe. The arrival of new products such as sugar, coffee, and cotton textiles had freed many Europeans' lives from their former limits, and this new-found abundance led them to readjust their thinking. Wanting even greater wealth, they became discontented with the old order's regulation of trade and livelihoods. Both ordinary people and the upper classes proposed changing society, adding to the calls from Enlightenment thinkers whom the Scientific Revolution, the English Revolution, and global contact influenced to demand more rational government. Such ideas affected North American politicians, Caribbean activists, and creole reformers like Simon Bolivar, transforming them into revolutionaries. Thus, global trading connections played a key role both in creating the conditions that prompted the development of new ideas and in providing pathways for the spread of those ideas.

Indeed, the impulse for change extended far beyond the Atlantic world. In Ottoman-controlled Egypt, French revolutionary forces under the command of Napoleon Bonaparte invaded, claiming to bring new political ideas of liberty. A determined leader, Muhammad Ali, helped drive out the French and then promoted reform himself. As ideas of freedom took hold and as the increasingly ambitious Bonaparte decided to push into Russia, the old powers united to fight him. Long-established empires faced new, often grave challenges in this age of revolution and political change.

By 1830 the map of the world had changed, but that change came at a great cost. Alongside the birth of new nations and a growing belief in political reform, there had been widespread hardship and destruction. Soldiers died by the hundreds of thousands;

MAPPING THE WORLD

Wars and Revolutions in the Atlantic World, 1750–1830

Between 1775 and 1830 transplanted Europeans, their descendants, and their slaves and servants overwhelmed the Spanish, British, and French empires in the Western Hemisphere and created many independent nations. Europe and the Mediterranean also experienced revolutionary change as the ideas of just government and citizens' rights traveled the crossroads of the world and caused both transformation and turmoil.

ROUTES ▼

→ Voyages of Simon Bolivar, 1799–1816

→ Independence campaigns of Simon Bolivar, 1817–1825

- **1804** Haiti becomes independent from France
- **1815** Napoleon defeated at Waterloo; Congress of Vienna resettles the boundaries of European states
- **1822** Brazil becomes independent from Portugal

1810 — 1825 — 1840

- **1811** Simon Bolivar first takes up arms against Spain
- **1816** Argentina becomes independent from Spain
- **1817** Chile becomes independent from Spain
- **1821** Mexico and Peru become independent from Spain
- **1825** Bolivia becomes independent from Spain

civilians also perished because political and social change set them against one another. The breakdown of established kingdoms was the work of the warriors, the masses, and determined leaders, but this age of revolution crushed many. Napoleon Bonaparte was condemned to exile, and even so privileged a revolutionary as Bolivar died of utter exhaustion in 1830 just as the new nations of Latin America began their independent existence.

OVERVIEW QUESTIONS

The major global development in this chapter: The Atlantic revolutions and their short- and long-term significance.

As you read, consider:

1. What role did the Scientific Revolution and expanding global contacts play in the cultural and social movement known as the Enlightenment?
2. Why did prosperous and poor people alike join revolutions in the Americas and in France?
3. Why were the Atlantic revolutions so influential, even to the present day?

The Promise of Enlightenment

FOCUS
What were the major ideas of the Enlightenment and their impacts?

Intense rethinking of society, politics, and the workings of the economy was under way in Europe in the eighteenth century, spurred by the Scientific Revolution's call for observation and rational thinking. Travelers' and missionaries' reports from the rest of the world provided ideas about alternative forms of government and social organization. Those reports added to the questioning—already under way in Europe—of beliefs in a uniform, God-given order in all states of the world. New global products such as brightly printed cottons, lacquered furniture, and porcelain raised the issue of where the European artisans learning to produce all these goods fit in a supposedly unchanging social structure. How the social and political order should change inspired lively conversation in salons and cafés as well as profound philosophical reflection in books and essays. Even monarchs began rethinking how the state should be run and their own role in government reform.

A New World of Ideas

contract government A political theory that views government as stemming from the people, who agree to surrender a measure of personal freedom in return for a government that guarantees protection of citizens' rights and property.

Europeans in the eighteenth century had a great deal to think about. Science had challenged traditional views of nature and offered a new methodology for uncovering nature's laws. Changing techniques in agriculture and rising commerce led people to reflect on the meaning of greater abundance. Reports from around the world on foreign customs, ways of conducting government, and trade practices fueled intense discussion among Europeans. Moreover, participation in this intellectual ferment was not limited to the political and social elite. As literacy spread in Europe, ever more people were caught up in the debate over social, political, and economic change. These wide-ranging reconsiderations have come collectively to be called the Enlightenment.

John Locke

Some Enlightenment writers hammered away at the abuses of monarchies and proposed representative rule based on the consent of the governed that later became the foundation of many states. The will of a monarch is not the best basis for government, the English philosopher John Locke wrote late in the seventeenth century. Rather, he maintained, governments should be established rationally, by mutual consent of the governed. The idea of compact or **contract government** grew from Locke's philosophy that people were born free, equal, and rational, and that natural rights, including personal freedoms, were basic to all humans. In Locke's view, governments were formed when people made the rational choice to give up a measure of freedom and create institutions that could express the people's will, guarantee natural rights, and protect everyone's property. If a government failed to fulfill these purposes, it ceased to be legitimate and the people had the right to replace it. Locke's ideas had centered on the situation in England, where citizens and the Parliament had, over the course of the seventeenth century, twice ousted their king.

Voltaire and Montesquieu

In contrast to Locke, French writers Voltaire and Baron Louis Montesquieu criticized their own society's religious and political abuses by referring to the political situation elsewhere—in China and outside Europe. They conspicuously set their widely read writings in faraway lands or used wise foreigners as foils to show Europe's backwardness. A wealthy trained jurist, Montesquieu in *The Persian Letters* (1721) featured a Persian ruler visiting Europe and writing back home of the strange goings-on. The continent was full of magicians, Montesquieu's hero reports, such as those who could turn wine and wafers into flesh—a mocking reference to the Christian sacrament of communion. Voltaire, a successful author thrown several times into jail for insulting the authorities, portrayed worthy young men cruelly treated by their supposed betters, such as priests and kings, in his rollicking novels *Zadig* (1747) and *Candide* (1759). From a prosperous family, Voltaire asked for a society based on merit, not on aristocracy of birth: "There is nothing in Asia that resembles the European nobility: nowhere in the Orient does one find an order of citizens distinct from all the rest by their hereditary titles or by exemptions and privileges given them solely by their birth."[2] Voltaire did not have the story quite right, but other Enlightenment thinkers joined his call for reason, hard work, and opportunity in both economic life and politics.

Jean-Jacques Rousseau

Swiss-born Jean-Jacques Rousseau took up the theme of freedom and opportunity in his many influential writings. In *The Social Contract* (1762) he claimed that "man is born free," but because of despotic government "he is everywhere in chains." Moving beyond the form of government to the process of shaping the modern citizen, Rousseau's best-selling novel *Emile* (1762) describes the ways in which a young boy is educated to develop many practical skills. Instead of learning through rote memory, as was common, Emile learns such skills as carpentry and medicine by actually working at them, and he spends much time outdoors, getting in touch with nature by living a simple life away from corrupt civilization. Like China's Kangxi monarch, whom Enlightenment thinkers held up as a model, Emile becomes a polymath, that is, someone with a knowledge of many subjects and numerous skills—in this case, artisanal and agricultural techniques that could earn him a livelihood. At the end of his apprenticeship in nature, Emile has become the responsible citizen who can fend for himself and regulate his movements according to natural laws, not despotically imposed ones.

Adam Smith

Enlightenment thinkers also redesigned ideas about the economy. In 1776, Scottish philosopher Adam Smith published one of the most influential Enlightenment documents, *On the Wealth of Nations*. Citing China as an important example of how specialization of trades leads to prosperity, Smith proposed to free the economy from government monopolies and regulations. Merchants from South America to the Caribbean and Europe embraced the idea of freedom from mercantilist regulations that forced them to send goods exclusively through their national ports before trading them in other markets. This idea of **laissez faire** (French for "let alone") became part of the theory called **liberalism**, which endorsed economic and personal freedom guaranteed by the rule of law. Smith saw trade itself as benefiting an individual's character because it required cooperation with others in the process of exchanging goods. The virtues created by trade were more desirable

laissez faire An economic doctrine that advocates freeing economies from government intervention and control.

liberalism A political ideology that emphasizes free trade, individual rights, and the rule of law to protect rights as the best means for promoting social and economic improvement.

than the military swaggering and roughness of aristocratic lives, and he continually stressed that alongside individualism there needed to be concern for the well-being of the community as a whole. Slavery, he argued, was inefficient and ought to be done away with. Still other Enlightenment writers said that a middle-class way of life promoted sensibility, love of family, thrift, and hard work—again, in stark contrast to the unfeeling, promiscuous, and spendthrift habits these reformers saw in the behavior of the nobility.

Spread of Enlightenment Thought

As we have seen, Enlightenment thinkers explicitly drew on the knowledge of the world beyond Europe that global economic connections had allowed them to acquire. Such connections also made it possible for Enlightenment ideas to spread around the world. Some Japanese thinkers and officials were so interested in new ideas that they began "Dutch Studies," referring to the body of European information brought in by Dutch traders. They wanted to learn about recent breakthroughs in practical subjects as well as scientific practices based on rational observation and deduction. Chinese scholars, though not directly influenced by Enlightenment thought, were reflecting on issues of good government and the capacities of the individual within the imperial system. In contrast, future nation builders in the North American colonies—Benjamin Franklin, John Adams, and Thomas Jefferson—were steeped in both the practical and political sides of the Enlightenment, running businesses, designing buildings, conducting scientific experiments, and writing political documents.

The Public Sphere

Enlightenment thought had an impact on all of Western society—high and low, male and female. Population growth in cities such as Paris strained traditional work patterns and neighborhoods, causing old social structures to weaken and new ideas to flourish. Another cause of change was the initiative of women of the wealthier classes, who conducted salons—that is, meetings in their homes devoted to discussing the most recent issues and publicizing the newest books and findings. German Jewish women, often kept at a distance from Christian society, made a name for themselves by forming such groups. Along with coffeehouses in European and colonial cities, modeled on those in the Ottoman Empire, salons created a **public sphere** in which people could meet outside court circles to talk about current affairs. Together with the new public libraries, reading groups, and a host of scientific clubs that dotted the Atlantic world, they built new community bonds and laid the groundwork for responsible citizenship. Instead of a monarchical government single-handedly determining public policy, ordinary people in Europe and its colonies, relying on knowledge gained from public discussion, could express their opinions on the course of events and thereby undermine government attempts at censorship and traditional ideas about society.

The ideals of the Enlightenment were well represented in the *Encyclopedia* (1751–1772) of France's Denis Diderot. The celebrated work highlighted the contributions of ordinary working people, particularly artisans, to the overall improvement of the human condition; it contained dozens of technical drawings of practical machinery that could advance prosperity. The *Encyclopedia* described the freedoms and rights nature endowed on *all* people, not just aristocrats or religious authorities. Like Rousseau, Diderot maintained that in a natural state all people were born free and equal. French writer Olympe de Gouges further proposed that there was no difference among people of different skin colors. "How are the Whites different from [the Black] race? . . . Why do blonds not claim superiority over brunettes?" she asked in her "Reflections on Negroes" (1788). "Like all the different types of animals, plants, and minerals that nature has produced, people's color also varies."[3] Essayists in the *Encyclopedia* added that women too were born free and endowed with natural rights.

public sphere A cultural and political environment that emerged during the Enlightenment, where members of society gathered to discuss issues of the day.

Many of the working people of Europe's growing towns and cities responded enthusiastically to the ideas set forth by the leading philosophers of the Enlightenment, such as Voltaire and Rousseau. The French glassworker Jacques Ménétra, for example, acquired and also distributed these new antireligious and egalitarian ideas as he moved from city to town and village, installing glass windows. With some religious schooling and then an apprenticeship in his trade, Ménétra, like his fellow journeymen artisans, led this

Eighteenth-Century English Drawing Room

When drinking their tea imported from Asia, middle- and upper-class Europeans aimed for elegance, inspired by Asian tea rituals. They used porcelain, whose production European manufacturers had recently figured out, and an array of new furnishings such as the tea table on display here. These English tea-takers are wearing sparkling white muslin, probably imported from India, which produced high-quality cloth that Europeans valued above cotton from anywhere else, including, as we will see in the next chapter, the new European industrial mills. (Private Collection/Bridgeman Art Library.)

kind of mobile life as a young man before establishing his own shop in Paris. During the course of his travels, he provided news of the Parisian thinkers to artisans along his route. In his autobiography—one of the few written by an ordinary European worker—he referred to Jean-Jacques Rousseau and gossiped about aristocrats. Young journeymen like Ménétra helped spread news of politics and current ideas before the coming of mass media, making the Enlightenment an affair not only of the well-born in salons but also of many average people.

Enlightenment and the Old Order

Enlightened Rulers

Despite its critique of monarchs, church officials, and the aristocracy, "Enlightenment" was a watchword of some of Europe's most powerful rulers. "Enlightened" rulers came to sense that more rational government could actually strengthen their regimes, for example by increasing governmental efficiency and increasing tax revenues. Thus, instead of touting his divine legacy, Prussian king Frederick the Great (r. 1740–1786) called a ruler someone who would "work efficiently for the good of the state" rather than "live in lazy luxury, enriching himself by the labor of the people."[4] A musician and poet, Frederick studied several languages, collected Chinese porcelain, and wrote librettos for operas, some of them about toleration. For him, Enlightenment made monarchs stronger. Spreading to Russia, the Enlightenment moved Catherine the Great (r. 1762–1796) to sponsor the writing of a dictionary of the Russian language, to correspond with learned thinkers such as Diderot, and to work to improve the education of girls. Additionally, Catherine's goal was to put a stop to aristocrats' "idle time spent in luxury and other vices corrupting to the morals," as she put it, and instead transform the nobility into active and informed administrators of her far-flung empire and its diverse peoples[5] (see Seeing the Past: Portrait of Catherine the Great).

The Spanish monarchy in the eighteenth century likewise instituted a series of policy changes called the Bourbon Reforms, so named because many of them aimed to make the monarchy—headed by the Bourbon dynasty—financially sound by taxing the colonies

Portrait of Catherine the Great

Catherine the Great as the Roman Goddess Minerva
(Hillwood Estate, Museum & Gardens; Photo by Ed Owen.)

Catherine the Great was a monarch of towering ability and ambition. Although her regime was known for smashing peasant uprisings, it also promoted the arts and knowledge. Even as her armies conquered some two hundred thousand square miles of territory and added it to the Russian Empire, Catherine commissioned the first dictionary of the Russian language and communicated with the greatest thinkers of the Enlightenment. While sponsoring education, she tried to reform her government to increase its power. In this regard, Enlightenment was not just about the fine arts but also about generally raising the economic and political profile of the monarchy through rationally devised policies.

Although Enlightenment thinkers often referred to the excellent customs and the rational policies of non-Western monarchs of their day—especially those in China—they also prized classical Greece and Rome for their democratic and republican forms of government. In this spirit of classical enthusiasm, monarchs were sometimes depicted as mythical figures, despite the often dark side to their regimes. For this image, a skilled Parisian craftsperson of the 1760s chose Minerva—Roman goddess of both war and wisdom—as the figure closest to the celebrated Catherine. The luxurious detail on this round box assures us that it was destined for an aristocratic palace, perhaps that of the monarch herself.

EXAMINING THE EVIDENCE

1. **What does this depiction of the empress as Minerva tell you about the society over which Catherine ruled?**
2. **How does this image of leadership compare with others you have seen, including those of U.S. presidents? How do you account for the differences? For the similarities?**

more efficiently. Following Enlightenment calls for rational and secular policies, Spain's rulers also attempted to limit the church's independence. Often opposing slavery and promoting better treatment of native peoples, the Jesuit order, for instance, had many followers in Spain's "New World" empire. Thus, the order was an alternate source of allegiance, and the monarchy outlawed it.

Leaders of the Spanish colonies adopted many Enlightenment ideas, including scientific farming and improvements in mining—both of them subjects dear to forward-looking thinkers who read publications such as the *Encyclopedia*. In Mexico, reformers saw the education of each woman as central to building responsible government. As one local journalist put it, under a mother's care the young citizen "grows, is nourished, and acquires his first notions of Good and Evil. [Therefore] women have even more reason to be enlightened than men."[6] In this view, motherhood was not a simple biological act but a livelihood critical to maintaining a strong national life.

Justification of Slavery

European prosperity depended on the productivity of slaves in the colonies, and wealthy slave owners used the Enlightenment fascination with nature to devise scientific explanations justifying the oppressive system. Though many Enlightenment thinkers such as Olympe de Gouges wanted equality for "noble savages," in slave owners' minds Africans were less than human and thus rightly subject to exploitation. Scientists captured Africans for study and came up with a list of their biological differences from whites and their similarities to animals, contributing to a sense of racial inferiority as a "scientific fact." Others justified race-based slavery in terms of character: blacks were, one British observer explained, "conceited, proud, indolent and very artful"—a rationale for harsh plantation discipline.[7] Thus, some strands of Enlightenment thought helped buyers and sellers of Africans and native Americans argue that slavery was useful and rational, especially because slaves could produce wealth and help society as a whole make progress.

Popular Revolts in an Age of Enlightenment

Pugachev Rebellion

Enlightened officials hoped to improve government at a time of popular uprising in many parts of the world. In Russia, people throughout society came to protest serfdom's irrationality and unfairness. One aristocrat believed that such unfairness "spread a plague in the hearts of the common people."[8] In 1773 the discontent of many serfs crystallized around Emel'ian Ivanovich Pugachev, once an officer in the Russian army, who claimed to be Peter III, the dead husband of Catherine. Tens of thousands of peasants, joined by rebellious workers, serf soldiers in Catherine's overworked armies, and Muslim minorities rose up, calling for the restoration of Pugachev, alias Peter, to the throne. Pugachev promised them great riches for their support. Serfs responded by plundering noble estates and killing aristocrats. They justified revolt in slogans and songs: "O woe to us slaves living for the masters. . . . how shameful and insulting / That another who is not worthy to be equal with us / Has so many of us in his power."[9] The rebellion was put down only with difficulty. Once Catherine's forces captured Pugachev, they cut off his arms and legs, then his head, and finally hacked his body to pieces—just punishment, nobles believed, for the crimes of this "monster" against the monarchy and upper classes.

Pugachev Uprising in Russia, 1773

Latin American Uprisings

Uprisings among the urban poor, farmworkers, and slaves also occurred in the Caribbean and other parts of the Western Hemisphere. Over the course of the eighteenth century the Latin American population grew rapidly and cities expanded. Rebels protested harsh conditions, which included their enslavement and only grew worse with Spain's demand for more revenue. Some native peoples envisioned the complete expulsion of the Spaniards or the overthrow of the wealthy creoles, who owned estates and plantations. Between 1780 and 1783, several different groups in Peru attempted to restore Inca power and end the increased burden of taxation under the Bourbon Reforms. The charismatic trader and wealthy landowner Tupac Amaru II (TOO-pack a-MAH-roo), an indigenous leader who took his name from the Inca leader of the late sixteenth century, led tens of thousands in the region of Tinta against corrupt local leadership and then against the administration of the region as a whole. Eventually captured by the authorities, Tupac Amaru II had his tongue cut out, was drawn and quartered by four horses, and was finally beheaded—after first watching the execution of most of his family. Rebellions continued nonetheless.

Revolution in North America

FOCUS

What factors lay behind the war between North American colonists and Great Britain?

The Atlantic world was part of a global trading network. Thus, Europeans in North America, participating in global livelihoods as merchants, fishermen, and sailors, were exposed to ideas and goods from around the world. A Boston newspaper in the 1720s advertised the sale of Moroccan leather, Indian chintz and muslin fabrics, South American mahogany, and Asian tea. Sending out lumber, dried fish, tobacco, and furs, the British colonies grew prosperous and cosmopolitan, interesting themselves in all facets of the Enlightenment and commercial growth.

Many enlightened North American colonists came to resent Britain's attempts to tax and rule them more efficiently, and people from various walks of life soon rebelled against what they saw as government contempt for their own rights as English people. Amid growing wealth and intellectual ferment, North American colonists along the Atlantic seaboard came to forge an independent nation—the future United States of America.

The British Empire and the Colonial Crisis 1764–1775

In the eighteenth century European states continued to wage increasingly costly wars for global trade and influence. Where governments were poorly run and taxes did not cover the huge military debt, as in the case of France, financial disaster loomed. The expense of the Seven Years' War of 1756–1763 was enormous as, for the first time in history, Europeans fought to gain influence in South Asia, the Philippines, the Caribbean, and North America. Ultimately beating both the French and the Spanish, Britain received all of French Canada and Florida at the end of the war (see Map 23.1). It hoped to boost colonial taxation to recoup its expenses and pay the costs of administering its empire.

Taxation Without Representation

In 1764 the British Parliament raised taxes on molasses with the Sugar Act, and in the following year it passed the Stamp Act, which taxed printed material and legal documents—all of them important to colonists' everyday lives. The Townshend Acts of 1767 put duties on other useful commodities, such as paper, glass, and paint, resulting in increasingly radical protests. Driven by England's own history of revolution and by the new political theories, some colonial activists insisted that if they were going to be taxed, they needed direct representation in the English Parliament, which they currently lacked. This argument followed Locke's theory of the social contract: a government where citizens were not represented had no right to take their property in taxes. With a literacy rate of 70 percent among men and 40 percent among women in the North American colonies—among the highest rates anywhere—new ideas about government and reports of British misdeeds spread rapidly, especially among townspeople.

The Birth of the United States 1775–1789

When yet another tax was placed on prized imported tea, a group of Bostonians, disguised as native Americans, dumped a load of tea into the harbor in December 1773. The British government responded to the "Boston Tea Party" by closing the seaport's thriving harbor, while colonial representatives gathered for an all-colony Continental Congress that resulted in a coordinated boycott of British goods.

U.S. Declaration of Independence

Tensions escalated. In April 1775 artisans and farmers in Lexington and Concord fought British troops sent to confiscate a stockpile of ammunition from rebellious colonists. On July 4, 1776, the Continental Congress issued its "Declaration of Independence," a short, dramatic document written largely by Thomas Jefferson that aimed—like the Enlightenment itself—to convert its readers to the side of reason in matters of government. The Declaration argued that the monarchy was tyrannical and had forfeited its right to rule. It went on to articulate an Enlightenment doctrine of rights—the famous rights of "life, liberty, and the pursuit of happiness." Some of the rebel colonists likened themselves to "slaves" lacking individual freedom, drawing a parallel—even though Declaration author Thomas Jefferson was himself a slave owner—with slave rebels across the Western world.

The War of Independence

The British sent a powerful army and navy to defeat the colonists. British forces burned coastal towns and occupied New York, Philadelphia, and other crucial centers of commerce and government. George Washington of Virginia headed the Continental Army. His forces suffered from lack of clothing, food, pay, and efficient recruiting. Yet the British deployed their larger armies in battle formation, whereas colonists were effective at guerrilla warfare, sniping at the invaders from behind trees and using bows and arrows if they lacked guns. Others joined in: colonial women fed armies in their vicinity, knitted and sewed clothing, and cared for the wounded. Critical help arrived from countries interested in blocking

MAP 23.1

Colonial Crisis and Revolution in North America, 1754–1789

The American Revolution soon followed the Seven Years' War, which had left Great Britain dominant in North America but with a hefty war debt to pay. To help cover the debt, the British government raised taxes on its North American colonies. Many of these colonists, however, were steeped in the ideas of the Enlightenment, and they found the new taxation oppressive and considered it a violation both of the rights of Englishmen and of the social contract between king and subjects. From the imposition of the Stamp Act to the battles of Lexington and Concord the colonists resisted, and with the British surrender at Yorktown in 1781 they won their independence.

British expansionism, foremost among these France but also Spain and the Netherlands. Substantial assistance from the French under the Marquis de Lafayette ultimately brought the British down at Yorktown, where they surrendered their army in 1781 (see again Map 23.1).

The U.S. Constitution

Growing immigration had made the United States ethnically diverse well before its founding. Uprisings and disputes over trade and taxation followed the 1781 victory, showing that a strong **federation**, or union of states, was needed. The Articles of Confederation, drawn up in 1777 as a provisional constitution, however, proved weak because they gave the central government few powers. As the newly independent thirteen states pursued their own interests under the Articles of Confederation in the aftermath of the war, the "frail and tottering edifice [of the loosely aligned thirteen states] seems ready to fall upon our heads and crush us beneath its ruins," as Alexander Hamilton, Washington's trusted aide during the War of Independence, put it.[10] In 1787, a Constitutional Convention met

federation A union of equal and sovereign states rather than a thoroughly integrated nation.

in Philadelphia to draft a new constitution. Two-thirds of the delegates were educated lawyers, grounded intellectually in Enlightenment thought, but there were some of humble beginnings: a delegate from Connecticut had worked as a shoemaker before becoming a merchant, for example. Most, however, were men of property. Indeed, George Washington, who presided over the meeting, not only had a substantial plantation (like others in the group) but also was the owner of hundreds of slaves.

The Constitution reflected the broad understanding of just government shared by these propertied men. In it, the founders enshrined the contract theory of government from the Enlightenment with its opening words: "We the people of the United States in order to form a more perfect union." However, the document also reflected the authors' material interests. One of their primary motives in creating a strong government was to protect what they saw as a central individual right, the right to private property. The authors did not agree on every point, even when it came to private property. What, for example, should the Constitution say about slaves, individuals who were themselves property? Should slavery be acknowledged, as many of the representatives from the southern states wanted, or should it be abolished, as major participants such as Alexander Hamilton of New York believed? Born in the Caribbean of a poor family, Hamilton was a bookkeeper as a young teenager—a job that gave him valuable connections with merchant families in North America, who helped him relocate to New York City, where he attended Columbia College and then studied law. His roots in the Caribbean made him abhor the slave system. "The existence of slavery," he wrote, "makes us fancy many things that are founded neither in reason or experience."[11]

Hamilton was to lose this argument. The new Constitution, formally adopted in 1789, echoed the aims of the revolution and the rights of individuals—except slaves and women. It guaranteed the ownership of property and fostered commerce and the spirit of industry by providing stable laws. Its banking structure promised reliability in the international credit markets, and it advanced U.S. involvement with the global economy by lifting restrictions on production, commerce, and business life. The political rights given to the substantial minority—the enfranchised white men—by the U.S. Constitution and by state

Samuel Jennings, *Liberty Displaying the Arts and Sciences* (1792)

Enlightenment writers debated whether the ideals of liberty and equality should apply to everyone regardless of race, condition of servitude, and gender. This painting, commissioned early in U.S. history to urge the abolition of slavery, shows Liberty with the Cap of Liberty on a staff next to her; she is displaying Enlightenment accomplishments in the arts and sciences to freed slaves. Although in the United States and elsewhere Liberty was usually depicted as a woman, the principles of equal citizenship expressed in the Constitution and the Declaration of Independence did not apply to most women, African Americans, or native Americans. (The Library Company of Philadelphia.)

law inspired this burst of activity, innovation, and enterprise. To achieve the Constitution, the founders, as men of the Enlightenment, negotiated, made concessions, and came to hard-fought agreements. The U.S. Constitution thus became a monument to consensus politics and to the form of government called a **republic**. When the heated disputes were over and the Constitution finally framed, George Washington wrote to the Marquis de Lafayette in France that achieving the document was "little short of a miracle."

The French Revolution and the Napoleonic Empire

FOCUS
What changes emerged from the French Revolution and Napoleon's reign?

In 1780, on the eve of victory in its War of Independence, the fledgling United States had only about 2.7 million people, but its triumph had a powerful impact on the far larger population in Europe. "The [French] nation has been awakened by our revolution," Ambassador Thomas Jefferson wrote in 1788 to President George Washington, "they feel their strength, they are enlightened."[12] More directly, the cost of French participation in global warfare with Britain, including the North American War of Independence, hastened the collapse of the monarchy. France's taxation policy put the cost of warfare on the poor and exempted the wealthy from paying their share. In 1789, less than a decade after the victory at Yorktown, the French people took matters into their own hands, ultimately ousting the king and launching a republic. The French Revolution resonated far and wide, and under the French conqueror Napoleon Bonaparte, revolutionary principles advanced across Europe and beyond, even as Europe's monarchs struggled to halt the march of "liberty, equality, fraternity."

From Monarchy to Republic 1789–1792

Having borrowed recklessly (as had his predecessors) to pursue wars and princely living, the French monarch Louis XVI (r. 1774–1793) in 1787 met with a firm "no" when he asked for more loans from bankers and financial help from the aristocracy. The king was forced to summon the Estates General—a representative body that had not met since 1614—to the royal palace at Versailles to bail out the government. Members of the Estates General arrived at their meeting in May 1789, carrying lists of grievances from people of all occupations and walks of life, who had met in local gatherings across France to help representatives prepare for their momentous assembly.

Formation of the National Assembly

There were several competing agendas at the meeting of the Estates General: those of the monarchy to repair its finances; those of the nobility to take power from the king; and those of the common people, who at the time were suffering from crop failures, heavy taxation, governmental restraints on trade, and a slowdown in business because of bad harvests. The meeting quickly broke down when representatives of the middle classes and common people left the general meeting. They were joined by sympathetic, reform-minded aristocrats and clergymen such as Abbé Sieyès, who asked what this mass of commoners meant to the kingdom. "Everything," he responded to his own question. "What has it been until now in the political order? Nothing."[13] These representatives declared themselves a National Assembly of "citizens" of France, not the lowly subjects of a king. The National Assembly included the lawyers and officials who had represented most of the people in 1789 as well as reform-minded deputies from the clergy and a substantial number of nobles.

Storming of the Bastille

Soon much of France was overwhelmed by enthusiasm for this new government based on citizen consent. On July 14, 1789, crowds in Paris stormed the Bastille, a notorious prison where people could be incarcerated simply at the king's orders. The liberation of the Bastille by the people of Paris so symbolized the French Revolution that it became France's national holiday, just as the Declaration of Independence on July 4 eventually made that Independence Day in the United States.

republic A political system in which the interests of all citizens are represented in the government.

Declaration of the Rights of Man and of the Citizen

In its first years, the revolution was shaped by Enlightenment principles. Strong citizen protest also motivated the legislators of the National Assembly, who like U.S. revolutionary leaders were mostly from the propertied classes. With peasants rioting in the countryside against the unfair rule of aristocratic landowners, in August 1789 the nobility surrendered its privileges, such as its exemption from taxation. Later that month the National Assembly issued the "Declaration of the Rights of Man and of the Citizen," a stirring announcement of the basic rights possessed by each new citizen, including rights to free speech, to own property, and to be safe from arbitrary acts of the state. Soon, Olympe de Gouges would issue her own "Declaration of the Rights of Woman and the Female Citizen," declaring, "Woman is born free and lives equal to man in her rights."

Power to the People

In October 1789, the market women of Paris, protesting the soaring cost of food, marched to the palace of Versailles twelve miles away and captured the royal family, bringing it to live "with the people" in the city. In so doing, they showed that monarchs existed to serve the people—and that kings ignored this fact at their own peril. The government passed laws reducing the power of the clergy and abolishing the guild system and other institutions that would restrain trade. Suddenly people could pursue the jobs they wanted on their own terms outside guild restrictions. The liberal Enlightenment program of freedom for the person and for trade and property was now accomplished, pushed by enthusiastic demonstrations by newly empowered citizens.

These early acts of the French Revolution stirred the hearts and minds of many. Women petitioned for a range of rights, and for a time the power of the husband over his

Women's March to Versailles

Although the French Revolution began with the ceremonial meeting of the Estates General in May 1789, people from many walks of life soon became directly involved in the drive for fundamental change. That October, after the people of Paris had liberated the notorious Bastille prison, the market women of the city marched to the royal palace at Versailles. Joined by men who came from Paris to reinforce them, they captured the king and his family. This engraving shows the crowds escorting the monarch back to the city of Paris, where they could keep an eye on him. (The Art Archive/Marc Charmet.)

wife was eliminated. Across the English Channel, poet William Wordsworth captured the rush of youthful belief that through newly active citizens the world would be reborn: "Bliss was it in that dawn to be alive, / But to be young was very heaven!" The Declaration of the Rights of Man and of the Citizen inspired the addition of a Bill of Rights to the U.S. Constitution, which outlined the essential rights, such as freedom of speech, that the government could never overturn. English author Mary Wollstonecraft penned *A Vindication of the Rights of Man* (1790) in defense of the revolution.

Mary Wollstonecraft

Two years later Wollstonecraft wrote *A Vindication of the Rights of Woman*, a globally influential work that saw men's privileges over women as similar to the French aristocracy's privileges over the peasantry. Current laws in Britain made men into a privileged aristocracy that took women's property and wages on marriage, thus denying women their rights. Wollstonecraft knew all this from bitter experience. Born into a well-to-do family, her brother not only inherited most of the family estate but also confiscated his sisters' inheritances for himself. Destitute, they had to earn a living without having been trained to do so. Wollstonecraft first became a governess and then a journalist, whose classic works protested that the legal privileges of men allowed them to impoverish women.

War, Terror, and Resistance 1792–1799

War Against France and Execution of the King

As revolutionary fervor spread across national borders, the monarchs and nobility of Europe scrambled to survive. In the spring of 1792 the royal houses of Austria and Prussia declared war on France. Wartime brought to power the lawyer Maximilien Robespierre, leader in the popular Jacobin club, a political group that hoped to sweep away all institutions from the oppressive past. In the face of total defeat by Austria and Prussia and the counterrevolutionary efforts of Louis XVI, Robespierre and other politicians became convinced that it was time to do away with the monarchy, that the nation had to become a republic if the revolution were to survive. Patriotic holidays to replace religious ones, dishes with revolutionary slogans, an entirely new calendar, and new laws making the family more egalitarian turned the country upside down. Workshops were set up for the unemployed to earn a living by making war goods, and all citizens were urged to give their energy to help the war effort. In 1793 both King Louis XVI and Queen Marie Antoinette were executed by guillotine—an "enlightened" mode of execution because it killed swiftly and reduced suffering. France stood on the threshold of total transformation.

The Terror

Claiming that there could be no rights in wartime, Robespierre and the newly created Committee of Public Safety stamped out free speech, squashed the various women's clubs that had sprung up to gain the rights of citizenship, and executed people such as Olympe de Gouges whom they judged to be traitors to the republic. This was the Terror, during which the government murdered people from all classes and livelihoods—from the highest to the lowest—because enemies of the republic, the government claimed, lurked on all rungs of the social ladder. To justify its actions, the Committee of Public Safety turned to Rousseau's idea of the **general will**. Rousseau's unique interpretation of the social contract maintained that once agreement among citizens had created a state, that state acted with a higher wisdom with which truly loyal citizens could not disagree, especially in wartime. The "general will" justified the Terror's mass executions and the suspension of individual rights and even free thought. The concept was one of the French Revolution's most powerful revolutionary legacies, enacted not only by totalitarian regimes in the twentieth century but even by democracies during times of stress.

By 1794, largely because the war was turning in France's favor, moderate and propertied politicians were able to regain public support and overthrew Robespierre and the Committee of Public Safety. At the same time, France's revolutionary armies went on the offensive, taking the idea of rights, constitutions, and republicanism to countries such as Austria that had tried to stop the revolution. French pride, based on a belief in the superiority of a republican form of government and full, equal citizenship for men, blossomed,

general will The political concept that once agreement among citizens creates a state, that state is endowed with a higher wisdom about policies with which virtuous citizens could not disagree.

especially among citizen-soldiers who found upward mobility in the revolutionary army. No one took more advantage of this opportunity than a newly minted officer, the young Napoleon Bonaparte (1769–1821).

Napoleon's Reign 1799–1815

Napoleon's Rise to Power

Napoleon Bonaparte, born into a modest Corsican family, became commander in chief of the French revolutionary army in Italy at the age of twenty-seven. A student of Enlightenment thought and an avid reader of history throughout his life, Napoleon had the good fortune to enter the army just as its aristocratic officers were fleeing the revolution in France by moving to other countries. Rising to power through the ranks, he attempted the conquest of Egypt in 1798 but escaped the country as he began to lose the campaign. He returned to France months later, in 1799. There he used the uncertain political scene to establish himself first as co-consul and then, in 1804, as emperor. "As in Rome, it took a dictator to save the Republic,"[14] Napoleon said of the repression that followed his takeover. He reconciled France with the Catholic Church and even called back to his court some of the exiled aristocracy to help add grandeur to his regime.

The Napoleonic Code

Yet Napoleon solidified many revolutionary changes, notably those concerning citizenship and the right to private property, as outlined in the Code Napoleon (1803–1804), a new set of basic laws. The Code set rules for property, ending restrictions on sales of the nobility's land and establishing rules for assets such as bonds, stocks, and mortgages. The Code thus advanced prosperity by providing secure laws for commercial, industrial, and agricultural livelihoods; Napoleon's founding of national schools for teachers, engineers, and the military served this end too. In the realm of family law, however, the Code reversed gains made by women during the revolution by making the wages and other property of married women the legal property of their husbands, by forbidding them to appear as witnesses in court, and by not allowing them to be guardians of their own children. Financial impoverishment gave women no choices in life but to remain loyal wives—principles that Napoleon's triumphant armies spread through Europe and that encouraged imitators around the world. Instead of respecting the equality of women suggested by some Enlightenment thinkers, Napoleon enforced Rousseau's idea that women should raise the next generation of citizens but not be equal citizens themselves.

Napoleon's Military Campaigns

Maintaining his grip by keeping the nation at war and plundering other countries, Napoleon launched a series of successful wars against Spain, the German states, and Italy (see Map 23.2). Then, in 1812, he made a disastrous attempt to invade and conquer Russia. The Russian army, the Russian people, and deadly winter conditions combined to deal Napoleon a catastrophic defeat. After that, a coalition of German, Russian, Austrian, and British forces defeated Napoleon twice more, once in Paris in 1814 and then, in a victory that crushed Napoleon's forces, at Waterloo in 1815.

Congress of Vienna

At the Congress of Vienna (1814–1815), the coalition resettled the boundaries of European states. In doing so, many of Europe's rulers sought to overturn revolutionary and Napoleonic reforms to restore their old regimes. It was far too late to stamp out the principles of constitutional government and natural rights, however. Although monarchs (including France's) were restored to their thrones in 1815, there were now limitations on their powers. Moreover, Napoleon's military campaigns, which spread principles of rights and citizenship, ensured the continuation of these new values in people's minds and helped upset power arrangements around the world.

Muhammad Ali and the Revolutionary Spirit in Egypt

Despite Napoleon's ultimate defeat, the revolutionary legacy fomented reform activity for more rational government not only across Europe but also outside it. When the French revolutionary armies under Napoleon invaded Egypt in 1798, they faced the forces of the Ottoman Empire, whose administration, like that of other great land-based empires, was in decline. From time to time a modernizing sultan came to power hoping to enact reforms. The entrenched powers of the janissaries (elite troops) and ulamas (Muslim authorities), however, usually put a stop to such efforts. The similarly entrenched Mamluk (MAM-luke) military force that ran the Egyptian government increasingly alienated landlords and other elites with its demands for more taxes.

Napoleon and Egypt

MAP 23.2 Napoleonic Europe, 1796–1815

Under Napoleon the military scene across Europe was tumultuous and bloody until 1815, when the allied forces of Austria, Prussia, Russia, and Great Britain finally defeated the French emperor's "Grand Army." French forces brought revolutionary ideas and aroused national feeling. Like many empires, Napoleon's suffered from overreach; after its defeat, the victors redrew the political map of Europe to ensure a balance of power across the continent.

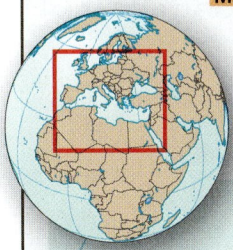

Napoleon Celebrates the Birthday of Muhammad

Napoleon's invasion of Egypt simultaneously brutalized and tried to accommodate Egyptians. The French army ransacked homes and public buildings, but Napoleon himself made sympathetic gestures such as the celebration in 1799 of the birth of the Prophet Muhammad depicted here. Though they labeled the French as hypocrites, some Egyptians welcomed the books and scientific drawings Napoleon made available to them in the name of Enlightenment. (Private Collection/Roger-Viollet, Paris/ Bridgeman Art Library.)

To some among these elites, the Atlantic revolutions provided a wealth of ideas for reform. Napoleon entered the country not only accompanied by a huge team of doctors, artists, scientists, and other learned men, but also armed with proposals for more enlightened rule. Amid combined resistance from the Mamluks, Ottomans, and British, who aimed to stop the French, Napoleon and the French army departed Egypt. Nonetheless, they left behind rising interest in European ideas, political innovation, and technology. No one was a better student and imitator than Muhammad Ali, often called the founder of modern Egypt.

Muhammad Ali

An officer in the Ottoman forces, Muhammad Ali had worked his way up the military ranks during the anti-French campaign. Born in the Ottoman Balkans (present-day Albania), Muhammad Ali began his career as a merchant before the Ottoman army drafted him as part of the Albanian quota of young men owed to the Ottomans. Muhammad Ali's rise to power was based on military accomplishments, but also on the negotiating skills he learned as a merchant. As a politician he exchanged favors with ordinary people and persuaded wealthy traders and soldiers alike to support his ouster of the hated Mamluks.

Appointed viceroy in 1805, Muhammad Ali set out to modernize Egypt, hiring French and other European administrators, technicians, and military men to advise him. Illiterate until he was forty-seven, he had many works translated into Arabic, the translations being read to him as they progressed. One major work, a translation of Italian political theorist Machiavelli's *The Prince*, he cut short because the message was "commonplace," Muhammad Ali reportedly announced. "I see clearly that I have nothing to learn from Machiavelli. I know many more tricks than he knew."[15] He advanced economic specialization in the country, sponsoring the large-scale production of cotton by several hundred thousand slaves while discouraging agriculture that was not for the market. Centralization of government, founding of public schools, improvement of transportation, and tighter bureaucratic control of Islam rounded out Muhammad Ali's reforms. His death in 1849 left his dream to make Egypt fully independent of the Ottomans unfulfilled, but like Napoleon he proved successful in applying the rational programs of the age.

Revolution Continued in the Western Hemisphere

FOCUS

What were the motives and methods of revolutionaries in the Caribbean and Latin America?

Such was the strength of late eighteenth-century global contacts that news of the French and American revolutions quickly spread to other parts of the Atlantic world. In the Western Hemisphere, revolutions broke out on the island of Hispaniola, motivating slave revolts elsewhere and arousing fear among whites. In Latin America, rebellion erupted not only among slaves and oppressed workers but also among middle- and upper-class creoles such as Simon Bolivar who wanted independence from Spain and Portugal. The Napoleonic Wars disturbed global trade, adding further to discontent and swelling the calls for political change. Soon concerted uprisings of peoples—rich, working-class, free peasants, and slaves—rose to fight for freedom in the Caribbean and across Latin America.

Revolution in Haiti 1791–1804

News of the French Revolution spread to the Caribbean island of Hispaniola, where the sugar plantations and coffee farms enriched merchants, plantation owners, and sugar refiners—whites and free blacks alike. The western part of the island was the French colony of Saint-Domingue (san-doe-MANGH, modern Haiti). The eastern part of Hispaniola was Santo Domingo (modern Dominican Republic), a colony of Spain. Saint-Domingue was the wealthiest colony in the region, in part because the newly independent United States could now purchase sugar from French rather than British plantations, and it did so from Saint-Domingue. This thriving trade inspired investors and merchants in France to pour vast sums into expanding production there.

As we saw in Chapter 22, Caribbean slaves lived under inhumane conditions. The hot, humid climate made laborious work punishing and kept their life span short. Some committed suicide; women used plant medicines to induce abortions and prevent bearing children who would live in misery. Slaves also developed community bonds to sustain them. The spirit of community and resistance arose from the daily trade of vegetables grown by the slaves in their small garden plots, from the use of a common language made up of French and various African dialects, and from joint participation in Vodou—a religious tradition observed by slaves on the islands.

Solidarity and suffering made the Caribbean ripe for revolution. Slave uprisings took place regularly, and individual slaves escaped into the forests and hills to create new communities of independent people, as they did across the Hispanic world. Added to this, the Caribbean—like the entire Atlantic region—was a crossroads of ideas. Among those ideas were freedom and human rights, circulating not only among African and North American slaves but also among the several thousand free blacks and mulattos in Haiti, who constituted some 30 percent of the slave owners in the region. When their white counterparts passed legislation putting them at political and economic disadvantage despite their success as plantation owners and traders, these free blacks founded the Society for Friends of the Blacks in 1788 and used it to lobby enlightened politicians in Paris for equality. When the French Revolution broke out in 1789, their demands grew louder. "You must return to these oppressed citizens," a group of free blacks entreated the National Assembly in October 1789, "the rights that have been unjustly stripped from them." In the face of continuing white hostility, they became, as one free black put it in 1790, "more committed than ever to uphold [our rights] with the last drop of our blood."[16]

The slaves were roused by news of revolution too. Rumors that French revolutionaries had freed them spread among the slaves, and in 1791 an organized slave uprising erupted in Saint-Domingue (see Map 23.3). From a cluster of leaders, the free black Pierre-Dominique Toussaint Louverture (too-SAN loo-ver-CHURE) emerged as the most able military commander. The slave revolt moved from success to success, and an enthusiastic French official sent to calm the scene did quite the opposite of what the planters wanted: he issued

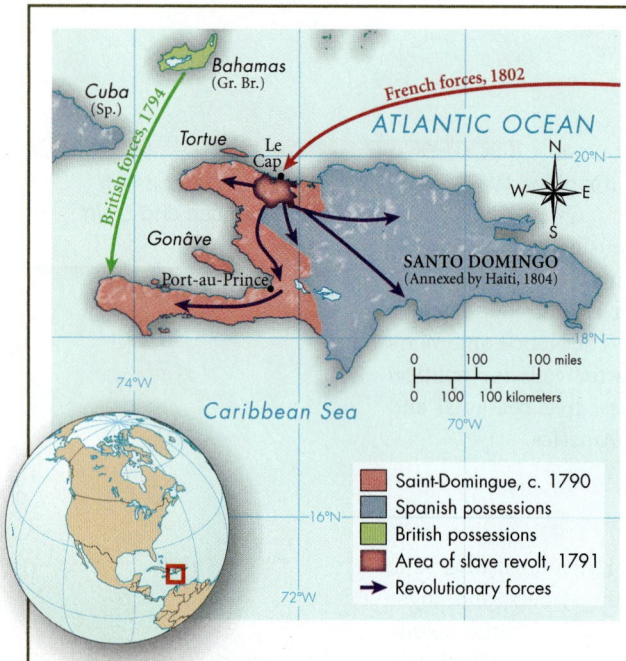

MAP 23.3 Haitian Rebellion and Independence, 1791–1804

The French colony of Saint-Domingue was a global crossroads for the sale of slaves and the sugar they produced. Commerce brought with it the flow of new ideas from around the world, whereas slavery produced not only grievances but solidarity. Even free blacks faced racism, and the Enlightenment ideas of human rights and dignity inspired them to protest. Soon after the French Revolution broke out in 1789, slaves in Saint-Domingue revolted and ultimately declared themselves the independent nation of Haiti.

a proclamation in 1793 granting slaves their freedom. In 1794, against the wishes of plantation owners and merchants—both black and white—the French revolutionary government formally declared that blacks had rights equal to those of whites. This news quickly passed across the Caribbean and Latin America, sparking further uprisings and rebellions against European rulers.

Conditions in Saint-Domingue evolved rapidly as Toussaint, himself a former slave and one grateful to France for its support of black equality, joined the French in driving back the British and Spanish, who hoped to conquer the French portion of the island for themselves. The black plantation owners refused to cooperate politically or economically with ex-slaves, and civil war broke out. In 1800 Toussaint defeated them too and issued a series of stiff reforms. Although slaves were free, they were to return to the sugar plantations, Toussaint legislated, and for their work they would receive a quarter of the profit from sugar production. The owners would receive another fourth, and the government would receive half.

By this time, however, Napoleon had come to power in France. Answering the appeal of Saint-Domingue plantation owners—who wanted far more profit than 25 percent—he determined to "pursue the rebels without mercy [and] flush them out," thereby regaining the upper hand in the colony.[17] The campaign led to the capture of Toussaint, who died in jail in 1803. With all blacks now uniting against any French takeover, however, the invading army suffered huge losses—some 50,000 of an army of 58,000—many of them from yellow fever. On January 1, 1804, the black generals who defeated the French proclaimed the independent republic of Haiti.

Revolutions in Latin America 1810–1830

The thirst for change gripped people in other empires. In Spain's Latin American empire discontent among artisans, agricultural workers, and slaves, along with rivalries among creoles and Spanish-born officials sent from the homeland, erupted under the pressures of the Napoleonic conquest of the Iberian peninsula in 1808. "It is now time to overthrow the [Spanish] yoke," a group of rebels in La Paz declared in 1809. "It is now time to declare the principle of liberty in these miserable colonies."[18] This spirit swept the Spanish lands, as the government back home in Europe crumbled.

Impact of the Napoleonic Wars

When Napoleon invaded Spain and Portugal in 1807, he sent the ruling dynasties packing to give his own family control. With British help, the Portuguese monarch fled to Brazil in hopes of ruling the empire from the colonies, while in Spain the monarch was replaced by Napoleon's brother Joseph. Guerrilla warfare erupted against the French while Spanish activists also organized **juntas** (HUN-tahs), or ruling councils, around the country despite French rule. In 1808, a national junta unveiled a broad program for reform. In the Spanish colonies, political confusion set in as news of the junta's plan for a constitution-based government spread. Some creole leaders welcomed the planned constitution, but other creoles in business and agriculture sensed an opportunity not simply for constitutional reform but for ousting officials from Spain altogether. Like imperial rulers elsewhere, the Spanish kings had come to treat their colonies as cash cows, milking them dry to pay for a lavish way of life in Europe. In the disorder brought on by the Napoleonic invasions and the appearance of reform-minded leaders in Spain, colonial leaders saw an opportunity to end these heavy burdens.

junta A ruling council.

The Napoleonic Wars opened up other avenues to economic and political change. Because Spain was allied with Britain in the wars against Napoleon, the people in the Spanish colonies had new contacts and new economic opportunities. Like Britain, Spain had formerly tried to prevent its colonies from manufacturing their own goods or trading directly with other countries. All goods were to be carried in Spanish vessels. Trade-minded local creoles resented these restrictions, as well as the privileged place of Spanish traders and the monopoly on good jobs enjoyed by Spanish aristocrats. The wars upset this state of affairs, throwing open ports to British vessels carrying both new ideas and exciting new products—both of them benefits of unrestricted trade. Mule drivers, parish priests, and market people also spread global news, alerting neighborhoods in distant towns to the possibility for change. Aspiring leaders saw a situation full of potential for new prosperity and freedom. Their struggles for independence would last until 1830 (see Map 23.4).

Toussaint Louverture

In 1791, Toussaint Louverture, a freed slave and slave owner, joined a slave revolt that erupted in Saint-Domingue, the prosperous sugar colony of France in the Caribbean. Louverture, shown here in his general's uniform, possessed strong military skills and soon became the leader of the Haitian Revolution, writing the constitution of the fledgling nation and working to defeat the Spanish, British, and French, who in turn sought to take the former colony for themselves. Ironically, although he modeled his new nation on French ideals of freedom and citizenship, Louverture re-enslaved many Haitians. He died in a French prison in 1803. (Private Collection/ Bridgeman Art Library.)

Reformers and rebels sprang into action throughout Latin America. In the lucrative colony of Mexico, Father Miguel Hidalgo, a Mexican priest trained in Enlightenment thought by the Jesuits and exiled by the Spanish to a rural parish because of his ideas, opened a campaign against colonial rule in 1810. His soldiers were his parishioners, most of them native Americans who worked as day laborers for the Spanish and creoles. The collapse of silver mining and the soaring prices of food made them desperate. Calling for the complete ouster of Spaniards, they wanted their jobs and their standard of living restored. Hidalgo's army swelled to some sixty thousand fighters, who hoped to get paid or fed as they fought. Drawn from the popular classes, the average fighter, in the opinion of the Mexican viceroy, was a "robber, assassin, and libertine."[19] Yet most of Hidalgo's followers were motivated by simple outrage at the poverty and oppression they faced—not by robbery or lust. They slaughtered entire contingents of Spaniards, creoles, and anyone else who stood in their path.

Father Hidalgo was captured and executed in 1811, but other armies appeared under the leadership of mulattos, mestizos (mixed-blood people of native American and European ancestry), and well-born creoles, who wanted the Spanish out and opportunity reborn. These armies—most notably that under the humbly born mestizo priest, Father José Maria Morelos—carried the uprising to the west of Mexico, using guerrilla tactics and living off the support of legions of women, who provisioned and tended the troops. The Spanish, however, were able to turn other native Americans, slaves, and mestizos against creole-led armies by pointing out that creoles owned the exploitative large farms. By 1815 the Spanish had put an end to this first stage of the Mexican drive for independence and had executed its leaders—adding to the hatred of colonialism that many felt.

Amid ongoing attacks from bandits and personal armies, new leadership emerged in Mexico, one that was more capable of victory. The key to its success lay in creoles' efforts to set aside their prejudices to unite with the native masses. Creoles adopted a nationalist sensibility, accepting the idea to distinguish *all* those inhabitants of Mexico born in the New World—the *Americanos*—from those born in Spain. Continued guerrilla fighting eroded the institutions of Spanish rule in Mexico, but the decisive move came when the creole leader Augustin de Iturbide (ee-tur-BEE-deh) allied his forces with Vicente Guerrero (goo-RER-eh), a leader of the popular armies, himself a mestizo and thus heir to the

MAP 23.4

Revolutions in Latin America, 1810–1830

The Spanish government, influenced by Enlightenment ideas about rational government, attempted to streamline its rule and enhance colonial profitability. As revolution rolled across the Atlantic world, colonial subjects in Latin America were equally affected by Enlightenment ideas about liberty and the opportunities it would bring. Revolutions in Latin America were prolonged, however, and they were wide-ranging, bringing in people from many walks of life and ethnicities as well as soldiers from different parts of the world—all motivated by the potential for revolutionary transformation.

Independence for Mexico

Morelos legacy of native rights. Iturbide had once served the Spanish as an army officer, winning battles and collecting tribute for the government. As was so often the case, his creole birth blocked his advance in the Spanish colony, despite his record. Resentment of unearned Spanish privilege made him a natural ally of people who were also held back by what the Spanish saw as low birth—native American, black, mestizo, or mulatto. Iturbide's and Guerrero's forces reached an agreement for a constitutional monarchy independent of Spain. In 1821, the three hundredth anniversary of the Spanish conquest of Mexico, Iturbide entered Mexico City as Spanish rule disintegrated. Yet it was not this event but rather the start of Father Hidalgo's uprising of the common people on September 16, 1810 that came to mark Mexico's Day of Independence.

Across South America similar independent rebel armies sprang up, most of them controlled by a local strongman, or *caudillo* (kauh-DEE-yoh), who was able to raise armies from people of all classes and ethnicities. Such a caudillo was José Gervasio Artigas in Uruguay. Artigas was a rancher, cattle thief, and, by virtue of having his own army, a regional peacekeeper. While keeping peace locally, the *caudillos* had as many problems getting along with one another as they did enduring Spanish rule. One quality these creoles shared, however, was their contempt for native Americans, Africans, mulattos, and mestizos. Simon Bolivar mustered caudillo support to liberate Venezuela in 1811, but at the time he firmly believed that slavery could be maintained in the fight for national independence.

Independence for Peru

Nonetheless, with the Spanish monarch's return to power after the defeat of Napoleon in 1815, it became clear that creoles in Latin America needed to ally themselves with oppressed workers, agricultural laborers, and the *llaneros* (yah-NEH-rows), or local cowboys, of all races (see Lives and Livelihoods: The Cowboy Way of Life). Bolivar made himself one with the llaneros, demonstrating that his troops were militarily fit and daring riders; he called for the forging of a Gran Colombia—a united nation like the United States, composed of all the liberated lands. To create such a state, the foreign-born Spanish must be ousted for good. Increasing Spanish oppression and the appeal to all "Americans" did some good, enabling Bolivar, with the help of black troops, to take Bogotá, Caracas, and Quito by 1822. In the meantime Argentinean general José de San Martin was conquering Buenos Aires, western Argentina, and Chile, moving into Peru in 1818. His armies bogged down in Peru, however, leaving the final task of ousting the Spanish to Bolivar, whose armies finally took Lima in 1823 and upper Peru or Bolivia in 1825 (see again Map 23.4). Both San Martin and Bolivar had originally seen no conflict between their own freedom and the existence of slavery, but as the need for slave support became obvious, Bolivar declared it "madness that a revolution for liberty should try to maintain slavery."[20] To get the support of the vast number of slaves, many liberation leaders promised and awarded slave soldiers their emancipation, either immediately as a way of attracting fighters or after the wars as a reward for victory.

Independence for Brazil

Brazil gained its independence from Portugal more tranquilly than the Spanish colonies did from Spain, and with little change in the social situation: slavery and the bureaucracy alike were left intact. The ruling family, safe in Brazil, was summoned back to Portugal at the end of the Napoleonic Wars, but the king left his son Pedro behind in the capital of Rio de Janeiro. Pedro proceeded to cooperate with business and other leaders and in 1822 declared Brazil independent of Portugal and made himself king. With the masses set

Upper-Class Woman and Her Slaves in Eighteenth-Century Brazil

Many aristocrats and wealthy landowners in prerevolutionary South America followed European customs in such matters as display of class privileges. For instance, in Europe servants wore uniforms or livery, as do these slaves as they carry their upper-class mistress in a sedan chair and follow her on foot. Aristocratic status was often evident in the number of people accompanying a noble person, but these slaves also show the variety in slave livelihoods. (J. Bedmar/Iberfoto/The Image Works.)

The Cowboy Way of Life

Gauchos

Gauchos lived away from towns, cities, and settled ranches. Like cowboys, their North American counterparts, gauchos prided themselves on a range of skills with wild horses and other animals. In this nineteenth-century colored etching, a gaucho hurls a rope with a ball on its end to capture a rhea by entangling its legs in the rope. As South America developed commerce, manufacturing, and modern industry, the gaucho came to symbolize the independent spirit of the young nations. (akg-images.)

One of the most important livelihoods in the Western Hemisphere was that of cowboys or cattle hunters, who differed from the later settled ranchers for whom cowboys came to work. Called *gauchos* in Argentina, *llaneros* in Venezuela and Colombia, and *vaqueros* in Mexico, cowboys rode the prairies rounding up the wild horses and cattle that grazed there. They created their livelihood from scratch, for only after 1494 when Columbus first introduced cattle into the Caribbean did cattle spread across both North and South America. As the livestock multiplied, cowboys hunted down the wild animals and slaughtered them. Cowboys developed an entire range of skills, making lassos, for example, from horses' tails. But their most lucrative products were animal hides and byproducts such as leather and tallow for candle-making.

These herdsmen, similar to those on the Asian steppes, were usually nomadic, with their own customs and ways of life. Living as far as possible from cities and the centers of government, they aimed to keep their independence and to escape government regulation, which increased under the Bourbon Reforms. Cowboys in all areas usually refused to ride mares as an unmanly practice and generally prided themselves on maintaining the rough, masculine ways of frontiersmen. Enterprising landowners, however, set up vast ranches and challenged the claims of the gauchos, llaneros, and vaqueros, who saw wild horses as their own. Settled ranchers hired their own cattle tenders and then encouraged the government to see the independent cowboys as "cattle rustlers" and thieves.

Their independent way of life eventually led nation builders to mythologize gauchos, llaneros, and other cowboys as symbols of freedom for the nation as a whole. However, cowboys played a more direct role in both politics and nation building in the nineteenth century. Their experience with horses made them valuable fighters on both sides in the war for Latin American independence, and their survival skills helped them endure the rough conditions of battle.

QUESTIONS TO CONSIDER

1. **For what reasons would some gauchos and llaneros ally themselves with upper-class creoles in the Latin American independence movements?**
2. **Why have cowboys become such icons in both North and South America?**

For Further Information:

Loy, R. Philip. *Westerns and American Culture, 1930–1955*. 2001.
Oliven, Ruben George. *Tradition Matters: Modern Gaucho Identity in Brazil*. 1996.
Reding, Nick. *The Last Cowboys at the End of the World: The Last Gauchos of Patagonia*. 2001.
Slatta, Richard W. *Gauchos and the Vanishing Frontier*. 1983.

against Portuguese foreigners, there was widespread rejoicing at independence even without major social change. A frontier society like the United States, Brazil beckoned entrepreneurs, adventurers, and exiles from around the world as a land of opportunity.

Consequences of Independence

For the most part, however, the new Latin American countries had been so devastated by years of exploitation, misrule, banditry, and armed uprising that except in Brazil, economies lay in shambles. Instead of effecting social reform that would have encouraged economic initiative, most new governments worked to ensure creole dominance, often refusing the promised slave emancipation. In 1799 a Spanish bishop-elect had noted the "great conflict of interests and the hostility which invariably prevails between those who have nothing and those who have everything."[21] Independence did not transform this situation, and thus the popular forces that would have promoted innovation and increased activity at the grassroots did not materialize as effectively as in the newly independent United States.

New Ideologies and Revolutionary Legacies

The revolutions in the Americas and Europe achieved independence for some states but deliberately failed to bring full and free citizenship to slaves, women, and a range of indentured and oppressed peoples. Nonetheless, they left aspirations for the economic opportunity and personal freedom that define the term *liberalism*. Inspired by Enlightenment principles, revolutionaries sought to create centralized nation-states ruled under a constitution as opposed to monarchical governments given to arbitrary rulings by aristocrats and princes. In the early days of both the North American and French republics, this faith in a unified nation of like-minded peoples, which came to be known as **nationalism**, went hand in hand with liberalism. The idea was that the unified rule of law under a single nation, as embodied in the U.S. Constitution and the Declaration of the Rights of Man and of the Citizen, would guarantee constitutional rights and economic growth through free trade. Latin American leaders such as Bolivar had much less faith in all the people of the nation being ready for participation in government (see Reading the Past: Simon Bolivar on Latin American Independence).

The definition of nationalism became more complicated even as it was being born. For one thing, a host of opponents to the new governments of the United States and France believed that time-honored monarchical traditions were a better guarantee of a peaceful society than constitutions and republics. Such thought was called **conservatism**, and many prominent conservatives across Europe and the Americas argued the case for tradition, continuity, and gradual reform based on practical experience. Appalled by the violence and bloodshed of the French Revolution, Edmund Burke of England attacked Enlightenment ideas of a social contract, citizenship, and new fangled constitutions as destructive to the wisdom of the ages.

Like conservatism, **romanticism**—a philosophical and artistic movement that glorified nature, emotion, and the imagination—emerged partly in reaction to the Enlightenment's reliance on reason, especially after the violent excesses of the French Revolution. Closely related to early nationalism, romanticism was also a response to the political turmoil of the Napoleonic Wars. There thus grew up a romantic nationalism, especially in territories such as the German states. Romantic nationalists revered language and traditions as sources of a common feeling among peoples—for instance, among all the German peoples. "Perfect laws are the beautiful and free forms of the interior life of a nation," wrote one German jurist, criticizing reformers' desire to take the Napoleonic Code as a model for change. For him, the Napoleonic Code had not "come out of the life of the German nation."[22] Romantic nationalists took less pride in law codes, well-defined citizenship, and civic rights than in their ancient past and shared cultural experience.

To make the revolutionary legacy more complicated yet, Napoleon Bonaparte and Simon Bolivar ultimately became romantic heroes to rich and poor alike, even though they represented Enlightenment ideals of social mobility, consistent systems of laws, a rational approach to government, and economic modernizing. "My wife and I," said one distillery worker in southern France in 1822, "have the emperor in our guts."[23] The many poets,

nationalism A belief in the importance of one's nation, stemming from its unique laws, language, traditions, and history.

conservatism A political philosophy emphasizing the continuation of traditional institutions and opposition to sudden change in the established order.

romanticism A European philosophical and artistic movement of the late eighteenth and early nineteenth centuries that valued feeling over reason and glorified traditional customs, nature, and the imagination.

READING THE PAST

Simon Bolivar on Latin American Independence

Simon Bolivar was a heroic "Liberator" to some observers, an authoritarian creole to others. Some of these contradictory images come from Bolivar's own views of the situation in Latin America. This document is from Bolivar's "Letter from Jamaica," written in exile after his 1815 flight from Spanish forces. In it Bolivar expresses his thoughts about liberation from the Spanish and the possibilities for representative government thereafter.

> The position of the inhabitants of the American hemisphere has for centuries been purely passive, its political role nonexistent. We are still at a level lower than slavery, and for that reason it is more difficult for us to raise ourselves to attain the enjoyment of freedom. . . . States are enslaved because of either the nature or the abuse of their constitutions; a people is therefore enslaved when the government by its essential nature or by its vices tramples on and usurps the rights of the citizens or subjects. . . .
>
> As long as our countrymen do not acquire the political capacities and virtues that distinguish our brothers of the north, fully democratic systems, far from working to our advantage, will, I fear, bring about our downfall. Unfortunately, these traits, to the extent to which they are required, do not appear to be within our reach. On the contrary, we are dominated by the vices acquired during the rule of a nation like Spain, which has only distinguished itself in brutality, ambition, vindictiveness, and greed. . . .
>
> South Americans have tried to create liberal, even perfect, institutions, doubtless out of that instinct which all men have to attain the greatest happiness possible, which necessarily follows in civil societies founded on the principles of justice, liberty, and equality. But can we maintain in proper balance the difficult charge of a republic? Is it conceivable that a newly liberated people can soar to the height of freedom, . . . without falling into an abyss? Such a marvel is inconceivable and never before seen.

Source: Carta de Jamaica, September 6, 1815, in *Escritos políticos*. Selección e introd., de Graciela Soriano (Madrid: Alianza Editorial, 1969). Translated by Donald R. Kelley.

EXAMINING THE EVIDENCE

1. How does Bolivar characterize Spanish rule?
2. How does he think this rule has affected his contemporaries' capacity for self-government?
3. What seem to be the political options left to Latin Americans once they have obtained their independence?

musicians, and artists influenced by romanticism earned their livelihoods not only by glorifying feelings instead of reason but by spreading the myth of Napoleon and Simon Bolivar as superhuman rulers who overcame horrific obstacles to become conquerors. These powerful, if conflicting, ideas—liberalism, nationalism, conservatism, and romanticism—resonated down through the next centuries, shaping both local and global politics.

COUNTERPOINT

Religious Revival in a Secular Age

FOCUS

What trends in Enlightenment and revolutionary society did religious revival challenge?

As we have seen in this chapter, in the challenge to long-established empires, some peoples declared their sovereignty and set up states in opposition to centuries-old forms of rulership. In the influential cases of France and the United States, the principle of a secular state—one tied to no particular religion—flourished, supported by the Enlightenment idea that reason rather than faith should determine social, political, and economic regulations. The French under Robespierre devised national festivals to substitute for religious holidays and even, at the height of revolutionary fervor, converted churches into "temples of reason." But secularism did not prevail everywhere, and movements arose that countered the weakening of religious belief or its supposedly empty ritual. In Europe and North America, great surges of religious fervor took hold of people's daily lives, and in the Arabian peninsula reformers sought to restore Muslims to the fundamental teachings of Islam.

Christianity's Great Awakening

The Great Awakening

The spirit of Christian revival first took shape in Prussia, where Lutherans had called for a renewal of faith in the late seventeenth century. As Protestant revival spread across the European continent, people joined new evangelical churches, most of them focused on sharpening the inward experience of faith. In the middle of the eighteenth century, a wave of revivals that historians term the "Great Awakening" took place throughout Britain and the North American colonies. Emotional orators such as the English preachers John Wesley and George Whitefield appeared at large rallies, rousing the faithful to break off from the sterile ritual of established churches and to join new communities of faith such as Methodism, the evangelical Protestant church founded by Wesley and characterized by active concern with social welfare and public morals. Some observers were appalled by the sight of worshipers literally weeping at the perils of damnation; in the words of one, the Great Awakening was "horrible beyond expression."[24] Nonetheless, in the middle colonies of British North America alone, some 550 new Protestant congregations were organized between 1740 and 1770.

New Churches and the State

Beginning in around 1800, the United States experienced a Second Great Awakening, where thousands at a time flocked to revival meetings. Describing the scene, one commentator wrote that "some of the people were singing, others praying, some praying for mercy," as they testified to their faith in the face of the growth of science, rationalism, and emotional coldness in the old churches. At the same time, African American slaves were also fervent believers, finding in religion evidence of their humanity (see Reading the Past: Phillis Wheatley, "On Being Brought from Africa to America"). Religion later provided arguments for an end to slavery and were part of a rising democratic impulse among people who together addressed their comments directly and emotionally to God. Despite the surge in religious enthusiasm, governments such as that of the United States declined to proclaim an official faith because of their people's religious diversity and because of Enlightenment thinkers' suspicion of churches as institutions.

Government and Religion Allied

In some instances, ties between government and religion became stronger, not weaker. In the Arabian peninsula an eighteenth-century religious reformer, Muhammad ibn Abd al-Wahhabi developed a strong alliance with Muhammad ibn Sa'ud, the head of a small market town. Ibn Abd al-Wahhabi called on Muslims to return to the tenets of Islam, most importantly the worship of the single god, Allah. He felt that Islam had been betrayed by an overemphasis on the Prophet Muhammad and other human saints. At the time, in fact, people worshiped local fortunetell-

Mecca and Wahhabism

Wahhabis fought for a purified Islamic faith, one that eliminated the common practice in the Middle East and elsewhere in the Muslim world of worshiping at religious shrines and the tombs of saints. They destroyed the tombs of the Prophet Muhammad's family but were stopped from overturning the tomb of the Prophet himself. Because the pilgrimage to Mecca was one of the five "pillars" of the faith, Mecca itself, depicted here, remained a center of religious devotion that grew in importance as Islam spread around the world. (Popular Traditions Museum, Damascus/Giraudon/Bridgeman Art Library.)

READING THE PAST

Phillis Wheatley, "On Being Brought from Africa to America"

Born in Senegal in 1853, Phillis Wheatley was seven when she was sold into slavery to a Boston family, who educated her along with their children. Wheatley published celebrated poetry while a slave, becoming a sensation in New England and even traveling to England in 1773. A voyager to three continents, Wheatley was a true child of the Atlantic world. This celebrated poem, written while she was a teenager, contains a host of ideas and images about slavery and her own condition. As you read, consider why this short verse might pose problems for some modern readers.

'Twas mercy brought me from my Pagan land,
Taught my benighted soul to understand
That there's a God, that there's a Saviour too:
Once I redemption neither sought now knew,
Some view our sable race with scornful eye,
"Their colour is a diabolic die."
Remember, Christians, Negroes, black as Cain,
May be refin'd, and join th' angelic train.

EXAMINING THE EVIDENCE

1. **In what ways does this poem reflect Enlightenment thought?**
2. **How does it relate to the Great Awakening?**
3. **Which ideas in the poem might present-day critics condemn? Which ideas might they praise?**

Arabia, 1802–1807

Wahhabi-Sa'ud Alliance

ers and healers as well as graves, rocks, and trees. One traveler found Arabs "so negligent of religion" that they were "generally considered infidels." This was certainly the opinion of ibn Abd al-Wahhabi and his followers, who declared these departures from the tenets of Islam to be paganism itself. He got help in his quest to return Arabs to the basic principles of Islam not only from his large and active following but from the house of Sa'ud—the town's leading family. Unity of worship would come with political unity, led in ibn Abd al-Wahhabi's mind by the Sa'uds. They would unite the various tribes under a purified Islamic practice, realizing al-Wahhabi's belief that "Arab" meant Muslim.

Muslims, if they are physically able, are instructed to make a pilgrimage to Mecca during their lifetime as one of their basic obligations. The Wahhabis, as the reformer's followers came to be called (at first, by their enemies), were determined to take control of Mecca for the Sa'uds and for their cause of Islamic fundamentalism. In 1802, making their first attempt, they destroyed all mosques dedicated to the worship of Muhammad. Being connected with the Sa'uds put real muscle to the Wahhabis' religious fervor, and in 1807 they finally wrenched the religious sites of Mecca and Medina from Ottoman control. Although the Ottomans would regain possession in 1840, the alliance between the Sa'uds and the Wahhabis remained, to become ever more powerful in the twentieth century as the discovery of oil in the region fortified the Sa'uds and the Wahhabis along with them.[25]

Conclusion

This period saw widespread challenges to centuries-old empires in the Americas, Europe, the Caribbean, West Asia, and Egypt. The most direct of these challenges came from the popular uprisings known as the Atlantic revolutions. In these revolutions, state power and rigid social structures impinged on people's lives by promoting high taxes and controlling commerce. Deepening poverty and frustrated ambition afflicted ordinary folk, whether in

France or in Peru, causing both riots and political activism. These economic conditions awakened some revolutionaries. Others were inspired to push for political reform by Enlightenment ideas about government based on individual rights and the rational rule of law rather than on inherited privilege and notions of a divine order. Simon Bolivar was one such secular-minded revolutionary and state-builder. Other political actors, such as the Sa'ud family of the Arabian peninsula, drew on religious fervor in their state-building, forming a counterpoint to the general trend.

Independence in the Western Hemisphere affected the entire world. As frontier societies, North American and Latin American countries served as magnets for European investment and for people searching for better livelihoods. Still, countless people of all classes and ethnicities who participated in the uprisings in the Atlantic world benefited not at all or in the most limited way. Slavery remained entrenched in some countries; women, free blacks, and other people of color were usually disqualified from participating in politics. As representative government developed, it too was uneven, especially in Latin America, where a creole elite dominated the new nations.

These political revolutions nonetheless formed a platform for further social and economic change, and we remember them for their powerful and enduring influence. In the short term, the revolutions created conditions for heightened manufacturing and eventually the Industrial Revolution. In the long term, they gave citizens confidence to use their freedom. "It is harder to release a nation from servitude than to enslave a free nation," Bolivar had written, and in this respect the age of revolutions nurtured aspirations and opened up opportunities.

NOTES

1. Luis Peru de Lacroix, *Diario de Cucuramanga* (Caracas: Comité ejecutivo del Bicentenario de Simon Bolivar, 1982), 67, quoted in Charles Minguet, ed., *Simon Bolivar: Unité impossible* (Paris: La Découverte, 1983), 13.
2. Voltaire, *Essai sur les moeurs*, 3:179.
3. Quoted in Hilda L. Smith and Berenice A. Carroll, eds., *Women's Political and Social Thought* (Bloomington: Indiana University Press, 2000), 133.
4. "Political Testament," in George I. Mosse et al., eds., *Europe in Review* (Chicago: Rand McNally and Co., 1957), 111–112.
5. Quoted in Richard Wortman, *Scenarios of Power: Myth and Ceremony in Russian Monarchy, From Peter the Great to the Death of Nicholas I* (Princeton, NJ: Princeton University Press, 1995), 130.
6. *Seminario Económico de México*, 1811, quoted in Silvia Marina Arrom, *The Women of Mexico City, 1790–1857* (Palo Alto, CA: Stanford University Press, 1985), 18.
7. Edward Long, quoted in Barbara Bush, *Slave Women in the Caribbean, 1650–1838* (London: Heinemann, 1990), 15, 51.
8. Quoted in Paul Dukes, ed. and trans., *Russia Under Catherine the Great: Select Documents on Government and Society* (Newtonville, MA: Priental Research Partners, 1978), 112.
9. Dukes, *Russia Under Catherine the Great*, 112, 115.
10. Alexander Hamilton, *Federalist Papers*, Number 15.
11. Letter to John Jay, March 14, 1779, http://www.c250.columbia.edu/c250_celebrates/remarkable_columbians/alexander_hamilton.html.
12. Quoted in Ron Chernow, *Alexander Hamilton* (New York: Penguin, 2004), 316.
13. Quoted in Lynn Hunt, *The French Revolution and Human Rights: A Brief Documentary History* (Boston: Bedford/St. Martins, 1996), 65.
14. Quoted in Annie Jourdain, *Napoléon: Héros, Imperator, Mécène* (Paris: Aubier, 1998), 34.
15. Quoted in Albert Hourani, *Arabic Thought in the Liberal Age, 1798–1939* (London: Oxford University Press, 1962), "Address to the National Assembly, to Our Lords the Representatives of the Nation," quoted in Laurent Dubois and John D. Garrigus, eds., *Slave Revolution in the Caribbean, 1789–1804: A Brief History with Documents* (Boston: Bedford/St. Martins, 2005), 69.
16. Quoted Dubois and Garrigus, *Slave Revolution*, 77.
17. "Notes [from Napoleon Bonaparte] to Serve as Instructions to Give to the Captain General Leclerc," quoted in Dubois and Garrigus, *Slave Revolution*, 176.
18. "Proclamation of 1809," quoted in Peter Bakewell, *A History of Latin America: Empires and Sequels, 1450–1930* (Oxford, U.K.: Blackwell, 1997), 362.
19. Juan Ruiz de Apodaca, quoted in Richard Boyer and Geoffrey Spurling, eds., *Colonial Lives: Documents on Latin American History, 1550–1850* (New York: Oxford University Press, 2000), 305.
20. Quoted in George Reid Andrews, *Afro-Latin America, 1800–2000* (New York: Oxford University Press, 2004), 57.

21. Quoted in John Lynch, "The Origins of Spanish American Independence," in *The Cambridge History of Latin America* (Cambridge, U.K.: Cambridge University Press, 1985), 3:32.
22. Quoted in Martyn Lyons, *Napoleon Bonaparte and the Legacy of the French Revolution* (London: Macmillan, 1994), 232.
23. Quoted in Lyons, *Napoleon Bonaparte*, v.
24. William Briggs, quoted in Phyllis Mack, *Heart Religion in the British Enlightenment: Gender and Emotion in Early Methodism* (New York: Cambridge University Press, 2008), 2.
25. John Esposito, *Islam, the Straight Path* (New York: Oxford University Press, 1991).

RESOURCES FOR RESEARCH

The Promise of Enlightenment

The Enlightenment had a global reach, sparking interest in South America and Japan as well as in Europe. Scientific curiosity among a range of people, as featured in Schiffer's book, led to ongoing experimentation.

Dalton, Susan. *Engendering the Republic of Letters: Reconnecting Public and Private Spheres*. 2003.

Gorbatov, Inna. *Catherine the Great and the French Philosophers of the Enlightenment: Montesquieu, Voltaire, Rousseau, Diderot and Grimm*. 2005.

Rowe, William T. *Saving the World: Chen Hongmou and Elite Consciousness in Eighteenth Century China*. 2001.

Schiffer, Michael B. *Drawing the Lightning Down: Benjamin Franklin and Electrical Technology in the Age of Enlightenment*. 2003.

Stein, Stanley J., and Barbara H. Stein. *Apogee of Empire: Spain and New Spain in the Age of Charles III, 1759–1789*. 2003.

Revolution in North America

The revolution in North America engaged the European powers, not only Britain but also France and Spain, as Elliott's masterful work shows. Linda Kerber highlights the many aspects of North American women's involvement as participants as well as symbols of liberty and rights.

Appleby, Joyce. *Inheriting the Revolution: The First Generation of Americans*. 2004.

Elliott, John H. *Empires of the Atlantic World: Britain and Spain in America, 1492–1830*. 2006.

Kerber, Linda. *Women of the Republic: Intellect and Ideology in the American Revolution*. 1986.

Middlekauff, Robert. *The Glorious Cause: The American Revolution, 1763–1789*. 2005.

Wood, Gordon S. *Revolutionary Characters: What Made the Founders Different?* 2006.

The French Revolution and the Napoleonic Empire

More than the American Revolution, this was the uprising heard round the world, and it has given rise to exciting studies of many kinds. The Web site at George Mason University has one of the most comprehensive online presentations of documents, images, and songs from the French Revolution.

French Revolution: http://chnm.gmu.edu/revolution/.

Hunt, Lynn. *Inventing Human Rights: A History*. 2007.

Marsot, Afaf Lutfi Al-Sayyid. *Egypt in the Reign of Muhammad Ali*. 1984.

Napoleonic Empire: http://www.bbc.co.uk/history/historic_figures/bonaparte_napoleon.shtml.

Shovlin, John. *The Political Economy of Virtue: Luxury, Patriotism, and the Origins of the French Revolution*. 2006.

Todd, Janet. *Mary Wollstonecraft: A Life*. 2000.

Revolution Continued in the Western Hemisphere

As revolution continued in the Atlantic world, the Caribbean and Latin America saw a wave of uprisings. Dubois movingly describes the causes and conduct of revolution in Haiti; the State University of New York/Albany maintains an excellent Web site on it.

Dubois, Laurent. *Avengers of the New World: The Story of the Haitian Revolution*. 2004.

Haitian revolution: http://www.albany.edu/~js3980/haitian-revolution.html.

Masur, Gerard. *Simón Bólivar*. 2006.

Morgan, Jennifer. *Laboring Women: Reproduction and Gender in New World Slavery*. 2004.

Van Young, Eric. *The Other Rebellion: Popular Violence, Ideology, and the Mexican Struggle for Independence, 1810–1821*. 2001.

COUNTERPOINT: Religious Revival in a Secular Age

The religious fervor that accompanied the age of reason is well chronicled in the works below.

Mack, Phyllis. *Heart Religion in the British Enlightenment: Gender and Emotion in Early Methodism*. 2008.

May, Cedrick. *Evangelism and Resistance in the Black Atlantic, 1760–1835*. 2008.

Qadhi, Abu Ammar Yasir. *A Critical Study of Shirk: Being a Translation and Commentary of Muhammad b. Abd al-Wahhab's Kashf al-Shubuhat*. 2002.

Vassiliev, Alexei. *A History of Saudi Arabia*. 1998.

▶ **For additional primary sources from this period**, see *Sources of Crossroads and Cultures*.

▶ **For Web sites, images, and documents related to topics in this chapter**, see Make History at bedfordstmartins.com/smith.

REVIEW

Online Study Guide
bedfordstmartins.com/smith

The major global development in this chapter ▶ The Atlantic revolutions and their short- and long-term significance.

IMPORTANT EVENTS

1751–1772	Publication of the *Encyclopedia*
1762	Jean-Jacques Rousseau publishes *The Social Contract* and *Emile*
1775–1781	Revolution in North America
1776	Adam Smith, *The Wealth of Nations*
1789	U.S. Constitution formally adopted; revolution begins in France
1791	Revolution begins in Haiti
1792	France declared a republic; Mary Wollstonecraft writes *A Vindication of the Rights of Woman*
1799	Napoleon comes to power
1804	Haiti becomes independent from France
1811	Simon Bolivar first takes up arms against Spain
1815	Napoleon defeated at Waterloo; Congress of Vienna resettles the boundaries of European states
1816	Argentina becomes independent from Spain
1817	Chile becomes independent from Spain
1821	Mexico and Peru become independent from Spain
1822	Brazil becomes independent from Portugal
1825	Bolivia becomes independent from Spain

KEY TERMS

conservatism (p. 783)
contract government (p. 762)
federation (p. 769)
general will (p. 773)
junta (p. 778)
laissez faire (p. 763)
liberalism (p. 763)
nationalism (p. 783)
public sphere (p. 764)
republic (p. 771)
romanticism (p. 783)

CHAPTER OVERVIEW QUESTIONS

1. What role did the Scientific Revolution and expanding global contacts play in the cultural and social movement known as the Enlightenment?
2. Why did prosperous and poor people alike join revolutions in the Americas and in France?
3. Why were the Atlantic revolutions so influential, even to the present day?

SECTION FOCUS QUESTIONS

1. What were the major ideas of the Enlightenment and their impacts?
2. What factors lay behind the war between North American colonists and Great Britain?
3. What changes emerged from the French Revolution and Napoleon's reign?
4. What were the motives and methods of revolutionaries in the Caribbean and Latin America?
5. What trends in Enlightenment and revolutionary society did religious revival challenge?

MAKING CONNECTIONS

1. What was the relationship between the Enlightenment and the political revolutions of the late eighteenth and early nineteenth centuries?
2. What are the common challenges that centuries-old empires faced during this period?
3. What makes Napoleon a significant historical figure?
4. Why was there so much bloodshed in the various efforts to achieve political and social change?

24

AT A CROSSROADS ▲

An artist from an elite samurai family, Kiyochika Kobayashi was so fascinated by technology and industry that in 1879 he placed a train front and center in this moonlit scene set in Takanawa Ushimachi, just outside of Tokyo. Earlier woodprints had portrayed the town as a slum called Oxtown with garbage strewn about its roads, but in this artist's eyes Takanawa Ushimachi became a prosperous, indeed alluring crossroads, thanks to the arrival of the railroad. Kiyochika changed the style of Japanese woodcuts by introducing into more traditional Japanese scenes such elements as clocks, cameras, electric lighting, and the massive cannons churned out by industry. (Santa Barbara Museum of Art, Gift of Dr. and Mrs. Roland A. Way.)

Industry and Everyday Life

1750–1900

As a seven-year-old in 1799, Robert Blincoe started working in a cotton mill outside the town of Nottingham, in central England. Robert was an orphan, and with others from his London orphanage he was sent to the mill. The idea was to have the orphans contribute to England's prosperity and learn the value of hard work, but it was not certain that Robert would even survive to adulthood. As his group of orphans reached the mill, he heard onlookers in the town mutter, "God help the poor wretches."[1] Robert soon found out why. He watched as his fellow child workers wasted away from the long hours and meager food, and he looked on in horror as the orphan Mary Richards was caught up in the machinery: he "heard the bones of her arms, legs, thighs, etc successively snap . . . her head appeared dashed to pieces, . . . her blood thrown about like water from a twirled mop."[2] Robert himself had to stand on a box to tend the machinery, but due to his small size he was less productive than the managers wanted, and he was constantly beaten. Robert's situation grew worse when his group was sent to another mill. The hours were even longer and the pace of work faster, and older workers tortured Robert, putting hot pitch into a blazing metal bowl and placing it on his head until his hair came off and his scalp was burned. Only when Robert reached age twenty-one, his entire body scarred for life from beatings, was he released from his grim "apprenticeship."

Robert Blincoe was a survivor of the Industrial Revolution—a change in the production of goods that substituted mechanical force for human energy. Beginning in Britain around 1750, European factories churned out machine-made products—first textiles and later manufactured items from sewing machines to automobiles—that came to replace

The Industrial Revolution Begins, 1750–1830

FOCUS What were the main causes of the Industrial Revolution?

Industrialization After 1830

FOCUS How did industrialization spread, and what steps did nations and manufacturers take to meet its challenges?

The Industrial Revolution and the World

FOCUS How did industrialization affect societies in China, South and West Asia, and Africa?

Industry and Society

FOCUS How did industrialization affect people's everyday lives and livelihoods?

The Culture of Industry

FOCUS How did writers and artists respond to the new industrial world?

COUNTERPOINT: African Women and Slave Agriculture

FOCUS What contributions did African women agricultural workers make to industrial development?

BACKSTORY

As we saw in Chapter 23, between 1750 and 1830 popular uprisings led to a revolutionary wave across the Atlantic world. Throwing off old political systems, revolutionaries also aimed to unchain their economies by eliminating stifling restrictions on manufacturing and commerce imposed by guilds and governments. Free global trade advanced further with the end of British control of the United States and Spanish control of much of Latin America. During the same period, slavery came under attack as an immoral institution that denied human beings equal rights and prevented a free labor force from developing. As Enlightenment ideas for good government flourished, reformers pushed to replace traditional aristocratic and monarchical privileges with rational codes of law. Free trade and free labor, promoted by enlightened laws and policies, helped bring dramatic changes to the global economy, most notably the unparalleled increase in productivity called the Industrial Revolution.

▪ **c. 1750** Industrialization begins in Great Britain

▪ **1769** James Watt creates the modern steam engine

▪ **1803** Denmark becomes the first Western country to abolish the slave trade

First Atlantic crossing by a steamship **1819** ▪

1750 1775 1800

1780s–1790s Interchangeability of parts developed in France

George Stephenson puts a steam engine on a carriage on rails, inventing the locomotive **1814** ▪

higher-quality but more expensive artisanal goods. Agriculture continued to dominate the world economy, and farms such as those in Africa, worked largely by women, saw innovations in cultivation and irrigation techniques, as we will see in the Counterpoint to this chapter. In the twentieth century, industry would outstrip agriculture as the leading economic sector and the major source of employment in much of Europe and the United States, and eventually in other parts of the globe.

The Industrial Revolution transformed the livelihoods of tens of millions of people in the nineteenth century in a variety of ways. After his release, Robert Blincoe grabbed at opportunity, setting up a grocery store and even establishing a small factory of his own. The course of industrialization was thus ragged, offering both danger and advantage. Some were driven into factories where conditions were often dangerous and even criminal. Where countries industrialized, a working class arose to tend machines in the factories. These workers' lives were soon strikingly different from those of the artisans with whom they competed. The efficient new weaving machines gave jobs to some, but they impoverished artisans, such as the Indian and European handloom weavers who continued to follow traditional manufacturing methods. Industry also influenced agriculture around the world. Factories consumed more raw materials, and an increasing number of workers in cities no longer grew their own food, depending instead on distant farmers. With the global spread of industry, art, music, philosophy, and political thought echoed the transformation, as writers and painters described this new world in their art and theorists analyzed their new societies. Whether a region had comparatively few factories, as in India and South America, or a dense network of them, as in Britain, patterns of work and everyday life changed—and not always for the better, as Robert Blincoe's case shows.

MAPPING THE WORLD

The Spread of Industrialization

The world remained more agricultural than industrial in 1900. As the twentieth century opened, however, the Industrial Revolution that originated in eighteenth-century Britain was driving industry to ever higher peaks. Among its globally significant consequences was the decline of the slave trade and slavery itself, which had previously greatly increased the world's productivity.

ROUTES ▼

- Major sea trade route, c. 1775
- African slave trade, to 1860
- Railroad, c. 1914

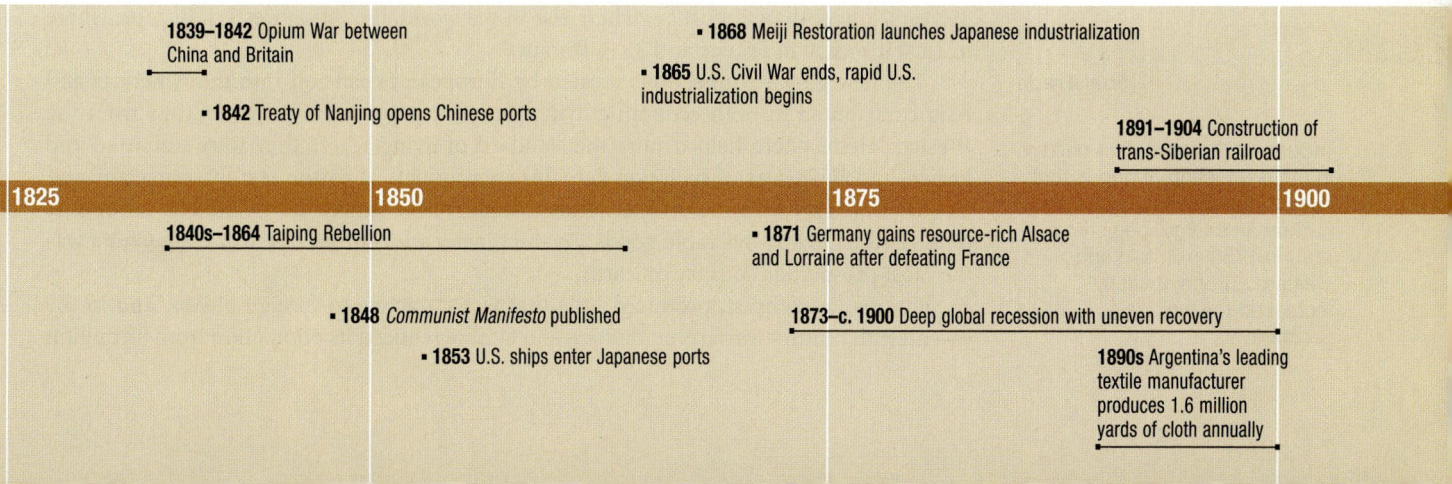

OVERVIEW QUESTIONS

The major global development in this chapter: The Industrial Revolution and its impact on societies and cultures throughout the world.

As you read, consider:

1. In what ways did the Industrial Revolution change people's work lives and ideas?
2. How did the Industrial Revolution benefit people, and what problems did it create?
3. How and where did industrial production develop, and how did it affect society and politics?

The Industrial Revolution Begins 1750–1830

FOCUS
What were the main causes of the Industrial Revolution?

The **Industrial Revolution** unfolded first in Britain and western Europe, eventually tipping the balance of global power to favor the West. The coming of mechanization expanded productivity as never before. Many historians believe the only transformation as important was the rise of settled agriculture thousands of years earlier. The Industrial Revolution had global roots, occurring in the context of worldwide trade, economic inventiveness, and agricultural improvement. Although Britain led in industry, the economies of Qing (ching) China and India were larger until almost 1900, when Britain surpassed them in overall productivity. A burning question for historians is how, in a climate of worldwide industriousness, Britain came to the forefront of the great industrial transformation.

The Global Roots of Industrialization

Industriousness and Population Growth

The Industrial Revolution took place amid a surge in productive activity. Industriousness rose, as people worked longer hours and tinkered to find new ways to make goods, developing thousands of new inventions in the process. In Qing China from the mid-1650s to 1800, productivity increased along with population, which soared from 160 million people in 1700 to 350 million in 1800. The dynamic economy improved many people's lifestyles and life expectancy, and encouraged people to work harder to acquire the new products constantly entering the market. Chinese life expectancy increased to the range of 34 to 39 years, longer than almost anywhere else in the world, including western Europe, where in 1800 it was 30 in France and 35 in Britain.

Global Trade

The new global connections created by European expansion into the Americas and Asia contributed to both economic dynamism and population growth. Crops from the Western Hemisphere helped raise the standard of living where they were imported and grown, and awareness of such popular Chinese products as cotton textiles, porcelain, and lacquer ware spread through international trade. Silver flowed into China as Europeans purchased its highly desirable goods. As the nineteenth century opened, Qing China was the most prosperous country on earth.

Europe, in contrast, produced little that was attractive to foreign buyers, and in the seventeenth century warfare, epidemics, and famine reduced its population from 85 million

Industrial Revolution A change in the production of goods that substituted mechanical power for human energy, beginning around 1750 in Britain and western Europe; it vastly increased the world's productivity.

MAP 24.1 Industrialization in Europe, c. 1900

Beginning in the workshops of England's tinkerers, industrialization spread across western Europe to Germany and then to Russia. The presence of raw materials such as coal and iron ore sparked industrial development, but so did curiosity and inventiveness. Sweden, for example, lacks mineral resources, so its people harnessed water power to develop electricity. Industrialization would remain uneven into the twenty-first century, however, and this imbalance often led to deadly political conflict.

to 80 million. After 1700, however, Europe's population surged, more than doubling by 1800, thanks to global trade that introduced nutritious foods and other useful goods. Population growth put pressure on British energy resources, especially fuel and food. With their populations rising rapidly, both Britain and China faced the limits of artisanal productivity and natural resources. The Industrial Revolution allowed the British to be the first to surpass those limits (see Map 24.1).

Great Britain: A Culture of Experimentation

Why did the Industrial Revolution happen when it did, and why did it happen in Britain first? After all, many regions have the coal, iron deposits, and other resources that allowed the British to make and power the first modern machines. Moreover, bursts of economic innovation have occurred at many times and in many places.

It was not just resources, however, that propelled Britain to the industrial forefront. As we saw in Chapter 20, the Scientific Revolution had fostered both new reliance on direct observation and deep curiosity about the world. Before the rise of industry, the British and other Europeans traveled the globe, which exposed them to technological developments from other societies. From China, for example, they learned about such implements as seed drills and winnowing machines to process grain. Publications like the *Encyclopedia*, composed in France during the Enlightenment and widely read in Europe (see Chapter 23), included mechanical designs from around the world, making them available to a public increasingly eager to tinker and experiment. Global trade and exchange, the Scientific Revolution, and the Enlightenment thus formed the backdrop for the Industrial Revolution. The massive expansion in productivity was initially not about theoretical science, however, but about trial and error—which especially flourished in Britain.

Artisans and Tinkerers

British artisans produced some of the early machinery of the Industrial Revolution. Britain had a particularly well-developed culture of experimentation and, as its population grew, the country's curious and industrious craftspeople worked to supply the surging population, to meet the shortage in energy due to declining wood supplies, and to devise products that the world might want to buy. "The age," wrote critic Samuel Johnson, "is running mad after innovation."[3] From aristocrats to artisans, the British latched onto news of successful experiments both at home and abroad. They tinkered with air pumps, clocks, and telescopes. European craftspeople worked hard to copy the new goods imported from China, India, and other countries. From the sixteenth century on, for example, European consumers bought hundreds of thousands of foreign porcelain pieces, leading would-be manufacturers in the Netherlands, France, and the German states to try to figure out the process of porcelain production. They finally succeeded early in the 1700s. Despite inventive activity across Europe, it was England that soon pulled ahead (see Reading the Past: Industry Comes to the British Countryside).

Wedgwood China

Josiah Wedgwood, the eighteenth-century English potter-turned-industrialist who founded a company still prosperous today, worked day and night to figure out the ingredients, formulas, and processes necessary to make "china"—that is, inexpensive, heat-resistant dishware patterned after China's renowned but costly and fragile porcelain. Wedgwood copied designs from around the world to brighten his dishware, but he is best known for his "Wedgwood blue" products, which were directly inspired by China's famed blue-and-white patterns. In this 1810 example, Wedgwood designers had fashioned a product that could compete with Chinese manufactures in the global marketplace. (Cotehele House, Cornwall, UK/Bridgeman Art Library.)

One English innovator who stands out is Josiah Wedgwood (1730–1795), founder of the Wedgwood dishware firm that still exists. Wedgwood developed a range of new processes, colors, and designs, expanding his business and making it a model for large-scale production. He grew up in a family that produced rough, traditional kinds of pottery on a very small scale. As a poor, younger son with an inquisitive mind, he used his bent for experimentation to devise many different types of ceramics. Helped by his wife and by the personal wealth she invested in the company, Wedgwood kept meticulous records of his five thousand experiments with "china" (so called because Chinese porcelain set the standard for ceramic production). He traveled widely in Britain, his agents searched the world for the right grade of clay to compete with Asian products, and he copied Asian designs unashamedly. Hence, in Wedgwood, the distinctive British culture of artisanal experimentation came together with the materials and inspiration provided by new global connections; the result was industrial innovation.

Life was not always easy for Wedgwood: an accident on a business trip eventually required that his leg be amputated. This setback only made him more determined to succeed. Born into poverty, he became the acclaimed manufacturer of fine dishes for British monarchs and for Catherine the Great of Russia, and he died one of the wealthiest men in his country. Wedgwood's fortune and spirit of experimentation passed down to his grandson Charles Darwin, who proposed the theory of evolution.

World Trade and the Rise of Industry

Global shipping, developed over three centuries, became ever more central to industrial progress in the eighteenth and nineteenth centuries. As population rose in Europe and as England, France, and other European countries

READING THE PAST

Industry Comes to the British Countryside

Industrialization transformed the human landscape and natural environment. In this passage from a promotional brochure, George Perry, co-owner of an ironworks in Coalbrookdale, England, describes how industrialization had changed the town by 1758. Dozens of travelers through the British countryside made similar observations as they noted the rise of industry in the eighteenth and nineteenth centuries and its complicated effects.

> In the year One Thousand Seven Hundred, the whole Village consisted of only One furnace, Five Dwelling Houses, and a Forge or two. About Forty years ago the present Iron-foundry was establish'd, and since that time its Trade and Buildings are so far increas'd that it contains at least Four Hundred and Fifty inhabitants, and finds employment for more than Five Hundred People, including all the several Occupations that are connected with the Works. . . .
>
> THIS place affords a number of delightful prospects. . . . Some of the Hills are cover'd with Verdure [greenery], others overgrown with Wood, and some again are naked and barren. These, with a View of a fine fertile Country, Water'd by the Severn [River], all contribute to form as agreeable a Variety to the Eye, as can well be conceiv'd. The Beauty of the scene is in the meantime greatly increas'd by a new view of the Dale itself. Pillars of Flame and smoke rising to vast height, large Reservoirs of Water, and a number of Engines in motion, never fail to raise the admiration of strangers, tho' it must be confess'd these things join'd to the murmuring of the Waterfalls, the noise of the Machines, and the roaring of the Furnaces, are apt to occasion a kind of Horror in those who happen to arrive in a dark Night. UPON the whole, there are perhaps few Places where rural prospects, and Scenes of hurry and Business are so happily united as at COALBROOKDALE.

Source: Prospectus for "A View of the Upperworks of Coalbrook Dale" (1758) by George Perry. Quoted in Sally and David Dugan, *The Day the World Took Off: The Roots of the Industrial Revolution* (London: Macmillan, 2000), 44.

EXAMINING THE EVIDENCE

1. **What is Perry's opinion of the industrial world in which he lives?**
2. **How might other people have viewed the industrial landscape differently?**
3. **Compare Perry's observations of Coalbrookdale with the story of Robert Blincoe that opens this chapter. Which do you think more accurately describes the effects of industrialization, and why?**

fought wars worldwide over trade, they needed more resources to supply people at home and far-flung armies and navies. To supply industry and feed the growing number of urban workers, global shipping brought grain from North America, wood from Canada and Russia, cotton from Egypt and the United States, and eventually meat from Australia. Imports and Europe's own produce fed urban workers. Foreign commodities such as tea, coffee, chocolate, and opium derivatives, which the lower classes were just coming to use in the nineteenth century, helped them endure the rigors of industry. Thus, dense global trade networks and raw materials produced by workers from around the world were critical to the Industrial Revolution.

Slavery and Industry

Slaves produced many elements crucial to industrial success. Eleven million Africans captured on the continent were sold into slavery in the Americas, raising capital to invest in commerce and industry. The slaves themselves produced low-cost agricultural products such as sugar and rice that enriched global traders and provided critical components in Atlantic trade networks (see Counterpoint: African Women and Slave Agriculture). Cheaper foodstuffs cut the expenses of factory owners, who justified low wages by pointing out that working families' costs had decreased. To clothe their slaves, wealthy African and American owners bought inexpensive factory-made textiles pumped out by British machines. In the northern United States, slave ironworkers were put to work building the metallurgical business, and in the Western Hemisphere generally slaves' skills played a crucial role in producing copper and tin for factory use. They also worked to produce raw materials such as cotton. Had free labor alone been used in these processes, some historians believe, the higher cost of raw materials and food would have slowed development of global trade and the pace of experiments with factories and machines.

The Technology of Industry

Mechanizing Textile Production

New technology was a final ingredient in the effort to meet the needs of a growing and increasingly interconnected population. In the eighteenth century, clever British inventors devised tools such as the flying shuttle (1733) to speed the weaving of textiles by individuals working at home. This, in turn, led to improvements in spinning to meet the increased demand for thread created by more efficient weavers. The spinning jenny, invented in about 1765 by craftsman James Hargreaves and named, it is said, after his wife or daughter, allowed an individual worker, using just the power of her hand, to spin not one bobbin of thread, but up to 120 at once. At about the same time, Richard Arkwright and partners invented the water frame, another kind of spinning machine that used water power. When hand-driven spinning machines could be linked to a central power source such as water, many could be placed in a single building. Thus, the world's first factories arose from the pressure to increase production of English cloth for the growing global market.

The Steam Engine Breakthrough

Still another, even more important breakthrough arose when steam engines were harnessed to both spinning and weaving machines. Steam engines could power a vast number of machines, which drew more people out of home textile production and into factories. Almost two thousand people worked in the British factories of Richard Arkwright alone. Although born in poverty, by the time of his death in 1792, Arkwright was a wealthy man who owned mills across England and Scotland. Industrial spies infiltrated these factories and sent their mechanical and organizational secrets to businessmen in Belgium, northern France, the United States, and elsewhere. The most dramatic innovation in European textiles was thus the adaptation of mechanized spinning and weaving machines to the mass production of cheap cotton, which in turn clothed a swelling global workforce.

The steam engine proved to be a pivotal piece of technology not just for textiles, but for the Industrial Revolution as a whole. It was used first in the gold and silver mining industry, then in textile production, and finally in driving trains and steamboats. The steam engine had been invented earlier in China, and was used there and elsewhere to pump water from mines. It was improved throughout the eighteenth century in Britain. In 1765, James Watt, a Scottish craftsman, figured out how to make the steam engine more practical, fuel-efficient, and powerful—"Cheap as well as good" was how he put it.[4] A slew of ideas for using and improving the engine followed, and in 1814, British engineer George Stephenson placed the machine in a carriage on rails, inventing the locomotive. The first steam-powered ship crossed the Atlantic soon after, in 1819.

Interchangeability of Parts

The **interchangeability of parts** was a final critical aspect of the Industrial Revolution. The many wars Europeans fought over global trade and influence in the eighteenth and early nineteenth centuries produced incredible demand for less expensive weapons and more of them. By 1790 French gunsmith Honoré Blanc, experimenting with tools and gauges, had produced guns with fully interchangeable parts. This lowered the cost per weapon and made repair possible for merchants and soldiers based in any part of the world. The goal was to "assure uniformity [of output], acceleration of work, and economy of price," as a government official in charge of weaponry put it in 1781.[5] By the early nineteenth century Blanc was producing 10,000 muskets a year. The idea of interchangeability in weaponry and machinery was crucial to the unfolding Industrial Revolution.

Industrialization After 1830

FOCUS

How did industrialization spread, and what steps did nations and manufacturers take to meet its challenges?

One striking feature of industrialization is its spread within countries, across regions, and around the world. Although threatened workers and fearful rulers have from time to time resisted industrialization, it has proved impossible to stop. Industrialization brings ongoing efficiencies, which have proven important to meet the needs of a growing global population. From its birth in England and western Europe, entrepreneurs across the continent advanced the industrial system, as did innovators in the United States. Japan did not

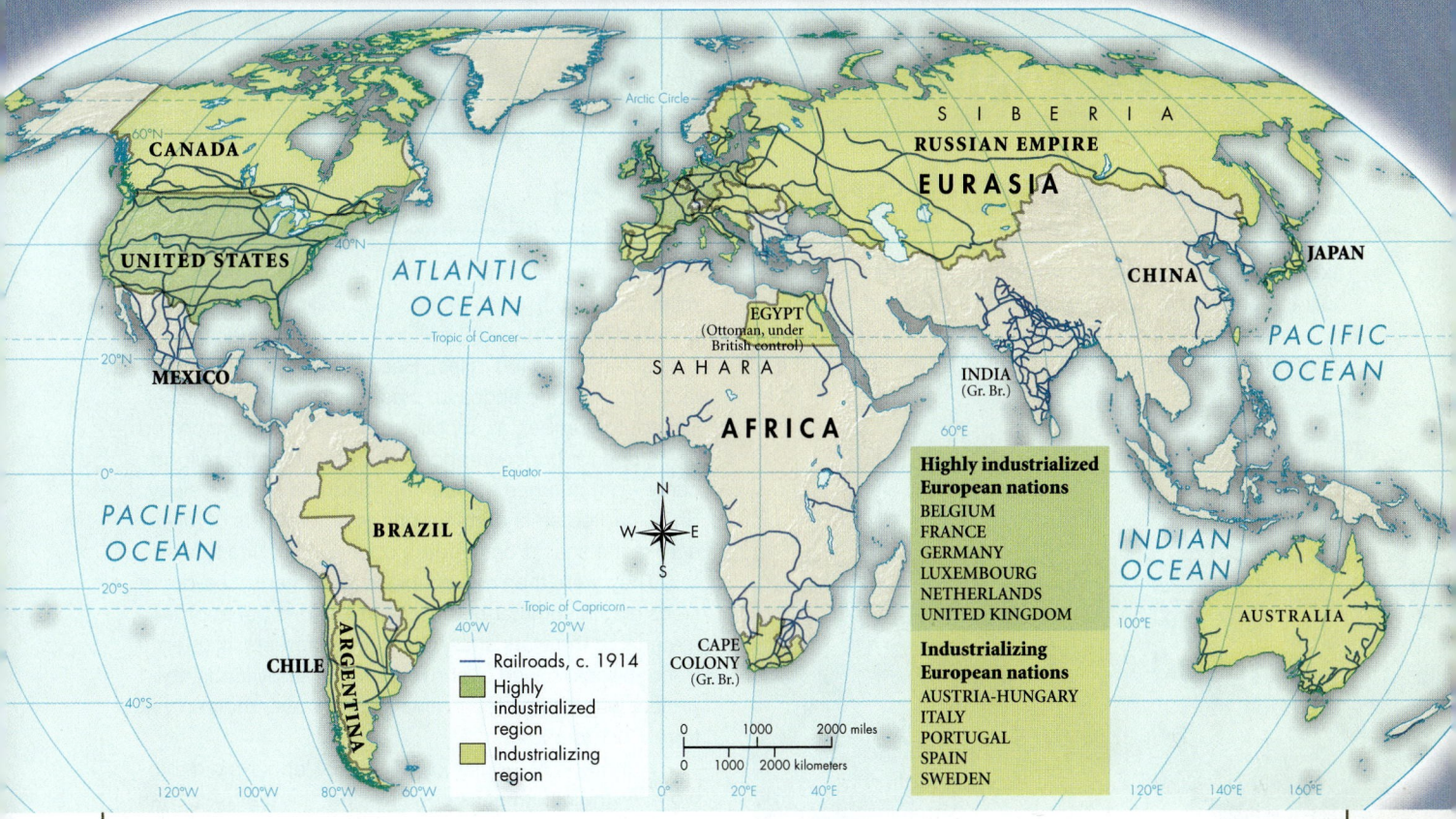

MAP 24.2

The Spread of Railroads, c. 1900

The spread of railroads throughout the world fostered industrialization because it required tracks, engines and railroad cars, and railway stations, which were increasingly made of iron, steel, and glass. Railroads generated economic growth beyond the building of trains and tracks, however. Entire cities grew up around railroad hubs, which attracted new migrants—not just hard-working builders but also professionals and service workers to fill the needs of the growing population. Railroads transported goods, turned handsome profits, promoted the fantasy world of tourism and travel, and almost immediately made warfare faster paced and more lethal.

industrialize until after 1870, but then it embraced technology enthusiastically. In many other countries, some enterprising individuals started factories, but full-scale industrialization across regions usually came later (see Map 24.2). Outside of Europe and the United States thorough industrialization generally did not develop until the twentieth century. Even though industry developed unevenly in different places, it affected the wider world by increasing demand for raw materials and creating new livelihoods.

Industrial Innovation Gathers Speed

By the end of the eighteenth century, entrepreneurs from the United States and across Europe joined British innovators, and the nineteenth century was one of widespread industrial, technological, and commercial innovation. Steam engines moved inexpensive manufactured goods on a growing network of railroads and shipping lanes, creating a host of new jobs outside of factory work (see Lives and Livelihoods: Builders of the Trans-Siberian Railroad). Around railroad hubs, for example, towns and cities filled with railroad and other workers who needed manufactured and agricultural goods. An increasing number of stores sold a soaring variety of products, ranging from the lowly cherry pitter to the reaping machine and bicycle, all of them proof of snowballing innovation in the nineteenth century.

Although independent craftsmen-tinkerers created the first machines, such as the spinning jenny and water frame, sophisticated engineers were more critical to later revolutionary technologies. In 1885 the German engineer Karl Benz devised a workable gasoline

interchangeability of parts
A late-eighteenth-century technological breakthrough in which machine and implement parts were standardized, allowing for mass production and easy repair.

LIVES AND LIVELIHOODS

Builders of the Trans-Siberian Railroad

Axes, saws, and wheelbarrows—these were the tools that built the greatest railway project ever undertaken. Stretching across Siberia from Moscow in the west to Vladivostok on the Sea of Japan (see again Map 24.2), the scale of the trans-Siberian railroad was enormous by any measure: miles laid (5700), earth moved (100 million cubic yards), rail installed (more than 100 million tons), and bridges and tunnels constructed (60 miles). Because this remote wilderness lacked roads, the endeavor was difficult and expensive. Except for lumber, all supplies needed to be transported. Cut stone for bridge supports and gravel for the railbed came from quarries sometimes hundreds of miles away. Ships carried steel parts for bridges thousands of miles across the seas, from Odessa on the Black Sea to Vladivostok. They were then moved inland. In winter horse-drawn sleds and in summer horse-drawn wagons transported material to the work sites. Cut through forests, blasted through rock, raised over rivers and swampy lands, the project was completed in nine sections over thirteen years from 1891 to 1904.

Convict Railroad Workers in Siberia, 1895
The tsarist government of Russia mobilized hundreds of thousands of workers to build the trans-Siberian railroad, the main line of which took thirteen years (1891–1904) to complete. Convicts provided essential manpower, and this image shows their housing and conditions of life. The labor entailed moving mountains of soil and rock and bringing in lumber and iron track, all without benefit of machinery and in the harsh Siberian climate. (Corbis.)

Hundreds of thousands of manual laborers did the work. At the height of its construction, the trans-Siberian employed as many as ninety thousand workers on each of its original nine sections. Many were recruited by contractors who scoured Russian cities and villages for hefty men. Prisoners and soldiers were forced to work on the project. Around the large work sites, the army and police stood guard to prevent disruption as the grueling, dangerous labor progressed. The government set up state liquor stores near work camps to appease laborers in their off-hours.

Doing the job quickly and cheaply was the government's top priority. Worker safety was of little concern, and casualties were many among the unskilled workforce. Cutting through forests to lay rail and dynamiting through hills to construct tunnels took thousands of lives. The anonymous dead lived on only in poetry:

The New Inventors: Engineers

engine, and six years later France's Armand Peugeot constructed the first automobile. Benz produced his first car two years later in 1893. After 1880, electricity became more available, providing power to light everything from private homes to government office buildings. The Eiffel Tower in Paris, constructed for the International Exhibit of 1889 and for decades the tallest structure in the world, was a monument to the age's engineering wizardry; visitors rode to its summit in electric elevators. In 1900 the tower's system of electric lights dazzled nighttime strollers.

Innovations in Machinery and Chemicals

To fuel this explosive growth, the leading industrial nations mined and produced massive quantities of coal, iron, and steel during the second half of the century. Output by the major European iron producers increased from 11 million to 23 million tons in the 1870s and 1880s alone. Steel output grew just as impressively in the same decades, from half a million to 11 million tons. Manufacturers used the metal to build more than 100,000 locomotives that pulled trains, transporting 2 billion people annually.

Historians sometimes contrast two periods of the Industrial Revolution. In the first, in the eighteenth and early nineteenth centuries, innovations in textile machinery

The way is straight, the embankment narrow,

Telegraph poles, rails, bridges,

And everywhere on both sides are Russian bones—. . .

Brothers! You remember our reward!

Fated to be strewn in the earth.[1]

The only apparent safety precaution was forbidding prisoners to work with explosives.

Other kinds of livelihoods developed around the railroad: its planning and design preoccupied Russia's ablest engineers, and the skilled aspects of its construction attracted stonemasons and other master builders from foreign lands. Financiers from around the world and producers of raw materials from as far away as the United States participated as well. Construction began in May 1891 when Nicholas, heir to the Russian throne, drove the first golden spike into the ground at Vladivostok.

Minister of Finance Sergei Witte maintained that the railroad would make Russia the dominant global market in the world: "The silk, tea, and fur trade for Europe, and the manufacturing and other trade for the Far East, will likely be concentrated in Moscow, which will become the hub of the world's transit movement," he predicted.[2] Long after the line's completion the trans-Siberian railroad provided good jobs for railway workers in Siberia. In settlements along the rail line, business thrived, and cities such as Novisibersk opened scores of new opportunities for service workers supporting railroad personnel.

The trans-Siberian railroad did indeed transform the livelihoods of the empire as a whole. The government sent some 5 million peasants from western Russia to Siberia between 1890 and 1914. The massive migration was intended to extend Russian power across the empire's vast expanse. The government designated millions of acres of land—populated at the time by the nomadic Asian foragers and herders—for Russian, Ukrainian, and Belorussian settlers. Russian bureaucrats hoped that as the peasants intermingled with indigenous peoples, the non-Russian ethnic groups would become "Russianized." They thus justified occupation on grounds similar to those the U.S. government used to justify white settlers' migration westward and takeover of American Indian lands. The completion of the longest railroad line in the world meant that hundreds of nomadic tribes lost hunting lands and pasturage that were the basis of their livelihoods, and the population of Siberia soared with the influx of farmers. Russia would never be the same.

1. Nicholai Nekrasov, quoted in J. N. Westwood, *A History of the Russian Railways* (London: George Allen and Unwin, 1964), 33.
2. Quoted in Stephen G. Marks, *Road to Power: The Trans-Siberian Railroad and the Colonization of Asian Russia, 1850–1917* (London: I. B. Tauris, 1991), 117.

QUESTIONS TO CONSIDER

1. **What jobs were needed to construct the trans-Siberian railroad, and how were workers treated?**
2. **How did the railroad affect livelihoods other than those directly connected with its construction?**
3. **How would you balance the human costs of building the railroad with the human opportunities it created?**
4. **What changes did the trans-Siberian railroad bring to Russia?**

powered by steam energy predominated. The second, in the later nineteenth century, concentrated on heavy industrial products and electrical and oil power. This was indeed the pattern in Britain, but as other areas industrialized, textile factories and blast furnaces were built simultaneously. Moreover, the number of small workshops grew faster than the number of factories, though factories dominated production. Although industrialization reduced household production in traditional crafts such as weaving, livelihoods pursued at home—called **outwork**—persisted in garment making, metalwork, and such "finishing trades" as metal polishing. In fact, factory production fostered "industriousness" more than ever, and factory, small workshop, and home enterprise have coexisted down to the present.

Industrial innovations in machinery and chemicals also transformed agriculture. Chemical fertilizers boosted crop yields, and reapers and threshers mechanized harvesting. In the 1870s, Sweden produced a cream separator, a first step toward mechanizing dairy farming. Wire fencing and barbed wire replaced more labor-intensive wooden fencing and stone walls, allowing large-scale cattle-raising. Refrigerated railroad cars and

outwork A method of manufacturing in which raw or semifinished materials are distributed to households where they are further processed or completed.

steamships, developed between the 1840s and 1870 in several countries, allowed fruits, vegetables, dairy products, and meat to be transported without spoiling, increasing the size and diversity of the urban food supply.

Challenge to British Dominance

Although Great Britain maintained its high industrial output throughout the second half of the 1800s and profited from a multitude of worldwide investments, other countries began to narrow Britain's industrial advantage. The United States industrialized rapidly after its Civil War (discussed in Chapter 25) ended in 1865, and Japan joined in after 1870. Argentina, Brazil, Chile, and Mexico gained industries at varying rates between 1870 and 1914, producing textiles, beer, soap, cigarettes, and an array of other products. In Argentina, the introduction of cigarette-rolling machinery allowed the National Tobacco Company's twenty-eight hundred workers to turn out four hundred thousand cigarettes per day by the end of the 1890s. In the same decade, its leading textile company produced 1.6 million yards of cloth annually. Industry—if not full-scale industrialization—circled the globe.

Germany

Two countries in particular began to surpass Britain in research, technical education, innovation, and growth rates: Germany and the United States. Germany's burst of industrial energy occurred after its states unified as a result of the Franco-Prussian War of 1870–1871 (discussed in Chapter 25). At this time, Germany took the French territories of Alsace and Lorraine with their textile industries, mineral deposits, and metallurgical factories. Investing heavily in research, German businesses began to mass-produce goods such as railroad stock and weapons, which other countries had pioneered in manufacturing. Germany also spent as much money on education as on its military in the 1870s and 1880s, producing highly skilled engineers and technical workers who made Germany's electrical and chemical engineering capabilities soar.

The United States

After its Civil War, the United States began to exploit its vast natural resources intensively, including coal, ores, gold, and oil. The value of U.S. industrial goods vaulted from $5 billion in 1880 to $13 billion in 1900. Whereas German accomplishments relied heavily on state promotion of industrial efforts, U.S. growth depended on innovative individuals, such as Andrew Carnegie in iron and steel and John D. Rockefeller in oil. As the nineteenth century came to a close, then, Britain struggled to keep ahead of its industrial competitors.

Industrialization in Japan

Foundation of Industriousness

Between 1750 and 1850 merchants, peasant producers, artisans, and even samurai warriors laid the foundation for Japan's industrialization. They engaged in brisk commerce, especially with the East and Southeast Asian mainland. Japan exported its sophisticated pottery—some 2 million pieces to Southeast Asia alone in the first decade of the nineteenth century—and it imported books, clocks, and small precision implements, especially from China. Internal trade increased too. Businessmen and farmers produced sake, silk, paper, and other commodities required by Japan's vast network of regional lords, the daimyo, and their retainers, the samurai. By law, the daimyo traveled from their own lands to the court at Edo for long periods every year, and they spent lavishly to support the travels of their large entourages. Japan's roads were clogged with traffic in people and goods (see Seeing the Past: Japan's Industrious Society).

The samurai of this era were what we might describe today as underemployed. After two centuries of peace under the Tokugawa Shogunate (see Chapter 21), there were many more samurai than the country needed for administration and defense. To occupy their time, some samurai studied the new findings in the botany, chemistry, and engineering coming from China and Europe. They experimented with electricity, created important devices such as thermometers that helped improve silkworm breeding, and awaited Dutch ships in the port of Nagasaki with their information from around the world. Craft-based innovation produced new kinds of seeds, new varieties of silkworms, and improvements

SEEING THE PAST

Japan's Industrious Society

Hiroshige, *Nihon-bashi*, from the series, *Fifty-three Stations on the Tokaido* (Road to Tokyo) (Brooklyn Museum/Corbis.)

Famed Japanese artist Ando Hiroshige (1797–1858) is best known for his prints of nature and for his several series about work life in early-nineteenth-century Japan. In these works, Hiroshige combined his great print-making skills with knowledge of Dutch and other Western art. The exchange went both ways, as Western artists borrowed from Hiroshige in return. Impressionists were especially drawn to his focus on daily life and his vibrant use of color. Later, Hiroshige's serial method and drawing technique influenced the creators of comic strips.

Hiroshige depicted the many livelihoods of Japan in some of his works. In particular he showed commercial life on the road to Edo (now Tokyo), the capital of Japan, before it industrialized. The road is clogged with busy people loaded with goods and supplies. Collectively, Hiroshige's drawings show a remarkably active commercial and productive life, demonstrating the prevailing view among historians today that many parts of the world enjoyed "industrious" economies in the seventeenth through the nineteenth centuries that laid the essential groundwork for full industrialization.

EXAMINING THE EVIDENCE

1. **What attitude toward work comes through in this print?**
2. **How does it contrast with the attitude displayed in the document on pages 815 and 816 by Mexican women workers?**

in their already highly technical looms. The inventive Japanese were more than ready to take advantage of Western machinery when the opportunity arose.

Merchants were also an economic force. As in Europe they supplied peasant families with looms and other machines for spinning and weaving at home. Under the Tokugawa regime, production was labor-intensive, and government encouraged these impressive levels of industriousness. Notable innovations took place in cotton and silk production and in manufacturing goods such as coins from precious metal, but output was limited. Japanese innovators aimed to replace this system with Western-style factory or mass production, beginning with textiles, guns, railroads, and steamships. It had become clear that, as one Japanese administrator wrote in 1868, "machinery is the basis of wealth."[6]

The final motive for change was concern about Western ships seeking access to Japanese ports and trade. Seeing outsiders as potential agents of social and political unrest, the Japanese had long restricted the flow of foreigners into the country. In the nineteenth century, however, they experienced for themselves the inroads they had seen Westerners make in China during the Opium War (discussed later in this chapter). In 1853 Commodore Matthew Perry steamed into Edo (now Tokyo) Bay and demanded diplomatic negotiations with the emperor. Some samurai urged resistance, but senior officials knew how defenseless the city would be against naval bombardment. The next year Perry signed an agreement on behalf of the United States under which Japan would open its ports on a regular basis.

Turn to Industry

Both individual Japanese and the government adjusted rapidly to the presence of these competitors. They were motivated in good part by the desire to learn the skills that would allow them to protect Japan through industrial prosperity and military strength. Inventors adapted European mechanical designs, using the country's wealth of skilled workers to make everything from steam engines to telegraph machines. The state sent delegations to Europe and the United States with the goal of "swiftly seizing upon the strengths of the Western industrial arts," as the minister of industry wrote in 1873.[7] By the early 1870s the reformed central government known as the Meiji Restoration (see Chapter 25) had overseen the laying of thousands of miles of railroad and telegraph lines, and by the early twentieth century the country had some 32,000 factories, many of them small; 5400 steam engines; and 2700 machines run by electricity. Although it is often said that Japan industrialized at state direction, a more accurate picture shows an effective mixture of state, local, and individual initiatives based on a foundation of industriousness. This combination eventually led to Japan's central role in the world economy.

Industrializing Japan, c. 1870–1900

Economic Crises and Solutions

Industry and the expansion of the global economy brought uneven prosperity to the world and seesawing booms and busts, especially in the second half of the nineteenth century. Because global trade bound industrialized western Europe to international markets, a recession—by today's definition, a period of negative economic growth lasting six months or longer—could simultaneously affect the economies of such diverse regions as Germany, Australia, South Africa, California, Argentina, Newfoundland, and the West Indies. At the time, economists, industrialists, and government officials did not clearly understand the workings of industrial and interconnected economies. When a stubborn recession struck in the 1870s and lasted in some places until the end of the century, they were stunned.

Late-Nineteenth-Century Recession

One reason for the recession of the 1870s was the skyrocketing start-up costs of new enterprises. Compared to steel and iron factories, the earliest textile mills had required little capital. After midcentury, industries became what modern economists call capital-intensive rather than labor-intensive: to grow, companies had to buy expensive machinery, not just hire more workers. This was especially true in developing countries such as those in Latin America, where the need to import machinery and hire foreign technicians added to costs.

Second, increased productivity in both agriculture and industry led to rapid price declines. Improved transportation allowed the expanding production of meat and grain in the United States, Australia, and Argentina to reach distant global markets rapidly, driving down prices. Wheat, for example, dropped to one-third its 1870 price by the 1890s. Consumers, however, did not always benefit from this persistent decrease in prices, or deflation, because employers slashed wages and unemployment rose during economic downturns. When this occurred, consumers just stopped purchasing manufactured goods.

Thus, a third major reason for the recession was underconsumption of manufactured products. Industrialists had made their fortunes by emphasizing production, not consumption. "Let the producers be many," went a Japanese saying, "and the consumers be few."[8] This attitude was disastrous because many goods were not sold, and the result was that prices for raw materials collapsed globally. People lost their land, jobs, and businesses, with consequences ranging from long stretches of unemployment to bankruptcy.

Governments and Businesses Respond

In response to these conditions, governments around the world took action to boost consumption and control markets and prices. New laws protected innovation through more secure patents and spurred development of the limited-liability corporation, which protected investors from personal responsibility, or liability, for a firm's debt. **Limited liability** greatly increased investor confidence in financing business ventures. As prices fell in the 1870s and 1880s, governments broke any commitments they had made to free trade. They imposed tariffs (taxes) on imported agricultural and manufactured goods to boost sales of domestic products. Latin American countries levied tariffs that were some five times those in Europe. Without this protection from cheap European goods, a Mexican official predicted, new industries would "be annihilated by foreign competition."[9]

Business people also took steps to end the economic turmoil. They advanced the development of **stock markets**, which financed the growth of industry by selling shares or part ownership in companies to individual shareholders. In an international economy linked by telegraph, telephone, railways, and steamships, the London Stock Exchange was a center of this financial activity. In 1882 it traded industrial shares worth £54 million, a value that surged to £443 million by 1900, dramatically increasing the capital individuals made available to industry. At the same time, firms in single industries banded together in **cartels** to control prices and competition. One German coal cartel founded in 1893 dominated more than 95 percent of coal production in Germany. Thus, business owners deliberately blocked open competition to ensure profitability and economic stability.

Rise of Managers and the "White-Collar" Service Sector

Another way to address the economic crisis was to add managerial expertise. In the late 1800s, industrialists began to hire others to run their increasingly complex day-to-day operations, which was a revolutionary change in business practices. A generation and more earlier, factory owners such as Richard Arkwright had been directly involved in every aspect of the business and often ran their firms through trial and error. Now, separate managers specializing in sales and distribution, finance, and purchasing made decisions. The rise of the manager was part of the emergence of a "white-collar" service sector of office workers, with managers (generally male) at the high end of the pay scale and secretaries, file clerks, and typists (increasingly female) at the low end. These office workers were essential to guide the flow of business information that managers needed to make profits. Banks needed tellers and clerks, just as railroads, insurance companies, and government-run telegraph and telephone companies needed armies of white-collar employees.

The Department Store

A final solution to the economic crisis was the development of consumer capitalism, sparked by the recognition that underconsumption of manufactured goods had directly led to the late-nineteenth-century recession. The principal institution for boosting consumption was the department store, which daring entrepreneurs founded after midcentury to promote sales of manufactured products. Department stores gathered an impressive variety of goods in one place, in imitation of the Middle Eastern bazaar and the large Asian merchant houses, and they eventually replaced many of the single-item stores to which people were accustomed. Buenos Aires alone had seven major department stores, among them Gath y Chaves (GOT e shah-VEZ), which by 1900 had grown to occupy a multistoried building of 13,000-plus square feet, and which tripled its space five years later. From the Mitsui family in Tokyo to the Bloomingdales in New York, entrepreneurs set up institutions for mass consumerism, and some, such as Harrods of London, established branches around the world.

Just as factories led workers to greater productivity, these modern palaces aimed to stimulate more consumer purchases. Luxury items like plush rugs and ornate draperies spilled over railings in glamorous disarray. Shoppers no longer bargained over prices; instead they reacted to sales, a new marketing technique that could incite a buying frenzy. Department stores also launched their own industrial ventures to meet consumer needs: Gath y Chaves began a line of ready-to-wear clothing, recognizing that busy urban workers no longer had time to make their own. Women explained their often lengthy trips to these stores as necessary to a healthy home and family life. Stores hired attractive salesgirls, another variety of service worker, to lure customers to buy. Shopping was not only an urban phenomenon: glossy mail-order catalogs from the Bon Marché in Paris and Sears, Roebuck in the United States arrived regularly in rural areas to help farmers buy the products

limited liability Legal protection for investors from personal responsibility for a firm's finances.

stock market A site for buying and selling financial interests, or stock, in businesses; examples include the London and Hong Kong stock exchanges.

cartel A group of independent business organizations in a single industry formed to control production and prices.

Gath y Chaves Department Store

The first department stores, such as this one in Buenos Aires, Argentina, were built to resemble palaces and present the possibility of luxury to everyone. Shoppers could walk on lush carpets, climb stately marble staircases, and purchase or imagine buying the items displayed from around the world. By assembling an array of goods once sold in individual small stores, the department store was revolutionary because it focused on increasing consumption rather than driving production, as industry had done. The first department stores were the direct ancestors of today's megastores and Internet shopping.

of industry. Thus, department stores were both commercial crossroads where urban shoppers could purchase a wide variety of manufactured goods from around the world and a means of connecting otherwise isolated rural consumers to the industrial marketplace.

The Industrial Revolution and the World

FOCUS

How did industrialization affect societies in China, South and West Asia, and Africa?

The Industrial Revolution transformed life in many parts of the world, even those with few factories of their own. Increased industrial development caused hardships for economies outside the West, eventually tipping trade balances and ultimately political power. The once-dominant economies of China, India, and the Ottoman Empire declined due to the Industrial Revolution, despite the real wealth that some local merchants, landowners, and entrepreneurs created for themselves. The Industrial Revolution allowed Western nations to pull ahead of these former world leaders.

Western nations used their powerful and increasingly reliable weaponry to open trade. Like Japan, other nations in the early nineteenth century were often unwilling to trade with Europe, which was widely seen as both uncivilized and a source of inferior goods. Even an English man, commenting on the high quality of a shawl from India, agreed, "I have never seen a European shawl I would use, even if it were given to me as a present."[10] This attitude, common not just in England but around the world, led Europeans and Americans alike to use threats of violence to open markets. Europe's immense industrial productivity demanded outlets for manufactured goods, its factories needed raw materials, and its growing population of industrial workers depended on foreign food and stimulants.

Reaction abroad to these demands and needs was mixed. Some governments, merchants, and producers around the world saw that there was money to be made from trading in Western products, setting up their own factories, and adopting technology. Others saw only danger to local artisanal economies and to the political status quo. In the long run, the rise of industry changed lives and livelihoods everywhere, not only because of the interconnected economic consequences of rising productivity, but because the industrialized West was willing to use violence to gain access to raw materials and to open new markets for manufactured goods.

The Slow Disintegration of Qing China

At the beginning of the industrial era, Qing China was the wealthiest and most productive country in the world, its prosperity built on the silver that flooded China in exchange for its cottons, porcelains, and other coveted items (see Map 24.3). Yet the Qing Empire was facing difficult problems, and the Industrial Revolution only compounded them. Revolutionary upheavals in North and South America and the Napoleonic Wars in France suddenly stopped the flow of silver and curtailed trade, eating away at the source of China's wealth and strangling job opportunities. On world markets, cheap industrial European goods competed with Chinese products, and social unrest erupted among the affected workers. Commercial rivalry soon turned to war.

Europeans had grown dependent on a variety of products from India and China, especially tea. The five chests of tea Europeans had purchased annually in the 1680s had soared to more than 23 million pounds by 1800. At the time this meant a severe trade imbalance for Europe, whose cheap but inferior textiles did not appeal to the Indians and Chinese.

By the 1820s, however, the British had found something the Chinese would buy—opium. Grown legally in British-controlled India, opium was smuggled into China, where its import and sale were illegal. So great was the demand for opium in China that even after buying tea the British merchants and smugglers turned a handsome profit. China's big payout in silver caused a drain on its economy, and Chinese officials worried that opium use was out of control. A Chinese government official charged with ending the illegal trade commanded the British to turn over all the opium they possessed; he burned what they surrendered. Determined to force opium on the Chinese, the British sent a fleet to China to keep the opium market open.

The Opium War

In the Opium War (1839–1842) that followed, Western firepower won decisive victories, and with the 1842 Treaty of Nanjing, China agreed to pay the British an indemnity (or fine), allow British diplomats access to the country, open five ports to trade, and reduce tariffs (see again Map 24.3). The treaty shifted power to Europeans, forcing the Chinese to deal with them as full trading partners and respected diplomats. The opium trade was legalized, making fortunes for British merchants and paving the way for other goods to enter China.

The Opium War made life difficult for Chinese workers. During the conflict, many lost their jobs as dockworkers, tea exporters, and commercial agents. A severe depression followed the war's end, and floods and famines between 1846 and 1848 compounded the hardships. In the late 1840s peasant religious leader Hong Xiuquan (hung she-o-chew-on) built a following among the underemployed and unemployed. Hong had failed to get the career he desperately wanted—a place in the prestigious Chinese civil service. He first tried to pass the nationwide civil service exam in 1836, and like others flunked this initial try. As Hong failed successive attempts to pass the exam, he fell feverishly ill and had religious visions that convinced him he was the brother of Jesus.

By 1850, his charismatic preaching of his version of Christianity had attracted some 20,000 disciples. Hong's social message promised a better future: he promoted work for all, equality of the sexes, and communal living, which appealed to hard-pressed ordinary people. It emphasized industriousness: "The diligent husbandman will be rewarded and the idle husbandman punished."[11] Like some of the Christian missionaries infiltrating China, Hong asked his followers to give up alcohol and opium and reject oppressive customs such as foot binding as first steps toward a more prosperous future. Hong's movement envisioned a perfect society—the Heavenly Kingdom of Peace, or Taiping Tianguo—and it began to move in vast armies across the country, ultimately gathering millions of adherents.

MAP 24.3

Qing China, 1830–1911

Qing officials knew that opium was dragging China's people into addiction, but the resulting Opium War with Britain to restrict the supply only made matters worse. Led by the British, Europeans forced open Chinese ports, destroyed historic Chinese cities, and helped create uprisings such as the Taiping Rebellion. While its officials debated how to protect the Qing Empire's mighty legacy of conquest and productivity, China maintained its vigorous trade in porcelain and other manufactured goods.

The Taiping Rebellion

To most Chinese, social discontent and economic distress were evidence that their rulers had lost "the Mandate of Heaven," their political legitimacy. The Taiping Rebellion accelerated the crisis of the Qing government, already weakened by the European economic and military assault. At this critical juncture, however, the movement's leaders began to quarrel among themselves and adopt a lavish lifestyle, which weakened the rebellion. The Hunan militia ultimately defeated the Taiping in 1864 under the leadership of the emperor's appointee, the scholar-official Zeng Guofan (zung gwoh-FAN). Hong himself died that year in the final siege of Nanjing.

The lesson learned by some intellectuals and officials—notably Zeng Guofan—was the value of Westernization, by which they meant modernizing the military, promoting technological education, and expanding industrialization. This led in the 1870s to the opening of mines and the development of textile industries, railroads, and the telegraph.

Weighing Opium in India

Opium grown in India went mostly to the Chinese market, though some found its way to Europe through Middle Eastern middlemen. Opium cured headaches, sleeplessness, and general aches and pains, but consumers in both Asia and Europe also welcomed the euphoric feeling of well-being the drug created. Many Chinese and European people became addicted, among them such famous Western artists as novelist Sir Walter Scott, poet Elizabeth Barrett Browning, and composer Hector Berlioz. British merchants and the British government, however, were concerned not with addiction but with sales, profits, and a favorable balance of payments. In the Opium Wars they crushed Chinese resistance with the help of their new steamships and industrially produced guns. (The Art Archive/ Victoria and Albert Museum London/Eileen Tweedy.)

However, the Dowager Empress Cixi, who had seized power during the uprising, focused more on maintaining imperial control of the government than on Western-style modernization. It was unclear which impulse would triumph.

Competition in West and South Asia

Since early modern times, the Ottoman Empire in West Asia had profited from its extensive system of textile manufacture—one so far-reaching that Europeans, Africans, and Asians had long coveted its silks, dyes, fine cottons, and woven rugs. As Western industrial powers sent inferior but less expensive thread, yarn, and woven cloth to markets around the world, it changed the balance of trade. As prices dropped, artisans spinning and weaving at home suffered, working longer hours just to earn a living wage. Textile manufacturing had traditionally been done in the home during winter to provide income during the agricultural off-season. These artisanal ways persisted, but in the last third of the nineteenth century some carpet factories were established across the Ottoman lands. Young unmarried girls, who were less expensive to hire than men and worked for just three or four years (that is, long enough to earn a dowry to attract a husband), replaced lifelong artisans. The Industrial Revolution altered centuries-old work patterns and left many Ottoman subjects, in the words of a British traveler, "ragged beyond belief."[12]

Although the Industrial Revolution hurt craftworkers globally, it boosted the fortunes of other workers. After 1815, the ruler of Egypt, Muhammad Ali, set his subjects to mastering the industry's "strange machinery," and he eventually exempted workers in silk factories from service in the army.[13] Ottoman merchants prospered, as did owners of large estates who could send cotton and other agricultural products to markets around the world on railroads and steamships. New jobs opened up: in 1911 there were thirteen thousand railroad workers in the empire, and thousands more had helped construct the lines. In the Ottoman Empire, regional rulers such as Muhammad Ali who recognized the need for modern skills founded engineering schools and expanded technical education. The Industrial Revolution opened opportunities for some even as it made life more difficult for others.

Industrializing India, c. 1857–1900

When Europe's cheap, lower-quality textiles flooded world markets, including those of the Indian subcontinent, the cut-rate competition hurt India's skilled spinners, weavers, and dyers. Furthermore, Britain taxed the textiles Indian craftsmen produced, tilting the economic playing field in favor of British goods. Even so, as in the Ottoman Empire, some in India's lively commercial economy adapted well. In Bengal between the 1830s and 1860s, entrepreneur Dwarkanath Tagore teamed up with British engineers and officials to found raw silk firms, coal mines, steamship companies, and an array of other businesses that made his family fabulously wealthy. The first textile factory started in Bombay in 1853, and by 1914 India had the fourth-largest textile industry and the fourth-longest railway system in the world. Some business people made fortunes. Yet the coming of industry hurt many of the region's independent artisans. The country did not industrialize enough to give them all factory jobs or business employment, and many returned to the countryside. As a result, India grew more rural as the West became more urban.

Besides textiles, India exported such manufactured goods as iron, steel, and jute, which contributed approximately 10 percent of the country's gross national product. Entrepreneurs such as Jamsetji Tata competed globally, founding a dynasty based first in textiles, then in iron and steel, and continuing in the twentieth century with airplanes and software. Yet the British presence was powerful. The East India Company and the British government filled their pockets by imposing high taxes and taking more than their share of the region's prosperity. Moreover, although the British improved the Indian infrastructure, building the rail system, for example, the benefits of such improvements were not spread evenly. By making it easier to extract and then sell agricultural goods on the world market, they favored large Indian landowners.

A New Course for Africa

Industrialization had long-term consequences for Africa as well. During the nineteenth century, the Atlantic slave trade declined quickly due to mounting protests against slavery and the growth of more profitable economic activities. As Denmark (1803) and Britain (1807) abolished the international slave trade, power in West Africa shifted away from the local rulers and traders who profited from it, and toward those who could provide raw materials to Western industry (see Map 24.4).

The Antislavery Movement

Since the Enlightenment, abolitionists had called for an end to the slave trade and to slavery itself. The antislavery message, often crafted by white religious leaders and blacks themselves, invoked Christian morality and the ideas of natural rights that had shaped the revolutions in the Atlantic world. In England, former slaves were eloquent participants in the antislavery movement, which expanded in the early nineteenth century to include international conferences. As the trade in humans was progressively outlawed, abolitionists worked to end slavery completely, a goal achieved in the Western Hemisphere in 1888 when Brazil became the last country in the Americas to outlaw it. Even after 1888, however, slavery continued in many parts of the world, including Africa and Asia.

The rationale for ending slavery also had an economic dimension, and many merchants, financiers, and workers supported the abolitionist movement. The price of slaves had risen during the eighteenth century, so the use of slaves became less profitable. Plantation owners, thinking that natural increase could supply them with slaves cheaply, tried to force slave women to have more children. Industrialists recognized that it was more profitable if Africans worked in Africa to produce raw materials such as palm oil and cotton. Factory workers supported abolition because they regarded slaves as cheap competition in the labor market. Free labor became a widely accepted ideology in industrial areas.

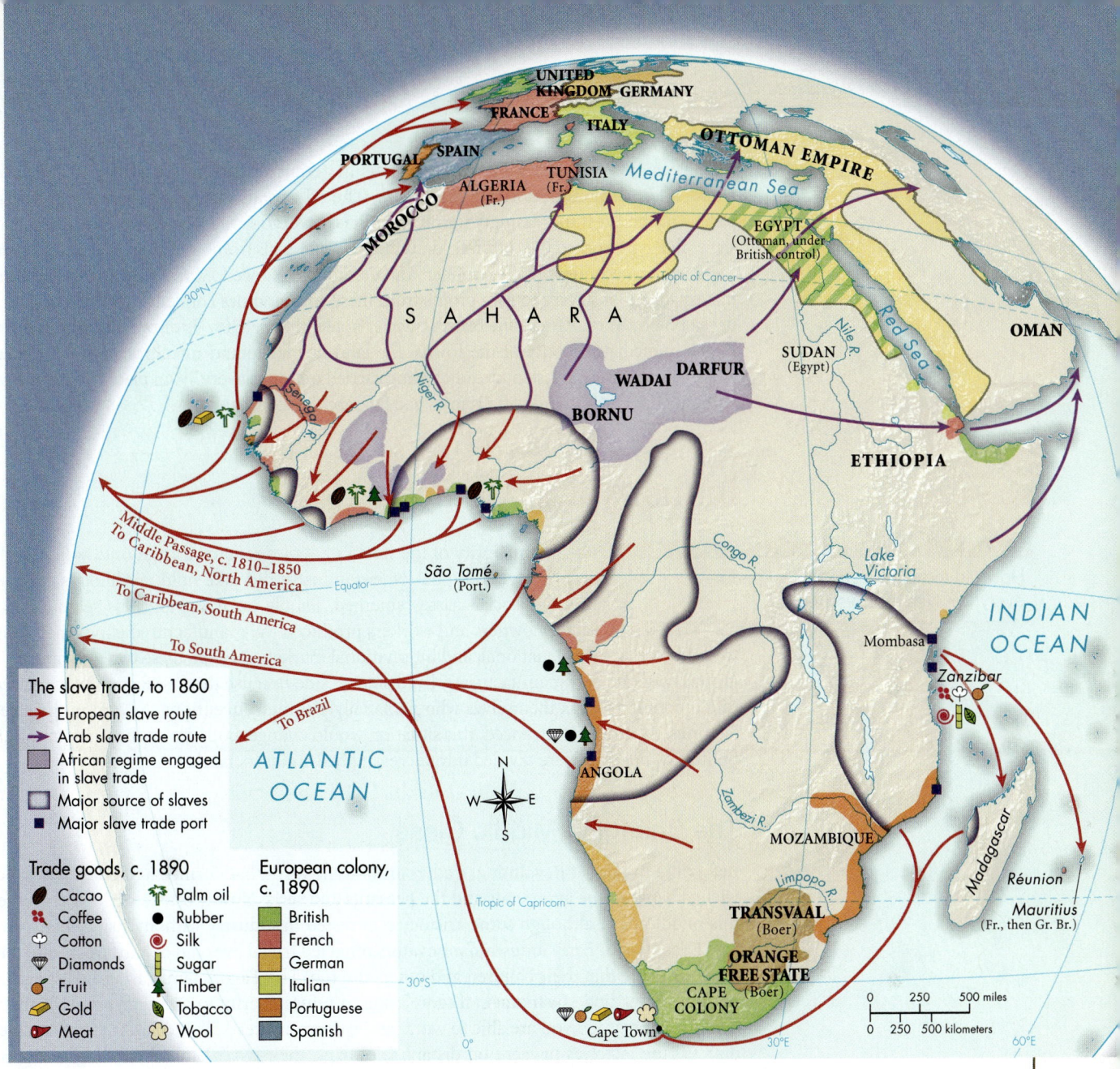

MAP 24.4 **Africa, 1750–1880**

African leaders built their wealth by selling captured warriors and civilians from neighboring states into slavery. After Great Britain abolished slavery in 1807, African business people continued the trade from different locations far from the British forces off the West African coast. As slavery further declined in the West, the Africans adapted once more, keeping their captives for themselves to provide raw materials for Western industrialists.

Expanding Slavery Within Africa

The decline of profits from the Atlantic slave trade threw some African elites into economic crisis. Many quickly adapted, simply moving the slave trade south to supply markets in Brazil and elsewhere. Slavers arriving in West African ports learned to load ships and depart in some 100 minutes to escape British surveillance. In the course of the nineteenth century, even as Europeans worked to abolish the trade, approximately 3.5 million slaves were taken from West Africa alone to sell in the Atlantic world. African rulers and business people used slaves to increase their efforts to provide raw materials for global manufacturing. They expanded slavery within Africa, waging war and kidnapping to capture slaves for their own use. For fear of enslavement, "One could not go to another town's sector of the market without being led by an armed elder," one Nigerian man recalled.[14]

Slaves in West Africa produced various materials for the textile industry: gum, redwood, and palm oil to lubricate machinery. The oil was also used to produce soap, which people in the West increasingly found essential to everyday life. Hundreds of thousands of slaves in Egypt worked the cotton fields. Other raw materials from Africa, such as gold, boosted the European economy; coffee, rubber, and diamonds followed. Many historians believe that the expansion of slavery to gain profits from these commodities condemned Africa to underdevelopment. West Africa, one British traveler noted in the 1830s, "is disorganized, and except in the immediate vicinity of the towns, the land lies waste and uncultivated, the wretched natives living under constant dread of being carried off into slavery."[15] In places both with and without factory labor, industrialization had far-reaching consequences.

Industry and Society

FOCUS

How did industrialization affect people's everyday lives and livelihoods?

The vast majority of the world's peoples remained rural until well into the twentieth century, but where industry did take hold, livelihoods changed and new social classes emerged. People were less and less self-sufficient. Factory owners and workers produced the manufactured goods that began to flood local, regional, national, and international markets. At first, these two growing social groups, workers and manufacturers, lived side by side because the first factory owners were often modest artisans themselves who personally put their inventions to work in their new factories. As industry advanced, this situation would change: both groups became important politically, but they were divided into increasingly distinct social classes.

The Changing Middle Class

Before the Industrial Revolution, traders around the world had formed a middle class, sandwiched between the aristocrats and the peasants and serfs. Now most factory owners joined this middle class, although some aristocrats invested in industry without losing their privileged class status. Early industrial innovators often led frugal lives full of hard work, and they tried to ensure that their children and others did too. The Tagore family in India thrived on hard work, leading Dwarkanath Tagore's son to refuse charity to a beggar-priest: "I shan't give you money. . . . you are able to work, and earn your bread."[16] While early businessmen directed the factories or went on distant sales trips, their wives often tended the accounts, dealt with subcontractors, supervised workers (especially if they were female), and organized shipments of finished goods. As factories grew and their owners became prosperous, they became society's leaders, rising far above the humble status of their workers. Leaders of industry built large houses and began to consume more goods, including luxuries. They removed their wives from factory supervision and from the working world, beginning what historians term a "cult of domesticity" for women that signaled a family's prosperity. These economic leaders have collectively been called the *bourgeoisie*, a French term for the middle-class groups at the center of the Industrial Revolution.

The Middle Class Promotes Progress

As we have seen, with the march of industry, scientists and engineers in research laboratories and universities replaced amateur tinkerers as industrial innovators. As part of the state's commitment to building national wealth, public monies often funded scientific research, which was increasingly expensive. The middle class grew to include those whose empirical and scientific knowledge benefited industrial society, and professionalization occurred in other fields as well. Doctors, lawyers, professors, and journalists—all of whom drew on the scientific method and objective analysis in their work—gained prestige as they served the wider population of industrial society.

Such prosperous men of the evolving middle class founded a range of societies and clubs to create solidarity and foster the exchange of knowledge. In Japan in 1876, the city fathers of Kanazawa opened an industrial museum to spread technical knowledge more widely among the public. Wealthy citizens around the world founded art, history, and science museums during these industrial years and worked to improve city life. "Reserve large areas for football, hockey, and parks," Indian industrialist Jamsetji Tata advised urban renovators. "Earmark areas for Hindu temples, Mohammedan mosques, and Christian churches."[17]

Well-to-do women banded together to provide baby clothes for newborn children and other goods to impoverished workers. Indian reformer Savithribai Phule, married at age nine, joined her husband in aiding the lowest-caste "Untouchables," despite mounting criticism and threats of violence against her. She founded schools for the girls of the Untouchable caste, claiming to feel "immeasurably happy" with her volunteer work. "Besides, it also demonstrates the horizons to which a human being can reach out," she wrote.[18] As industrialization and rapid urban growth disturbed centuries-old ways of life, these institutions, in the words of one English official, promoted "the protection of their [industrialists'] property" by reducing worker misery. Good works also helped to unite the middle classes in the face of challenges from those with "anti-social and revolutionary principles."[19]

An East Indian Middle-Class Family

Sometime in the late nineteenth century, this middle-class family donned their best clothes and sat for this formal portrait. The father may have worked for the British government or been an independent merchant or factory owner. Nevertheless, the British dominated the subcontinent politically, economically, and culturally. This family wore fashionable Western clothing, although some of the women adapted their outfits by adding elements of the traditional sari to their dress. (Dinodia Photos.)

The New Working Class

While the middle classes enjoyed increased comfort and prosperity, industrial workers led work lives governed by the machine, the factory whistle, and eventually the time clock of the office or department store. Initially, many industrial workers, whether in the United States, Japan, Britain, or Argentina, were young, unmarried women whose families no longer needed them on farms, which now took fewer hands to run. Factories were magnets, offering steady wages and, often, supervised living quarters. Women and children were paid less than men, reducing labor costs, and this trend continued as industry spread. Despite the low pay, many women found factory work far preferable to domestic service as maids, where they were on call twenty-four hours a day. After her husband died in 1910, the Mexican widow Marcela Bernal del Viuda de Torres left her young sons to live with relatives and took her two daughters to Mexico City to find work for all three in its thriving factories. Marcela, like the underemployed around the world, sought opportunity. As she said when explaining the move to her daughters, "I'm sure not going to let you end up as maids."[20]

Working Conditions

The worker's day was often long, grueling, and unsafe in the early days of industry, as Robert Blincoe witnessed firsthand. In 1844 England limited women's work to twelve hours per day, but in Japan men and women worked fourteen to seventeen hours a day even late in the century. They tended machines while they ate meals and usually had just half a day off per week. Machines lacked even minimal safety features, leading to amputated limbs, punctured eyes, torn-off scalps, and other crippling injuries. A Japanese observer described cotton workers in urban factories as "pale and exhausted with faces like invalids. . . . young girls with the lifeblood sucked out of them."[21]

Workers' health deteriorated in many cities, and critics said it was because the lower classes, as one British observer put it as early as 1795, lived "crowded in offensive, dark, damp and incommodious habitations, a too fertile source of disease."[22] The lure of industrial work swelled urban populations to the breaking point. There was not enough housing, and sanitary facilities were almost nonexistent. Europe's cities were usually surrounded by medieval walls, which limited their natural expansion, and humid factories nurtured disease. Wherever workers were crowded together, epidemics of deadly cholera might erupt, as happened, for example, in the camps housing thousands of Indian railroad builders. Deaths from tuberculosis and pneumonia soared. In its early days, industry's human costs were clear.

Fighting the Industrial Advance

Many people resisted the introduction of laborsaving machines into their towns and villages. Handloom weavers saw their livelihoods slipping away, and agricultural workers resented mechanization's threat to their livelihoods. Some handicraft workers—notably the Luddites (named after their leader, Ned Ludd), who attacked whole factories in northern England in 1812 and after—smashed the new machines, which they believed were putting them out of work. In the countryside, day laborers left menacing notes for those who introduced threshing machines, such as: "If providing you dont pull down your messhenes . . . we will burn down your barns and you in them this is the last notis."[23] The British government mobilized its armies to protect the new system from protesters. It executed and imprisoned many, and sent large numbers to populate Australia and New Zealand—which industrialized in turn.

Under the older values of city life, artisans mutually supported one another, but that system weakened. As rural folk migrated to cities in search of industrial jobs, workers were often strangers to one another. Between 1820 and 1840 the Russian government of Poland deemed that Lodz would become a textile center, for example, and thousands of migrant workers from the countryside and fledgling industrialists from several parts of Europe quickly moved there. Chinese migrated to the Caribbean to service the sugar industry, and South Asians took their commercial and other skills to East Africa. Single young people or widows migrating from the countryside lived beyond the reach of their families and old community networks. Prostitution soared, as did venereal disease and illegitimacy. Thus, as industrialization created dense networks of new economic connections throughout the world, it contributed to the breakdown of social connections in local communities.

Industrialization brought people's everyday lives into a mechanical orbit and changed the rhythms of earning a livelihood. No longer did sunrise and sunset determine the beginning and end of the workday. Now the clock, perfected in the early modern period to measure

Child Labor in Britain

Although the exploitation of children is still a feature of industrialization, the use of child labor by early industrialists was especially harsh, as the life of Robert Blincoe testifies and as this late-nineteenth-century illustration of children at work in the mines demonstrates. After these children were lowered side by side into claustrophobic conditions, they faced the rough job of physically hauling carts of coal out of the mines through narrow passageways. Like their adult counterparts, they suffered from coal dust and extremes of heat and cold. It is little wonder that even liberal British politicians of the time, who wanted no interference from government in business, agreed to governmental investigation and regulation of mining conditions. After parliamentary hearings on mine work, children's work and that of women who worked in and near the mines were regulated. (Photo: akg-images.)

even in seconds, set the hours for work of many kinds. Factory whistles signaled the start of the workday, while stopwatches timed the pace of work. The ongoing march of the machine, rather than the seasons, determined people's movements and organized their labor. Industrialists imposed heavy fines on anyone late by even a minute. With alcohol a prominent feature of life in a world where there was no safe water or milk supply, however, drunkenness sometimes undermined the strict discipline industrialists hoped to impose.

The Sexual Division of Labor

Factory Workers

The Industrial Revolution ushered in major changes in the sexual division of labor. Industrialists and manufacturers followed the tradition of dividing work along gender lines; now, however, the division was generally arbitrary. In some factory towns the weavers were all men, and women performed some processes in finishing the woven cloth. In other places, women tended the looms, and men only repaired and maintained the machines. Women's work in factories, even though it might be identical to men's, was said to require less skill; it always received lower pay. Men dreaded the introduction of women into a factory, which could signal that the owner intended to save on wages by cutting men's jobs. Sometimes the wife or daughter in an artisanal family went to work in a factory because the husband's work as a shoemaker or handloom weaver no longer paid enough to support the household. In such cases the husband's independent identity as handloom weaver or shoemaker may have been a proud one, providing freedom from the oversight of a foreman and an industrialist. His wife, however, may have surrendered her freedom to earn the extra income that permitted him to maintain his.

The vast majority of women, both unmarried and married, worked to support their families or themselves. Factory owners and supervisors often demanded sexual favors from women as the price of employment. The foreman supervising Adelheid Popp, a factory worker in late-nineteenth-century Germany, demanded kisses in exchange for higher wages. She quit the job, but others did not have such freedom. "Even the decent jobs, for example, those in banks," one Russian woman complained, "are rarely available unless one first grants favors to the director, the manager, or some other individual."[24] It was normal for supervisors to select one favorite woman, take her as a mistress, and then fire her once he tired of the relationship. Domestic service, which expanded with the rising prosperity of the middle class, was thought to be safer for young women, but many a housemaid fell victim to fathers and sons in middle-class families, who were regular harassers of working women. If these sexual relations became known, the women would be fired, and pregnant servants quickly lost their jobs. This is why Marcela de Torres feared for her daughters.

White-Collar Workers

The new white-collar sector advanced the sexual division of labor. Cost-conscious employers looking for workers with mathematical, reading, and writing skills gladly offered jobs to women. Since respectable lower-middle-class women had few other employment options, businesses in the service sector paid women much less than men for the same work, as in factories. As women increasingly filled lower-level white collar jobs, all sectors of the industrial economy perpetuated the idea that women were simply worth less than men and should receive lower wages (see Reading the Past: Mexican Women on Strike).

The Culture of Industry

FOCUS

How did writers and artists respond to the new industrial world?

Writers, artists, and ordinary people alike responded to the dramatic new sights and unexpected changes of industrialization. The railroad and expanded trade spread local customs, creating greater variety in everyday life and contributing to developing regional and national cultures. In Japan, for example, sashimi and sushi, once known in only a few fishing towns, became popular dishes across the nation. Better communication networks helped the spread of knowledge, and technological improvements helped knowledge flourish: gas lighting

READING THE PAST

Mexican Women on Strike

As industrialization progressed, factory workers increasingly responded to the harsh conditions of industrialization by organizing unions and banding together to strike. They directed their demands to factory owners and government officials, and they sought support from their fellow citizens. For instance, in 1881, women cigarette workers in Mexico City wrote a letter to a magazine for elite women in which they suggested that poverty might lead them to prostitution. At the same time, women cigar workers posted this placard around Mexico City to explain their strike against the factory owners.

> Oppression by the Capitalist!
>
> Until October 2, 1881, we used to make 2185 cigars for four reales [Mexican money], and now they have increased the number of cigars and lowered our salary. On October 3, 1881, through the mediation of El Congreso Obrero [The Congress of Workers], we agreed to make 2304 cigars for four reales. It is not possible for us to make more. We have to work from six in the morning until nine at night. . . . We don't have one hour left to take care of our domestic chores, and not a minute for education. The capitalists are suffocating us. In spite of such hard work, we still live in great poverty. What are our brother-workers going to do? What are the representatives of the Mexican press going to do? We need protection, protection for working women!

Source: Susie S. Porter, *Working Women in Mexico City: Public Discourses and Material Conditions, 1879–1931* (Tucson: University of Arizona Press, 2003), 80.

EXAMINING THE EVIDENCE

1. **What major concerns do the women announce in this placard?**
2. **To what specific groups is the placard addressed? Why did the strikers single out these groups?**

extended reading deep into the night, for example, and railroads exposed more travelers than ever to ideas far from home. The increased productivity associated with industrialization eventually led to more leisure time, and streams of workers entered cafés, dance halls, and parks to enjoy their new free time. Such changes in everyday life led to a torrent of artistic and literary reflections on the dramatic new industrial world.

Socialism and Marxism

In some, industry inspired optimism. For such thinkers, the rational calculation and technological progress that had produced industry raised the possibility that a perfect society could be created. A group of French and British thinkers, the "utopian socialists," spread this faith around the world. Their goal was to improve society as a whole, not just for the individual—hence the term **socialism**. They believed that rational planning would lead to social and political perfection—that is, to utopia—and to prove their point they often lived in communes where daily life could be as precisely organized as it was in the factory. The inefficient nuclear family became obsolete in their communes, where large numbers of people worked together to finish necessary tasks efficiently. At a time when many people still held monarchs and leisured aristocrats in the highest esteem, **utopian socialism** valued technicians and engineers as future rulers of nations.

socialism A social and political ideology dating from the early nineteenth century that stresses the need to maintain social harmony through communities based on cooperation rather than competition; in Marxist terms, a classless society of workers who collectively control the production of goods necessary for life.

utopian socialism A goal of certain French and British thinkers early in the nineteenth century, who envisioned the creation of a perfect society through cooperation and social planning.

materialism In Marxist terms, the idea that the organization of society derives from the organization of production.

Two middle-class German theorists—the lawyer and economist Karl Marx (1818–1883) and the wealthy industrialist Friedrich Engels (1820–1895)—had completely different ideas on how to best organize society. Although they shared the utopian socialists' appreciation of science, they saw the new industrial order as unjust and oppressive. In the 1840s they began to analyze the life of workers, publishing their results in Engels's *The Condition of the Working Class in England* (1844). In 1848 they published *The Communist Manifesto*, which became the bible of modern socialism. Marx elaborated on what he called "scientific socialism" in his most important work, *Das Kapital* (Capital), published between 1867 and 1894.

Marx held that the fundamental organization of any society derived from the relationships built into work, or what he called, simply, production. This idea, known as **materialism**, was that a society's structure was built on the class relationships that stemmed from production—such as those between serf and medieval lord, slave and master, or worker and factory owner. Marx referred to these systems—feudalism, slavery, and **capitalism**, respectively—as modes of production. In the industrial era, people were in one of two classes: the workers, or **proletariat**, and the owners, or capitalists (also the **bourgeoisie**, in Marxist terms), who owned the means of production—the land, machines, factories, and other forms of wealth. Rejecting the eighteenth-century liberal focus on individual rights, he held that the cause of the inequality between classes such as the proletariat and the capitalists was the owners' control of the means of production. When capitalist control disappeared, as Marx was certain it would, a classless society of workers would arise.

Economic liberals such as Adam Smith thought the free market would ultimately produce balance and a harmony of interests among people in all classes of society. Marx, however, believed that the workers' economic oppression by their bosses inevitably caused conflict. He predicted that as workers became aware of their oppression they would unite in revolt against their capitalist exploiters. Their revolt—not reform or legislation—would be the mechanism for worldwide historical change. The proletariat would overthrow capitalism, and socialism would reign. The moment for revolt, Marx thought, was near. "The proletarians have nothing to lose but their chains. They have a world to win. WORKING MEN OF ALL COUNTRIES, UNITE!" So ends *The Communist Manifesto.*

Marx never precisely described the classless society, but he believed it would involve workers' control of production in large factories. In a socialist society, private ownership of the means of production would end. This in turn would end the need for a state, whose only function, Marx claimed, was to protect the propertied classes. Like many male intellectuals in Europe, Marx devoted little analysis to inequalities based on race and gender. He did conclude, however, that women's lives would automatically improve under socialism. The possibility of achieving socialism inspired workers around the world. As we will see in later chapters, Marxist ideas shaped both the Russian Revolution of 1917 and the Chinese Revolution of 1949.

Industry and the Arts

The new industrial world inspired artists as well as intellectuals. Some celebrated industry, welcoming the artistic influences from far-off places that it made possible. Japanese woodblocks showed trains racing through a countryside of blossoming cherries. Hiroshige's prints depicting roads teeming with industrious people influenced Western artists to turn from mythical topics and great historic scenes to the subject matter of ordinary working lives (see again Seeing the Past: Japan's Industrious Society). Deeply influenced by the color, line, and delicacy of Japanese art as well as by its focus on scenes of ordinary daily life, French painters such as Claude Monet pioneered the artistic style known as "impressionism," so called for the artists' effort to capture a single moment by focusing on how the ever-changing light and color transformed everyday sights. Industry contributed to the new style as factories produced products that allowed Western painters to use a wider, more intense spectrum of colors.

Other Western artists interpreted the Industrial Revolution differently, focusing instead on the grim working conditions brought about by wrenching change. One was Germany's Käthe Kollwitz, whose woodcuts realistically depict starving artisans. British author Charles Dickens wrote of the dark side of industrialization in popular novels that even reached a Japanese audience. Among them was *Oliver Twist* (1837–1839), which many scholars speculate was based in part on the life of Robert Blincoe. *Uncle Tom's Cabin* (1852), U.S. writer Harriet Beecher Stowe's shocking tale of slave life in the American South, influenced some in the Russian nobility to lobby for freeing the serfs.

Even musical forms showed the impact of the Industrial Revolution. Utopian socialists composed music celebrating the railroad and the sounds of industry. Concert halls, like factories, became bigger to accommodate the increasing urban population, and orchestras grew larger and included more instruments to produce a massive sound. Military bands marched through the widening streets of capital cities. Their increasing precision and noise matched that of the new machines and the precise movements of the industrial workers tending them.

capitalism An economic system in which the means of production—machines, factories, land, and other forms of wealth—are privately owned.

proletariat Under capitalism, those who work without owning the means of production.

bourgeoisie Originally a term meaning the urban middle class; Marx defined it as the owners of the means of production under capitalism.

Workers Going Home at the Lehrter Railroad Station, 1897

German artist Käthe Kollwitz came from a family of socially active reformers and was married to the doctor Karl Kollwitz, who worked among the poor. "My real motive for choosing my subjects almost exclusively from the life of the workers was that only such subjects gave me in a simple and unqualified way what I felt to be beautiful," she wrote. Kollwitz spent her entire artistic career depicting the struggles of ordinary men and women, as in this image of workers going home exhausted after a day of hard labor. Many in the upper classes, including the German Kaiser, disapproved of such sordid subjects, but they are now considered to be among the most important art of modern times. (Käthe Kollwitz, *Workers on the Way Home at the Lehrter Station* (NT 146) 1897–1899 Brush and watercolor with accents in white Käthe Kollwitz Museum Köln © 2011 Artists Rights Society (ARS), New York/ VG Bild-Kunst, Bonn.)

COUNTERPOINT

African Women and Slave Agriculture

FOCUS

What contributions did African women agricultural workers make to industrial development?

The story of the Industrial Revolution often centers on individual inventors and the laborsaving machinery they pioneered. But entire groups, many of them anonymous and uncelebrated, piloted advances critical to industrialization. A good example comes from Africa, which nineteenth-century Europeans and Americans often regarded as a continent full of unskilled people; they used this perspective to justify both their enslavement and discrimination against all people of color. Africans, however, were foremost among the collective innovators of their day.

Women and Farming in Africa

Many of these unnamed inventors were women, who have dominated African farming both as cultivators of their own land or as slaves on African plantations. Armies of male slaves kidnapped individuals or captured entire communities of neighboring peoples for regional leaders to sell or enslave in turn. Male slaves also served in urban commerce, working as artisans, porters, and traders. Women slaves largely did agricultural work to feed the slave armies and other male slaves. Some slave men hunted such prized commodities as elephant tusks, which were fashioned into piano keys, gun handles, combs, and other objects characteristic of middle-class lives around the world. Women slaves also served as domestic servants and concubines for African elites.

Women's agricultural labor supported African life. When they married, women received land to provide for themselves and their children. Free and slave women alike could themselves own slaves to increase their agricultural productivity. As farm workers, women served as a counterpoint to independent and free male farmers, peasants and large landowners alike. In Africa it was women, either as independent farmers or more usually

Nayemwezi Women Pounding Sorghum, 1864
As industrialization advanced around the world, women in Africa were central to its agricultural foundation, as this drawing shows. They planted, weeded, and harvested major crops such as sorghum, a grass whose kernels were pounded into flour and whose stalks were pressed to produce a sweet syrup. Sorghum is native to Africa, and there is evidence that slave women brought it, along with rice and other crops, to the North American colonies, and that these crops fed both industrial workers and local slaves. (Photo: akg-images.)

as slave laborers, who introduced new varieties of seeds, new tools for farming, and more productive farming techniques. Today it is estimated that African women grow some 80 percent of all agricultural produce on the continent.

Rice Cultivation

On the west coast of Africa, although men participated in some aspects of rice farming, rice cultivation was known as "women's sweat." Women developed complex systems for cultivating the important rice crop, especially a variety called "red" rice. To control water supplies, they installed canals, sluices, and embankments, depending on whether they were capturing water from rain, tides, or floods. They reaped bountiful harvests through this manipulation of the environment.[25]

Women Slaves in the North American South

Many landowners in South Carolina and Georgia prized West African slave women, considering them "choice cargo" because of their knowledge of rice cultivation. In fact, it was slaves from West Africa who established the "red" rice variety as a preferred crop on American plantations and provided the initial technological systems for growing it. This rice was so important to the U.S. South's developing commercial economy that Thomas Jefferson, for one, sought more information about it. Its main advantage, he learned, was that if cultivated according to African techniques of water management, it could be grown outside of swamps. The more usual practice of cultivating rice in standing water "sweeps off numbers of the inhabitants with pestilential fevers,"[26] according to Jefferson, so a growing system that eliminated the threat of disease was advantageous.

Spread of Agricultural Technologies from Africa to the U.S. South

Jefferson, like some other American planters, never succeeded in cultivating red rice. The first African rice to be widely grown in North America was fragile, demanding special skills that planters, such as Jefferson, usually lacked. In contrast, West African women possessed an extensive knowledge of this and other forms of agriculture and passed this knowledge down through their families.

Slavers added these women to their cargo along with unhusked rice and many other plants and seeds. When they arrived in the United States, the technological knowledge to grow them moved from Africans to Europeans, not the other way around. In this regard West African women farmers form a counterpoint to the celebrated inventors of machines. Although they have been overlooked in history books, they created wealth for their owners, most of whom in the early days of rice cultivation were adventurers with little knowledge of how to grow these crops. Their story of the introduction of rice to North America, the perfection of seeds, and the complex technology of irrigation and processing that helped feed a growing workforce has seemed less heroic than that of an individual who invented one laborsaving machine.

Conclusion

The Industrial Revolution changed not only the world economy but the lives and livelihoods of tens of millions of people, from workers and manufacturers to the politicians trying to organize rapidly changing societies. By replacing simple machines operated by human energy with complex machines powered by steam engines, mechanization expanded productivity almost beyond measure. The results were both grim and liberating. Industrial laborers such as mill worker Robert Blincoe suffered abuse, and the flow of cheap goods from industrial countries drove down prices and threw artisans around the world into poverty. Slavery not only flourished but also allowed industry to advance. Unsung slave women spread rice cultivation to help feed the growing world population of workers. The new patterns of work in large factories transformed the rhythm of labor and the texture of urban life, and cities grew rapidly with the influx of migrants from the countryside and from other regions of the world. Political ideas and the arts also changed with the rise of industry and with the continuing global expansion of trade. Movements to end slavery and to create free workers succeeded in Europe and many parts of the Western Hemisphere.

Debate continues about whether industry was a force for good, but even opponents at the time saw that industrial life liberated people from the hardships and restrictions of rural life and gave them access to a wider array of inexpensive goods. Some theorists, such as Marx and Engels, believed that solidarity would grow among a global working class no longer isolated on individual farms, while artists depicted these new workers with paint and pen—occasionally romanticizing their productivity but more often presenting the poverty that accompanied industrialization. The middle and working classes that developed with industrialization led different lives even within the same industrial cities, but they often joined in a major global movement of the time—the development of the political form called the nation-state that increasingly shaped industrial society. As we will see in the next chapter, it was a form that spread around the world alongside industrialization and ushered in other conflicts and advances of the modern era.

NOTES

1. James R. Simmons Jr., ed., *Factory Lives: Four Nineteenth-Century Working-Class Autobiographies* (Peterborough, Ontario: Broadview, 2007), 110.
2. Ibid., 123.
3. Quoted in Brian Dolan, *Wedgwood: The First Tycoon* (New York: Viking, 2004), 54.
4. Quoted in Sally and David Dugan, *The Day the World Took Off: The Roots of the Industrial Revolution* (London: Macmillan, 2000), 54.
5. Quoted in Ken Alder, *Engineering the Revolution: Arms and Enlightenment in France, 1763–1815* (Princeton, NJ: Princeton University Press, 1997), 223.

6. Quoted in Tessa Morris-Suzuki, *The Technological Transformation of Japan from the Seventeenth to the Twenty-First Century* (Cambridge, U.K.: Cambridge University Press, 1994), 65.
7. Quoted in ibid., 73.
8. Quoted in T. R. Havens, "Early Modern Farm Ideology and Japanese Agriculture," in *Meiji Japan: Political, Economic and Social History*, ed. Peter Kornicki, 4 vols. (Routledge: New York, 1998), 1:235.
9. Quoted in Edward Beatty, *Institutions and Investment: The Political Basis of Industrialization in Mexico Before 1911* (Stanford: Stanford University Press, 2001), 59.
10. Thomas Munro, quoted in Romash Chunder Dutt, *The Economic History of India* (Delhi: Low Price, 1990 [orig. pub. 1902–1904]), 185–186.
11. "The Land System of the Heavenly Dynasty" (1853), quoted in *China: Readings in the History of China from the Opium War to the Present*, ed. J. Mason Gentzler (New York: Praeger, 1977), 56.
12. Quoted in Michael E. Meeker, *A Nation of Empire: The Ottoman Legacy of Turkish Modernity* (Berkeley: University of California Press, 2002), 103.
13. Afaf Lutfi Al-Sayyid Marsot, *Egypt in the Reign of Muhammad Ali* (Cambridge: Cambridge University Press, 1984), 169–171.
14. Quoted in Carolyn Brown, *"We Were All Slaves": African Miners, Culture, and Resistance at the Enugu Government Colliery* (Portsmouth, NH: Heinemann, 2003), 36.
15. Mr. Laird, quoted in Joseph Inicori, *Africans and the Industrial Revolution in England: A Study in International Trade and Economic Development* (New York: Cambridge University Press, 2002), 394.
16. Debendranath Tagore, quoted in Blair B. Kling, *Partner in Empire: Dwarkanath Tagore and the Age of Enterprise in Eastern India* (Berkeley: University of California Press, 1976), 184.
17. Quoted on the Tata Group Web site, http://www.tata.com/0_about_us/history/pioneers/quotable.htm.
18. Quoted in Susie Tharu and K. Lalita, eds., *Women Writing in India: 600 B.C. to the Early Twentieth Century*, 2 vols. (London: Pandora, 1991), 1:214.
19. Quoted in Caroline Arscott, "'Without Distinction of Party': The Polytechnic Exhibitions in Leeds, 1839–1945," in *The Culture of Capital: Art, Power, and the Nineteenth-Century Middle Class*, ed. Janet Wolff and John Seed (Manchester, U.K.: Manchester University Press, 1988), 145.
20. Quoted in Susie Porter, *Working Women in Mexico City: Public Discourse and Material Conditions, 1879–1931* (Tucson: University of Arizona Press, 2003), 3–4.
21. Quoted in E. Patricia Tsrumi, *Factory Girls: Women in the Thread Mills of Meiji Japan* (Princeton, NJ: Princeton University Press, 1990), 139.
22. Quoted in Ivy Pinchbeck, *Women Workers and the Industrial Revolution, 1750–1850* (London: Virago, 1981 [orig. pub. 1930]), 195.
23. Quoted in Eric Hobsbawm and George Rudé, *Captain Swing: A Social History of the Great English Agricultural Uprising of 1830* (New York: Norton, 1968), 208.
24. Quoted in Victoria E. Bonnell, *The Russian Worker: Life and Labor Under the Tsarist Regime* (Berkeley: University of California Press, 1983), 197.
25. Judith A. Carney, *Black Rice: The African Origins of Rice Cultivation in the Americas* (Cambridge, MA: Harvard University Press, 2001), 31.
26. Ibid., 147.

RESOURCES FOR RESEARCH

The Industrial Revolution Begins, 1750–1830

World history allows us to think differently about the Industrial Revolution, understanding it less as a radical departure and more as a burst of productivity and inventiveness taking place in many parts of the world. Bezis-Selfa's and Dolan's books depict the day-to-day toil of workers and manufacturers.

Bayly, C. A. *The Birth of the Modern World, 1780–1914: Global Connections and Comparisons*. 2004.

Bezis-Selfa, John. *Forging America: Ironworkers, Adventurers, and the Industrious Revolution*. 2004.

Clark, Gregory. *A Farewell to Alms: A Brief Economic History of the World*. 2007.

Dolan, Brian. *Wedgwood: The First Tycoon*. 2004.

Inikori, Joseph. *Africans and the Industrial Revolution in England: A Study in International Trade and Economic Development*. 2002.

Industrialization After 1830

Countries industrialized in different ways, though they often experienced similar problems. Morris-Suzuki and D'Costa show in exciting detail the road to industrialization in Japan and Argentina.

Beatty, Edward. *Institutions and Investment: The Political Basis of Industrialization in Mexico Before 1911*. 2001.

D'Costa, Anthony. *The Long March to Capitalism: Embourgeoisement, Internationalization, and Industrial Transformation in India*. 2005.

Morris-Suzuki, Tessa. *The Technological Transformation of Japan*. 1994.

Rappaport, Erica. *Shopping for Pleasure: Women in the Making of London's West End*. 2000.

Rocchi, Fernando. *Chimneys in the Desert: Industrialization in Argentina During the Export Boom Years*. 2006.

The Industrial Revolution and the World

Just as global innovation and trade provided much of the impetus for the Industrial Revolution, industrialists' efforts to sell their goods changed local and regional economies around the world. The books below describe the consequences for a variety of countries.

Bello, David Anthony. *Opium and the Limits of Empire: Drug Prohibition in the Chinese Interior, 1729–1850.* 2005.

Goswami, Manu. *Producing India: From Colonial Economy to National Space.* 2004.

Meeker, Michael E. *A Nation of Empire: The Ottoman Legacy of Turkish Modernity.* 2002.

Reilly, Thomas H. *The Taiping Heavenly Kingdom: Rebellion and the Blasphemy of Empire.* 2004.

Shepherd, Verene A. *A Maharani's Misery: Narratives of a Passage from India to the Caribbean.* 2002.

Industry and Society

The idea that a middle class arose during the Industrial Revolution is disputed, because world historians acknowledge that for centuries there had been merchants sandwiched between princes and peasants. At the same time, many believe that industrialist workers followed industrial rhythms and saw the world differently from their predecessors. For a real-life example of the opportunities seized by one striving industrialist, see the PBS Web site on Andrew Carnegie.

Banerjee, Swapna M. *Men, Women, and Domestics: Articulating Middle-Class Identity in Colonial Bengal.* 2004.

Igler, David. *Industrial Cowboys: Miller and Lux and the Transformation of the Far West, 1850–1920.* 2001.

Morgan, Kenneth. *The Birth of Industrial Britain: Social Change, 1750–1850.* 2004.

Porter, Susie. *Working Women in Mexico City: Public Discourses and Material Conditions, 1879–1931.* 2003.

Public Broadcasting Service. *American Experience*, "Andrew Carnegie." http://www.pbs.org/wgbh/amex/carnegie/.

The Culture of Industry

Those in the world of art and ideas responded to the sights and sounds of industry. The Metropolitan Museum of Art's Web site has many links to specific instances of cultural exchange during the nineteenth century, including the one listed on Japan's influence on the West during industrialization.

Callen, Anthea. *The Art of Impressionism: Painting Technique and the Making of Modernity.* 2000.

Izzard, Sebastian. *Hiroshige/Eisen: The Sixty-Nine Stations of the Kisokaido.* 2008.

Megill, Allan. *Karl Marx: The Burden of Reason.* 2002.

Metropolitan Museum of Art. *Timeline of Art History*, "Japonisme." http://www.metmuseum.org/toah/hd/jpon/hd_jpon.htm.

Peskin, Lawrence. *The Intellectual Origins of Early American Industry.* 2003.

COUNTERPOINT: African Women and Slave Agriculture

The unsung innovators of the past are in the process of being discovered. Carney looks at the West African women and men who brought rice cultivation, processing, and cooking to the U.S. South.

Carney, Judith A. *Black Rice: The African Origins of Rice Cultivation in the Americas.* 2001.

Carney, Judith A., and Richard N. Rosomoff. *In the Shadow of Slavery: Africa's Botanical Legacy in the Atlantic World.* 2009.

Hoerder, Dirk. *Cultures in Contact: World Migrations in the Second Millennium.* 2002.

▶ **For additional primary sources from this period**, see *Sources of Crossroads and Cultures.*

▶ **For Web sites, images, and documents related to topics in this chapter**, see Make History at bedfordstmartins.com/smith.

REVIEW

Online Study Guide
bedfordstmartins.com/smith

The major global development in this chapter ▶ The Industrial Revolution and its impact on societies and cultures throughout the world.

IMPORTANT EVENTS

c. 1750	Industrialization begins in Great Britain
1769	James Watt creates the modern steam engine
1780s–1790s	Interchangeability of parts developed in France
1803	Denmark becomes the first Western country to abolish the slave trade
1814	George Stephenson puts a steam engine on a carriage on rails, inventing the locomotive
1819	First Atlantic crossing by a steamship
1839–1842	Opium War between China and Britain
1842	Treaty of Nanjing opens Chinese ports
1848	*Communist Manifesto* published
1853	U.S. ships enter Japanese ports
1840s–1864	Taiping Rebellion
1865	U.S. Civil War ends, rapid U.S. industrialization begins
1868	Meiji Restoration launches Japanese industrialization
1871	Germany gains resource-rich Alsace and Lorraine after defeating France
1873–c. 1900	Deep global recession with uneven recovery
1890s	Argentina's leading textile manufacturer produces 1.6 million yards of cloth annually
1891–1904	Construction of trans-Siberian railroad

KEY TERMS

bourgeoisie (p. 817)
capitalism (p. 817)
cartel (p. 805)
Industrial Revolution (p. 794)
interchangeability of parts (p. 799)
limited liability (p. 805)
materialism (p. 816)
outwork (p. 801)
proletariat (p. 817)
socialism (p. 816)
stock market (p. 805)
utopian socialism (p. 816)

CHAPTER OVERVIEW QUESTIONS

1. In what ways did the Industrial Revolution change people's work lives and ideas?
2. How did the Industrial Revolution benefit people, and what problems did it create?
3. How and where did industrial production develop, and how did it affect society and politics?

SECTION FOCUS QUESTIONS

1. What were the main causes of the Industrial Revolution?
2. How did industrialization spread, and what steps did nations and manufacturers take to meet its challenges?
3. How did industrialization affect societies in China, South and West Asia, and Africa?
4. How did industrialization affect people's everyday lives and livelihoods?
5. How did writers and artists respond to the new industrial world?
6. What contributions did African women agricultural workers make to industrial development?

MAKING CONNECTIONS

1. How did the Scientific Revolution (see Chapter 20) and the Enlightenment (see Chapter 23) contribute to industrialization?
2. How did industrialization in the United States and in Japan differ, and why?
3. What was the role of slavery in industrial development?
4. In what ways was the Industrial Revolution a world event?

25

AT A CROSSROADS ▲

The Meiji Restoration of 1868 was the foundation of Japanese nation building and industrialization. Its Charter Oath, the founding document of Japan's new regime, is shown here being read in the presence of the emperor. The Charter Oath established the rule of law over "evil customs" of the past and opened the door to freedom in livelihoods. It also called on the Japanese to scour the world for new findings and advances, making Japan a crossroads of nation building and economic development. (Art Resource, NY.)

The Rise of Modern Nation-States

1850–1900

In 1862 Matsuo Taseko, a prosperous Japanese peasant, packed a few possessions and, leaving her family behind, made her way to the capital at Kyoto. The trip was an unusual one for a woman to make on her own, and even more so because of its goal: to overthrow the country's civilian leadership. Taseko belonged to a group of conservative activists eager to restore the power of the Japanese emperor, who for centuries had played second fiddle to the Tokugawa shogun, or first minister. So subordinate was the emperor that he received just 5 percent of the government's revenues while the shogun took 25 percent. To those in Taseko's group, the shogun's position was a reversal of the natural order. In a proper world, decision-making and revenue should have been the other way around. "Despicable charlatans," she called the shogun's administration. Even worse to Taseko was the presence of foreigners in the country's port cities, notably the Americans and British, who had demanded in the 1850s that Japan open its harbors to global trade. Taseko wrote this poem about them:

> The superficial
> foreign barbarians
> pile up mountains
> of silver,
> but even I, who am not
> a brave warrior
> from the land of the rising sun,
> I do not want their money,
> I would rather be poor.[1]

Modernizing Nations

FOCUS How did some states transform themselves into modern nations?

Emerging Powers: The United States and Japan

FOCUS How did the United States and Japan make their governments politically and economically powerful in the nineteenth century?

The Culture of Nations

FOCUS What part did culture play in forging a national identity?

COUNTERPOINT: Outsiders Inside the Nation-State

FOCUS Which groups were excluded from full participation in the nation-state, and why?

BACKSTORY

As we saw in Chapter 24, throughout the nineteenth century Europe and the United States industrialized rapidly, if unevenly, allowing the West to catch up economically with India and China. Industrialization offered a host of advantages to the West. Both Europe and the United States excelled in producing weaponry, which made them especially successful in opening trade and gaining diplomatic power. Industrializing nations engaged in increasingly global commerce, enjoyed greater productivity, and developed dense networks of swift transportation. As the West's newly industrialized states extended their power around the world, industrialization also produced internal transformations. It gave rise to new social classes and new occupations, swelling the middle and working classes and giving both a stake in the growing prosperity of their nations. These groups had the awareness, and some of them the wealth, to challenge the political and social values of kings and the aristocracy, sometimes overthrowing existing political institutions entirely and at other times working to modify them.

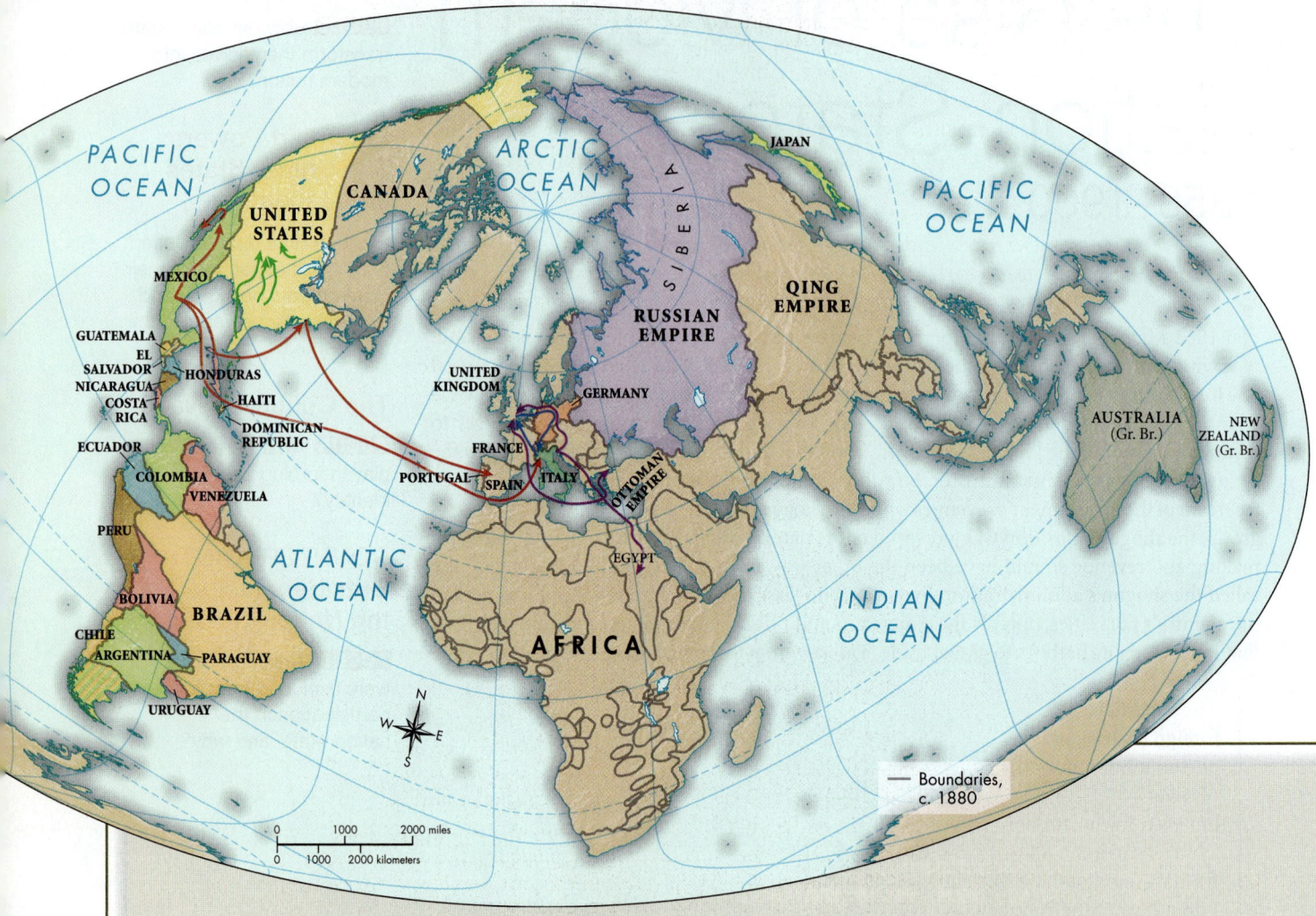

1833–1855 Mexican caudillo Santa Anna serves at intervals to lead the government

1846–1848 Mexican-American War

1853–1856 Crimean War

1859–1870 Unification of Italy

1861–1865 U.S. Civil War

▪ **1863** Emancipation Proclamation in the United States

1840 | 1850 | 1860 | 1870

Walt Whitman, *Leaves of Grass* **1855** ▪

1860s Height of opera singer Angela Peralta's career

Emancipation of the serfs in Russia **1861** ▪

Meiji Restoration of Japan **1868** ▪

Unification of Germany **1866–1871**

Beginning in 1862 members of Taseko's conservative group, aiming to free Japan from outside influences and to restore the emperor, took part in a virtual civil war with reformers who wanted trade, the latest technology, and a modern nation-state. Assassinations, riots, and street violence plagued the country, causing Taseko herself, who was sometimes seen as a spy by political opponents, to go into hiding in the spring of 1863 and eventually to return to her hometown. By 1868 the reformers had restored the emperor to his central position in a nation-building revolution that became known as the Meiji Restoration.

The Meiji Restoration was primarily the work of propertied individuals who wanted to update Japan's government and economy. It was part of a global nineteenth-century trend toward building strong states whose people felt bound together as part of a single political unity. In Latin America, leaders in Mexico, Argentina, and other states struggled to develop national institutions and to create connections between the central government and local elites. In Europe the nation-states of Germany and Italy unified amid economic ferment and calls for social and political reform. The United States fought a destructive civil war and killed and displaced native Americans to create a mighty nation-state stretching thousands of miles. Russia freed its serfs and reformed its legal and military systems—reforms designed to make it more competitive in a modernizing and global economic system.

Historians sometimes treat the rise of powerful nation-states and the sense of national identity among peoples as part of an inevitable process. However, it was not: as Italy and Germany were forming unified nations and Latin Americans were developing notions of modern citizenship, millions of individuals in the Austrian Empire, Africa, and Oceania, for example, held on to local identities based on village life or ethnic ties. Moreover, many

MAPPING THE WORLD

Nation-States, c. 1880

In many cases, but not all, industrial growth and revolutionary uprisings often led kingdoms to develop into nation-states. Around the world, nations reformed their administrative structures, created more effective armies, and encouraged national spirit. From Russia to Australia and across the Western Hemisphere, war and the seizure of native peoples' lands accompanied the rise of the nation-state.

ROUTES ▼

- → Forced migrations of Native Americans, 1832–1835
- → Travels of Florence Nightingale, 1820–1855
- → Travels of Camillo di Cavour, 1830–1838
- → Travels of Angela Peralta, 1862–1883

1880s Popular uprisings in Japan

▪ **1889** Brazilian emperor Pedro II abdicates and republic is installed

1880 1890 1900

▪ **1881** Young rebels assassinate Alexander II of Russia

▪ **1888** Emancipation of slaves in Brazil

1872–1876 Fukuzawa Yukichi, *Encouragement of Learning*

rulers had no interest in political and economic reforms, preferring to embrace tradition rather than change.

Other once-powerful states labored unsuccessfully to meet the challenges of global trade, rising population, and the growing industrial power of Europe. The Ottoman sultans found it difficult to modernize their administration of a complex empire; local governors such as the rulers of Egypt modernized cities, transportation, and other facilities on their own. China likewise failed to reform its governmental structures sufficiently to fight off the inroads made by the European powers, even though segments of its population were pushing for modern institutions and growing rich by dealing with the West.

Matsuo was a traditionalist—eager to restore the emperor to power and to rid Japan of outside influence. Although she was a peasant, she was well educated. Broader education also contributed to nation building as people circulated and debated political and philosophical writings, poetry, and other works. People came to be united not only by new institutions, but also by a common culture. However, modern nation-states also denied certain people within their borders full citizenship. Immigrants, women, and the conquered local peoples of Australia and the United States worked and paid taxes, for example, but they did not enjoy full equality and rights such as being able to vote. People hotly debated who did and did not belong to the nation, and Matsuo Taseko engaged in such debates, fighting for ideals that were centuries old. Even though she longed for an older way of doing things, she participated in the development of "the public"—that is, a wide arena of concerns and values that went beyond individual or family interests to create a shared national way of life. Thus, the era of nation building saw many forms of nation-states taking shape, all of them influenced by the public voices of many different people.

OVERVIEW QUESTIONS

The major global development in this chapter: The causes and consequences of nation building in the nineteenth century.

As you read, consider:

1. Why did nation-states become so important to people in the nineteenth century?
2. What was the role of war in the rise of the nation-state?
3. What was the role of ordinary people in nation building?
4. Are nation-states still important today, and are there still outsiders inside nations?

Modernizing Nations

FOCUS

How did some states transform themselves into modern nations?

Politicians of this time and the citizens who backed them worked to bring varied peoples into cohesive nations and to develop more effective governments. This was an age of national growth and nation building when states industrialized and politicians changed the nature of government. To prosper in a more competitive and connected economic world, some even created entirely new entities, as occurred in Italy and Germany. Even where industry was slower to thrive, nation building occurred. People in the newly independent nations of Latin America began to develop a sense of themselves as citizens with common values. In Eurasia the mighty Russian Empire instituted dramatic reforms as part of a nationalizing effort after being decisively beaten in the Crimean War. What emerged from these efforts was a political and cultural form—the nation-state—that has shaped the course of modern world history, both for good and for ill.

"What Is a Nation?"

In an 1882 lecture, French writer Ernest Renan asked, "What is a nation?" The concept was a new one, and subject to debate. Nations came to be seen as political units in which citizens feel an allegiance to one another and are active in the government or state that represents them. Thus *nation-state* and *nation* are often treated as synonyms. A **nation** differs dramatically from a kingdom. A princely kingdom is the personal domain of a monarch, who sees people as subjects to be governed, not as active citizens with a political voice. Despite differences in their form, nations rely on the allegiance of a wide range of people within their geographic borders, who as citizens demand the rule of law and involvement in government. This active civic voice was essential to the rise of modern nations. Facing an enemy from without, people proudly protected the nation—that is, themselves and their community—as patriotic soldiers rather than military recruits forced to defend royal interests, as in a kingdom. Although women did not take up arms and lacked political rights, they too began to consider themselves active contributors to a nation's well-being, rearing young children to be virtuous citizens and volunteering their efforts in times of trouble.

In the nineteenth century and thereafter, politicians sought to mobilize whole populations to build powerful nation-states. Some waged external and civil wars in hopes of creating or maintaining national unity. The U.S. Civil War, for example, can be seen as a war for national unity waged by the North against the South. Other wars were fought to force outlying states to join a powerful military state permanently; this happened with Prussia, which formed the core of the new Germany. Historians have called the development of the nation-state a modernizing influence because the unity it created helped economic development spread over a wider territory. The nation-state also aided economic expansion by eliminating tariffs among cities and localities and by working to replace disruptive regional armies with a single fighting force operating to advance national, not local, power. Nation builders hoped to provide effective, centralized institutions—constitutions, bureaucracies, laws, and common military, education, and transportation systems. Theirs was a multifaceted undertaking in which centralizing authorities sought to challenge local identities and strengthen the connections and loyalties that bound populations together.

Latin American Nation Building

After the regions of South and Central America gained independence from Spain and Portugal early in the nineteenth century, they did not generally develop efficient or smoothly functioning democracies, but they did lay the groundwork for nation-states. Wars between states and civil wars between supporters of centralization and those wanting regional self-rule affected nation-building efforts. Although some people of individual nations were developing a sense of themselves as citizens, Latin American nation building was complex and often difficult (see Map 25.1).

Brazil Takes the Lead

Brazil's dominant ruler for more than five decades was the emperor Pedro II (r. 1831–1889)—a committed nation builder. "I have no rights; all I have is a power resulting from birth and chance," he claimed. "It is my duty to use it for the welfare, the progress, and the liberty of my people."[2] Pedro II tried to centralize government by gaining dominance over the wealthy landowning families and factions that controlled the countryside. As the capital of Rio de Janeiro prospered, Brazil fought a war against Paraguay

nation A sovereign political entity and defined territory of modern times representing a supposedly united people.

MAP 25.1

Latin America, c. 1900

The new nations of Latin America worked to create effective governments and engage citizens in the nation-building process. Like the new United States of America to the north, these nations often fought with their neighbors to expand boundaries and crushed native Americans to gain their lands. Simultaneously they created important institutions, such as systems of law, education, and culture, that would both enhance government power and advance citizens' capabilities.

(1864–1870), which built allegiance to the central government. A firm believer that nation building depended on legal equality and opportunity, Pedro surrounded himself with people of all races. He ended the slave trade in 1850, partly in response to the growing voice of people of color expressed through their newspapers and clubs. Brazil ended slavery altogether in 1888, and it also tried to eliminate hierarchies based on skin color and racial ancestry. In its openness to change, Brazil seemed to be ahead of all its neighbors. It produced one of the greatest Latin American writers, Joachim Machado de Assis (ma-KA-do day ah-SEES). Of African descent, Machado de Assis's masterful novels do not portray a rosy society of the sort that Pedro hoped for. They are full of satire, as Machado explores the worlds of the old moneyed classes, the new bureaucracies of the rising nation-state, and the outsider status of women—all shaped by the legacy of slavery.

Nation Versus Region

National cohesion quickly fell apart in Brazil. The emancipation of Brazil's slaves enraged plantation and mine owners in the countryside, who relied on cheap slave labor for their profits. Believers in small government, hierarchical social arrangements including slavery, and regional autonomy, they billed themselves as "federalists" and "liberals."

Brazilian Plantation Workers
Pedro II freed Brazil's slaves in 1888 as part of his nation-building efforts, believing that modern, unified nations needed to integrate all races into citizenship. Once regional leaders overthrew his monarchy, however, the weakened national authority could not protect newly freed workers from exploitation. The lack of protection for workers and the free hand given large landowners produced a huge disparity between the upper classes, who were virtually omnipotent, and impoverished ordinary people such as these workers on a manioc plantation in the 1890s. (The Art Archive/Museu Nacional de Belas Artes Rio de Janeiro Brazil/Gianni Dagli Orti.)

In 1889 they overthrew Pedro's centralizing monarchy, returning power to provincial governments that they themselves controlled. Under the landlords' rule, movement toward a strong, tolerant nation-state seemed to go backward. As one newspaper complained in 1890 of the takeover, "In Brazil there are no more citizens; we are all slaves!"[3]

In fact, most of Latin America was shaped by the bold, powerful landowners in the countryside, who controlled the production of minerals, coffee, sugar, and other commodities sold on the global market. Such men believed that their wealth and power rested on the liberal, eighteenth-century belief in minimal government and the building of individual wealth. They felt that any policy or reform that challenged these principles should be resisted at all costs. In an age of nation building, their stance against strong centralized institutions went against the prevailing trend and kept individual states in turmoil. Almost every Latin American state experienced this contest between centralization and **federalism**.

Caudillos

Many wealthy landowners were themselves strongmen with their own armies, but there were also independent military leaders, *caudillos*, men at the head of unofficial bands of warriors who controlled the countryside by force. Caudillos ruled regions so far removed from the capital cities that they functioned as a law unto themselves. They gathered the support of peasants, workers, and the poor by offering protection in a turbulent countryside where the peasantry on large estates was intensely exploited.

Some caudillos stabilized the central government by acting as temporary dictators. General Antonio Lopez de Santa Anna was the quintessential caudillo. In Mexico, the period from the 1830s to 1855 is called the "Age of Santa Anna" because he wielded so much personal influence. In this period, conservatives favored the rule of large landowners, while the Catholic Church battled reformers who championed individual rights, foreign investment, and trade. During their disputes Santa Anna, who was called "Defender of the Homeland," was summoned some dozen times to head the government and stabilize the nation between 1833 and 1855. During this time of instability Mexico lost much of its territory to the United States in the Mexican-American War (1846–1848). Nonetheless, the

federalism A form of government in which power and administration are located in regions such as provinces and states rather than in a centralized administration.

caudillo remained an important figure in Latin American nation building, and at times even rescued nations from dissolution.

Although caudillos could mobilize masses of workers and peasants to political causes, gradually governments built state institutions such as national armies and military schools to train nationally oriented officers. Governments also took control of infrastructure such as railroads and ports along Latin America's extensive coastline. In the second half of the nineteenth century, state bureaucracies grew as the educated middle class came to fill government offices. Regional economic interests gave way to national economic interests; for instance, local tariffs exacted by the different regions of a nation gave way to tariffs collected at national borders.

A Sense of Citizenship

During the struggles to construct new, centralized governments, many people in individual Latin American countries developed a sense of belonging and citizenship that was crucial to nation building. José Gregorio Paz Soldán, a judge in Peru, had first supported slavery in the new republic but soon became an ardent supporter of liberty and equal treatment for all, commenting that "The Indians are no more savage or ferocious than other people who have been attracted to a social and civilized life."[4] Paz Soldán wanted solidarity among citizens of all classes. Employers, he urged, should give laborers "a salary and good treatment."[5] The Peruvian constitution of 1828 stated that "All citizens may be admitted to public employment, without any difference except that of their talents and virtues."[6] The qualifications for participating in the nation were in theory the same for everyone, uniting people of different ethnicities and classes instead of dividing them as the Spanish monarchy had done by giving preference to the Spanish-born.

Even in Cuba, where the Spanish crown still ruled, people came to believe in a common citizenship characteristic of an independent nation-state. Free blacks in Havana protested their exclusion from service in the militia because of their race, citing their commonality with other citizens. "Mulattoes and blacks, we are the ones who practice the mechanical arts to the highest degree of perfection, to the admiration and wonder of professors from other enlightened nations. We own property—houses that we live in with our families, workshops, and buildings to rent out to those who need them. We have farms and slaves in the same proportions as those other members of the people of Havana who possess such property."[7] The Spanish put down the protest, but they could not quell the sense of citizenship that gave rise to it.

After independence, cities in Latin American countries had thriving political clubs, mutual aid societies, newspapers and journals, and economic organizations that concerned themselves not only with the welfare of the community but with the nation as a whole. Although a nation might have a dictatorial ruler or a corrupt administration, commercial groups took part in public debate over building a strong national economy, and mutual aid societies focused on well-being in neighborhoods. "Clubs have enabled us to replace tyranny with liberty," was the opinion of one Mexican newspaper in 1855. "They have provided the government with a way to become acquainted with public opinion, and this is the reason we support them."[8] People became immersed in the public affairs of their nation as never before. Thus, the connections among citizens that were central to the nation-state were not solely the product of state policies imposed from the top down. They were also created from the bottom up by citizens themselves.

The Russian Empire's New Course

Other countries that seemed unlikely to embrace the institutions and values of modern nation-states were often transformed by events, such as peasant uprisings, inefficiencies, low productivity, and the revelation of internal problems from external defeat. The Russian Empire, for example, modernized its institutions when wartime defeat dramatically revealed the need for change. In the 1800s, Russia continued its centuries-old expansionism into Asia and the Middle East. Just as the British aimed for inroads in China, Tsar Nicholas I wanted to absorb much of the Ottoman Empire, which was fast becoming known as "the sick man of Europe" because of the disintegrating administration of its lands. As Russia grew more aggressive, war erupted in October 1853. The Crimean War (1853–1856) began as a conflict between the Russian and Ottoman empires but ended as a war with long-lasting consequences for Russia, much of Europe, and, indeed, for the world (see Map 25.2).

The war disrupted Europe's balance of power, as France and Great Britain, enemies for more than a century, united in declaring war on Russia to defend the Ottoman Empire's sovereignty. Their goal was to maintain power in the global economy by securing their full access to the eastern Mediterranean. British and French troops landed in the Crimea in September 1854 and waged a long siege of the Russian naval base at Sevastopol on the Black Sea. The war coincided with the continuing spread of the Industrial Revolution, which introduced powerful new technologies into warfare: the railroad, shell-firing cannon, breech-loading rifles, steam-powered ships, and the telegraph. With the telegraph and increased press coverage, the relationship of the home front to the battlefront changed. Home audiences received news from the Crimean front lines more rapidly and in more detail than ever before, intensifying national unity and thus nation building across Europe.

Despite the new weaponry, Sevastopol fell only after a year of savage and costly combat. Generals on both sides were incompetent, and governments failed to provide combatants with even minimal supplies, sanitation, and medical care. A million men died, more than two-thirds from disease and starvation. The casualties resulting from incompetence and poor sanitation showed that nations needed strong institutions. London reformer Florence Nightingale seized the moment to escape the confines of middle-class domesticity by organizing a battlefield nursing service to care for British troops. Through her tough-minded organization of nursing units, she pioneered nursing as a profession and also better sanitary conditions both in armies and in society in general. After the war, she contributed to nation building by publishing statistical studies showing that national effectiveness depended on public health and a scientifically prepared and centrally directed military.

MAP 25.2 The Crimean War and Postwar Settlement, 1853–1856

The Crimean War has been called senseless, but it was rich in consequences. By splitting the conservative alliance between Austria and Russia that had effectively kept France and indeed all of Europe in check, it opened the way for ambitious politicians in Italy and Germany to unify their fragmented states into two strong nations. Additionally, its defeat caused Russia to free the serfs and institute significant reforms; the Ottoman Empire continued to attempt modern nation building as well.

The war exposed Russia's weakness and transformed the global balance of power. With casualties mounting, Tsar Alexander II (r. 1855–1881) asked for peace. As a result of the peace treaty of 1856, the Black Sea was declared neutral waters and Russia lost its claim to protect Christians in Ottoman lands. Austria's and Russia's grip on European affairs weakened, making way for the rise of new regional and global powers. The defeat forced the authoritarian Russian state to embark on a long-overdue renovation of the empire.

Serfdom in Russia

When Russia lost the Crimean War, the educated public, including some government officials, found the poor performance of serf-conscripted armies to be a disgrace. When a son was conscripted into the Russian army for the regular twenty-five-year term, parents held funerals because the army experience was so long and brutal and the chance of returning alive so slight. The system of serf labor was also seen as an intolerable liability for a country that needed economic and institutional modernization to be an effective nation-state on the world stage. The Russian economy had stagnated compared with western

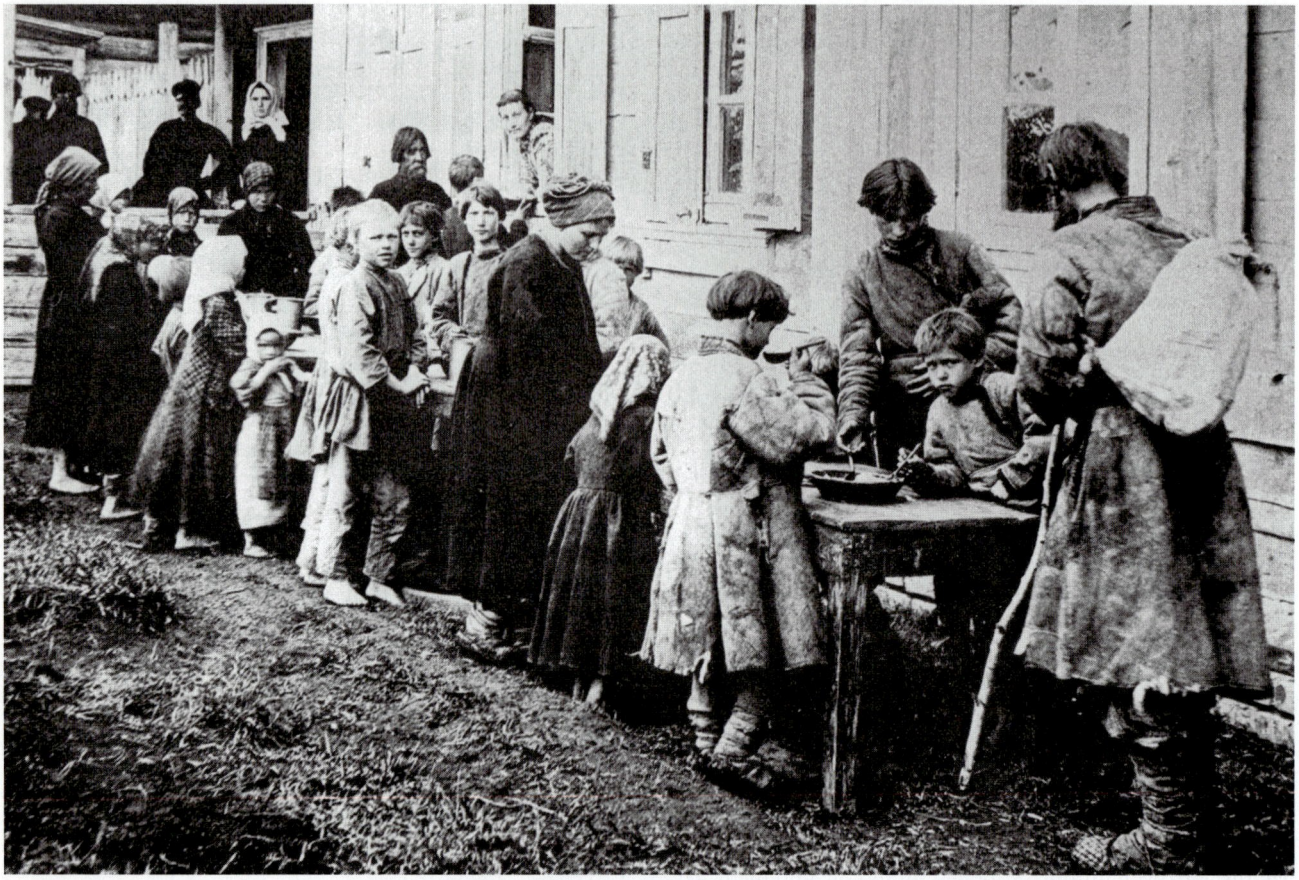

Russian Peasants at a Soup Kitchen

Even after emancipation from serfdom in 1861 and other reforms that followed, Russian peasants were hard-pressed to earn a living. As a condition of emancipation, they were burdened with debt for farmland and could not migrate freely in search of greater opportunity. Tensions in the countryside grew, alleviated only by acts of charity and relief programs, such as the soup kitchen shown here. (©Sovfoto.)

Europe. Old-fashioned farming techniques led to worn-out soil and food shortages. For serfs, everyday life brought constant toil and obedience to flighty or cruel masters, who could marry them off at will or rent them out at great distances from home.

Challenges to serfdom had begun to grow during the decades before the Crimean War. Serf defiance ranged from malingering while at forced labor to small uprisings. Works of art such as novelist Ivan Turgenev's *A Hunter's Sketches* (1852) contributed to a spirit of reform with their sympathetic portrayals of serfs and frank depiction of brutal masters: "O Lord Jesus Christ!" one of his characters thunders. "Am I not free to use my slaves as I wish?"[9] But other inspiration came from serf artists and writers—the lucky ones among the serf population who were assigned artistic tasks such as piano tuning, fine cabinetry, or portrait painting on estates; some even became highly educated.

One of these was Alexander Nikitenko, born a serf in 1804. His father had been sent to sing in one of Russia's famous boys' choirs by his owner, a great landowner. Enraged at being returned to the estate still a serf, Nikitenko's father, who had learned to read while in the choir, made sure that his son received a good education. Alexander also fumed at the injustice of his serf condition, especially as he became known as one of the most learned young men in the land. In the late 1830s, a powerful Russian prince obtained Nikitenko's freedom, allowing him to become a high government official. Educated serfs such as Nikitenko were among the most bitter and vocal advocates of change (see Reading the Past: The Russian People Under Serfdom).

READING THE PAST

The Russian People Under Serfdom

Alexander Nikitenko gained his freedom from serfdom after proving himself a learned and conscientious teacher as well as an outstanding manager of households and general man of all work. Many serfs were accomplished; their achievements included painting and traveling in troupes of actors and singers, which brought Russians in contact with one another across vast spaces. Like Nikitenko, some of these serfs reached national eminence and came to be celebrated, but Nikitenko felt the degradation of serfdom long after he was free. These excerpts from his autobiography, first published in 1824, concern the early nineteenth century when he was between six and ten years old. They do not reflect the thinking of a child, however; Nikitenko observed serfdom for decades while honing this account of his life.

> The peasants suffered beneath the yoke of serfdom. If a master was wealthy and owned several thousand serfs, they suffered less oppression because most of them were tenant farmers. . . . On the other hand, small [landowners] literally sucked out the strength of unfortunates in their power. Neither time nor land was at their disposal. . . . In addition, sometimes there was inhuman treatment, and often cruelty was accompanied by debauchery. . . .
>
> People could be bought and sold wholesale or in small numbers, by families, or singly like bulls and sheep. . . . Tsar Alexander I, during the humanitarian phase of his reign, talked about improving the lot of his serf-subjects, but attempts to limit the [landowners'] power vanished without a trace. The nobility wanted to live in luxury befitting its station. . . .
>
> [E]veryone bore the burdens generated by the People's War [Napoleon's 1812 invasion] without complaint. They supplied and equipped recruits at great personal expense. Yet I did not detect in their conversations a sign of deep interest in the events of the time. Evidently everyone was interested solely in their own affairs. The mention of Napoleon's name evoked awe rather than hate. The nonchalant attitude of our community toward the disaster hanging over Russia was startling. This may have been due in part to the distance of the theater of war. . . .
>
> But I think the main reason was apathy, characteristic of a people estranged from participation in society's affairs, as Russians were then. They were not accustomed to discussion [of] what went on around them and unconditionally obeyed the orders of the authorities.

Source: Alexander Nikitenko, *Up from Serfdom: My Childhood and Youth in Russia 1804–1824*, trans. Helen Saltz Jacobson (New Haven: Yale University Press, 2001), 54–56, 75.

EXAMINING THE EVIDENCE

1. **How does Nikitenko characterize Russian serfs?**
2. **How did serfdom affect the Russian people and state more generally?**
3. **What was the mood of the Russian people as a nation facing the Napoleonic invasion of 1812? How might the emancipation of the serfs in 1861 have changed that mood?**

Emancipation of the Serfs

Faced with Russia's dire situation, Alexander II proved more flexible than his predecessors in modernizing society. Better educated and more widely traveled, he ushered in what came to be known as the Great Reforms, granting Russians new rights from above as a way to ensure that violent action from below would not force change. The most dramatic reform was the emancipation of almost 50 million serfs beginning in 1861. Under the terms of emancipation, communities of former serfs, headed by male village elders, were given their personal freedom and grants of land. Each community, called a ***mir*** (mihr), was given full power to distribute this land among its members and to direct their own economic activity. Thus, although the serfs were free, the requirements of communal landowning and decision-making held back individuals with new ideas and those who wanted to find opportunity elsewhere. Nonetheless, millions surely received this news as former serf Alexander Nikitenko did: "with an inexpressible feeling of joy."[10] Ending serfdom and slavery was often the foundation for creating citizens and for nation building.

mir In Russia, the organization of land and former serfs following the emancipation of the serfs.

The state awarded peasant communities some 13 percent less land than they had tilled under serfdom, forced them to "redeem" or pay the government for this land in long-term loans, and in fact awarded the best land to the nobility. Although some landowners experimented with modern farming techniques, which made Russia the largest grain-exporting nation by 1900, the conditions of emancipation held Russian agriculture back. Nevertheless, idealistic reformers believed the emancipation of the serfs, whom the nobility once treated virtually as livestock, had produced miraculous results. As one writer put it, "The people are without any exaggeration transfigured from head to foot. . . . The look, the walk, the speech, everything is changed."

Other Nation-Building Reforms

The state also reformed local administration, the judiciary, and the military. The government set up ***zemstvos*** (ZEHMST-vohs), regional councils through which aristocrats could revive neglected public institutions for education, public health, and welfare. As aristocrats gained responsibility for local well-being, some became invested in Russia's health as a nation. Judicial reform in 1864 gave all Russians, even former serfs, access to modern civil courts, where ordinary people for the first time benefited from the principle of equality of all persons, regardless of social rank, under a unified set of laws. Military reform followed in 1874 when the government ended the twenty-five-year term of conscription, substituting a six-year term and devoting more attention to education, efficiency, and the humane treatment of recruits. These changes improved the fitness of Russian soldiers, helping them identify with the nation as a whole.

Limits of the Great Reforms

Alexander's reforms encouraged modernizers and gave many in the upper classes a more worldly outlook, but nation building also diminished the personal prerogatives of the nobility, leaving its authority generally weakened and sparking intergenerational rebellion. "An epidemic seemed to seize upon [noble] children . . . an epidemic of fleeing from the parental roof," one observer noted. Rejecting aristocratic values, youthful rebels from the upper class valued practical activity and sometimes identified with peasants and workers. Some formed communes, where they joined together in cooperative living to do humble manual labor. Others turned to higher education, especially the sciences, to gain modern knowledge. Rebellious daughters of the nobility flouted parental expectations by cropping their hair short, wearing black, and escaping from home through marriages in name only so they could study medicine and the sciences in European universities.

This repudiation of traditional society led Turgenev to label radical youth as *nihilists* (from the Latin for "nothing"), meaning people who lack belief in any values whatsoever. In fact, these individual rebellions showed a spirit of defiance percolating in Russian society that would soon fuel assassinations, including that of the reformer Alexander II in 1881, and ultimately produce the revolutions that would shape the world in the next century. For the time being, the tsarist regime only partially succeeded in developing the administrative, economic, and civic institutions that were strengthening nation-states elsewhere. The tsar and his inner circle held tightly to the reins of government, slowing the development of consensus politics and modern citizenship.

A Unified Italy and a United Germany

With the European powers divided over the Crimean War of 1853 to 1856, politicians in the German and Italian states took advantage of the opportunity to unify their respective countries. In 1848 workers, students, and professionals had revolted in many of the individual Italian and German states, hoping to reform and unify their countries. Despite their failure, the issue of unification simmered until two practical but visionary leaders took charge: Camillo di Cavour of the kingdom of Piedmont-Sardinia in the economically modernizing north of Italy, and Otto von Bismarck from the prosperous agrarian kingdom of Prussia. Both depended on modern railroads, strong armies, and power diplomacy to transform disunited states into coherent nations with a presence on the world stage.

Italy

The architect of the new Italy was Camillo di Cavour, prime minister of the kingdom of Piedmont-Sardinia from 1852 until his death in 1861. A rebel in his youth, the young

Cavour had conducted agricultural experiments on his aristocratic father's land. He organized steamship companies, played the stock market, and inhaled the fresh air of modernization during his travels to Paris and London. Cavour promoted economic development rather than democratic uprising as the means to achieve a united Italy. As prime minister, he helped develop a healthy Piedmontese economy, a modern army, and a liberal political climate to anchor Piedmont's drive to unite the Italian states.

To achieve this goal, however, Piedmont would have to confront Austria, which governed the provinces of Lombardy and Venetia and had a strong influence on most of the peninsula. Realizing that Austria was too powerful for Piedmont to take on by itself, Cavour first got a promise of help from France and then provoked the Austrians to invade northern Italy in April 1859. Nationalists seeking unity and political liberals seeking constitutions and modern institutions in Tuscany and other central Italian states joined the Piedmontese cause. Using the newly built Piedmontese railroad to move troops, the French and Piedmontese armies achieved rapid victories in the north. In May 1860, Giuseppe Garibaldi, an inspired guerrilla fighter and veteran of the revolutions of 1848, set sail from Genoa to liberate Sicily with a thousand red-shirted volunteers, many of them teenage boys and half from the urban working class, "splendid in the dress and cap of the student, and in the more humble dress of the bricklayer, the carpenter, and the [blacksmith]," as Garibaldi himself put it.[11]

Unification of Italy, 1859–1870

Across the Sicilian countryside peasant revolts against landlords and the corrupt government were under way in anticipation of ***Risorgimento***, the "rebirth" of a strong Italian state. Anger in the countryside was so violent against these oppressors that the farmers massacred opponents, leaving them to be "devoured by dogs . . . torn to pieces by their own brothers with a fury which would have horrified the hyenas."[12] Successfully mastering the scene in the south, Garibaldi threw his support to Piedmont-Sardinia's leadership. In 1861, the kingdom of Italy was proclaimed. Exhausted by a decade of overwork, Cavour soon died, but despite huge difficulties such as poverty in the south, many citizens of the new country took pride in the Italian nation and came to see themselves as one people.

Germany

A momentous act of nation building, for both Europe and the world, was the creation of a united Germany in 1871. The Prussian state brought an array of cities and kingdoms under its control within a single decade by using both the conservative military to wage war on behalf of unification and the liberal businessmen's enthusiasm for the profits to be gained from a single national market. The newly unified Germany prospered, continuing to consolidate its economic might as business people small and large enjoyed a bigger market to pursue profits. Its growing industrial and commercial wealth would make Germany the foremost power on the European continent by the end of the nineteenth century.

The architect of a unified Germany was Otto von Bismarck, the Prussian minister-president. Bismarck came from landed nobility on his father's side; his mother's family included high-ranking bureaucrats and middle-class intellectuals. As a university student, the young Bismarck had gambled and womanized; he was interested in only one course, on the economic foundations of politics. After failing in the civil service he worked to modernize operations on his family's estates while leading an otherwise rowdy life. His marriage to a pious Lutheran woman worked a transformation and gave him new purpose: to establish Prussia as a respected and dominant power.

In 1862, the king of Prussia appointed Bismarck prime minister in hopes that he would block the growing power of the liberals, who were the reformers and modernizers in the Prussian parliament, and instead build the army over their objections. Bismarck

zemstvo Regional council of the Russian nobility established after the emancipation of the serfs to deal with education and local welfare issues.

Risorgimento Italian for "rebirth," a nineteenth-century rallying cry for the unification of the Italian states.

Unification of Germany, 1866–1871

indeed managed to ram through programs to build the army despite the opposition's belief in parliamentary control. His brand of nation building was based on ***realpolitik***—a political strategy of hard-headed realism, armed might, and rapid industrial and commercial development. "Germany looks not to Prussia's liberalism, but to its power," he preached. "The great questions of the day will not be settled by speeches and majority decisions . . . but by iron and blood."

After his triumph over the parliament, Bismarck led Prussia into a series of victorious wars, against Denmark in 1864, against Austria in 1866, and, finally, against France in 1870. His victory over Austria-Hungary, which claimed to be the leader of the disunited German states, allowed Bismarck to create a North German Confederation led by Prussia. Prussia's swift victory over France persuaded all the German states to unify under Prussia's leadership. In January 1871, the king of Prussia was proclaimed the Kaiser, or emperor, of a new, imperial Germany.

Despite the growing wealth of liberal business people, the constitution of the newly unified empire ensured the continued political dominance of the aristocracy and monarchy. The Kaiser, who also remained Prussia's king, controlled the military and appointed Bismarck to the powerful position of chancellor for the Reich (empire). Bismarck balanced the right to vote, which the constitution granted to men, with an unequal electoral system in Prussia, which continued to be the dominant state within the German Empire. In the Prussian system, votes from the upper classes counted more than those from the lower. Bismarck's nation-building deals worked, allowing Germany, even more than Italy, to focus its national energy on industrial growth and power politics. Europe would never be the same.

Emerging Powers: The United States and Japan

FOCUS

How did the United States and Japan make their governments politically and economically powerful in the nineteenth century?

Two other newcomers, the United States and Japan, were also eager for global wealth and influence. These two states built national power in the nineteenth century and drastically reformed their societies and political structures to industrialize and to make their governments more focused and effective. By 1900 the United States and Japan were beginning to rival the great European powers as nation building promoted their economic strength and pumped ordinary people's ambitions.

Expansion and Consolidation of the United States

The United States went from a cluster of states hugging the eastern seaboard in the eighteenth century to a growing power in the nineteenth century. Like Germany and Italy, it did so through warfare. Confronted with the pressures of migration and the demands for raw materials, it fought Mexico and Indian peoples in order to seize their resources and land. It also engaged in a devastating civil war over issues arising from the brisk global trade in cotton, slaves, and—increasingly—industrial products. The series of wars the United States pursued in the nineteenth century expanded its territory and unified a rambunctious nation of adventurers, immigrants, farmers, ranchers, miners, entrepreneurs, and industrial innovators. Amid all this turmoil, the nation built up its common institutions, such as schools and transportation networks, and widened its global connections.

realpolitik A practical, tough-minded approach to politics, wielded most famously by Otto von Bismarck in Germany.

Westward Expansion and Manifest Destiny

U.S. settlers continued to push westward in the nineteenth century, seeking more land to profit from the global trade in raw materials, particularly cotton. They drove into Mexican territory in the continent's southwest, where struggles for control of both trade and territory resulted in sporadic warfare. Between 1846 and 1848 the United States first provoked and then won a war with Mexico over land in Mexico's north, and as a result almost doubled its territory, annexing Texas as well as large portions of California and the Southwest (see Map 25.3). Simultaneously, immigrants from around the world flocked to California and later to other places where gold was discovered. Americans came to see this western expansion as part of the nation's **Manifest Destiny**—that is, the belief that white Americans had a God-given right to control the entire continent no matter how many native Americans were killed or displaced.

Manifest Destiny The nineteenth-century doctrine that the United States had the right and duty to expand throughout the North American continent.

MAP 25.3 U.S. Civil War and Westward Expansion

U.S. nation building advanced through the war with Mexico, the Civil War, and ongoing battles to take the land of native Americans. Calls for unity during wartime and appeals asserting the superiority of white Americans welded the country together both politically and culturally. These shared values helped the United States forge ahead economically, with innovation coming to justify U.S. claims to being more advanced than those whose property the expanding nation took.

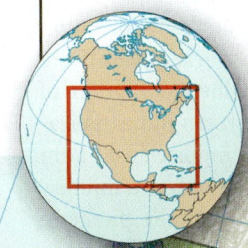

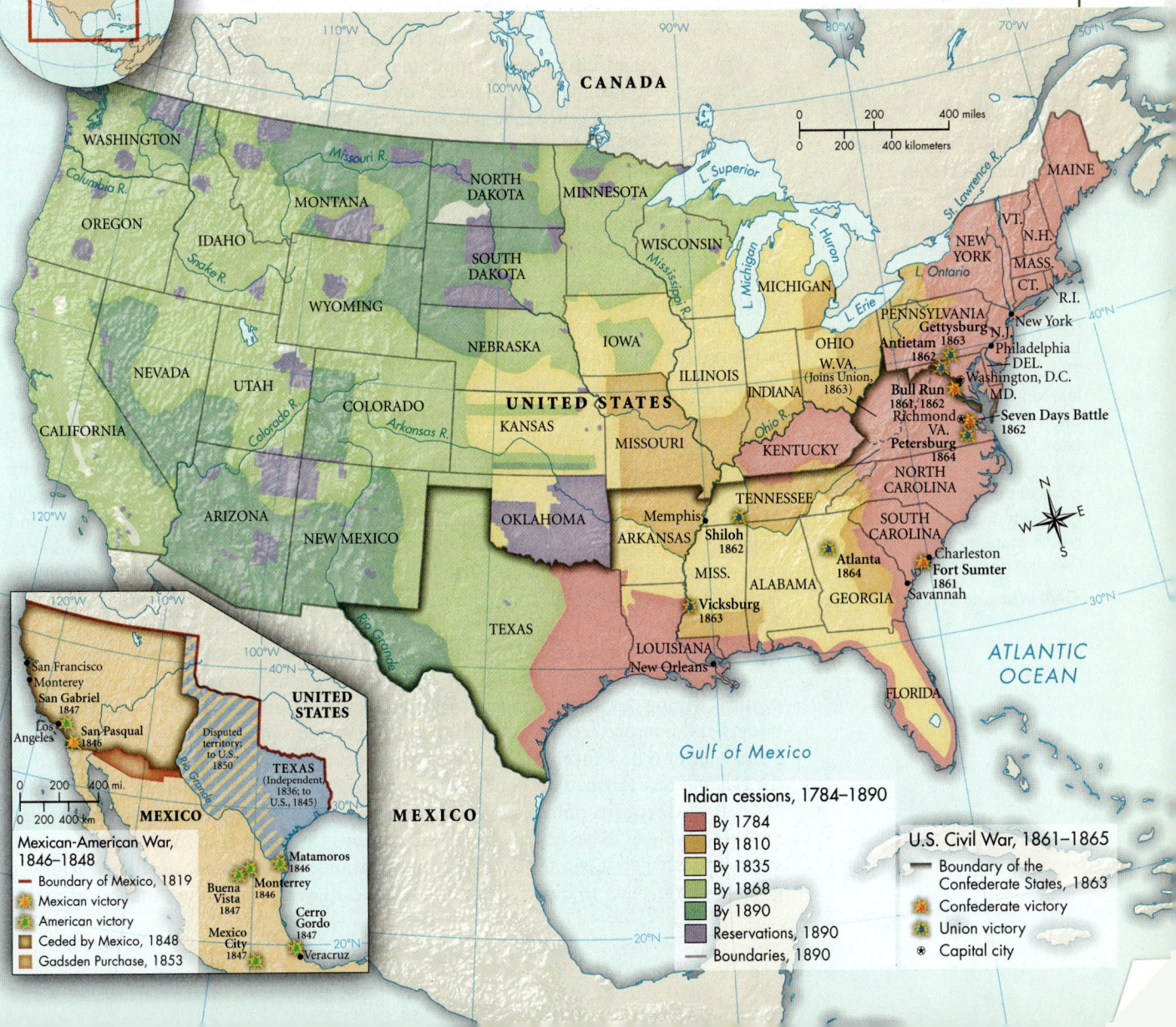

English Porcelain Statue of Abraham Lincoln

Although the British generally backed the Confederate cause because they needed southern cotton for its textile industry, the Staffordshire porcelain company issued this statue on Abraham Lincoln's inauguration in 1861. The oddly regal garment Lincoln is wearing and the highly decorated horse he is riding were based on an earlier representation of King George III. Portrayals of political heroes such as Lincoln grew with the spread of the nation-state. (The Art Archive/Private Collection/Eileen Tweedy.)

Civil War and Reconstruction

Politicians and citizens alike argued over the status of the new western lands. The greatest quarrels came over the expansion of slavery to the new territories, and the main issue was livelihoods. Should the West be settled by free white farmers, or could southern plantation owners bring in their slaves, against whose unpaid labor white farmers could not compete? Like some Latin American nation builders, many saw equal legal status of citizens as essential to a thriving nation, but others disagreed so strongly that the country became polarized. In the North, where abolitionists had a strong organization to fight against slavery, the new Republican Party called for "free soil, free labor, free men." However, few Republicans backed the abolitionists' demand for an immediate end to slavery in the South. In the months following Republican Abraham Lincoln's election to the presidency in 1860, most of the southern slaveholding states seceded to form the Confederate States of America.

Under Lincoln's leadership the North fought the South in a civil war from 1861 to 1865 to uphold the union. Lincoln did not initially aim to abolish slavery, but in January 1863 his Emancipation Proclamation came into force as a wartime measure officially freeing all slaves in the Confederate States and turning the war into a fight not only for union but for the end of slavery—thus creating a pool of workers who were entirely free *and* connecting nation building to the liberal program of rights and opportunity. While the war dragged on, northern industrialization flourished: "Believe me," remarked one Pennsylvania industrialist, "I am not eager for peace."[13] The North's superior industrial strength and military might ultimately overpowered the South, and in April 1865 the prostrate Confederacy surrendered. For Lincoln, the victory was short-lived. Within days a Confederate sympathizer had assassinated the president.

During the postwar period known as Reconstruction (1865–1877), constitutional amendments ended slavery and granted the rights of citizenship and voting to black males. For a time under Reconstruction, the newly liberated slaves received land and education, and some served in government or moved up in the world of business and work. The way was open for continent-wide industrial expansion and commercial agriculture, based on a free labor force, common rights for citizens, and migration from virtually every continent. The country would soon become a thriving nation-state.

A final piece of the nation-building effort in the United States was crushing the various native American peoples by forcibly taking their North American homelands or killing them to open up resources for whites. "Manifest Destiny" became a strong post-Civil War rallying cry. In the 1820s the state of Georgia simply took the land of the Cherokees, a group of native Americans who had a constitution and practiced settled farming, forcing them to migrate westward along the "Trail of Tears"—so named because of the number of deaths along the way. Pushed from the east coast westward by European settlers in the seventeenth century, tens of thousands of North American Indians had moved onto the Great Plains by the end of the eighteenth century. Numerous other native Americans had settled there far earlier in farming communities. Many were horse traders and herders of an estimated 40 million buffalo, exchanging goods with communities in New Mexico to the south and the British and French to the north. "There was always fat meat, glad singing, and much dancing in our villages," one Crow woman remembered of her people's mid-nineteenth-century prosperity.[14]

All that was before Europeans moved onto the Plains themselves in the nineteenth century, wiping out the buffalo and spreading European diseases widely, through Indian traders and interpreters. The Mandan tribes numbered some 15,000 in 1750; a hundred years later only 138 survived. Hundreds of thousands of native Americans perished as the U.S. military finished the conquest, carrying out government orders to drive remaining native Americans onto reservations in Oklahoma and other states, where they had no right to vote or to participate in U.S. institutions (see again Map 25.3). As one Apache survivor described it, whites considered reservations "a good place for the Apaches—a good place for them to die."[15] For white Americans at the time, the conquest of native

Americans across the continent helped industry thrive, helped immigrants find new livelihoods, and helped the nation to unify.

Dramatic Change in Japan

When the United States forced the opening of Japan to foreigners in the 1850s, it disturbed the country's peace and, as the activism of Matsuo Taseko shows, threw Japan into political turmoil. Strange, unruly white men walked the streets of port cities, and Western emissaries made demands on the government. All the same, even some of Japan's provincial rulers sensed the excitement and opportunity. There was money to be made, local notables suspected, and they resented the Tokugawa shogun's control of trade with the foreigners and thus his monopoly on profits. More conservative leaders found the break with the tradition of relative isolation an affront to Japan's greatness, and they were willing to use violence to suppress Japanese contact with the outside world. For example, conservatives assassinated an official who accepted trade treaties with foreigners and murdered a scholar who used a Western saddle on his horse. Such traditionalists shared Matsuo Taseko's desire to drive the "barbarians" from Japan and return the Japanese people to their traditions.

The furor over political and economic life led to a dramatic realignment of power in Japan. Many of the provincial rulers adopted the goal of restoring the emperor Komei to the full dignity of his office. The emperor was their "jewel," and Japanese of almost all political positions now unified around him. By late 1867, support for the shogun's long-standing power had dwindled to virtually nothing, and he was forced to resign.

Sioux Women Line Up for Rations

Nation building allowed many citizens to prosper because of the rule of law and new rights and opportunities. For many others, however, nation building was a disaster. Whereas once the Sioux had prospered, by the 1890s they were confined to small sections of the continent that was their homeland. Native Americans were the last group given the vote in the United States, although romanticized portrayals of native Americans who aided the European colonists as well as tales of native American "savagery" became staples of U.S. nation-building lore. (Denver Public Library. Western History Collection, photo by C.G. Morledge, Call number X-31445.)

Meiji Restoration

The restoration of power to the emperor did not, however, bring with it a straightforward return to Japanese isolation as conservatives such as Matsuo Taseko had hoped. Although a series of shoguns had recognized the importance of relationships with the West, Emperor Komei had been against it. Conveniently for the modernizers, he fell ill and died as the shogunate collapsed, leaving the throne to his fifteen-year-old son, Mutsuhito (r. 1868–1912). The resulting new government revived the imperial house and gave priority to Westernization and the shogun's more open, global policies—largely to protect Japan from further inroads by foreigners. Having fought to gain influence, the victorious, reform-minded elites crafted an assembly of high-ranking men such as themselves to determine the laws, making imperial rule much less than absolute. The government announced the "Meiji Restoration"—*Meiji* means "enlightened rule"—as a combination of "Western science and Eastern values" offering both innovation and restoration. Thus, the revival of imperial power partly masked the reality of revolutionary change. Japan would be transformed by its new relationship with the West, but its leaders hoped that by embracing aspects of Westernization they could control that transformation, ensuring that the process would serve Japan's interests, and not those of the West (see Map 25.4).

MAP 25.4 Japan, c. 1860–1889

Japan's rapid development of a more modern administration and economy cost many people their livelihoods, most notably the samurai. The changes the new government imposed during the Meiji Restoration of 1868 stirred uprisings and peasant revolts, particularly because Western nations appeared to be forcing Japan open with the goal of foreign domination.

The Meiji government stabilized itself through a series of necessary changes. A pressing issue was overturning the older decentralization of power embodied in the system of local lords, the daimyo, and their loyal retainers, the samurai. The government successfully centralized power by forcing the daimyo to surrender their political and economic control of the countryside and giving them large payments or positions in the new government instead. The tens of thousands of samurai, who became unemployed once their local lords had no need for them, were potentially troublesome members of the new social order—a good many of them had no skills at all, except roughhousing. The government bought them off with pensions and later with government bonds. The samurai's status further declined as some of the most prominent politicians toured the world to gain ideas for modernization and concluded that a centralized conscript army would be far more reliable than Japan's traditional, samurai-based forces. Whereas the samurai mostly relied on a code of individual heroism, a national, conscript army was a disciplined fighting mass trained to cooperate in the use of modern weaponry. As a result of these findings, Japan instituted universal military conscription. It simultaneously created a hereditary nobility, as in Europe, and limited the powers of elected representatives who might come from the people. These last changes, enshrined in the constitution of 1889, showed that despite centralization, the government would not be fully based on republican institutions or popular rule.

The first two decades of the Meiji Restoration were tumultuous. Discontent and disorder persisted, as people from many walks of life remade the economy. The first to revolt were the displaced samurai, followed by farmers such as Matsuo Taseko, merchants, and countless others who had fought to bring back the emperor and face down the "barbarian" challenge. Now the same people struggled for the recognition of what were called "People's Rights" within the imperial system. They drafted constitutions of their own that laid out the fundamental powers of the people who, after all, were the building blocks of the nation. When their constitutions were ignored by the government during these first two decades of Meiji rule, they took up arms.

Social Unrest and Rebellion

Throughout the early Meiji period, people of the rural lower classes launched a series of rebellions. They found themselves squeezed by high taxes, intended to finance Japan's modernization and industrialization, and by a drop in agricultural prices that resulted from increased global competition. The new officials of the Meiji government, instead of respecting those on the land, seemed to inflict them with hardship even as cities were thriving. In Chichibu outside Tokyo, one resident expressed his despair: "The wind blows, / The rain falls, / Young men die. The groans of poverty / Flutter like flags in the wind."[16] In 1884, an army of eight thousand peasants in Chichibu began fighting for the people's rights, fully believing that they could force the central government to negotiate. In the Chichibu uprising, the armed populace talked about "deposing evil rulers" and "changing the mandate" as part of the program of ousting corrupt officials. Government forces smashed the uprising, imprisoning and executing many participants. Meiji officials attributed the uprising to criminals, but in fact this revolt, like others occurring across Japan, showed that successful nation building required more attention to the needs of the Japanese population as a whole. In the decades to come, Japan would continue on the difficult path to the creation of a modern nation-state.

The Culture of Nations

FOCUS

What part did culture play in forging a national identity?

History, music, art, and other cultural works helped peoples forge national identities and built bonds across regions and localities. National cultures sometimes focused on reviving a country's literary past and celebrating long-dead authors' works. In other instances, people invented customs such as special dress or songs that over time came to be seen as "traditional." Still other peoples prized their nation's modernity, and citizens traveled miles to experience fast-paced new technology like the railroad or to see for themselves modern new structures such as the Eiffel Tower in Paris. Widely circulated books and newspapers for the masses also brought people together in national and even global unity. Cultural leaders such as composers, artists, editors, and even some university professors shaped the attitudes and experiences of a growing number of citizens, uniting them around shared knowledge and artistic achievement.

The Culture of Tradition

In the early days of the Meiji Restoration, Matsuo Taseko was invited to the home of a prince, where she heard a Western organ played. Taseko was appalled at the declining appreciation for Japan's own instruments and sent a poem to the princess. "In Japan / the koto cannot be quick / but I ask you not to listen gladly / to this barbarian harp / no matter how clever it is."[17] Taseko's nationalism was built on imitating the past and indeed protecting it from outside influences and from cultural mixture such as the playing of a Western instrument. She herself wrote hundreds of poems modeled on those from earlier centuries. In the culture of tradition, one followed not only the form but even the exact words of earlier poetry. As public schools developed, children across the nation recited poetic masterpieces from the past as a way to create and to participate in a national culture.

Forging National Unity

Leaders of monarchies, republics, and empires became symbols of national unity. Taseko carefully guarded gifts from the emperor to show to her closest friends and to pass down to her children and grandchildren as emblems of patriotism. Monarchs' and presidents' portraits appeared on dishware and on household walls and adorned public

SEEING THE PAST

The Korean Flag

The Korean Flag
(Tetra Images/Corbis.)

Flags existed in ancient times to distinguish regiments of an army, as was the case with Egyptian standards. Over the centuries, most flags continued to be standards for armies, but they also became important symbols of the nation. Designing a single flag around which citizens of an entire country could rally became a crucial part of the process of nation building. Colors were carefully chosen to represent virtues such as courage and purity, and figures like lions, eagles, stars, and the sun were selected to portray a nation's strength and magnificence.

In the 1880s, as China, Russia, and Japan greedily eyed Korea for conquest, the kings of Korea adopted the more impressive title of emperor, and they also designed a flag. Its central figure represents the balance of yin and yang in the cosmos, while the four corners indicate the elements—fire, water, earth, and air—and the four seasons. After Japan had defeated both China and Russia (discussed in Chapter 26), it established a protectorate over Korea in 1905 and then annexed it in 1910, replacing the Korean flag with its own. On the defeat of Japan in World War II, the nineteenth-century flag became the standard of South Korea.

EXAMINING THE EVIDENCE

1. **What makes this flag or any flag distinctive to the nation?**
2. **Compare the Korean flag with the U.S. flag. What do the differences reveal about the political culture and national identity of each country?**

spaces such as schools and office buildings, thus providing a unifying symbol. National flags were designed to serve a similar purpose (see Seeing the Past: The Korean Flag). Royal births were widely reported in the press, and in Britain, for example, officials carefully staged royal marriages, birthdays, and funerals as public ceremonies, which were not only viewed by the growing urban population but also commemorated with the new photographic technology. Nishimiya Hide, daughter of a samurai and lady-in-waiting to a member of the high Japanese nobility, found a way to use her knowledge of court traditions after the samurai and grand nobility had lost their leading role. She supported herself in part under the Meiji Restoration by teaching court ceremonies from an earlier time to members of the new elite.

Writing and teaching history became a popular way to legitimate nations (see Lives and Livelihoods: Historians of the Nation-State). The public latched onto the story of the rise of the nation-state from its origins as a princely kingdom to its current modern might. Historical pageantry was popular in the nineteenth century in the form of parades, theater, and the revival of rituals at shrines. Governments erected monuments in the capital and other cities to celebrate great moments in the nation's past; these suggested the nation's durability and antiquity, even though many nations were actually quite new. Official histories eventually integrated the story of native peoples to build pride in the nation's progress from barbarism to civilization. Governments built museums to house collections of national documents, coins, and other treasure, but also native artifacts such as baskets, arrowheads, and beadwork to illustrate the "primitive" condition before the nation took shape.

Romanticizing the Past

The reality of nation building was brutal, producing hundreds of thousands of casualties and entailing real suffering, but the stories of nation building told by artists and writers were often romantic and inspiring. From the late nineteenth century to the present, authors and artists have presented accounts of the birth of Latin American nations, the Meiji Restoration, and the U.S. Civil War as glamorous, heart-throbbing adventures. Towering heroes such as Simon Bolivar and their selfless officers and families were portrayed as sacrificing for a greater good—the nation. The idea of "founding fathers" erased the fact that people lived in the region before the nation-state appeared, and appeals to ancient gods and goddesses supported claims of a nation-state's eternal existence. Biographies of nation builders became popular reading from the nineteenth century on, which helped replace people's local identities with a shared national culture.

Westernization

The power of the nation-state fostered world trade, of both goods and ideas. Readers in East Asia and South America, for example, studied works by contemporary Western writers such as the Englishmen John Stuart Mill and Charles Darwin and the Russian novelist Fyodor Dostoevsky. The eighteenth-century French social and political theorist Jean-Jacques Rousseau was especially popular among reformers and modernizers for his ideas of the social contract and natural rights. Rapid steamships carried potential leaders from Asia, Africa, and South America to Europe for their education, and sometimes to the United States for firsthand observation of popular government and nation building. Japanese leaders were among those who identified military power as the foundation of Western success, and they visited Europe, especially Germany, and the United States to learn about new weaponry and modern military training techniques. Influences went in many directions: young Chinese people who wanted their nation to modernize studied in Japan, which was increasingly seen as strong and modern.

Recasting Western Culture

Back home, reformers popularized ideas from the West. Sometimes writers modified Western theories to suit the local situation. Japanese author and educator Fukuzawa Yukichi came from an impoverished samurai family but quickly achieved fame and fortune through his innovative reform message. Best-selling works such as *Encouragement of Learning* (1872–1876) made people aware of current thinking in the West. Fukuzawa maintained, like Rousseau, that the entire population created the state, agreeing to a social contract through a constitution, and that they entered this contract from a position of complete equality—a totally novel concept for the Japanese. Fukuzawa's theory differed from much of Western constitutional thought, however, when it maintained that once people had agreed to the formation of a state, they surrendered their right to criticize or protest. In this way, he recast Western liberal theory into a form that suited the Meiji Restoration, justifying reform but also fortifying an authoritarian, emperor-centered state.

Angela Peralta was a Mexican opera performer whose popularization of European operas helped build her country's national culture. Born in 1845, at a time when Mexicans were already wild about opera, she took audiences to new heights of rapture with her renditions of the most difficult European operas. Described as "angelic in voice and in name," Peralta sang across Europe and in Egypt. Her real triumphs, however, occurred in Mexico, where she traveled from city to city mobbed by fans—"an incomparable woman," they called her—and spreading her fame and the culture of opera. News of Peralta's comings and goings passed from city to village and back to other cities, uniting Mexicans culturally, as Santa Anna and other rulers were trying to do politically. By the time of her death from yellow fever at the age of thirty-seven, many a theater owner had become wealthy from her performances, and opera had received such a boost that Mexican composers began writing operas about Aztec princesses and other Mexican peoples, creating "national" traditions

LIVES AND LIVELIHOODS

Historians of the Nation-State

With the rise of the nation-state, the study of history became a profession in the nineteenth century. Historians—whether in Japan, Latin America, Europe, or North America—set out to collect the major documents that legitimated the rise of the unified nation-state. They concerned themselves above all with the story of institutional development, the formation of states and governments, and the expansion of imperial power. The tradition of official history writing went way back in China to the Han dynasty; in the eighteenth century, the Chinese emperors charged court historians with the job of celebrating their conquests to the west. Nineteenth-century nation builders appointed professional historians, trained in the study of the past, to posts in prestigious universities, where they were to research and write true, verifiable accounts of the national past.

The model of the new professional historian arose in Germany, and Leopold von Ranke and his followers became the most honored historians of their day, even in foreign lands. Merchants actually stood outside Ranke's classroom to sell his photograph to admiring students. Ranke was swept up by the enthusiasm for unity that gripped the German states. Nations drew individuals together, and he believed in a strong central government. He aimed in his investigation and verification of documents to provide an objective account of Germany's development over the centuries. Ranke had his disciples, such as Heinrich von Treitschke, who even as a supposedly dispassionate scholar lectured to his students about the genius of the German nation: "It is for us to stand together in manly discipline and self restraint, and to pass on the bulwark of our unity, the German kingdom, to our sons." These professional historians often advised rulers while they usually kept from their classrooms the same groups of people kept from citizenship—women and many people of color.

Source: Quoted in Andreas Dorpalen, *Heinrich von Treitschke* (New Haven, CT: Yale University Press, 1957), 156.

Leopold von Ranke

Historians wrote the story of a nation, giving it a solid foundation in facts and research. The most enduring figure in the professionalization of history is Leopold von Ranke, who took the writing of history out of the hands of amateurs and put it into those of university-trained scholars. Ranke wrote histories of Prussia and of Germany, basing his work on archival and documentary research and thus reinforcing the idea of the nation itself as true, reliable, and authoritative. (bpk, Berlin/Nationalgalerie, Staatliche Museen, Berlin/Andres Kilger/Art Resource, NY.)

QUESTIONS TO CONSIDER

1. **Why did nation-states promote history as a profession?**
2. **Compare this textbook with the description of Ranke's historical writing. What differences and similarities do you perceive, and what do these suggest about history as a field of study?**

through a Western cultural form. Her tombstone reads: "She sang like no one has ever sung in this world."[18]

National Institutions

Institutional innovations helped consolidate and modernize the state. Citizens took pride in the modernization of their cities, especially capital cities such as Cairo, Tokyo, and Paris. Bureaucrats undertook efforts to improve sanitation, medicine, and other institutions to promote public health. Reformers recognized public education as a crucial ingredient of national development. A Japanese law of 1872, for example, mandated universal education so that in the modernized Meiji state there would be "no community with an illiterate family nor a family with an illiterate person."[19] Improved facilities, whether public transportation or cultural institutions such as opera houses, theaters, and museums, testified to a nation's power and greatness.

Ordinary persons in agrarian societies based on traditional rhythms of planting and harvest were often illiterate and untutored. The nation-state was based on citizen participation and required a more literate population with a common culture and common skills and ideals. China had long offered more widespread education than elsewhere because for centuries the positions of government officials had required literacy and extensive training. Nationally minded reformers sought not only to imitate the Chinese tradition of an educated officialdom but also to expand education more generally as the foundation of strong nations. Although he ruled an agrarian state, the emperor Pedro II of Brazil established a record number of schools as part of his commitment to nation building. When he came to power in 1831, the capital of Rio de Janeiro had 16 primary schools; when he abdicated in 1889, the number had climbed to 118. Schools built a sense of common purpose. "We must constantly strive to work diligently at our tasks," a third-grade Japanese textbook of 1892 instructed, "and, when an emergency arises, defend our nation."[20]

French emperor Napoleon I (r. 1803–1815) was among the first to see the importance of science, math, and engineering to national power, and he ordered the development of high-level technical schools to teach advanced skills such as engineering. Thereafter secondary and postsecondary education advanced across Europe and the United States. Universities added modern subjects such as science and math to the list of prestigious courses in the second half of the century, reshaping the curriculum to make it better serve the national interest in a competitive global environment.

Angela Peralta

Mexican singer Angela Peralta was famed in her time for her range as a soprano and for the delicate beauty of her voice—"like the trill of a goldfinch," one critic noted in his diary. Peralta sang before kings and emperors and performed in the major opera houses of Europe. She toured Mexico itself, becoming an icon as she helped build a shared culture for its people. (Library of Congress Prints and Photographs DivisionLC-USZ62-132102.)

Reformers bucked tradition when they opened public schools for girls and young women. Across the globe these activists touted the education of women as key to modernization, because ignorant or illiterate mothers would give children a poor start. By contrast, the educated mother, instructed in both national culture and practical skills, provided a living example of the cultured citizen and had the capacity to begin the educational process for preschool offspring (see Reading the Past: "Good Wives, Wise Mothers" Build Japan). Primary, secondary, and even university education for young women developed in the second half of the nineteenth century in most parts of the world. These changes were hotly contested, however; often, the education of women was seen as the final blow in the collapse of tradition.

Public Education

Cultural Unity

Another tactic of nation building was to foster a uniform culture and uniform beliefs. The Russian Empire, comprising more than a hundred ethnicities, sought to reduce the threat of future rebellion by forcing all its ethnic groups, from Poles to Afghans, to adopt the Russian language and culture and to worship in the Russian Orthodox church. When resistance to this "Russification" mounted, the government showed some leniency to encourage continued acceptance of the nation-state. Across Latin America, plantation owners had tolerated the many different religious practices that African slaves had brought with them because the differences, it was thought, would keep slaves divided and less likely to rebel.

With independence, however, nation builders in some countries tried to impose greater control over religious life, seeking to replace loyalty to religion with loyalty to

READING THE PAST

"Good Wives, Wise Mothers" Build Japan

In 1874 a group of reformers, many of them samurai, established a new Japanese journal, *Meiroku Zasshi*, to bring readers knowledge of Western philosophy, science, and customs—among them current attitudes toward women. Nakamura Masanao, of samurai background, brought to Japanese readers the new idea that mothers should actively raise their children as part of nation building. By 1900 the slogan "good wives, wise mothers" dominated the national ideology about women, making women's connection to children and love for their husbands part of patriotism.

> Thus we must invariably have fine mothers if we want effectively to advance the people to the area of enlightenment and to alter their customs and conditions for the good. If the mothers are superb, they can have superb children, and Japan can become a splendid country in later generations. We can then have people trained in religious and moral education as well as in the sciences and arts whose intellects are advanced, whose minds are elevated, and whose conduct is high. . . .
>
> Now to develop fine mothers, there is nothing better than to educate daughters. . . . It is then not excessive even to say that the foundations for [a man's] virtues of bravery, endurance, and perseverance of a later day were laid while he was still playing in his cradle and receiving his mother's milk. To fear harm from equal rights for men and women is no more than to fear that the uneducated woman will sit on her husband. This anxiety would not exist if women honored Divine Providence, respected noble sentiments, admired the arts, appreciated science, and helped their husbands, and if husbands and wives mutually loved and respected each other.
>
> Aside from the matter of equal rights, the training of men and women should be equal and not of two types. If we desire to preserve an extremely high and extremely pure level among human beings as a whole, we should accord both men and women the same type of upbringing and enable them to progress equally. . . . A wife possessed of a feeling of deep love will bring her husband ease and happiness and encourage him to exert himself in enterprises useful to the country.

Source: Meiroku Zasshi: Journal of the Japanese Enlightenment, trans. and ed. William Reynolds Braisted (Cambridge, MA: Harvard University Press, 1976), 401–403.

EXAMINING THE EVIDENCE

1. **What are the groups of people that Nakamura identifies?**
2. **How are they supposed to support the nation?**
3. **How do men and women compare in their standing in the nation?**

the nation-state. Latin American officials made Carnival celebrations less African and more uniformly Spanish. In Germany in the 1870s, Otto von Bismarck sought to build cultural unity by striking out against Catholicism; he expelled the Jesuits, increased the government's power over the clergy, and introduced obligatory civil marriage. His *Kulturkampf*, or culture war, aimed to weaken allegiance to religion and to redirect it to the German nation. German Catholics and other citizens rebelled at this attack on freedom of religion, but overall Bismarck's achievements fostered a strong sense of German identity, especially because an excellent public school system served the cause of cultural uniformity.

Support of Multiculturalism

Some nations built their common ideology around multiculturalism, which allowed citizens to take pride in their diversity or regional strengths. In the United States, for instance, the poet Walt Whitman's *Leaves of Grass* (1855) celebrated the many types of ordinary people working across the country. African Americans developed powerful musical forms such as blues and jazz from the African tradition of the *griot* (or oral poet) and the sounds, rhythms, and tonalities of African and local music. Many Americans increasingly saw this music as part of American rather than African heritage. In Japan, even as a Shinto religion was declared to be the "traditional" Japanese faith, religious pluralism existed, and cultural leaders announced that this pluralism was part of the nation's cultural evolution. Although multiple religious and cultural traditions were allowed, they argued, the Japanese should nonetheless choose the highest form of religion and culture—which was none other than Shintoism—and Japanese forms of poetry such as the brief verses called haiku. Controversies over culture persisted over the course of nation building down to the present, but these debates can also bring people together around the search for consensus.

COUNTERPOINT

Outsiders Inside the Nation-State

FOCUS

Which groups were excluded from full participation in the nation-state, and why?

Defining who was a true Brazilian, Russian, Japanese, or other citizen was an essential part of the process of nation building. Nation-states saw no contradiction between the ideal of universal membership and the exclusion of certain people from political participation and thus full citizenship. Sometimes these people—native Americans, for example—were those who had resisted nation building, often because it threatened their livelihoods, took their land, and devalued their beliefs. Other outsiders, notably women, often had helped in nation building from the start but were still excluded. Nation building created a body of "we's," insiders who felt their citizenship most keenly when they discriminated against a set of "they's," the outsiders.

People of Color

Native Peoples

From Japan to South America, nation-building efforts had a devastating effect on indigenous peoples. Settlers in South America, Australia, New Zealand, and Siberia treated native peoples—who had lived in the territory for centuries and even for millennia—as remnants of barbarism. "In point of fact," the *New York World* told its readers in 1874, "the country never belonged to the Indians in any other sense than it belonged to the wolves and bears, which white settlers shoot without mercy."[21] Indigenous civilization was dismissed, even when settlement usually depended on learning the skills and receiving aid in food and medicine from local peoples. Native peoples generally lived within national borders but without the rights of citizens. In the United States they were excluded from voting and full protection of the law until 1924, and in Peru Indians paid an extra tax, which constituted almost half of Peru's national income. The Australian and Canadian governments took native children from their families, sending them to live in white homes or in boarding schools to be "civilized." Russian officials simply moved settlers into the far reaches of Siberia and displaced reindeer herders in the name of strengthening the nation. As an article in one U.S. newspaper argued, settlers "are the people who develop a country; who carry a civilization with them."[22]

Ethnic and racial thinking justified exploitation in the name of civilized nation building, even though the people exploited were subject to the nation's laws and taxes. Japanese nation builders taught that the Ainu peoples on the country's outer islands were dirty and disheveled; their tattoos and physical features were judged as hideous. The caste systems of the Spanish Empire and of Brazil ranked people of pure European blood highest and those of native or African blood lowest; those of mixed blood fell in the middle. Whether it was the mother or father, a free or unfree parent, who had the darker skin could also alter one's status. In the long run, however, the hierarchy was simple: the darker the skin, the lower the person.

Former U.S. Slaves

In the United States the withdrawal of Union troops from the South in 1877 marked the end of Reconstruction and the withdrawal of the rights to citizenship given to black men in the Fourteenth Amendment to the Constitution. Southerners passed "Jim Crow" laws segregating blacks from whites in public places and effectively disenfranchising them with a variety of regulations. The Ku Klux Klan, a paramilitary group of white Southerners, terrorized blacks and lynched and mutilated black men, whom they falsely accused of raping white women. Unprotected by U.S. laws, blacks fought back in ways both brave and subtle. One woman took as her goal in life keeping her daughter from the common livelihood for African American girls and women of domestic service in a white family, "for [Southern men] consider the colored girl their special prey."[23] The exclusion of blacks and native Americans from rights became a unifying ideal for many white Americans.

Women

From Italy and Germany to the United States, and in the case of Matsuo Taseko, Japan, women joined the effort to create and preserve strong nation-states. "I am a U.S. soldier," wrote Clara Barton, nurse on a U.S. Civil War battlefield.[24] Women such as Barton were subject to the laws and taxes of the nation-state, but they too were denied rights of citizenship, including the right to vote, to own property, and to participate in public life. In countries as distant from one another as Japan and France, the government made it a crime for women to participate in political meetings under pain of arrest and imprisonment. Rape, other forms of physical abuse, and inequality of wages (and sometimes no wages at all) were seen as normal treatment for women.

Nonetheless, women became central to national myths of origin. In almost every modernizing country, the self-sacrifice of women to their nation or family was held up as a common model for citizenship. Just as women put aside their self-interest when being "good wives, wise mothers," as the new, nationalist Japanese slogan went, so women sacrificed their personal interests to strengthen the nation, even if this meant accepting beatings and the taxation and confiscation of their property by men and governments. Countries such as the United States, France, and Germany took mythical women—in these examples, Columbia, Marianne, and Germania—as their symbols on coins and other official artifacts even as they denied women the rights of citizenship.

Frederick Douglass

Frederick Douglass was an escaped slave, journalist, and civil rights pioneer of the nineteenth century. His goal was freedom for slaves and civil rights for all, and as such he became a hero to all outsiders down to the present day. As outsiders have been integrated, national histories make heroes of them to build a portrait of the nation as all-encompassing and based on mass participation of its citizenry. (National Portrait Gallery, Smithsonian Institution/Art Resource, NY.)

Begum Rokeya Sakhawat Hossain

Begum Rokeya Sakhawat Hossain was an outsider to political life, as women generally lived in seclusion from society. In 1905 this Muslim woman, born in present-day Bangladesh, wrote an unusual short story that described what a nation—"Ladyland," she called it—would be like if women ruled with their brains instead of men ruling with their muscle. Ladyland ran smoothly because the women harnessed high-tech solar power; men remained safely tucked away in seclusion the way women had once been.

The Struggle for Citizens' Rights

Throughout the nineteenth century, reformers asserted the rights of native peoples, former slaves, and women. Juan Manuel de Rosas, the powerful caudillo of Buenos Aires, Argentina, and its countryside, combated prejudices against people of Indian and African ancestry by incorporating them into his armies, promoting them to high ranks in the military, and giving them farms for their service. He built a loyal following, not through discrimination, but through nondiscrimination. In the United States, Frederick Douglass had been an abolitionist before the Civil War; after it he worked for the rights of freed black men. Ida B. Wells, U.S. newspaper woman and daughter of a former slave, campaigned in the late nineteenth century to end segregation of public facilities and, more forcefully and dangerously, to stop the lynching of black men. "I felt I owed it to myself and to my race to tell the whole truth now," Wells explained in her autobiography.[25] She received death threats and was forced to go into hiding. Across Latin America and the United States reformers worked, often for free, with native peoples, freed slaves, and poverty-stricken urban dwellers to build solidarity, provide education, and teach new work skills—all in the name of improving the nation by improving conditions within it.

Simultaneously, however, minorities such as African Americans in the United States and former slaves in the Caribbean began to see the source of their common nationality not as the Western Hemisphere, which to them was a place of captivity, but as Africa. By the end of the century **pan-Africanism**, an ideology that stresses the common bonds of all people of African descent, had taken root. Similarly, Jews, who were discriminated against in many parts of the world, also fought back with thoughts of building a nation of their own where they would have full rights. "Why should we be any less worthy than any other . . . people?" one Jewish leader asked. "What about our nation, our language, our land?" Jewish intellectuals began drawing upon Jewish folklore, language, customs, and history to establish a national identity parallel to that of other Europeans. By the late nineteenth century, a nationalist movement called **Zionism**, led by Hungarian-born writer Theodor Herzl, advocated the migration of Jews to their ancestral homeland of Palestine and the creation there of a Jewish nation-state.

Because rising nation-states refused women a whole series of rights, activists began lobbying for women's full citizenship. As the Chinese moved toward a program of national strengthening, activists denounced foot-binding and the lack of education for women. Activists often blamed men directly—"the basest of roughs," one German doctor called

pan-Africanism Originating in the late nineteenth century, an ideology that stresses the bonds of all people of African descent, both on the African continent and beyond.

Zionism A movement that began in the late nineteenth century among European Jews to form a Jewish state.

them.[26] In the United States the leading activists among a wide variety of mostly white women's organizations were Susan B. Anthony and Elizabeth Cady Stanton; black feminists included Sojourner Truth and Maria Cooper, who worked for the more complicated ends of both racial and gender equality. In 1903 the most militant of suffrage movements arose in England; there Emmeline Pankhurst and her daughters founded the Women's Social and Political Union in the belief that women would accomplish nothing unless they threatened men's property. In 1907, WSPU members staged parades in English cities, and in 1909 they began a campaign of violence, blowing up railroad stations, slashing works of art, and chaining themselves to the gates of Parliament.

When nationalist movements became strong in India, Egypt, the Middle East, and China, activist women focused on gaining rights and equality within an independent nation. Although these groups often looked to Western **suffragists** for some of their ideas, European suffragists were themselves inspired by non-Western women's less restrictive clothing, ownership of property, and recognized political roles. Latin American activists were also vocal, concerning themselves with education, the status of children, and the legal rights of women. Feminism thus became a global movement as women's writings, fictional and nonfictional, were translated across national boundaries and women from around the world met at international suffrage meetings. By 1904 feminist organizations from countries on almost all continents joined to form the International Woman Suffrage Alliance. International connections among feminist, African, and African American groups showed the ways in which national movements for citizenship took shape within a global context. The goal of most, however, was no longer to be an outsider to the nation by gaining full insider rights.

Conclusion

Regions throughout the world witnessed revolutionary change in the second half of the nineteenth century as leaders joined with ordinary people to create strong, centralized nation-states. Sometimes these striving nations, such as many in Latin America, simultaneously felt the strong, divisive forces of regionalism. The United States experienced a devastating civil war over competing political and economic systems that threatened to divide the country in two. In Russia, fear of revolution made that government change policies, liberating the serfs as a way to strengthen the state. But Russia remained an autocracy that failed to listen to the voice of the people—even the wealthy ones. This meant that fundamental flaws, unrecognized at the time, were woven into its nation-building efforts, which around the world were promoting access to education; urban improvements in sanitation, transport, and communications; and the development of public institutions such as museums and libraries.

Though it became increasingly central to nation building in the nineteenth century, nationalism ultimately became a destructive force. Critics add that the widespread discrimination against "outsiders" such as women and people of other races and ethnicities is unfortunately a characteristic of how nation-states create unity among those privileged to be its citizens. Nation building did not happen everywhere, nor did it proceed evenly. It did not eliminate monarchies and empires, although, as Matsuo Taseko witnessed, it changed them. Nation builders around the world recognized that, given the global web of trade, communications, and industrialization, the nation-state was an effective means of focusing political, economic, and military power, even becoming a tool for moving beyond the nation-state to create far-flung empires. Those who lacked the concentrated force of the nation-state were ripe for colonization rather than independence and prosperity.

suffragist An activist on behalf of the vote for women.

NOTES

1. Anne Walthall, *The Weak Body of a Useless Woman: Matsuo Taseko and the Meiji Restoration* (Chicago: University of Chicago Press, 1998), 98, 107.
2. Quoted in John Armstrong Crow, *The Epic of Latin America*, 4th ed. (Berkeley: University of California Press, 1992), 542.
3. Quoted in George Reid Andrews, *Afro-Latin America, 1800–2000* (New York: Oxford University Press, 2004), 113.
4. Quoted in Sarah C. Chambers, *From Subjects to Citizens: Honor, Gender, and Politics in Arequipa, Peru, 1780–1854* (University Park: Pennsylvania State University Press, 1999), 234–235.
5. Ibid.
6. Quoted in ibid., 184.
7. Quoted in Andrews, *Afro-Latin America*, 107, 181.
8. *El Republicano*, October 29, 1855, quoted in Carlos Froment, *Democracy in Latin America, 1760–1900: Civic Selfhood and Public Life in Mexico and Peru* (Chicago: University of Chicago Press, 2003), 155.
9. Quoted in Richard Stites, *Serfdom, Society, and the Arts in Imperial Russia: The Pleasure and the Power* (New Haven, CT: Yale University Press, 2005), 38.
10. "Alexander Nikitenko Responds to the Emancipation of the Serfs, 1861," http://artsci.shu.edu/reesp/documents/nikitenko.htm.
11. Quoted in Jasper Ridley, *Garibaldi* (London: St. Martins, 2001), 443.
12. Ibid., 448.
13. Quoted in James L. Roark et al., *The American Promise: A History of the United States*, 4th ed. (Boston: Bedford/St. Martins, 2009), 537.
14. Quoted in Frank Linderman, *Pretty-shield, Medicine Woman of the Crows* (Lincoln: University of Nebraska Press, 1972), 83.
15. Daklugie quoted in Colin G. Calloway, *First Peoples: A Documentary Survey of American Indian History*, 3d ed. (Boston: Bedford/St. Martins, 2008), 312.
16. Quoted in Mikiso Hane, *Peasants, Rebels, and Outcastes: The Underside of Modern Japan* (New York: Pantheon, 1982), 24.
17. Walthall, *The Weak Body of a Useless Woman*, 269.
18. Quoted in Ronald H. Dolkart, "Angela Peralta: A Mexican Diva," in Judith Ewell and William H. Beezley, eds., *The Human Tradition in Latin America: The Nineteenth Century* (Wilmington, DE: Scholarly Resources, 1989), 165, 167, 173.
19. Quoted in Irokawa Daikichi, *The Culture of the Meiji Period*, ed. and trans. Marius B. Jansen (Princeton, NJ: Princeton University Press, 1985), 56.
20. Quoted in Mikiso Hane, *Peasants, Rebels, and Outcastes*, 58.
21. Quoted in Richard Slotkin, *The Fatal Environment: The Myth of the Frontier in an Age of Industrialization* (Norman: University of Oklahoma Press, 1985), 339.
22. Ibid., 347.
23. "The Race Problem: An Autobiography: A Southern Colored Woman," *The Independent* 56 (1904): 586–589.
24. Quoted in Stephen Oates, *A Woman of Valor: Clara Barton and the Civil War* (New York: Free Press, 1994), 157–158.
25. Ida B. Wells, *Crusade for Justice: The Autobiography of Ida B. Wells*, ed. Alfreda M. Duster (Chicago: University of Chicago Press, 1970), 49.
26. Grete Meisel-Hess, *The Sexual Crisis*, trans. Eden and Cedar Paul (New York: The Critic and Guide Company, 1917), 6.

RESOURCES FOR RESEARCH

Modernizing Nations

Nations modernized and built their strength in different ways, but one common trend involved upgrading the education and general welfare of a wider segment of the population. Froment's book describes popular movements and official policies that worked toward that change.

Blackbourn, David. *Fontana History of Germany, 1780–1918: The Long Nineteenth Century*. 1997.

Froment, Carlos. *Democracy in Latin America, 1760–1900: Civic Selfhood and Public Life in Mexico and Peru*. 2003.

Mexican-American War, 1846–1848. Kera. PBS Online. www.pbs.org/kera/usmexicanwar/.

Meyer, Michael C., and William H. Beezley. *Oxford History of Mexico*. 2000.

*Nikitenko, Alexander. *Up from Serfdom: My Childhood and Youth in Russia, 1804–1824*. Translated by Helen Saltz Jacobson. 2001.

Emerging Powers: The United States and Japan

Two surprising newcomers on the nineteenth-century international stage were the United States and Japan, whose rise to prominence was full of struggle and bloodshed, as described in these works.

Faust, Drew Gilpin. *This Republic of Suffering: Death and the American Civil War*. 2008.

Foner, Eric. *The Fiery Trial: Abraham Lincoln and American Slavery*. 2010.

Keene, Donald. *Emperor of Japan: Meiji and His World, 1852–1912*. 2002.

Love, Eric T. L. *Race over Empire: Racism and U.S. Imperialism, 1865–1900*. 2005.

Walthall, Anne. *The Weak Body of a Useless Woman: Matsuo Taseko and the Meiji Restoration*. 1998.

The Culture of Nations

Culture was an integral part of creating a national identity. Stites's book shows how serf artists shaped not only the culture of the Russian Empire but its national politics.

Andrews, George Reid. *Afro-Latin America, 1800–2000*. 2004.

Huffman, James L. *Creating a Public: People and Press in Meiji Japan*. 1997.

Marchand, Suzanne, and David Lindenfeld, eds. *Germany at the Fin de Siècle: Culture, Politics, and Ideas*. 2004.

Stites, Richard. *Serfdom, Society, and the Arts in Imperial Russia: The Pleasure and the Power*. 2005.

Walthall, Anne, ed. *The Human Tradition in Modern Japan*. 2004.

COUNTERPOINT: Outsiders Inside the Nation-State

In an age when nations were defining themselves, outsiders to the nation were those who lived within its boundaries but were kept from full citizenship. The battles for full rights continue to this day, especially as citizenship becomes global rather than national.

Bay, Mia. *To Tell the Truth Freely: The Life of Ida B. Wells*. 2009.

Calloway, Colin G. *First Peoples: A Documentary Survey of American Indian Peoples*. 2011.

*Douglass, Frederick. *Narrative of the Life of Frederick Douglass, an American Slave, Written by Himself*. 1993.

Lowy, Dina. *The Japanese "New Woman": Images of Gender and Modernity*. 2007.

Lynch, John. *Argentine Caudillo: Juan Manuel de Rosas*. 2001.

* Primary source.

▶ **For additional primary sources from this period**, see *Sources of Crossroads and Cultures*.

▶ **For Web sites, images, and documents related to topics in this chapter**, see Make History at bedfordstmartins.com/smith.

REVIEW

Online Study Guide
bedfordstmartins.com/smith

The major global development in this chapter ▶ The causes and consequences of nation building in the nineteenth century.

IMPORTANT EVENTS

1833–1855	Mexican caudillo Santa Anna serves at intervals to lead the government
1846–1848	Mexican-American War
1853–1856	Crimean War
1855	Walt Whitman, *Leaves of Grass*
1859–1870	Unification of Italy
1860s	Height of opera singer Angela Peralta's career
1861	Emancipation of the serfs in Russia
1861–1865	U.S. Civil War
1863	Emancipation Proclamation in the United States
1866–1871	Unification of Germany
1868	Meiji Restoration of Japan
1872–1876	Fukuzawa Yukichi, *Encouragement of Learning*
1880s	Popular uprisings in Japan
1881	Young rebels assassinate Alexander II of Russia
1888	Emancipation of slaves in Brazil
1889	Brazilian emperor Pedro II abdicates and republic is installed

KEY TERMS

federalism (p. 831)
Manifest Destiny (p. 839)
mir (p. 835)
nation (p. 829)
pan-Africanism (p. 851)
realpolitik (p. 838)
Risorgimento (p. 837)
suffragist (p. 852)
zemstvo (p. 837)
Zionism (p. 851)

CHAPTER OVERVIEW QUESTIONS

1. Why did nation-states become so important to people in the nineteenth century?
2. What was the role of war in the rise of the nation-state?
3. What was the role of ordinary people in nation building?
4. Are nation-states still important today, and are there still outsiders inside nations?

SECTION FOCUS QUESTIONS

1. How did some states transform themselves into modern nations?
2. How did the United States and Japan make their governments politically and economically powerful in the nineteenth century?
3. What part did culture play in forging a national identity?
4. What groups were excluded from full participation in the nation-state, and why?

MAKING CONNECTIONS

1. How did the spread of industrialization (see Chapter 24) affect the rise of modern nation-states?
2. What was the legacy of slavery in the new nations? Did it make a difference to nation building that some states—Germany and Italy, for example—did not have large numbers of slaves in their homelands?
3. Why did Russia fail to offer rights to citizens equal to those offered by Western nations?

26

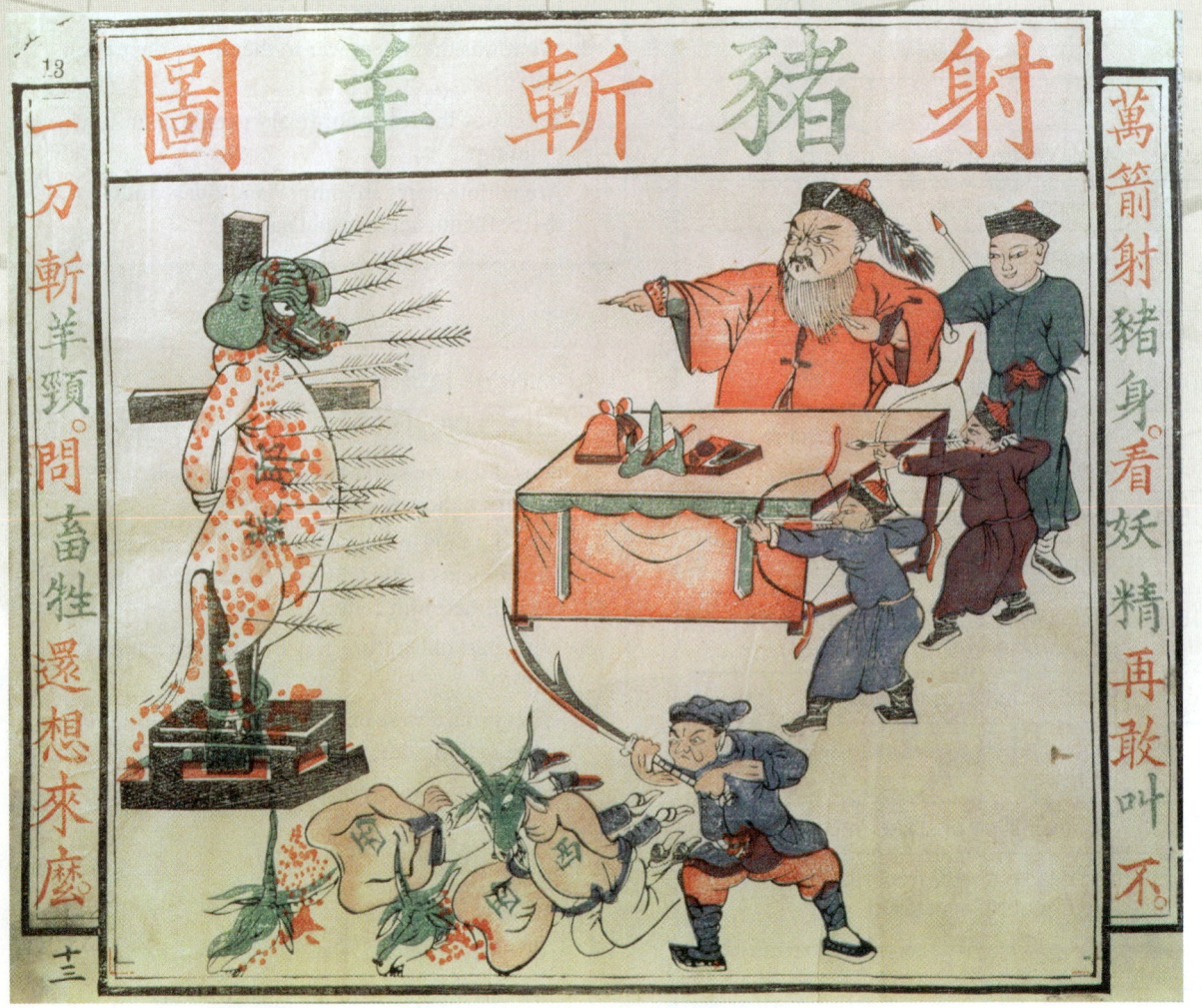

AT A CROSSROADS ▲

By 1900 China had become a crossroads of global ambitions. Japan, the United States, and the European powers had begun to exploit its markets and resources and in some cases to convert its population to Christianity. At the time, China was also a crossroads of famine and want, leading subjects of the Qing Empire to see their distress as the result of foreign inroads. The Chinese rebels known as the Boxers, illustrated here, were determined to "Kill the Pig"—that is, foreign missionaries, diplomats, and merchants. Armies from the foreign powers invaded China, suppressed the Boxers, rampaged across Chinese cities and farms, and further plundered the country's wealth. (Private Collection /Bridgeman Art Library.)

Imperial Order and Disorder

1850–1914

"Here come the foreign devils," a little boy shouted in 1900 in the northern Chinese city of Tianjin, "that's why we don't have any rain."[1] It was a time of intense drought in the region, and the Chinese were starving. Seedlings dried up in the fields, leaving peasants with time on their hands and with hunger killing both body and spirit. Many blamed the foreigners from Britain, Germany, Japan, and other parts of the world for these problems. On December 31, 1899, a British missionary, one of the many sent to convert the Chinese to Christianity, was assassinated in Shandong, an eastern province of China. By the summer of 1900, not only missionaries but also the German ambassador, European businessmen, and Chinese converts to Christianity by the thousands were being killed in antiforeign uprisings that came to be known as the Boxer Rebellion. The rebels believed that they were acting in self-defense, protecting their homeland from outsiders whose presence had brought the drought and the resulting hardship, devastation, and death.

Europeans had been fascinated by China for centuries. It had long been the most important power in the world with a tradition of excellence in philosophy, art, and literature; it was also the source of prized porcelain, silks, and cottons. In fact, it was the desire to gain a direct connection to the wealth and resources of Asia that had prompted early modern European expansion. The Japanese, too, had borrowed much from the Chinese, whose political and religious ideas played a key role in Japan's development. Nonetheless, in the nineteenth century the European powers, along with Japan and the expansionist United States, had come to see China—and most of the rest of the world—as areas to be dominated. Individual nation-states could increase their strength by gaining access to China's raw materials and cheap labor, and there was money to be made by seizing its taxes and financing development projects such as railroads. Britain, France, the Netherlands, Germany, Russia, Japan, and the United States all shared an impulse to control the wealth and, increasingly, even the governments of other regions of the world. In the second half

Building Empires

FOCUS What motivated the imperialists, and how did they impose their control over other nations?

Imperial Society

FOCUS How did imperialism change lives and livelihoods around the world?

Culture in an Imperial Age

FOCUS How did artists and writers respond to the age of empire?

Imperial Contests at the Dawn of the Twentieth Century

FOCUS What were the main issues in the contests over empire, and what were the results of these contests?

COUNTERPOINT: The West Copies from the World

FOCUS How did non-Western and colonized lands shape Western culture and society?

BACKSTORY

As we saw in Chapter 25, in the nineteenth century a number of states improved their governing institutions, expanded their bureaucracies, and attempted to build a shared sense of national identity in their often diverse populations. States also began to devote more attention to public education, seeing an educated population as a source of national strength. The drive to increase national power was a prime motive for commercial and military expansion, an outgrowth of state efforts to gain control of resources, markets, and strategic locations around the world. As states jostled with one another for power, their rivalries were increasingly played out in a competition for possessions outside of the nation-state's boundaries.

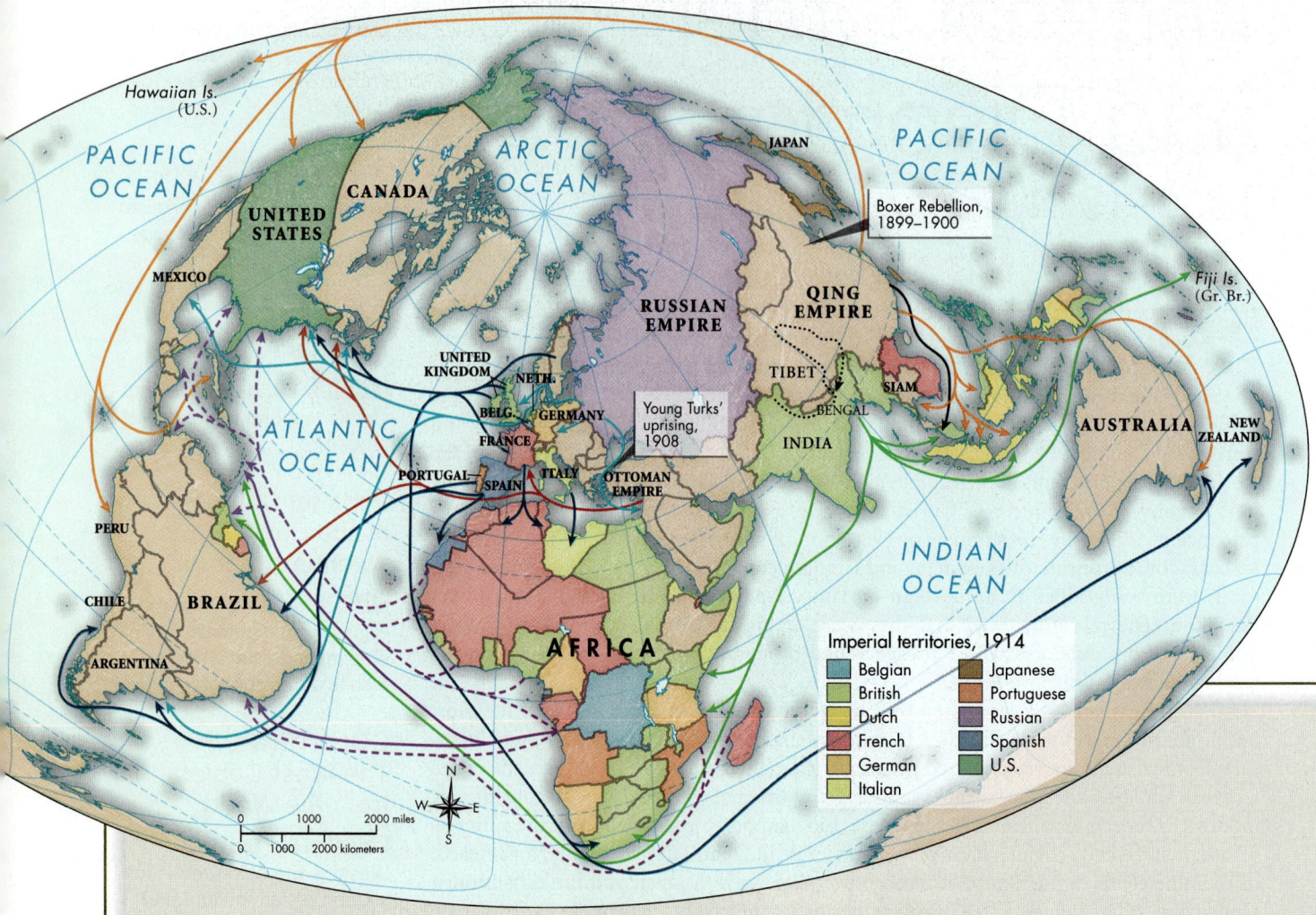

c. 1840–1900 Global migration because of indenture, imperial opportunity, and harsh environmental conditions

▪ **1857** Indian Uprising against the British

British Parliament declares Victoria empress of India **1876** ▪

Britain takes over Egypt **1882**

1850 1860 1870 1880

▪ **1869** Suez Canal completed

c. 1860–1900 Impressionism flourishes in the European arts, borrowing many non-Western techniques of the nineteenth century the word *imperialism* was used to describe this impulse toward global domination.

In the rush to dominate, these competing nations changed their tune, many claiming that they were bringing civilization and order to backward peoples of the world. Despite that promise, imperialism in China and elsewhere around the globe brought massive bloodshed and disorder, much of it inflicted by the imperialists themselves on those who would not bow to their rule. Empire builders in Asia, Africa, and the Mediterranean basin focused so exclusively on extracting wealth that they let the maintenance of traditional but crucial systems such as irrigation deteriorate because they did not yield immediate profit. The result was starvation and suffering. Imperialist inroads inspired heartfelt resistance, often increasing the bloodshed. Many in the colonies were inspired by some of the imperialists' accomplishments, including the creation of powerful nation-states and guarantees of liberal ideals such as self-determination and human rights. Even though such guarantees were hardly given to colonized peoples, the very existence of these ideals led many to fight for their freedom.

In the course of imperialism and the globalization of trade and finance that accompanied it, society and culture changed. Poets and artists reacted to the whirl of imperial activity around them, sometimes deploring the changes and at other times seizing on ideas from other cultures to spark their creativity. Tens of millions of people migrated either to find opportunity within empires or to escape the misery at home that imperialism brought. As they left their homes to take up livelihoods in other parts of the world, these migrants

MAPPING THE WORLD

The Spread of Imperialism, 1850–1914

The world's peoples interacted more in the late nineteenth century because of the spread of empire and increases in migration and travel. Behind this movement of peoples were the quest for opportunity and freedom, and also ambition and greed. Occasionally those driving imperialism had philanthropic and scientific motives, but imperialists often used naked violence to achieve their ends.

ROUTES ▼

Mass migrations, 1850–1910

- African slaves, c. 1800–1860
- African, c. 1840–1910
- Chinese
- European Jewish
- Other European
- Indian
- Lebanese

- Travels of Khaw Soo Cheang, c. 1820
- Travels of Nain Singh, 1873–1875

1884–1885 European nations carve up Africa at the Berlin Conference

1894–1895 Sino-Japanese War

1900 Sigmund Freud, *The Interpretation of Dreams*

1910 Japan annexes Korea

1890 1900 1910

c. 1870–1914 European powers, Japan, and the United States extend formal and informal control over Asia, Africa, and parts of Latin America

Spanish-American War **1898**

1899–1902 South African War

1899–1900 Boxer Rebellion in China

1904–1905 Russo-Japanese War

1908 Young Turks' uprising against the Ottoman Empire

created new communities, such as the Chinese in Singapore and San Francisco and the Lebanese in Rio de Janeiro and Montreal. Thus, imperialism brought wrenching change as well as new opportunity for peoples throughout the world while pulling societies, willingly or not, into ever-closer contact. The Boxer Rebellion against the "foreign devils" was but one expression of the complex enterprise of imperialism.

OVERVIEW QUESTIONS

The major global development in this chapter: The accelerated competition among nineteenth-century nation-states for empire.

As you read, consider:

1. What are the arguments for and against imperialism?
2. How and why did some local peoples assist imperialists who took over their own countries?
3. Which were the major imperialist powers, and what made them so capable of conquest?
4. How did imperialism change the lives of people in the conquering countries and in the colonies?

Building Empires

FOCUS
What motivated the imperialists, and how did they impose their control over other nations?

The nineteenth century was an age of imperialism, a time when nations around the world built both formal and informal empires. The British government formally took over the governments of South Asian states, ending the East India Company's domination of the region through trade, taxation, and military might. It incorporated India into Britain politically and declared Queen Victoria empress. After midcentury, other nations instituted direct rule of areas once linked to them by trade alone. They sent soldiers and more settlers to distant lands and expanded their foreign office bureaucracies. Such takeovers—often called the "**new imperialism**" in contrast to the trader-based domination of preceding centuries—promoted both individual wealth and national power, albeit funded by ordinary taxpayers. The new imperialism was not, however, simply a story of violence inflicted by foreigners aiming for political and economic domination. Conquering nations provided social and cultural services such as schools to reflect the imperial power's values. In many instances local chieftains, merchants, and cultural leaders helped imperialists make their inroads abroad.

new imperialism The takeover in the second half of the nineteenth century of foreign lands by Western powers and Japan, which entailed political control as well as economic domination.

globalization A variety of behaviors and processes, such as trade, warfare, travel, and the spread of culture, that link the world's peoples.

Imperialism: What Is It?

Imperialism is associated with the domination that European powers, Japan, and the United States began to exercise over much of the rest of the world in the second half of the nineteenth century. The term is used to describe the ambitions, conquests, and power exercised over the trade, taxation, and governments of other states and their peoples—somewhat similar to the way in which the word **globalization** is used today to describe a variety of behaviors and processes that link the world's peoples. There had been empires throughout history, but the new imperialism of the nineteenth and twentieth centuries was both more and less than empire. The word connotes not just formally claimed territory, indirectly ruled lands, and economic domination, but even the strong desire to possess territory. Although modern imperialism motivated both governmental and private actions right through World War II, it was never a coherent system or a consistent set of practices. It also describes a control that was never complete and that colonized peoples constantly contested.

Colonization and Colonialism

One important feature of modern imperialism was colonization, that is, the creation of settlements in foreign territories intended to dominate the land and its native peoples and to take its wealth. Colonization shaped the Roman Empire and others, including the later Spanish and Portuguese empires of the sixteenth century, and it remained a prominent part of the new imperialism. Colonization, it was believed, could secure distant territories at less expense than armies would require; it could train a foreign population in the imperial power's culture; in some cases, it could alleviate crowding in the mother country. **Colonialism** is the term for the system that dominated people in these ways.

Imperial Motivations

A second feature of imperialism was the range of motivations behind it. Some national leaders saw more extensive landholdings in and of themselves as a major ingredient of national strength; others saw the wealth that could be siphoned off to strengthen nations. Business leaders aimed to make money in underdeveloped areas by building harbors, railroads, and roads, while merchants wanted to increase commerce and thus profits through imperial networks. "Business" or "informal" imperialism based on foreign investment, commerce, and manufacturing could also exist without political rule. Britain, and later the United States, exerted considerable power over Latin American states through investments in and control of key industries. **Business imperialism** included economic domination of sugar, coffee, and other plantation agriculture in many parts of the world. Finally, many envisioned imperialism as an almost saintly undertaking. As one French economist put it in 1891, taking over countries would bring civilization to "barbarous and savage tribes, some enduring wars without end and destructive ways of life, others knowing nothing of the arts and having so few habits of work and invention that they have no way of knowing how to get riches from the land."[2]

For the Spanish and Portuguese, who saw firsthand the immense accomplishment and wealth of American peoples, their own superiority rested on their Catholic faith. Increasingly, Christianity blended with racism to justify domination. In the second half of the nineteenth century, new "scientific" theories of race reinforced this sense of cultural superiority. The ideas of European scientists and doctors—especially those of Charles Darwin, the English naturalist who developed the theory of evolution—appealed to imperialists. Darwin himself, along with people later called Social Darwinists, explicitly stated that nonwhites, women, and members of the working class were less highly evolved than white men and therefore in need of domination. This inferiority was affirmed by a number of bogus measurements in the nineteenth century, such as the size of the cranium. Scientific racism was not confined to whites: the Japanese considered themselves far in advance of native peoples such as the Ainu who lived far from the capital, and of foreigners such as the Koreans.

Confident of their superiority, imperialists proposed that they would uplift and liberate the people they conquered from their own backwardness. Paradoxically, cultural pride prompted some "civilizers" such as missionaries to support the most brutal military measures to accomplish their goals. Thus, the building of schools and churches occurred alongside massacres of local people who would not turn over their property, animals, or houses. Forcing others to accept cultural values such as Christian belief was also part of imperialism.

colonialism The establishment of settler communities in areas ruled by foreign powers.

business imperialism The domination of foreign economies without military or political rule.

Takeover in Asia

Great Britain, the era's mightiest colonial power, made a dramatic change of course by instituting governmental control of India while the Russians and British were also in constant struggle to rule Central Asia and the French and Dutch struggled with local peoples

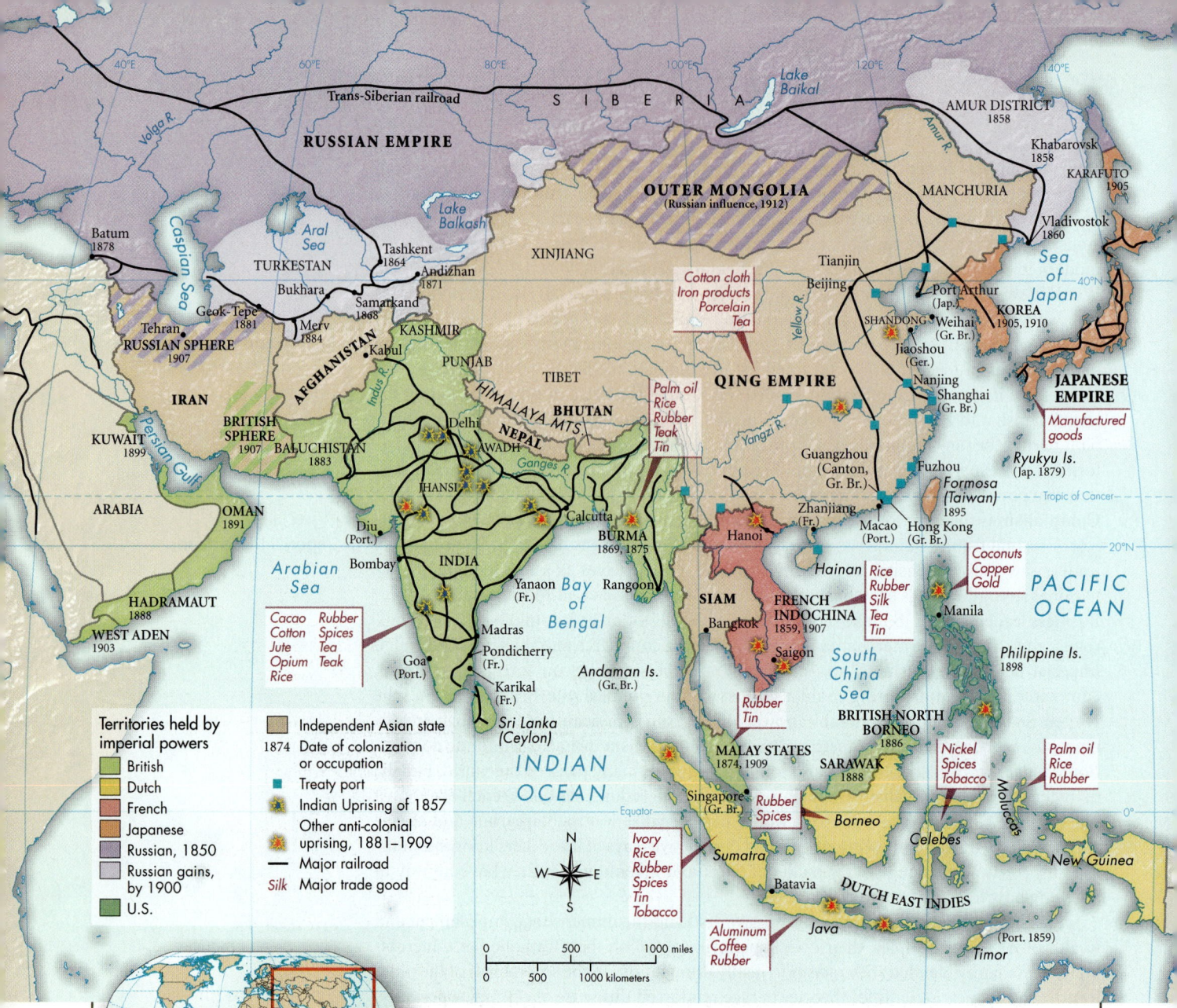

MAP 26.1

Imperial Division of Asia, c. 1850–1900

The Western powers and Japan expanded their influence in Asia in the second half of the nineteenth century and in the early twentieth. They built railroads and used steamboats and increasingly destructive weaponry to accomplish their ends. They also made deals with local rulers and merchants who stood to profit by collaborating with imperialists. Generally, farmers and urban artisans fared the worst under imperialism because their livelihoods were either threatened or complicated by the imperialists' demands on local economies.

for empire in Southeast Asia. The contest in Central Asia has been called the "Great Game," but that hardly conveys the destruction inflicted on local peoples and on the imperialists themselves—all in the name of advancing the nation by forging an empire (see Map 26.1).

The British in India

Since the eighteenth century and especially after the loss of Britain's thirteen North American colonies, the East India Company had expanded its reach to become the major tax collector for the Mughal emperor, princes, and other ruling officers on the subcontinent. The Company became the acting ruler of some of these Indian territories and later built railroads throughout the countryside to make commerce and revenue collecting more efficient. In 1856, wanting more revenue and control, the Company took over the wealthy northern kingdom of Awadh, contrary to formal treaties with the king about his sovereignty.

For Indians whose wealth and livelihoods derived from their connections with the Company, this event was of little importance. Outside of this small segment of the population, however, the takeover of Awadh fueled already rising anger over excessive taxation and the Company's increasingly high-handed ways. In 1857, Indian troops serving the Company, known as *sepoys*, heard rumors that the new Enfield rifles they were to use had cartridges greased with cow and pig fat, forbidden to Hindus (for whom cows are sacred) and Muslims (for whom pigs are unclean). The soldiers believed that they were deliberately being made impure and that the cartridges were part of a plot to convert them to Christianity. Spurred by the economic grievances of the peasant classes from which most of them sprang, the soldiers massacred their British officers and then conquered the Indian capital at Delhi, reinstating the emperor and declaring the independence of the Indian people.

Rebellions spread to the general populace, justified, so the emperor explained, by "the tyranny and oppression of the infidel and treacherous English." The Rani (Queen) Lakshmibai, widow of the ruler of the state of Jhansi in central India, led a separate military revolt when the East India Company tried to take over her lands, but she was only one among many to do so. The British had trouble motivating recruits to put down the uprisings. "All black men are one," said a newly recruited soldier, who vowed he would not fight the rebels.[3] Eventually British-led forces from other regions crushed the Indian Uprising of 1857, as this widespread revolt is now called. In the aftermath of the uprising, the British government substituted its control for that of the Company and in 1876 declared Queen Victoria the empress of India.

The British constructed India as a single colony formed from independent kingdoms and small princely territories, but in practice this apparent unity was partial at best. Many states remained semi-independent. Paradoxically, the British "unification" of India contributed to growing nationalist sentiment among Indian elites. It was in this context that, in 1885, wealthy and well-educated Indians created the Indian National Congress, an organization aiming to bring about reform, obtain rights and representation in the British government, and eventually gain independence.

The British and Russians in Central Asia

British success in South Asia was part of a struggle for trade and empire that made entire continents a battlefield of competing interests and warring armies. In Central Asia, Russian and British armies blasted former centers of Silk Road trade into ruins and slaughtered Afghan resisters during decades of destructive conflict. After the fall of Kabul to British forces in 1842, a commander set his men loose on the city's population to avenge the killing of British soldiers and civilians by Afghani resisters. The Russian general who took the fortress of Geok-Tepe in modern Turkmenistan let his troops steal, rape, and butcher its inhabitants. He justified the sixteen thousand dead by saying, "The duration of peace is in direct proportion to the slaughter you inflict upon the enemy."[4] Publicly hanging only a few ringleaders of the rebellion, he explained, inspired further resistance to takeovers, whereas a reputation for massive killings would create fear—and thus obedience.

Imperial moves inspired countermoves. The British added to their holdings in Asia partly to block Russian and French expansion. Russia absorbed the small Muslim states of West and Central Asia, including Turkestan; some provinces of Afghanistan; and extending into the Ottoman Empire, Persia, northern India, and China, often encountering British competition but mostly fighting local peoples. Russia built the trans-Siberian railroad to help integrate Siberia—once considered a distant colony—into an expanding Russian Empire. Once completed, the new rail line helped transport settlers and soldiers into the region (see again Map 26.1).

From India the British military pushed to the east, moving into Burma in 1869 and taking the Malay peninsula in 1874. The presence of British troops guaranteed the order necessary to expand railroads for greater access to interior markets and more efficient extraction of raw materials—tin, oil, rice, teak, and rubber. The environmental consequences were severe as the British built factories and leased forests in the north of Burma to private companies that stripped them bare, "denuding the country," as one official put it, "to its great and lasting loss."[5] Famine and drought followed this ecological nightmare, weakening the local population and making it easier to annex Burma in 1875.

The French in Southeast Asia

In the 1860s the French were establishing their own control in Cochin China (modern southern Vietnam). Missionaries in the area, ambitious French naval officers stationed in Asia, native officials looking for work, and even some local peoples making profits from European trade urged the French government on. After sending in troops, France used favorable treaties (backed by the threat of military action) to create the Union of Indochina from the ancient states of Cambodia, Tonkin, Annam, and Cochin China in 1887 (the latter three constitute the modern nation of Vietnam). Rubber plantations and other money-making projects followed. Laos was added to Indochina in 1893.

Like the British in India, the French brought some Western innovations to the societies they conquered. Modern agricultural projects spurred rapid growth in the food supply. The French also improved sanitation and public health in Indochina. Such changes proved a mixed blessing, however, because they led to population growth that strained resources. Furthermore, French landowners and traders siphoned off the profits from economic development. The French also transformed cities such as Saigon by constructing tree-lined boulevards inspired by those in Paris. French literature, theater, and art were popular with colonial officials and upper-class Indochinese alike. Nonetheless, in the countryside ordinary Vietnamese saw things differently. As one peasant protested to the governor general in 1907, "the French are treating us like animals, looking at us like wood and stone."[6] Such treatment, combined with the exposure of native elites to Western ideas of "the rights of man," helped produce an Indochinese nationalist movement.

Europeans Scramble for Africa

North Africa

Imperialism often involved seizures of people's lands and goods after their military defeat. In Africa, however, the cruelty was notorious, as Europeans trained their sights on the continent in the second half of the nineteenth century. European conquest of the continent began with North Africa, and then moved on to sub-Saharan Africa with its rich supplies of raw materials such as palm oil, cotton, diamonds, cacao, and rubber (see Map 26.2, page 866). With its empire in India, Britain additionally hoped to keep the southern and eastern coasts of Africa secure for stopover ports on the route to Asia. While North Africa had commercial value, the Mediterranean as a whole was most important for its strategic location.

Modernization Projects in Egypt, c. 1910

French emperor Napoleon III, remembering his uncle's campaign in Egypt, helped sponsor the building of the Suez Canal, which would connect the Mediterranean with the Red Sea and the Indian Ocean and thus dramatically shorten the route from Europe to Asia. The canal was completed in 1869, and beginning with Muhammad Ali, Egypt's enterprising rulers made Cairo into a bustling city, boosting commerce and manufacturing and attracting European capital investment. In an effort to further enhance the connections between Egypt's economy and the rest of the world, Egyptian businessmen and government officials supported the construction of thousands of miles of railroad track, the improvement of harbors, and the installation of telegraph systems. Many of these ventures were paid for with money borrowed from European lenders at far higher rates of interest than Europeans paid. Nonetheless, many Egyptian elites believed that such modernization projects were essential to their country's future and, therefore, that an Egyptian-European financial alliance was necessary, whatever its cost.

Albert Rieger, *Suez Canal* (1864)

Workers from around the Mediterranean labored on the Suez Canal, which the French designed to connect the Mediterranean to the Red Sea and thus speed up commerce with Asia. The British saw the Suez Canal, completed in 1869, as important to protecting its Asian empire, and by 1882 they had taken over Egypt not only to control the canal but also to guarantee British financial investments in the canal and in other Egyptian modernization projects. The Suez Canal remains a major world crossroads to this day. (The Art Archive/Museo Civico Revoltella Trieste/Collection Dagli Orti.)

The alliance turned sour when Great Britain and France, eager to control business with Egypt, took over the Egyptian treasury with the excuse that they needed to guarantee loans that the Egyptian government found itself hard-pressed to repay. In 1882, after striking a deal with the French, the British invaded and essentially took control of the government, an act they claimed was necessary to put down those Egyptian nationalists who protested the seizure of the treasury. Soon Cairo had the air of "an English town," as one Egyptian local put it.[7] The English, in alliance with local entrepreneurs, shifted the Egyptian economy from a system based on multiple crops—a system that maintained the country's self-sufficiency—to one that emphasized the production of a few highly marketable crops, notably cotton and wheat, which were especially useful to the English. As the colonial powers and Egyptian elites grew rich, the bulk of the rural population, their livelihoods transformed, barely eked out an existence.

Meanwhile the French army, driving into the North African hinterland, occupied all of Algeria by 1870 and then neighboring Tunisia in 1881. As elsewhere, French rule in North Africa was aided by the attraction of local people to European trade and technology. Merchants and local leaders cooperated in building railroads, sought bank loans from the French, and sent their children to European-style schools. They became "evolved"—as the French called those who adopted European ways. Many local peoples, however, resisted French intrusions, attacking soldiers and settlers. Others died from European-spread diseases. By 1872, the native population in Algeria had declined by more than 20 percent from five years earlier.

Sub-Saharan Africa

In the 1880s, European governments raced to the African interior, both playing to local elites' self-interest and using military force to overwhelm resistance. The French, Belgians, Portuguese, Italians, and Germans jockeyed to dominate peoples, land, and resources—"the magnificent cake of Africa," as King Leopold II of Belgium (r. 1865–1909) put it. Driven by almost unparalleled greed, Leopold claimed the Congo region of central Africa, thereby initiating competition with France for that territory and inflicting on its peoples unspeakable acts of cruelty. German chancellor Otto von Bismarck established

MAP 26.2

Imperial Division of Africa, c. 1880–1914

Though some Africans profited, most suffered from contacts with Europeans, which increased after the mid-nineteenth century, largely because the use of quinine cut down health risks for the invaders. Environmental factors also aided Europeans in their new pursuit of actual colonies on the continent. Where famine and drought failed to make Africans submit, the Europeans' outright brutality put down often stubborn resistance.

German control over Cameroon and a section of East Africa. Faced with stiff competition for African territory, the British spent millions of pounds attempting to take over the continent militarily "from Cairo to Cape Town," as the slogan went. The French cemented their hold on large portions of western Africa (see again Map 26.2).

Environmental disasters, regional tensions, and African rulers themselves scrambling for resources and territory helped the would-be conquerors. In 1882 the king of Daboya in northern Ghana explained his treaty with the British in these terms: "I want to keep off all my enemies and none to be able to stand before me."[8] The king expected guns and military backing from the British should it be necessary. The European powers put so much stake in the ability of local rulers to collect taxes and in the loyalty of African police and soldiers for maintaining order that during the 1890s, Germans in imperial Tanzania kept only one hundred military personnel to guard the entire territory.

Resistance in South Africa

The Zulu had maintained a powerful kingdom in southern Africa since early in the nineteenth century. Using excellent camouflage and stealthy movements, they consistently resisted the British, despite being outgunned. Finally, in the Anglo-Zulu War of 1879, they were defeated, and their king Cetshwayo was held and interrogated in an effort to prove he was a dictatorial savage and thus inferior to British rulers. Note that this painting makes it appear as if the British heroically fought dozens of Zulu individually. In fact, by the final battles the British were launching tens of thousands of African and European troops against the Zulu. (The Print Collector/HIP/The Image Works.)

South Africa

Violent struggle occurred for control of southern Africa, where farmers of European descent and immigrant prospectors, rather than military personnel, battled the Xhosa (KOH-suh), Zulu, and other African peoples for the frontier regions of Transvaal, Natal, the Orange Free State, Rhodesia, and the Cape Colony. Although the Dutch were the first Europeans to settle the area permanently, the British had gained control by 1815. Thereafter descendants of the Dutch, called *Boers* (Dutch for "farmers"), were joined by British immigrants in their fight to seize farmland and mineral resources from natives. British businessman and politician Cecil Rhodes, sent to South Africa for his health at age seventeen, just as diamonds were being discovered, cornered the diamond market and claimed a huge amount of African territory with the help of official charters from the British government, all before he turned forty. Pushing hundreds of miles into the interior of southern Africa (a region soon to be named Rhodesia after him), Rhodes moved into gold mining too. His ambition for Britain and for himself was boundless: "I contend that we are the finest race in the world," he explained, "and that the more of the world we inhabit the better it is."

The Berlin Conference

The scramble for Africa intensified tensions among the imperial powers, leading to a conference of European nations in 1884. Statesmen from the fourteen nations represented at the Berlin Conference echoed Rhodes's racial pride; as representatives of a "superior" civilization, they considered themselves fully entitled to determine the fate of the African continent. To resolve territorial disputes, they decided that any nation that controlled a settlement along the African coast was also guaranteed the rights to the corresponding interior territory. This agreement led to the linear dissection of the continent, a process that ignored the actual territorial borders of some 70 percent of Africa's ethnic groups. In theory the meeting was supposed to reduce bloodshed and temper ambitions in Africa, but European leaders remained more committed than ever to expanding their power. Newspaper reports of daring conquests only stirred up citizens to demand more imperialist excitement.

Japan's Imperial Agenda

Japan escaped the "new" European imperialism by rapidly transforming into a modern industrial nation with its own imperial agenda. The Japanese, unlike China, endorsed technology and the quest for colonies. In contrast to Europe where there was often heated debate about imperial conquest, the Meiji regime insisted on unity: "All classes high and low shall unite in vigorously promoting the economy and welfare of the nation," ran one of its statements. By 1894, Japan had become powerful enough to force traders to accept its terms for commerce and diplomatic relations. Then, it went further.

The Sino-Japanese War

To expand its influence and resource base, the Meiji government entered the imperial fray by invading the Chinese island of Formosa (present-day Taiwan) in 1874. In 1876, Japan forced unequal trading treaties on China-dominated Korea. Further Japanese encroachments in Korea led to the 1894 Sino-Japanese War. Modern military technology carried Japan to a swift victory that left the once powerful Qing China humiliated and Japan the colonial overlord of Taiwan and Korea. The European powers, alarmed at Japanese expansion, forced it to relinquish many gains, a move that outraged Japanese nationalists. Tensions between Japan and Russia continued to escalate over the course of the 1890s. The extension of the trans-Siberian railroad through Manchuria and the arrival of millions of Russian settlers accelerated Russian expansion into East and South Asia. Russia sponsored anti-Japanese groups in Korea, making the Korean peninsula appear, as a Japanese military leader put it, like "a dagger thrust at the heart of Japan." As we will see, war soon erupted between the Russians and Japanese, showing the deadly potential for conflict among imperial rivals.

The Sino-Japanese War, 1894

Technology, Environment, and the Imperial Advantage

Imperialists were helped immeasurably by both industrial technology and a series of ecological disasters that weakened Asian and African societies. Powerful guns, railroads, steamships, and medicines greatly accelerated imperial conquest. The gunboats that forced the Chinese to open their borders to opium played the same role in forcing African ethnic groups to give up their rights and independence. Improvements to the breech-loading rifle and the development of the machine gun, or "repeater," between 1862 and 1880 dramatically increased firepower. "The whites did not seize their enemy as we do by the body, but thundered from afar," claimed one resister at the 1898 Battle of Obdurman in Sudan, where the British, losing fifty men, mowed down some twenty-five thousand Africans with machine guns (see again Map 26.2). "Death raged everywhere—like the death vomited forth from the tempest," as one African put it. Railroads sped troops and weapons to wherever there was resistance and thus cemented imperial domination.

Industrial Technology

Environmental Disaster

The ecological balance of power changed too. Whereas once the tropical climate had given Africans an advantage, quinine extracted from cinchona bark from the Andes protected Europeans from the deadly tropical disease malaria, which had once made Africa the "White Man's Grave." Disastrously for Africans and Asians, El Niño weather currents of the last quarter of the nineteenth century brought drought that resulted in deadly famine across a wide swath of both continents. Mysore, India, one official wrote, contained "none but the dead and the dying."[9] Desperate for food, the population began resorting to theft, eating the dead, and, if they had the energy, rioting against big landowners and tax collectors. It was amid environmental catastrophe that Europeans seized land and cattle and generally expanded their holdings. "Europeans," one African man observed at the time, "track famine like a sky full of vultures."[10] The Chinese Boxers could not have said it better.

Imperial Society

FOCUS
How did imperialism change lives and livelihoods around the world?

Imperialism brought closer connections among peoples far distant from one another, through trade, migration, and warfare. These interactions reshaped societies around the world—both for good and for ill. In the colonies, violence and disorder increased because of the imperialists' heavy taxation, theft of property, and intrusion on everyday life. Migration and the rapid spread of disease added to the burdens of colonial societies. However, imperialists were only able to dominate distant colonies and informally held areas such as China with the help of local people, many of whom profited from the economic opportunities such as new jobs and new technologies that imperial globalization offered. Thus, imperialism was full of paradox and contradiction.

Changing Conditions of Everyday Life

Citizens paid heavy taxes to maintain empires, which usually cost the country as a whole more than it gained. In trade, manufacturing, and international banking, however, individual business people reaped profits. For certain businesses, colonies provided crucial protected markets: late in the century, for instance, French colonies bought 65 percent of France's exports of soap and 41 percent of its metallurgical exports. People in port cities around the world had better jobs because of imperialism. Other segments of the population, however, simply paid the taxes to cover the costs of imperialism, without reward. Many had to leave home and family behind to seek jobs—whether in mines, on newly opened farmland, or in the factories springing up around the world. Imperial interactions changed local life for native peoples, often making it unhealthy and oppressive for many and bringing stupendous wealth to the few.

Working with and for the Imperialists

Networks of guides and translators were among those who dealt successfully with imperialists from Europe, Japan, and the United States, just as their ancestors centuries earlier had dealt with Mongols or Mughals. Nain Singh was the principal of a village school in the Himalayas, but the expanding British Empire transformed his life. Talented and knowledgeable about the vast, uncharted region that included Tibet, Nain Singh took a job with the British colonial service. There he learned to take measured steps of thirty-three inches in order to map terrain, to take the temperature of water so as to chart altitudes, and to speak many languages. After several years of training, Nain Singh attached himself to caravans, posing as a Buddhist pilgrim or a merchant. In fact, he was a British spy against Russia in the contest for control of Central Asia. In that capacity, he charted the forbidden region of Tibet and even spent time in the forbidden Tibetan capital, Lhasa, where he met the Dalai Lama. At great personal risk and sacrifice, intrepid local travelers such as Nain Singh acquired the geographic knowledge on which imperialists depended.

Local elites served the imperialists as soldiers and administrators in both India and Africa, and others helped ward off foreign competition. Khaw Soo Cheang left his home in China for Thailand in the 1820s, beginning his career as a fruit vendor but ending it as a

Nain Singh

Indian explorer Nain Singh worked for the British as a spy and a guide in Central Asia. His livelihood shows how imperialism created complicated relationships between the colonizers and the colonized. Tens of thousands of local Asians and Africans served in European armies, civil service jobs, and commercial and industrial ventures. For most local people, however, the relationship was far from equal, and many such employees testified to being treated with contempt and even physical violence. (TopFoto/The Image Works.)

magnate in the shipping and mining business. He also became an official of the Thai government and handed down his position to his five sons, who efficiently managed the southern states, collected taxes, and made important improvements to roads, mines, and public buildings. As Khaw's family initiatives flourished, Khaw's sons and daughters married into the wealthy world of regional shippers and other businessmen; the sons partnered with Europeans and Australians in their ventures, making the area profitable under Khaw control. A British official complained of the lack of opportunity in a region where, as he described it, a Khaw "has his finger in every pie"; in so doing the family had effectively immunized the region from full-scale intervention by outsiders.[11] There were many ways to work with imperialism.

Under imperialism a system of indirect rule often emerged, one that used local officials, chiefs, and princes to enforce imperial laws and keep order. In India, the best-known example, a few thousand British officials supervised close to half a million local civilian and military employees, who were paid far less than British employees would have been. Other powers adopted similar systems. Indirect rule reduced the cost of empire and invested local officials in the imperial project. As elsewhere, British civil servants attacked Indian cultural practices, such as female infanticide, child marriage, and *sati*, a widow's self-immolation on her husband's funeral pyre. Some in the upper classes of colonized countries were attracted to Japanese reforms and Western ideals—"the lofty tree of liberty," as one high Tunisian official praised them—and to notions of a scientifically ordered society.[12]

The vast majority of colonized peoples, however, were exploited. For example, to prevent superior Indian textiles from competing with British cloth, the government worked to close down Indian manufacturing centers and force artisans to become day laborers producing raw materials such as wheat and cotton. On land seized from peasants, imperialists and local business people set up plantations and opened mines in Africa and Asia. Once self-sufficient farmers became landless workers, either on their former lands or wherever labor was needed, not only in their home region but around the world, as cash agriculture became an instrument of imperial rule. A British governor of the Gold Coast in Africa put the matter succinctly in 1886: the British would "rule the country as if there were no inhabitants," as if local traditions of political and economic life did not exist. By confiscating land for tea, cotton, or rubber plantations, Europeans forced native peoples to work for them to earn a living. The agents of Leopold II of Belgium chopped off hands or simply shot Africans who did not provide their quota of rubber. "All of us wanted only one thing," reported a foreign worker in a Belgian Congo mine, "to terminate our contract and return to our country—we were so frightened by the number of people who died each day"[13] (see Reading the Past: Rubber Workers in the Congo). Subsistence agriculture based on growing a variety of crops and raising animals that supported families declined around the world, and communities were undermined as men left their homes to work in mines or on plantations to earn cash to pay imperial taxes.

Social Disorder

Imperialists brought not just economic but social disorder, upsetting established patterns of life. Even though some local people profited from the presence of outsiders, whom they often viewed as barbarians, other locals were victims of theft or physical abuse. While earlier merchants, administrators, and sailors had arrived without families and mingled with the local population, in the late nineteenth century governments began sending wives and children to accompany colonial officials, often clearing local people out of desirable urban neighborhoods to make room for European families. Women from Europe and the United States appeared in public in Western garb, which was unwelcome in Muslim regions where segregation of the sexes was a strong social norm. As men left their families

Rubber Workers in the Congo

In 1896 American manager Edgar Canisius began working for the Belgians in the Congo Free State, where rubber was harvested by forced labor. Canisius was thus part of the global workforce at the turn of the century, as were the inhabitants of Congo, who labored for a distant king—Leopold II of Belgium. After describing the atrocities the Belgians inflicted on Congolese whose harvest fell the slightest bit short of the quota, he noted the punishing work process itself. Canisius's report on his time in the Congo was published early in the twentieth century.

> The Congo native, when about to gather rubber, generally goes with his fellow villagers far into the jungle. Then, having formed a rough, shelterless camp, he begins his search for the creepers [rubber vines that wind themselves around other trees]. Having found one of sufficient size, he cuts with his knife a number of incisions in the bark, and, hanging a small earthenware pot below the vine, allows the sap to slowly trickle into it. Should the creeper have been already tapped, the man must climb into the supporting tree at more or less personal risk and make an incision in the vine high above the ground where the sap has not been exhausted. . . . Not infrequently the natives slumber on their lofty perches, and, falling to the ground, become victims of the white man's greed. Few Africans will imperil their lives in rubber-gathering unless under compulsion. . . .
>
> Each tribe has only a limited extent of forest which it can call its exclusive domain, and it consequently very frequently happens, when their own "bush" is worked out, that natives from one village penetrate the territory of the other in defiance of tribal usage. Such an invasion is naturally resented by their neighbors, who, equally pressed no doubt by circumstances and the white man, are themselves experiencing difficulty in making up the quota of rubber definitely fixed for each village, and a deficient production of which may entail dire punishment and even death. In consequence, disputes arise between villages which heretofore, perhaps for quite a long period, have been at peace; and then come wars, involving more or less loss of life, destruction and cannibalism. Natives, I may add, have often come to me with bitter laments over the disappearance of their brothers after accidents when rubber-gathering, or the attacks of leopards or hostile tribesmen.

Source: Edgar Canisius, "A Campaign Amongst Cannibals," in Captain Guy Burrows, *The Curse of Central Africa* (London: R. A. Everett and Co., 1903), 74–80, quoted in Robert O. Collins, ed., *Central and South African History*, vol. 3, *African History: Text and Readings.* (New York: Markus Wiener, 1990), 111–112.

EXAMINING THE EVIDENCE

1. **What were the conditions of life for those gathering rubber in the Congo?**
2. **What were rubber gatherers' attitudes in the face of their task?**
3. **What were the consequences of rubber gathering for the individual, the community, and the region at large?**

to work in mines, on urban docks, or on plantations, imperialists recruited local women into prostitution around these new workplaces.

Missionaries brought another kind of disorder, as the Boxer Rebellion demonstrated. European missionaries rushed to newly secured areas of Africa and Asia. A woman missionary working among the Tibetans reflected a common view when she remarked that the native peoples were "going down, down into hell, and there is no one but me . . . to witness for Jesus amongst them." In addition to their often unwanted arrival into native communities, missionaries fought among themselves, drawing locals into conflicts that sometimes led to military intervention and the expansion of imperial control. Women missionaries often found their new settings liberating as they left the domestic confines of their homelands for societies where they faced fewer restrictions. Their empowerment made some of them feel entitled to change local people's lives, and most earnestly hoped to improve daily life abroad. Christian missions attracted followers, upsetting local patterns of living.

Imperialists also disordered the traditional landscape, not only with large plantations in rural areas but also with administrative buildings, theaters, and schools, designed in styles of the so-called mother country (see Seeing the Past: Imperial Architecture in Saigon). Wide

Imperial Architecture in Saigon

An Imperial Cityscape: Saigon (ND/Roger-Viollet/The Image Works.)

Not only did imperialism take the wealth of foreign regions and the labor of their inhabitants, but the imperial powers also attempted to impose their own culture and values on subjected lands. One way of doing this was building monuments to imperial rulers and transforming cities according to Western ideas of proper urban architecture. The French filled the Vietnamese city of Saigon, for example, with the same wide boulevards found in Paris and with buildings such as cafés, private dwellings, and government offices that resembled those in Paris as well.

EXAMINING THE EVIDENCE

1. **What does this photograph reveal about changing livelihoods in imperial Saigon?**
2. **Why would local residents welcome this grand hotel in the French style? Why would they object to it?**

boulevards allowed passage of fine carriages—and also military parades that demonstrated the empire's power.

Everyday Resistance and Accommodation

Those in contact with imperialists practiced everyday resistance such as slowdowns at work or petty theft. Indian merchants used traditional tactics to block tax increases: they closed up shop and left town by the thousands. African merchants protested conditions around ports that seemed to favor imperial traders. In Freetown, Sierra Leone, local merchants found that the pathway to the customs house was constructed to block their goods from entering while providing the European merchants direct access for their wares. Their protests forced European officials to negotiate and ultimately change the port's arrangements. There was also accommodation: the British employed Sikhs in the colonial army because of their warrior skills and bravery in battle. But they wanted the Sikhs to control their hair, which they kept long for religious reasons. Sikh soldiers complied to keep their good jobs by adopting a turban as part of their uniform, making it a proud symbol of their separate identity. Missionaries also had to adapt when, as the price for attending church, local people wanted lessons in the colonial culture, languages, and practical skills such as Western science and math.

Although resistance sometimes led to compromise, it often prompted violent repression. In early-twentieth-century German East Africa, local people refused to pay taxes. "We do not owe you anything. We have no debt to you. If you as a stranger want to stay in this country, you will have to ask us."[14] In this case resistance was met with force: in 1907, the Germans massacred these East Africans, seizing their food supplies and leaving survivors to die of starvation. Highly organized resistance usually met with brutal mass repression, making subtle opposition a better choice.

Medicine, Science, and Well-Being in the Colonies

Imperialism changed the life of local people in myriad ways. It crucially affected health and well-being, which declined on some fronts and improved on others. Trains efficiently transported food crops away from the colonies, and equally efficiently transmitted diseases from railroad hub to railroad hub, often leaving local people both hungry and sick. Simultaneously, colonial agents introduced modern health and hygiene programs; the contradictory agendas of imperialists affected local life in complex and profound ways.

Spread of Famine and Disease

Famine, made worse by the policies of imperial powers, helped empire builders expand their holdings. During the El Niño conditions of the late nineteenth century, when weather disturbances in the tropical Pacific dried up farming lands in Asia, Africa, and parts of Brazil, acreage that was once green and productive turned brown and hard. Rivers and shallow wells dried up, making safe water and fresh food unavailable. When such conditions had occurred before, traditional rulers in India, China, and the Ottoman Empire had sent aid and cut taxes. Instead of relenting on taxes during this disaster, the Europeans redoubled their efforts to collect them, sending in tax collectors "whip in hand." As British officials announced in India: "The revenue must at all costs be gathered in."[15] Those who could not pay lost their lands, which were then given to wealthy local peoples or Europeans; colonial agents then shipped these newly landless people to plantations and mines, saving them from starvation by forcing them to work in semislavery. The plantation owners' profits in the Caribbean and elsewhere soared with the arrival of this virtually cost-free labor.

Similarly, government policies going back centuries had ensured that reservoirs and irrigation systems collected scarce water to save for droughts. The British in India, however, had no interest in such projects. Maintaining irrigation systems cost money, and the British were in India to make money. In the Qing Empire as well, with foreign powers in control of revenue collection as a result of the Opium War, taxes were no longer used for upkeep of the reservoirs, irrigation systems, or even waterways that might have transported aid to stricken regions. Imperialist neglect further devastated both agriculture and the environment.

Industrialization worsened the situation. As people in drought-stricken areas lost their ability to buy goods, including food, imperialists made fortunes, using trains to carry grain out of poor regions and store it until shortages led to rising prices and bigger profits. As trains moved back and forth among regions, they helped spread diseases to weakened people. Mortality rates soared as smallpox, influenza, typhus, cholera, and other lethal diseases worked their way through China, India, and other areas. Influential Europeans believed that no relief should be provided because any relaxation of laissez-faire principles would simply spoil recipients of aid. Lord Lytton, viceroy of India during the 1870s, spent handsomely for grand ceremonials celebrating the ascension of Britain's Queen Victoria to the imperial throne of India, yet he refused to send food to the starving, calling the cost of such aid harmful to the economy as a whole. According to Lytton, people who wanted to restore the water storage infrastructure were "irrigation quacks," and those proposing to give food to the starving were "humanitarian hysterics." When some citizens in the imperial countries became so ashamed at the photos of skeletal Indians and Chinese that they set up relief funds, colonial governors—most of them strict believers in laissez faire—diverted these funds to colonial wars in Afghanistan, South Africa, and elsewhere to expand imperialism.

Science and Hygiene

At the same time, the imperial powers aimed to transform local life with new public health programs, in large part to protect their own soldiers and officials. Governments set up scientific stations to study and adapt local plant life to serve imperial interests. Simultaneously, foreign doctors ordered that entire villages be burned to the ground when contagious diseases were found in a single household. Europeans also worked to increase hospital births in the colonies as a way to build the colonial workforce. (By contrast, the vast majority of European women still gave birth at home.) Hospitalization of expectant mothers undermined local customs and sociability and ruined the livelihoods of midwives and other healers. Sometimes changes that were not directly related to public health were explained in hygienic terms: the wide boulevards that destroyed neighborhoods and changed the face of cities opened infested areas to sunlight and cleaner conditions, for example. Local people created their own stories to accompany medical explanations. In African lore, the vampire, with its bloodsucking habit, reflected the natives' concern about colonial doctors who took blood. In other countries, such as China, those interested in change translated books on Western hygienic methods.

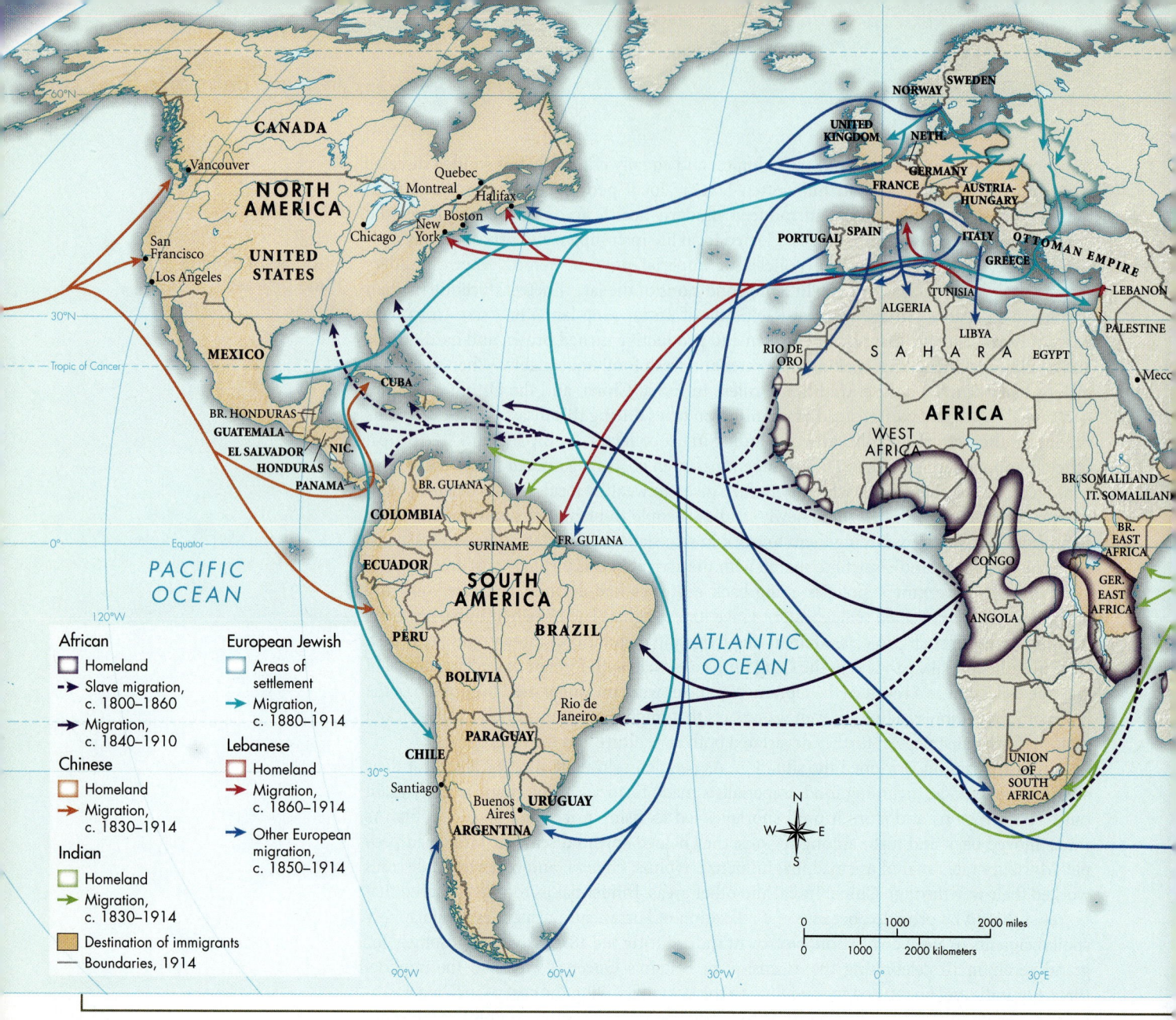

Migrants and Diasporas

The global expansion of industry and empire brought with it mass migration in the second half of the nineteenth century (see Map 26.3). In some cases, people moved because imperialists offered jobs outside their homelands. Others migrated simply because conditions at home were so bad: millions left the rural areas of Europe to escape persecution, crop failures, and eventually the hardship caused by global competition in agriculture. In Asia, Africa, and Latin America, people migrated regionally to cacao, rubber, coffee, and other plantations in response to the demands of imperialists that they pay new taxes and the lure of steady jobs.

Regional Migration

Both industrialization and imperialism affected the movement of people in search of livelihoods. Migrants left rural areas for industrialized cities, swelling their population to the bursting point. Migrants sometimes returned to the countryside at harvest time. Temporary migrants to the cities worked as masons, rickshaw drivers, or factory hands to supplement declining income from agriculture; in the winter, those remaining on the land turned to cottage industries producing a variety of goods, including bricks, pottery, lace, and locks. In Africa, dense networks of trade took Africans, Arabs, and Indians hundreds

MAP 26.3

Global Migration, c. 1800–1910

People were on the move during these decades for many different reasons. Most were concerned with finding better livelihoods, or finding any livelihood. The formal ending of the slave trade and then slavery itself led underemployed people from Asia and Africa to migrate as indentured servants, which many saw as a new type of slavery. Europeans migrated from rural areas because the global trade in grain drove down prices for produce; others, however, hoped to escape religious and personal persecution on the continent while simultaneously finding new means of support.

and even thousands of miles in caravans packed with goods. These temporary migrations were often interrupted to pay tribute to traditional rulers—not necessarily to imperialists. Yet in the colonies regional migration was also coercive and tested family ties.

Global Migration

Europeans, Asians, and Africans alike followed a pattern of global migration, moving well beyond their national borders to countries where land was being taken from native peoples to give to white settlers, or where imperialism created new job opportunities (see Lives and Livelihoods: Indentured Laborers). In parts of Europe, China, and India, for example, the land simply could not produce enough to support rapidly expanding populations, especially when drought, agricultural diseases, and famine struck. Millions of rural Jews, especially from eastern Europe, left their villages for economic reasons to populate many regions of the world, but Russian Jews also fled in the face of vicious anti-Semitic **pogroms**. In the course of such state-approved riots, Russian mobs brutally attacked Jewish communities, destroying homes and businesses and even murdering some Jews. "People who saw such things never smiled anymore, no matter how long they lived," recalled one Russian Jewish woman who migrated to the United States in the early 1890s.

pogrom A systematic attack on Jews, as carried out, for example, in the late-nineteenth-century Russian Empire.

News of commercial, agricultural, and industrial opportunity, often from recruiting agents working for governments or businesses, determined destinations. Railroads and steamships

LIVES AND LIVELIHOODS

Indentured Laborers

After slavery declined in many countries during the first half of the nineteenth century, owners of plantations, mines, and refineries complained that they needed more workers. Agents began to scour the countryside of colonized regions—especially where there was famine and other economic distress—to find workers to transport to other parts of the world. By the system of indenture, workers were cajoled or forced to sign contracts that obliged them to work for five to seven years in distant lands. Between 1830 and the outbreak of World War I in 1914, some 1.5 million Indians served as indentured laborers on European-owned plantations. Transported to Mauritania, British Guiana, Fiji, Trinidad, Guadeloupe, and Natal, to name a few destinations, their goal was to earn enough money to return home with some kind of savings.

An African Indentured Servant

The end of slavery left global business people searching for ways to secure cheap labor for plantations around the world. One source was indentured labor, a system in which agents scoured regions for underemployed workers who would serve an extended term of labor, usually in a far-off land. India, China, and West Africa thus provided workers for sugar and other plantations in the Pacific and Caribbean—to name a few destinations. This photograph shows an indentured servant planting coconut trees on Fiji, one of the Solomon Islands. Today, these regions have a rich heritage of multiculturalism in large part because of the traditions indentured laborers brought with them. (Art Media/Heritage/The Image Works.)

made journeys across and out of Asia and Europe more affordable and faster, even though most workers traveled in steerage. Once established in their new countries, migrants frequently sent money back home, and thus remained part of the family economy. They might use the funds they earned to educate a younger brother or set up a daughter or son in a small business, thus contributing to advancement. Nationalists in eastern and central Europe bemoaned the loss of ethnic vigor as the young and active departed, but peasants everywhere welcomed the arrival of "magic" income from their overseas kin. The connection between migrants and their homelands was not, therefore, completely severed by their departure. In fact, migration helped create new connections among distant parts of the world.

Migration to another part of the world did, however, often mean the end to the old way of life for the migrants themselves. Working men and women immediately had to learn new languages and civic practices and to compete for jobs in growing cities where they formed the cheapest pool of labor, often working in factories or sweatshops. Most of the first Chinese and Indian migrants were men, but when women migrants arrived with their husbands, they stayed at home and tended to associate with others like themselves, preserving traditional ways in dress and housekeeping. Their children and husbands,

"A new form of slavery," a British aristocrat and opponent called the system of indentured servitude that European powers developed after ending the slave trade. Indentured laborers endured horrendous conditions cutting sugarcane, growing other cash crops, or working in mines. "I haven't had food for three days, my body is weak, my throat is parched," reported one worker in Fiji. Another worker in the Fiji cane fields said, "We were whipped for small mistakes. If you woke up late, i.e. later than three A.M., you got whipped. No matter whether there was rain or thunder you had to work . . . otherwise we were abused and beaten up." Even those whose working conditions were somewhat better found themselves without any basic cultural institutions: "There are no temples, no festivals, no idols, . . . no schools for our children, who receive no education of any kind," an Indian indentured worker in Guadeloupe wrote in 1884. "It seems to us that animals are better treated than us in this colony."

Indentured workers kept in touch with their home culture through missionaries from India itself, adopting the ancient texts of the *Ramayana*—a tale of exile and deliverance—as their spiritual sustenance. Some African indentured laborers traveled back and forth between the Caribbean and the West African coast, even serving as recruiters after one term on the plantations. Many indentured laborers never returned to their homeland, however, constituting extensive diasporas far from Africa and South Asia. Nonetheless, they maintained many traditions: performing scenes from the *Ramayana*, for example, remains a joyous public celebration in Trinidad today. Indentured workers also transported African religions and rituals, which are still influential in binding descendants of these workers to the African continent.

Source: Quoted in Marina Carter and Khal Torabully, *Coolitude: An Anthology of the Indian Labour Diaspora* (London: Anthem Press, 2002), 90–91, 110.

QUESTIONS TO CONSIDER

1. How does the system of indentured servitude compare to slavery?
2. How did Africans and others help in the system of indentured labor, and why might they have cooperated?
3. What is the cultural legacy of indentured servitude?

For Further Information:

Carter, Marina, and Khal Torabully. *Coolitude: An Anthology of the Indian Labour Diaspora*. 2002.
Kale, Madhavi. *Fragments of Empire: Capital, Slavery, and Indian Indentured Labor Migration in the British Caribbean*. 1998.

forced to remake their lives in the schools and factories of their adopted land, were more likely to embrace the new and search out opportunity.

Global Diasporas

As migrants from extended families or the same region settled near one another, they formed ethnic **diasporas**, clusters of people who shared an ethnic identity. Continuing enslavement of Africans, Russians, and others created the harshest diasporas, but imperialism also encouraged diasporas born of opportunity. For example, the British persuaded skilled Chinese traders to settle in Singapore, and thousands of them migrated—usually without establishing permanent attachments—to build this commercial city virtually from scratch (see again Map 26.3). Other Chinese settled around the world, depending for their success on global networks to supply goods and thereby maintaining close ties to their ancestral roots. The same was true of the Lebanese diaspora to France, the United States, Argentina, and Brazil. Many of these migrants were Christians who wanted to make money in trade without having to deal with Ottoman restrictions on non-Muslims. Thus they moved to areas of opportunity, expecting to prosper and eventually to return home. In fact, historians estimate that in the early twentieth century as many as 40 percent of these Lebanese migrants found their way back—mostly to the area around Beirut—for at least a period, if not permanently.

diaspora The dispersal of a population, often resulting in large settlements in different parts of the world.

Migrants even proved influential in politics back home. The "Song of Revolution" of the turn of the century called on members of the Chinese diaspora to help overthrow the Manchu dynasty and reform the Qing Empire: "What use is the cumulation of silver cash? / Why not use it to eject the Manchus? / Ten thousand each from you isn't much / To buy cannons and guns and ship them inland."[16]

Culture in an Imperial Age

FOCUS
How did artists and writers respond to the age of empire?

The imperial age led to new ways of thought and changing norms around the world. Exposure to new environments inspired scientists and led to fresh discoveries. Ordinary people adjusted their ideas and habits to suit new city neighborhoods. Books and art from around the world inspired artists and writers as they produced works that reflected on life in the imperial age. Global contacts sparked debates over gender roles and interest in alternative ways of life. Accelerating cultural change produced what is called "modernism" in the arts—a style based on sometimes disturbing transformations in artistic expression. In fact, we may interpret spreading modernity in the realm of behavior and culture as part of globalization.

The Culture of Everyday Life

Migration from countryside to city in an age of empire meant that people transplanted rural habits and cultural life to urban settings. Bengali women who migrated to Calcutta to work as potters, basketmakers, dyers, and occasionally as factory workers, for example, celebrated their holidays in traditional ways, singing and dancing to stories of the gods and goddesses. They amused city folk with their country poetry at weddings and births, poetry that often featured tales of seduction, jealousy, and betrayal. Drug-smoking husbands and lovers who stole women's possessions were a favorite topic:

> My tears dry up in my eyes,
> I go around making merry. I'm writing in pain,
> Yet I act coy
> Swinging my hips.[17]

Such popular amusement outraged Calcutta's elites, who now preferred British middle-class norms for "civilized" female behavior. In their view, women who performed in public, such as actresses or singers, were prostitutes. Certain middle-class attitudes became standard among many Bengalis and elites in other parts of the world. As a result, the number of women performers in Calcutta declined drastically, from over seventeen thousand in the 1870s to three thousand in 1890.

In other places, local leaders were able to maintain cultural values and patterns of life. In West Africa, the French allowed Islam to flourish and used religious leaders to maintain the peace even as the region lost its economic and political independence. In turn, religious leaders preached the doctrine of accommodation to French rule. "Support the French government totally," the Sufi leader Malik Sy urged in the early twentieth century. "God has given special victory, grace, and favor to the French. He has chosen them to protect our persons and property."[18] In West Africa, France financed pilgrimages to Mecca for Muslim leaders and local officials and supported the building of mosques and the observance of Islamic law.

Urbanization and globalization remained powerful forces, breaking down traditional customs. The development of the mass media—particularly the newspaper—made millions of readers aware of other ways of doing things. Photography displayed the triumphs of technology for viewers around the world, making railroads appear even more modern by juxtaposing their images with photos of "savages," whether from the U.S. West or Oceania.

Indian Woman Dancing with Musicians

Indian women traditionally danced on many occasions and in both public and private celebrations. One popular dance was the pot dance, which revolved around the imagery of a full container whose contents must be protected: any spillage would symbolize the emptying of one's own or one's family's being. Many in the growing Indian middle class came to see these dancers, whose entire bodies were in motion, as overly sexual and bordering on barbaric. (The British Library/HIP/The Image Works.)

To build circulation, Western journalists puffed up the triumphs of "explorers" and roused readers' emotions with lurid stories of the global trade in women and girls. In celebrations of such holidays as "Empire Day" in Britain and in imperial ceremonies in South Asia and Africa, people around the world participated in an invented global culture that seemed to endorse empire. Monuments and portraits of conquerors and rulers were aimed at reshaping local loyalties into imperial ones.

Clothing traveled the world too. When French painter Paul Gauguin arrived in Tahiti late in the nineteenth century, he noted that local women had already adopted Western-style dresses with long sleeves and high necks. Chinese women had their portraits painted wearing perky Western straw hats adorned with feathers. Traditional patterns of thought and behavior loosened their hold on everyday life, especially in the world's teeming cities.

Art and Empire

The arts felt influences from empire. Japanese, Indian, Chinese, and Latin American artists adapted Western techniques that they learned of through training in Western art schools and the increasing availability of photographs. Simultaneously, writers across the globe read one another's works. Global celebrities such as Rabindranath Tagore emerged. Tagore, who won the Nobel Prize for literature in 1913, was educated in Bengal and in London, but backed by the enormous wealth of his grandfather, a financier, he was able to travel the world at leisure while composing poems, songs, short stories, and other works of prose. In his works, Tagore commented on the difficult lives of Bengali peasants while emphasizing Indian nationalism and education in Western knowledge. This ability to consider and often integrate different cultural traditions is called **cosmopolitanism**.

Similarly aware of world developments and foreign educated, Soseki Natsumi, called the greatest writer of the Meiji period, wove insights on local Japanese life as it modernized into his novels and journalism. Soseki's *Botchan* (*Little Master*, 1906) focused on a cranky youth—a "misfit" in the Meiji world—who had been educated in math and science and sent to the provinces to teach. He insults his colleagues, no one more than an art teacher who wears a French-style smock and floppy bow tie around his neck, affecting the attitude

cosmopolitanism The merging or acceptance of a variety of national and ethnic values and traditions.

The Durbar for Edward VII in Delhi, India

Lavish celebrations and rituals were invented to cement imperial relationships between rulers and ruled. Held at the very end of 1902 and into 1903, this durbar—a formal state reception given by Indian princes for a British sovereign—marked the ascension of Edward VII to the imperial throne and thus to rule over India. Maharajahs and other local dignitaries attended, riding elephants and wearing luxurious clothing and jewels, appearing to accept this foreign ruler. Such ceremonies masked the violence with which the British and other imperial powers attempted to rule and the ever-present resistance to these foreign invaders. (Getty Images.)

of a Western artist. Soseki railed against consumers of Western-style journalism, especially readers who gobbled up news of fires, murders, and accidents with the idea that they were now in touch with a Western kind of reality. In Soseki's view, this foreign habit actually cut them off from a deeper reality. At the same time, he transformed Japanese literature by probing the psychology of his characters as writers in the West did. The leading writers of Asia were thus engaged with styles and worldviews brought from afar by imperialism and globalization.

Western literature traveled the world, arousing both acclaim and controversy. The Norwegian playwright Henrik Ibsen's *A Doll's House* (1879), a drama about a woman who leaves a loveless marriage, riveted global audiences. It influenced many to think that their countries' modernization required changes in the situation of women. Inspired by the play, Japanese women started a feminist movement; some Chinese women campaigned to eliminate foot-binding. Similarly, women in Ottoman countries abandoned their veils in the belief that it would help free their countries if they looked more Western. Under the influence of imperialism and globalization, literature influenced rebellion against the West even as it promoted the adoption of Western values and cultural patterns.

Imperial Contests at the Dawn of the Twentieth Century

FOCUS

What were the main issues in the contests over empire, and what were the results of these contests?

Although cultural influences were shaping city life and traveling around the world, imperialism was increasingly chaotic and deadly at the start of the twentieth century. Large-scale rebellions by ordinary people fighting against imperial domination, such as the Boxer Rebellion, became more common. Competition among the imperial powers themselves was also heating up as their ambitions swelled. The United States and Japan pursued global empire more vigorously in these years, fighting successful wars against older empires. International politics became menacing and imperial nerves were on edge, especially as military spending grew amid competition for power.

Clashes for Imperial Control

After centuries of global expansion, imperial adventure soured for empires both old and new. Some of this trouble arose from newcomers to imperial competition, such as Japan and the United States, both of which took territory and expanded their markets at the turn of the century, defeating older rivals. Empires faced constant challenges to their survival: as empires were competing among themselves for influence, the colonized and otherwise oppressed people were fighting back with increasing vigor.

The South African War

The British experienced an unexpected setback to their imperial ambitions in 1896, when Cecil Rhodes, by then prime minister of the Cape Colony at Africa's southern tip, directed a raid on Johannesburg to stir up trouble between the Boers, descendants of early Dutch settlers, and the more recent immigrants from Britain who had come to southern Africa in search of gold. Rhodes hoped the raid would justify a British takeover of the Transvaal and the Orange Free State, which the Boers independently controlled. The Boers unexpectedly won, leading the British to wage the South African (or Boer) War directly against the Transvaal and the Orange Free State. As journalists reported on appalling bloodshed, rampant disease, and the unfit condition of the average British soldier, citizens back home were stunned. The British herded the Boers into a shocking and unfamiliar institution—the concentration camp, which became the graveyard of tens of thousands of women and children. Britain finally defeated the Boers in 1902 and annexed the area, but the cost of war in money, loss of life, and public morale was enormous.

Native Africans, who mostly had supported the British with the thought that they were more civilized and law-abiding than the Boers, were quickly disillusioned. Soon after the annexation, the government of South Africa passed a series of laws appropriating African-owned lands for whites, depriving Africans of free movement, and imposing an entire range of restrictions on their lives. It was the foundation for the policy of racial segregation and discrimination that would be called apartheid. "We expected deliverance," one local chieftain commented bitterly on postwar British policy, "whereas we have gone deeper into bond[age]."[19]

The Spanish-American War

At about the time the British were fighting the Boer War, Spain lost Cuba, Puerto Rico, and the Philippines to the United States, which defeated it in the Spanish-American War of 1898. As Spanish imperial power declined, the Spanish government tried to support itself by raising taxes to exorbitant levels on its remaining colonies. Meanwhile, the United States, a newcomer to imperialism overseas, had been killing native Americans and driving them from their lands since the seventeenth century. In addition it had asserted its diplomatic influence in the Western Hemisphere in the Monroe Doctrine (1823), purchased Alaska in 1867, and annexed Hawaii in 1898 at the urgings of missionaries and businessmen, who had set up plantations on the islands (see Reading the Past: The United States Overthrows the Hawaiian Queen).

Before the Spanish-American War, both Cuba and the Philippines had vigorous independence movements backed by all classes of people. Expansionist-minded Theodore Roosevelt, then assistant secretary of the navy, and the inflammatory daily press goaded the U.S. government to help the independence movements with armed force. However, after its swift victory over Spain the United States annexed Puerto Rico and Guam and bought the Philippines from its former ruler. In theory, Cuba remained independent, but U.S. businesses virtually controlled its sugar-exporting economy—a clear example of business imperialism. The lesson for the imperial powers was the unpredictability of empire. After that, the triumphant United States, encouraged by British poet Rudyard Kipling to "take up the white man's burden" by bringing the benefits of Western civilization to the Philippines, waged a bloody war against the Filipinos, who wanted independence, not simply a different imperial ruler. Reports of American brutality in the Philippines, where some twenty

The Spanish-American War, 1898

READING THE PAST

The United States Overthrows the Hawaiian Queen

U.S. businessmen set themselves up in the Hawaiian Islands, establishing lucrative sugar plantations and other agricultural enterprises. With government support, they then worked to undermine the ruling monarchy, calling themselves the Committee of Safety. After imprisoning the Hawaiian queen under house arrest in 1893, they forced her to abdicate in a document that gave no indication of the trickery and violence behind their deeds. In this passage from her memoir of 1898, Queen Liliuokalani describes the threats that led to her abdication. The men she cites were members of the Committee.

> For the first few days nothing occurred to disturb the quiet of my apartments save the tread of the sentry. On the fourth day I received a visit from Mr. Paul Neumann, who asked me if, in the event that it should be decided that all the principal parties to the revolt must pay for it with their lives, I was prepared to die? I replied to this in the affirmative, telling him I had no anxiety for myself, and felt no dread of death. He then told me that six others besides myself had been selected to be shot for treason, but that he would call again, and let me know further about our fate. . . .
>
> About the 22d of January a paper was handed to me by Mr. Wilson, which, on examination, proved to be a purported act of abdication for me to sign. . . . For myself, I would have chosen death rather than to have signed it; but it was represented to me that by my signing this paper all the persons who had been arrested, all my people now in trouble by reason of their love and loyalty towards me, would be immediately released. Think of my position—sick, a lone woman in prison, scarcely knowing who was my friend, or who listened to my words only to betray me, without legal advice or friendly counsel, and the stream of blood ready to flow unless it was stayed by my pen.
>
> My persecutors have stated, and at that time compelled me to state, that this paper was signed and acknowledged by me after consultation with my friends whose names appear at the foot of it as witnesses. Not the least opportunity was given to me to confer with anyone; but for the purpose of making it appear to the outside world that I was under the guidance of others, friends who had known me well in better days were brought into the place of my imprisonment, and stood around to see a signature affixed by me. . . . Then the following individuals witnessed my subscription of the signature which was demanded of me: William G. Irwin, H. A. Widemann, Samuel Parker, S. Kalua Kookano, Charles B. Wilson, and Paul Neumann. . . .
>
> So far from the presence of these persons being evidence of a voluntary act on my part, was it not an assurance to me that they, too, knew that, unless I did the will of my jailers, what Mr. Neumann had threatened would be performed, and six prominent citizens immediately put to death. I so regarded it then, and I still believe that murder was the alternative. Be this as it may, it is certainly happier for me to reflect to-day that there is not a drop of the blood of my subjects, friends or foes, upon my soul.

Source: Liliuokalani, *Hawaii's Story by Hawaii's Queen* (Boston: Lothrop, Lee, and Shepard,1898), http://digital.library.upenn.edu/women/liliuokalani/hawaii/hawaii.html.

EXAMINING THE EVIDENCE

1. **Why do you think that Queen Liliuokalani wrote this memoir?**
2. **What attitudes do you sense behind the actions of those who wanted to take over her lands and resources?**
3. **How does the queen portray herself in the face of these adversaries?**

thousand freedom fighters and several hundred thousand civilians died, disillusioned the Western public, who liked to imagine native peoples joyously welcoming the bearers of civilization.

The Russo-Japanese War

The Japanese vigorously pursued empire, defeating China and then trouncing Russia—both of them Japan's rivals for influence in the Far East. Angered by Russian expansion in Manchuria, the Japanese attacked tsarist forces at Port Arthur in 1904 (see Map 26.4). Casualties were once again fearsome, as powerful new weaponry such as machine guns mowed down combatants on both sides. To the astonishment of the world, the Japanese completely destroyed the Russian fleet in the 1905 Battle of Tsushima Strait. The victory was the first by a non-European nation over a European great power in the modern age. As one

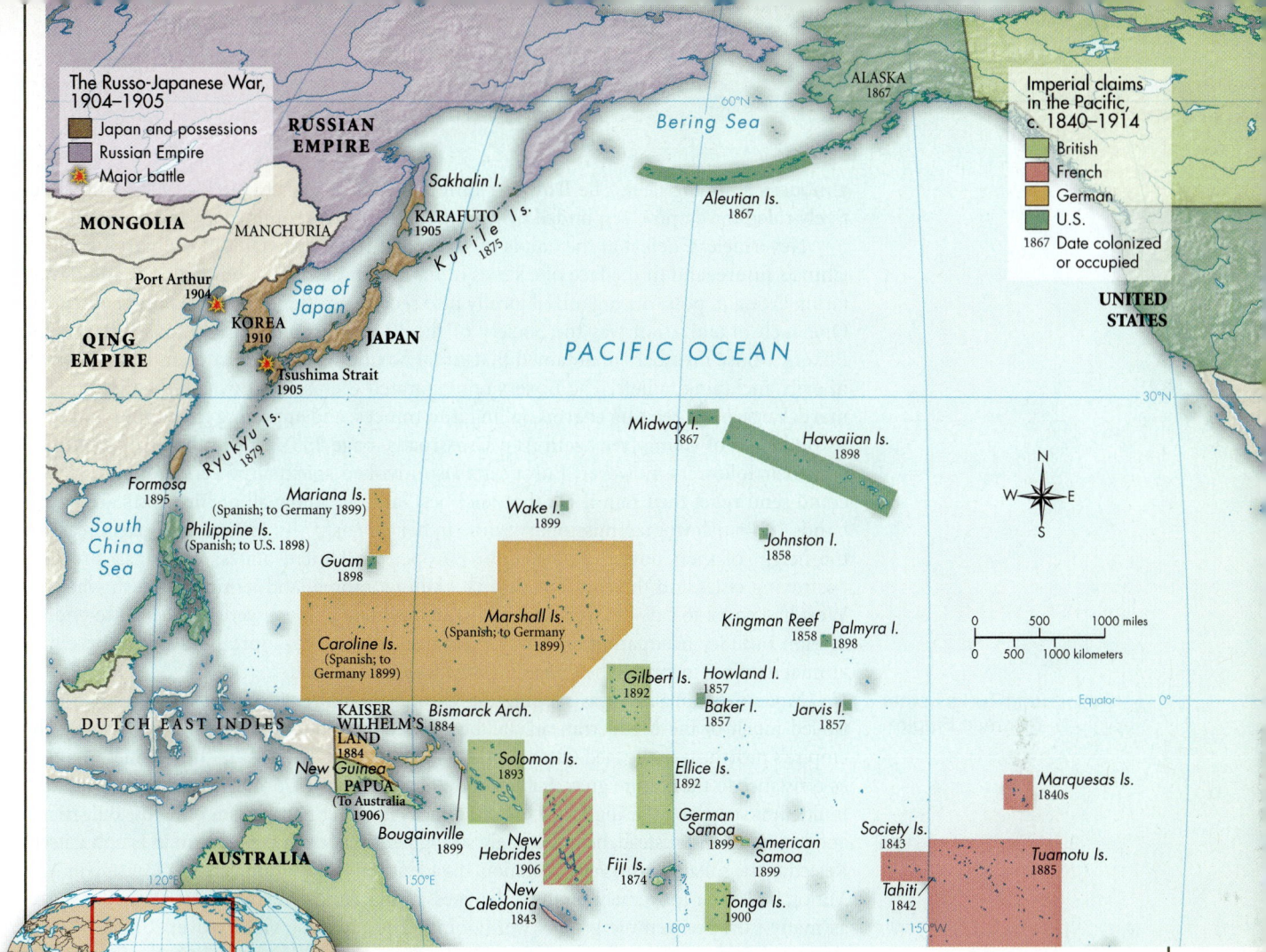

MAP 26.4

Imperialism in the Pacific, c. 1840–1914

European and Japanese imperialists sent their traders, missionaries, military, and adventurers to China, Southeast Asia, and the Pacific Islands. They savagely put down the Boxer Rebellion, a Chinese uprising. The outbreak of the Sino-Japanese and Russo-Japanese wars showed that imperial ambitions could lead to international warfare among the powers, with unpredictable results.

English general ominously observed of the Russian defeat, "I have today seen the most stupendous spectacle it is possible for the mortal brain to conceive—Asia advancing, Europe falling back." Japan went on to annex Korea in 1910 and to eye other areas for colonization. Russia itself erupted in the Revolution of 1905, forcing the tsar to institute a weak form of parliament, the Duma. The double blow of military defeat by Japan and social revolution exposed Russia's internal weaknesses, especially the widespread discontent of ordinary people.

Growing Resistance to Foreign Domination

The Japanese military victory over two important dynasties—the Qing in China and the Romanov in Russia—reverberated around the world. People under foreign domination responded to Japan's victory with enthusiasm and hope, believing that if a small non-Western nation such as Japan could defeat a Western power, they too could defeat outside forces.

Boxers in China

In China, students, elites, and ordinary people felt humiliated by the 1895 defeat by Japan and the forced economic concessions to Western powers that followed. Students demanded reform, presenting a memorandum asking for modern institutions such as an efficient tax system and national railroad, postal, and banking networks. The memo insisted that the government sponsor technology and commerce, the latter through creating a modern shipping fleet. The Dowager Empress Cixi (kee-shee) (1835–1908), who effectively ruled the empire, responded by having the reformers rounded up and executed.

Nevertheless, defeat at the hands of Japan had rocked the faith of ordinary people in China's future, and in the face of a series of natural disasters, including floods and devastating drought, peasants organized locally into secret societies to restore Chinese integrity. One such organization was the Society of the Righteous and Harmonious Fists, or the Boxers, whose members maintained that ritual boxing would protect them from a variety of evils, including bullets. The Boxers reinvigorated themselves through the discipline of martial arts, often reciting charms, falling into trances, and appealing to the gods and spirits on behalf of China (see again At a Crossroads, page 856). Facing these young Boxers and their followers, however, Europeans also invoked spiritual powers: "We know God could send relief thru rain if He thot [*sic*] best, and we know all our interests are in His hands," a British woman missionary wrote in her journal.[20] By 1900 as the Boxers reached the height of their power, troops from Europe, the United States, and Japan invaded, destroying cities and the countryside alike, killing, raping, and looting to crush what the West had come to call "the yellow peril." The defeated Chinese were compelled to endure foreign military occupation and to pay a huge indemnity—more than twice the entire annual national income. The Qing dynasty faced its downfall.

Young Turks in the Ottoman Empire

Modern nationalism was sapping the Ottoman Empire, which for centuries had controlled much of the Mediterranean. In the nineteenth century, rebellions in several of the empire's provinces challenged Ottoman rule, and more erupted early in the twentieth century as resistance to the empire grew. Sultan Abdul Hamid II (r. 1876–1909) tried to revitalize the multiethnic empire by using Islam to counteract the rising nationalism of Serbs, Bulgarians, and Macedonians. Instead, he unwittingly strengthened Turkish nationalism in Istanbul itself. Rejecting the sultan's pan-Islamic solution, dissident Turks, the dominant ethnic group in Asia Minor, built their movement on the uniqueness of the Turkish culture, history, and language, as many European ethnic groups were doing. The Japanese victory over Russia in 1905 electrified Turkish nationalists with the vision of a modern Turkey becoming "the Japan of the Middle East," as they put it. In 1908, a group calling itself the Young Turks took control of the government in Istanbul, which had been fatally weakened by nationalist agitation and by the empire's economic dependence on Western financiers and businessmen.

The Young Turks' triumph motivated other groups in the Middle East and the Balkans to demand an end to Ottoman domination in their regions. These groups adopted Western values and platforms, and some, such as the Egyptians, had strong contingents of feminist

Young Turks

The Young Turks formed a group committed to the modernization of the Ottoman Empire—one of the longest imperial reigns in history. By the early twentieth century, the Young Turks had grown impatient with declining Ottoman power and, trained in western European military strategies and tactics, sought a complete overhaul of Ottoman institutions, economy, and culture. Complete success would not come, however, until after World War I, when officers in the defeated Ottoman army beat back Allied and Greek attempts to take over Turkey. (Mary Evans/Grenville Collins/The Image Works.)

nationalists who mobilized women to become modern and work for independence. But the Young Turks, now in control of the Ottoman government and often aided by European powers with financial and political interests in the region, brutally tried to repress movements in Egypt, Syria, and the Balkans modeled after their own nationalist success.

Further Blows Against Empire

Resistance to empire grew everywhere in the wake of the Japanese victory. In India, the fervently anti-British Hindu leader, B. G. Tilak, preached outright noncooperation. "We shall not give them assistance to collect revenue and keep peace. We shall not assist them in fighting beyond the frontiers or outside India with Indian blood and money." Tilak promoted Hindu customs, asserted the distinctiveness of Hindu values, and inspired violent rebellion in his followers. This brand of nationalism broke with that of the Indian National Congress, which was based on assimilating to British culture and promoting gradual change. Trying to repress Tilak, the British sponsored the Muslim League, a rival nationalist group, to divide Muslim nationalists from Hindus in the Congress.

Violence escalated, and inhabitants of the colonies—rulers and ruled alike—were often on edge. Imperial powers responded to growing resistance with harsh crackdowns. In German East Africa, colonial forces crushed native resistance in 1905 with a scorched-earth policy of destroying homes, livestock, and food, eventually killing more than one hundred thousand Africans there. Having set up police surveillance in colonies around the world, the French closed the University of Hanoi, executed Indochinese intellectuals, and deported thousands of suspected nationalists in an extreme attempt to maintain their grip on Indochina. A French general stationed there summed up the fears of many colonial rulers in the new century. "The gravest fact of our actual political situation in Indochina is not the recent trouble in Tonkin [or] the plots undertaken against us but in the muted but growing hatred that our subjects show toward us." Imperialists were right to worry.

COUNTERPOINT

The West Copies from the World

In the late nineteenth century, Western political thought, technology, and science were increasingly triumphant around the world. At the same time, however, interest in non-Western religion, art, and literature was growing in the West. Thus, alongside the political and military rule of the imperialist powers, cultural exchange flourished.

FOCUS

How did non-Western and colonized lands shape Western culture and society?

Changes in the Arts

Art from around the world resonated in the imaginations of Western artists. The most striking changes came in the work of impressionist painters such as Claude Monet and Vincent Van Gogh. As Japanese woodcuts came on the European market, Monet painted water lilies, Japanese bridges, and trailing wisteria vines, all of them gracefully depicted and seeming to shimmer in the light. The concept of the fleetingness of situations came from a centuries-old Japanese concept—*mono no aware*, serenity before and sensitivity to the fleetingness of life. The color, line, and delicacy of Japanese art, which many impressionists collected, is also evident in the work of the American expatriate Mary Cassatt. Cassatt was known for her paintings of women and children, which were strongly influenced by similar Japanese prints that she owned. Van Gogh filled the backgrounds of portraits with copies of intensely colored Japanese prints, even imitating classic Japanese woodcuts.

With increased global contact, poetry, music, dance, and literature changed in Europe and the United States, never to return to their preimperialism forms. The translation of haiku poetry influenced Western poets to give up formal meter, simplify their verse, and surrender lofty subjects in favor of the everyday topics of Japanese rhyme. William Butler Yeats, in his attempts to create an authentic Irish literature, copied themes and images from Japanese Noh and

Vincent Van Gogh, *Flowering Plum Tree* (1887)

Western culture soaked up influences from afar, whether in the fine arts or in practices of everyday life. By the late nineteenth century, ordinary people drank chocolate, tea, and coffee and filled their gardens with non-native plants that had become naturalized to the West. Western artists' indebtedness to non-Western styles is epitomized in this painting by Dutch painter Vincent Van Gogh, who modeled this work on a print by Hiroshige (see page 803). The brief flowering of trees so dear to the Japanese represented the fleetingness of life, and impressionists built their entire style on capturing the rapid changes in light. (akg-images.)

kabuki plays and, rejecting the ornate classical patterns of English poetry, stripped his verses of all embellishment. Yeats was but one of many who followed this path. Composers such as Claude Debussy largely abandoned centuries of Western musical patterns to create modern music based on sounds from around the world that Europeans encountered during their travels or at world fairs. In the same way, choreographers studied steps and movements practiced around the world to develop modern dance, a new way of performing that rejected the formality of classical Western ballet.

Expansion of Ideas

Outside the arts, Viennese physician Sigmund Freud, trained as a neurologist, led the West in the study of the human mind. Freud practiced telepathy (communication through means other than the senses), hypnosis, and dream therapies—all developed from ideas and therapies used in Africa and Asia. Dreams, he explained in *The Interpretation of Dreams* (1900), reveal an unseen, repressed part of the personality—the "unconscious," where all sorts of desires are more or less hidden. His new science for the treatment of mental disturbances, called **psychoanalysis**, centered on the "talking cure," that is, discussing one's dreams to uncover the reasons for mental problems. Freud read anthropological literature about the practices of witch doctors and shamans, coming up with ideas for his "talking cure" and for understanding fetishes such as fixations on shoes, gloves, or other ordinary objects.

Other Western intellectuals studied Hinduism, Buddhism, African religions, and many other bodies of thought and culture to develop new ideas. For example, at the beginning of the twentieth century, discussions of sexuality in the West expanded beyond biblically defined boundaries. South Asian ideas about reincarnation inspired the thought that the physical indications of a person's sex were merely temporary because an eternal self without sex was reborn across time in differently sexed bodies. So-called homosexuality and transgendering were explained by this process. People began discussing sexuality as variable, using ideas that came from beyond the West and that continue to be influential to this day.

Lifestyles Transformed

In Europe and the United States, people began to live in efficiently designed single-family homes styled after the Indian bungalow; they had porches and verandas, and they often decorated their homes with palms, bamboo furniture, and textiles of Asian or African designs. European cookbooks carried recipes for curry and cakes made from an array of global products, such as sugar, chocolate, vanilla, and coconut. Women joined men in wearing slimmer, more informal clothing, much of it modeled on non-Western styles. Late in the nineteenth century, women adopted looser "reform clothing"—kimono-like garments or those modeled after Middle Eastern caftans—and they began following Asian and African women in not wearing corsets.

To get and stay in shape, Westerners, who had generally not thought in such terms, began to exercise more. Men kept fit by practicing martial arts, all of which came from outside Europe

psychoanalysis A psychiatric therapy developed by Sigmund Freud; some elements, such as dream interpretation, were influenced by Freud's knowledge of African and Asian practices.

and the United States. Even as national and international tensions were heating up and as the West thought itself superior in all things, Western military schools were using Sun Tzu's *The Art of War*, a Chinese classic from the sixth century B.C.E., in their courses on strategy. Despite the power of Western imperialism, ideas never followed a one-way street from West to East. Rather, imperialism was, among much else, a crossroads for ideas to travel in many directions.

Conclusion

The nineteenth century is called an age of imperialism because of the growing contest among Western nation-states to dominate the world's peoples politically and economically. New technology springing from ongoing industrialization helped people and ideas move more rapidly around the world, enabling the exercise of political and military power as well as cultural and economic exchange. Western technology gave its agents a real advantage in developing wealth globally and controlling the flow of resources. New forms of oppression such as indentured servitude developed; plantation agriculture increasingly replaced self-sufficient farming; and environmental catastrophes weakened societies and helped imperialism spread. Imperialism was complex. Some colonized peoples prospered by participating in the system and simultaneously developed goals such as national independence, based on the Western values of rights and freedom that were denied them.

Newly powerful countries vied with established ones for a share of world influence, fueling the "new" imperialism's explosive potential. Although global expansion led to increased wealth for some individuals and states, events such as China's Boxer Rebellion demonstrated that it brought violence and insecurity to most ordinary people and to governments. Imperial competition made the world more dangerous, as did the drive even within Europe to gain territory from the weakening Ottoman Empire. Thus, global and local battles raged during this period. Although it was meant to stabilize international politics, imperialism intensified distrust and insecurity among the powers. When global and local political ambitions met, as they did in the second decade of the twentieth century, catastrophic violence followed.

NOTES

1. Quoted in Paul A. Cohen, *History in Three Keys: The Boxers as Event, Experience, and Myth* (New York: Columbia University Press, 1997), 86–87.
2. Paul Leroy-Beaulieu, quoted in *Histoire de la colonisation française* (Paris: Fayard, 1991), 2:149.
3. Quoted in Rudrangshu Mukherjee, "The Sepoy Mutinies Revisited," in *War and Society in Colonial India, 1807–1945*, ed. Kaushik Roy (Delhi: Oxford University Press, 2006), 121.
4. General Skobelev, quoted in Peter Hopkirk, *The Great Game: The Struggle for Empire in Central Asia* (New York: Kodansha International, 1992), 407.
5. Quoted in Charles Lee Keeton, *King Thebaw and the Ecological Rape of Burma: The Political and Commercial Struggle Between British India and French Indo-China in Burma, 1878–1886* (Delhi, India: Manohar Book Service, 1974), 202.
6. Phan Chau Trinh, in Truong Buu Lam, *Colonialism Experienced: Vietnamese Writing on Colonialism, 1900–1931* (Ann Arbor: University of Michigan Press, 2000), 130.
7. William Morton Fullerton, *In Cairo*, quoted in Max Rodenbeck, *Cairo: The City Victorious* (New York: Knopf, 1999), 136.
8. Letter from the King of Daboya to Governor of the Gold Coast, 8 July 1892, quoted in A. Adu Boahen, *African Perspectives on Colonialism* (Baltimore, MD: Johns Hopkins University Press, 1987), 37.
9. Quoted in Mike Davis, *Late Victorian Holocausts: El Niño Famines and the Making of the Third World* (London: Verso, 2001), 46.
10. Davis, *Late Victorian Holocausts*, 139.
11. Quoted in Jennifer W. Cushman, *Family and State: The Formation of a Sino-Thai Tin-Mining Dynasty, 1797–1832* (Singapore: Oxford University Press, 1991), 62.
12. Khayr al-Din al-Tunisi, "The Surest Path to Knowledge Concerning the Condition of Countries," quoted in *Colonial Rule in Africa: Readings from Primary Sources*, ed. Bruce Fetter (Madison: University of Wisconsin Press, 1979), 57.
13. Quoted in Bruce Fetter, ed., *Colonial Rule in Africa*, 117.

14. Quoted in Robert O. Collins, ed., *Eastern African History*, vol. 2, *African History: Text and Readings* (New York: Markus Wiener Publishing, 1990), 124.
15. Quoted in Davis, *Late Victorian Holocausts*, 31, 57, 172.
16. "Song of Revolution," in Gungwu Wang, *Community and Nation: China, Southeast Asia and Australia* (St. Leonards, Australia: Allen and Unwin, 1992), 10.
17. Quoted in Sumanta Banerjee, "Women's Popular Culture in Nineteenth Century Bengal," in *Recasting Women: Essays in Indian Colonial History*, ed. Kumkum Sangari and Sudesh Vaid (New Brunswick, NJ: Rutgers University Press, 1990), 142.
18. Quoted in David Robinson, *Muslim Societies and French Colonial Authorities in Senegal and Mauritania, 1880–1920* (Athens: Ohio University Press, 2000), 204.
19. Chief Segale, quoted in Peter Warwick, *Black People and the South African War, 1899–1902* (Cambridge, U.K.: Cambridge University Press, 1983), 177.
20. Quoted in Cohen, *History in Three Keys*, 80.

RESOURCES FOR RESEARCH

Building Empires

There are many debates about the motivations for empire. Cain and Hopkins dispute the view that industrialists backed imperialism to provide them with markets, arguing instead that financial and other service providers were the major advocates of colonies. Steinmetz interestingly shows German imperialism as inconsistent, varying from one area to another, and he suggests that all colonies were similarly run, depending on the imperialists' evaluations of a particular region's culture.

Burbank, Jane, and Frederick Cooper. *Empires in World History: Power and the Politics of Difference*. 2010.

Cain, P. J., and A. G. Hopkins. *British Imperialism, 1688–2000*. 2002.

Feifer, George. *Breaking Open Japan: Commodore Perry, Lord Abe and the American Imperialism of 1853*. 2006.

Steinmetz, George. *The Devil's Handwriting: Precoloniality and the German Colonial State in Qingdao, Samoa, and Southwest Africa*. 2004.

Sunderland, Willard. *Taming the Wild Field: Colonization and Empire on the Russian Steppe*. 2004.

Imperial Society

Imperial powers showed their dominance through the exercise of military but also political and social power.

Armstrong, Charles K., et al., eds. *Korea at the Center: Dynamics of Regionalism in Northeast Asia*. 2006.

Carter, Marina, and Khal Torabully. *Coolitude: An Anthology of the Indian Labour Diaspora*. 2002.

Davis, Mike. *Late Victorian Holocausts: El Niño Famines and the Making of the Third World*. 2001.

Maugubane, Zine. *Bringing the Empire Home: Race, Class, and Gender in Britain and Colonial South Africa*. 2004.

Sahadeo, Jeff. *Russian Colonial Society in Tashkent, 1865–1923*. 2007.

Culture in an Imperial Age

The imperialists shaped colonial customs and attitudes, claiming to bring a superior civilization to their subjects.

Adas, Michael. *Dominance by Design: Technological Imperatives and America's Civilizing Mission*. 2006.

Berenson, Edward. *Heroes of Empire: Five Charismatic Men and the Conquest of Africa*. 2011.

Jansen, Marius B. *The Making of Modern Japan*. 2000.

Lowy, Dina. *The Japanese "New Woman": Images of Gender and Modernity*. 2007.

Robinson, David. *Muslim Societies and French Colonial Authorities in Senegal and Mauritania, 1880–1920*. 2000.

Imperial Contests at the Dawn of the Twentieth Century

The start of the twentieth century was a time of increasing global conflict. Several of the following authors describe the range of this conflict and the main issues in each example.

Cohen, Paul A. *History in Three Keys: The Boxers as Event, Experience, and Myth*. 1997.

Hobson, Rolf. *Imperialism at Sea: Naval Strategic Thought, the Ideology of Sea Power, and the Tirpitz Plan, 1875–1914*. 2002.

Parsons, Timothy. *The Rule of Empires: Those Who Built Them, Those Who Endured Them, and Why They Always Fall*. 2010.

Silbey, David J. *A War of Frontier and Empire: The Philippine-American War, 1899–1902*. 2007.

South African War. The Anglo-Boer War Museum maintains a helpful Web site. http://www.anglo-boer.co.za/.

Counterpoint: The West Copies from the World

As these works reveal, cultural exchange flourished alongside the rule of the imperialists.

Baas, Jacquelynn. *Smile of the Buddha: Eastern Philosophy and Western Art from Monet to Today*. 2005.

Brower, M. Brady. *Unruly Spirits: The Science of Psychic Phenomena in Modern France*. 2010.

Dixon, Joy. *Divine Feminine: Theosophy and Feminism in England*. 2001.

Treitel, Corinne. *A Science for the Soul: Occultism and the Genesis of the German Modern*. 2004.

▶ **For additional primary sources from this period**, see *Sources of Crossroads and Cultures*.

▶ **For Web sites, images, and documents related to topics in this chapter**, see Make History at bedfordstmartins.com/smith.

REVIEW

Online Study Guide
bedfordstmartins.com/smith

The major global development in this chapter ▶ The accelerated competition among nineteenth-century nation-states for empire.

IMPORTANT EVENTS

c. 1840–1910	Global migration because of indenture, imperial opportunity, and harsh environmental conditions
1857	Indian Uprising against the British
c. 1860–1900	Impressionism flourishes in the European arts, borrowing many non-Western techniques
1869	Suez Canal completed
c. 1870–1914	European powers, Japan, and the United States extend formal and informal control over Asia, Africa, and parts of Latin America
1876	British Parliament declares Victoria empress of India
1882	Britain takes over Egypt
1884–1885	European nations carve up Africa at the Berlin Conference
1894–1895	Sino-Japanese War
1898	Spanish-American War
1899–1900	Boxer Rebellion in China
1899–1902	South African War
1900	Sigmund Freud, *The Interpretation of Dreams*
1904–1905	Russo-Japanese War
1908	Young Turks' uprising against the Ottoman Empire
1910	Japan annexes Korea

KEY TERMS

business imperialism (p. 861)
colonialism (p. 861)
cosmopolitanism (p. 879)
diaspora (p. 877)
globalization (p. 860)
new imperialism (p. 860)
pogrom (p. 875)
psychoanalysis (p. 886)

CHAPTER OVERVIEW QUESTIONS

1. What are the arguments for and against imperialism?
2. How and why did some local peoples assist imperialists who took over their own countries?
3. Which were the major imperialist powers, and what made them so capable of conquest?
4. How did imperialism change the lives of people in the conquering countries and in the colonies?

SECTION FOCUS QUESTIONS

1. What motivated the imperialists, and how did they impose their control over other nations?
2. How did imperialism change lives and livelihoods around the world?
3. How did artists and writers respond to the age of empire?
4. What were the main issues in the contests over empire, and what were the results of these contests?
5. How did non-Western and colonized lands shape Western culture and society?

MAKING CONNECTIONS

1. How are the Industrial Revolution (see Chapter 24) and imperialism connected?
2. How are nation building (see Chapter 25) and imperialism connected?
3. In what ways might the globalization connected with imperialism undermine nation building?
4. Recall the empires discussed in Part 3. What were the key differences between empires in the early modern period and modern empires of the nineteenth century?

27

AT A CROSSROADS ▲

Diego Rivera spent most of the Mexican Revolution in Europe, where he learned a range of classical Western styles of painting. The bloodshed of the revolution and World War I and the coming of communism to Russia and elsewhere inspired him to become a communist and to take up the cause of oppressed native American peasants and workers on his return to Mexico. This mural, *Blood of the Revolutionary Martyrs Fertilizing the Earth* (1927), reflects the traditional Mexican idea that martyrdom makes the earth fertile. Rivera's strong belief in the value of workers and representations of this brutal era in human history make his art a crossroads of politics and cultural styles. The martyrs represented are peasant rebel leader Emiliano Zapata (right) and his follower Otilio Montano (left). (Schalkwijk/Art Resource, NY. /© 2011 Banco de México Diego Rivera Frida Kahlo Museums Trust, Mexico, D.F./ARS, NY.)

Wars, Revolutions, and the Birth of Mass Society

1910–1929

The rebel leader Emiliano Zapata was a dandy, wearing blinding white shirts and fitted black pants adorned with silver. Before 1910 he had worked the land of his part-Indian family in central Mexico, where small farmers such as Zapata struggled—usually unsuccessfully—to block the takeover of their traditional lands by big hacienda (plantation) owners producing sugar and other commodities for the global market. Zapata grew and sold watermelons, prospering by comparison with others in his village. A fighter against the takeover of local land, in 1910 he was galvanized by the call for revolution against the corrupt regime of Porfirio Diaz, a key ally of the big landowners. Gathering a peasant army, Zapata swept through central Mexico, motivating his followers with the slogan "It is better to die on your feet than live on your knees." During the long revolutionary struggle, Zapata became known as a shrewd, rational political leader, but he also provoked an emotional response: peasants who had never seen him boosted their spirits during the decade-long Mexican Revolution with cries of "Viva [Long Live] Zapata!"

By 1920, the Mexican Revolution had killed between 1 and 2 million people, some by rifles, machine guns, and bombs and others by disease, but it was just one of several lethal cataclysms in that decade. Between 1910 and 1920, tens of millions fought and died. In cities and villages, farms and battlefields around the world grew the grim sense that in this new century war would never end and that ordinary people would be endlessly called upon to support the slaughter. After Mexico, China erupted in revolution in 1911, throwing

Revolutions, Local Wars, and World War

FOCUS What factors contributed to the wars of the early twentieth century?

Revolution in Russia and the End of World War I

FOCUS Why did the Russian Revolution take place, and what changes did it produce in Russian politics and daily life?

Postwar Global Politics

FOCUS What were the major outcomes of the peacemaking process and postwar conditions?

An Age of the Masses

FOCUS How did the rise of mass society affect politics, culture, and everyday life around the world?

COUNTERPOINT: A Golden Age for Argentineans

FOCUS In what ways did Argentina's history differ from that of countries caught up in World War I?

BACKSTORY

The competition among Western powers heated up in the second half of the nineteenth century, fueled by the drive for overseas expansion known as imperialism (see Chapter 26). European nations used the economic and military advantages that resulted from industrialization to take direct and indirect control of territories in Asia, Africa, and Latin America. Newcomers Japan and the United States joined the race for empire, and many other states pursued policies intended to produce political centralization and national unification. Resistance to both new and old empires and to political elites mounted during these years, even as imperialism multiplied the connections among the world's peoples and intensified the pace of cultural and economic exchange. Both competition for power and resistance to existing power structures contributed to the violence that marked the early twentieth century. The application of industrial technology to warfare made conflicts between and within states more destructive than ever.

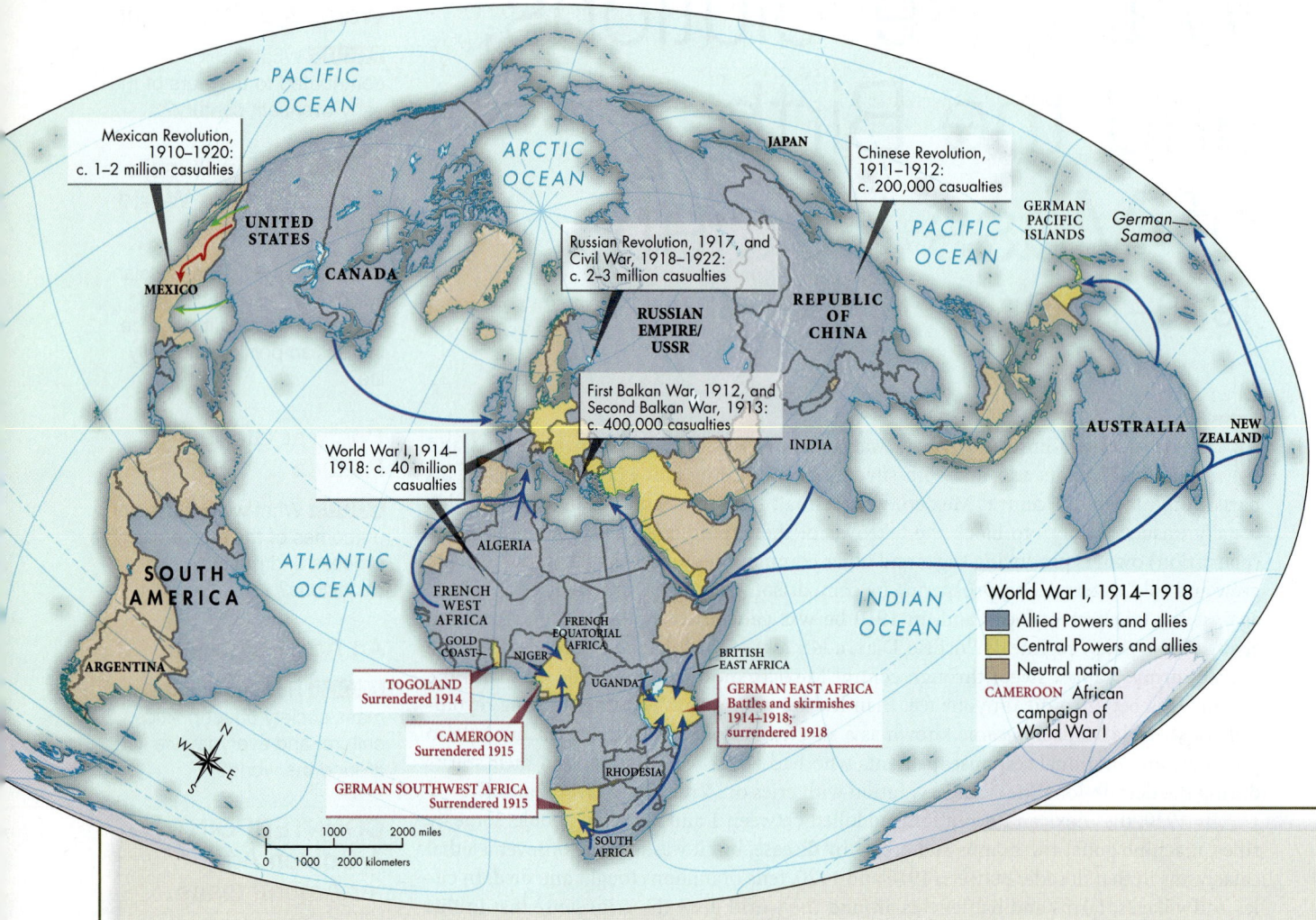

- **1910** Mexican Revolution begins
- **1911–1912** Revolutionaries overthrow Qing dynasty in China
- **1912** First Balkan War
- **1913** Second Balkan War
- **1914** World War I begins
- Russian Revolution begins; United States enters World War I; Lenin returns to Russia **1917**
- **1918** Bolsheviks take full control of Russian government; Treaty of Brest-Litovsk; armistice ends World War I
- Treaties comprising Peace of Paris signed, including the Treaty of Versailles with Germany **1919–1920**
- Lenin introduces New Economic Policy in Russia **1921**
- Germany forms Weimar Republic; May 4th movement in China **1919**

1910 | 1915 | 1920

off the Qing dynasty, and in 1912 and 1913 a host of Balkan peoples challenged the Ottoman and Austro-Hungarian empires. Their struggle led to World War I, which lasted from 1914 to 1918 and in turn spawned further wars and revolutions—most notably the Russian Revolution and the civil war that followed. The legacy of these conflicts shaped the rest of the century, and stories of soldiers' bravery—like that of Emiliano Zapata—filled the popular imagination through novels, films, and the new medium of radio.

These wars occurred on the crossroads of global trade and international politics. The Mexican Revolution, which was partly a struggle over U.S. control of the Mexican economy, led to American intervention, and even the peasant leader Emiliano Zapata corresponded with foreign leaders. The fall of the Qing left the future of a vast region in question and increased the interest of imperial powers in taking more of China's land and resources for themselves. World War I was a global war, fought not only on the European continent but in the Middle East, Africa, and the Pacific, as the powers pursued the goal of imperial expansion. All of these wars brought the masses into global politics, not only as soldiers but also as producers of the technology and supplies that soldiers needed. None of these wars, however, settled problems or restored social order as the combatants hoped. Instead, the Mexican Revolution destroyed the country's economy, while World War I produced political cataclysm, overturning the Russian, German, Ottoman, and Austro-Hungarian empires and changing the global balance of power. The Mexican Revolution, the fall of the Qing, World War I, and the Russian Revolution helped define early-twentieth-century history, and political uprisings continued into the 1920s, giving rise in turn to mass society.

Mass politics after the wars depended on mass culture, urbanization, and growing productivity, based on the postwar explosion of technology. Urban people from China to Argentina experienced the "Roaring Twenties," snapping up new consumer goods, drinking in the entertainment provided by films and radio, and relishing new personal freedoms. Modern communication technologies such as radio provided enjoyment, but they

MAPPING THE WORLD

Wars and Revolutions, 1910–1929

Wars and revolutions circled the globe in the early twentieth century. Areas where empire and imperial influence were at stake were especially hard hit, including a broad sweep of Eurasia. This era of local and global conflict brought dramatic political and other change, notably the fall of imperial dynasties, the exchange of colonial holdings and territory, and a stark toll in deaths from military campaigns, famine, and an influenza pandemic.

ROUTES ▼

- Route of colonial and British Commonwealth troops in support of Allied Powers, 1914–1918
- Route of U.S. forces during the Mexican Revolution, 1914–1916
- Route of Pancho Villa, 1913–1916

▪ **1922** Civil war ends in Russia; Mussolini comes to power in Italy

1925 1930

▪ **1923** Founding of the independent republic of Turkey under Mustafa Kemal; formation of Union of Soviet Socialist Republics

1920s Mohandas Gandhi's nonviolent movement for India independence attracts millions; mass culture flourishes in film and publishing industries; growth of radio transmissions; technology increases global productivity also spread political ideologies more widely than ever before. Some of these became the core of mass nationalist politics—some evil, like fascism, and some aimed at helping ordinary people, like the reform program of Emiliano Zapata.

OVERVIEW QUESTIONS

The major global development in this chapter: The wars of the decade 1910 to 1920 and their role in the creation of mass culture and society.

As you read, consider:

1. Why did the Mexican Revolution, the Chinese Revolution, World War I, and the Russian Revolution cause so much change far from the battlefield?
2. How did these wars help produce mass culture and society?
3. What role did technology play in these developments?

Revolutions, Local Wars, and World War

FOCUS
What factors contributed to the wars of the early twentieth century?

The Mexican Revolution, the Chinese Revolution, and the Balkan wars opened one of the bloodiest decades in human history. The reasons for the violence were many and complex. Some fought to overthrow corrupt leaders, others to free their nations from outside threats, and still others to win the international competition for power and wealth. The conflicts of the early twentieth century did not always produce the social, economic, and political outcomes that had originally inspired individuals and nations to take up arms. Though some nations gained new territory, the fighting did not produce stability and order, but rather sowed the seeds for a new round of conflict and upheaval.

Revolutionaries and Warriors: Mexico, China, and the Balkans

The tensions created by imperialism and modern state-building were apparent in many parts of the world by 1910. In Mexico liberal reformers and peasant leaders, backed by local armies, attempted to reform a corrupt political order, while in China modernizers threw off the power of the Qing. In 1913 Balkan countries waged war against the weakening Ottoman Empire to claim more land and resources. When the victors fought against one another later that year, the chaos provoked further turmoil. In 1914, what some have called the Third Balkan War erupted, a regional conflict that sparked the global cataclysm of World War I.

The Mexican Revolution

In 1910, liberal Mexican reformers headed by the wealthy landowner Francisco Madero began a drive to force the dictator Porfirio Diaz from office. Diaz saw himself as a modernizer. During his forty years in power, Mexico had built some twelve thousand miles of railroads, and its mines yielded increasing amounts of lead, copper, and zinc. However, only a handful of wealthy families and foreign investors reaped the riches of Mexico's development. By encouraging the concentration of agricultural lands in the hands of a few, Diaz's policies had impoverished village people. By 1900, just 1 percent of the population held 85 percent of the land, much of it seized by the government for the wealthy. Compounding Mexican landlessness was the government's policy of granting huge tracts of this confiscated land for cattle-raising and mining to U.S. companies, which further hurt the prospects of ordinary citizens. Madero and his well-off friends were political reformers, seeking a more open political system and the rule of law, but peasants and workers, who were often paid in goods instead of cash, had survival on their minds.

Given this bleak situation, peasant armies arose to work for land reform—that is, for social, not just political, change—as conflict erupted on many fronts. Zapata described their situation and their goals: "Considering that for the great majority, villages and citizens of Mexico possess not even the land that they work and that they cannot ameliorate their condition in the slightest . . . because the land, the mountains, and the water are in the hands of a very small number, the following is decreed: one-third of all monopolies will be expropriated . . . and distributed to those villages and citizens who are now prevented from having their traditional rights to the land prevail."[1] In the north, butcher and landowner Pancho Villa headed another popular army that fought for the entire decade against U.S. citizens and others who were taking over local land and resources. Complicating the revolution was simple factional fighting for local and regional power.

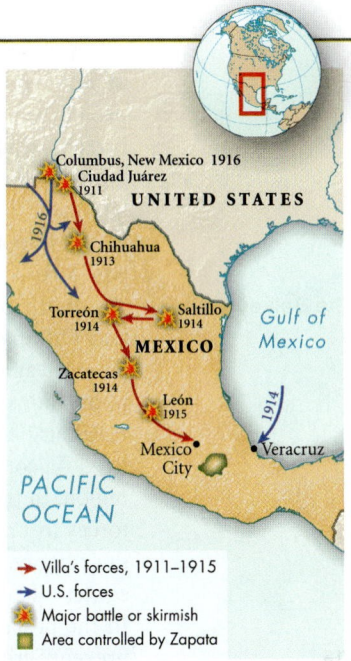

The Mexican Revolution, 1910–1911

The cause of the people was so strong, however, that in the end, long after the ouster of Diaz in 1911 and amid assassinations of leaders, including Zapata, the Mexican government announced land reform in its Constitution of 1917. The story of the hundreds of thousands of common warriors, many of them of Indian or mixed blood like Zapata, giving their lives for fundamental reform would inspire generations of Mexican writers and artists. The lasting cultural impact of this struggle is exemplified in the mural art of Diego Rivera, whose huge depictions of the Mexican Revolution were meant to show the masses their own past heroism and inspire them to remain committed to social justice.

The Chinese Revolution

As we saw in Chapter 26, the combination of Japan's lightning defeat of China in the Sino-Japanese War (1894) and the Boxer Rebellion (1899–1900) thoroughly discredited the Qing dynasty. These humiliating events ushered in a wave of reform, some of it sponsored by the Qing administration itself. Schools, urban planning, and women's rights all filled the agenda of reformers. Behind the flurry of change, modernizing businessmen, professionals, and intellectuals sensed that the Manchu dynasty was dangerously outdated and needed to be replaced by new rulers drawn from the Chinese people themselves. Influenced by Western ideas of evolution, reformers likened the Manchus, who descended from northern nomads, to undeveloped peoples of past times who "lived in dens and wore pelts."[2] In 1911 to 1912 a group of revolutionaries organized as the **Guomindang** (gwo-min-DAHNG), or Nationalist Party, overthrew the long-lived dynasty and declared China a republic. Their leader, the medical doctor Sun Yatsen (soon yot-SEN), who like many proponents of change had been educated outside of China, used a cluster of Western ideas in his slogan "nationalism, democracy, and socialism." However, he interpreted these ideas in the context of long-standing Chinese values. For example, whereas Marxist socialists called for an end to private property, Sun's socialism was based in such traditional charitable thinking as the view that all people should have enough food. Sun's Guomindang called for the revival of the Chinese belief in correct behavior between governors and the governed, economic and social reform in line with scientific theories, and the end of foreign domination over China.

Sun's stirring leadership helped set China on a modernizing course, but he was not a capable administrator and quickly resigned in favor of a powerful former Qing general, Yuan Shikai (yoo-ahn shee-KI). Yuan was no democrat, however, and in 1916 he broke with the Nationalists to declare the foundation of a new imperial dynasty. When regional generals rejected Yuan's imperial claims, formed their own armies, and began to act as warlords, the country descended into a decade of chaos.

Guomindang The Chinese nationalist party founded by Sun Yatsen that overthrew the Qing dynasty and fought to rule mainland China from 1911 to 1949.

Yet aspirations for a new way of life continued to grow, university life flourished, and literature became pointedly directed toward the need to modernize China. Reform-minded people were inspired by author Lu Xun, whose novella *The True Story of Ah Q* (1921–1922) presents what Lu called the typical Chinese, arrogant no matter how pathetic his station in life and full of useless maxims: "If a woman walks alone on the street, she must want to seduce bad men." Such backward thinking on Ah Q's part threatens his survival in modern times, just as China, in Lu's view, was held back by out-of-date ideas and the blindness of leaders who focused on China's glorious past and ignored the problems of its troubled present.

The Balkan Wars

In the Balkans politicians whipped up ethnic nationalism to challenge both Habsburg and Ottoman power. Greece, Serbia, Bulgaria, Romania, and Montenegro had recently emerged as autonomous states, almost all of them home to ethnically and religiously diverse populations. These small states sought strength as modern nations by taking Ottoman and Habsburg territory in which others from their own imagined majority ethnic group lived—a complicated desire, given the historic intermingling of ethnicities throughout the region. In the First Balkan War, in 1912, Serbia, Bulgaria, Greece, and Montenegro joined forces to break off Macedonia and Albania from the Ottomans. The victors divided up their booty, but they soon turned against one another. Serbia, Greece, and Montenegro contested Bulgarian gains in the Second Balkan War in 1913 and won a quick victory. In the peace treaty that followed the fighting, an alarmed Austria-Hungary managed to prevent Serbia from gaining parts of Albania, further inflaming Serb grievances toward the dual monarchy. Many Serbs dreamed of crushing Austria-Hungary with the help of their powerful Slavic ally Russia, a dream the Russian government did little to discourage. Thus, the nationalist aspirations of Slavic Serbs contributed to growing tensions between two great European powers, Austria-Hungary and Russia. Under these circumstances, events in the Balkans took on international importance.

Outbreak of World War I

The situation came to a head in June 1914 in the Habsburg-controlled Bosnian capital of Sarajevo when a Bosnian Serb, funded by the Serbian secret police, assassinated the heir to the Habsburg throne, Archduke Franz Ferdinand, and his wife Sophie. The young assassin hoped thereby to free his homeland from the Habsburgs and unite it with Serbia. According to its alliance with Germany, Austria-Hungary had the promise of full German support if it launched an offensive war to defeat the Serbians once and for all. So it issued a stern ultimatum: the Serbian government had just forty-eight hours in which to agree to demands that would amount to Austrian control of the Serbian state. When Serbia refused to meet one of these demands, Austria declared war on Serbia on July 28. Equipped with well-prepared war plans and armed to the teeth for war, the major European powers were eager to end the international tensions that existed among them over global, national, and even domestic issues. Thus, the origins of World War I lay in great-power interests in the Balkans, long-standing alliances and strategies for war among the powers, the buildup of military technologies, and a climate of rivalry for territory and influence. This so-called Third Balkan War proved to be more than any of the powers—or the world—bargained for.

Fighting World War I

World War I erupted in August 1914. On one side stood the Central Powers—Austria-Hungary and Germany—which had evolved from Bismarck's Triple Alliance of 1882 (see Chapter 25). On the other side were the Allies—France, Great Britain, and Russia—which had emerged as a bloc from an alliance between France and Great Britain that became the Triple Entente when Russia joined in 1907. In 1915, Italy, originally part of Bismarck's Triple Alliance, went over to the Entente (or Allies) in hopes of making postwar gains. As the fighting spread to the combatants' overseas colonies and non-European powers took sides, the war became a global conflict. Japan, eager to extend its empire into China, soon joined the Allies, while the Ottoman Empire united with the Central Powers against its traditional enemy, Russia (see Map 27.1, page 898). In time, the United States would enter the war as well, contributing to the Allied victory.

The Blueprint for War

The antagonists hungered for the same power and prosperity that inspired imperialism. Germany hoped to acquire a far-flung empire by annexing Russian territory, parts of Belgium, France, and Luxembourg, and even Austria-Hungary. Austria-Hungary aimed to rebuild its power, which was under attack from the competing nationalist movements within its borders and by Serbs and other Slavs outside them. Russia wanted to reassert its great-power position as protector of the Slavs by adding all of Poland to the Russian Empire and by controlling other Slavic peoples. The French, too, craved territory, especially the return of Alsace and Lorraine, lost after the Franco-Prussian War of 1870 to 1871 (discussed in Chapter 25). The British sought to secure their world empire by defeating its competitors. The secret Treaty of London (1915) promised Italy territory in Africa, Anatolia (modern Turkey), and the Balkans in return for joining the Allies.

In August 1914, armies had at their disposal machine guns and rifles, airplanes, battleships, submarines, and cars, railroads, and other motorized transport. Newer technologies such as chlorine gas, tanks, and bombs would develop between 1914 and 1918. Nonetheless, officers on both sides held to a nineteenth-century strategy, the "cult of the offensive," in which continuous spirited attacks and flashing sabers and bayonets would be decisive. The colonies of the European powers were to provide massive assistance to wage such offensives. Some 1 million Africans, another 2 million Indians, and more than a million members of the British Commonwealth countries, notably Canada, Australia, and New Zealand, served on the battlefronts, while the imperial powers conscripted uncounted numbers of colonists as forced laborers. In the face of massive firepower, the outdated "cult of the offensive" would cost millions of these lives.

The Battlefronts, 1914–1916

The first months of the war crushed hopes of quick victory. All the major armies mobilized rapidly. The Germans were guided by a strategy devised by Alfred von Schlieffen, a former chief of the general staff. The Schlieffen Plan outlined a way to avoid a two-front war by concentrating on one foe at a time. It called for a rapid and concentrated blow to the west against France, accompanied by a light holding action to the east against France's ally, Russia. According to the plan, France would be defeated in six weeks, and only then would German forces be concentrated against Russia, which, the Germans believed, would mobilize slowly. The attack on France began in the summer of 1914 and proceeded through Belgium, but there it met unexpected and spirited resistance, slowing the German advance and allowing British and French troops to reach the northern front. In massive battles neither side could defeat the other, and casualties were in the millions. The unprecedented firepower of modern weaponry turned what was supposed to be an offensive war of movement into a stationary, defensive stalemate along a line of trenches that stretched from the North Sea through Belgium and northern France to Switzerland. Deep within trenches dug along this front, millions of soldiers lived in nightmarish shelters.

Meanwhile, on the eastern front, the massive Russian army, some 12 million strong, mobilized more quickly than expected, driving into German territory by mid-August. The Russian generals believed that no matter how ill equipped their army was, no army could stand up to their massive numbers. Russian success was short-lived, however. The Germans crushed the tsar's army in East Prussia in the fall of 1914 and then turned south to Galicia. Victory against Russia emboldened the commanding generals to demand and get more troops for the eastern front. Nonetheless, by year's end Germany had failed to knock out the Russians and was bogged down in the very two-front war its military planners had taken such pains to avoid (see again Map 27.1).

War at sea proved equally indecisive. When the Allies blockaded ports to prevent supplies from reaching Germany and Austria-Hungary, the Germans responded with an intensive submarine, or U-boat ("underwater boat"), campaign against both Allied and neutral shipping. Despite U.S. deaths, President Woodrow Wilson maintained a policy of neutrality, and Germany, unwilling to provoke Wilson further, called off unrestricted submarine warfare—that is, attacks on neutral shipping. Throughout 1915 the British hoped to knock out the Ottomans and open ports to Russia by attacking at

MAP 27.1

World War I in Europe and the Middle East, 1914–1918

World War I transformed many parts of Europe and the Middle East into wastelands because of the increasingly devastating weaponry. Farmlands were put out of commission for years, and livestock near battlefields was decimated. On the western front the damage was mostly confined to northern France, but on the eastern front the destructive power was mobile as armies crossed some areas several times. An effective blockade added to the hunger that central and eastern Europeans suffered as the war came to an end in 1918.

the Dardanelles Strait. At Gallipoli, casualty rates for both sides of 50 to 60 percent only yielded stalemate. "A miserable time," one Irish soldier called Gallipoli, as his comrades from New Zealand, Australia, and elsewhere in the empire had their heads blown off and their limbs smashed to pulp. Horrific suffering in this single battle

The Dead of World War I
Even as the death toll mounted during World War I, politicians and crowned heads of state across Europe refused to give up the idea of victory. For most soldiers, this political decision meant ongoing suffering in the trenches and, for millions, hysteria, crippling wounds, or death. The bones of the unburied were collected from the battlefield as shown here in Verdun, for placement in ossuaries, at the war's end. (Bettmann/Corbis.)

strengthened Australia's and New Zealand's will to break with British leadership, which had led them into the tragedy.

Both sides refused a negotiated peace: "No peace before England is defeated and destroyed," Kaiser William II railed against his cousin, Britain's King George V. "Only amidst the ruins of London will I forgive Georgy." French leaders called for a "war to the death." General staffs on both sides continued to prepare fierce attacks: after heavy artillery pounded enemy trenches and gun emplacements, troops obeyed the order to go "over the top" by scrambling out of their trenches and into battle, usually to be mowed down by machine-gun fire from the tens of thousands of defenders in their own trenches. On the western front, casualties of one hundred thousand and more for a single campaign became commonplace. In 1916, in an effort to break French morale, the Germans launched massive assaults on the fortress at Verdun, firing as many as a million shells in a single day during the attack. Combined French and German losses totaled close to a million men, whose anonymous bones today fill a vast shrine at the site.

The Soldiers' War

Had the military leaders thoroughly dominated the scene, historians judge, all armies would have been utterly demolished in nonstop offensives by the end of 1915. Yet ordinary soldiers in this war were not automatons, and in the face of what seemed to them suicidal orders, soldiers on both sides sometimes refused to engage in battle. Enemies facing each other across the trenches frequently ate their meals in peace, even though the trenches were within hand-grenade reach. Right up to the closing year of the war, soldiers fraternized with the "enemy," playing an occasional game of soccer, exchanging mementos, and entering into silent agreements not to fight. A British veteran of the trenches explained to a new recruit that the Germans "don't want to fight any more than we do, so there's a kind of understanding between us. Don't fire at us and we'll not fire at you." Male bonding aided survival: soldiers picked lice from one another's bodies and clothes and came to love one another, sometimes even passionately.

Troops from Asian and African colonies, taken like the European whites from their everyday lives, often had different experiences, especially because colonial soldiers were often put in the front ranks where the risks were greatest. Many suffered from the rigors of a totally unfamiliar climate and strange food, as well as from their encounter with Western war technology. Colonial troops' perspectives changed as they saw their "masters" completely undone and "uncivilized." For when fighting did break out, trenches became a veritable hell of shelling and sniping, flying body parts, rotting cadavers, and blinding gas. "I am greatly distressed in mind," one South Asian soldier wrote to his family, echoing the hopelessness that so many soldiers felt on seeing their comrades lose hands, feet, and entire limbs.[3] Colonizers and colonized could alike be reduced to hysteria through the sheer stress and violence of battle; others became cynical. "It might be me tomorrow," a young British soldier wrote his mother in 1916. "Who cares?"

Civilians at War: The Home Front

World War I quickly became a "**total war**," one in which all of the resources of each nation were harnessed to the war effort and lines between the home front and the battlefield were blurred. Civilians manufactured the machine guns, poisonous gases, bombs, airplanes, and eventually tanks that were the backbone of technological warfare. Increased and well-organized production of coffins, canes, wheelchairs, and artificial limbs was also a wartime necessity. Because their efforts were vital to military success, civilians were required to work overtime and sacrifice for victory. To supply the battlefront efficiently, governments took over the operation of the economy and suppressed dissent.

Politics Suspended

Initially, political parties in each combatant nation put aside their differences. For decades socialist parties had preached that "the worker has no country" and that nationalism was mere ideology meant to keep workers disunited and obedient to their employers. In August 1914, however, most socialists backed the war, trading worker solidarity for national unity in a time of crisis. Although many feminists were opposed to war, the British suffrage leader Emmeline Pankhurst was hardly alone in also becoming a militant nationalist. "What is the use of fighting for a vote if we have not got a country to vote in?" she asked. Others hoped that the spirit of nationalism could end prejudices. "In the German fatherland there are no longer any Christians and Jews, any believers and disbelievers, there are only Germans," one rabbi proudly announced. National leaders stressed ending political division in the name of victory: "I no longer recognize [political] parties," Kaiser William II declared on August 4, 1914. "I recognize only Germans." Governments mobilized the masses on the home front to endure long hours and food shortages with large doses of propaganda that promoted patriotism by demonizing the enemy (see Seeing the Past: Wartime Propaganda). New laws made it a crime to criticize official policies. For a time, it seemed as if old barriers would be broken down and new bonds formed among the citizens of each nation.

As the war dragged on, social and political tensions returned, and some individuals and groups began to lobby for peace. In 1915, activists in the international women's movement met in The Hague to call for an end to war. "We can no longer endure . . . brute force as the only solution of international disputes," declared Dutch physician Aletta Jacobs. Some socialists moved to neutral countries such as Switzerland to work for a negotiated peace settlement.

The Civilians' War

The requirements of total war upset the social and political order. In the early days of fighting many women lost their jobs when luxury shops, textile factories, and other nonmilitary establishments closed. Wartime conditions, however, soon created new opportunities for women workers. As men left the workplace to join the fighting, women moved into a variety of high-paying jobs, including munitions production, metallurgy, and services like streetcar conducting and ambulance driving. Workingmen often protested that women, in the words of one metalworker, were "sending men to the slaughter" and robbing them of their role as breadwinner. Many people, including some women, objected to women's loss of femininity, as workers cut their hair short and wore utilitarian slacks and streamlined clothing. "The feminine in me decreased more and more, and I did not know

total war The vital involvement of civilians in the war industry, the blurring of home and battle fronts, and the use of industrial weaponry to destroy an enemy.

SEEING THE PAST

Wartime Propaganda

The French Are Using Monkeys: A German Magazine Cover
(Christel Gerstenberg/Corbis.)

Will Germany Take Over the World?: An Australian Poster
(K.J. Historical/Corbis.)

Propaganda agencies within governments on both sides in World War I touted the war as a patriotic mission to resist villainous enemies. They used both film and print to turn people who formerly saw themselves as neighbors into hate-filled enemies. British propagandists fabricated atrocities that the German "Huns" supposedly committed against Belgians, and German propaganda warned that French African troops would rape German women if Germany were defeated. Efforts were often clumsy: a British film, *The Battle of the Somme* (1916), so obviously sanitized the war's horrors that soldiers in the audience roared with laughter, though civilians found it riveting.

Brightly colored propaganda posters, representing the best lithographic technology, were pasted to walls and placed in windows. Government experts hired the best graphic artists to execute their carefully chosen themes. In the image on the left, German propagandists picked up on the widespread use of African soldiers in the French army to make their point, depicting the enemy in this magazine cover as monkeys. "The Ersatz Battalion—Senegal" speaks to the effectiveness of the enemy. By contrast, an Australian artist drew the Allied poster on the right representing the German enemy with a frightening face and its hands dripping blood.

EXAMINING THE EVIDENCE

1. What accounts for these specific representations of the enemy?
2. How would the audience respond to each representation, and how would the images have aroused commitment to the war?
3. Alongside this type of caricature was sentimental wartime propaganda depicting brave soldiers, faithful wives, and children in need of their hardy fathers' and other male protection. Why was there such variety in propaganda, and which type of image would you judge to be most effective?

whether to be sad or glad about this," wrote one Russian nurse about putting on rough male clothing for the battlefield. Despite some alarm, a "new woman" with different clothing, a respectable job, and new responsibilities for supporting her family was emerging in great numbers from the war.

Rising social tensions revolved around issues of class as well as gender. Workers toiled longer hours eating less, while many in the upper classes bought abundant food and fashionable clothing on the black market (outside the official system of rationing). Governments allowed many businesses to keep raising prices and thus earn higher profits than ever, practices that caused the cost of living to surge and thus contributed to social strife. Shortages of staples such as bread, sugar, and meat caused hardships everywhere. A German roof-workers' association pleaded for relief: "We can no longer go on. Our children are starving." Civilians in occupied areas and in such colonies as German East Africa suffered oppressive conditions, facing harsh forced labor along with skyrocketing taxes and prices. Thus, even though political debate officially stopped during the war, the prolonged conflict created political grievances among people worldwide.

Revolution in Russia and the End of World War I

FOCUS

Why did the Russian Revolution take place, and what changes did it produce in Russian politics and daily life?

By 1917 the situation was becoming desperate for everyone—politicians, the military, and civilians. In February of that year, the German government, responding to public anger over mounting casualties, resumed unrestricted submarine warfare—a move that brought the United States into the war two months later, after German U-boats had sunk several American ships. Meanwhile, as prices soared, tenants across Europe conducted rent strikes, and factory hands and white-collar workers alike walked off the job. In the spring of 1917, French soldiers mutinied against further offensives, while in Russia, wartime protest turned into outright revolution.

Revolution in Russia

Of all the warring nations, Russia sustained the greatest number of casualties—7.5 million by 1917. Unlike other heads of state, Tsar Nicholas II failed to unify his government or his people. Nicholas was capable of making patriotic gestures, such as changing the German-sounding name of St. Petersburg to Petrograd, but he stubbornly insisted on conducting the war himself instead of using experienced and knowledgeable officials. "Is this stupidity or treason?" one member of the Russian Duma asked of the ineffective wartime effort. In March 1917, crowds of working women and civilians commemorating International Women's Day swarmed the streets of Petrograd and began looting shops for food. Other workers, furious at the government's inability to provide basic necessities, joined them. Many in the army defected, angered by the massive casualties caused by their substandard weapons. Nicholas abdicated that same month, bringing the three-hundred-year-old Romanov dynasty to an abrupt end.

The Provisional Government

Politicians from the old Duma formed a new ruling entity called the Provisional Government. At first hopes were high that under the Provisional Government, as one revolutionary poet put it, "our false, filthy, boring, hideous life should become a just, pure, merry, and beautiful life." However, the abdication of the tsar did not end internal conflict in Russia. Instead, the Russian Revolution unleashed social and political forces that had been building for decades. Spontaneously elected **soviets**—councils of workers and soldiers—campaigned to end favor of the wealthy and urged concern for workers and the poor. The peasantry, another force competing for power, began to seize aristocratic estates. Meanwhile, the Provisional Government seemed unwilling to end the war and unable to improve living conditions.

soviet A council of workers and soldiers elected to represent the people in the Russian revolutions of 1905 and 1917.

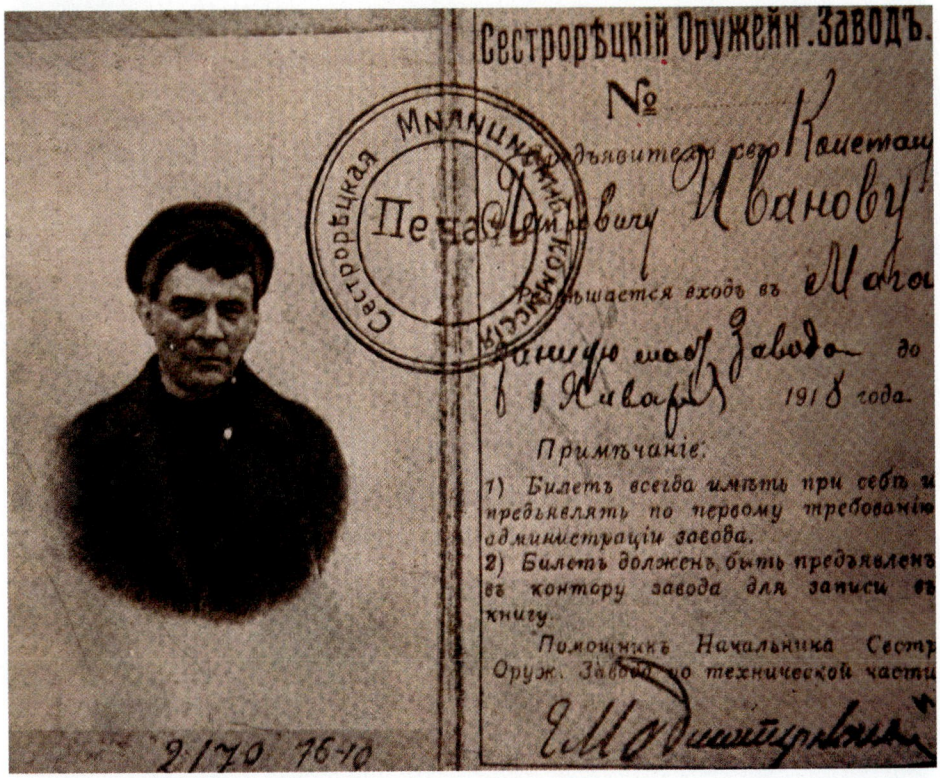

Lenin's False Identity Papers, 1917

Before the Russian Revolution began in 1917, Bolshevik leader V. I. Lenin had lived in forced exile, agitated among the Social Democrats in foreign lands, and preached loudly against World War I. During the Russian Revolution itself, he used many disguises and false identity papers such as the one shown here to escape notice by the Provisional Government, which he worked to bring down. By the autumn of 1917, the war was still going so badly for Russia and inflicted so much additional suffering that the Bolsheviks were able to take power. (Private Collection/The Stapleton Collection/Bridgeman Art Library.)

In April 1917, Vladimir Ilyich Lenin, leader of a faction of the Russian Socialist Party, returned from exile in Siberia, his safe rail transportation provided by the Germans, who hoped that Lenin might further weaken the Russian war effort. Son of a prominent provincial official, Lenin nonetheless lived his life as a revolutionary, beginning political activism while at university and then becoming a political organizer of Marxist and working-class groups across Europe. Among his principles was the belief that the Russian people needed to be led by an elite group of revolutionaries—not by the masses themselves. Those belonging to Lenin's faction were called **Bolsheviks**. On returning to Russia, Lenin quickly called on his countrymen to withdraw from World War 1, for the soviets to seize power on behalf of workers and poor peasants, and for all private land to be nationalized. The Bolsheviks challenged the Provisional Government with the slogans "All power to the soviets!" and "Peace, land, and bread!" In contrast, the Provisional Government—like governments across Europe—continued to seek popular support through battlefield victories, even as the Russian army continued to suffer staggering losses.

The Bolshevik Takeover

In November 1917, the Bolsheviks seized power in the name of the soviets. When in January 1918 elections for a constituent assembly failed to give the Bolsheviks a majority, the party took over the government by force. Observing Marxist doctrine, the Bolsheviks abolished private property, nationalizing factories in order to restore productivity. The new government asked Germany for peace and agreed to the Treaty of Brest-Litovsk (March 1918), which placed vast regions of the Russian Empire under German occupation (see again Map 27.1). Because the loss of millions of square miles put Petrograd at risk, the Bolsheviks relocated the capital to Moscow. To distinguish themselves from the socialists or Social Democrats who had voted for the disastrous war in 1914, the Bolsheviks formally adopted the name Communists, taken from Marx's writings. Lenin agreed to the huge loss of territory not only because he had promised to bring peace to Russia, but because he believed the rest of Europe would soon rebel and overthrow the capitalist order.

Opposition to Bolshevik policies swiftly formed and soon mushroomed into full-fledged civil war. The pro-Bolsheviks (or "Reds") faced an array of antirevolutionary forces

Bolshevik A faction of the Russian Socialist Party that advocated control of revolutionary activity by a disciplined group of the party elite instead of by the working class as a whole; renamed "Communist" by Lenin following the Russian Revolution.

Civil War

(the "Whites"). Among the Whites, the tsarist military leadership, composed of many aristocratic landlords, was joined by non-Russian-nationality groups eager to regain independence. Russia's former allies, notably the United States, Britain, France, and Japan, landed troops in the country, hoping to defeat the Bolsheviks. The Whites failed, however, because instead of conducting a united effort, the individual groups competed with one another: the pro-tsarist forces, for example, wanted a restored empire, whereas the nationality groups such as the Ukrainians and Lithuanians wanted freedom as individual nation-states.

In contrast, the Bolsheviks had a more unified leadership that essentially reshaped Marxism. Leon Trotsky, Bolshevik commissar of war, built a highly disciplined army by ending the democratic procedures, such as the election of officers, that had originally attracted soldiers to Bolshevism. The Cheka (secret police) set up detention camps for political opponents and often shot them without trial. The expansion of the Cheka, Red Army, and bureaucracy undermined the promise of Marxism that revolution would bring a "withering away" of the state.

Finally, the Bolsheviks organized revolutionary Marxism worldwide. In March 1919, they founded the **Comintern** (Communist International), a centrally run organization dedicated to preaching communism globally. By mid-1921, the Red Army had secured the Crimea, the Caucasus, and the Muslim borderlands in Central Asia, and in 1922 the Japanese withdrew from Siberia—the last of the foreign invaders to leave—ending the civil war. The Bolsheviks were now in charge of a state, the Union of Soviet Socialist Republics (USSR), as multiethnic as the former Russian Empire. In the meantime, civil war had brought Russia only unprecedented disease, hunger, and death. Nonetheless, people around the world saw in Soviet communism the promise of an improved life for the masses.

Ending the War: 1918

Although Russia was out of World War I by the spring of 1918, much of the rest of the world remained mired in the brutal conflict. Relying on Arab, African, and Indian troops, the British took Baghdad in 1917 as well as Palestine, Lebanon, and Syria from the Ottomans (see again Map 27.1). In sub-Saharan Africa, more than a million Kenyans and Tanzanians were conscripted by the Europeans to fight a vicious campaign for control of East Africa. African troops serving the imperial powers died by the thousands, as did the civilian population whose resources were confiscated and villages burned by competing powers. The Japanese seized German holdings in China to enlarge their influence on the mainland.

Allied Victory

In the spring of 1918 the Central Powers made one final attempt to smash through the Allied lines, but by then the British and French had started making limited but effective use of tanks that could withstand machine-gun fire. In the summer of 1918, the Allies, now fortified by U.S. troops, pushed back the Germans all along the western front and headed toward Germany. In an effort to shift the blame for defeat away from themselves, the German military leaders who had been running the country allowed a civilian government to form and ask for peace. After the war, the generals would claim that weak-willed civilians had dealt the military a "stab in the back," forcing Germany to surrender when victory was still possible. As the Central Powers collapsed on all fronts and mutinies and rebellions broke out across Germany, on November 11, 1918, delegates from the two sides signed an armistice ending the war.

Comintern An international organization of workers established by the Bolsheviks to spread communism worldwide.

Fourteen Points A proposal by U.S. president Woodrow Wilson for peace during World War I based on "settlement" rather than "victory" and on the self-determination of peoples.

In the course of four years, civilization had been sorely tested, if not shattered. Conservative figures put the battlefield toll at a minimum of 10 million dead and 30 million wounded, incapacitated, or eventually to die of their wounds. In every European combatant country, industrial and agricultural production had plummeted, and much of the reduced output had been put to military use. From 1918 to 1919, the weakened global population suffered an influenza epidemic that left as many as 100 million more dead. "They carried the dead people on mule-drawn carts without even being in boxes," one fighter in Pancho Villa's army reported of the flu in Mexico. "Many poor people left their small children as orphans . . . without father, without mother, without anything."[4] The influenza pandemic only added to the horrifying fact that total war had drained society of resources and population and had sown the seeds of future catastrophes.

Postwar Global Politics

FOCUS

What were the major outcomes of the peacemaking process and postwar conditions?

Across Europe, civilians and returning soldiers rose in protest after the war. Even as peace talks began in 1919, the red flag of socialist revolution flew from the city hall in Glasgow, Scotland, while in cities of the collapsing Austro-Hungarian Empire, workers set up soviet-like councils to reshape politics. The conduct of the war—including forced labor—damaged Western claims to be more advanced than other parts of the world, causing a surging resistance to colonialism even as the victorious Allies took steps to secure and expand their empires. Such was the highly charged backdrop for peacemaking.

The Paris Peace Conference
1919–1920

The Paris Peace Conference opened in January 1919 with the leaders of the United States, Great Britain, and France dominating the proceedings. Western leaders worried about communism spreading far beyond Russia's borders and about pressure from their angry citizens, who demanded revenge. France, for example, had lost 1.3 million people—almost an entire generation of young men, more than a million buildings, and thousands of miles of railroad lines and roads had been destroyed while the war was fought on French soil. The British slogan "Hang the Kaiser!" captured the public mood. Italian officials arrived on the scene demanding the territory promised to them in the 1915 Treaty of London. Meanwhile U.S. president Woodrow Wilson, head of the growing world power that had contributed to the Allied victory, had his own agenda. His **Fourteen Points**, the peace proposal on which the truce had been based, were steeped in the language of freedom and called for open diplomacy, an "open-minded" settlement of colonial issues, and the self-determination of peoples—meaning the right of national groups to have autonomy if they wanted it. Amid disagreements over the need to punish the Central Powers or to prevent too harsh or humiliating a peace, representatives from Middle Eastern states, Japan, and other deeply interested parties lobbied for fair treatment from the victorious powers. World War I had drawn in non-European peoples from around the world, and now, having fought in the war, they wanted a say in the peace.

Paris Peace Conference, 1918

Allied heads of state, diplomats, military personnel, and policy experts dominated the peace conference that opened in Paris in 1918. Also attending were a variety of other participants in the war seeking a just peace, national independence, or special acknowledgment of their ethnic or other interest group. Among these were leaders from the Middle East, who had rallied their own armed forces to fight for the Allies on the promise of postwar independence. Their small presence in this picture symbolizes the utter disregard for those promises in the Peace of Paris settlement. (The Art Archive/Domenica del Corriere/Collection Dagli Orti.)

MAP 27.2

The Peace of Paris in Central and Eastern Europe, 1920

Where mighty empires had once reigned over central and eastern Europe, new states appeared and new forms of government replaced dynastic rule. These small states were generally fragile due to their very novelty, postwar economic difficulties, and the need to modernize agriculture and to develop industrial capacity. Their citizens faced more powerful neighbors—Germany and the Soviet Union—whose aspirations to expand would soon menace the region's security.

The Peace of Paris Treaties

After six months, the Allies produced the Peace of Paris (1919–1920), composed of a cluster of individual treaties. The treaties separated Austria from Hungary, reduced Hungary by almost two-thirds of its inhabitants and three-quarters of its territory, and broke up the Ottoman Empire. The Habsburg Empire was replaced by a group of small, internally divided, and relatively weak states: Czechoslovakia, Poland, and the Kingdom of the Serbs, Croats, and Slovenes, soon renamed Yugoslavia. Austria and Hungary were both left reeling at their loss of territory and resources (see Map 27.2).

The settlement with Germany, the Treaty of Versailles (named after the palace where the treaty was signed), was the centerpiece of the Peace of Paris. France recovered Alsace and Lorraine, and Germany was ordered to pay substantial reparations for civilian damage during the war—terms that would cripple the German economy. It was also directed to give up its colonies, reduce its army, stop manufacturing offensive weapons, and deliver a large amount of free coal each year to Belgium and France. The average German saw in the terms of the Treaty of Versailles an unmerited humiliation of "war guilt" that was compounded by Article 231 of the treaty, which assigned "responsibility" for the war to "the aggression of Germany and her allies." Germany, a powerful nation, was branded an outcast in the global community.

League of Nations

Besides redrawing the map of Europe, the diplomats created the **League of Nations**, an organization whose members had a joint responsibility for maintaining peace through negotiation—a principle called **collective security**, which was to replace the divisive secrecy of prewar power politics. In Woodrow Wilson's vision, the League would peacefully guide the world toward disarmament, arbitrate its members' disputes, and monitor labor conditions around the world. However, the U.S. Senate, in an embarrassing defeat for the president, both failed to ratify the peace settlement and refused to join the League. Moreover, both Germany and Russia initially were excluded from the League and were thus blocked from participating in international consensus-building with the forty-two founding member nations. The absence of these three major powers weakened the League as a global peacekeeper from the outset.

League of Nations The international organization set up following World War I to maintain peace by arbitrating disputes and promoting collective security.

collective security The system of international diplomacy, especially involving the peaceful resolution of disputes, established by the League of Nations.

The end to imperialism was at the top of many non-Western representatives' agenda, but they were to be denied. The covenant, or charter, of the League of Nations organized the new administration of the surrendered colonies and territories of Germany and the Ottoman Empire through a system of mandates (see Map 27.3). The European powers

MAP 27.3

The Mandate System in Africa and the Middle East, 1924

Instead of granting Middle Eastern and African peoples the promised rights and independence that had brought them into the war, the Allies scooped up former territories controlled by the Germans and the Ottomans and converted them into "mandates"—in effect, colonies. The growing importance of oil and of other resources lay behind this seizure of control.

Mandate System

exercised political control over mandated territory, but some local leaders retained limited authority. The League covenant justified the **mandate system** as providing governance by "advanced nations" over territories "not yet able to stand by themselves under the strenuous conditions of the modern world."

Not surprisingly, the people of the new mandates were furious. Sharif Husayn ibn Ali had mobilized a substantial force to wage war against the Ottomans because of agreements with Britain for an independent Syria. His son Faisal was humiliated in Paris when it became clear that no such independence was forthcoming. On his return to the Middle East Faisal called on the crowds to "choose either to be slaves or masters of your own destiny."[5] Rebellions against France and Britain erupted in the Middle East, but they were put down. Outside of the Middle East, opponents of colonialism redoubled their organizational efforts in such movements as pan-Africanism, whose members now held regular international meetings with the goal of promoting solidarity among blacks everywhere and, eventually, a vast self-governing union of all African peoples. "Never again will the darker people of the world occupy just the place they had before," the African American leader W.E.B. Du Bois predicted in 1918. The postwar settlements, like the war itself, contributed to renewed activism among colonial peoples around the world.

Struggles for Reform and Independence

In the aftermath of war many of the world's peoples took advantage of Western weakness to seek independence from outside domination. These struggles occurred in remnants of the Ottoman Empire, China, India, and Africa. In the face of such determination, imperial powers from Japan to Britain not only resisted loosening their domination, but often resorted to violence to maintain and expand their empires.

Turkey Emerges from the Ottoman Empire

The Allied invasion of the Ottoman Empire caused chaos and suffering from Anatolia through Syria, Lebanon, and Egypt. Allied blockades during the war led to widespread starvation, and Allied agents provoked rebellion against the Ottoman grip to weaken the empire. From 1915 to 1916 the Ottoman leadership carried out the mass deportation of unknown numbers—estimates range from 300 thousand to 1.5 million—of Armenians in the empire, claiming that they were spying and plotting with the Russians to revolt in wartime. Armenians were rounded up and sent on marches into the desert to perish. Their considerable property was stolen, and their fellow villagers moved into abandoned Armenian homes. Witnesses based in the region sent horrifying reports around the world, but the Ottoman position was that "the Armenians have only themselves to blame." They were, in the words of one official, "a menace to the Turkish race."[6]

Once the war was over and the Ottoman Empire disbanded, determined Turkish military officers resisted the continuing presence of the Allies, who were inciting the Greeks to seize Ottoman lands. Led by General Mustafa Kemal, the remnants of the Ottoman army traveled the countryside calling for a democratically elected national assembly to represent the voice of the people. Kemal preached an anti-imperialist message in the face of the British occupation of Istanbul: "All we want is to save our country from sharing the fate of India and Egypt."[7] He and his followers also pushed for the primacy of ethnic Turks, despite the presence of many ethnic groups who had lived together for centuries. A war of independence broke out as the Allies tried to suppress the Turkish reformers and bring about a partition of Anatolia, but the spirit of nationalism proved too strong. Kemal, who later took the name Atatürk ("first among Turks"), led the Turks to found an independent republic in 1923 (see Map 27.4).

After victory in 1923, Kemal became head of the government. From the beginning he worked to bring the region into the orbit of Western modernity and to craft a capitalist economy. "A nation must be strong in spirit, knowledge, science and morals," he announced.[8] In an effort to Westernize Turkish culture and the new Turkish state, Kemal moved the capital from Istanbul to Ankara in 1923, officially changed the ancient Greek name *Constantinople* to the Turkish *Istanbul* in 1930, mandated Western dress for men

mandate system A system of regional control over former Ottoman lands awarded by the League of Nations' charter to the victors in World War I.

MAP 27.4

Turkey Under Mustafa Kemal, 1923

With Allied support and military assistance, Greece invaded Turkey after World War I in an attempt to take it over. Armenia also attacked. Turkish nationalists under the command of Mustafa Kemal defeated both groups despite a British drive to control Istanbul and the Dardanelles Strait. The United States backed its wartime allies without success. In 1923 the Ottoman Empire was dissolved, Turkey was declared an independent republic, and Kemal—or Atatürk ("first among Turks")—became its first president.

and women, introduced the Latin alphabet, and abolished polygamy. Ordinary people reacted to their world being turned topsy-turvy: "It's a Christian hat," a barber warned to a young soldier sporting a Western-style hat as part of his uniform. "If a Muslim puts such a shocking thing on his head the good God will surely punish him."[9] In 1936, women received the vote and were made eligible to serve in the parliament.

Reform in Turkey, 1923

Like many colonized countries and those seeking to free themselves from Western control, Turkey under Atatürk considered the condition of women an important element of modernization. Atatürk decreed that women and men alike should dress in Western clothes, receive a secular education, and switch from the Arabic to the Latin alphabet. There was much for the citizens of the new Turkey to learn and unlearn; women were at the center of this nation-building process, as we see in this image from a Turkish classroom. (Gamma-Keystone via Getty Images.)

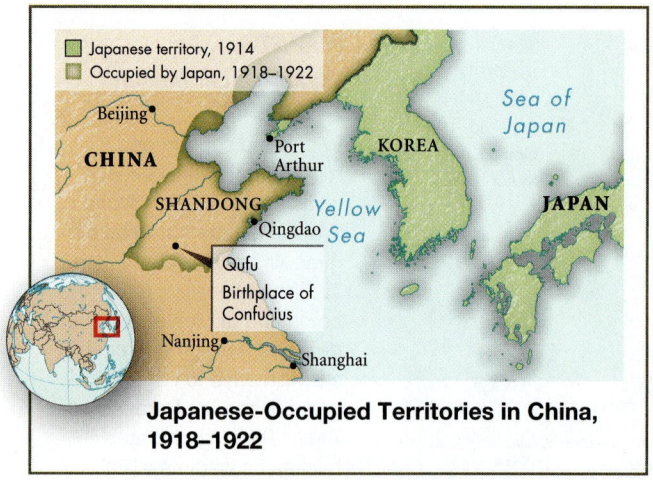

Japanese-Occupied Territories in China, 1918–1922

In China, the course of nation building stalled after the overthrow of the Qing dynasty in 1912, but the results of World War I gave it a new boost. People from many walks of life were outraged by Japan's 1915 takeover of Germany's sphere of influence in China, which included the birthplace of Confucius. The Allies' legal endorsement of that takeover, announced on May 4, 1919, galvanized student protest. Carrying signs that read, "China Belongs to the Chinese," they were joined by dockworkers, business people, and others from different walks of life. Among the middle and educated classes, the May 4th movement also targeted Chinese traditions—from Confucian values such as patriarchal control of women and the young to educational "backwardness"—as responsible for China's treatment on the world stage. Although they detested imperialism, some of these reformers came to see the value of Christian institutions that offered training in Western languages, modern science, and political theory. Like the leaders of the new Turkey and Meiji Japan, they had come to see selective Westernization as key to independence.

China Seeks a Modern Government

Many other Chinese, however, turned away from the West. Students and workers declared that Western leaders at the Paris conference were "still selfish and militaristic and that they were all great liars," as one student put it.[10] Some adopted an alternative—communism—just as the Soviet Union sent aid to the Chinese Communist Party with instructions that it should help Sun Yatsen's nationalist party, the Guomindang, to help organize and politicize the people (see Reading the Past: Communism Spreads in China). Politicization led to strikes, but also to tensions between Communists and the Guomindang, which had been taken over by the military leader Jiang Jieshi (Chiang Kai-Shek) after the death of Sun in 1925. Jiang led his troops to put down warlords to the north as the beginning of reunification. As he took the cities of Nanjing and Shanghai, his followers murdered the Communists in hopes of stopping their influence for good. Jiang then turned to mobilizing his countrymen for modernization.

Ireland Demands Independence

War and its aftermath inspired other attempts at liberation from combatant countries. In Ireland, pro-independence activists attacked government buildings in Dublin on Easter Monday 1916, in an effort to gain Irish freedom from Britain. Ill-prepared, their Easter rebellion was easily defeated and many of them were executed. Demands for home rule only intensified, and in January 1919, republican leaders proclaimed Ireland's independence from Britain. Instead of granting it, the British government sent in the "Black and Tans," a volunteer army of demobilized soldiers—so called for the color of their uniforms. Terror reigned in Ireland, as both the pro-independence forces and the Black and Tans waged guerrilla warfare, taking hostages, blowing up buildings, and even shooting into crowds at soccer matches. By 1921 public outrage at the violence forced the British to negotiate a treaty. The Irish Free State was declared a self-governing dominion owing allegiance to the British crown. Northern Ireland, a group of six northern counties containing many Protestants, gained a separate status as a self-governing British territory with representation in the British Parliament. Partial independence and the rights of religious minorities remained contentious issues, producing violence for decades thereafter.

Ireland, 1921

Colonized peoples rose up after the war in virtually every empire. Those who had fought expected the rights that European politicians and military recruiters had solemnly promised in exchange for service. Instead, they met worsening conditions at home. "Is our reward to have our tax raised . . . and for our ownership of land to be called

Communism Spreads in China

Communism was one alternative for middle- and upper-class Chinese reformers angry that the Western powers had given part of their country to Japan at the Peace of Paris. In this passage, P'eng P'ai, son of a prosperous landowning family, recounts the creation in the early 1920s of the Hai-Feng Peasant Union in the early 1920s based on Communist ideas. P'eng P'ai himself had much to learn about building a mass movement. At first he searched out peasant activists while wearing a fancy, Western-style white suit and a white hat; most of the peasants fled. After changing his clothing to simpler attire, P'eng had greater success. The Peasant Union grew to more than twenty thousand out of a population of one hundred thousand and undertook a range of activities to protect peasant livelihoods. Below are some of the Union's activities.

> [W]e found that some peasants would try to get others' land to till, and landlords would increase rent and change tenants. So the Union drew up some regulations to prevent such incidents.
>
> 1. Unless permission is given by the member and by the Union, no one may encroach on a member's rented land.
> 2. Unless a member relinquishes his lease and the Union gives its permission, no one may rent the land already rented to a member of the Union. Violators are subject to severe punishment.
> 3. In case a landlord takes back his land from a member by means of increasing the rent, and as a result a member's livelihood is in danger, he may ask for help from the Union, which will either persuade nearby members to allow him to till part of their land, or will introduce him to another trade.
>
> After the regulations were publicized, there was no longer any competition for land among our members, and the landlords also were afraid to raise the rent of members of the Union. . . .
>
> Soon it was Chinese New Year of 1923. Dragon dancers and music troupes from all the villages came to celebrate, and the Union organized a New Year's Festival for all peasants in Hai-Feng. . . . More than six thousand members and three thousand non-members participated and the banners of each village's bands, dragon dancers, and music troupes danced in the open air. . . . The speakers . . . pointed out that before the proletarian revolution was realized, there could be no joyous New Year, for New Year's Day was a time for the exploiters to oppress us and to demand us to pay our debts. We were now united in our hardships, not in joy. However, this was an opportunity in which we might demonstrate our strength to our enemies and awaken the spirit of revolution in ourselves. We were prepared for a battle with our enemies. This was the reason why, on the one hand, we felt weighed down by our emotions, but on the other hand elated.
>
> On that day, we issued two thousand new membership cards, and received over four hundred dollars in dues.

Patricia Buckley Ebrey. Adapted with permission of Free Press, a division of Simon & Schuster, Inc., from *Chinese Civilization and Society: A Sourcebook* by Patricia Buckley Ebrey. Copyright © 1981 by The Free Press. All rights reserved.

Source: Patricia B. Ebrey, ed., *Chinese Civilization and Society: A Sourcebook* (New York: Free Press, 1981), 273, 276.

EXAMINING THE EVIDENCE

1. **What types of activities did the Hai-Feng Peasant Union sponsor, and why did these activities prove effective?**
2. **What would lead peasants to fear the Union, and what would make them want to join it?**
3. **What insight into mass movements does this document provide?**

into question?" one group of East Africans asked in 1921 (see Reading the Past: Léopold Sédar Senghor, "To the Senegalese Soldiers Who Died for France").[11]

Protesting Colonization

Rebellions mostly met a brutal response. Fearful of losing India, British forces shot into crowds of protesters at Amritsar in 1919 and put down revolts in Egypt and Iran in the early 1920s. The Dutch jailed political leaders in Indonesia; the French punished Indochinese nationalists; and in 1929 the British crushed Ibo women's tax protest. Maintaining empires abroad was crucial to covering debts incurred during World War I, spurring colonial rule to become more brutal in the face of protest.

Léopold Sédar Senghor, "To the Senegalese Soldiers Who Died for France"

Among the colonial troops in World War I were the Senegalese Sharpshooters, who fought on the side of their French imperial masters. Though the Senegalese riflemen served on the front lines, they received little credit from the French and were even forced to march around, rather than through, villages so that white citizens would not have to set eyes on black soldiers. They were immortalized in a poem by Léopold Sédar Senghor, who himself fought in the French colonial forces and who became the first president of an independent Senegal in 1960. Among the thousands of poems memorializing World War I, the one from which this excerpt was taken also served as Senegal's national anthem after liberation.

They put flowers on tombs and warm the Unknown Soldier.
But you, my dark brothers, no one calls your names.
. . .
Listen to me, Senegalese soldiers, in the solitude of the black ground
And of death, in your deaf and blind solitude,
More than I in my dark skin in the depths of the Province,
Without even the warmth of your comrades lying close to you,
As in the trenches back then or the village palavers [conversations] long ago,
. . .
We bring you, listen to us, we who spelled your names
In the months of your deaths, we bring you,
In these fearful days without memory,
The friendship of your age-mates.
Ah! If I could one day sing in a voice glowing like embers,
If I could praise the friendship of comrades as fervent
And delicate as entrails, as strong as tendons.
Listen to us, you Dead stretched out in water as far as
The northern and eastern fields.
Receive this red earth, under a summer sun this soil
Reddened with the blood of white hosts
Receive the salute of your black comrades,
Senegalese soldiers
WHO DIED FOR THE REPUBLIC!

Source: Léopold Sédar Senghor, *The Collected Poetry*, trans. Melvin Dixon (Charlottesville: University Press of Virginia, 1991), 46–47.

EXAMINING THE EVIDENCE

1. **What emotions and values does Senghor express in this poem?**
2. **What views of World War I does the poem reveal?**
3. **Why do you think Senghor wrote this poem, and for whom?**
4. **Why would this poem about a specific group of people fighting on behalf of imperial powers become the national anthem of an independent country?**

Postwar Imperial Expansion

Amid protest, imperialism reached its high tide in the 1920s and 1930s. Britain and France, enjoying control of Germany's African colonies and former Ottoman lands in the Middle East, were at the height of their global power. A new generation of adventurers headed for Middle Eastern and Indonesian oil fields, as the importance of oil increased along with the number of automobiles, airplanes, trucks, ships, and oil-heated homes. Investors from the United States and elsewhere grabbed land in the Caribbean and across Latin America, cornering markets in sugar, cocoa, and tropical fruit that were becoming a regular part of the Western diet. Competition for territory and business was alive and well.

The balance of power among the imperial nations was shifting, however. The most important change was Japan's growing competitiveness for markets, resources, and influence. During the war, Japanese output of industrial goods such as ships and metal grew some 40 percent because the Western powers outsourced their wartime needs for such products. As Japan took shipping, financial, and other business from Britain and France, its prosperity skyrocketed and officials touted its success as the key to an Asia free from Westerners. Ardently nationalist, the Japanese government was not yet strong enough to challenge Western powers militarily. Thus, although outraged at Wilson's abrupt rejection (with British backing) of a nondiscrimination clause in the charter of the League of Nations put forward by the Japanese, Japan cooperated in the Anglo-American-dominated peace, even agreeing both to restore Chinese possessions and to keep a ratio of English, American, and Japanese shipbuilding at 5:5:3 respectively. "Rolls Royce, Rolls Royce, Ford," a Japanese official commented bitterly.[12] This bitterness ultimately festered into war.

An Age of the Masses

FOCUS

How did the rise of mass society affect politics, culture, and everyday life around the world?

War and revolutions demonstrated the centrality of the masses to modern life. With the collapse of autocratic governments from China to Germany, the sense of democratic potential based on mass participation grew. The condition of women came to symbolize the strength of the masses, which was reflected in the extension of the vote to many Western women during the 1920s. Modernizing the economy—a goal of many countries after the war—meant developing mass consumerism, while modern technology provided mass entertainment and news across the globe. By the end of the decade, a handful of political leaders were adopting new media to mobilize their citizenry.

Mass Society

The development of mass society was a global phenomenon, fueled by the growing connections among economies. Urbanization surged in Asia, Latin America, Africa, and the United States as populations exploded and rural people migrated to cities in search of work. Global population, aided by the spread of medicine and improved sanitation, also soared. Tokyo had some 3.5 million inhabitants in 1920, New York 5.5 million, and Shanghai over 2 million. Calcutta's population quadrupled to 1.8 million from the late nineteenth century to 1920. City life was fast paced, brimming with trams, buses, and automobiles; in China rickshaws with cushioned wheels pulled by fast young men replaced the leisurely sedan chair as the conveyance of choice. Tall buildings lifted skylines, first in New York with its much-admired Chrysler and Empire State buildings, but soon in cities throughout the world. New urban cultural livelihoods arose, such as performing jazz and managing nightclubs. Across the globe class distinctions were blurred in the confusion of city life. Outside city centers, wealthy suburbs and exclusive beachside retreats flourished, such as that near the city of Bombay, India, started by the Tata family of industrialists (whom we met in Chapter 24). This mass society centered in cities depended on economic modernization—most notably, mass production and its byproduct, mass unionization.

Mass Production

Trade revived in the 1920s, and wartime innovations spurred new industries and created new jobs making cars, electrical products, and synthetic goods for peacetime use. The prewar pattern of mergers and cartels continued after 1918, giving rise to multinational food-processing firms such as Nestlé in Switzerland and global petroleum enterprises such as Royal Dutch Shell. Owners of these large manufacturing conglomerates wielded more financial and political power than entire small countries. By the late 1920s, many in Asia and Europe had survived the wild economic swings of the immediate postwar years to enjoy renewed economic growth.

Among economic leaders, the United States had become the trendsetter in modernization. Businessmen from around the world made pilgrimages to Henry Ford's Detroit assembly line, which by 1929 produced a Ford automobile every ten seconds. Ford claimed that this miracle of productivity resulted in a lower cost of living and increased purchasing power for workers, and indeed some 17 million cars were on U.S. streets by 1925. The new livelihood of scientific manager also played a part, as efficiency experts developed methods to streamline workers' tasks and motions for maximum productivity. Despite the rewards, many workers found the emphasis on efficiency inhumane, with restrictions on time and motion so severe that often they were allowed to use the bathroom only on a fixed schedule.

"When I left the factory, it followed me," wrote one French automobile worker. "In my dreams I was a machine."

Increased Unionization

As industry spread, the number of people in unions increased around the world, with both skilled and unskilled workers organizing to advance their collective interests. Sometimes the reasons for joining were basic: local workers on the French railroads in West Africa complained of "unsanitary food seasoned with dried fish and full of worms" and began unionizing.[13] White-collar workers and government clerks also had large, effective unions. Where male workers' jobs were threatened by laborsaving machinery, unions usually agreed with employers that women should receive lower wages, saving scarce high-paying jobs for men. Under these circumstances, women's participation in union activity was proportionally lower than men's.

Because they could mobilize masses of people, unions played a key role in politics, as they demonstrated when unionized workers in China struck against Britain's control of Hong Kong. "Down with imperialism!" was one of their cries, and they forced merchants to show that their goods did not originate in Britain.[14] India's ongoing industrialization during the war provided jobs, but in the postwar period some 125,000 Bombay textile workers were among those who struck to get their share of the profits. The British sent airplanes to attack strikers, first strafing civilians in 1920s India. As labor flexed its muscle around the world, union members blocked coups against Germany's newly elected democratic government, the Weimar Republic, and organized a general strike in Great Britain in the 1920s.

Changing Class Distinctions

Modernization and rising global productivity affected traditional social divisions. Advances in industrialization boosted the size of the modern middle class by expanding the need for managers and professionals and for skilled workers in new jobs. Often these opportunities reduced the influence of traditional elites and made society more complex in colonized areas such as India, where a modern working class and financial and industrialist classes grew alongside caste and religious divisions. Reformers such as those in China's May 4th movement pointed to the irrationality of traditional patterns of deference within families.

Class and racial prescriptions were also breaking down as a result of the war: men of all classes and ethnicities had served in distant trenches together and were even buried in common graves. As a result of the war, daughters around the world supported themselves in jobs, and their mothers did their own housework because people who once worked as servants could now earn more money in factories. A middle-class "look" became common around the world, promoted by global advertising that appealed to consumers with vivid images of sleek, modern styles.

The "New Woman"

One emblem of postwar modernity in most parts of the world was the "new woman," the "modern girl," or the "flapper," as she was called in the United States. In the 1920s many women around the world cut their hair, abandoned traditional clothes such as kimonos, smoked, had money of their own from working in the service sector, and went out unchaperoned, even dancing with men. Zhu Su'e, born in 1901 to a banking family in Changzhou, China, unbound her feet as a teenager and then left home in 1921 to study in Shanghai. She graduated from law school, married for love instead of having a traditional arranged marriage, and continued her career: "I understood that you must be able to earn money in order to be independent."[15] As an attorney, she often helped women in oppressive marriages, guiding them to become independent and educated. Attempts to impose "modern" standards were often rejected, however. When activists in the USSR urged Muslim women to remove their veils and change their way of life, fervent Muslims often attacked both the activists and the women who followed their advice.

Culture for the Masses

Wartime propaganda had aimed to unite classes, races, and countries against a common enemy. In the 1920s, phonographs, the radio, and film continued the development of mass or standardized culture. Print media, cheaper and more widely distributed to an increasingly literate global population, showed people what to buy and what to wear.

Mass media had the potential to create an informed citizenry, enhance democracy, and promote liberation in the colonies. Paradoxically, it also provided tools for dictatorship. Authoritarian rulers in the Soviet Union, Italy, Japan, and elsewhere were coming to see the advantage of mobilizing the masses through the control of information and culture.

By the 1920s, film flourished around the world, with Shanghai and Hong Kong joining the United States, Europe, and South Asia as important centers of production and regional distribution (see Lives and Livelihoods: The Film Industry). In India, where movie theaters had sprung up at the start of the century in Madras and Bombay, movies retelling the *Mahabharata* and history films on the story of the Taj Mahal developed Indians' sense of a common heritage. Bolshevik leaders underwrote the innovative work of director Sergei Eisenstein, whose films *Potemkin* (1925) and *Ten Days That Shook the World* (1927–1928) presented a Bolshevik view of history to Soviet and many international audiences, spreading standard Communist values. Films also showed the shared predicaments of ordinary people, helping to standardize behavior. Popular comedies of the 1920s and 1930s such as the Shanghai hits *Three Modern Women* (1933) and *New Woman* (1934) showed women viewers the ways of flappers.

Miss Brazil in Texas, 1929

Healthful sports and exercise, feats of daring, and a growing consumerism all signaled postwar revival in many parts of the world. In this photograph, Miss Brazil—an example of the new, modern woman with her trim clothing and cosmetically enhanced face—has traveled to the United States to participate in a beauty contest. International beauty contests introduced consumers around the world to global styles in fashion and self-presentation. (The Granger Collection, New York.)

Cinematic portrayals also played to postwar fantasies and fears, as threats to class and caste systems shaped movie plots from India to the United States. Impersonators, "gold diggers," and con artists abounded. The plight of gangsters appealed to veterans of revolutions and wars, who had seen that the modern world sometimes placed little value on life. English actor and producer Charlie Chaplin in *Little Tramp* (1914–1915) won international popularity as the defeated hero, the anonymous modern man, trying to keep his dignity in a mechanical world. Sporting events such as cricket, boxing, and martial arts were internationalized, and clips from matches were shown as newsreels before featured movies. As popular films and books crossed national borders, a cosmopolitan, global culture flourished.

Film and Radio

Radio was an even newer medium. Developed from the Italian inventor Guglielmo Marconi's wireless technology, radio broadcasts in the first half of the 1920s were heard by mass audiences in public halls (much like film theaters) and featured orchestras and song followed by audience discussion. The radio quickly became a relatively inexpensive consumer item, allowing public events to penetrate private homes. Specialized programming for men (such as sports reporting) and for women (such as advice on home management) soon followed. By the 1930s, politicians used radio to reach the masses wherever they might be—even alone at home.

Mass Marketing

The print media—newspapers and magazines—grew in popularity, and their advertising promoted mass consumption of modern conveniences such as electric clothes washers and irons. Mass marketing encouraged new personal habits, presenting mass-produced razors and deodorants as essential to modern hygiene. Politicians joined in as modernizers: Jiang Jieshi and Bolshevik leaders alike promoted toothpaste and toothbrushing as part of nationbuilding. "New woman" Rilda Marta of South Africa traveled to the United

LIVES AND LIVELIHOODS

The Film Industry

Butterfly Hu and Chinese Cinema

By the 1920s films were made and distributed throughout the world. *Twin Sisters* (1933), a product of Shanghai's bustling film industry, focused on the plight of twin sisters—raised apart with utterly different personalities—both played by the Chinese star Butterfly Hu. So easily could distant parts of the world now speak across cultural borders that the movie was a box office hit in China, Southeast Asia, Japan, and western Europe. (Still from "Zi Mei Hua" (Twin Sisters), directed by Zheng Zhengqiu.)

The development of the film industry worldwide from the late nineteenth century on led to the creation of dozens of new livelihoods. Although early films often were the work of a single author-director-cameraman, by the 1920s opportunities for new careers opened up as moviegoing became a mass phenomenon after World War I and as filmmaking itself came to involve many more jobs. Among the most notable new livelihoods were those of screenwriter, cameraman, art editor, and film financier, along with less-renowned jobs for stuntmen, animal trainers, baby actors, and in the United States especially,

States to learn about African American cosmetics and on her return advocated the subtle use of lipstick and rouge: "The key to Happiness and Success is a good appearance," she proclaimed. "You are often judged by how you look."[16] A multibillion-dollar global cosmetics industry sprang up almost overnight, and women from Tokyo to Buenos Aires bought their products to imitate the appearance of film celebrities.

Mobilizing the Masses

The 1920s saw the rise of politicians mobilizing the masses for their political causes. When the Bolsheviks encountered opposition to their rule, for example, they began massive propaganda efforts to bring communism to villages and cities, peasants and workers, and Muslims, Christians, and Jews alike. So successful were these efforts that people around the world came to believe that the USSR was an ideal state, a utopia. In the colonies and mandates, leaders like Mohandas Gandhi in India and groups such as the Muslim Brotherhood in Egypt mobilized the masses around spiritual teachings. In Italy, where postwar resentment simmered, Benito Mussolini first staged a coup and then consolidated his rule with mass propaganda.

Gandhi's Movement in India

From the beginning of the twentieth century, Indian leaders objected to British rule of their country and urged boycotts of British products. Indian activist Mohandas Gandhi (1869–1948) transformed this cause into a nonviolent mass movement that appealed to film censors. The Chinese focus on martial arts in film increased the number of jobs for and prominence of these experts. Before the "talkies," films with sound, were invented in the 1930s, silent movies featured pianists who provided mood-setting music and soloists who entertained the audience during intermission. In Japan the work of the *benshi* was to explain throughout the film the action on the screen, sometimes even singing and dancing as part of the job.

From Southeast Asia to Central America, lavish cinema houses attracted hundreds of millions of weekly viewers, the majority of them women. The importance of the cinema house itself gave jobs to architects, construction workers, and even the elegant usher, who in some countries accompanied viewers to their seats in exchange for a tip. With India producing some fifteen hundred films of its own between 1912 and 1927, the need for all the accoutrements of film viewing provided a rich array of livelihoods.

In the 1920s the "star" system developed, turning performers from humble backgrounds in burlesque or comedy into national, even global, celebrities. In Japan's thriving film industry, almost all stars were men, who played both male and female roles as they had done in kabuki and Noh theater (discussed in Chapter 21). By contrast, in China, the highest-paid star was the actress Butterfly Hu, who made her film debut in 1925 and starred in the first "talkie," *Sing Song Red Peony*, in 1930. Butterfly Hu also filled the pages of the print media as she became a style setter in terms of fashion and grooming. Hu, like other stars, was promoted by professional publicists and hired agents and managers, still other new livelihoods. Media entrepreneurs earned a handsome living founding magazines and engaging Hu and others to sell products. New lines of work opened for journalists to provide gossip about film celebrities, biographies of directors, and reviews of films. Celebrity for a few men and women in the film industry spawned hundreds of new livelihoods across mass culture.

QUESTIONS TO CONSIDER

1. **What skills did those working in the film industry need, and to what extent were they new?**
2. **What accounts for the popularity of cinema in these decades?**
3. **In what ways was film important to global culture and the world economy?**

For Further Information:

Grieveson, Lee, and Peter Krämer, eds. *The Silent Cinema Reader*. 2004.
Sklar, Robert. *A World History of Film*. 2002.
Wada-Marciano, Mitsuyo. *Nippon Modern: Japanese Cinema of the 1920s and 1930s*. 2008.
Zhang, Yingjin. *Cinema and Urban Culture in Shanghai, 1922–1943*. 1999.

millions. Born of middle-class parents in a village on the west coast of India, Gandhi studied law in England and then began practice in the Indian community in South Africa. The racism he experienced there made him determined to liberate the Indian masses from British imperialism. When he returned to India permanently in 1915, he began a full-time drive for Hind Swaraj (HIHND swah-RAJ), or Indian Home Rule, to escape the violent, even genocidal values of Westerners engaged in world war. Using the media and making speeches, he challenged the view that Britain was "civilized" and thus worthy of respect. To Gandhi's way of thinking his fellow citizens had the story backward. South Asia had a very long tradition of civilization, he pointed out, while Britain and other Western countries, above all the United States, valued only one thing: material wealth. "Many problems can be solved," Gandhi wrote early in his career, "by remembering that money is their God."[17]

Gandhi envisioned a nonviolent return to an India of small self-sufficient communities in which people grew their own food and spun the cloth for their own clothes. Rejecting the modernization brought by factories and railroads, he dressed in a simple loincloth and shawl made from cloth he had woven himself. For Gandhi, the root cause of India's subjection was that Indian merchants had handed the country over to "Satanic" Western values and turned away from the Indian goals of contemplation and humility. He opposed scientific developments such as birth control and rejected the modern sensibility that wanted to eliminate the caste system.

Sheikh Hassan al-Banna, Founder of the Muslim Brotherhood

Sheikh Hassan al-Banna founded the Muslim Brotherhood in 1928 and worked to make it a mass movement that would revive the standing of Islam and Muslim culture in the world. Dismayed at the respect given Western culture and the power of the West's economy, al-Banna built his organization as a counterweight. His commitment to anticolonialism and Islamic values made him an enemy of the West's allies in the Middle East; they had him assassinated in 1949. (AFP/Getty Images.)

In rejecting the West, Gandhi's resembled another potent organization for the empowerment of ordinary people—the Muslim Brotherhood, founded in Egypt in 1928. This organization called for a return to Islam along with a rejection of the secular, "modern" mindset. "Islam is the solution" was the Brotherhood's watchword as it sought to end British influence in the country. Like Gandhi's movement, the Muslim Brotherhood would grow in mass appeal.

In contrast, communism promised a shining future and a modern, technological culture. The reality was that workers' living conditions declined while Communist Party supervisors enjoyed a privileged life. In the early 1920s, workers, sailors, and peasant bands alike revolted against harsh Bolshevik policies toward ordinary people. The government had many of the rebels shot, but as production dropped to 13 percent of its prewar output, Lenin changed course. His **New Economic Policy** compromised with capitalism by allowing peasants to sell their grain freely and entrepreneurs to engage in trade and keep the profits. More food soon became available, and some peasants and merchants did indeed prosper.

Nonetheless, grassroots opposition drove the Bolsheviks to make communism not just a political ideology but a cultural reality that would guide the masses' daily lives and reshape their thoughts. Party leaders invaded the countryside to set up classes on a variety of political subjects, and volunteers pushed the importance of literacy—on the eve of World War I, less than half the people in the USSR could read. As commissar for public welfare, Aleksandra Kollontai promoted birth-control education, classes in "domestic science," and the establishment of day care for children of working parents. To advance literacy, she wrote simply worded novels about love and work in the new socialist state. The government tried to develop a mass proletarian culture through workers' universities, a workers' theater, and workers' publishing. For many, it worked: as one teacher and worker on a veterinary farm wrote in her diary, "I have discovered a new world for me in Marxism. I read with deep interest."[18]

Authoritarian rule came as well to Italy, though of a different nature from communism. Benito Mussolini (1883–1945) came to power as a mass hero. Since the late nineteenth century, some Europeans had come to blame their parliaments for economic ills. Thus many Italians were enthusiastic when Mussolini, a socialist journalist who had turned to the radical right, built a personal army called the "Black Shirts" of veterans and the unemployed and used it to overturn parliamentary government. In 1922, his supporters, known as Fascists, started a march on Rome, leading to Mussolini's appointment as prime minister. Although in theory he ruled with the consent of the masses, Mussolini consolidated his power by making criticism of the state a criminal offense, violently attacking opposition, and beating up striking workers. Yet the sight of hundreds of Black Shirts marching through the streets like disciplined soldiers signaled to many Italians that their country was ordered and modern.

New Economic Policy Lenin's compromise with capitalism that allowed peasants to sell their grain on the market and entrepreneurs to engage in trade and keep the profits.

fascism A political movement originating in postwar Italy under Mussolini that stressed the primacy of the state over the individual and the importance of violence and warfare in making nations strong.

Besides violence, Mussolini used mass propaganda and the media to promote traditional values and prejudices, though **fascism**, unlike communism, was never an organized set of principles, except for the principle that the state had supremacy over the people. Peasant men huddled around radios to hear him call for a "battle of wheat" to enhance farm productivity on behalf of the state. Peasant women worshiped him for

REVIEW

Online Study Guide
bedfordstmartins.com/smith

The major global development in this chapter ▶ The wars of the decade 1910 to 1920 and their role in the creation of mass culture and society.

IMPORTANT EVENTS

1910	Mexican Revolution begins
1911–1912	Revolutionaries overthrow Qing dynasty in China
1912	First Balkan War
1913	Second Balkan War
1914	World War I begins
1917	Russian Revolution begins; United States enters World War I; Lenin returns to Russia
1918	Bolsheviks take full control of Russian government; Treaty of Brest-Litovsk; armistice ends World War I
1919	Germany forms Weimar Republic; May 4th movement in China
1919–1920	Treaties comprising Peace of Paris signed, including the Treaty of Versailles with Germany
1920s	Mohandas Gandhi's nonviolent movement for India independence attracts millions; mass culture flourishes in film and publishing industries; growth of radio transmissions; technology increases global productivity
1921	Lenin introduces New Economic Policy in Russia
1922	Civil war ends in Russia; Mussolini comes to power in Italy
1923	Founding of the independent republic of Turkey under Mustafa Kemal; formation of Union of Soviet Socialist Republics

KEY TERMS

Bolshevik (p. 903)
collective security (p. 907)
Comintern (p. 904)
fascism (p. 918)
Fourteen Points (p. 904)
Guomindang (p. 895)
League of Nations (p. 907)
mandate system (p. 908)
New Economic Policy (p. 918)
soviet (p. 902)
total war (p. 900)

CHAPTER OVERVIEW QUESTIONS

1. Why did the Mexican Revolution, the Chinese Revolution, World War I, and the Russian Revolution cause so much change far from the battlefield?
2. How did these wars help produce mass culture and society?
3. What role did technology play in these developments?

SECTION FOCUS QUESTIONS

1. What factors contributed to the wars of the early twentieth century?
2. Why did the Russian Revolution take place, and what changes did it produce in Russian politics and daily life?
3. What were the major outcomes of the peacemaking process and postwar conditions?
4. How did the rise of mass society affect politics, culture, and everyday life around the world?
5. In what ways did Argentina's history differ from that of countries caught up in World War I?

MAKING CONNECTIONS

1. In what ways did conditions at the end of World War I differ from those expected at the outbreak of the war?
2. Consider the empires discussed in Chapter 26. How did they change in the 1920s, and why?
3. How did World War I affect work and livelihoods?
4. How did the mass political movements that emerged during and after the war differ from one another?

28

AT A CROSSROADS ▲

This photograph of a Nazi rally held in 1938 in Nuremberg reveals how young people, among others, admired Hitler and all that he stood for: quick fixes to a depressed economy and the promise of renewed global power. His rhetoric of hatred rallied Germans across the social order to envision a better future once their nation had been purified of enemies such as Jews, who were actually their neighbors and fellow Germans. Popular support for Hitler's violent bigotry has made historians aware that the history of Nazism is not just the story of one charismatic leader, but also of the masses whose devotion was the source of his power. (bpk, Berlin/Art Resource, NY.)

Global Catastrophe: The Great Depression and World War II

1929–1945

Eva Kantorowsky worked as a secretary and teacher of English in Shanghai during World War II. A cosmopolitan city, Shanghai attracted refugees from war-torn Europe from the 1930s on, especially those fleeing Adolf Hitler's brutal Nazi regime in Germany. Eva Kantorowsky was one of these, helped by her uncle's successful acquisition of three exit visas so that she, her mother, and her father—a rabbi in Berlin—could make their way across two continents to China in 1940. They left only after Eva's father had been repeatedly beaten by the Nazis. Their reluctance to leave Germany had another cause: Eva's uncle had neglected to get an exit visa for her brother Hans, who, the uncle mistakenly thought, had already left the country. After World War II ended in 1945, Eva's family received the crushing news that Hans had died in Auschwitz, murdered along with millions of fellow Jews as well as Slavs, Roma ("gypsies"), and other persecuted groups, in the genocide the Nazis hoped would purify their empire.

Eva Kantorowsky escaped this genocide—the Holocaust—and survived the most destructive war in world history. World War II, with a death toll of some one hundred

1929: The Great Depression Begins

FOCUS What was the global impact of both the Great Depression and the attempts to overcome it?

Militarizing the Masses in the 1930s

FOCUS How did dictatorships and democracies attempt to mobilize the masses?

Global War, 1937–1945

FOCUS How did World War II progress on the battlefront and the home front?

From Allied Victory to the Cold War, 1943–1945

FOCUS How did the Allied victory unfold, and what were the causes of that victory?

COUNTERPOINT: Nonviolence and Pacifism in an Age of War

FOCUS In what ways did peace movements serve as a countertrend to events in the period from 1929 to 1945?

BACKSTORY

As we saw in Chapter 27, in 1918 World War I ended, and with it fell four major empires: the Ottoman, Russian, Austro-Hungarian, and German. The victorious Western powers took the colonies and other lands of the defeated German and Ottoman empires, expanding the "new imperialism" (see Chapter 26). Significant changes in the nature of government and in the relationship between governments and their peoples accompanied the new geopolitical order. In countries around the world, governments grew larger and more powerful, taking advantage of the new mass media to promote a uniform culture that stressed the central importance of patriotism and national identity. In the political and economic turmoil that followed the war, the same mass media contributed to the rise of stridently nationalist dictators. When a worldwide depression struck in the late 1920s, these dictators, backed by modern bureaucracies and military technology, grew more dangerous. Intent on expanding their nation's boundaries and empires, they posed a grave threat to world peace.

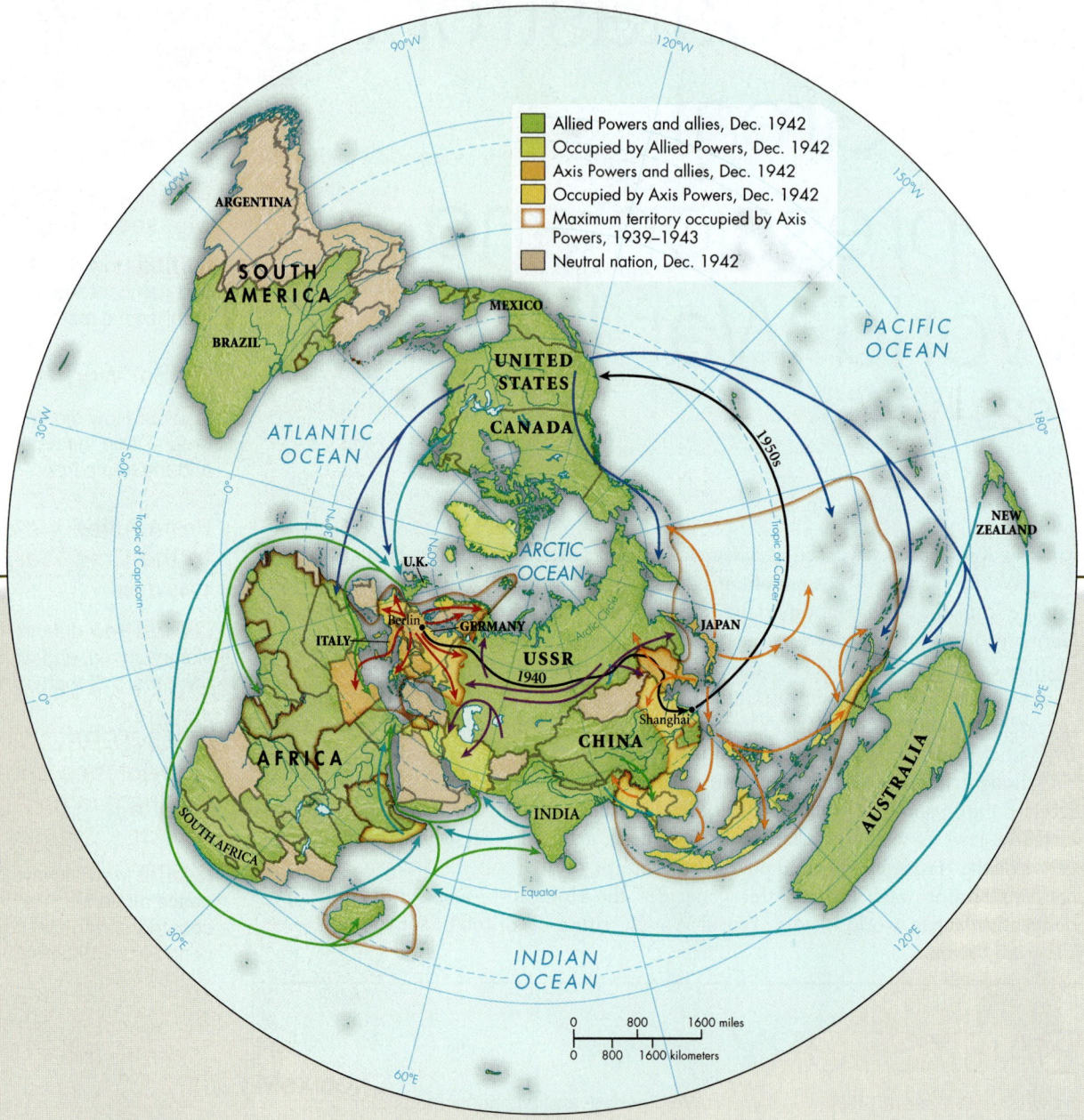

1920s Collapse of commodity prices around the world

Crash of the U.S. stock market; global depression begins; Stalin's "liquidation of the kulaks" **1929**

Nuremberg Laws against the Jews in Germany; Italy invades Ethiopia **1935**

Purges and show trials begin in USSR **1936**

1920 | 1925 | 1930 | 1935

1930s Sweden begins setting up welfare state

Gandhi's Salt March **1930**

Chinese Communists begin Long March **1934**

Japan invades Manchuria **1931**

Hitler comes to power in Germany and ends representative government **1933** million people, capped off a decade of suffering that began with the Great Depression of the 1930s, a global economic catastrophe that was sparked by the crash of the U.S. stock market in 1929. The crash opened a tragic era in world history, a time when people around the world were connected by their shared experience of economic hardship, war, and genocide. The Great Depression intensified social protest throughout the world. In Japan, China, Italy, Germany, and across Latin America, strongmen took power and militarized the masses, promising that disciplined obedience would end their troubles. Adolf Hitler roused the German masses to pursue national greatness by scorning democracy and scapegoating "inferior" and "menacing" Jews such as the Kantorowsky family. Joseph Stalin believed that the Soviet Union's rapid industrialization was worth the lives of the millions of citizens who died remaking their nation in the 1930s. For militaristic authoritarian regimes around the world, human rights and democratic institutions were nothing more than obstacles to national greatness.

Elected leaders in established democracies reacted ineffectively to the depression and the militarism it spawned. The League of Nations, formed after World War I to preserve world peace, ignored Japan's aggression in China, Italy's in Ethiopia, and Germany's in Europe. Whether in China or central Europe, aggression followed aggression until Hitler's invasion of Poland in 1939 and Japan's bombing of Pearl Harbor in 1941 finally pushed the democracies to declare war. By the end of 1941, Great Britain, France, the Soviet

MAPPING THE WORLD

World War II, 1937–1945

The Great Depression spread economic hardship, which was compounded by the advance of militarism and empire. Japan's drive to expand its empire early in the 1930s was followed by Italy's campaigns for empire in Africa and the German takeover of central and eastern Europe. These aspiring powers used increasingly formidable weaponry, lightning speed, and massive attacks on civilians. The culmination was World War II, which broke out in 1937 in East Asia and 1939 in Europe, ending only in 1945. The Great Depression and World War II stand out in human history as an era of unprecedented suffering.

ROUTES ▼

Troop movements during World War II

Axis offensive, 1939–1942

→ German

→ Japanese

Allied counteroffensive to front lines, 1942–1945

→ British

→ British colonial and Commonwealth

→ Soviet

→ U.S.

→ Probable travels of Eva Kantorowsky, 1940–1950s

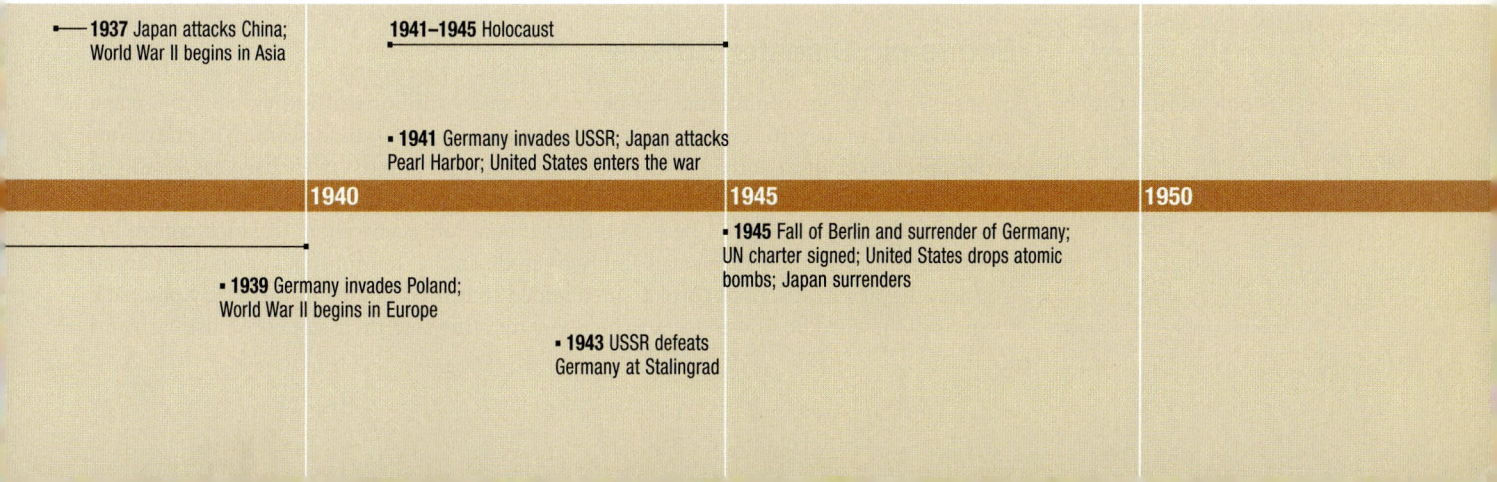

Union, and the United States were locked in combat with Germany, Italy, and Japan. The coalition that formed to stop Germany and its partners was an uneasy one, however, and by the end of the war the world's reigning military superpowers, the United States and the Soviet Union, regarded each other with deep distrust born of ideological differences. As hot war turned to cold war after 1945, tens of millions more became homeless refugees, among them Eva Kantorowsky. In this most destructive war in human history, however, she was among the lucky ones: global migration helped her survive. The dense network of economic and political connections that had made the Great Depression a global event and drawn the world into war also provided routes for some individuals to escape persecution and suffering in their home countries.

OVERVIEW QUESTIONS

The major global development in this chapter: The causes and outcomes of the Great Depression and World War II.

As you read, consider:

1. How did ordinary people react to the Great Depression, and how did their reactions differ from country to country?
2. Why were dictators and antidemocratic leaders able to come to power in the 1930s, and how did all countries—autocratic and democratic alike—militarize the masses?
3. How are the Great Depression and World War II related historical events?

1929: The Great Depression Begins

FOCUS
What was the global impact of both the Great Depression and the attempts to overcome it?

A rapid decline in agricultural prices in the 1920s followed by the U.S. stock market crash of 1929 threw tens of millions out of work and wrecked the prospects of rural people worldwide. Economic depression spread from continent to continent as commerce and investment in industry declined, social life and gender roles were upset, and the birthrate plummeted. People everywhere, from farmers to industrial workers, saw their livelihoods destroyed. Despair turned to outrage, as many rose up in rebellion, embracing militaristic solutions to their nation's problems.

Economic Disaster Strikes

U.S. Stock Market Crash

In the 1920s, U.S. corporations and banks as well as millions of individual Americans invested their money (often borrowed) in the stock market, which seemed to churn out endless profits. Confident that stock prices would continue to rise, they used easy credit to buy shares in companies based on electric, automotive, and other new technologies. At the end of the decade, the Federal Reserve Bank—the nation's central bank, which controlled financial policy—tightened the availability of credit in an attempt to stabilize the market. To meet the new restrictions, brokers demanded that their clients immediately pay back the money they had borrowed to buy stock. As investors sold their stocks to raise cash and repay their loans, the wave of selling caused prices on the stock market to collapse. Between early October and mid-November 1929, the value of businesses listed on the U.S. stock market—and thus of people's investments through the stocks they owned in those businesses—dropped nearly two-thirds, from $87 billion to $30 billion. Individuals lost their money, and a breakdown of the economy as a whole followed.

Global Economic Collapse

The stock market crash helped spark the global economic collapse known as the **Great Depression**, because the United States, a leading international creditor, had financed the economic growth of the previous five years by lending money for business development around the world. Suddenly strapped themselves, U.S. financiers cut back drastically on loans and called in debts, weakening banks and industry at home and abroad. Creditors to newly created industries in India, for example, demanded repayment of loans and refused to finance further expansion. In Europe, the lack of credit and the decline in consumer buying caused businesses to close, workers to be laid off, and the European economy to slump. By 1933, almost 6 million German workers, or about one-third of the workforce, were unemployed, and many others were underemployed. The effects of the economic collapse were uneven, however: a few Latin American countries were able to expand domestic consumption enough at least partially to offset lost sales abroad.

In general, though, rural and urban folk alike suffered as tens of millions lost their livelihoods. For farmers, times had been tough for years. In the 1920s, technological innovation and a number of other factors combined to produce record crops and, consequently, falling farm prices. Canada, Australia, Argentina, and the United States had increased their production of wheat while World War I was raging in Europe; they did not cut back when the war ended and Europe became productive again. In the mid-1920s the price of wheat collapsed. Prices for other consumables, such as coffee and sugar, also tumbled, creating dire consequences in Africa, Asia, and some Latin American countries as large-scale farmers—either local magnates or white settlers—bought up the land of struggling small producers. Prices fell even for commodities such as rice, for which there was not a surplus, until by 1931 farmers were receiving 50 percent less for their crops than they had a few years earlier. As a result, rural consumption of manufactured goods dropped too. Thus, problems in agriculture were directly connected to industrial decline.

Government Response

Government responses to the crisis made a bad situation worse. Great Britain went off the gold standard, which had the effect of depreciating its currency, thus making imports more expensive and cutting the sales of its trading partners. Other countries followed suit, blocking imports with high tariffs in hopes of sparking purchases of domestically produced goods. Measures such as cutting budgets were also part of accepted economic theory at the time, but reductions in spending only further undermined demand, leading to more business failures and higher unemployment. Governments in Latin America and eastern Europe often ignored the farmers' plight as they poured available funds into industrialization—a policy that increased tensions in rural society.

One solution for the imperial powers was to increase economic exploitation in the colonies. World War I and postwar investment had generated economic growth, a rising population, and explosive urbanization outside of Europe. Between 1920 and 1940, Calcutta ballooned from 1.8 million to 3.4 million residents and Saigon from 180,000 to 256,000, making them more attractive as markets and sources of tax revenue. Now the imperial powers demanded that colonial subjects pay higher taxes, no matter how desperate the local peoples' plight, to compensate for falling revenues back home. In the Belgian Congo, local farmers paid a per-person tax—called a poll or head tax—equivalent to one-sixth of their crops in the 1920s and one-fourth in the 1930s. Britain took its domestic economy off the gold standard, but it forced colonies such as India to pay taxes and other charges in gold. India's farmers stripped the subcontinent of its stores of gold to turn in every scrap of the precious metal, including women's jewelry, to meet British demands. During hard times, most imperial powers were able to shift at least some of their financial burden to their colonial subjects in Asia and Africa.

Great Depression The economic crisis of the 1930s that began in agricultural regions through a severe drop in commodity prices in the 1920s and then, with the U.S. stock market crash of 1929, spread to industrial countries.

READING THE PAST

Promoting Business in the Great Depression

Winifred Tete-Ansa was an innovative businessman in Nigeria and the Gold Coast. He set up a cooperative so that Gold Coast cocoa growers could market their own products outside the imperial system. Then he established a bank to finance African-owned businesses such as trade in mahogany, palm oil, and other local commodities because European-owned banks would not. In 1930, at a time of economic depression and growing opposition to colonialism, Tete-Ansa explained to African Americans in this prospectus why he had started a bank to help finance African trade cooperatives. He urged these readers to contribute financially to his work.

> Picture a land one-eighth as large as the United States and with a population one-fifth as great, where the people grow three-fifths of the world's cocoa supply. . . .
>
> By the time this vast business has reached the ultimate consumer, over half a billion dollars have changed hands, and enormous profits have accrued to those of the white race who have furnished the necessary capital and directed the labor of thousands of the Negro race. A reasonable earning power on wealth of some five billion of dollars is thus developed, and the greater portion of these earnings go [*sic*] to the members of the white race. . . .
>
> Realize, if you will, the cities to be built and rebuilt, harbors to be developed, rivers to be harnessed, power to be developed and transmitted, railroads to be built, trains to be run, the cities to be lighted, water to be piped, sanitary arrangements to be installed and metals to be found and processed, the engines, motors, shafting, buildings necessary to turn the potential of raw products into highly saleable commodities at a higher price. . . .
>
> We of West Africa have taken the natural advantages of our country and have now fashioned them into a sphere of opportunity. On account of the vast area, the enormous number of our race habitant there and the sound foundation for progress that we have built, it now forms the most important sphere of opportunity for industrial success of the Negro and by the Negro; and a well-built, well-lubricated vehicle to carry on toward industrial emancipation.
>
> This vehicle needs capital to furnish it power to propel itself, and passengers to occupy its seats. We have provided the driver to direct it and the roads for it to travel. It is to be hoped that you, Negroes of America, will help furnish this power and the passengers for this journey to the Industrial Precedence of the Race.

Source: Winifred Tete-Ansa, *Africa at Work* (n.p., 1930), 78, 86–87.

EXAMINING THE EVIDENCE

1. **What kind of global vision does Tete-Ansa present?**
2. **How would you describe his approach to colonialism?**
3. **How does he address the problem of livelihoods in hard times for Africans?**

Social Effects of the Great Depression

The Great Depression caused enormous hardship for many, but its social and economic effects were complex and not entirely negative. Despite the economic crisis, modernization proceeded, whether in the form of building new roads in Africa or bringing electricity to the Soviet Union (see Reading the Past: Promoting Business in the Great Depression). Wealthy individual Chinese living abroad poured money into modernizing their homeland, investing in profitable development projects. Bordering English slums, one British observer in the mid-1930s noticed, were "filling stations and factories that look like exhibition buildings, giant cinemas and dance halls and cafés, bungalows with tiny garages, cocktail bars, Woolworth's [and] swimming pools." Municipal and national governments modernized sanitation, and running water, electricity, and sewage pipes were installed in many homes throughout the world for the first time. New factories manufactured synthetic fabrics, new electrical products such as stoves, and improved automobiles.

The Fortunate

Despite oft-repeated stories of thousands of ruined stockbrokers committing suicide, many in the upper classes prospered during the Great Depression. In Kenya, southern

Indochina, and elsewhere, large landowners evicted tenants who were unable to pay their rents and replaced them with cheaper day laborers. Moneylenders in India and Burma loaned peasants money to pay their rising taxes—due before the harvest. When agricultural prices fell early in the 1930s, some could not repay these loans, and moneylenders and large landowners alike took over the peasants' lands. Moreover, whereas rising tariffs, the turn to self-sufficiency, and the loss of foreign markets such as Britain hurt many international traders, merchants engaged in domestic trade managed to survive. Colombia, Brazil, Chile, Mexico, and Argentina actually showed either rising production or increased exports by 1932–1933. Throughout the Great Depression arms manufacturers made huge profits as nations such as Germany militarized. The majority of Europeans and Americans had jobs throughout the 1930s, and those with steady employment benefited from the drastic drop in consumer prices.

The Destitute

Even employed people, however, saw the millions of others around them struggling for a bare existence. In Cuba, where sugar prices collapsed, workers who did not lose their jobs were no longer paid, but simply fed a meal of "black or *caritas* beans, with their accompanying scum of weevils and worms . . . garbage that had no market," as one sugar worker described the food.[1] Because of the slump in agricultural prices, Japanese farmers were often reduced to eating tree bark, grass, and acorns and even gave up working: "Better to remain idle and eat less than work hard and eat more than can be earned," was the motto of some.[2] In towns with heavy industry, sometimes more than half the population was out of work. In a 1932 school assignment, a German youth wrote: "My father has been out of work for two-and-a-half years. He thinks that I'll never find a job." Under these conditions, a storm cloud of fear, resentment, and hopelessness settled over many parts of the globe.

Gender Relations

Economic catastrophe strained social stability and upset gender relations. The collapse of prices for rice and raw silk made some Japanese peasants so desperate that they sold their daughters into prostitution. As taxes increased in Africa, men migrated to regions hundreds of miles from their families in search of better jobs, weakening family ties. In urban areas of Europe and the United States unemployed men stayed home all day, increasing the tension in small, overcrowded apartments. Men who stayed at home sometimes took over housekeeping chores, but others found this "women's work" emasculating. Women around the world could often find low-paying jobs doing laundry and other domestic service; some brewed and marketed beer and prepared foods from their homes. As many women became breadwinners, albeit for low wages, men could be seen standing on street corners begging—a reversal of gender expectations that fueled discontent.

Rural men also faced the erosion of patriarchal authority, which was once central to overseeing farm labor and allocating property among heirs. Some lost their land entirely, and others had fewer children because of the economic slump. Mandatory education—and thus more years of required schooling—reduced family income and increased expenses for parents. Working-class children no longer earned wages to contribute to household income and were no longer available to help the family in other ways; instead they cost money while they went to school. Family-planning centers opened to help working people reduce family size in hard times. In a wide variety of ways, hard times disrupted the most fundamental human connections–the relationships among family members.

Protesting Poverty

The Great Depression produced rising protest by the unemployed. Often led by activists trained in the USSR, Communist parties flourished in the Chinese countryside, Indochina, the United States, Latin America, and across Europe, because they helped organize strikes and promised to end joblessness and exploitation. Mexican artist Diego Rivera captured the experiences of ordinary working people and the appeal of communism to them in huge murals he painted for public buildings. These massive paintings featured workers in factories and on farms, with portraits of Marx, Lenin, and Trotsky prominently intermingled with those of ordinary laborers. Union members in cities as distant as Shanghai, Detroit,

Diego Rivera, *Man at the Crossroads* (1934)
Communism and socialism appealed to workers both as ideologies and as political movements during the Great Depression, because they focused on ordinary people's needs. Mexican artist Diego Rivera had no love for the Soviet Union, yet he also considered communism to be an answer to the plight of native Americans and the oppressed around the world. In this mural, painted for Rockefeller Center in New York City but then torn down because of its image of Lenin, workers from many walks of life and ethnicities flock to the red flag and the message of Marx, Trotsky, and Lenin. (The Art Archive/Museo del Palacio de Bellas Artes Mexico/Dagli Orti.)

and Paris took to the streets to demand relief. In 1935, women textile workers in Medellin, Colombia, rose in angry protest about low wages and the insulting behavior of bosses. "Look, they'd go after the companies or whatever it was with rocks," said one woman of the strikers. "It was rough, it was bitter," she added.[3] Union leaders turned their wrath on big business. "Revolutions grow out of the depths of hunger," warned William Green, head of the American Federation of Labor, in 1931. For their part, governments and even factory owners responded with guns: police in Kobe, Japan, fought dockworkers, and government troops joined in crushing the demonstrators. U.S. automobile magnate Henry Ford turned his private police force on unemployed workers outside one of his plants, killing four of them and wounding far more. During the Great Depression, the masses had to defend their lives as well as their livelihoods.

Economic distress added to smoldering grievances in the colonies. As prices on commodities such as coffee, tin, and copper sank, colonial farmers withheld their produce from imperial wholesalers. Farmers in Ghana, for example, refused to sell cocoa in the 1930s. Discontent ran deep across the Middle East and Asia as well, fueled by the injustices of the World War I peace settlement, increasing colonial taxation, and hard economic times. General strikes rocked Palestine and India in 1936 and 1937, respectively. Their resolve fortified by bitter experiences, by the example of Japan's rising power, and by their own industrial development, colonial peoples roused themselves in an effort to overturn the imperial order.

Western-educated native leaders such as Ho Chi Minh, founder of the Indochinese Communist Party, led popular movements to contest their people's subjection. In 1930 the French government brutally crushed the peasant uprising Ho led. During the 1930s millions more working people came to follow Mohandas Gandhi, the charismatic leader of the Indian independence movement. The British jailed Gandhi repeatedly, stirred up Hindu-Muslim antagonism, and massacred protesters. Britain, France, and other European countries were quick to use their military might to put down colonial uprisings in an effort to preserve their empires. At the same time, however, they were slow to recognize a much greater threat to their well-being. As totalitarianism spread across Europe, the Western democracies responded with little more than words.

Imperialist Response to Popular Uprisings

Militarizing the Masses in the 1930s

FOCUS
How did dictatorships and democracies attempt to mobilize the masses?

Representative government collapsed in many countries under the sheer weight of social and economic crisis. Japanese military men promoted overseas conquest as a solution to the depression, and even poor peasants donated funds to Japan's military cause. After 1929, Italy's Benito Mussolini, the Soviet Union's Joseph Stalin, and Germany's Adolf Hitler gained vast support for their regimes by mobilizing the masses in ways that had previously been attempted only in times of war. This common commitment to the use of political violence has led historians to apply the term **totalitarianism** to the Fascist, Communist, and Nazi regimes of the 1930s. The term refers to highly centralized systems of government that attempt to control society and ensure obedience through a single party and police terror. Many citizens admired Mussolini, Stalin, and Hitler for the discipline they brought to social and economic life, and overlooked the brutal side of totalitarian government. Unity and soldier-like obedience—not individual rights and open debate—were seen as keys to recovery.

To mobilize the masses, politicians also appealed to racist sentiment. "Superior" peoples were selfishly failing to flourish and breed, they charged, while growing numbers of "inferior" peoples were seeking to take their place. For the Japanese, the Chinese and Koreans were the "inferiors"; for Germans, Jews were the enemy and all others were inferiors. In the United States, some politicians built popular support by scapegoating Mexican Americans and other minorities. Targeting an enemy—whether fellow citizens of different faiths, colors, or ethnicities, or an entire country—enabled popular leaders to mobilize the masses to fight this internal or external enemy instead of building national unity around democratically solving economic problems.

The Rise of Stalinism

Joseph Stalin, who succeeded Lenin in 1929, led the astonishing transformation of the USSR in the 1930s from a predominantly agricultural society into a formidable industrial power. In 1929 Stalin ended Lenin's New Economic Policy, which (as we saw in Chapter 27) combined elements of Marxism and capitalism, and replaced it with the first of several **five-year plans** intended to mobilize Soviet citizens to industrialize the nation. Stalin's economic transformations reduced individual freedom and cost the lives of millions.

Transforming the Economy and Society

Stalin outlined a program for massive increases in the output of coal, iron ore, steel, and industrial goods over successive five-year periods. Without an end to economic backwardness, Stalin warned, "the advanced countries . . . will crush us." He thus established **central economic planning**, a policy of government direction of the economy, as used in World War I and increasingly favored by economists and industrialists around the world. Between 1929 and 1940, the number of Soviet workers in industry, construction, and transport grew from 4.6 million to 12.6 million, and production soared. Stalin's first five-year plan helped make the USSR a leading industrial nation, and one that was ultimately able to withstand the test of world war.

Central planning created a new elite class of bureaucrats and industrial officials, who dominated Soviet workers, forcing them to leave the countryside to work in state-run factories. While Communist officials enjoyed benefits such as country homes and luxurious vacations, untrained workers from the countryside were herded into barracklike dwellings or tents and endured dangerous factory conditions. Still, many believed in the promise of communism and took pride in learning new skills: "We mastered this profession—completely new to us—with great pleasure," a female lathe operator recalled. They tolerated intense suffering because, as one worker put it, "Man himself is being rebuilt." Nonetheless, new workers often lacked the technical education necessary to achieve the goals prescribed by the five-year plan, and official lying about productivity became a regular practice.

The Soviet government also drastically changed conditions on the land. Faced with peasants' refusal simply to turn over their grain to the government, Stalin called for the "liquidation of the kulaks" (koo-LAHKS). The word *kulak*, which literally means "fist," was first an insulting Soviet term for a prosperous peasant, but it came to apply to any independent farmer. One Russian remembered believing kulaks were "bloodsuckers, cattle, swine, loathsome, repulsive: they had no souls; they stank," and were "enemies of the state." Party workers robbed farmers of their possessions, left them to starve, or even murdered them outright. Confiscated kulak land formed the basis of the new collective farms,

totalitarianism A single-party form of government emerging after World War I in which the ruling political party seeks to control all parts of the social, cultural, economic, and political lives of the population, typically making use of mass communication and violence to instill its ideology and maintain power.

five-year plan One of the centralized programs for economic development instituted by Joseph Stalin in the USSR and copied by Adolf Hitler in Germany; these plans set production priorities and targets for individual industries and agriculture.

central economic planning A policy of government direction of the economy, established during World War I and increasingly used in peacetime.

Socialist Realist Art

The early days of the Bolshevik Revolution witnessed experimentation in social and sexual relationships and in the arts. Under Stalin the government sponsored the official artistic style called "socialist realism"; it featured smiling workers with glowing complexions who radiated a sense of supreme happiness. Often taken as hypocritical, given the actual living conditions in the Soviet Union, socialist realist art in fact looked to the future—what socialist society would be when it reached the state of perfection for which everyone should strive and sacrifice. (akg-images/Michael Teller.)

where the remaining peasants were forced to live and to share facilities and modern machinery. Traditional peasant life was brought to a violent end as the social and economic connections that bound rural residents to one another and to society at large were redrawn.

The result of the Communist experiment with collective farming was mass starvation, as Soviet grain harvests declined from 83 million tons in 1930 to 67 million in 1934. Economic failure became a political issue, and Stalin blamed the crisis not on inexperienced workers but on enemies of communism. He instituted **purges**—that is, state-approved violence that included widespread arrests, imprisonments in labor camps, and executions. Beginning in 1936, a series of "show trials" based on trumped-up charges and fabricated evidence resulted in the conviction and execution of former Bolshevik leaders and thousands of military officers for conspiring against the USSR. Simultaneously, the government expanded the system of lethal prison camps—called the *Gulag*, an acronym for the department that ran the camps—to stretch several thousand miles from Moscow to Siberia. Prisoners did every kind of work, from digging canals to building apartment complexes in Moscow. With 1 million dying annually from the harsh conditions, the casualties of the Soviet system far exceeded those in Nazi Germany in the 1930s.

Militarization in the 1930s curtailed personal freedom. As the population declined from famine, purges, and a rapid drop in the birthrate in the 1930s, the USSR ended the reproductive freedom of the early revolutionary years, restricting access to birth-control information and abortion and criminalizing homosexuality. Yet because of state programs, women across the Soviet Union made gains in literacy and received better health care. Positions in the lower ranks of the Communist Party opened to women as the purges continued, and women increasingly were accepted into the professions. Still, the burden on women was great. After working long hours in factories, they had to stand in line for scarce consumer goods and perform all household and child-care tasks.

Stalin used artists and writers—"engineers of the soul," he called them—to help mobilize the masses. In return for housing, office space, and secretarial help, the "comrade artist" adhered to the official style of "socialist realism," which depicted workers as full of rosy emotions—a rosiness reflecting less communist reality than its promises for future fulfillment. Some artists, such as the poet Anna Akhmatova (ahk-MAH-toh-vah), protested the harsh Soviet reality. "Stars of death stood above us, and Russia, / In her innocence, twisted in pain / Under blood-spattered boots," wrote Akhmatova of the 1930s, as she stood in line outside a Soviet prison, waiting for news of her son, who was being held there. Once a prosperous and celebrated writer, Akhmatova was reduced to living off the generosity of her friends as a result of her resistance.

Despite such notable exceptions, Stalin triumphantly militarized the masses in his warlike campaign to industrialize in the 1930s, becoming to them, as one worker put it, "a god on earth."[4] Admirers from around the world headed to the USSR to see the "workers' paradise" for themselves and to learn how to mobilize mass support in other countries.

purge In the USSR in the 1930s, one of a series of attacks on citizens accused of being enemies of the state.

Japanese Expansionism

The Great Depression struck Japan's economy as it was recovering from a catastrophic earthquake that had killed more than 140,000 people and laid waste to both the capital of Tokyo and the bustling port city of Yokohama. The earthquake sparked murders—led by the military—of Korean and Chinese workers in the area as somehow responsible for the devastation. In 1925, men over the age of twenty-five had received the vote and the young Hirohito (heer-oh-HEE-toh) had become emperor, but the economic downturn and social unrest made Japan unstable.

An ambitious military, impatient with Japan's weak democratic institutions, sought control of the government, as did politicians favoring improved representative government. A modernizing economy and growing world trade had unleashed social change, and reformers challenged traditional values such as women's obedience. Author Junichiro Tanizaki captured the clash of old and new worldviews in novels such as *Naomi* (1924–1925), in which an engineer is totally obsessed with an independent "new woman," and *The Makioka Sisters* (1943–1948), some of whose protagonists struggle to protect tradition amid relentless change.

The Japanese military won out over the liberal politicians. Military leaders offered their own solution to the depressed conditions of workers, peasants, and business people: conquer nearby regions to provide new farmlands and create markets. Japanese peasants, hampered in the pursuit of their livelihoods, would settle new areas such as Manchuria, while business people would benefit from a larger pool of consumers, workers, and raw materials in annexed lands. Viewing China and the Western powers as obstacles to Japan's prosperity, Japan's military leaders promoted the idea that the military was an institution unto itself, an "emperor's army" not subject to civilian control, and that it would bring about a new world order and the fulfillment of Japan's destiny. By the 1930s, Emperor Hirohito and his advisers had built public support for a militaristic imperial system. Renewed military vigor was seen as key to Japan's claims to racial superiority and its entitlement to the lands of people they considered "inferior"—such as the Chinese. Such claims linked Japan with Germany and Italy in the 1930s, setting the stage for a menacing global alliance.

MAP 28.1 Japanese Expansion, 1931–1942

Japan's rise as a modern industrial power began in the nineteenth century with the Meiji Restoration. Like most powers and would-be powers, its leaders believed that the nation should dominate others to create its own empire. Expansion in the 1930s was intended to cap the earlier annexation of Taiwan and Korea and lead to the conquest of much of Asia, bringing the island nation enormous new territory and resources.

The Manchurian Incident

The Japanese army took the lead in making these claims a reality: in September 1931 it blew up a Japanese-owned train in the Chinese province of Manchuria and made the incident look like an attack on Japan by placing corpses dressed in official Chinese uniforms alongside the tracks. The military then used the explosion as an excuse to invade the territory, set up a puppet government, and push farther into China (see Map 28.1). Journalists back in Japan rallied the public to condemn Chinese aggression and support expansion into China. China appealed to the League of Nations in protest. Although the League condemned the invasion, it imposed no penalties or economic sanctions against Japan. Meanwhile the Japanese army dealt with the democratic opposition by simply assassinating them.

China's New Life Movement

The Chinese did not sit idly by in the face of Japan's invasion. In 1934 Jiang Jieshi (Chiang Kai-shek) introduced the "New Life" Movement, whose aim was "to militarize the

Jiang Jieshi and Mai-ling Soong

Jiang Jieshi took control of the Nationalist government in China and campaigned to promote regular exercise and hygiene as part of his modernization efforts. At the time of this 1927 photograph, Mai-ling Soong, from one of China's wealthiest families and sister-in-law of Sun Yatsen, was Jiang's fiancée. Having crossed the globe, she represented the "new woman" with her U.S. college education, unbound feet, and Western clothing. (Bettmann/Corbis.)

life of the people" and to make them "willing to sacrifice for the nation at all times."[5] The New Life Movement was inspired by European fascist militarism, with its promise of national unity, but the program also promoted discipline in everyday life through cleanliness and exercise. Some nationalist reformers saw the position of women as key to modernizing and strengthening China. Traditions such as foot-binding were attacked as old-fashioned, and by the mid-1930s there were some six thousand institutions of higher education for women in China. To Jiang, national unity demanded mobilization on the political level against the Chinese Communist Party—not the Japanese. Ultimately, however, Jiang was forced to join the Communists in fighting the Japanese instead of fighting one another.

Mobilization of the Masses in Japan

Japanese army leaders, countering increasing Chinese unity and purpose, mobilized their own people, using the mass media to create a "people's patriotism" among poor farmers and factory workers. In 1933, the film *Japan in the National Emergency* depicted the utopian mission of Japan "to create an ideal land in East Asia" where under Japanese leadership the races would harmoniously join together. Decadent Western culture—notably its racism, the film claimed—showed that Japan as a whole needed to turn away from the West and return to protecting the "sacred spirit" of the nation.[6] Propagandists encouraged Japanese citizens to renounce individual rights: "even in our private lives we always remember to unite with the emperor and serve the state."[7] Labor unions supported militarization, pressing impoverished workers to contribute funds for the military. By 1937, Japan's government was spending 47 percent of its budget on weaponry, thanks to the successful mobilization of people from all classes.

Hitler's Rise to Power

Mass politics reached terrifying proportions in Germany when Adolf Hitler finally achieved his goal of overthrowing German democracy. In his book *Mein Kampf* ("My Struggle," 1925), he laid out his vision of "scientific" anti-Semitism and the rebirth of the German "race," a vision he attempted to implement through his leadership of the Nazi

Party (National Socialist German Workers' Party). When the Great Depression struck Germany, the Nazis began to outstrip their rivals in elections, thanks in part to support from some big businessmen and the press. Hitler's election as chancellor in 1933 launched twelve years of violent Nazi rule.

Appeal of Nazism

Foremost among the Nazis' supporters were idealistic youth, who believed that Germany could recapture its former glory only if Hitler took control, and also white-collar workers and the lower middle class, who were still hurting from the postwar inflation that had destroyed their savings. By targeting all their parliamentary opponents as a single, monolithic group of "Bolshevik" enemies, the Nazis won wide approval for confronting those they accused of causing the depression. Many thought it was time to replace democratic government with a bold new leader who would take on these enemies militarily, without concern for constitutions, laws, or individual rights.

Hitler devised modern propaganda techniques to build his appeal. Thousands of recordings of Hitler's speeches and other Nazi souvenir items circulated among the public, and Nazi rallies were masterpieces of mass spectacle. Hitler, however, viewed the masses with contempt: "The receptivity of the great masses is very limited, their intelligence is small. In consequence of these facts, all effective propaganda must be limited to a very few points and must harp on those in slogans." Germany's power brokers from the military, industry, and the state bureaucracy, fearing the Communists for their opposition to private property, saw to it that Hitler legally became chancellor in 1933. Millions celebrated. "My father went down to the cellar and brought up our best bottles of wine. . . . And my mother wept for joy," one German recalled. "Now everything will be all right," she said.

Repression in the Nazi State

Hitler took command brutally and forcibly closed down representative government. Nazis suspended civil rights, imposed censorship of the press, and prohibited meetings of the political parties. Hitler made his aims clear: "I have set myself one task, namely to sweep those parties out of Germany." Storm troopers—the private Nazi army that existed in addition to Germany's regular forces—so harassed democratic politicians that at the end of March 1933 intimidated delegates let pass the Enabling Act, which suspended the constitution for four years and allowed Nazi laws to take effect without parliamentary approval. The elite SS (*Schutzstaffel*) was yet another military organization, and along with the Gestapo, or political police, it enforced complete obedience to Nazism. These organizations had vast powers to arrest Communists, Jews, homosexuals, and activists and either executed them or imprisoned them in concentration camps, the first of which opened at Dachau near Munich in March 1933.

The Nazis knew that their power depended on improving economic conditions and, in that context, the government pursued pump priming, that is, stimulating the economy by investing in public works projects such as constructing tanks, airplanes, and highways. Unemployment declined from a peak of almost 6 million in 1932 to 1.6 million by 1936. The Nazi Party closed down labor unions, and government managers classified jobs and set pay levels, rating women's jobs lower than men's regardless of the level of expertise required. The belief grew that Hitler was working an economic miracle.

The Nazi government took control of all aspects of everyday life, including gender roles. A law encouraged Aryans (those people legally defined as racially German) to have children by providing loans to Aryan newlyweds, but only if the wife left the workforce. Nazi marriage programs enforced both racial and gender ideology; women were supposed to be subordinate so men would feel tough and industrious despite military defeat and economic depression. A woman "joyfully sacrifices and fulfills her fate," one Nazi leader explained. Censorship flourished. Radio broadcasts were clogged with propaganda; book-burnings destroyed works by Jews, socialists, homosexuals, and modernist writers. Hitler claimed to be rebuilding the harmonious community destroyed by modernity even as his government used very modern tools of surveillance and big government programs to enforce the Nazi program. For millions of Germans, however, Nazi rule brought anything but harmony and well-being.

Nazi Racism

The Nazis defined Jews as an inferior "race" dangerous to the superior Aryan "race" and as responsible for both Germany's defeat in World War I and the economic crisis that followed. National Socialism, Hitler insisted in a 1938 speech, was not based on old fashioned anti-Semitism but on "the greatest of scientific knowledge." Jews were "vermin," "parasites," and "Bolsheviks," whom the Germans had to eliminate. In 1935, the Nuremberg Laws deprived Jews of citizenship and prohibited marriage between Jews and other Germans. Whereas women defined as Aryan had increasing difficulty obtaining abortions or birth-control information, these were readily available to Jews and other outcast groups. In the name of improving the Aryan race, doctors in the late 1930s helped organize the T4 project, which used carbon monoxide poisoning and other means to kill two hundred thousand "inferior" people—especially the handicapped.

Jews were forced into slave labor, evicted from their apartments, and prevented from buying most clothing and food. In 1938, a Jewish teenager, reacting to the harassment of his parents, killed a German official. In retaliation, Nazis attacked synagogues, smashed windows of Jewish-owned stores, and threw more than twenty thousand Jews—including Eva Kantorowski's father—into prisons and work camps. The night of November 9–10 became known as *Kristallnacht* (kris-TAHL-nahkt), or the Night of Broken Glass. Faced with this relentless persecution, by 1939 more than half of Germany's five hundred thousand Jews had emigrated. Hitler mobilized the masses by targeting an enemy—the Jews—not just in wartime but in peacetime, not outside the country but within it. Persecution of the Jews brought Germans new financial resources as they simply stole Jewish property and took Jewish jobs.

Democracies Mobilize

Facing the double-barreled assault of economic depression and totalitarian aggression, democracies rallied in support of freedom, individuals' rights, and citizens' well-being, though they often limited their efforts to whites. In the eyes of many, however, representative government appeared feeble compared with totalitarian leaders' military style of mobilizing the masses. Democracy was difficult to support in tough economic times, but as the depression wore on, some governments—notably the United States and Sweden—undertook bold experiments to solve social and economic crises while still maintaining democratic politics.

The United States

In the early days of the depression, U.S. lawmakers opposed giving direct aid to the unemployed and even used military force to put down a demonstration by jobless veterans in the nation's capital. Government policy changed, however, after Franklin Delano Roosevelt was elected president in 1932. Roosevelt pushed through a torrent of legislation: relief for businesses, price supports for struggling farmers, and public works programs for the unemployed. The Social Security Act of 1935 set up a fund to which employers and employees contributed to provide retirement and other benefits for citizens. Like other successful politicians of the 1930s and thereafter, Roosevelt used the new mass media expertly, especially in his radio series of "fireside chats" to the American people. In sharp contrast to Mussolini and Hitler, Roosevelt—with the able assistance of his wife Eleanor—aimed to build faith in democracy rather than denounce it: "We Americans of today . . . are characters in the living book of democracy," he told a group of teenagers in 1939. The president's bold programs and successful use of the media kept the masses, even those facing racial discrimination, mobilized to believe in a democratic future.

Sweden

Sweden's response to the crisis of the 1930s became a model for the postwar welfare state. The Swedish government turned its economy around by instituting social welfare programs and central planning of the economy. It devalued its currency to make Swedish exports more attractive. Pump-priming projects increased Swedish productivity by 20 percent between 1929 and 1935, a period when other democracies were floundering. Government programs also addressed the population problem, but without the racism and coercion of totalitarianism. One architect of the program to boost childbirth was the activist Alva Myrdal (MEER-dahl), a young sociologist and leading member of parliament. Myrdal's mother had been so against modern education that she forbade library books in the house, claiming that they promoted diseases. Myrdal made it to university, but after her topics for a doctoral dissertation were rejected, she turned to activism, promoting causes such as "voluntary parenthood" and improved work opportunities for women—even married ones. Following Myrdal's lead, the Swedish government started a loan program for married couples in 1937 and introduced prenatal care, free childbirth in a hospital, and subsidized housing for large families. Because all families—rural and urban, poor or prosperous—received these benefits, there was widespread support for this experiment with developing a welfare state alongside democracy. Alva Myrdal went on to become ambassador to India, a tireless worker for the United Nations and world peace, and a Nobel Prize recipient.

France

Like Germany, France faced economic and political turmoil and only narrowly avoided a fascist takeover. Deputies with opposing views frequently came to blows in the Chamber of Deputies, and right-wing paramilitary groups took to the streets, attracting the unemployed, students, and veterans to demonstrations against representative government. The growing attraction of fascism shocked French liberals, socialists, and Communists into an antifascist coalition known as the Popular Front. This alliance was made possible when Stalin allowed Communist parties, whose policies he determined, to join in the protection of democracy rather than work to destroy it. For just over a year in 1936–1937 and again very briefly in 1938, the French Popular Front, headed by socialist leader Léon Blum, led the government. Like American and Swedish reformers, the Popular Front enacted welfare benefits and mandatory two-week paid vacations for workers. Bankers and industrialists greeted Blum's costly programs by sending their savings out of the country, however, leaving France financially strapped and the government mortally wounded. "Better Hitler than Blum" was the slogan of the upper classes, and the Popular Front fell. The collapse of the antifascist Popular Front showed the difficulties of democratic societies facing economic crisis and the revival of militarism.

Cultural Mobilization in the West

Democratic cultural life also fought the lure of fascism. During its brief existence, the Popular Front encouraged the masses to celebrate democratic holidays such as Bastille Day with new enthusiasm. Artists made films, wrote novels, and produced art that celebrated ordinary people and captured their everyday struggles. In Charlie Chaplin's film *Modern Times* (1936), his famous character, the Little Tramp, was a worker in a modern factory molded by his monotonous job to believe that even his co-workers' bodies needed mechanical adjustment. Viewers laughed with him instead of growing resentful. Heroines in immensely popular musical comedies behaved bravely, pulling their men out of the depths of despair and thus away from fascist temptation. In the film *Keep Smiling* (1938), for example, British comedienne Gracie Fields portrayed a spunky working-class woman who remained cheerful despite the challenges of living in hard times.

Novelists affirmed human rights and the dignity of the poor in the face of dictatorial pomp and bombast. In a series of novels based on the biblical figure Joseph, German writer and Nobel Prize winner Thomas Mann conveyed the conflict between humane values and barbarism. The fourth volume, *Joseph the Provider* (1944), praised Joseph's welfare state, in which the granaries are full and the rich pay taxes so the poor might live decent lives. Chinese author Pa Chin used his widely influential novel *Family* (1931) to criticize the dictatorial powers of traditional patriarchy, which destroyed humane values and loving relationships. In one of her last works, *Three Guineas* (1938), English writer Virginia Woolf abandoned the experimental novel in favor of a direct attack on militarism, poverty, and the oppression of women, showing that these were interconnected parts of the single, dangerous worldview of the 1930s.

Global War 1937–1945

The depression intensified competition among nations as politicians sought to expand their country's access to land, markets, and resources. Mobilizing the masses around national and military might, Hitler, Mussolini, and Japan's military leaders marched the world toward another catastrophic war.

FOCUS

How did World War II progress on the battlefront and the home front?

Democratic statesmen hoped that sanctions imposed by the League of Nations would stop new aggression, but military assaults escalated with Japan's invasion of China and the outbreak of war in 1937. An era of destruction opened that at war's end left some 100 million of the world's peoples dead and tens of millions more starving and homeless.

Europe's Road to War

The surge in global imperialism that occurred during the 1930s has shaped international politics to the present day. Hitler's harsh anti-Jewish policies drove increasing numbers of European Jews to migrate to Palestine, bringing clashes between Palestinians and Jewish newcomers. Western imperialist powers, including Britain, France, the United States, and the Netherlands, increased their exploitation of resource-rich regions outside their borders amid mounting local resentment. The most severe challenge to the global order, however, came from Germany, Italy, and Japan, whose authoritarian regimes and drive for empire became ever bolder.

Uncontested Aggression

Like Japanese leaders, Hitler and Mussolini presented their countries as "have-nots" and demanded more power, resources, and land. Hitler's agenda included gaining more *Lebensraum* (LAY-buns-rowm), or living space, in which supposedly superior "Aryans" could thrive. This space would be taken from the "inferior" Slavic peoples, who would be moved to Siberia or would serve as slaves. In 1935 Hitler loudly rejected the Treaty of Versailles's limitations on German military strength and openly began rearming. In the same year, Mussolini invaded Ethiopia, one of the few African states not overwhelmed by European imperialism. "The Roman legionnaires are again on the march," one Italian soldier exulted at this colonial adventure. Despite the resistance of the poorly equipped Ethiopians, their capital, Addis Ababa, fell in the spring of 1936. The League of Nations voted to impose sanctions against Italy, but Britain and France opposed any embargo on oil, suggesting a lack of will to fight aggression.

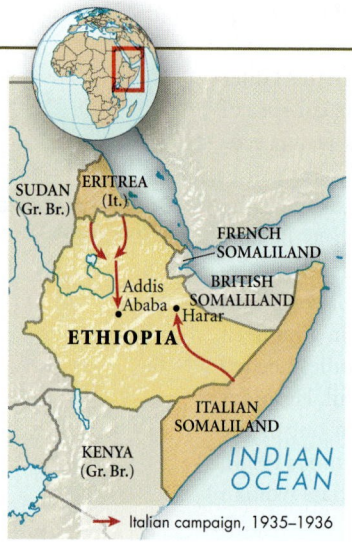

Italian Invasion of Ethiopia, 1935–1936

Nazi territorial expansion began with the annexation of Austria in 1938 (see Map 28.2). Aiming to unite all German peoples, Hitler's troops entered Austria, and the enthusiasm of Nazi sympathizers there made Germany's actions appear to support Wilsonian "self-determination." Nazis generated support in Austria by building factories to solve the unemployment problem and by reawakening Austrians' sense that they belonged once more to a mighty empire. Hitler turned next to Czechoslovakia and its rich resources. Hitler gambled correctly that the other Western powers would not interfere with any takeover if he could convince them that this was his last territorial claim. In the fall of 1938, British Prime Minister Neville Chamberlain, French Premier Édouard Daladier, and Mussolini met with Hitler in Munich, Germany, and, despite strong Czech opposition, agreed to allow Germany's claim to the Sudetenland (sue-DAY-ten-lahnd)—the German-populated border region of Czechoslovakia. Their strategy was to make concessions for grievances (in this case, injustices to Germany in the Peace of Paris), a policy called **appeasement**. As Europe outside of Czechoslovakia rejoiced, Chamberlain announced that he had secured "peace in our time" for a continent fearing another devastating war. Appeasement proved a failure: in March 1939, Hitler invaded the rest of Czechoslovakia.

The Fall of Central Europe

The Early Years of the War 1937–1943

While this expansion was unfolding, the first phase of World War II had begun in East Asia. In 1937, the Japanese military, after skirmishes around Beijing, attacked Shanghai, justifying its offensive as the first step in liberating the region from Western imperialism (see again Map 28.1). Moving to capture major cities along the coast, the Japanese army

appeasement The strategy of preventing a war by making concessions to aggressors.

MAP 28.2

Nazi Expansion, 1933–1939

Like Japan's expansion, Germany's conquests in the 1930s resulted from greed and the conviction that its superior people deserved the wealth of others. Throughout the 1930s the Nazis stole the possessions of German Jews—rich and poor—and then advanced across central and eastern Europe to seize the property of Jews and Slavs along with the gold and other wealth of conquered nations. Other European powers, committed to empire themselves, allowed this initial expansion to go unchallenged.

took the Chinese capital of Nanjing, massacring hundreds of thousands of Chinese in the "Rape of Nanjing," an atrocity so named because of the special brutality toward girls and women before they were killed. Japan's invasion of China marked the Asian beginnings of World War II.

Despite the slaughter, many in the West continued to believe that the highly militarized and industrialized Japanese were more fit to rule China than the Chinese themselves. In 1938, the Japanese government described its expansionism as the foundation for a "New Order" in Asia, the **Greater East Asia Co-Prosperity Sphere** that Japan would use to help free Asians and indeed the world from the oppressive white race. In reality, however, the Japanese made enormous demands on Asians for resources while treating Chinese and Koreans with brutality (see Reading the Past: "Comfort Women" in World War II).

As the Japanese fought to conquer China, Hitler launched an all-out attack on Poland on September 1, 1939. The way was prepared a week earlier on August 23, 1939, when Germany and the USSR signed a nonaggression agreement—the Nazi-Soviet Pact—providing that if one country became embroiled in war, the other country would remain neutral. Feeling confident, German forces let loose an overpowering *Blitzkrieg* ("lightning war"), a stunning and concentrated onslaught of airplanes, tanks, and motorized infantry, to defeat the ill-equipped Polish defenders with overwhelming speed. Allowing the army

Greater East Asia Co-Prosperity Sphere A region of Asian states to be dominated by Japan, and in theory, to benefit from Japan's superior civilization.

READING THE PAST

"Comfort Women" in World War II

Oh Omok was sixteen when she left home in Chongup, Korea, in 1937 to take up a new livelihood: that, she was told, of a factory worker in Japan. Instead, like thousands of other young Korean women, she ended up in a military brothel. This is a small part of her story, among the mildest of those gathered in the 1990s from former "comfort women" and meticulously documented by researchers.

> At first I delivered food for the soldiers and had to serve the rank and file, to have sex with them. . . . On receiving orders we were called to the appropriate unit and served five or six men a day. At times we would serve up to ten. We served the soldiers in very small rooms with floors covered with Japanese-style mats, *tatami*. . . . When the soldiers were away on an expedition it was nice and quiet, but once they returned we had to serve many of them. Then they would come to our rooms in a continuous stream. I wept a lot in the early days. Some soldiers tried to comfort me saying "*kawaisoni*" or "*naitara ikanyo*," which meant something like "you poor thing" and "don't cry." Some of the soldiers would hit me because I didn't understand their language. If we displeased them in the slightest way they shouted at us and beat us: "*bakayaro*" or "*kisamayaro*," "you idiot" and "you bastard." I realized that I must do whatever they wanted of me if I wished to survive.
>
> The soldiers used condoms. We had to have a medical examination for venereal infections once a week. Those infected took medicine and were injected with "No. 606" [a medicine regularly injected into the forced sex workers, often with bad side effects]. Sometime later, I became quite close to a Lieutenant Morimoto, who arranged for Okhui [a friend of Oh Omok] and me to receive only high-ranking officers. Once we began to exclusively serve lieutenants and second lieutenants, our lives became much easier.

Source: Keith Howard, ed., *True Stories of the Korean Comfort Women: Testimonies Compiled by the Korean Council for Women Drafted for Military Sexual Slavery by Japan and the Research Association on the Women Drafted for Military Sexual Slavery by Japan*, trans. Young Joo Lee (London: Cassell, 1995), 66–67.

EXAMINING THE EVIDENCE

1. **How would you describe Oh Omok's attitude toward her situation?**
2. **How might her experience as a "comfort woman" shape her ideas about gender and class relations?**

The German Onslaught

to conserve supplies, the Blitzkrieg assured Germans at home that the human costs of conquest would be low. On September 17, 1939, the Soviets invaded Poland from the east, and the victors then divided the country according to secret provisions in the Nazi-Soviet Pact (see again Map 28.2). Within Germany, Hitler called for defense of the fatherland against the "warlike menace" of world Jewry.

In April 1940, the Blitzkrieg crushed Denmark and Norway; Belgium, the Netherlands, and France fell in May and June (see Map 28.3). Stalin meanwhile annexed the Baltic states of Estonia, Latvia, and Lithuania. As Winston Churchill, an early advocate of resistance, took over as prime minister, Hitler ordered the bombardment of Britain. Churchill, another savvy orator, rallied the British people by radio to protect the ideals of liberty with their "blood, toil, tears, and sweat." In the Battle of Britain, or the Blitz as the British called it, the Luftwaffe (German air force) bombed homes, public buildings, harbors, weapons depots, and factories. Britain poured resources into anti-aircraft weapons, its highly successful code-detecting group called Ultra, and further development of radar. By year's end, the British airplane industry was outproducing the Germans by 50 percent.

By the fall of 1940, German air losses had driven Hitler to abandon his planned conquest of Britain. Forcing Hungary, Romania, and Bulgaria to become its allies, Germany gained access to more food and oil. In violation of the Nazi-Soviet Pact, Hitler launched an all-out campaign in June 1941 against what he called the "center of judeobolshevism"—the Soviet Union. Deployed along a two-thousand-mile front, 3 million German and other Axis troops quickly penetrated Soviet lines and killed, captured, or wounded more than

MAP 28.3

World War II in Europe, North Africa, and the Soviet Union, 1939–1945

War in the European theater was horrendous because increasingly powerful bombers, tanks, and artillery were unleashed on soldiers and civilians alike. After its initial success in the spring of 1940, Germany was so ideologically driven that it pursued its military ambitions even after failing in the Battle of Britain and then in the war against the Soviet Union. Meanwhile, the Allies outproduced the Axis powers by a wide margin and lavishly used their own heavy weapons to achieve a final victory in May 1945. By then, much of the European continent and parts of the Middle East and North Africa had been reduced to rubble.

half of the 4.5 million Soviet soldiers defending the borders. As the campaign continued along the far-flung battlefront, the Soviet people fought back. Because Hitler feared that equipping his army for Russian conditions would suggest to civilians that a prolonged war lay in store, the Nazi soldiers were unprepared for the onset of winter. In this way, Hitler

MAP 28.4

World War II in the Pacific, 1937–1945

The "Europe first" strategy of the Allies permitted Japan a comparatively free hand in the Pacific. Japan's victories were short-lived, however, despite the determined efforts of its civilians and military to sacrifice everything for victory. The many conquered peoples of the Pacific suffered mightily under Japanese rule, performing forced labor, serving as sex slaves, and bearing the brunt of the final Allied push to defeat the Axis in the Pacific.

preserved the average citizen's confidence in German might, but at the cost of undermining the actual effectiveness of his army.

War Intensifies in the Pacific

Allies The alliance of Great Britain, France, the Soviet Union, and the United States and their coalition partners in World War II.

Axis The alliance of Italy, Germany, and Japan and their client states in World War II.

As Japan swiftly captured British colonies in Asia and invaded French Indochina for its raw materials, the United States stopped supplying Japan with essential industrial goods. The Japanese government decided it should settle matters with the West, and in December 1941, its planes bombed American naval and air bases at Pearl Harbor in Hawaii and then destroyed a fleet of airplanes in the Philippines. President Roosevelt summoned the Congress to declare war on Japan. By spring 1942, the Japanese had conquered Guam, the Philippines, Malaya, Burma, Indonesia, Singapore, and much of the southwestern Pacific (see Map 28.4). As had happened with Germany's expansionist drive, the victories strengthened the appeal of the Japanese military's imperial ideology. "The era of democracy is finished," the foreign minister announced confidently.[8] Japanese officials portrayed Emperor Hirohito as the pan-Asian monarch who would liberate Asians everywhere.

Germany and Italy quickly joined Japan and declared war on the United States—an appropriate enemy, Hitler proclaimed, as it was "half Judaized and the other half Negrified." The United States was ambivalent toward the Soviet Union despite Hitler's attack, and Stalin reciprocated the mistrust. Nonetheless, the Soviet Union joined with Great Britain, the Free French (an exile government based in London), and the United States to form the Grand Alliance. Twenty other countries joined this group of nations to form a coalition—known collectively as the **Allies**—who fought the **Axis** powers of Germany, Italy, and Japan. In the long run the Allies held distinct advantages in terms of manpower and access to resources, given the extensive terrain they controlled, but both sides faced the bloodiest fight in world history (see Lives and Livelihoods: Soldiers and Soldiering).

War and the World's Civilians

Victory in World War II depended on industrial productivity geared toward total war and mass killings. From the Rape of Nanjing to the horrors of the Holocaust, far more civilians than soldiers died in World War II. The Axis and the Allies alike bombed cities to destroy civilians' will to resist—a debatable tactic since it often inspired defiance rather than surrender. The Allied firebombing of Dresden and Tokyo alone killed tens of thousands of civilians, but Axis attacks caused far more civilian deaths. Chinese civilians, not Chinese soldiers, were the target of the Rape of Nanjing, and British people, not British soldiers, were the target of the Battle of Britain. Mass slaughter had a rationale behind it: in a total war, workers were as important as soldiers because they manufactured the tools of war. Neither Japan nor Germany took the resources and civilian morale of its enemies into full account, however.

The new "master races" believed it was their mission to rid the world of subhumans and then repopulate it themselves. As the German army swept through eastern Europe, it slaughtered Jews, Communists, Slavs, and others whom Nazi ideology deemed "racial inferiors" and enemies. The number of deliberately murdered civilian victims in China alone is estimated to be at least 2.5 million, with untold millions murdered elsewhere in the region. Some 3 million Japanese were then relocated as "civilizers" in conquered areas of East Asia, while "racially pure" Germans took over farms and homes in Poland and elsewhere. To lessen resistance, German occupiers tested the reading skills of those captured with the promise that they could avoid hard labor. Instead, those who could read were lined up and shot as potential rebel leaders.

The extermination of Jews became a special focus of the Nazis. Crowded into urban ghettos, stripped of their possessions, and living on minimal rations, countless eastern European Jews died of starvation and disease—the Nazis' initial plan for reducing the Jewish population. Soon the Nazis put into operation the "Final Solution," their bureaucratic plan for the extermination of all of Europe's Jews by rounding them up for transport to death camps. Soldiers, ordinary civilians, police, scientists, and doctors—all participated in the **Holocaust**. Extermination camps were developed specifically for the purposes of mass murder, though some, like Auschwitz-Birkenau in Poland, served as both death and labor camps. Captives, among them Hans Kantorowsky, were herded into gas chambers where they were killed by lethal gas, and then the corpses were burned in specially designed crematoria. As of 1943, Auschwitz had the capacity to burn 1.7 million bodies per year.

Major Concentration Camps and Extermination Sites in Europe

Holocaust The genocidal murder of some 6 million Jews by the Germans during World War II in an attempt to exterminate European Jewry.

For all their anti-Semitic bluster, the Nazis took pains to hide the true purpose of the camps. Those not chosen for immediate murder in the camps had their heads shaved,

LIVES AND LIVELIHOODS

Soldiers and Soldiering

African American Sailors in World War II

The U.S. military offered African Americans opportunity as well as danger in the struggle to defeat fascism. Even as they themselves faced discrimination in the armed forces, many saw the war as a campaign to promote universal rights and to defeat the forces of racism and ethnic supremacy. Having participated in the great moral victory of defeating violent bigotry abroad, they often joined the civil rights campaign after the war to defeat violent bigotry at home. (Bettmann/Corbis.)

Between 1930 and 1945 tens of millions of men and women worldwide became soldiers, joining both regular armies and paramilitary groups such as those run by the Chinese Communist Party and the German National Socialist (Nazi) Party. In 1927, for example, Mao Zedong, a young leader among Chinese Communists, helped decide that the groups should become a "Red Army" rather than organize into a traditional army. This paramilitary group marched northward through rural regions of China, adding recruits and ministering to the needs of peasants even as it indoctrinated them and took their resources. The German Nazi and Italian fascist paramilitary groups inflicted violence on strikers, on Communists, and, in the case of the Nazis, on Jews. During tough economic times, when jobs in the civilian workforce were lacking, men found a livelihood in paramilitary armies.

Thus, well before World War II, there was active soldiering and warfare. Indeed, many people wondered if war ever really ended. In the deadly Chaco War (1932–1935) between Bolivia and Paraguay to increase territory, especially where oil exploration was taking place, teenage boys were drafted. One Bolivian survivor, drafted at age fifteen, recalled, "We had the luck to have bad commanders. They didn't lead us. . . . They sent all the soldiers to the front, and they stayed behind. They didn't give us a single thing to eat nor a single

The Holocaust

were disinfected, and then given prison garments—many of them so thin and tattered that they offered no protection against winter cold and rain. So began life in "a living hell," as one survivor wrote of the starvation, overwork, and disease. In the name of advancing "racial science," doctors in German concentration camps performed unbelievably cruel medical experiments and operations with no anesthesia on pregnant women, twins, and other innocent people. But prisoners developed strategies for survival, forging friendships that sustained them. Thanks to the food and favors he received from fellow prisoners, wrote Auschwitz survivor Primo Levi, "I managed not to forget that I myself was a man." In the end, 6 million Jews, the vast majority from eastern Europe, along with a mosaic of thing to drink. . . . For this simple reason [soldiers] collapsed . . . they died."[1]

The highest ranks of the military were generally staffed by social elites and treated well. In China, Jiang Jieshi, from a relatively prosperous family, attended Baoding Military Academy. He then trained in Japan, where high levels of literacy and knowledge of the classics were central, so officers usually came from homes that were cultured. In the United States, movie stars and children from the highest ranks of society, including the sons and daughters of senators and millionaires, volunteered for World War II and were often placed in less dangerous regions. Ordinary members of the infantry, however, were on the frontlines, where the most common activity was digging, especially the foxholes in which they lived and protected themselves.

For many, political belief was a major factor in warfare. "The only thing that keeps me always on my feet and always ready: faith in God and in the Duce," one Italian soldier wrote from the front. From their training, Japanese soldiers came to believe "we are all samurai now," and an Australian soldier observed that whatever the character of the individual Japanese soldier, "good or bad, kind or sadistic, they had one supreme virtue . . . a courage that I believe to be unequalled in our time."[2]

There were failures in instilling belief, however. After their increasing exploitation during the depression, Africans often hid from recruiters and village chiefs in charge of wartime forced labor. In Southern Rhodesia, they used colonial ideology to justify their draft-dodging: "We are women. The White people are our menfolk to whom we look for guidance and protection. We have never had the courage or the ability to fight in war."[3]

War was a grim experience for most—they might face starvation in prison camps, epidemic disease, horrific wounds, wrenching physical and mental torture, suicide, cannibalism, and death. Yet soldiers' lives also had a bright side based on the loyal comradeship that developed during combat. Many professed not to fight for a cause but for the well-being of those fighting alongside them, and others found love and support on ships, in hospitals, and on the battlefield. Some believed that the military offered opportunity, among them African Americans, even though many had grown cynical when their efforts in World War I brought no relief from lynching, job discrimination, and open racism more generally. Soldiers might gain new technological skills and even find wholly new livelihoods to pursue in the future.

1. Cristobal Arancibia, quoted in "Cristobal Arancibia: The Life of a Bolivian Peasant During the Chaco War, 1932–1935," ed. W. H. Beezley and J. Ewell, *Human Tradition in Latin America: The Twentieth Century* (Wilmington, DE: Scholarly Resources, 1987), 97.
2. Quoted in John Keegan, *Soldiers: A History of Men in Battle* (New York: Viking Penguin, 1986), 51.
3. Quoted in David Johnson, *World War II and the Scramble for Labour in Colonial Zimbabwe, 1939–1948* (Harare: University of Zimbabwe Press, 2000), 18.

QUESTIONS TO CONSIDER

1. **What specific advantages did soldiers from many walks of life see in joining the military?**
2. **How would you describe soldiers' lives from 1930 to 1945, and how did they vary?**
3. **What were the class dimensions of the military?**

For Further Information:

Cottam, Kazimiera Janina. *Soviet Airwomen in Combat in World War II*. 1983.
Johnson, David. *World War II and the Scramble for Labour in Colonial Zimbabwe, 1939–1948*. 2000.
Keegan, John. *Soldiers: A History of Men in Battle*. 1986.
Montgomerie, Deborah. *Love in a Time of War: Letter-Writing in the Second World War*. 2005.

millions of Roma, homosexuals, Slavs, and others, were murdered in the Nazis' organized, genocidal fury.

Societies at War

The Axis countries remained at a disadvantage throughout the war despite their early conquests. Although the war accelerated economic production some 300 percent between 1940 and 1944 in all belligerent countries, the Allies produced more than three times as much as the Axis in 1943 alone. Even while some of its lands were occupied and many of its cities besieged, the Soviet Union increased its production of weapons. Both Japan and Germany made the most of their lower capacity, with such tactics as Japan's suicide, or *kamikaze*, attacks in the last months of the war. Hitler had to prevent wartime shortages

The Warsaw Ghetto, 1943
From the 1930s on, the Nazis considered Jews and others to be both dangerous enemies and inferiors unworthy of living; they drove them into ghettos, confiscated their property, took away their livelihoods, and deprived them of food and fuel. Despite being confined to these ghettos, residents learned of the ongoing Holocaust, and in 1943 the people of the Warsaw ghetto staged an uprising. Those shown here were taken prisoner, and the uprising was brutally put down. (SZ Photo/ Bridgeman Art Library.)

because he had come to power promising to end economic suffering, not increase it. Japanese propaganda, however, persuaded civilians to endure extreme scarcity for the sake of the nation. The use of millions of forced laborers and resources from occupied areas reduced Axis deprivation.

Allied governments were overwhelmingly successful in generating civilian participation, especially among women. Soviet women constituted more than half the workforce by war's end. They dug massive antitank trenches around Moscow and other threatened cities, and eight hundred thousand volunteered for the military, even serving as pilots. As the Germans invaded, Soviet citizens moved entire factories eastward. In Germany and Italy, where government policy particularly exalted motherhood and kept women from the best-paying jobs, officials began to realize that women were desperately needed in offices and factories. Japanese women rushed to help, but even changing the propaganda to stress that they should take jobs did not convince German women to join the low-paid female workforce.

Even more than in World War I, propaganda saturated society in movie theaters and on the radio. People were glued to their radios for war news, but much of it was tightly controlled. Japan, like Germany, generally withheld news of defeats and large numbers of casualties to maintain civilian support. The antireligious Soviet government found radio programming from the Russian Orthodox clergy that boosted patriotism, and Japanese propagandists taught that both the war and the emperor were sacred. Filmmakers—subject to censorship unless their films conveyed the "right" message, including racial thinking—encouraged patriotism with stories of aviation heroes and faithful wives left behind. The German government continued to advertise ugly caricatures of Jews, Slavs, and Roma; Allied propaganda depicted Germans as gorillas and "Japs" as uncivilized, insectlike fanatics.

Such characterizations eased the way for the USSR to uproot Muslims and minority ethnic groups as potential Nazi collaborators and for the U.S. government to force citizens of Japanese origin into its own concentration camps. Fred Korematsu, born in Oakland,

California in 1919, was one U.S. citizen of Japanese descent who refused to leave his home on the grounds that only a handful of Americans of Italian and German descent were similarly interned. Korematsu was arrested and ultimately sent to a camp surrounded by barbed wire, machine guns, and watchtowers. Like that of many interned Japanese Americans, his family's property was taken and sold and he was left to find odd jobs, but he continued to fight his removal to a concentration camp and became a pioneer for civil rights.

Colonized peoples were drawn into the war through conscription into the armies and forced labor. Some 2 million Indian men served the Allied cause, as did several hundred thousand Africans, even as governments stripped their families of resources. To prevent Japanese confiscation of Indian resources, the British withdrew all shipping from Bengali ports, leaving the region with no food deliveries. "When I was nine years old we had the Bengal famine," one Indian remembered. "The victims suddenly emerged in millions—it seemed from absolutely nowhere, dying in incredible numbers."[9] Some 3 to 7 million Bengali civilians died of starvation—a British-inflicted Holocaust, as many have called it. Among the peoples of the great powers, Soviet children and old people were at the greatest risk of starvation; an adolescent alive during the siege of Leningrad would probably have been among the 1 million residents of the city who starved to death. Where there were resources, bureaucrats around the war-torn world regulated the production and distribution of food, clothing, and household products, all of which were of lower quality than before the war.

Forced Labor in Vietnam

Japan promised the colonized peoples of the world—especially those in Asia—that Japanese rule would bring liberation and real benefits to those who had been dominated by the Western powers. The reality was usually quite different. Korean, Chinese, and other women were made to serve as sex slaves to members of the Japanese military, and other civilians were forced to provide manual labor, such as these Vietnamese women digging what appears to be a trench to defend the military against tanks and other enemy vehicles. (bpk, Berlin/Art Resource, NY.)

Collaboration

Collaboration with Axis conquerors was common among colonial people who had suffered the racist oppression of the Western powers. As the Japanese swept through the Pacific and parts of East Asia, they conscripted local men into their army; many volunteered willingly. Subhas Bose, educated in England and accepted into the Indian Civil Service, quit his post in 1921 and became a prominent member of the Indian Congress Party, spending time in British prisons for his activities. When World War II broke out and the British refused to grant India home rule, he went over to the Axis side and recruited an all-Indian army to fight the British in South Asia. "Gandhi wants to change human beings, and all I want to do is free India," Bose maintained, as he fought on Japan's side.[10] Throughout the Axis-occupied areas of Europe, collaborationist leaders such as Philippe Pétain in France and Vidkun Quisling in Norway provided workers and equipment for the Axis cause. Many an ordinary person moved up the economic ladder by spying for the Axis powers and working for the occupiers.

Resistance

Resistance to the Axis also began early in the war. Escaping France in 1940, General Charles de Gaulle from his haven in London directed the Free French government, resisters on the continent, and Free French military—a mixed organization of troops of colonized Asians and Africans and soldiers and volunteers from France and other occupied

Colonial Recruits in World War II

Colonial forces played as significant a role in World War II as they had in World War I. They participated by the millions in armies, and both the Axis and the Allies drove colonized people under their control into forced labor. Often colonized peoples used the war to work against their imperial masters. These North African soldiers, who were probably under the rule of the French before the war, appear to have joined forces with the Germans as they chat with an officer. (akg-images/ullstein bild.)

countries. Other resisters, called partisans, planned assassinations of collaborators and enemy officers and bombed bridges and rail lines. Although the Catholic Church officially supported Mussolini, Catholic and Protestant clergy and their parishioners were among those who set up resistance networks, often hiding Jews and political suspects. Ordinary people also fought back through everyday activities. Homemakers circulated newsletters urging demonstrations at prisons where civilians were detained and in marketplaces where food was rationed. Jews rose up against their Nazi captors in Warsaw in 1943 but were mercilessly butchered. Resisters played on stereotypes: women often carried weapons to assassination sites and seduced and murdered enemy officers. "Naturally the Germans didn't think that a woman could have carried a bomb," explained one female Italian resister, "so this became the woman's task."[11]

From Allied Victory to the Cold War 1943–1945

FOCUS

How did the Allied victory unfold, and what were the causes of that victory?

Allied victory began to look certain by 1943, even though tough fighting still lay ahead. The Allies crashed through German lines in the east, south, and west of Europe, while war in the Pacific turned in the Allies' favor, despite the Japanese policy of resistance to the death. In a series of wartime meetings, Churchill, Stalin, and Roosevelt—nicknamed the Big Three—planned the peace that they expected to achieve, including the creation of a new organization called the United Nations to prevent another war. On the eve of victory, however, distrust among the Allies was about to provoke yet another struggle for supremacy—the Cold War between the United States and the Soviet Union.

The Axis Defeated

Germany and Italy Crushed

The Battle of Stalingrad in 1942–1943 marked a turning point in the war in Europe. In August 1942 the German army began a siege of this city, whose capture would give Germany access to Soviet oil. The fighting dragged on much longer than the Germans expected, and when winter arrived, the German army was ill-equipped to deal with harsh conditions. After months of ferocious fighting, in February 1943, the Soviet army captured the ninety thousand Germans who survived the freezing cold and near-constant combat. Meanwhile, the British army in North Africa faced off against German troops under General Erwin Rommel. Skilled in the new kind of mobile warfare, Rommel let his tanks move hundreds of miles from supply lines. He could not, however, overcome Allied access to secret German communication codes, and this access ultimately helped the Allies capture Morocco and Algeria in the fall of 1942. After driving Rommel out of Africa, the Allies landed in Sicily in July 1943. A slow, bitter fight for the Italian peninsula followed, lasting until April 1945, when Allied forces finally triumphed. After Italy's liberation, partisans shot Mussolini and his mistress and hung their dead bodies for public display.

The victory at Stalingrad marked the beginning of the Soviet drive westward, during which the Soviets still bore the brunt of the Nazi war machine. British and U.S. warplanes bombed German cities, and on June 6, 1944, known as D-Day, combined Allied forces attacked the heavily fortified French beaches of Normandy and then fought their way through the German-held territory of western France. Meanwhile the Soviets took Poland, Bulgaria, Romania, and finally Hungary during the winter of 1944–1945. As the military vice tightened, Hitler refused to spare the German people by surrendering. Instead, he committed suicide with his wife, Eva Braun, as the Soviet army took Berlin in April. Germany finally surrendered on May 8, 1945.

Turning the Tide in the Pacific

The Allies had followed a "Europe first" strategy for conducting the war, but had nonetheless steadily pursued the Japanese in the Pacific. In 1942, Allied forces destroyed some of Japan's formidable naval power in battles at Midway Island and Guadalcanal (see again Map 28.4). Japan lacked the capacity to recoup losses of ships or of manpower, while the Allies had not only their own productive power but access to materiel manufactured in Australia, India, and elsewhere around the world. The Allies stormed one Pacific island after another, gaining more bases from which to cut off Japanese supply lines and launch bombers toward Japan. In response to kamikaze attacks and the suicidal resistance of soldiers and civilians alike, the Allies stepped up their bombing of major cities, killing some 120,000 civilians in its spring 1945 firebombing of Tokyo.

The Atomic Bomb

Meanwhile a U.S.-based international team of more than one hundred thousand workers, including scientists, technicians, and other staff, had secretly developed the atomic bomb. The Japanese practice of fighting to the last man rather than surrendering persuaded Allied military leaders that the defeat of Japan might cost the lives of hundreds of thousands of Allied soldiers (and even more Japanese). On August 6, 1945, the U.S. government unleashed the new atomic weapon on Hiroshima. Three days later a second bomb was dropped on Nagasaki. The two bombings killed 140,000 people instantly; tens of thousands died later from burns, radiation poisoning, and other wounds. Hardliners in the Japanese military wanted to continue the war, but on August 15, 1945, Japan surrendered.

Postwar Plans and Uncertainties

Although the fighting had ended, conditions for lasting peace were poor at best. Japan, Europe, and large parts of East Asia and the Pacific lay in ruins. Governments and social order in many parts of the world were fragile if not totally broken. An estimated 100 million people had died in the war, and perhaps an equal number were homeless refugees, wandering the devastated land in search of food and shelter. Forced into armies or labor camps for war production, colonial peoples were in full rebellion or close to it. For a second time in three decades, they had seen their imperial masters killing one another, slaughtered by the very technology that was supposed to make Western civilization superior (see Seeing the Past: Technological Warfare: Civilization or Barbarism?). With their respect for empire undone, it was only a matter of time before colonized peoples would mount battles of their own for independence.

SEEING THE PAST

Technological Warfare: Civilization or Barbarism?

Hiroshima, September 2, 1945 (Bettmann/Corbis.)

This photograph of Hiroshima, Japan, shows the near-total destruction that resulted from the dropping of the first atomic bomb on August 6, 1945. The atomic bomb was the work of the world's top scientists during World War II, and its development resulted from the theories of brilliant people like Albert Einstein. So too, other increasingly sophisticated weaponry and methods for mass killing paralleled the great advances in a number of scientific fields. For some two centuries, the West characterized its scientific achievements as the hallmark of advanced civilization and viewed as backward those countries without them. It continued to make such claims as increasingly powerful nuclear weapons were tested in the Pacific and on the Asian continent, resulting in the annihilation of entire islands and the destruction of the environment. The visual and other evidence from Hiroshima can lead us to reflect to what degree the ability to destroy more lives than ever before and with less effort is a mark of high civilization or of barbarism.

EXAMINING THE EVIDENCE

1. **How is a moral argument for the atomic bomb possible?**
2. **How would you situate the atomic bomb and its use during World War II in the scientific and intellectual history of the West?**

The United Nations

Amid chaos, a wartime agreement led to the founding of the **United Nations** (UN). Franklin Roosevelt coined the term *United Nations* for the alliance of twenty-six countries formed on January 1, 1942, to fight the Axis. With the weakening of the League of Nations during the 1930s and its collapse after the outbreak of war, international institutions for collective security were absent, giving the formation of the United Nations a new urgency and the term a new meaning. In 1944, even as the war proceeded, delegates from the Big Three plus China met in Washington, D.C., to draw up plans for the UN. As a result of this often-ignored wartime conference, in June 1945, before the war was over, representatives from fifty countries signed the UN charter, setting the conditions for peaceful international cooperation. It remained to be seen whether this new organization would be more successful than its predecessor at maintaining world peace.

The Cold War

As the world sought to recover, a new struggle called the Cold War was taking root between the world's two military powers—the United States and the Soviet Union. At war's end, Stalin continued to see the world as hostile to his nation; the United States abruptly cut off many aid programs to the starving Soviet Union. In the face of this hostility, Stalin believed that Soviet security depended on not just a temporary military occupation of eastern Europe and Germany but a permanent "buffer zone" of European states loyal to the USSR as a safeguard against a revived Germany in particular and the anti-Soviet Western states more generally. Across the Atlantic, President Harry S. Truman, who had succeeded Roosevelt after his death in April 1945, saw the initial temporary occupation as the beginning of an era of permanent Communist expansion, especially since the Soviets were setting up friendly governments in the areas of eastern Europe they had liberated. By 1946, members of the U.S. State Department were describing Stalin as a "neurotic"

United Nations The international organization of nations established at the end of World War II to replace the League of Nations and to promote diplomacy and the peaceful settlement of disputes for countries worldwide.

Asian ruler prepared to continue the centuries-old Russian thirst for world domination. For his part, Stalin claimed that "it was the Soviet army that won" World War II and warned Anglo-American forces not to continue moving eastward. In a March 1946 speech, former British Prime Minister Churchill warned that an "iron curtain" had fallen across Europe, cutting off the East from the West and dividing the world into two hostile camps.

As the Cold War came to inflame global politics, it affected the world's peoples as World War II had done. Eva Kantorowsky was again ensnared as she and her family, like many of Shanghai's refugees, tried to emigrate to the United States. But many Americans, even though they had fought against Hitler, remained anti-Semitic, and the U.S. Congress passed legislation blocking the immigration of Jewish refugees after the war. Jews were Communists, members of Congress claimed, echoing Nazi ideology as they played the Cold War card. Eva eventually arrived in the United States despite the growing intensity of the Cold War.

COUNTERPOINT

Nonviolence and Pacifism in an Age of War

FOCUS

In what ways did peace movements serve as a countertrend to events in the period from 1929 to 1945?

The wars of the twentieth century—hot and cold—focused the attention of peoples throughout the world on the exercise of military power. Leading nations from Germany and Japan to the Soviet Union and the United States saw military capacity as the measure of national greatness. Some activists and ordinary people, however, realized that nonviolent tactics could be powerful and effective tools to undermine colonialism and the doctrine of total war. Traditional modes of resistance shaped some efforts, while religious precepts underlay others.

Traditional Tactics: The Example of Nigerian Women

In 1929, women in British-controlled Nigeria rebelled at the new tax the government tried to impose on them as part of its effort to resolve economic problems in England. They painted their bodies and sang and danced in the nude outside the homes of local tax collectors, who attacked and even burned some of the women's houses. Their method was called "sitting on a man," because it was generally used against rulings by men that the women considered unjust. British officials justified shooting the women, killing fifty-three of them, by calling the women's behavior irrational and dangerous. Throughout the 1930s and up into the 1980s, women in Nigeria used traditional nonviolent tactics, including removing all their clothing, to protest low prices for their palm products and the exploitative practices of oil companies in their region.

The women of Nigeria eventually became national heroes of the movement for independence, and other pacifist traditions were mobilized during the 1920s and 1930s as well. Jainism, an ancient South Asian religion, held to the belief in *ahimsa*—the idea of doing no harm—and other Asian religions adopted this belief, leading many to become pacifists.

Gandhi and Civil Disobedience

In the 1920s and 1930s, practitioners of peaceful protest adopted an approach that came to be variously called **civil disobedience** or nonviolent resistance. Mohandas Gandhi, for one, led his followers in 1930 on a twenty-three-day "Salt March" to break the law giving the British a monopoly on salt—a necessity of life that exists freely in nature. Professing to model his tactics on those of the British suffragists and the teachings of Jesus, Buddha, and other spiritual leaders, Gandhi's nonviolent protest highlighted India's difference

civil disobedience A political strategy of deliberately but peacefully breaking the law to protest oppression and obtain political change.

Mohandas Gandhi and Nonviolence

Indian leader Mohandas (Mahatma "great souled one") Gandhi led a mass movement, but his followers flocked to him because of a message entirely different from those of Mussolini and Hitler. Gandhi was neither bombastic nor wedded to material and militaristic display. Instead he denounced the violence and materialism of the West, preferring *Satyagraha*—soulforce—to physical conflict, and spinning by hand to parading tanks and rockets. (The Art Archive/Kharbine-Tapabor/Collection NB.)

from militaristic, even genocidal Westerners, as he noted in more than one of his writings. He called his strategy *Satyagraha* (SAH-ty-ah-GRAH-hah)—truth and firmness—and rejected the view that his tactics were "passive." Rather, such acts as taking salt and then being beaten or arrested (as Gandhi was) demanded incredible discipline to remain opposed but at the same time nonviolent.

Pacifism, including the tactics of Gandhi, unfolded with real conviction both during the pre–World War I arms race and with even greater fervor in the aftermath of World War I. Feminists played key roles in the development of the Women's International League for Peace and Freedom after that war, and religious groups in many parts of the world contested what they saw as a new militarism developing in the interwar years. Many of these groups remained firmly pacifistic even with the rise of fascism, and were ridiculed either as deluded or as traitors. British novelist George Orwell called all pacifists in the 1930s "objectively fascist." After World War II, civil rights activists in the United States embraced nonviolence and civil disobedience. In the 1950s and early 1960s they "sat in" to desegregate lunch counters, buses, and public facilities that were closed to them, even as officials whipped, hosed, and murdered them. Many still see committed pacifists as deluded thinkers or as traitors to the nation-state, but none can deny that for some causes pacifists have been remarkably effective.

Conclusion

The Great Depression, which destroyed the lives and livelihoods of millions of people throughout the world, created conditions in which dictators and authoritarian rulers thrived because they promised to restore national greatness and prosperity. Mobilized by the mass media, people turned from the representative institutions that were accused of failing them and supported militaristic leaders who offered hope of a brighter future. Authoritarian leaders used aggression and violence to gain support, but others—both nonviolent resisters in the colonies and those with vivid memories of World War I—took up pacifism or a strategy of nonviolent civil disobedience to achieve their objectives, objectives that included the overthrow of authoritarian leaders.

Leaders of the Western democracies, hoping to avoid another war, permitted Hitler and Mussolini to menace Europe unimpeded throughout the 1930s. In Asia, the Japanese military convinced citizens that the nation deserved an extensive empire and that white domination must be ended. The coalition that formed to stop Germany, Italy, and Japan was an uneasy confederation among the Allied powers of France, Britain, the Soviet Union, and the United States. At the war's end, Europe's economies were shattered, its population reduced, its colonies on the verge of independence, its peoples starving and homeless. Occupied by the victorious U.S. Army, Japan was similarly devastated, as were large swaths of North Africa, Asia, and the Pacific Islands. People who had been dislocated by the war—such as Eva Kantorowsky and her family—were dislocated once again. The massive death and destruction of the war ended Europe's global dominance. Now the Soviet Union and the United States reigned as the world's superpowers, with the newly formed United Nations, a global organization, the only potential check on the two nations' unprecedented power.

In the decades following World War II, the United States and the Soviet Union competed for power and influence in every corner of the globe, seeing every local and regional development through the prism of the Cold War ideological split. Amid this growing divide, World War II brought another notable change: millions of people determined as a result of their experience of global war that colonialism, whether that of the French, British, or Japanese, would not long survive.

NOTES

1. Ana Núñez Machin, quoted in Angel Santana Suárez ,"Angel Santana Suárez: Cuban Sugar Worker," in *The Human Tradition in Latin America: The Twentieth Century*, ed. William H. Beezley and Judith Ewell (Wilmington, DE: Scholarly Resources, 1987), 85, 86.
2. Quoted in Piers Brendon, *The Dark Valley: A Panorama of the 1930s* (London: Jonathan Cape, 2000), 175.
3. Quoted in Ann Farnsworth-Alvear, *Dulcinea in the Factory: Myths, Morals, Men, and Women in Colombia's Industrial Experiment, 1905–1960* (Durham, NC: Duke University Press, 2000), 124, 125.
4. Edvard Radzinsky, *Stalin: The First In-Depth Biography Based on Explosive New Documents from Russia's Secret Archives*, trans. H. T. Willetts (New York: Doubleday, 1996), 363.
5. Jiang Jieshi, quoted in Patricia Buckley Ebrey, *Cambridge Illustrated History of China* (Cambridge, U.K.: Cambridge University Press, 1996), 277.
6. Herbert Bix, *Hirohito and the Making of Modern Japan* (New York: HarperCollins, 2000), 274–276.
7. Quoted in Bix, *Hirohito*, 315.
8. Matsuoka Yosuke, quoted in Bix, *Hirohito*, 374.
9. Amartya Sen, "Interview," *Journal of Economic Perspectives* (1994).
10. Quoted in *The Washington Post*, May 23, 2005.
11. Carla Capponi, interviewed in Shelley Saywell, *Women in War: From World War II to El Salvador* (New York: Penguin, 1986), 82.

RESOURCES FOR RESEARCH

1929: The Great Depression Begins

The Great Depression was a global event, affecting peasants and farmers, factory workers and shopkeepers, and the upper classes. Balderston and Rothermund provide excellent surveys of the worldwide impact.

Balderston, Theo. *The World Economy and National Economies in the Interwar Slump*. 2003.

Brendon, Piers. *The Dark Valley: A Panorama of the 1930s*. 2000.

Feinstein, Charles H., et al. *The World Economy Between the World Wars*. 2008.

Rothermund, Dietmar. *The Global Impact of the Great Depression, 1929–1939*. 1996.

Vernon, James. *Modernity's Hunger: How Imperial Britain Created and Failed to Solve the Problem of Hunger in the Modern World*. 2006.

Militarizing the Masses in the 1930s

Many postwar politicians promised relief of economic hardship through military conquest and discipline. Regimented parades and other displays of military power attracted mass audiences. Kushner's book captures the unfolding of those promises in the case of Japan in Manchuria.

Hammer, Joshua. *Yokohama Burning: The Deadly 1923 Earthquake and Fire That Helped Forge the Path to World War II.* 2006.

Kaplan, Marion. *Between Dignity and Despair: Jewish Life in Nazi Germany.* 1998.

Kushner, Barak. *The Thought War: Japanese Imperial Propaganda.* 2006.

Naimark, Norman. *Stalin's Genocides.* 2010.

* Pa, Chin. *Family.* 1931.

Wildt, Michael. *An Uncompromising Generation: The Nazi Leadership of the Reich Security Main Office.* 2009.

Global War, 1937–1945

The scholarship on World War II is extensive. These works cover facets of global warfare.

Browning, Christopher. *Remembering Survival: Inside a Nazi Slave Labor Camp.* 2010.

Fyne, Robert. *Long Ago and Far Away: Hollywood and the Second World War.* 2008.

Johnson, David. *World War II and the Scramble for Labour in Colonial Zimbabwe, 1939–1948.* 2000.

Peattie, Mark R. *Sunburst: The Rise of Japanese Naval Air Power, 1909–1940.* 2002.

St. Andrews University in Scotland provides a number of links to sources for the diplomatic history of the origins of World War II: http://www.st-andrews.ac.uk/~pv/courses/prewar/resources.html.

Weinberg, Gerhard L. *A World at Arms: A Global History of World War II.* 2005.

From Allied Victory to the Cold War, 1943–1945

Among the many fascinating books about the war is Spector's account of the conflict's end in Asia, where Japanese soldiers and conquered peoples did not believe the war had ended and where in many cases the Allies enlisted remnants of the Japanese army to crush independence movements.

Bucur, Maria. *Heroes and Victims: Remembering War in Twentieth-Century Romania.* 2009.

Krylova, Anna. *Soviet Women in Combat: A History of Violence on the Eastern Front.* 2010.

Miner, Steven Merritt. *Stalin's Holy War: Religion, Nationalism, and Alliance Politics, 1941–1945.* 2003.

Rhodes, Richard. *Arsenals of Folly: The Making of the Nuclear Arms Race.* 2007.

Spector, Ronald H. *In the Ruins of Empire: The Japanese Surrender and the Battle for Postwar Asia.* 2007.

COUNTERPOINT: Nonviolence and Pacifism in an Age of War

Pacifism and nonviolent resistance were global phenomena. The anthology of Brock and Socknat provides a look at worldwide pacifism in the interwar years.

Allman, Jean, Susan Geiger, and Nakanyike Musisi, eds. *Women in African Colonial Histories.* 2002.

Brock, Peter, and Thomas P. Socknat, eds. *Challenge to Mars: Essays on Pacifism from 1918 to 1945.* 1999.

Matera, Marc, Misty L. Bastian, and Susan Kingsley Kent. *The Women's War of 1929: Gender and Violence in Colonial Nigeria.* 2011.

Siegel, Mona. *The Moral Disarmament of France: Education, Pacifism, and Patriotism, 1914–1940.* 2004.

Tidrick, Kathryn. *Gandhi: A Political and Spiritual Life.* 2007.

* Primary source.

▶ **For additional primary sources from this period**, see *Sources of Crossroads and Cultures*.

▶ **For Web sites, images, and documents related to topics in this chapter**, see Make History at bedfordstmartins.com/smith.

REVIEW

Online Study Guide
bedfordstmartins.com/smith

The major global development in this chapter ▶ The causes and outcomes of the Great Depression and World War II.

IMPORTANT EVENTS

1920s	Collapse of commodity prices around the world
1929	Crash of the U.S. stock market; global depression begins; Stalin's "liquidation of the kulaks"
1930	Gandhi's Salt March
1930s	Sweden begins setting up welfare state
1931	Japan invades Manchuria
1933	Hitler comes to power in Germany and ends representative government
1934	Chinese Communists begin Long March
1935	Nuremberg Laws against the Jews in Germany; Italy invades Ethiopia
1936	Purges and show trials begin in USSR
1937	Japan attacks China; World War II begins in Asia
1939	Germany invades Poland; World War II begins in Europe
1941	Germany invades USSR; Japan attacks Pearl Harbor; United States enters the war
1941–1945	Holocaust
1943	USSR defeats Germany at Stalingrad
1945	Fall of Berlin and surrender of Germany; UN charter signed; United States drops atomic bombs; Japan surrenders

KEY TERMS

Allies (p. 944)
appeasement (p. 940)
Axis (p. 944)
central economic planning (p. 933)
civil disobedience (p. 953)
five-year plan (p. 933)
Great Depression (p. 929)
Greater East Asia Co-Prosperity Sphere (p. 941)
Holocaust (p. 945)
purge (p. 934)
totalitarianism (p. 933)
United Nations (p. 952)

CHAPTER OVERVIEW QUESTIONS

1. How did ordinary people react to the Great Depression, and how did their reactions differ from country to country?
2. Why were dictators and antidemocratic leaders able to come to power in the 1930s, and how did all countries—autocratic and democratic alike—militarize the masses?
3. How are the Great Depression and World War II related historical events?

SECTION FOCUS QUESTIONS

1. What was the global impact of both the Great Depression and the attempts to overcome it?
2. How did dictatorships and democracies attempt to mobilize the masses?
3. How did World War II progress on the battlefront and the home front?
4. How did the Allied victory unfold, and what were the causes of that victory?
5. In what ways did peace movements serve as a countertrend to events in the period from 1929 to 1945?

MAKING CONNECTIONS

1. What are the main differences between World War I (see Chapter 27) and World War II?
2. In what specific ways did World Wars I and II affect the African and Asian colonies of the imperial powers?
3. How do the strengths and weaknesses of the Allies and the Axis compare?
4. How would you describe the importance of World War II not only to the unfolding of history but also to present-day concerns?

29

AT A CROSSROADS ▶

In 1957 Ghana became the first sub-Saharan nation to free itself from imperial rule. This woman celebrates not only Ghana's freedom but also its president, Kwame Nkrumah, who had led the campaign of civil disobedience against the British. Her clothing displays emblems of liberation, including Nkrumah's image—a preview of what would become the popular use of political heroes' faces on T-shirts and banners in the 1960s. At the time, Ghana marked a crossroads in global and African politics, as its leader and those who followed him advocated pan-Africanism and a political activism similar to that of Indian nationalist and spiritual leader Mohandas Gandhi. (Universal Images Group/SuperStock.)

The Emergence of New Nations in a Cold War World

1945–1970

During the early 1950s, on the first Thursday of the month, everyday life in Cairo and other major cities of the Arab world came to a standstill. Patrons of cafés huddled around the radio, and cabdrivers discharged their customers and dashed home to catch the broadcast. All were eager to tune in to a program featuring singer Umm Kulthum. Kulthum's repertoire included traditional desert songs, religious verses, and romantic ballads. Born at the beginning of the twentieth century, she began her career as a child disguised as a boy because girls were not supposed to perform in public. Singing verses from the Qur'an in her strong voice, she enraptured local audiences and her fame spread. By the 1950s she had become a national phenomenon, "the voice of Egypt" for the newly independent republic. In the words of one fan, her singing "shows our ordinary life." Even Egypt's leader Gamal Abdel Nasser, who in 1952 finally instituted a government totally free from British supervision, recognized the power of Umm Kulthum's popularity. He broadcast his speeches just before her program aired to link himself to her appeal. Traveling widely through the Middle East, Umm Kulthum used her vocal talent to encourage Arab-speaking people as a whole to celebrate their own culture as another way of shaking off the European powers.

The creation of a fully independent Egyptian republic was just one of the acts of liberation in the postwar world. From the Middle East through Africa and Asia, independence

World Politics and the Cold War

FOCUS Why was the Cold War waged, and how did it reshape world politics?

Decolonization and the Birth of Nations

FOCUS How did colonized peoples achieve their independence from the imperialist powers after World War II?

World Recovery in the 1950s and 1960s

FOCUS What were the major elements of recovery in different parts of the world in the decades following World War II?

Cultural Dynamism amid Cold War

FOCUS How did the experience of world war, decolonization, and Cold War affect cultural life and thought?

COUNTERPOINT: The Bandung Conference, 1955

FOCUS How did the Bandung Conference and its aims represent an alternative to the Cold War division of the globe?

BACKSTORY

As we saw in Chapter 28, imperial rivalries played a key role in the outbreak of World War II, the most destructive conflict in human history. By the time the war was over, as many as 100 million people had died, countries around the world lay in ruin, and the imperial system that had helped produce the war was in disarray. The chaos and confusion of the postwar world gave rise to a new set of global political trends. The formation of organizations such as the United Nations reflected new levels of cooperation among nations. At the same time, rising nationalism among colonized peoples sparked the process of decolonization. Finally, the Cold War between the United States and the Soviet Union shaped politics around the world and posed an unprecedented threat to world peace. These trends, along with the rising level of technological sophistication and the yearning of people around the world for peace and prosperity, would play major roles in defining the postwar world, a world that was more closely connected than ever before.

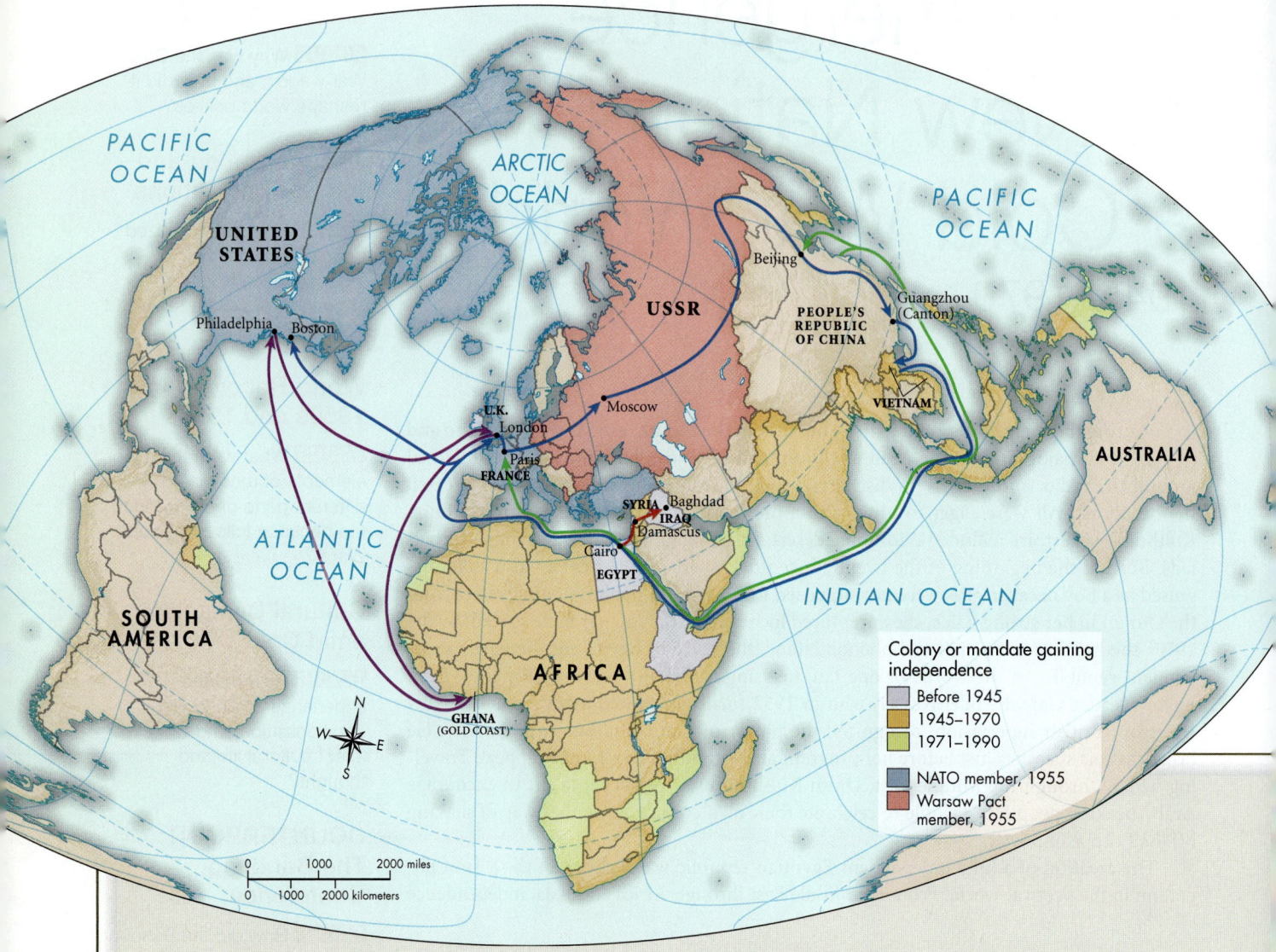

- **1945** World War II ends
- **1947** India and Pakistan win independence
- **1948** Israel gains independence
- **1948–1949** Arab-Israeli War
- **1949** Communists take control of China; Western powers form NATO; USSR detonates atomic bomb
- **1949** Indonesia gains independence
- **1950–1953** Korean War
- **1952** Egypt achieves full independence under Nasser
- **1953** Death of Stalin
- **1954** Vietnamese defeat French army at Dien Bien Phu
- **1956** Khrushchev denounces Stalin; Suez crisis; revolution in Hungary
- **1957** USSR launches *Sputnik*
- **1958** Khrushchev forces Boris Pasternak to refuse Nobel Prize in Literature
- Construction of the Berlin Wall **1961**

1945 1950 1955 1960

movements toppled colonial governments that attempted to revive their control after World War II. Workers, professionals, veterans, and other activists took up arms to drive out British, French, Dutch, Belgian, and U.S. forces. **Decolonization** was followed by the difficult process of nation building. In addition to creating government structures, newly independent states had to rebuild roads destroyed in the war, erect public buildings, and create systems for educating citizens and maintaining their health. In sum, the destruction of the colonial system created the opportunity, and the necessity, for formerly colonized peoples to rebuild and redefine the connections among citizens and the relationship between newly independent nations and the rest of the world. Like Umm Kulthum, talented patriots throughout the Middle East, Asia, Africa, and Latin America devoted their livelihoods and capabilities to advancing this cause.

Postcolonial nation building took place in a vastly changed world. The old European-dominated international order was gone, replaced by the rivalry between the United States and the Soviet Union for control of a world in which many traditional political and economic systems had collapsed. The nuclear arsenals of these two "superpowers," a term coined in 1947, grew massively in the 1950s, but they were enemies who did not fight outright—at least not on their own soil. Instead, they preferred to confront each other in the developing world. The U.S.-USSR rivalry, known as the **Cold War**, set the so-called communist East against the democratic, capitalist West. When the United States discovered Soviet missile sites on the island of Cuba in 1962, the Cold War rivals took the world to the brink of nuclear disaster.

Yet there was a surge of optimistic activism after World War II. The birth of new nations and the defeat of authoritarian militarism inspired hope that life would become fairer and that people everywhere would gain the freedom to determine their own fate. Revolutionary-minded thinkers poured out new political theories, while novelists explored the often-harsh realities of independence. In rebuilding, some politicians championed the

decolonization The process of freeing regions from imperial control and creating independent nations.

Cold War The rivalry between the Soviet Union and the United States that followed World War II and shaped world politics between 1945 and 1989.

MAPPING THE WORLD

Independence Movements and New Nations

Earlier movements for freedom from colonialism were reinvigorated at the end of World War II; the Axis and Allied powers had been exhausted by this unprecedented conflict, and some were bankrupt. Independent nations emerged from the remnants of imperialism, some of them only after violent struggles with their rulers. These independent nations, however, faced a novel global situation—a bipolar world dominated by the Soviet Union and the United States and faced with a possible nuclear holocaust. This potentially disastrous confrontation was called the Cold War.

ROUTES ▼

- Travels of Ho Chi Minh, c. 1912–1941
- Travels of Kwame Nkrumah, c. 1930–1947
- Travels of Umm Kulthum, c. 1932
- Travels of Wu Guanzhong, c. 1947–1950

1962 Algeria wins independence; Cuban Missile Crisis

1965 1970 1975

c. 1966–1976 Mao Zedong's "Cultural Revolution"

well-being of their nation's citizens. Vast nation-building projects took shape; the welfare state expanded; and by the end of the 1950s economic rebirth, stimulated in part by the Cold War, had made many regions grow more rapidly than ever before. In many places, however, people caught up in events precipitated by Cold War rivalries faced a grim, and often deadly, reality. In the 1950s and 1960s, at the same time that Egyptian singer Umm Kulthum invigorated Arabs about the region's future, youthful followers of China's Mao Zedong banded together to bring about a "cultural revolution" that would transform society, killing and torturing millions of their fellow citizens in its name. The search for freedom thus differed drastically from place to place in this age of Cold War extremes.

OVERVIEW QUESTIONS

The major global development in this chapter: The political transformations of the postwar world and their social and cultural consequences.

As you read, consider:

1. How did the Cold War affect the superpowers and the world beyond them?
2. How did the Cold War shape everyday lives and goals?
3. Why did colonial nationalism revive in the postwar world, and how did decolonization affect society and culture?
4. Why did the model of a welfare state emerge after World War II, and how did this development affect ordinary people?

World Politics and the Cold War

FOCUS

Why was the Cold War waged, and how did it reshape world politics?

In 1945, Europe's world leadership ended and the reign of the United States and the Soviet Union as the world's new superpowers began. The United States, its territory virtually untouched in the war, had become the world's economic giant, and the Soviet Union, despite suffering immense destruction, had developed enormous military might. Occupying Europe as part of the victorious alliance against Nazism and fascism, the two superpowers came to use Germany—at the heart of the continent and its politics—to divide Europe in two. By the late 1940s, the USSR had imposed communist rule throughout most of eastern Europe, while the United States poured vast amounts of money, personnel, and military equipment into western Europe and parts of Asia, Africa, and Latin America to win the allegiance of new and old nations in those areas. Both superpowers maintained dense networks of spies and conducted plots, assassinations, and other undercover operations around the world. Unwilling to confront each other head-on, they fought **proxy wars** in smaller, contained areas such as Korea, while amassing huge stockpiles of weapons—including nuclear missiles and bombs—that could annihilate the world.

proxy war During the Cold War, a conflict in another part of the world backed by the USSR or the United States as part of their rivalry.

The New Superpowers

The situation of the two superpowers in 1945 could not have been more different. The United States was the richest country in the world. Its industrial output had increased a

The United States

remarkable 15 percent annually between 1940 and 1944, a rate of growth that was reflected in workers' wages. By 1947, the United States controlled almost two-thirds of the world's gold bullion and more than half of its commercial shipping. Casting aside its post–World War I policy of nonintervention, the United States embraced its position as global leader and negotiated collective security agreements with many nations. Americans had learned about the world while tracking the progress of World War II; hundreds of thousands of American soldiers, government officials, and relief workers gained direct experience of Europe, Africa, and Asia. Although some Americans feared a postwar depression and nuclear annihilation, continued spending on industrial and military research, a baby boom, suburban housing development, and rising consumer purchases kept the economy buoyant, and most Americans were optimistic about their futures.

The Soviet Union

The Soviets emerged from the war with a well-justified sense of accomplishment. Withstanding horrendous losses, they had successfully resisted the most massive onslaught ever launched against a modern nation. Soviet citizens believed that a victory that had cost the USSR tens of millions of lives would improve everyday conditions and continue the war's relatively relaxed politics. "Life will become pleasant," one writer prophesied at war's end. "There will be much coming and going, and a lot of contacts with the West." In the 1930s, the Soviets had industrialized their nation, and in the 1940s they had defeated Nazism. With these achievements behind them, many expected an end to decades of hardship and looked forward to building a new, more open Soviet society.

Taking a very different view of the situation, Stalin moved ruthlessly to reassert control. In 1946, his new five-year plan increased production goals and mandated more stringent collectivization of agriculture. Stalin cut back the army by two-thirds to beef up the labor force, and also turned his attention to the low birthrate brought about by wartime conditions. He introduced an intense propaganda campaign emphasizing that working women should hold down jobs and also fulfill their "true nature" by producing many children.

The Cold War Unfolds 1945–1962

The Cold War, the political, economic, and ideological competition between the United States and the Soviet Union, would afflict the world for more than four decades, with lingering effects even today. Its origins remain a matter of debate. Some historians point to consistent U.S., British, and French hostility that began with the Bolshevik Revolution in 1917 and continued through World War II. Others stress Stalin's aggressive policies, notably the Nazi-Soviet alliance in 1939 and his quick claims on the Baltic states and Polish territory when World War II broke out. Even during that war, suspicions among the Allies ran deep. Stalin felt that Churchill and Roosevelt, as part of their anticommunist policy, were deliberately letting the USSR bear the brunt of Hitler's onslaught on Europe. Some Americans believed that dropping the atomic bomb on Japan would also frighten the Soviets away from seizing more land. As early as 1946, the U.S. State Department described Stalin as continuing the centuries-old Russian thirst for "world domination." In late August 1949, the USSR tested its own atom bomb, and from then on the superpowers built and stockpiled ever-more-sophisticated nuclear weapons, including hydrogen and neutron bombs. From this point on, the conflict between the superpowers carried with it the threat of global annihilation.

The Truman Doctrine and the Marshall Plan

The United States acknowledged Soviet influence in areas the USSR occupied, but worried that the Soviets were intent on spreading communism around the world. The difficulties of postwar life in western and southern Europe made communist programs promising better conditions attractive to workers, and communist leadership in the resistance movements of World War II gave the party a powerful appeal. When in 1947 communist insurgents threatened to overrun the right-wing monarchy the British had installed in Greece, U.S. President Harry S. Truman announced what quickly became known as the Truman Doctrine, the countering of political crises that might lead to communist rule with economic and military aid. Fearing that Americans would balk at backing an antidemocratic Greece, the U.S. Congress

American Aid to Tokyo's Orphans

In addition to the homelessness, disease, and starvation caused by the war, many of Japan's citizens lost their families in the atomic- and fire-bombings. As part of the Cold War effort to win allies, the United States hurried to make things better for those most in need—including defeated enemies such as Japan and Germany—by giving them aid. These orphans in Tokyo are photographed gratefully receiving this aid. What in this image suggests both a humanitarian and a propaganda purpose to such aid programs? (Bettmann/Corbis.)

agreed to the program only if Truman would "scare the hell out of the country," as one member of Congress put it. Truman thus promoted a massive aid program as necessary to prevent global Soviet conquest, warning that "the seeds of totalitarian regimes are nurtured by misery and want."[1] As the Communists backed off in Greece, the Truman Doctrine began the U.S. Cold War policy of **containment**—the attempt to keep communism from spreading.

The Truman Doctrine was quickly followed by enactment of the European Recovery Program, popularly called the Marshall Plan, a program of massive U.S. economic aid to Europe. Announced by Secretary of State George C. Marshall in 1947, the Marshall Plan claimed to be directed not "against any country or doctrine but against hunger, poverty, desperation, and chaos." Stalin, however, saw it as a U.S. political trick that caught him without resources to offer similar economic aid to the Soviet satellite countries and thus designed to open avenues to American influence in eastern Europe. By the early 1950s, the United States had sent western Europe more than $12 billion in food, equipment, and services, and it sent the same amount to Japan alone, helping even former enemies to rebuild and thus stay in the U.S. orbit.

Taking advantage of its military occupation of the region, the Soviet Union turned its military occupation of eastern Europe into a buffer zone of satellite states directed by "people's governments." In such Soviet-allied states as Poland, Czechoslovakia, and Hungary, Stalin enforced collectivized agriculture, centralized industrialization, and the nationalization of private property. In Hungary, for example, communists seized and reapportioned all estates over twelve hundred acres. Land redistribution won the support of the poorer peasants, but enforced collectivization of farming was a brutal process for many. Others felt that ultimately their lives and their children's lives had improved. "Before we peasants were dirty and poor, we worked like dogs. . . . Was that a good life? No sir, it wasn't. . . . I was a miserable sharecropper and my son is an engineer," said one Romanian peasant.

Modernization of production in the Soviet bloc opened new technical and bureaucratic careers, but economic development in the satellite states remained slow because the USSR bought goods from these satellite states at bargain prices and sold to them at exorbitant ones. Despite this inequity, people's livelihoods changed dramatically, as they moved to cities to receive better education, health care, and jobs, albeit at the price of severe political repression. They also experienced intense immersion in Russian rather than their own national cultures.

Germany Divided

Cold War competition led to the division of Germany. The terms of Allied agreements reached at Yalta in 1945 provided for the division of Germany and its capital city, Berlin, into four zones, each of which was occupied by one of the four principal victors in World War II—the United States, the Soviet Union, Britain, and France (see Map 29.1). The agreements provided for economic coordination among the zones, with agricultural surplus from Soviet-occupied areas feeding urban populations in the Western-controlled zones; in turn, industrial goods would be sent to the USSR. The Soviets upset this plan and instead sent equipment and dismantled industries from its zone to the Soviet Union. They transported skilled workers, engineers, and scientists to the USSR to work as virtual slave laborers. In response, France, Britain, and the United States agreed to merge their zones

containment The U.S. policy developed during the Cold War to prevent the spread of communism.

into a West German state that would serve as a buffer against the Soviets. The Soviets then created an East German state to act as a buffer against the West German state.

On June 24, 1948, Soviet troops blockaded Germany's capital, Berlin, located more than one hundred miles deep in the Soviet zone. The Soviets declared all of Berlin part of their zone of occupation and, expecting to starve the city into submission, refused to allow highway, railroad, and barge traffic into West Berlin. Instead of handing over Berlin, the United States flew in millions of tons of provisions to the city that just three years earlier had been the capital of the Nazi state. During the winter of 1948–1949, the Berlin airlift—"Operation Vittles," U.S. pilots called it—even funneled coal to the city to warm some 2 million isolated Berliners. The blockade was lifted in May 1949 and West Berlin remained tied to the West—a symbol of freedom to many. More than a decade later, in the summer of 1961, the East German government began construction of the Berlin Wall. The divided city had served, embarrassingly to the Soviets, as an escape route by which some 3 million people had fled to the freer, more prosperous West.

MAP 29.1 Divided Germany

Temporarily divided among the Allied powers, postwar Germany was caught in the tentacles of Cold War politics. By 1949, the former industrial center of Europe had been divided into two nations, commonly called East and West Germany. Deep in the Soviet-dominated eastern sector was the once-vibrant city of Berlin, itself divided east and west.

The People's Republic of China 1949

At the same time that the conflict between the superpowers in Europe was heating up, the Cold War entered a new phase with the triumph of Chinese Communist forces over the Nationalists in 1949. Before, during, and after World War II, the Nationalist government led by Jiang Jieshi (Chiang Kai-shek) and his unpopular armies had fought to eliminate rival communist forces to consolidate the Nationalist regime. With varying degrees of success, the United States and its allies did much both to prop up Jiang and to force these two Chinese enemy factions to concentrate on defeating Japan during World War II instead of annihilating one another. Once the war was over, however, the Nationalists and Communists went at each other once more.

Mao Zedong and the Communist Victory

In 1949, Mao Zedong (MOW zuh-DOONG) and his army of Communists won. From a prosperous peasant family, Mao had little in common with the farmers whom he targeted for support. He never worked as an agricultural laborer but rather spent his entire life as a politician, taking advantage of the opportunities for advancement created by the fluid conditions of modern nation building in China. At the outset he gravitated toward communism with USSR financial support. Once in power, Mao announced that Chinese communism in the new People's Republic of China would focus above all on the welfare of the peasantry rather than the industrial proletariat. Mao's government instituted social reforms such as civil equality for women and at the same time copied Soviet collectivization, rapid industrialization, and brutal repression of the privileged classes. Jiang and many of his Nationalist forces were forced to the island of Taiwan, where they refused to accept the legitimacy of Mao's communist government. With Jiang supported by the United States, Cold War fires spread to East Asia.

Proxy Wars and Cold War Alliances

The Chinese Communists' victory over the Nationalists in 1949 spurred both superpowers not only to increase their involvement in Asian politics but to form alliances with nations around the world, pulling much of the globe into the Cold War. Africa and Latin America

LIVES AND LIVELIHOODS

Cosmonauts and Astronauts

Soviet Leaders Honor Yuri Gagarin and Valentina Tereshkova

Soviet cosmonauts, like U.S. astronauts, were heroes not only in their own countries but in their Cold War blocs. The Soviets made these two cosmonauts special heroes: Gagarin (second from the left) because he was the first man in space, and Tereshkova because she was the first woman in space and represented the equality for women said to exist only in the Soviet bloc. Even today, one can find mementos of these heroes on T-shirts and caps across the former Soviet Union, reminders of the Cold War. (akg-images/RIA Nowosti.)

The space race gave rise to many new livelihoods, but none more celebrated than that of cosmonaut and astronaut, as space travelers were called in the USSR and United States, respectively. As an occupation, it attracted people of both genders and all ethnicities and classes. The parents of cosmonaut Yuri Gagarin, the first person in space, worked on a communist collective farm, and Gagarin himself labored in a foundry before the Soviet government selected him for technical education and eventual training as a pilot. His small stature, 5 feet 2 inches, helped him fit into the small cockpit of the first manned spacecraft—*Vostok I*. Television programs and films celebrate pioneers of space travel, both real and imaginary, and even today in small villages in eastern Europe one can buy T-shirts with pictures of Gagarin and other space heroes. The enduring human fascination with voyages and the longing to travel beyond the earth was on its way to being satisfied during these years.

felt the Cold War's impact as guerrilla fighters, spies, and activists for both sides blanketed their regions. The Cold War even reached into space: in 1957, the Soviets successfully launched the first artificial earth satellite, *Sputnik*, and in 1961 they put the first cosmonaut, Yuri Gagarin, in orbit around the earth. The Soviets' edge in space technology shocked the Western bloc as the superpowers continued their rivalries on the ground with more traditional weapons (see Lives and Livelihoods: Cosmonauts and Astronauts).

The Korean War

The two superpowers faced off indirectly in Korea, which after World War II had been divided into two nations, North and South Korea. After border skirmishes by both sides, in 1950 the North Koreans, supported by the Soviet Union, invaded the U.S.-backed South. The United States maneuvered the UN Security Council into approving a "police action" against the North, and UN forces quickly drove well into North Korean territory, where they were met by the Chinese army supported by Soviet planes. Fighting continued for another two and a half years, with 3 million civilian deaths, but the war remained a stalemate. The opposing sides finally agreed to a settlement in 1953 that changed nothing: Korea would remain divided as before. The United States increased its military spending from

After the successful 1957 launch of *Sputnik*, the Soviets' edge in space so shocked the Western bloc that it motivated the creation in 1958 of the U.S. National Aeronautics and Space Administration (NASA). U.S. astronauts followed Gagarin, and like him became heroes: astronaut John Glenn, for example, served as a U.S. senator. Despite the dominance of the superpowers in space, citizens of some thirty-five countries, including Afghanistan, Belgium, Brazil, China, Cuba, Malaysia, Mexico, and Saudi Arabia, contributed their citizens to the world's various space programs. In addition, individual countries such as China, Brazil, and Iran recognized that capabilities in space were needed to participate in satellite technology and to create an independent military capability. Brazil, with the most developed space program in Latin America, began its work with sounding rockets in 1964. As countries beyond the superpowers initiated their own programs and cooperated with multinational ventures, livelihoods in space multiplied, including monitoring and spying on other nations' space capabilities.

Trained space travelers are generally drawn from the ranks of jet pilots (like Gagarin) and space engineers, with mathematicians and scientists added to oversee the execution of experiments in space. Recently, teachers and space tourists have joined the ranks of those more explicitly trained for space, to give these costly and time-consuming programs more widespread appeal. Whatever their backgrounds and missions on the spacecraft, however, candidates for space travel undergo rigorous instruction in experiencing weightlessness, enduring space environments, and other space techniques. Participants in multinational space ventures also need to speak other languages well to communicate, and thus they undergo extensive language training.

Space travel is one of the more dangerous livelihoods created since the end of World War II. Not only have dozens of trained astronauts and cosmonauts died, but so have ground workers involved in space programs. In 2003, twenty-one workers and scientists died in a rocket explosion at Brazil's space site, and the next year six people in India's space program were killed when a rocket motor burst into flames. Yuri Gagarin himself died in 1968 during a jet training flight.

QUESTIONS TO CONSIDER

1. **What roles did astronauts and cosmonauts play in the Cold War?**
2. **Why did so many countries besides the superpowers begin their own space programs?**
3. **What livelihoods are comparable to those of astronaut and cosmonaut?**

For Further Information:

Brzezinski, Matthew. *Red Moon Rising: Sputnik and the Hidden Rivalries that Ignited the Space Age*. 2007.
De Groot, Gerard. *Dark Side of the Moon: The Magnificent Madness of the American Lunar Quest*. 2006.
Dickson, Paul. *Sputnik: The Shock of the Century*. 2001.
Wolfe, Tom. *The Right Stuff*. 1979.

$10.9 billion in 1948 to almost $60 billion in 1953 to "contain" the global threat of communist expansion. The fear that communist regimes would be established in decolonizing areas led U.S. President Dwight Eisenhower to characterize Asian countries as a row of dominoes: "You knock over the first one and what will happen is that it will go over [to communism] very quickly."[2] Thus, the Cold War mentality helped create a perception of connections between global developments, even in cases where those connections did not really exist.

Viewing the Cold War as a global conflict, the USSR and the United States formed competing military alliances that split most of the world into two opposing camps. In 1949 the United States, Canada, and their European allies formed the **North Atlantic Treaty Organization** (NATO). NATO provided a unified military force for its member countries. In 1955, after the United States forced France and Britain to invite West Germany to join NATO, the Soviet Union retaliated by establishing its own military organization, commonly called the **Warsaw Pact**, which included Albania, Bulgaria, Czechoslovakia, East Germany, Hungary, Poland, and Romania. These two massive regional alliances formed the military muscle for Cold War politics in Europe and replaced the individual might of the European powers (see Map 29.2).

North Atlantic Treaty Organization A Cold War alliance formed in 1949 among the United States, its western European allies, and Canada.

Warsaw Pact A Cold War alliance formed in 1955 among the Soviet Union and its eastern European satellite states.

MAP 29.2

Regional Alliances, 1948–1955

As the Cold War advanced, the United States and the Soviet Union divided the world into regional alliances, which were pitted against one another like the two superpowers themselves. With help from the superpowers, or sometimes on their own, individual members of these alliances rearmed and even built their own nuclear capacity. Military budgets soared, nowhere more than in the USSR and the United States, both of which also took the Cold War into space.

Regional Alliances

Even though the most heated Cold War activity seemed to center on Europe, the largest and earliest regional alliance was far away. In 1948, some twenty-one nations from the Western Hemisphere banded together to form the **Organization of American States** (OAS). To strengthen the alliance as a Cold War vehicle, the United States gave individual Latin American countries of the OAS greater economic assistance as well as military aid and training for officers. U.S. aid guaranteed Latin American military regimes' increased prestige and power over civilians and prevented movements for democracy from succeeding. The expansion of the Cold War to Asia prompted the creation of an Asian counterpart to NATO. Established in 1954, the **Southeast Asia Treaty Organization** (SEATO) included Pakistan, Thailand, the Philippines, Britain, Australia, New Zealand, France, and the United States. Collectively, the new organizations reflected the determination of the United States to pull as much of the world as possible into its orbit.

Organization of American States An alliance formed in 1948 among nations in the Western Hemisphere.

Southeast Asia Treaty Organization A Cold War coalition of U.S. Asian allies formed in 1954.

One Latin American nation, however, refused to align with the United States. In 1959 a revolution in Cuba brought to power the young Fidel Castro. Born in 1926 to the owner of a large plantation and his housekeeper, Castro as a child played with others far less privileged than he, and he saw up close the ways of the local poor. Soon, however, the boy was separated from his poorer friends and given an elite education, leading eventually to law school. At the university, Castro was a political leader, and eventually he became a major opposition figure in Cuban politics. In 1959 Castro's forces overthrew the island's corrupt regime, which was controlled in large part by U.S. sugar interests and the mob. Peasants and well-educated guerrilla fighters like Castro banded together to end the economic plunder not only of the Cuban island but of individual workers. After being rebuffed by the United States, Castro, initially opposed to communist organizations, turned to the Soviet Union for aid to rebuild the country.

Revolution in Cuba

Cuba's connection to the Soviet Union frightened American decision makers, including John F. Kennedy. Elected U.S. president in 1960, Kennedy intensified the arms race and escalated the Cold War to a frightening pitch. In 1961 he authorized an invasion of Cuba by CIA-trained Cuban exiles at the Bay of Pigs to overthrow Castro. The CIA had backed similar coups in Iran, where it overthrew a populist nationalist regime to install the Shah, and in Guatemala, where it devised an invasion by so-called exile forces who imposed a president friendly to U.S. interests. The Bay of Pigs invasion, however, failed miserably and humiliated the United States, as Castro's tiny air force sank U.S. ships and captured more than a thousand invaders.

Cuban Missile Crisis

Another incident involving Cuba brought the world even closer to the brink of nuclear war. In October 1962, the CIA reported the installation of launching pads for Soviet medium-range nuclear missiles in Cuba (see again Map 29.2). In response, Kennedy called for a blockade of Soviet ships headed for Cuba and threatened nuclear war if the installations were not removed. For several days, superpower leaders were acutely aware that the world hovered on the brink of nuclear disaster. A high Soviet official called his wife telling her to leave Moscow immediately; men in Kennedy's cabinet reported looking at the sunset, believing it to be the last they would see. Then, between October 25 and 27, Nikita Khrushchev, Stalin's successor, and Kennedy negotiated an end to the crisis. The two leaders, who had looked deeply into the nuclear future, clearly feared what they saw.

Decolonization and the Birth of Nations

FOCUS

How did colonized peoples achieve their independence from the imperialist powers after World War II?

In World War II colonized peoples had been on the frontlines defending the West. They had witnessed the full barbarism of the imperial powers' warfare—and also the West's weaknesses. "We felt that the British were not supermen as we used to think," one Singapore worker put it. Another was enraged at seeing "the same old arrogance that you saw before the war."[3] Excluded from victory parades and other ceremonies so the Allies could maintain the illusion of white supremacy, veterans from the colonies were determined to be free. Workers and farmers in Asia, Africa, and the Middle East felt that they too had borne the brunt of the war effort. People from many walks of life, often led by individuals experienced in warfare and steeped in Western nationalism, fought for liberation as the postwar period opened.

The path to independence was paved with difficulties. In Africa, a continent whose peoples spoke several thousand languages, the European conquerors' creation of administrative units such as "Nigeria" and "Rhodesia" had obliterated divisions based on ethnic ties and local cultures. Religion also played a complicated role in independence movements. In the Middle East and North Africa, pan-Arab and pan-Islamic movements might seem to have been unifying forces. Yet many Muslims were not Arab, not all Arabs were Muslim, and Islam itself encompassed many competing beliefs and sects. In India, Hindus, Sikhs, and Muslims battled one another, though they shared the goal of eliminating British rule. Differences in religious beliefs, ethnic groups, and cultural practices—many of them invented or promoted by the colonizers to divide and rule—overlapped and undermined political unity. Despite these complications, in the three decades after World War II colonized peoples succeeded in throwing off the imperial yoke, often to become entangled in the battle between the United States and the USSR for world supremacy.

The End of Empire in Asia

At the end of World War II, Asians demonstrated against the inflation, unemployment, and other harsh conditions the war had imposed on them, while politicians continued to mobilize this mass discontent against the colonial powers. White colonizers often fought back, but able leaders and ordinary people worked together to drive out foreign rulers. Slipping as the major imperial power, Britain in 1947 finally parted with India, the "jewel in its crown." As some half a billion Asians gained their independence, Britain's sole notable remaining colony was Hong Kong.

India

During World War II, soldiers, workers, and farm tenants actively protested conditions under colonialism, sometimes using Gandhi's tactic of civil disobedience and at other times attacking the workplaces of moneylenders and landlords. Britain had promised in the 1930s to grant India its independence, but postponed the plan when war broke out. Two million Indian veterans, who had participated in the war in the Middle East and Asia, joined forces with powerful Indian Congress politicians, many of whom had helped finance the British war effort by buying out British entrepreneurs short of cash. India was now one of Britain's major creditors, and Britain had to face the inevitable by granting the colony its independence.

Independent countries emerged along the lines of religious rivalries that Britain had fomented under colonialism as a strategy to divide and conquer. In 1947, political leaders agreed to partition British India into an independent India for Hindus and the new state of Pakistan for Muslims; both were artificial divisions, because there were people from many religions living together across the subcontinent. The new state of India, in fact, had the second largest Muslim population in the world after Indonesia. Ordinary people had violent reactions as **Partition** unfolded (see Map 29.3). A powerful religious minority—the Sikhs—bitterly resented receiving nothing. Because independence as determined by the British occurred along religious rather than secular lines, tensions exploded among opposing religious groups, who used partition to struggle for resources and power. Hundreds of thousands were massacred in the great shift of populations between India and Pakistan—"appalling sights," a journalist reported, as trains reached their destination filled with nothing but corpses and hospitals treated the wounded whose hands had been cut off.[4] Indian and Pakistani soldiers began fighting for control of Kashmir along the border between the two countries. In the midst of this tragic bloodshed, in 1948 a radical Hindu assassinated Gandhi, who had loudly championed religious reconciliation and a secular Indian democracy. Delayed by bitter feelings, a Constitution emerged for India that forced wealthy, autonomous Indian states into the union.

MAP 29.3 Partition of India, 1947

The British had whipped up religious antagonisms as part of their strategy of divide and conquer in India, and they used the same strategy in planning for decolonization. Thus, despite the commitment of Gandhi and other leaders to unity and religious toleration, Britain, along with some Indian leaders, arranged for a partition into a Muslim-dominated Pakistan and a Hindu-dominated India. Given the many religions in the region, the partition was a recipe for independence plagued by violence.

In Indonesia in the closing days of World War II, the Japanese, eager to foil the Dutch, allowed a group of nationalist leaders, headed by the Western-educated Achmed Sukarno, to declare Indonesia an independent state. Sukarno's distinctive nationalist vision brought all the islands of the archipelago into a unified nation. His task was complicated by three factors. First, Indonesia had a tradition of local princely rule, even under Dutch control. Second, from the beginning of the twentieth century Indonesians had built an array of organizations, including a variety of Islamic ones, that pushed for freedom from Dutch exploitation. Third, Allied military forces had helped the Dutch to reclaim their empire, and after the defeat of Japan they even enlisted the occupying Japanese troops to put down all movements for independence.

MAP 29.4

New States of Southeast Asia, 1945–1999

The French were determined to keep their empire in Southeast Asia, but their forces were handily defeated by the Vietnamese in 1954. Even as the Bandung Conference was held in Indonesia, the emerging nations of Southeast Asia became pivotal to the Cold War, as communist leader Ho Chi Minh stood steadfast in his vision for the region. One of the longest and most lethal proxy wars of the Cold War was fought in Vietnam, where genocide in neighboring Cambodia erupted adjacent to the war for liberation.

Indonesia

The popular forces of independence used **guerrilla warfare** that was unstoppable. In 1949 the Dutch conceded Indonesian independence, and in 1957 Sukarno, as head of the new state, legislated that all Dutch leave the country. Sukarno's policies entailed economic modernization and a cultural unity based on the belief in one God, whether Islamic, Christian, or other. Although the new Ministry of Religion fostered unity through Islamic institutions, sponsoring the building of mosques and institutions for Islamic welfare programs, ethnic, religious, and economic interests diverged and kept the archipelago involved in constant governmental struggle against dissenters. For a time, Sukarno himself was the mainstay of unity, becoming a charismatic leader by championing the power of newly independent countries (see Map 29.4).

Indochina

In Indochina nationalists struggled to prevent the postwar revival of French imperialism. From the 1930s on, their leader, Ho Chi Minh (hoe chee min), built a powerful organization, the Communist Viet Minh, to fight colonial rule. He began his career, however, by working aboard a French ocean liner, then taking jobs in London and Paris at the time of World War I, experiences that brought him in direct contact with white racism. Ho became interested in Marxism, which led him to Moscow and training as a political operative; he was first assigned to organizing strikers in China in the 1920s. Once head of the Viet Minh, he advocated the redistribution of land held by big landowners, especially in the rich agricultural area in southern Indochina where some six thousand owners held more than 60 percent of the land.

Partition The division of the Indian subcontinent into different states in 1947 and the violence accompanying it.

guerrilla warfare Unconventional combat, often undertaken by those who are not members of official armies.

During World War II, Ho worked to overthrow the Japanese, who had taken over Indochina, and at the end of the war, he declared Vietnam independent. The French, however, reasserted their control. Viet Minh peasant guerrillas ultimately forced the French to withdraw from the country after the bloody battle of Dien Bien Phu in 1954. Later that year the Geneva Conference—a meeting held in Switzerland to settle the war between the Indochinese and the French—carved out an independent Laos and divided Vietnam into North and South, each free from French control. Ho established a communist government in North Vietnam, and a noncommunist government was installed in South Vietnam (see again Map 29.4). Fearing that Ho would further the spread of communism in Asia, the United States supported the regime in South Vietnam, even its cancelling of elections in 1956 to prevent a communist victory. Ho and North Vietnam, in turn, received aid from both the Soviet Union and China.

The Struggle for Independence in the Middle East

By war's end in 1945, much of the world had become almost fully dependent on the Middle East's rich petroleum resources to fuel cars and airplanes, heat homes, and create products such as plastics. "The oil in this region is the greatest single prize in all history," as one geologist put it.[5] The Middle Eastern nations that emerged from their political domination by the European powers were thus economically and strategically important enough to maneuver between the Cold War rivals. At the same time, newly independent nations such as Syria, Lebanon, and Iraq struggled to develop a sure footing and autonomous identity. The legacy of the Holocaust complicated the political scene as the Western powers' commitment to secure a Jewish homeland in the Middle East stirred up Arab determination to hold onto their lands. From 1945 on, the Middle East was the scene of coups, power struggles, and ethnic and religious conflict, even as new nations were being born and older ones were strengthened by oil.

Israel

When World War II broke out, six hundred thousand Jewish settlers and twice as many Arabs lived, amid intermittent conflict, in British-controlled Palestine. In 1947, an exhausted Britain ceded the area to the United Nations to work out a settlement between the Jews and the Arabs. The UN voted to partition Palestine into an Arab region and a Jewish one, and in May 1948 Israelis proclaimed the new state of Israel. "The dream had come true," Golda Meir, future prime minister of Israel, remembered, but "too late to save those who had perished in the Holocaust."[6] Arguing that the UN had no right to award land to the Jewish minority in Palestine, five neighboring Arab states attacked Israel and were beaten. A UN-negotiated truce in 1949 to the Arab-Israeli War gave Israel even more territory than had been granted earlier. The result was that some two-thirds of Palestinian Arabs became stateless refugees and the war itself became but one more confrontation in a longer Arab-Israeli conflict over territory, rising Jewish immigration, and Palestinian rights to a homeland that continues to the present day.

The Arab-Israeli War of 1948–1949

Israel's neighbor, Egypt, had been a center of Allied efforts in North Africa and the Middle East during the war and demanded complete independence from British domination at the war's end. Britain, however, was determined to keep its control of Middle Eastern oil and Asian shipping through the Suez Canal, which was owned by a British-run company. Early in the 1950s the people of Cairo took to the streets, destroying flags of the puppet monarchy and other symbols of British rule. In 1952, army officer Gamal Abdel Nasser took part in the military ouster of the Egyptian king, a puppet of Britain's behind-the-scenes rule. The son of a postal inspector, Nasser rose quickly to become president of Egypt in 1956. As president, Nasser worked to improve the economic well-being of the peasants by redistributing land from the very wealthiest estates. Most notably, he faced down the European powers that wanted to keep control of Egyptian resources. A prime goal was reclaiming the Suez Canal, "where 120,000 of our sons had lost their lives in digging it [by force]," Nasser stated. In July 1956, after being denied a loan from the United States to build the projected Aswan Dam, he nationalized the Suez Canal so that Egypt would receive the income from tolls paid by those who used the canal. Nationalization of the Suez Canal sent Nasser's reputation soaring, making him the most popular and respected leader in the Arab world.

Egypt

Nasser's nationalization sent an angry tremor through the imperial powers, however. The Egyptians, Britain claimed, were hardly advanced enough as a people to run as complex an operation as the Suez Canal. Britain, with assistance from Israel and France, then invaded Egypt, bringing the Suez crisis to a head. American opposition made the British back down. Nasser's triumph in gaining the canal inspired confidence that the Middle East could confront the West and win.

New Nations in Africa

Displaced from their traditional agricultural livelihood during the war, many Africans flocked to cities such as Lagos and Nairobi, where they lived in shantytowns and survived by scavenging and doing menial labor for whites. After the war, struggling urban workers, including civil servants, professionals, and ordinary laborers, formed the core of the nationalist movement. High taxes imposed by white settlers gave added impetus to the decolonization movement. Another element in the drive toward independence was the transnational vision of Africans involved in trade and intellectual contact with the wider world. Leaders who had studied abroad were determined to have Western-style freedom.

Sub-Saharan Africa

In sub-Saharan Africa, these nationalists led increasingly discontented peoples to challenge the European imperialists. In the British-controlled Gold Coast of West Africa, Kwame Nkrumah (KWAH-may ehn-KROO-mah), formerly a poor school teacher, led the region's diverse inhabitants in Gandhian-style civil disobedience. A student in the United States in 1936, Nkrumah had been radicalized by Italy's invasion and defeat of Ethiopia. After the war, he joined a group of fellow West Africans in London, forging with them plans for liberation. Nkrumah returned to the Gold Coast, where he led protests that, despite determined British opposition, resulted in the formation of the independent country of Ghana in 1957 (see Seeing the Past: African Liberation on Cloth, page 975).

Nkrumah lobbied for the unity of all African states: "How except by our united efforts will the richest and still enslaved part of our continent be freed from colonial occupation . . . ?" he asked the heads of African governments in 1963 before all of Africa had been liberated.[7] But individual nation building was the order of the day. In the most populous African colony, Nigeria, workers and veterans recognized how important they were to Britain's postwar recovery and struck for higher wages, better working conditions, and greater respect. Respect did not come quickly: during a miners' strike in 1949 the British police commissioner ordered his troops to shoot because, he said, the miners were "dancing around and around" and chanting "We are all one."[8] Nonetheless, Nigeria gained its freedom in 1960 after the leaders of its many regional groups, unions, and political organizations reached agreement on a federal-style government. In these and other African states where the population was mostly black, independence came less violently than in mixed-race territory (see Map 29.5, page 974).

The numerous European settlers along Africa's eastern coast and in the southern and central areas of the continent violently resisted independence movements. In British East Africa, where white settlers ruled in splendor, the increasing mechanization of agriculture during the war drove blacks off the land. Displaced people filled cities like Nairobi or tried to eke out a living on infertile land. From the middle of World War II on, some of these displaced persons, including returning veterans, began forming secret political groups to oppose British rule. Violence erupted in the 1950s, when these rebels—including women who served as provisioners, messengers, and weapons stealers—tried to recover land from the whites. The rebels, who were mostly from the Kikuyu (kih-KOO-you) ethnic group, called themselves the Land and Freedom Army, but the whites referred to them as "Mau

MAP 29.5 New States in Africa and the Middle East, 1945–2011

To maintain their empires, the British, French, and Belgians fought lethal wars in Kenya, Algeria, and Congo, which featured brutal attacks against the local populations and killed tens of thousands. Inspired by their leaders, other African countries became independent relatively peacefully, although the costs of nation building were crushing in areas that had been so overexploited. The Middle East, in contrast, had enormous assets that drew the superpowers and other nations to compete fiercely for oil and control of the region's other assets, such as the Suez Canal.

Mau." The British responded by rounding up Kikuyus by the hundreds of thousands and placing them in secret concentration camps where conditions were so grim and mortality so high that the British deny their existence to this day. Nonetheless, despite the coordinated slaughter of an estimated 150,000 to 320,000 Kikuyus, the Land and Freedom Army finally wore the British down in costly military actions. Kenya gained formal independence in 1963.

North Africa

As the tide of liberation spread, colonial leaders in Tunisia, Morocco, and French West Africa successfully convinced France to leave peaceably, in large part because European settlers were few and there was little military involvement running these areas. Having earlier been declared an integral part of France, Algeria was another story altogether. In 1954 the newly formed Front for National Liberation (FLN) rose up, attacking French government buildings, radio stations, and utility plants. A radio station in Cairo announced the FLN's goal: the "restoration of the Algerian state, sovereign, democratic, and social, within the framework of the principles of Islam." The French sent in more than four hundred thousand troops to crush the uprising, determined to keep Algeria French and to guard the well-being of over 1 million European settlers.

SEEING THE PAST

African Liberation on Cloth

Nigerian Commemorative Textile (Textile Museum of Canada.)

Many African societies used commemorative textiles such as this vividly colored one from Nigeria to mark special occasions. Nations gaining their independence from the European powers issued such textiles in the 1960s and 1970s as they threw off imperial rule. This cloth clearly proclaims "Independence," but others presented the portraits of liberation heroes as they announced their freedom to the world. The textiles were immensely popular, hanging in homes and public buildings or serving as clothing (see At a Crossroads, page 958). Paradoxically, the independence textiles symbolized unity in the face of divisions among regions and ethnic groups within a country that had been artificially created by imperialist designs. In so doing, commemorative textiles, sometimes fashioned by women artisans, stood at the crossroads of pre-war and postwar world history.

EXAMINING THE EVIDENCE

1. **What was the purpose of these commemorative textiles?**
2. **What accounts for their popularity, given the many divisions among the peoples of new nations?**
3. **Why would some commemorative textiles feature brutal dictators?**

Neither side fought according to the rules of warfare: the French tortured native people, mutilating and then beheading them. The FLN fought a guerrilla war, fading into the mountains and countryside, while Algerian women, defying gender stereotypes, planted bombs in European cafés and carried weapons to assassination sites. Although France won the war with Algeria in military terms, the Algerian nationalists knew how to win the war of world opinion. Using modern public relations methods, they turned the United States and other influential nations against the French, convincing them that France stood in the way of Algerian economic development and the fight against communism. In 1962 Charles de Gaulle, leader of the Free French during World War II and new president of France, negotiated a settlement that resulted in independence for Algeria. Fearing retribution, hundreds of thousands of Europeans in Algeria as well as their Arab supporters fled to France. Having won its independence, Algeria, like the other newly independent states, now faced the challenge of establishing an effective, unified nation.

World Recovery in the 1950s and 1960s

FOCUS

What were the major elements of recovery in different parts of the world in the decades following World War II?

The struggles against colonialism and the ideological clash between the United States and the Soviet Union took place alongside remarkable economic growth and social change. Some parts of the world had prospered during the war. Latin America, for example, benefited from the wartime demand for raw materials and manufactured goods. Cuba's exports of sugar grew almost 300 percent between 1938 and the end of the war. The population of Latin America steadily grew. Other peoples, within a few decades after suffering the deprivation and devastation of total war, came to live longer lives and to enjoy a higher standard of living than ever before in history. In Europe this newfound prosperity was celebrated as an "economic miracle." As governments took increasing responsibility for the health and well-being of citizens, the menacing Cold War was also the backdrop for rapid development of the welfare state pioneered by Sweden (see Chapter 28).

Political changes fostered some of the movement toward economic growth. New nations faced the enormous task of building effective government. India, for example, had experienced the horrors of Partition and was additionally composed of more than five hundred small and several quite large states that had enjoyed local rule under the British. "We have to make [people] feel they are parts of India, not only politically but emotionally and otherwise, and that their future is tied up with India," the first prime minister, Jawaharlal Nehru (JAH-wa-HAR-lahl NAY-roo), wrote in 1955.[9] To build loyalty to new nations and the superpowers alike, governments often turned to expensive projects such as building dams, extending railroads, and electrifying rural areas—all of which contributed to the postwar pattern of economic growth.

Expanding Economic Prosperity

In the immediate aftermath of the war, governments in new and old nations alike diverted labor and capital into rebuilding infrastructure—transportation, communications, and industrial capacity. The scarcity of consumer goods sparked unrest in many parts of the world, but the influx of U.S. funds into nations worldwide as part of its Cold War mission fueled economic recovery. Food and consumer goods became more plentiful, and demand for them increased. The growth in production alleviated unemployment among those whose livelihoods the war had destroyed. Oil-rich countries imported people from many parts of Asia and Africa to perform menial labor: women from the Philippines, Indonesia, and the Caribbean were among those who migrated as nurses, nannies, and household help. Northern Europe, short of labor, arranged for "guest" workers to arrive from Sicily, Turkey, and North and sub-Saharan Africa to help rebuild cities. The outbreak of war in Korea in 1950 encouraged economic recovery in Japan and elsewhere. Korea itself, however, was devastated. The Cold War thus spurred economic advance in some parts of the world while labor shortages led to ongoing migration and further interconnectedness of peoples and livelihoods.

During the postwar recovery, wartime technology was adapted to civilian use, and military spending continued. Civilian travel expanded globally as nations organized their own air systems based on improved airplane technology. Developed to relieve wartime shortages, synthetic goods such as nylon now became part of peacetime civilian life. Factories churned out a vast assortment of electronics, and plastic products ranging from pipes to household goods and rainwear. In the climate of Cold War, governments ordered bombs, fighter planes, tanks, and missiles, and they continued to conduct military research. Governments in decolonized countries courted the superpowers to provide up-to-date weaponry to secure their rule against internal and external foes. The number of radios in homes grew steadily around the world, and by the 1960s television had become a widely popular consumer item and the source for a host of new occupations.

The Common Market

International cooperation and economic growth led to the creation in 1957 of the **European Economic Community** (EEC), known popularly as the Common Market, the foundation of the European Union of the 1990s. In 1957, Belgium, the Netherlands, Luxembourg, France, West Germany, and Italy established the EEC, which reduced tariffs among the six partners and worked to develop common trade policies. According to its founders, the EEC aimed to "prevent the race of nationalism, which is the true curse of the modern world." Increased cooperation produced great economic rewards for the six members, and it reduced the threat of war: the Italian economy, which had lagged behind that of France and Germany, boomed, and as additional countries joined from the 1970s on, many of them flourished too.

European Economic Community A consortium of European countries established in 1957 to promote free trade and economic cooperation among its members.

Rio de Janeiro
In 1946 Brazil threw off its dictatorship and became a democracy, embarking on a range of activities to modernize the nation. Among these was the construction of the Maracanã in Rio de Janeiro, the largest soccer stadium in the world at the time. Other modern urban construction followed, and as migrants arrived from rural areas Rio became Brazil's largest city. Many of those newcomers lived in shantytowns on the city's outskirts, shown in the lower left of this photograph. (akg-images/PictureContact.)

The Welfare State

Even as new nations came into being, the trend in postwar and postcolonial government was to intervene in people's everyday lives to improve social conditions and to prevent the political extremism and discontent of the 1930s. This policy of intervention became known as the **welfare state**, a term suggesting that, in addition to building their military power, states would guarantee a minimum level of well-being for their citizens. Postwar governments promoted both the advance of industry and the welfare of the general population with various forms of financial assistance. Imitating the sweeping Swedish programs of the 1930s, nations expanded or created family allowances, health-care and medical benefits, and programs for pregnant women. The combination of better material conditions and state provision of health care dramatically extended life expectancy. Contributing to the overall progress, the number of medical doctors and dentists soared between 1920 and 1950, and vaccines greatly reduced the global death toll from such diseases as tuberculosis, diphtheria, measles, and polio.

State initiatives in other areas also helped raise the standard of living. Government-built atomic power plants brought electrification to many more rural areas. States legislated for better conditions and more leisure time for workers and sponsored construction to alleviate housing shortages resulting from three decades of economic depression and war. Such efforts often drained the economies of newly independent countries. Moreover, despite the new construction, housing shortages persisted, and growing cities like Rio de Janeiro were surrounded by shantytowns. Nonetheless, the modernized appearance of many of the world's largest cities suggested that the century's two cataclysmic wars had swept away much that was old and traditional.

Welfare for Workers in Argentina

The welfare state became the backbone of politics in many regions. Juan Perón, a colonel in the Argentine army, became president in 1946 on a platform of welfare for workers and independence from the financial domination of Britain and the United States. During the war, as manufacturing jobs multiplied and migration to cities in search of industrial jobs swelled, Perón had forced American meatpacking plants around Buenos Aires to raise wages. Hundreds of thousands of workers backed Perón's array of economic benefits for "the shirtless ones," and his dramatic use of surplus government funds to buy out British-owned telephone companies and railroad lines was said to free Argentina from Western business imperialism domination. While Perón added to workers' wallets with rising social security and wages, his wife Eva, who was from the lower class, won their hearts. During the depression,

welfare state The postwar system of government-sponsored programs designed to provide citizens with basic standards of health care, housing, and income.

READING THE PAST

The Great Leap Forward in China

In 1949, life in China changed for most people because of the communist revolution that brought Mao Zedong to power. Kang Zhengguo was a student in the 1950s as the full weight of change began. His grandfather owned land and was a Buddhist leader; his father was a highly trained engineer. In this early passage from Zhengguo's memoir, he describes one of Mao's earliest programs, "The Great Leap Forward," when China was supposed to industrialize rapidly as the Soviets had done. Later parts of his memoir present bloody and terrifying incidents, including those that he himself endured.

> In 1958, the year of the Great Leap Forward, the nation became caught up in a frenzy of smelting "backyard steel." It was our "glorious mission" to donate scrap iron to this cause, so our school playground, like most other work units, was heaped with it, along with piles of burned charcoal. Some enthusiasts had tossed in their pots and pans or drawer handles for good measure, even if they were made of copper or tin. The student cafeteria had been temporarily converted into a foundry, equipped with a mighty blower that shook the classrooms with its roar and filled the air with a sooty purplish haze. Nobody seemed to have time for mundane pursuits like eating and sleeping. The upperclassmen manned the furnaces around the clock with holiday spirit, belting out all of their new songs and cheering for the molten "steel" as it poured out of the furnaces. Once it congealed into hard black slag, we deemed it a success and swathed it in bright red silk. Then, banging on drums and gongs and carrying big red paper placards that read "SURPASS ENGLAND AND CATCH UP TO AMERICA," we marched it triumphantly over to the district party committee.
>
> Classes were canceled more often than not, and even we younger students had to help out at the foundry.

Source: Kang Zhengguo, *Confessions: An Innocent Life in Communist China*, trans. Susan Wilf (New York: W. W. Norton, 2007), 14–15.

EXAMINING THE EVIDENCE

1. **What impression does this passage give you of the Great Leap Forward?**
2. **What is the place of politics in education, as suggested by this excerpt?**
3. **How would you describe the industrialization taking place during the Great Leap Forward?**
4. **How would you describe the student life?**

at the age of fifteen, she had migrated from the countryside to Buenos Aires, quickly leaving her poverty behind when she succeeded in radio and film. As Perón's wife, "Evita" joined him in providing the poor with housing, unemployment funds, and personal charity, which she virtually extorted from businesses. In exchange, the masses loyally supported the Peróns, even as the upper and middle classes stewed in silent protest. Eva Perón died from cancer at the age of thirty-two, leaving the Argentine masses heartbroken and the government strapped for funds to continue its welfare policies. In 1955, the military drove Perón out, reducing both the welfare state and the anti-American rhetoric.

Building and Rebuilding Communism

Two countries in particular bore the brunt of World War II in terms of population loss and outright destruction. The Soviet Union lost between 42 and 47 million people, new estimates suggest, while the Japanese invasion and more than a decade of civil war killed some 30 million people in China. Both Stalin and Mao Zedong were committed to rebuilding and modernizing their countries, and both revived the crushing methods that had served before to modernize and industrialize traditional peasant economies. An admirer of American industrial know-how, Stalin prodded all Soviet-bloc nations to match U.S. productivity. In China Mao had similar goals, and reaching them produced losses in both lives and jobs.

The Soviet Union

Stalin's death in 1953 created an opportunity to create a less repressive society in the USSR. Political prisoners in the labor camps pressed for reform, leading to the release of millions. Cold War competition and growing protests over shortages of food and other consumer items led the government to increase production of consumer goods. Nikita Khrushchev, an illiterate coal miner before the Bolshevik Revolution, outmaneuvered other rivals to become in 1955 the undisputed leader of the Soviet Union, but he did so without the usual executions. At a party congress in 1956, Khrushchev attacked the "cult of personality" Stalin had built about himself and announced that Stalinism did not equal socialism. The so-called Secret Speech—it was not published in the USSR but became widely known—sent tremors through hard-line Communist parties around the world.

In 1956, discontented Polish railroad workers successfully struck for better wages. Inspired by the Polish example, Hungarians rebelled later that year against forced collectivization and wage cutbacks, but the protest soon targeted the entire communist system. Tens of thousands of protesters filled the streets of Budapest, urged on both publicly and privately by the United States and its allies. When Hungary announced that it might leave the Warsaw Pact, Soviet troops moved in, killing tens of thousands and causing hundreds of thousands more to flee to the West. The U.S. refusal to act showed that, despite its rhetoric of "liberation," it would not risk World War III by military intervention in the Soviet sphere of influence.

Wu Guanzhong, *Willows on a Hillside*

Wu Guanzhong's studies in Europe influenced his art after his return to China to teach in Beijing in the 1950s. Forbidden to paint during the Cultural Revolution of the 1960s, Wu returned to his hybrid style, which mixed abstract representations from the West with Chinese styles that he modernized in his work. For many critics, Wu's work reflects both his own artistry and the influence of other contemporary artists, such as Jackson Pollock (see page 983). (Christie's Images/Corbis.)

In the People's Republic of China, Mao Zedong faced the problem of rebuilding a war-torn peasant society. Like Stalin, Mao saw modernization as the answer, but to keep Chinese communism and himself in power, Mao tacked back and forth, uncertain of what to do. In 1959 he initiated the **Great Leap Forward**, an economic plan intended to increase industrial production. The plan ordered country people to stop tending their farms and instead produce steel from their shovels, pots, and pans in their own small backyard furnaces (see Reading the Past: The Great Leap Forward in China). This decentralized plan of industrial production proved to be a disaster, as much of the do-it-yourself iron and steel was worthless. Meanwhile, the halting of agriculture resulted in massive famine. An estimated 30 million people died, and millions more went hungry. "Communism is not a dinner party," Mao remarked with grim irony, and his government touted the virtues of being thin. During this and other projects, livelihoods deteriorated and education was devalued in the name of participating in different communist schemes.

China

In the early 1960s, Mao's slipping popularity and rising threats from outside the country led to the brutal development known as the **Cultural Revolution**. To break the opposition that had emerged during the Great Leap Forward, Mao turned against his associates in the Communist Party, appealing to China's youth to reinvigorate the revolution. Brought up to revere Mao, young people responded to his call to rid society of the "four olds"—old customs, old habits, old culture, and old ideas. In Mao's name they destroyed artistic treasures and crushed individual lives, striking yet another blow at ordinary people's ability to pursue productive lives.

During the Cultural Revolution, any kind of skilled person was branded uncommunist and thus criminal, as seen in the experience of painter Wu Guanzhong. Wu went to Paris in 1947 on a government scholarship to learn the techniques of Western masters, but after three years Mao's administration summoned him back to teach in Beijing. By the mid-1950s, the Chinese leadership had come to see Wu's work, which mixed Chinese and Western

Great Leap Forward The Chinese communist program of the mid-1950s designed to push the country ahead of all others in industrial and other production.

Cultural Revolution The Chinese communist program of the 1960s and early 1970s carried out by Mao Zedong's youthful followers to remake Chinese thought, behavior, and everyday life.

styles, as a "poisonous weed." In their view, the only acceptable approach to art was Soviet-style socialist realism. Wu was removed from his prestigious teaching post and sent to farm in the countryside, where he was forbidden to paint or to talk to his wife, who accompanied him. In 1972 Wu was allowed to resume his artwork "for relaxation" one day a week, but he had trouble finding materials and came ultimately to describe himself as a "cow-dung painter." After Mao's death in 1976 the brutality of the Cultural Revolution eased. Wu Guanzhong's reputation as one of the world's outstanding artists was restored, and the skills of the Chinese people in artistic, agricultural, industrial, and other pursuits were once again valued.

Cultural Dynamism amid Cold War

FOCUS

How did the experience of world war, decolonization, and Cold War affect cultural life and thought?

As the Cold War unfolded, people around the world vigorously discussed the devastating World War II experience, the rationale for decolonization, and the dangers of the Cold War itself. Writers tried to understand the meaning of war and genocide. Literature exploring concepts of freedom and liberation poured out of Africa, Latin America, and Asia and reached the West, where oppressed minorities were likewise demanding better treatment. Thus, the postwar period was one of intense cultural ferment and unprecedented levels of cultural exchange within each Cold War bloc.

Confronting the Heritage of World War

In 1944, during the last months of the war, University of Tokyo professor Tanabe Hajime began a soul-searching book, turning to Buddhism for enlightenment. In *Philosophy as Matonetics* (the title refers to an act of repentant confession), Tanabe urged the Japanese to enter higher realms of wisdom as they faced defeat. His program for a return to Buddhist values allowed the Japanese to see in their defeat a lofty purpose, elevating them above the brute power politics of the Western victors. Such programs for exalting the wartime losers took place alongside intense indoctrination in democratic values and the dramatic trials of Axis leaders conducted at Nuremberg, Germany, in 1945 and in Tokyo, Japan, in 1946. Both sets of trials revealed a horrifying panorama of crimes and led to death sentences or long imprisonment for most of the defendants. These trials introduced the concept of "crimes against humanity" and an international politics based on demands for human rights.

Nonetheless, as civilians in the defeated Axis nations struggled with starvation, rape, and other postwar hardships, many Japanese and Germans came to believe that they were the main victims of the war. The Cold War helped reinforce that view. American officials themselves, eager to fight the communists, began to rely on the expertise of high-ranking Japanese militarists, fascists, and Nazis, overlooking war crimes as trivial when compared to the evil menace of the USSR. The work of Tanabe and others justified the speedy rehabilitation of the Axis powers, as the war temporarily came to be explained as one of idealism on both sides.

Memoirs of the death camps and tales of the resistance evoked a starkly different side of the events of the 1930s and 1940s. Anne Frank's *Diary of a Young Girl* (1947) was the poignant record of a German Jewish teenager hidden with her family for two years in the back of an Amsterdam warehouse before they were discovered and sent to concentration camps, where all died except Anne's father. Confronted with the small miseries of daily life and the grand evils of Nazism, Frank wrote that she never stopped believing that "people are really good at heart." Histories of the resistance addressed the public's need for inspiration after the savagery of World War II. After years of censorship and privation, Japanese publishers tapped a market thirsty for books by putting out moving collections of letters from soldiers that quickly became best sellers. Only phrase books teaching the language of the conquerors outsold the books of soldiers' letters. Filmmakers from around the world also depicted war, as memories and nightmares of World War II haunted the screen into the twenty-first century.

existentialism A philosophy prominent after World War II, developed primarily by French thinkers, that stresses the importance of active engagement with the world in the creation of an authentic existence.

By the end of the 1940s, **existentialism** had become popular among the cultural elites and students in universities around the world. This philosophy explored the meaning of human existence in a world where evil flourished. The principal theorists of existentialism, Frenchmen Jean-Paul Sartre and Albert Camus, wrote plays and essays in which they asked what "being" meant, given what they saw as the absence of God and the breakdown of morality under Nazism. Their answer was that "being," or existing, was not the automatic process either of God's creation or of birth into the natural world. Instead, through action and choice, the individual created an "authentic" or meaningful and valuable existence. As existentialists, Sartre and Camus emphasized political activism and resistance to totalitarianism.

In 1949, Simone de Beauvoir, Sartre's lifetime companion, published *The Second Sex*, the twentieth century's most influential work on the condition of women. Examining women's status as mothers, wives, and daughters, de Beauvoir concluded that most women had failed to take the kind of action necessary to lead authentic lives. Instead of acting based on their individual reasoning, they devoted themselves to reproduction and motherhood because it was a social expectation. Failing to create an authentic self through considered action, they had become its opposite—an object, or "Other," who followed cultural norms set by men. Translated into many languages, de Beauvoir's book asked women to change by creating their own freedom.

Frantz Fanon

Frantz Fanon was one of the most influential thinkers during anti-imperial liberation struggles of the 1950s. He justified the use of violence against colonizers by arguing that brute force was all the imperialists understood, and indeed it was what colonized peoples themselves understood best because of the violence regularly inflicted on them. He also raised the question of how one "decolonized" one's mind of such propagandistic notions as the superiority of whites and the inferiority of blacks. (© Abdelhamid Kahia/Kaha Studio.)

Liberation Culture

In decolonizing areas, thinkers mapped out new visions of how to construct the future. In the 1950s and 1960s Frantz Fanon, a black psychiatrist from the French Caribbean colony of Martinique, wrote that the mind of the colonized person had been traumatized by the brutal imposition of an alien culture. Ruled by guns, the colonized person knew only violence and would thus naturally decolonize by means of violence. Translated into many languages, Fanon's *Black Skin, White Masks* (1952) and *The Wretched of the Earth* (1961) posed the question of how to "decolonize" one's mind. South African writer Bessie Head, the daughter of a white mother and an African father, developed Fanon's themes in her novels. Her characters danced on the edge of madness because of their complicated identities springing from colonialism, clashing ethnicities, and education. A teacher in Head's novel *Maru* (1971) has an English education but is despised and disdained by other Africans because she belongs to the darkest-skinned group of Bushmen. Liberation culture characterized independence as something emotionally confusing for individuals, with the meaning of freedom remaining to be puzzled out.

The Spread of Ideas

Ideas about the meaning of liberation circled the world. Mao Zedong's "Little Red Book" contained brief maxims intended to guide hundreds of millions of postcolonial citizens. Fanon's ideas also circulated among Africans, North Americans, and Latin Americans. They intersected with those of Jamaica-born Marcus Garvey, who in the interwar years had promoted a "back to Africa" movement as the way for African Americans to escape racial discrimination in the United States. In the 1960s the physician and upper-class guerrilla warrior Che Guevara, though a Marxist, wrote of avoiding the centralized and dictatorial Marxism of both the USSR and China. His popular works advocated a compassionate Marxism based on an appreciation of the oppressed rather than on a determination to direct them.

The U.S. Civil Rights Movement

Inspired not only by their own situation in the United States but by decolonization movements throughout the world, African Americans intensified their agitation for civil rights in the 1950s. In principle, African American troops had fought to defeat the Nazi idea of white racial supremacy; now African Americans hoped to end ideas of white racial superiority in the United States. In 1954, the U.S. Supreme Court declared segregated education unconstitutional

The "New Look" for Women After World War II

Designers and marketers aimed to return women in the West to a state of hyperfemininity in the postwar world, even though women in war-torn areas often lacked the bare necessities. In some places, clothing and food were rationed into the early 1950s, making the attire shown here more a fantasy than a reality. (Bibliotheque des Arts Decoratifs, Paris/Archives Charmet/Bridgeman Art Library.)

in *Brown v. Board of Education*, a case initiated by the National Association for the Advancement of Colored People (NAACP). Over the course of the 1950s, many talented individuals emerged to lead the civil rights movement, foremost among them Martin Luther King, Jr., a minister from Georgia whose powerful oratory galvanized African Americans to peaceful resistance in the face of brutal white retaliation. By the 1960s, other activists came to follow thinkers such as Fanon, proclaiming "black power" to achieve rights through violence if necessary.

The Culture of Cold War

In the effort to win the Cold War, both sides poured vast sums of money into high and popular culture. The United States secretly channeled government money into foundations to promote favorable journalism around the world and to sponsor specific artists. In the USSR, official writers churned out spy stories, and espionage novels topped best seller lists as well in the West. *Casino Royale* (1953), by the British author Ian Fleming, introduced James Bond, British intelligence agent 007, who survived tests of wit and physical prowess at the hands of communist and other political villains. Soviet pilots would not take off for flights when the work of Yulian Simyonov, the Russian counterpart of Ian Fleming, was playing on radio or television. Daily reports of Soviets and Americans—fictional or real—facing one another down fed many of the world's fantasies and nightmares.

In postwar Europe and the United States, everyday life also revolved around the growing availability of material goods and household conveniences. A rising birthrate and a bustling youth culture encouraged spending on newly available goods. The advertising business boomed, confronting the thriftiness of the Great Depression and wartime with messages that described new products and encouraged the desire to buy them. These were the years when American-style consumerism came to stand for freedom and plenty versus the scarcity in the communist world. Women's magazines in the West publicized a "new look" that encouraged women to be sexy and feminine—unlike women in communist countries—and urged them to return to the "normal" life of domesticity and shopping. European communists debated the "Americanization" they saw taking place. Many wanted American products; nonetheless, Communist parties worked to get American products banned. The Communist Party in France, for example, led a successful campaign to ban Coca-Cola for a time in the 1950s, and the Soviets tried unsuccessfully to match the West's production of consumer goods.

Consumerism in the West

Spreading Cold War Culture

Radio was key to spreading Cold War culture and values; both the United States and the USSR used the medium to broadcast news and propaganda. During the late 1940s and early 1950s, the Voice of America, broadcasting in thirty-eight languages from one hundred transmitters, provided an alternative source of news for people around the world. The Soviet counterpart broadcast in Russian around the clock but initially spent much of its wattage jamming U.S. programming. Russian programs stressed a uniform communist culture and values. The United States, by contrast, emphasized diverse programming and promoted debate about current affairs—even while a U.S. senator, Joseph McCarthy, began a witch hunt for communists to win an election in 1950. Radio and television helped the events and developments of the Cold War acquire a far-reaching emotional impact: both the United States and USSR whipped up fear of enemies within, persecuting millions of citizens for allegedly favoring the opposing side. People heard reports of nuclear build-ups; in school, children rehearsed what to do in case of nuclear war; and families built bomb shelters in their backyards.

Abstract Expressionism

As leadership of the art world passed from Europe to the United States, art became part of the Cold War, along with consumer goods and books. **Abstract expressionism**, developed primarily by American artists, encompassed many diverse styles but often featured large canvasses depicting nonrepresentational forms in bold colors. Abstract expressionists spoke of the importance of the artist's self-discovery, spiritual growth, and sensations in the process of painting. American artist Jackson Pollock produced abstract works by dripping, spattering, and pouring paint. Dutch-born artist Willem de Kooning commented on his relationship with his canvas, "If I stretch my arms next to the rest of myself and wonder where my fingers are, that is all the space I need as a painter." Said to exemplify Western freedom, such painters were awarded commissions at the secret direction of the U.S. Central Intelligence Agency. Pro-Soviet critics in western Europe condemned abstract art as "an infantile sickness" and favored socialist realist art with "human content," showing the condition of the workers and the oppressed races in the United States. When a show of abstract art opened in the Soviet Union, Khrushchev yelled that it was "dog shit."

Official Communist Culture

The USSR promoted an official communist culture based on the socialist realist style highlighting the heroism of the working classes. The government sponsored classical training in ballet and music and harassed innovators in the arts. Communist culture emphasized Soviet successes, celebrating Soviet wartime victories and the USSR's progress toward Stalin's goal of economic modernization. Dissenters in the USSR were both feared and bullied. For example, Khrushchev forced Boris Pasternak to refuse the 1958 Nobel Prize in Literature because Pasternak's novel *Doctor Zhivago* (1957) cast doubt on the glory of the Bolshevik Revolution and affirmed the value of the individual. Yet Khrushchev himself made several trips to the West and was a more cosmopolitan, public figure than Stalin had been. With growing confidence and affluence, the Soviets concentrated their efforts on spreading official socialist culture and influence in Asia, Africa, and Latin America.

COUNTERPOINT

The Bandung Conference 1955

FOCUS

How did the Bandung Conference and its aims represent an alternative to the Cold War division of the globe?

In April 1955, Achmed Sukarno, who led the struggle for Indonesian independence from the Dutch, hosted a conference in Bandung, Indonesia, of emerging nations. The Bandung Conference, also known as the Asian-African Conference, was meant to ensure the independence of the emerging Asian and African nations despite the temptations of loans and military aid from the superpowers. The conference was thus a counterpoint to the seemingly global grip of the Cold War and the superpowers' hold on international politics.

abstract expressionism A postwar artistic style characterized by nonrepresentational forms and bold colors; often associated with the freedom of the Western world.

Cosponsored by Egypt, Indonesia, Burma, Sri Lanka, India, and Pakistan, the conference was attended by representatives from twenty-nine countries, most of them newly independent. They constituted a who's who of anticolonialism: Kwame Nkrumah of Ghana, Gamal Abdel Nasser of Egypt, Zhou Enlai of China, and Ho Chi Minh of Vietnam attended alongside Sukarno and Jawaharlal Nehru, prime minister of India. Activists throughout the world were inspired

The Bandung Conference
In 1955, leaders from Asia and Africa met in newly independent Indonesia at the Bandung Conference, with the goal of building unity among emerging nations. Participants listened to inspiring and hard-hitting speeches as they began a policy of "nonalignment" in the Cold War. This policy was a refusal to become pawns of the superpowers, but it was hard for many to maintain because the need for support was so great in regions devastated by imperial greed and total war. (AP Photo/Asia-Africa Museum, HO.)

by the independent, even defiant stand against the superpowers taken by the leaders gathered at Bandung. African American author Richard Wright, who attended the conference, was riveted by the meaning of such an assembly: "The despised, the insulted, the hurt, the dispossessed—in short, the underdogs of the human race were meeting. Here were class and racial and religious consciousness on a global scale. Who had thought of organizing such a meeting? And what had these nations in common? Nothing, it seemed to me, but what their past relationship to the Western world had made them feel. This meeting of the rejected was in itself a kind of judgment upon the Western world!"[10] Leaders at the conference, speakers noted, represented more than half the world's population.

Shared Goals

Issues discussed at the Bandung Conference included economic development outside the structures of colonialism, and the achievement of political well-being without following the dictates of either the Soviet Union or the United States. Nehru argued strongly for nonalignment, maintaining that nations affiliating with one side or another would lose their identity. Moreover, Nehru claimed, the superpowers had come to equate a nation's worth with its military power. To his mind this was evidence that "greatness sometimes brings quite false values, false standards. When they begin to think in terms of military strength—whether it be the United Kingdom, the Soviet Union, or the U.S.A.—then they are going away from the right track and the result of that will be that the overwhelming might of one country will conquer the world."[11] In India, Nehru tried to follow a middle course between the superpowers in his own economic policies, even though he simultaneously offered support to communist China.

Nehru had high hopes for Bandung, but he also had concerns that proper conditions such as first-rate accommodations and sanitary facilities be provided for delegates of the emerging nations to the conference. They needed to be recognized as valuable through their treatment, as they were at the meetings of the United Nations in New York. Nehru admired the more lofty goals of the UN, including the charter outlining a collective global authority that would adjudicate conflicts and provide military protection to any member threatened by aggression. Meetings of both the UN and emerging nations began shifting global issues away from superpower priorities. Human rights and economic inequities among developing countries and the West nudged their way into public consciousness.

Divisive Issues

Yet for all the desire to be an influential third force between the superpowers, serious issues divided participants at the Bandung Conference. For one, the legacy of mistrust between India and Pakistan grew increasingly bitter and violent over their rival claims to the state of Kashmir. The leaders at Bandung argued both in favor of nationalism and in support of movements that transcended nationalism, such as pan-Islam and pan-Africanism. Although the Bandung Conference did not yield an enduring world power bloc, it did articulate a position that after the end of the Cold War would evolve into the idea of a North-South divide. Those living in the northern half of the globe were wealthy compared with those in the south, impoverished because imperialism's legacy had relegated them to poorly remunerated production of commodities. In the 1950s and 1960s, however, the notable achievement of the Bandung Conference was that it strengthened the commitment of new nations to remain independent in the face of the superpowers' military and economic might.

Conclusion

The Cold War began the atomic age and transformed international power politics. The two new superpowers, the Soviet Union and the United States, each built massive atomic arsenals, replacing the former European leadership and facing off in a Cold War that menaced the entire world. The Cold War saturated everyday life, producing a culture of bomb shelters, spies, and witch-hunts. Yet within this atmosphere of division and nuclear rivalry an astonishing worldwide recovery occurred. New housing, transport, and industrial rebuilding—often sponsored by a burgeoning welfare state and using wartime technology—made many people healthier and more prosperous.

World War II promoted further discontent and activism—like that of Umm Kulthum—among the colonized peoples of the world and simultaneously loosened the grip of the colonial powers. From India to Ghana and Nigeria, colonial peoples, often led by Western-educated and nationalist politicians, won their independence and turned to nation building. Many, as in the case of Algeria and Kenya, had to take up arms against the brutality of the imperialists to become free. Nation building in newly independent states, however, turned out to be slow and halting, even though many of these nations also enjoyed a burst of postwar prosperity.

As the world grew overall in prosperity, its cultural life focused on eradicating the evils inflicted by the Axis and on surviving the atomic rivalry of the superpowers. Frantz Fanon and other thinkers developed theories to explain the struggles of decolonized peoples for their full independence. In the midst of postwar intellectual introspection and heated Cold War rhetoric, many came to wonder whether Cold War was really worth the threat of nuclear annihilation and whether there might be an alternative way of living as individuals and as a world community. Leaders of newly independent nations, through such activities as the Bandung Conference, promoted the idea of nonalignment with either superpower, but they often had difficulty overcoming their own differences, rivalries, and internal corruption. These hopes matured into a burst of technological creativity and further activism to improve the world—including putting an end to the Cold War.

NOTES

1. Harry S. Truman, "Truman Doctrine Speech," March 12, 1947.
2. Dwight D. Eisenhower, press conference, April 7, 1954.
3. Quoted in Ronald J. Spector, *In the Ruins of Empire: The Japanese Surrender and the Battle for Postwar Asia* (New York: Random House, 2007), 78.
4. Quoted in Alex von Tunzelmann, *Indian Summer: The Secret History of the End of an Empire* (New York: Henry Holt, 2007), 225.

5. Everette Lee DeGoyler, quoted in Daniel Yergin, *The Prize: The Epic Quest for Oil, Money, and Power* (New York: Simon and Schuster, 1991), 393.
6. Golda Meir, *My Life* (New York: Putnam, 1975).
7. "Africa Must Unite" (1963), quoted in Michael Hunt, *The World Transformed, 1945 to the Present* (Boston: Bedford/St. Martin's, 2004), 144.
8. Superintendent of Police Philip, quoted in Carolyn A. Brown, *"We Were All Slaves": African Miners, Culture, and Resistance at the Enugu Government Colliery* (Portsmouth, NH: Heinemann, 2003), 310.
9. Quoted in Judith M. Brown, *Nehru: A Political Life* (New Haven, CT: Yale University Press, 2003), 229.
10. Richard Wright, *The Color Curtain: A Report on the Bandung Conference* (Jackson, MS: Banner, 1995).
11. *Selected Works of Jawaharlal Nehru: 1 February–31 May 1955*. vol. 28.

RESOURCES FOR RESEARCH

World Politics and the Cold War

The Cold War replaced the great-power politics of the previous hundred years, making the world increasingly dangerous. Spector's history of the immediate postwar years in Asia shows the chaos and violence that provided the setting for the Cold War division of the world and the transformation of world politics.

Cumings, Bruce. *Korea's Place in the Sun: A Modern History*. 2005.
The Korean War Educator. http://www.koreanwar-educator.org.
Meisner, Maurice. *Mao Zedong: A Political and Intellectual Portrait*. 2007.
Skierka, Volker. *Fidel Castro: A Biography*. 2007.
Spector, Ronald H. *In the Ruins of Empire: The Japanese Surrender and the Battle for Postwar Asia*. 2007.
Statler, Kathryn, and Andrew Johns, eds. *The Eisenhower Administration, the Third World, and the Globalization of the Cold War*. 2006.

Decolonization and the Birth of Nations

New nations emerged in a variety of ways, with differing levels of violence and styles of leadership. Elkins's book starkly details the British torture and slaughter of Kenyans who wanted freedom.

Connelley, Matthew. *A Diplomatic Revolution: Algeria's Fight for Independence and the Origins of the Post–Cold War Era*. 2002.
Danielson, Virginia. *Umm Kulthum, Arabic Song, and Egyptian Society in the Twentieth Century*. 1998.
Duara, Prasenjit, ed. *Decolonization: Perspectives from Then and Now*. 2004.
Elkins, Caroline. *Imperial Reckoning: The Untold Story of Britain's Gulag in Kenya*. 2005.
Guha, Ramachandra. *India After Gandhi: The History of the World's Largest Democracy*. 2008.
Hyam, Ronald. *Britain's Declining Empire: The Road to Decolonisation, 1918–1968*. 2007.

World Recovery in the 1950s and 1960s

Recovering from the devastation of World War II and the trials of nation building was no easy task. Notable leaders of new nations worked to overcome poverty, illiteracy, and lingering factionalism. Brown's biography of Nehru provides a good example.

Allen, Larry. *The Global Economic System Since 1945*. 2005.
Brown, Judith M. *Nehru: A Political Life*. 2003.
Estévez-Abe, Margarita. *Welfare and Capitalism in Postwar Japan*. 2008.
Rhodes, Richard. *Arsenals of Folly: The Nuclear Arms Race*. 2007.
Sturgeon, Janet C. *Border Landscapes: The Politics of Akha Land Use in China and Thailand*. 2005.
Tignor, Robert. *W. Arthur Lewis and the Birth of Development Economics*. 2006.

Culture Dynamism amid Cold War

An array of thinkers and artists considered the birth of new nations amid immense postwar suffering. Frantz Fanon was one of the most influential theorists of decolonization of his time, but Cold War rivalries also led to cultural competition, as seen in Von Eschen's work.

Fanon, Frantz. *The Wretched of the Earth*. 1963 [orig. pub. 1961].
Hoerder, Dirk. *Cultures in Contact: World Migrations in the Second Millennium*. 2002.
Igarashi, Yoshikuni. *Bodies of Memory: Narratives of War in Postwar Japanese Culture, 1945–1970*. 2000.
Von Eschen, Penny. *Satchmo Blows Up the World: Jazz Ambassadors Play the Cold War*. 2005.
Wright, Michelle M. *Becoming Black: Creating Identity in the African Diaspora*. 2004.

COUNTERPOINT: The Bandung Conference, 1955

Taylor's people-oriented book provides the Indonesian background to Bandung and shows the stresses and strains of nation building amid postwar turbulence.

Jankowitz, Odile, and Karl Sauvant, eds. *The Third World Without Superpowers: Collected Documents of Non-Aligned Countries*. 1973–1993.
Legge, John David. *Sukarno: A Political Biography*. 2003.
Taylor, Jean Gelman. *Indonesia: Peoples and History*. 2003.
Wright, Richard. *The Color Curtain: A Report on the Bandung Conference*. 1995.

▶ **For additional primary sources from this period**, see *Sources of Crossroads and Cultures*.

▶ **For Web sites, images, and documents related to topics in this chapter**, see Make History at bedfordstmartins.com/smith.

REVIEW

Online Study Guide
bedfordstmartins.com/smith

The major global development in this chapter ▶ The political transformations of the postwar world and their social and cultural consequences.

IMPORTANT EVENTS

1945	World War II ends
1947	India and Pakistan win independence
1948	Israel gains independence
1948–1949	Arab-Israeli War
1949	Communists take control of China; Western powers form NATO; USSR detonates atomic bomb
1949	Indonesia gains independence
1950–1953	Korean War
1952	Egypt achieves full independence under Nasser
1953	Death of Stalin
1954	Vietnamese defeat French army at Dien Bien Phu
1956	Khrushchev denounces Stalin; Suez crisis; revolution in Hungary
1957	USSR launches *Sputnik*
1958	Khrushchev forces Boris Pasternak to refuse Nobel Prize in Literature
1961	Construction of the Berlin Wall
1962	Algeria wins independence; Cuban Missile Crisis
c. 1966–1976	Mao Zedong's "Cultural Revolution"

KEY TERMS

abstract expressionism (p. 983)
Cold War (p. 961)
containment (p. 964)
Cultural Revolution (p. 979)
decolonization (p. 961)
European Economic Community (p. 976)
existentialism (p. 980)
Great Leap Forward (p. 979)
guerrilla warfare (p. 971)
North Atlantic Treaty Organization (p. 967)
Organization of American States (p. 968)
Partition (p. 971)
proxy war (p. 962)
Southeast Asia Treaty Organization (p. 968)
Warsaw Pact (p. 967)
welfare state (p. 977)

CHAPTER OVERVIEW QUESTIONS

1. How did the Cold War affect the superpowers and the world beyond them?
2. How did the Cold War shape everyday lives and goals?
3. Why did colonial nationalism revive in the postwar world, and how did decolonization affect society and culture?
4. Why did the model of a welfare state emerge after World War II, and how did this development affect ordinary people?

SECTION FOCUS QUESTIONS

1. Why was the Cold War waged, and how did it reshape world politics?
2. How did colonized peoples achieve their independence from the imperialist powers after World War II?
3. What were the major elements of recovery in different parts of the world in the decades following World War II?
4. How did the experience of world war, decolonization, and Cold War affect cultural life and thought?
5. How did the Bandung Conference and its aims represent an alternative to the Cold War division of the globe?

MAKING CONNECTIONS

1. Recall Chapters 27 and 28. Why did economic well-being seem so much stronger a decade and longer after World War II than it had been after World War I?
2. Why did proxy wars play such a constant role in the Cold War? Some historians see these wars as part of a new imperialism. Do you agree?
3. What was the role of culture in shaping the Cold War?
4. What remnants of decolonization and the Cold War still affect life today?

AT A CROSSROADS ▶

This technician, working in 1962 in a telephone plant in Bangalore, India, stands at a crossroads of global technological innovation. Not only would satellites come to connect a range of communication devices such as telephones throughout the world, but telephones would evolve into such instruments as the iPhone, which would incorporate almost all other means of communication. By the twenty-first century, Bangalore itself would become a leader in global service work because of these and other innovations. (National Geographic/Getty Images.)

Technological Transformation and the End of Cold War

1960–1992

In 1973 the film *Bobby* opened to packed houses in cities across India. The film tells the story of Raj and Bobby, teenagers who fall in love after Raj returns to Bombay from boarding school. Infatuated with each other and the world, Bobby wears long chiffon scarves floating from her ponytail and Raj races around on his motorbike, both of them setting consumer trends among young Indians tired of postindependence seriousness. As Raj's wealthy industrialist father works to stop his son from marrying someone of a lower class, moviegoers cheered the young couple's determination to stay together, even as thugs kidnap them to obtain ransom money from the father. Rebellious young love, new fashions, and lots of song and dance filled *Bobby* and other hit Indian films, which helped "Bollywood," as the film industry centered in Bombay (Mumbai) came to be called, outpace Hollywood in ticket sales and popularity in the 1970s. Thanks to new video-recording technology, developed by the Japanese as a mass market item late in the 1970s, *Bobby* came to circulate worldwide, especially among South Asian fans who had migrated to Western countries.

Hundreds of Bollywood writers, composers, actors, designers, cameramen, editors, agents, and the other service workers who constituted an ever-growing segment of the global workforce contributed to the making of *Bobby*. Bollywood films represented the

Advances in Technology and Science

FOCUS What were the major postwar advances in technology and science, and why were they important?

Changes in the World Economy

FOCUS How did changes in the global economy affect livelihoods and family life?

Politics and Protest in an Age of Cold War

FOCUS What developments challenged the superpowers' dominance of world politics, and how did the superpowers attempt to address those challenges?

The End of the Cold War Order

FOCUS Why did the Cold War order come to an end?

COUNTERPOINT: Agrarian Peoples in a Technological Age

FOCUS How did some agrarian peoples resist the scientific and technological developments that threatened their ways of life?

BACKSTORY

As we saw in Chapter 29, by 1960 the two superpowers had pulled much of the world into the Cold War, using their considerable military and economic power to attract allies and counter each other's efforts. Their ability to extend their influence into developing countries rested on their successful adoption and application of the technological and industrial developments of the past two centuries. Since 1750 the Industrial Revolution (discussed in Chapter 24) had substituted mechanical energy for human power and then proceeded to develop electrical, chemical, and nuclear capacity. By the postwar period all of these technologies were being enhanced and democratized, widely improving civilian life. Those societies that could innovate, adapt, and then efficiently coordinate the use of these technologies moved ahead, as Japan and Western countries understood early on.

Arab-Israeli Six-Day War **1967** ▪

Vietnam War ends; Vietnam reunited **1975**

▪ **1957** USSR launches *Sputnik*

"Prague Spring" in Czechoslovakia **1968** ▪

▪ **1969** U.S. astronauts land on moon

1950 1960 1970

Betty Friedan, *The Feminine Mystique* **1963** ▪

U.S. president Richard Nixon visits China; SALT I agreement **1972** ▪

1973–1976 Aleksandr Solzhenitsyn, *Gulag Archipelago*

Arab-Israeli Yom Kippur War; OPEC raises oil prices and imposes embargo **1973** ▪

fantasies of an increasingly service-oriented population and those aspiring to join it. Across the world, sophisticated technology devised by highly educated service workers transmitted productions via satellite and circulated them on DVDs. In **postindustrial**, service-driven economies, institutions of higher education sprang up at a dizzying rate, drawing more students away from traditional families than ever before—among them bright-eyed young people like Raj and Bobby. The high-tech youthfulness and rebellion represented by *Bobby* and Bollywood were one aspect of the unsettled, dynamic social and economic environment of the late twentieth century.

Although Bollywood presented social and economic change in lighthearted fantasies, people were also making serious efforts to tackle the most pressing problems of modern society. The same young people targeted by the makers of Bollywood films joined a wide variety of activists to strike out against the effects of technology, as well as against war and the Cold War, social inequality and repression, and prevailing attitudes of racism and sexism. Many of these activists participated in grassroots protests against national dictatorships—in Latin America, for example—and against the way high-tech nations in general and the superpowers in particular were directing society. Between 1945 and 1990, more than one hundred major rebellions and civil wars erupted around the world as countries in both the Soviet and U.S. blocs headed toward political revolution. Whole nations—often with the young on the frontlines—challenged the superpowers' monopoly of international power. Agonizing wars in Vietnam and Afghanistan sapped the resources of the United States and the Soviet Union, respectively. Other states emerged to exercise surprising economic and military power as they grasped the reins of technology. The oil-producing states of the Middle East combined their efforts and reduced the export of oil to the leading industrial nations in the 1970s while also raising prices.

As the USSR failed to keep pace with high-tech innovation or to heed youthful calls for change, an invisible erosion of Soviet legitimacy took place, and soon a reform-minded leader—Mikhail Gorbachev—set the country on a new course. It was too late: in 1989, the

postindustrial An economy or society in which service work rather than manufacturing or agriculture predominates.

MAPPING THE WORLD

OPEC, Pacific Tigers, and World Migration

In the decades from 1960 to 1990, the world seemed bogged down in the Cold War order, but it was actually in tremendous flux. Technological change was transforming society and would continue to do so through the twenty-first century. Economic power was beginning to shift away from the West, and this shift would accelerate over the coming decades. Finally, under the influence of technology and global economic change, livelihoods became postindustrial in some areas and more attuned to manufacturing in formerly agricultural regions.

ROUTES ▼

- Major oil trade routes, c. 1975
- South Asian migrations, 1970–present
- Southeast Asian migrations, 1975–present
- Routes of Aleksandr Solzhenitsyn, 1945–1974

1978–1979 Islamic revolution in Iran

1978 World's first test-tube baby born

1985 Mikhail Gorbachev becomes Soviet leader, introduces new policies of perestroika and glasnost

1992 Soviet Union no longer exists

1980 1990 2000

1979–1989 Soviet war in Afghanistan

1980 Solidarity labor union organizes resistance to communism in Poland; Prime Minister Margaret Thatcher introduces neoliberal program in Britain

1989 Chinese students demonstrate at Tiananmen Square; communist regimes in eastern Europe fall

Soviet bloc collapsed, and by 1992 the USSR itself had dissolved. The dissolution of the Soviet bloc occurred in part as a result of the transformations in the rest of the world. Among these transformations were the growth of rapid global communications, revolutionary developments in technology, and the raised voices of educated young people like Raj and Bobby.

OVERVIEW QUESTIONS

The major global development in this chapter: The technological revolution of the late twentieth century and its impact on societies and political developments around the world.

As you read, consider:

1. How did the technological developments of these decades transform social and economic conditions?
2. What were the attitudes of young people toward technology and social change during these years, and how did they reflect the Cold War climate in which these changes occurred?
3. How did the technological developments influence the fall of communist regimes in Europe and the dissolution of the Soviet Union?
4. How did the scientific and technological developments of the second half of the twentieth century affect the waging—and the end—of the Cold War?

Advances in Technology and Science

FOCUS
What were the major postwar advances in technology and science, and why were they important?

Revolutionary developments in technology and science reshaped global society after World War II, if unevenly. Wartime technology adapted for civilian use—such as the massive development of nuclear power—continued to improve daily life and boost prosperity. The spread of technology allowed billions of people access to instantaneous radio and television news, to new forms of contraceptives to control reproduction, and to the advantages of computers. Satellites orbiting the earth reported weather conditions, relayed telephone signals, and collected military intelligence. While television, cassettes, and the computer changed politics, other gadgets such as Japanese-developed electric rice cookers and electronic games made life more pleasant for consumers. New forms of information technology allowed citizens to better understand conditions in other countries—knowledge that inspired people around the world to demand more from employers and politicians alike.

The Information Revolution

Information technology catalyzed social and political change in these postwar decades just as innovations in textile making and the spread of railroads had in the nineteenth century. In the first half of the twentieth century, mass journalism, film, and radio had begun to forge a more homogeneous society based on shared information and images; in the last third of the century, television, computers, and telecommunications made information even more accessible and linked once-remote towns to urban capitals on the other side of the globe. In effect, the new information technology acted as a new kind of crossroads, giving individuals access to the ideas, beliefs, and products of societies around the world.

Television

Americans embraced television in the 1950s; following the postwar recovery television became a major entertainment and communications medium in countries around the world. In many places the audience for newspapers and theater declined. "We devote more . . . hours per year to television than [to] any other single artifact," a French sociologist commented in 1969.[1] As with radio, many governments funded television broadcasting with tax dollars and initially controlled TV programming to tap its potential for sending political messages and to avoid what they perceived as the substandard fare offered by American commercial TV. The Indian official in charge of early television programming forbade pop music, for example, and some European countries broadcast mostly classical drama and news. Thus, states assumed a new obligation to organize their citizens' leisure time, thereby gaining more influence over daily life.

With the emergence of communications satellites and video recorders in the 1960s, state-sponsored television encountered competition. Satellite technology transmitted sports broadcasts and other programming to a worldwide audience. In 1969 the Sony Corporation of Japan introduced the first color videocassette recorder to the consumer market; it was widely purchased late in the 1970s. What statesmen and intellectuals considered the junk programming of the United States—soap operas, game shows, sitcoms—arrived dubbed in the native language. More interesting to Brazilians, however, were their own soap operas and those imported from Mexico. Although under the Brazilian dictatorship news was censored from the 1960s into the 1980s, soap operas seemed to show real life, and Mexican programming added to their pool of information. By the 1980s people migrating from one continent to another could keep in touch with their home culture by watching sporting events broadcast via satellite or viewing films such as *Bobby* on videocassettes.

East and west, television exercised a powerful political and cultural influence. Educational programming united the far-flung population of the USSR by broadcasting shows featuring Soviet specialties such as ballet. At the same time, with travel forbidden or too expensive for many people globally, shows about foreign lands were often the most popular. By late in the century even some of the poorest houses in remote African oases sported satellite dishes. Heads of state such as Fidel Castro in Cuba used the medium to maintain national leadership, often preempting regular programming to address fellow citizens. Because electoral success increasingly depended on a successful media image, politicians came to rely on media experts—a new service job—as much as they did policy experts.

Computers

Just as revolutionary as television, the computer reshaped work in science, defense, and industry and eventually came to affect everyday life. As large as a gymnasium in the 1940s, computing machines shrank to the size of an attaché case in the mid-1980s and became far less expensive and fantastically more powerful, thanks to the development of sophisticated digital electronic circuitry implanted on tiny silicon chips, which replaced the clumsy radio tubes used in 1940s and 1950s computers. Within a few decades, the computer could perform hundreds of millions of operations per second and the price of the integrated circuit at the heart of computer technology would fall to less than a dollar, allowing businesses and individuals access to computing power at a reasonable cost.

Computers changed the pace and patterns of work by speeding up tasks and making them easier. By performing many operations that skilled workers had once done themselves, they rendered many livelihoods obsolete. In garment making, for example, experienced workers no longer painstakingly figured out how to arrange patterns on cloth for maximum efficiency and economy. Instead, a computer gave instructions for the best positioning of pattern pieces, and workers, usually women, simply followed the machine's directions. In 1981 the French phone company launched a public Internet server, the Minitel—a forerunner of the World Wide Web—through which French users made dinner reservations, performed stock transactions, and gained information. As in earlier

Computer Programmers in the 1940s
Early computers were massive, and programming required plugging and unplugging multiple cables, as this photograph shows. Many women, such as these U.S. workers, were among the first programmers, perhaps because the process resembled large telephone operations. Technological advances brought increasing miniaturization of ever more powerful computers—a true knowledge revolution that advanced the development of postindustrial society and globalization. (Corbis.)

times, people could work in their homes, but technology now allowed them to be connected to a central mainframe.

Failure to profit from high-tech efficiencies could have dire political consequences, as we shall see. But debate raged over the social effects of computers. Whereas in the Industrial Revolution, machine capabilities had replaced human power, in the information revolution computer technology augmented brainpower. Many believed that computers would further expand mental life, providing, in the words of one scientist, "boundless opportunities . . . to resolve the puzzles of cosmology, of life, and of the society of man."[2] Others maintained that computers programmed people, reducing human capacity for inventiveness and problem solving. Widespread access to the Internet and World Wide Web in the 1990s provoked debates over privacy, property rights, and the transmission of pornography, debates that continue to the present day.

The Space Age

The Space Race

New information and computer technology both contributed to and grew out of another mid-twentieth century development—the space race. After the Soviets' launch of the satellite *Sputnik* in 1957, the space race took off. The competition produced increasingly complex space flights that tested humans' ability to survive space exploration and its effects. Astronauts walked in space, endured weeks (and later, months) in orbit, docked with other craft, fixed satellites, and carried out experiments for the military and private industry. Meanwhile, a series of unmanned rockets filled the earth's gravitational sphere with weather, television, intelligence, and other communications satellites. In July 1969, U.S. astronauts Neil Armstrong and Edwin "Buzz" Aldrin walked on the moon's surface—a climactic moment in the space race.

Global Communication

Although the space race grew out of Cold War rivalry, the space age also offered the possibility of global political cooperation and communication. The exploration of space by a single country came to involve the participation of other countries. In 1965, an international consortium headed by the United States launched the first commercial communications satellite, *Intelsat I*, and by 1969, with the launch of *Intelsat III* covering the Indian Ocean region, the entire world was linked via satellite. Although some 50 percent of satellites were for military and espionage purposes, the rest promoted international communication and were sustained by transnational collaboration: by the 1970s some 150 countries collaborated to maintain the global satellite system. Satellite transmission allowed 500 million people to watch live reporting from the moon in 1969, and in 1978 one billion fans—or one quarter of the world's population at the time—tuned in to the World Cup soccer game. Global linkages only grew in magnitude and importance over the next decades.

Scientific Advances

Lunar landings and experiments in space brought advances in pure science. For example, astronomers used mineral samples from the moon to calculate the age of the solar system with unprecedented precision. Unmanned spacecraft provided data on cosmic radiation, magnetic fields, and infrared sources. Utilizing a range of technology, including the radiotelescope, which depicted space by receiving, measuring, and calculating nonvisible rays, these findings reinforced the so-called big bang theory of the origins of the universe and brought other new information, such as data on the composition of other planets, to scientists around the world. Long before politicians resolved Cold War differences, scientists were sharing their knowledge of the universe.

A New Scientific Revolution

Sophisticated technologies extended to the life sciences, bringing dramatic health benefits and ultimately changing reproduction itself. In 1952, English molecular biologist Francis Crick and American biologist James Watson discovered the configuration of DNA, the material in a cell's chromosomes that carries hereditary information. Simultaneously, other scientists were working on "the pill"—an oral contraceptive for women that tapped more than a century of scientific work in the field of birth control. More breakthroughs lay ahead—ones that would revolutionize conception and make scientific duplication of species possible.

Understanding DNA

Crick and Watson, young men working as a team from laboratories in Cambridge, England, solved the mystery of the gene and thus of biological inheritance when they demonstrated the structure of DNA. They showed how the double helix of the DNA molecule splits in cellular reproduction to form the basis of each new cell. This genetic material, biologists concluded, provides the chemical pattern for an individual organism's life. Beginning in the 1960s, genetics and the new field of molecular biology progressed rapidly. Growing understanding of nucleic acids and proteins advanced knowledge of viruses and bacteria, leading to effective worldwide campaigns against polio, tetanus, syphilis, tuberculosis, and such dangerous childhood diseases as mumps and measles—boosting the world's population.

Understanding how DNA works allowed scientists both to alter the makeup of plants and to bypass natural animal reproduction in a process called cloning—obtaining the cells of an organism and dividing or reproducing them (in an exact copy) in a laboratory. The possibility of genetically altering species and even creating new variations (for instance, to control agricultural pests) led to concern about how such actions would affect the balance of nature. Adding to medical breakthroughs, in 1967 Dr. Christiaan Barnard of South Africa performed the first successful heart transplant, and U.S. doctors later developed an artificial heart. By the end of the twentieth century, transplant technology circled the globe. Critics questioned whether the enormous cost of new medical technology to save a few people might be better spent on improving basic medical and health care for the many.

Transforming Reproduction

Technology also influenced the most intimate areas of human relations—sexuality and procreation. In traditional societies, community and family norms dictated marital arrangements and sexual practices, in large part because too many or too few children threatened the crucial balance between population size and agricultural productivity. As societies industrialized and urbanized, however, not only did these considerations become less important, but the growing availability of reliable birth-control devices permitted young people to begin sexual relations earlier, with less risk of pregnancy. These trends accelerated in the 1960s when the birth-control pill, developed in a Mexican research institute and later mass-produced in the United States and tested on women in Puerto Rico and other developing areas, came on the Western market. By 1970, its use was spreading around the world. Millions also sought out voluntary surgical sterilization through tubal ligations and vasectomies. New techniques brought abortion, traditionally performed by amateurs, into the hands of medical professionals, making the procedure safe, though still controversial.

Childbirth and conception itself were similarly transformed. Whereas only a small minority of Western births took place in hospitals in 1920, more than 90 percent did by 1970 and this trend spread worldwide. Obstetricians performed much of the work midwives had once done. As pregnancy and birth became a medical process, innovative procedures and equipment made it possible to monitor women and fetuses throughout pregnancy, labor, and delivery. In 1978, the first "test-tube baby," Louise Brown, was born to an English couple. She had been conceived when her mother's eggs were fertilized with her father's sperm in a laboratory dish and then implanted in her mother's uterus—a complex process called *in vitro fertilization*. If a woman could not carry a child to term, the laboratory-fertilized embryo could be implanted in the uterus of a surrogate, or substitute, mother.

The Green Revolution

Science also helped boost grain harvests around the world. In Mexico City in the 1940s, a team of scientists led by Norman Borlaug experimented with blending Japanese strains of wheat with Mexican ones, devising hardier seeds that raised yields by some 70 percent. Borlaug became part of "an army of hunger fighters," as he called those who next worked to devise rice that would thrive in India, the Philippines, and other countries.[3]

Those most able to profit from the breakthrough, however, were large landowners who could afford the irrigation, fertilizers, and the new seeds themselves. High costs led many small farmers to fail. As a result of the **Green Revolution**, however, rural poverty nonetheless declined in countries such as India, where it fell from close to 50 percent of the population in the 1960s to 30 percent in the 1990s. Although technological innovation did not affect all societies to the same degree or in the same ways, the rate of scientific discovery and its overall impact on life around the world increased steadily in the late twentieth century. Moreover, as the century came to a close, Western nations lost their monopoly on scientific and industrial power.

Changes in the World Economy

FOCUS

How did changes in the global economy affect livelihoods and family life?

Beginning in the 1960s industrial and agrarian entrepreneurship and the development of technology rose dramatically outside the West, especially in Asia and the Middle East. Profits from both manufacturing and the sale of commodities soared during these years. In contrast, reshaped by the spread of technology, the economies of Western countries took what has been labeled a postindustrial course. Instead of being centered on industry and agriculture, the postindustrial economy emphasized intellectual work and the distribution of services such as health care and education. As Asia and Latin America in particular developed their manufacturing and service sectors in the last third of the century, the share in the world economy of the traditional industrial powers declined.

The Rising Pacific Economy

Green Revolution The application of DNA and other scientific knowledge to the production of seeds and fertilizers to raise agricultural productivity in developing parts of the world.

From Japan to Singapore, explosive productivity began to spread economic power through the Pacific region. Japan's government determined to oversee the nation's economic rebirth, with the Ministry of Trade and Industry announcing in 1959 a goal of "income doubling" within ten years. In an effort to strengthen its Cold War allies, the United States pumped some $12 billion into East Asian allies such as South Korea, contributing to its

MAP 30.1

The Pacific Tigers, c. 1960–1995

The Pacific tigers of East and Southeast Asia accelerated economic growth in the region by focusing on manufacturing in electronics and other rising industries. These countries promised industries around the world a supply of cheap labor—mostly female. Despite often horrific working conditions and consequent strikes and labor activism, long-term benefits often included higher rates of literacy, increased school attendance, and improved health.

economic dynamism. Japan, too, benefited from U.S. contracts it filled during the wars in Korea and Vietnam. By 1982, Asian Pacific nations accounted for 16.4 percent of global production, a figure that had doubled since the 1960s. China abandoned Mao's disastrous economic experiments in 1978, achieving economic growth rates of 8 percent by the mid-1990s. Japan and China joined the United States and Germany as the world's top trading nations, while South Korea, Taiwan, Singapore, and Hong Kong came to be called **Pacific tigers** for the ferocity of their growth in the 1980s and 1990s (see Map 30.1).

Japan led the way in developing innovative high-tech industries. In 1982, Japan had more than four times as many industrial robots in operation as the United States. Constant government spending on technological innovation paid off as buyers around the

Pacific tiger One of the East Asian economies with ferocious rates of growth in the 1980s and 1990s.

world snapped up automobiles, videocassettes, and computers from Japanese and other Asian Pacific companies. As the United States poured vast sums into Cold War military spending, the resulting profits from the Pacific Rim went to purchase U.S. government bonds, thus financing America's national debt. Forty years after its total defeat in World War II, Japan was bankrolling its former conqueror.

Multinational Corporations

One of the major innovations of the postindustrial era was the growing number of **multinational corporations**. These companies produced goods and services for a global market and conducted business worldwide, but unlike older international firms, they established major factories in countries other than their home base. For example, of the five hundred largest businesses in the United States in 1970, more than one hundred did over a quarter of their business abroad, with IBM operating in more than one hundred countries. Although the greatest number of multinationals in these years were U.S.-based corporations, European and Japanese firms such as Shell, Nestlé, Toshiba, and Sony also had a broad global scope.

Some multinational corporations had bigger revenues than entire nations, as they set up shop in whatever part of the world offered cheap labor. Many of their founders broke the rules of traditional business success. Soichiro Honda, founder of the postwar Honda corporation, had only contempt for the connections and diplomas that traditionally led to success in Japanese business. A former bicycle repairman, he pioneered in making low-cost motorcycles that by 1961 were selling one hundred thousand a month. "Other companies may not consider you to be the cream of the crop but we believe in you,"[4] he told new employees, urging them to speak their minds and to follow his adventure of setting up firms around the world (see Reading the Past: Japan Transforms Business Practices). Beginning in the 1960s, multinationals moved more of their operations to formerly colonized states to reduce labor costs, taxes, and regulations. Most multinational profits went to enrich foreign stockholders and thus looked to some like imperialism in a new form.

Global Changes in Work

New Manufacturing Areas

The new global economy brought about major changes in people's work lives as manufacturing jobs moved to different areas and a new type of working class emerged. A particularly significant change was the expansion of jobs in manufacturing, mining, and the extraction of natural resources outside the West. Brazil set up all sorts of manufacturing enterprises in the 1960s, including what would eventually become the successful production of automobiles. Jobs in electronics and the textile and clothing industries moved to other parts of the world while declining in the West. South Korea, for instance, built its economy in the 1960s and 1970s by attracting electronics firms with the promise that its female workers would accept low wages and benefits. In sweatshops in Central and South America, young women and even children helped support their families by making sneakers and other goods. In China, rural families chose which single daughters would be sent to work in European toy factories or Taiwanese textile plants located in China. These young women performed repetitive work, yet still learned to move from plant to plant to gain small advantages either in pay or conditions in the few years during which their families allowed them to leave the village. People learned new skills: "The first time I saw those English letters I was scared to death. I couldn't recognize them, so I copied them down and recited them at night," one young Chinese worker recalled of learning English.[5] With the influx of manufacturing jobs, educational standards rose, along with access to birth control and other medical care that improved health.

multinational corporation A company that produces goods and services for a global market and that operates businesses worldwide.

Change also occurred in the West, where the number of manufacturing workers who had once labored to exhaustion declined, a trend that slowly spread to the rest of the world. Resource depletion in coal mines, the substitution of foreign oil for coal and of plastics for steel, the growth of offshore manufacturing, and automation in industrial

Japan Transforms Business Practices

Alongside technological innovation from the 1960s on came a fundamental change in the way many multinational companies were run. Japan led the way, as it did in much innovation in these years, and its businessmen introduced new responsibilities for workers—a real break from the relationships between bosses and workers in the first two hundred years of the Industrial Revolution. Akio Morita was a cofounder of Sony, the Japanese electronics pioneer that quickly became a global corporation. Its founders ushered in the cutting-edge practice of spreading responsibility for innovation and productivity across the firm instead of confining it to the managerial ranks as had been the previous practice. Morita explained the concept in his autobiography *Made in Japan* (1986).

> A company will get nowhere if all of the thinking is left to management. Everybody in the company must contribute, and for the lower-level employees their contribution must be more than just manual labor. We insist that all of our employees contribute their minds. Today we get an average of eight suggestions a year from each of our employees, and most of the suggestions have to do with making their own jobs easier or their work more reliable or a process more efficient. Some people in the West scoff at the suggestion process, saying that it forces people to repeat the obvious, or that it indicates a lack of leadership by management. This attitude shows a lack of understanding. We don't force suggestions, and we take them seriously and implement the best ones. . . . After all, who could tell us better how to structure the work than the people who are doing it? . . .
>
> I always tell employees that they should not worry too much about what their superiors tell them. I say, "Go ahead without waiting for instructions." To the managers I say this is an important element in bringing out the ability and creativity of those below them. Young people have flexible and creative minds, so a manager should not try to cram preconceived ideas into them, because it may smother their originality before it gets a chance to bloom.
>
> In Japan, workers who spend a lot of time together develop an atmosphere of self-motivation, and it is the young employees who give the real impetus to this. Management officers, knowing that the company's ordinary business is being done by energetic and enthusiastic younger employees, can devote their time and effort to planning the future of the company. With this in mind, we think it is unwise and unnecessary to define individual responsibility too clearly.

Source: Akio Morita with Edwin M. Reingold and Mitsuko Shimomura, *Made in Japan: Akio Morita and Sony* (New York: E. P. Dutton, 1986), 149.

EXAMINING THE EVIDENCE

1. **What is Akio Morita's attitude toward employees in this statement?**
2. **What are the innovative aspects of his policies?**
3. **What role does Akio Morita see for young people in businesses?**
4. **How have industrial attitudes, as described in this excerpt, changed from those discussed in Chapter 24?**

Changes in the Workforce in the West

processes reduced the blue-collar workforce. Remaining blue-collar workers enjoyed improved conditions as work in manufacturing became cleaner and more mechanized than ever before. Huge new agribusinesses forced many struggling farmers to take different jobs. Governments, cooperatives, and planning agencies set production quotas and handled an array of marketing transactions for the modern farmer-entrepreneur.

Meanwhile, the ranks of service workers swelled with researchers, health-care and medical workers, technicians, planners, and government functionaries. Jobs in banks, insurance companies, and other financial institutions also surged because of the vast sums needed to finance technology and research. Entire categories of employees such as flight attendants found that much of their work focused on the psychological well-being of customers. Already by 1969, the percentage of service-sector employees had passed that of manufacturing workers in several industrialized countries: 61.1 percent versus 33.7 percent in the United States alone (see Lives and Livelihoods: Global Tourism).

Global Tourism

International Tourism Workers in Japan

These guides at the Imperial Palace in Japan are part of the vast global pool of service workers, whose fields range from medicine and health care to teaching, law, and personal service such as beautification and domestic help. Tourism workers number in the millions and are found in thousands of capital cities, historic locations, and sites of natural beauty. (Robert Holmes/Corbis.)

Mr. Ibrahim stands outside the hotel gates near the Great Pyramids of Giza looking for customers who might want a guide around the nearby city of Cairo. Friendly, speaking several languages, he asks passersby if they need directions or a ride into town in his car. Like him, women in Guatemala wait by bus and train stations with ponchos and other craft items they have made themselves in hopes that a tourist will buy something. Native Americans ring the main square of Santa Fe, New Mexico, with lavish displays of leatherwork, jewelry, and paintings. In Bamako, capital of Mali, Muhammad waits to do such services for visitors as finding a telephone, delivering a message, or guiding them around the museums. All of these workers make their living through the growing presence of tourists eager to visit every part of a shrinking world, and to make purchases when they get there. They are the uncounted laborers in one of the fastest-growing global livelihoods—tourism.

In 1841 Thomas Cook, a Baptist evangelist in Britain, arranged for a special train to take some six hundred people to a temperance rally. His belief was that going to a rally and then seeing the local sights was a far better way to spend time than frequenting cafés and taverns. Cook's enterprise was so financially successful that he made deals with trains and found lodging for ever-larger groups of travelers.

The Knowledge Economy

Research and education were the means by which nations now advanced their economic and military might. Common sense, hard work, and creative intuition had launched the earliest successes of the Industrial Revolution. By the late twentieth century, success in business or government demanded humanistic or technological expertise and ever-growing staffs of researchers. As one French official put it, "the accumulation of knowledge, not of wealth, . . . makes the difference" in the quest for power. Thus governments around the world expanded the welfare state's mandate for intensive development of educational and research facilities.

Research and Applied Science

Investment in research fueled economic leadership. The United States funneled more than 20 percent of its gross national product into research in the 1960s, in the process enticing many of the world's leading intellectuals and technicians to work in America—

In 1851 he provided package tours for people wanting to attend the Crystal Palace Exhibition in London—over one hundred thousand travelers from Yorkshire alone. Cook's Tours, the company he eventually founded, became so skilled in arranging long-distance travel that the government even hired it to move troops in such distant regions as Africa. With Cook's Tours, some say, tourism became an official line of work—and that was a century before the postwar boom in transportation and communication.

There have been travelers, pilgrims, and even tourists for thousands of years, using guides and drivers, porters, cooks, laundresses, and innkeepers to smooth the way. None of these could avail themselves of transport by air, of course, but in the twentieth century, flight went from being primarily a military phenomenon to one that involved tens of millions of consumers around the world after World War II. At that point the tourist industry grew to comprise employees of large multinational corporations such as airlines and banks. Transcontinental hotel chains employed so many different types of workers that postsecondary schools came to offer programs in hotel and restaurant management. These service workers made up the booming postindustrial economy of the late twentieth and early twenty-first centuries. The United Kingdom estimates tourism currently as one of its largest industries, generating approximately £74 billion annually and employing 2.1 million people in a variety of livelihoods, including those in hotels, restaurants, and tour companies. Still growing in the decolonized areas where women and children struggle to earn a living is sex tourism from wealthy societies such as western Europe and Japan.

Besides small-scale workers in tourism and large and vigorous multinational companies dealing with hundreds of thousands of people, tourism has generated livelihoods for bureaucrats, statisticians, and, increasingly, public relations experts, translators, and Web site designers. Every country and most cities had Web sites for tourists by the twenty-first century. The World Tourism Organization (WTO), which took shape in 1925 and became an agency of the UN in 1974, provided work for people who monitored, counted, and encouraged travel. Employees of the WTO, for example, have recently worked to boost tourism in eastern European countries and sub-Saharan Africa—all of these livelihoods developing the service sector still further.

QUESTIONS TO CONSIDER

1. **What is the range of service occupations you can connect to tourism?**
2. **What skills are necessary in the tourism industry, and how do these fit the knowledge-based, technological society of the postwar world?**
3. **Why do you think tourism has grown so dramatically since the time of Thomas Cook?**

For Further Information:

Baud, Michiel, and Annelou Ypeij, eds. *Cultural Tourism in Latin America: The Politics of Space and Imagery*. 2009.

Dallen, J. Timothy, and Gyan P. Nyaupane, eds. *Cultural Heritage and Tourism in the Developing World: A Regional Perspective*. 2009.

Segreto, Luciano, et al., eds. *Europe at the Seaside: The Economic History of Mass Tourism in the Mediterranean*. 2009.

the so-called brain drain. Soon, however, Japan was outpacing Western countries in research and new product development. Complex systems—for example, nuclear power generation with its many components, from scientific conceptualization to plant construction to the supervised disposal of radioactive waste—required intricate coordination and oversight. In the realm of space programs, weapons development, and economic policy, scientists and bureaucrats frequently made more crucial decisions than did elected politicians. Developing and developed nations alike set up special cities and research hubs where scientists lived and worked, but Soviet-bloc nations proved less successful at linking their considerable achievements in science and technology to actual applications because of bureaucratic red tape. In the 1960s, an astounding 40 percent of Soviet-bloc scientific findings became obsolete before the government approved them. Falsification of information in the Soviet system also hampered efforts to make technology work to the nation's benefit.

Growth in Higher Education

The new criteria for success fostered unprecedented global growth in education, especially in the size and number of universities and scientific institutes. The number of university students in South Korea soared from 11,358 in 1950 to 3.4 million by 2000. Countries set up networks of universities specifically to encourage the technical research that traditional elite universities often scorned and established schools to train high-level experts in administration. Meanwhile, institutions of higher learning added courses in business and management, information technology, and systems analysis. Students enrolled in schools outside their home nations as education became internationalized. In principle, education equalized avenues to success by basing them on talent instead of wealth, but in fact, broad societal leveling did not occur in many universities. So long as socioeconomic background remained a key factor in determining university attendance, universities would reinforce inequality, not reduce it.

Postindustrial Family Life

Just as education changed dramatically to meet the needs of postindustrial society, in urban areas family structure and parent-child relationships shifted significantly from what they had been a century earlier. A steady flow of migrants produced enormous variety in urban households. These varied from patriarchal households consisting of several generations to those headed by a single female parent, unmarried couples cohabitating, or traditionally married couples who had few or no children. Daily life within the urban family became increasingly mechanized. The wages that young Chinese workers earned enabled them to buy more consumer items, even in villages distant from cities, and radio and television often formed the basis of the household's common social life, yielding conversations from Australia to Chile about the plots of soap operas and the outcomes of sporting matches. By the end of the century, appliances became increasingly affordable and more households were able to own them. The increase of appliances within the home reduced the time women devoted to household work, but did not eliminate it, as the standards of cleanliness also increased. Still, the mechanization of domestic chores freed more women to work outside the home. Young women's wages went to finance the education of brothers, and working mothers supported the prolonged economic dependence of their children, who spent more years in school. Working mothers still, however, did the housework and provided child care almost entirely themselves.

***Bobby* and the Youth Revolution**

In the late 1960s and 1970s, young people around the globe asserted their rights to sexual freedom and independent private lives. The 1973 hit film *Bobby*, in which the main character rebelled by choosing a partner from a different social class, featured the youth culture of these years. Made at the height of postwar prosperity, just before the first oil embargo, the film also reflected youthful consumerism, as young people bought such items as motorcycles and up-to-date fashions. (RK FILMS LTD/Ronald Grant Archive/Mary Evans/The Image Works Editorial.)

Whereas early modern families organized labor, taught craft skills, and monitored reproductive behavior, the primary focus of the modern urban family was most often on psychological and financial assistance. Many children in industrialized regions did not enter the labor force until their twenties but instead attended school, thus requiring their parents' backing. Japanese parents doled out the most resources: they financed their children's after-school education beginning as early as the primary grades to give the children a competitive edge in exams, and ambitious parents never let their children do housework or hold part-time jobs. Parents could also rely on an array of psychologists and other service workers to counsel them.

Children and Teenagers

Most notably, modern society transformed teenagers' lives; they gained new roles as the most up-to-date consumers. Advertisers and industrialists saw youth as a multibillion-dollar market and wooed them with consumer items such as rock music recordings, electronic games, and eventually computers and iPods. Rock music celebrated youthful rebellion against adult culture in biting and often sexually explicit lyrics. This youth music, in the words of one 1960s Latin American commentator, was "a threat to the family."[6] Sex roles for the young did not change, however. Despite the popularity of a few individual women rockers, promoters focused on men, setting them up as idols surrounded by worshiping female groupies. Advanced technology and savvy marketing for global mass consumption contributed to a worldwide youth culture and a growing generation gap—phenomena depicted in the film *Bobby*.

A Sexual Revolution?

The global media helped spread knowledge of birth-control procedures and allowed for public discussion of sexual matters in many parts of the world. Although highly sexualized film, music, and journalism permeated the world, widespread use of birth control (by some 80 percent of the world's people at the end of the twentieth century) meant there was no corresponding rise in the birthrate—evidence of the increasing separation of sexuality from reproduction. Statistical surveys showed that regular sexual activity began at an ever-younger age, and people talked more openly about sex—another component of cultural change. Critics as early as the mid-1950s worried about the level of sexuality in media: "Reduce the sex appeal in [motion] pictures," one Indian official urged. "How can we progress in other matters if every young man is thinking of this [sex] stuff all the time?"[7] Finally, in a climate of increased publicity about sexuality, homosexual behavior became more open and accepted. Some media announced the arrival of a "sexual revolution," but many political voices denounced it as a particularly dangerous form of Westernization.

Politics and Protest in an Age of Cold War

FOCUS

What developments challenged the superpowers' dominance of world politics, and how did the superpowers attempt to address those challenges?

Scientific sophistication and high-tech military elevated the United States and the Soviet Union to the peak of their power in the 1960s. Simultaneously, however, other nations' aspirations for freedom and their own growing access to technology began to limit the superpowers' ability to shape world politics. Expanding European Common Market and Pacific Rim economies were innovative and had muscle of their own. People in eastern Europe had greater contact with the West via satellite and other technology and contested Soviet leadership. Elsewhere, people refused to endure superpower-backed dictatorships. At the same time, both superpowers discovered that there were limits to their ability to dictate the outcomes of foreign struggles, notably in Vietnam and Afghanistan. Thus, popular struggles around democratization, technology, and economic well-being strained the international political order of the Cold War.

Democracy and Dictatorship in Latin America

World War II and the early Cold War had boosted prosperity in many countries of Latin America, but a hefty percentage of profits went to multinational corporations that had taken control of resources and often shaped the economy around one or two crops such as coffee or bananas or raw materials such as copper. When prices for commodities dropped after the war, workers in undiversified economies suffered and activism grew. By providing aid to Cuba, the Soviet Union came to dominate the Cuban government, while the United States sent money and personnel to overthrow democratic leaders in Guatemala,

MAP 30.2

South and Central America, 1960–1992

During these years the wealth gap in South and Central America was one of the greatest in the world, as owners of businesses and vast plantations controlled wages and government policies to advance their own interests. Many of the businesses remained local, but the agricultural sector operated in the world market. By the mid-1990s, however, Latin American countries launched multinational corporations, and such corporations in Brazil and Mexico joined the ranks of the top one hundred transnational firms.

Chile, Nicaragua, and other Latin American nations with the aim of keeping communism at bay. Generous financing by the superpowers gave rise to repressive dictatorships allied to one side or the other in the Cold War. In many Latin American countries citizen activists protested against both economic difficulties in an increasingly technological world and foreign-backed political oppression (see Map 30.2).

Argentina

Dictatorships grew up across Latin America to crush democratic movements for change and to provide the kind of bureaucratic planning for a technology-driven economy that was helping Common Market countries advance. Argentineans, burdened by rising prices and wage freezes along with dictatorship, took their protests to the streets in the 1960s and early 1970s. In response, the Argentinean military, having taken over from Perón in 1955, launched what came to be known as "the dirty war," silencing critics through kidnapping, torture, and murder. Mothers of the Plaza de Mayo became celebrated for opposing the "dirty war." Beginning in April 1977, a group of women, whose relatives were among the "disappeared" ones, began meeting at three-thirty in the afternoon in the plaza that fronted important government buildings. Walking in silent protest around the bustling center where Argentineans gathered to chat or conduct business, the "Mothers"—women from all livelihoods and conditions—wordlessly demanded an account of their missing brothers, husbands, and children. Hebe de Bonafini, whose two sons had "disappeared," explained the change in her everyday existence: "My life had been the life of a housewife—washing, ironing, cooking, and bringing up my children, just like you're always taught to do, believing that everything else was nothing. . . . Then I realized that that wasn't everything, that I had another world too. You realize that you're in a world where you have to do a lot of things."[8] She became an activist, helping bring the human rights abuses of the Argentinean government to the attention of a global audience (see Reading the Past: Terror and Resistance in El Salvador).

The many protests against the Argentinean government, combined with a disastrous economic situation, led to the election of civilian Raúl Alfonsin to the presidency in 1983. Alfonsin tried to deal with the nation's economic troubles brought on by a lack of investment in industry, large public expenditures, and an unequal balance of payments, but his failure to solve these problems quickly and his decision to freeze wages led to the return of a military-backed candidate in 1989. But one thing had changed: the military's policy of torture and murder was ended—a crucial victory. "There's no more official torture here; there are no more 'disappeared,'" one reporter exclaimed of the more open political climate. "Whatever else may be happening, this is terribly terribly important."[9]

Chile

Brazil also took the Argentine route of dictatorship in the name of orderly technological development, but until the mid-1970s Chile remained democratic even as it experienced the chaotic postwar rush to the cities. In country and city alike, however, poverty remained pervasive. In 1970 Chileans elected socialist candidate Salvador Allende (ah-YEHN-day), whose platform for improving the economy included taking over the country's copper resources from foreign investors, notably many Americans. The U.S. fought back against both Allende's socialism and his potential to reduce U.S. economic interests, pouring vast sums into political opposition and sending CIA operatives to murder Allende's supporters in the military. Allende hoped to improve Chile's economic position, but the measures he used failed miserably. He mandated a wage increase, but he also imposed price controls that discouraged domestic manufacturers. Inexperienced bureaucrats could not make newly nationalized industries function either well enough or fast enough. As inflation soared, opposition to Allende mounted, much of it sponsored by the CIA. In 1973 Allende was murdered in a military coup.

Chile's multiple political parties depended on the support of people from different classes. Allende's had come from the working classes, whereas professionals and small shopkeepers backed more centrist parties. General Augusto Pinochet (pin-oh-CHET), who emerged to rule after the coup, ended this tradition of political participation, closing down the elected Congress and suspending the constitution. While working to stabilize the economy, Pinochet's government kidnapped and killed dissidents. Determined opponents, braving torture and facing murder, slowly gained a foothold and finally became strong enough to defeat Pinochet. Mothers for Life, one of the opposition groups, launched a series of demonstrations, sending letters to foreign embassies and the press: "We are Chilean women from a variety of fields: workers, professionals, students, peasants, artists, and housewives, women of all ages who have survived more than a decade of a system of

READING THE PAST

Terror and Resistance in El Salvador

In a number of Latin American countries, dictators came to power in the second half of the twentieth century, using the military and private armed forces to "disappear" those who opposed them. Teenage critics, protesters, relatives of protesters, and sympathetic Catholic clergy were kidnapped, tortured, raped, and most often killed, frequently with the assistance of the superpowers. In El Salvador, the disappearance of family members beginning in 1975 sparked the development of the CoMadres ("co-mothers"), a group of mostly peasant women who—like women in other Latin American nations—gave up their normal livelihoods to protest these conditions. In the face of the increasing number of disappeared and even the torture and rape of virtually all the "mothers" themselves, the group regularly marched in protest and collected information about the capture of family members—their own and others'. Here, one of the founders explains the protest movement to an American anthropologist.

> In the beginning of our struggle, it was an individual problem. But one began to discover that there were others in the same situation, and we realized we couldn't be isolated, that our struggle had to be collective. It had to be a group of people who participated in the same fight, in the same search, trying to discover the truth. . . .
>
> We borrowed from a march of mothers dressed in black during a march in 1922 to protest a massacre of male and female teachers. They went out into the street to protest the killing of their children. We borrowed our black dress from them. . . . Black signified the condolences and affliction we carry for each person killed. And the white headscarf represents the peace we are seeking—but it must be a peace with justice, not a peace with impunity! We also carry a red and white carnation: the red for the spilled blood, the white for the detained—disappeared and the green leaves, the hope for life. That is our complete dress. . . .
>
> Most of us at this time were from Christian-based communities. . . . Mons[eigneur] Romero would read our public letters out loud in his Sunday homily in the Cathedral so that the CoMadres became known nationally. One month before he was assassinated, I remember that Mons[eigneur] Romero gave us his blessing by telling us, "Ah, women, you are the Marys of today. . . . All of you are suffering the same loss, the same pain."

Source: Interviews conducted by Jennifer Schirmer, "The Seeking of Truth and the Gendering of Consciousness: The CoMadres of El Salvador and the CONAVIGUA Widows of Guatemala," in *"VIVA": Women and Popular Protest in Latin America*, ed. Sarah A. Radcliffe and Sallie Westwood (London: Routledge, 1993), 32–33, 36.

EXAMINING THE EVIDENCE

1. **What caused these women to leave their ordinary livelihoods to protest on a regular basis?**
2. **To what extent would you say that protest and the search for their children became a new livelihood for them?**
3. **Why did the CoMadres and similar groups of Latin American women activists become such a powerful symbol around the world?**

death. . . . We accuse the military regime of throwing our nation into the greatest crisis of history. . . . It is a crisis of the future, a crisis of life."[10] The Mothers for Life were hardly alone, and by 1988 a broad coalition of the Chilean people had swept Pinochet from office, bringing in a representative government and leaving him to face international tribunals for crimes against humanity. Thus, while global developments contributed to the rise of dictatorships in Latin America, some of the same developments made it possible for ordinary individuals to forge connections with sympathetic people around the world and to serve as models for others who wanted change.

Domestic Revolution and a Changing International Order

Political change surged around the world, undermining allies of both superpowers, upsetting the Cold War order, and generally highlighting the need to advance technologically, economically, and politically. In Spain, the death of dictator Francisco Franco in 1975

The Rule of Idi Amin in Uganda

New nations emerging from colonial rule were often plagued by dictatorships headed by the military leaders who fought the imperialists. Idi Amin took power in Uganda in 1971, and during his eight-year reign his forces murdered some five hundred thousand Ugandans, forcing many thousands more to flee the country to safe havens around the world. In this image of a public execution in 1973, a supposed guerrilla fighter becomes one of Amin's victims. (Mohamed Amin/Africa Media Online/The Image Works.)

ended more than three decades of authoritarian rule. Franco's handpicked successor, King Juan Carlos, surprisingly steered his nation to Western-style constitutional monarchy that ushered in Spain's economic modernization and membership in the Common Market. In Africa, brutal killers such as Idi Amin of Uganda were overthrown, and other dictators fell, making Cold War stability uncertain.

South Korea

In 1960 some thirty thousand South Korean university and high school students mounted a peaceful demonstration in Seoul to call for clean elections in their country. They stood before the presidential residence, where Syngman Rhee (SING-man REE), a U.S.-educated and U.S.-supported dictator, had ruled since before the Korean War. Playing the Cold War card, Rhee labeled any critic or democratic politician a communist and had that person arrested or assassinated. Rhee employed his usual tactics in response to the student protesters' call for honest democracy: the police fired into the crowd and killed and wounded hundreds. Citizen outrage caused the government to collapse and free elections brought to power leaders oriented toward openness and constitutional government.

In May 1961, however, Park Chung Hee, a major general in the military, overthrew the new democratic government and instituted a dictatorship, which the U.S. praised as "Korean-style democracy." Instead of democracy, however, Park opted to give Koreans economic growth, using repressive measures such as torture and imprisonment of critics as the government lured hi-tech multinationals to its shores. Student protests continued through the late 1960s and 1970s, and workers denounced the influence of General Motors and other foreign corporations even as the police beat them up. Working people fought the regime: textile worker Chon T'ae-il immolated himself in 1970, shouting as he died "Don't mistreat young girls," a reference to the fifteen-hour days with one day off per month worked by teenagers in unheated textile factories to meet the government's goals for economic development.[11] In 1979, Park ordered more severe police retaliation against demonstrators; opposing the directive, the head of the Korean CIA shot Park. A military junta took over, again with U.S. backing to keep South Korea loyal, and ruled until 1987, when a newly elected president, backed by the military, instituted reforms, including guarantees of civil rights and democratic procedures. It appeared that popular activism had finally brought greater democracy while technological advances made South Korea a looming economic power.

Vietnam

The Cold War remained a potent force in world politics as the United States became increasingly embroiled in Vietnam. After the Geneva settlement in 1954 formally ended French domination of the region, the United States escalated its commitment to the corrupt and incompetent leadership of noncommunist South Vietnam. North Vietnam, China, and the Soviet Union backed the rebel Vietcong, or South Vietnamese communists. The strength of the Vietcong seemed to grow daily, and by 1968, the United States had more than half a million soldiers in South Vietnam. Before the war ended in 1975, the United States would in its effort to defeat communism drop more bombs on North Vietnam than the Allies had launched on Germany and Japan combined during World War II.

The United States and the Vietnam War, c. 1968–1975

U.S. president Richard Nixon promised to bring peace to Southeast Asia. In 1970, however, he ordered U.S. troops also to invade Cambodia, the site of North Vietnamese bases. Americans erupted in protest, and political turmoil followed in Cambodia. The communist Khmer Rouge, led by Pol Pot, a zealot intent on returning the country to preindustrial conditions, took control in 1975 and launched genocidal murders of minority Vietnamese, Chinese, and political opponents that ultimately killed 21 percent of the population. As this brutal situation unfolded, the United States and North Vietnam agreed to peace in January 1973, but the fighting continued. In 1975, South Vietnam collapsed under a determined North Vietnamese offensive and Vietnam was forcibly reunited. The United States reeled from the defeat, having suffered the loss of some fifty-eight thousand young lives and countless billions of dollars, along with a serious blow to its international prestige. Vietnam had demonstrated that the awesome technological might of the United States did not always ensure an easy victory, or even any victory at all.

Lessons from the U.S. defeat in Vietnam did not stop the Soviet Union from becoming entangled with Islamic forces in Afghanistan when it unleashed its own high-tech military to support a communist coup against Afghanistan's government in 1979. Afghanis who saw their traditional way of life being threatened by communism's modernizing goals put up stiff resistance. By 1980, tens of thousands of Soviet troops were fighting in Afghanistan, using the USSR's most advanced missiles and artillery in an ultimately unsuccessful effort to overcome Muslim leaders. The United States, China, Saudi Arabia, and Pakistan provided aid to a group of Muslim resisters, some of whom later coalesced into the Taliban. After the Soviets pulled out of their own "Vietnam" in 1989, the fundamentalist Taliban movement took over in the 1990s, imposing strict rules said to represent true Islamic teachings and causing millions of political and religious refugees to flee the country. Involvement in the wars in Vietnam and Afghanistan undermined both superpowers, sapping them of resources despite their technological advantages over their enemies.

Afghanistan

Revolution in Iran

In Iran, religiously inspired protests by students, clerics, shopkeepers, and unemployed men in 1978 and 1979 brought to power the Islamic religious leader Ayatollah Ruhollah Khomeini (a-yat-ol-LAH ROOH-ol-LAH ko-MAY-nee). The uprising was directed against Shah Mohammed Reza Pahlavi (REH-zah PAH-lah-vee), whose repressive regime the United States supported to protect its oil interests. Employing audiocassettes to spread his message, Khomeini called for a transformation of the country into a truly Islamic society, proclaiming "Neither East, nor West, only the Islamic Republic." Overturning the Westernization policy of the deposed shah, Khomeini's regime required women to cover their bodies almost totally in special clothing, restricted their access to divorce, and eliminated a range of other rights. Islamic revolutionaries believed these restrictions would restore the pride and Islamic identity that imperialism had stripped from Middle Eastern men. Khomeini won widespread support among Shi'ite Muslims, who constituted the majority but had long been subordinate to Sunni Muslims.

In the autumn of 1979, supporters of Khomeini seized hostages at the American embassy in Tehran, keeping them captive until Ronald Reagan's inauguration in January 1981. U.S. paralysis in the face of Islamic militancy, following on the heels of defeat in Vietnam, showed the possibility of superpower decline (see Seeing the Past: The Iranian Revolution as Visual News).

The Soviet War in Afghanistan, 1979–1989

Activists Challenge the Superpowers

The Cold War, technological transformation, and bloody conflict gave rise to social activism that challenged the superpowers. Prosperity and the benefits of a high-tech, service-oriented economy made people eager for peace instead of the violence of war, just as those living in Latin American and South Korean dictatorships wanted to "take back the streets." Activists sought a fair chance to get education, jobs, and political influence. Students, blacks and other minorities, Soviet-bloc citizens, women, environmentalists, and homosexuals joined in what became increasingly fiery protests in the 1960s and 1970s. They protested the Cold War order that they believed denied an equal share of well-being and democracy for all.

Activism in the U.S. Bloc

African Americans in the United States led the way in demanding equal rights early in the 1960s, even as white segregationists murdered and maimed those attempting to integrate lunch counters, register black voters, or simply march on behalf of freedom. This violent racism was the weak link in the American claim to moral superiority in the Cold War, prompting President John F. Kennedy to introduce civil rights legislation, which, following Kennedy's assassination, was pushed through Congress in 1964 by his successor, Lyndon B. Johnson. This legislation forbade segregation in public facilities and created the Equal Employment Opportunity Commission to fight job discrimination based on "race, color, national origin, religion, and sex."

Despite the civil rights legislation, change came too slowly for some minority activists. Among those were César Chavez and Dolores Huerta, who in the 1960s led oppressed Mexican American migrant workers in the California grape agribusiness to nonviolent resistance in their struggle for their right to collective bargaining and for an end to discrimination. Chavez knew their plight firsthand—he had lived in miserable conditions as a son of migrant workers. A teacher had put a sign around his neck reading "I am a clown. I speak Spanish." Huerta, his co-organizer, had led a somewhat different life but was equally committed to the cause—"a firebrand," she was called. She had attended community college but faced racial discrimination as a Chicano despite her education.

Some African American activists, frustrated by the lack of any real change in their condition, turned militant, and urban riots erupted across the United States in 1965 and subsequent years. In 1968, civil rights leader Martin Luther King, Jr., was assassinated by a white racist. More than a hundred cities in the United States erupted in violence as African Americans vented their anguish and rage. Many felt they had more in common with decolonizing people than with Americans. They aimed for "black power," and some took up arms in the belief that, like decolonizing people elsewhere, they needed to protect themselves against the violent whites around them.

Young people, who had been critical of racism, the war in Vietnam, and the militaristic and environmentally harmful effects of technology, closed down classes in campuses around the world. In western Europe, students went on strike, invading administration offices to protest their inferior education and status. They called themselves a proletariat—an exploited working class in the new high-tech, service society—and, rejecting the Soviets, considered

SEEING THE PAST

The Iranian Revolution as Visual News

U.S. Hostages During the Iranian Revolution (Bettmann/Corbis.)

Supporters of the Ayatollah Khomeini (Abbas/Magnum Photos.)

The Iranian Revolution was a shock to the West and the world because it overthrew the ruler of a major Middle Eastern client state of the United States. Moreover, the Ayatollah Khomeini refused to ally the country with either of the superpowers because he saw them both as corrupt. In 1979, militant Iranian students stormed the U.S. Embassy in Tehran and took those in it hostage. With the development of satellite communications, images of current events circled the globe almost immediately, and newspapers and television repeatedly broadcast the two photographs shown here. The first photograph features the blindfolded hostages the day after their capture. In the second, women supporters of the hostage-taking hold their own demonstration before the U.S. Embassy to chastise the United States for backing the authoritarian rule of the Shah for so many years. The global news regularly portrayed women in Iran in this way.

EXAMINING THE EVIDENCE

1. **What responses might each of these two photographs individually have provoked in viewers? What responses might they have provoked when seen together?**
2. **What is the historic value of these photographs? What propagandistic goal might they have served?**

themselves part of a New Left. After French police beat up students, some 9 million French workers went on strike, calling not only for higher wages but also for participation in everyday decision making both in politics and in work life. With their long hair, communal living, and scorn for sexual chastity, students proclaimed their rejection of middle-class values.

Women around the world turned to feminist activism, calling for equal rights and an end to gender discrimination. Middle-class women eagerly responded to the international best seller *The Feminine Mystique* (1963) by American journalist Betty Friedan. Pointing to the stagnating talents of many housewives, Friedan helped organize the National Organization for Women in 1966 to lobby for equal pay and legal reforms. Women demonstrated on behalf of such issues as abortion rights, and they were soon joined by gays demanding the decriminalization of their sexuality. Many flouted social conventions in their attire and attitudes, speaking openly about taboo subjects such as their sexual feelings. African American women pointed to the "double jeopardy" of being "black and female." Women engaged in the civil rights and student movements soon realized that many of those protest organizations devalued women just as society at large did. As African American activist Angela Davis complained, women aiming for equality supposedly "wanted to rob [male protesters] of their manhood."[12]

Women's activism engendered some concrete changes. Just after the war, women in Chile and other Latin American countries had lobbied successfully for the vote. In Catholic Italy, feminists won the rights to divorce, to gain access to birth-control information, and to obtain legal abortions. The demand for protection from rape, incest, and battering became the focus of thousands of women's groups from the 1970s to the present, as they combated a long-held value in virtually every society—the inferiority of women.

Protests erupted in the Soviet bloc too, with students at a Czech May Day rally in 1967 publicly chanting, "The only good communist is a dead one." In 1967 the Czechoslovak Communist Party took up the cause of reform when Alexander Dubçek (DOOB-chehk), head of the Slovak branch of the party, called for more social and political openness, striking a chord among frustrated party officials, technocrats, and intellectuals. Arguing that socialism should have "a human face," Dubçek was made head of the entire party and quickly changed the communist style of government, ending censorship, instituting the secret ballot for party elections, and allowing competing political groups to form. The Prague Spring had begun—"an orgy of free expression," one Czech journalist called the almost nonstop political debate that followed.[15]

Mexico City Protest, 1968

Following World War II, a rising standard of living encouraged young people around the world to enter universities in greater numbers than ever before, which helped them see social and political ills more clearly. In Mexico City, which in the spring of 1968 was about to host the summer Olympics, university students protested police violence and government repression after the slaying of several high school students. They too were mowed down by the police. During the late 1960s and 1970s, reactions to student demonstrations varied worldwide. Notice in this photograph a common denominator of student protest across the world: emblems of rebellion such as the banner featuring the revolutionary Che Guevara. (Bettmann/Corbis.)

Dubçek was unsuccessful in devising policies acceptable to both the USSR and reform-minded Czechs, and in August 1968, Soviet tanks rolled into Prague in a massive show of antirevolutionary force. Citizens turned to sabotage to defend their new rights: they painted graffiti on the tanks and removed street signs to confuse invading troops. Illegal radio stations broadcast testimonials of resistance, and merchants refused to sell food or anything else to Soviet troops. These responses could not stop the determined Soviet leadership, and the moment of reform-minded change passed even as some students, like those in Korea, immolated themselves in protest.

Activism in the Soviet Bloc

Activists' protests challenged superpower dominance, but little turned out the way reformers had hoped. Governments in both the Soviet and U.S. blocs turned to conservative solutions: the Soviets announced the Brezhnev Doctrine, which stated that reform movements, as a "common problem" of all socialist countries, would face swift repression and that those countries in any case had only limited independence. In 1974, Brezhnev

The Superpowers Restore Order

expelled author Aleksandr Solzhenitsyn from the USSR after the first volume of Solzhenitsyn's *Gulag Archipelago* (1973–1976) was published in the U.S.-led bloc. Solzhenitsyn's story of the Gulag (the Soviet system of internment and forced-labor camps) documented the brutal conditions Soviet prisoners endured under Stalin and his successors. More than any other single work, the *Gulag Archipelago* disillusioned loyal communists around the world. Brezhnev also expelled feminists who dared speak about communist sexism, Jews who became scapegoats for the failures of the Soviet system, and other dissenters. The brain drain from the Soviet bloc was severe, enriching the rest of the world.

In the U.S. bloc the reaction against activists was different, though order was restored there too. A current of public opinion turned against young people with the idea that somehow they—not the defeat in Vietnam or government corruption—had brought the United States down. Protesters had opened all leadership to question, helping conservatives gain power in the name of bringing back traditional values. As order returned, some young reformers turned to open terrorism in the West. In this atmosphere of reform, reaction, and radicalization, the future of prosperity became uncertain.

The End of the Cold War Order

FOCUS
Why did the Cold War order come to an end?

During the 1970s the superpowers faced internal corruption, competition from oil-producing states and rising Asian economies, and the increasing costs of attempting to control the world beyond their borders. Oil-producing nations brought a crashing halt to postindustrial prosperity in the West even as innovation continued. In response, reformers Margaret Thatcher in Great Britain and Mikhail Gorbachev in the USSR began implementing strikingly new policies in the 1980s to get their economies moving, just as Latin American countries were turning away from dictatorship. In the Soviet bloc, however, restoring prosperity was virtually impossible because a corrupt and inefficient system failed to take full advantage of technology and an unpopular war drained scarce resources. Suddenly, in 1989, the Soviet Empire collapsed and the Cold War came to an abrupt end. The USSR itself slowly dissolved, finally disappearing by January 1, 1992.

A Shifting Balance of Global Power

The United States seemed to overcome all obstacles when in 1972 it achieved a foreign policy triumph over the USSR by opening diplomatic relations with the other communist giant—China. Almost immediately a Middle Eastern oil embargo hit the United States hard, and the relationship between the United States and the Middle East began to overtake the Cold War as a major issue in global politics. In this arena, technology and Cold War muscle gave no advantage.

The United States Reaches Out to China

In the midst of turmoil at home and the draining war in Vietnam, Henry Kissinger, Nixon's national security adviser, decided to take advantage of growing tensions between China and the Soviet Union. Kissinger's efforts to forge closer ties with this other communist power led Nixon to visit China in 1972, opening up the possibility of contact and exchange between the two very different great nations. Nixon's visit served the domestic interests of both the Nixon administration and the Chinese leadership. For Nixon, the visit represented a high-profile diplomatic victory at a time when his conduct of the war in Vietnam was increasingly unpopular. Within China, the meeting helped stop the brutality of Mao's Cultural Revolution while advancing the careers of Chinese pragmatists interested in technology and economic growth.

U.S.-Soviet Rapprochement

The diplomatic success also advanced U.S.-Soviet relations. Fearful of the Chinese diplomatic advantage and similarly confronted by popular protest, the Soviets made their own overtures to the U.S.-led bloc. In 1972, the superpowers signed the first Strategic Arms Limitation Treaty (SALT I), which set a cap on the number of antimissile defenses each country could have. In 1975, in the Helsinki accords on human rights, the Western bloc officially acknowledged Soviet territorial gains in World War II in exchange for the Soviets' guarantee of basic human rights.

The Politics of Oil

The Middle East's oil-producing nations dealt Western dominance and prosperity a major blow by withholding exports of oil. Tension between Israel and the Arab world provided the catalyst. On June 5, 1967, Israeli forces, responding to the buildup of Syrian, Egyptian, and other Arab armies on its border, seized Gaza and the Sinai peninsula from Egypt, the Golan Heights from Syria, and the West Bank from Jordan (see Map 30.3). Israel's stunning victory, which came to be called the Six-Day War, so humiliated the Arab states that it led them to forge common political and economic strategies. In 1973, Egypt and Syria attacked Israel on Yom Kippur, the most holy day in the Jewish calendar. Israel, with assistance from the United States, stopped the assault.

Having failed militarily, the Arab nations took economic action, striking at the West's weakest point—its enormous dependence on Middle Eastern oil. Arab member nations of **OPEC** (Organization of Petroleum Exporting Countries) quadrupled the price of its oil and imposed an embargo, cutting off all exports of oil to the United States in retaliation for U.S. support of Israel. For the first time since imperialism's heyday, the producers of raw materials—not the industrial powers—controlled the flow of commodities and set the prices. The West and many parts of the world now faced an oil crisis.

Throughout the 1970s, oil-dependent Westerners watched in astonishment as OPEC upset the balance of economic power, bringing about a recession in the West. The oil embargo and price hike caused a significant rise in unemployment in Europe and the United States,

OPEC A consortium of oil-producing countries in the Middle East established to control the production and distribution of oil.

MAP 30.3 The Middle East, 1967–1990

During the Cold War and later, the Middle East was a region of great promise and great peril. Its wealth in oil bolstered dictators in the region and gave jobs in its oil fields and cities to workers from around the world. Inequality in many of these countries was great because of the oligarchic control of resources, which created social and political tensions. Among those tensions, most persistent were the struggles between Israelis and Arabs, especially Palestinians, which led to virtually unceasing warfare, protests, and rebellions.

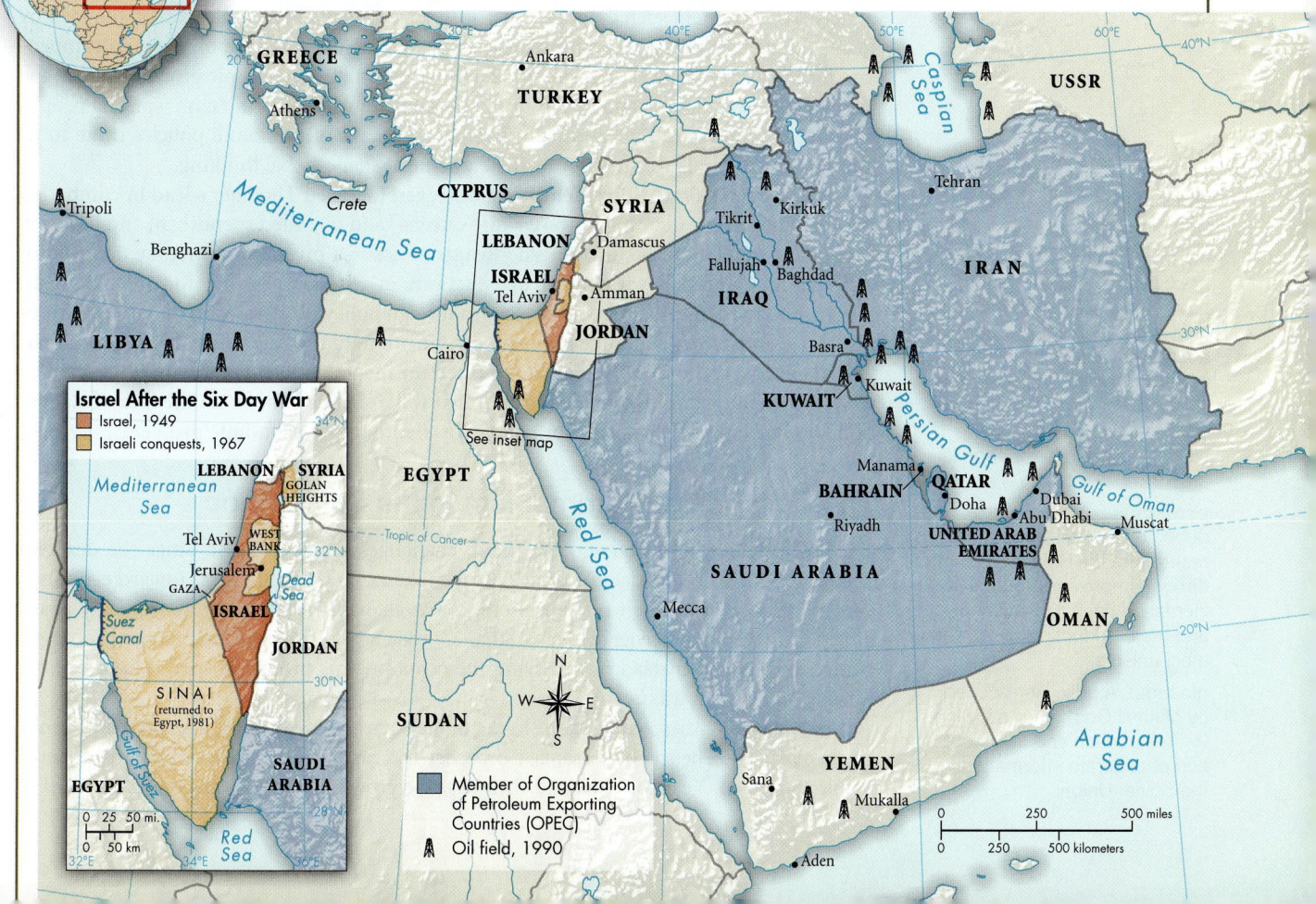

and by the mid-1970s inflation soared around the world. Skyrocketing interest rates discouraged both industrial investment and consumer buying. With prices, unemployment, and interest rates surging—an unusual combination of economic conditions dubbed **stagflation**—some came to realize that both energy resources and economic growth had limits. Western Europe and Japan drastically cut back on their oil dependence by undertaking conservation measures, improving public transportation, and raising the price of gasoline to encourage the development of fuel-efficient cars. But more was clearly needed.

A Change of Course in the West

At the beginning of the 1980s, stagflation and the realignment of global economic power forced noncommunist governments in the West to put their economic houses in order. Conservative politicians, who blamed welfare state programs for the West's economic problems, were handily elected in a number of countries. Tough times also intensified feelings that the unemployed and new immigrants from around the world were responsible for the economic downturn. An emphasis on competitiveness, individualism, and privilege replaced the twentieth-century trend of promoting economic democracy—a dramatic change of political course.

Thatcherism and Reaganomics

More than anyone else, Margaret Thatcher, the outspoken leader of Britain's Conservative Party and prime minister from 1979 to 1990, reshaped the West's political and economic ideas to meet the crisis. She called herself "a nineteenth-century liberal" in reference to the economic individualism that she wanted to restore. Believing that only more private enterprise could revive the sluggish British economy, the combative prime minister rejected the politics of consensus building, targeting unions and welfare recipients as enemies of British well-being.

The policies of Thatcherism were based on monetarist, or supply-side, economic theories, which state that inflation results when government pumps money into the economy at a rate higher than a nation's economic growth rate. Supply-siders thus advocate tight control of the money supply to keep prices from rising rapidly. They maintain that the economy as a whole flourishes when businesses grow and their prosperity "trickles down" throughout the society. To implement such theories, the British government cut income taxes on the wealthy to encourage new investment and increased sales taxes on everyday purchases to compensate for the lost revenue. The result was fairly successful, but economic growth came at the price of cuts to education and health programs and an increased burden on working people, who bore the brunt of the sales tax. Thatcher's package of economic policies came to be known as **neoliberalism**, and it immediately came to shape global thinking.

In the United States, President Ronald Reagan followed Thatcher's lead in combating the economic crisis. Blaming both "welfare queens" and so-called spendthrift and immoral liberals for stagflation, he introduced "Reaganomics"—a program of income tax cuts for the wealthy combined with massive reductions in federal spending for student loans, school lunch programs, and mass transit. In foreign policy, Reagan warned of the communist threat and demanded huge military spending to fight the "evil empire." The combination of tax cuts and military expansion pushed the federal budget deficit to $200 billion by 1986. Other western European leaders limited welfare-state benefits in the face of stagflation, though without blaming poor people for their nation's economic problems.

stagflation A surge in prices and interest rates combined with high unemployment and a slowdown in economic growth.

neoliberalism A theory first promoted by British prime minister Margaret Thatcher, calling for a return to nineteenth-century liberal principles, including the reduction of welfare-state programs and tax cuts for the wealthy to promote economic growth.

perestroika A policy introduced by Mikhail Gorbachev to restructure the Soviet economy through improved productivity, increased capital investment, and the introduction of market mechanisms.

glasnost A policy introduced by Mikhail Gorbachev allowing for free speech and the circulation of accurate information in the Soviet Union.

The Collapse of Communism in the Soviet Bloc

The Soviet Union faced far more difficult challenges than the West. Since the death of Stalin in 1953, Soviet leaders had periodically taken small, halting steps toward economic and political reform. Such reforms were, however, halfhearted and often quickly abandoned. In 1985 a new Soviet leader, Mikhail Gorbachev, introduced much more thoroughgoing reforms, but instead of fortifying the economy, his programs stirred up rebellion. The corrupt system was beyond cure.

Mikhail Gorbachev, who became leader of the Soviet Union in 1985, unexpectedly opened an era of change. The son of peasants, Gorbachev had firsthand experience of the costs of economic stagnation. Years of weak and then negative growth led to a deteriorating standard of

Gorbachev Attempts Reform

living. After working a full day, Soviet homemakers stood in long lines to obtain basic commodities. Alcoholism reached crisis levels, diminishing productivity and straining the nation's morale. Despite its tremendous agricultural potential, the USSR imported massive amounts of grain because 20 to 30 percent of homegrown grain rotted before it could be harvested or shipped to market, so great was the mismanagement of the state-directed economy. A massive and privileged party bureaucracy stifled effective use of technology, while Soviet military spending of 15 to 20 percent of the gross national product (more than double the U.S. proportion) further lowered living standards. A new generation came of age lacking the fear instilled by World War II or Stalin's purges. "They believe in nothing," a mother said of Soviet youth in 1984.

Gorbachev knew from experience and travels to western Europe that the Soviet system was not keeping up, and he quickly proposed several new programs. A crucial economic reform, ***perestroika*** ("restructuring"), aimed to reinvigorate the Soviet economy by encouraging more up-to-date technology and introducing such market features as prices and profits. Alongside economic change was the policy of ***glasnost*** (translated as "openness"), which called for disseminating "wide, prompt, and frank information" and for allowing Soviet citizens freer speech.

Glasnost stirred debate across the USSR and affected superpower relations as well. Television reporting adopted the outspoken methods of American investigative journalism, and newspapers, instead of publishing made-up letters praising the Soviet state, printed real ones complaining of shortages and abuse. One outraged "mother of two" protested that the cost-cutting policy of reusing syringes in hospitals was a source of AIDS. "Why should little kids have to pay for the criminal actions of our Ministry of Health?" she asked. "We saw television programs about U.S. racism," one young man reported, "but blacks there had cars, housing, and other goods that we didn't."[14] Gorbachev cut missile production, defusing the Cold War, and in early 1989 withdrew Soviet forces from the disastrous war in Afghanistan. By the end of the year the United States started to reduce its own vast military buildup.

Solidarity Protests in Poland, 1981–1983

Rebellion in Poland

Even before Gorbachev's reforms of the mid-1980s unleashed free speech in the USSR, dissent had risen across the Soviet bloc. In the summer of 1980, Poles had reacted to rising food prices by going on strike and forming an independent labor movement called **Solidarity** under the leadership of electrician Lech Walesa and crane operator Anna Walentynowicz. The organization attracted much of the adult population, including a million members of the Communist Party. Waving Polish flags and parading giant portraits of the Virgin Mary and Pope John Paul II—a Polish native—Solidarity workers occupied factories in protest against inflation, the scarcity of food, and the deteriorating conditions of everyday life. The scarcity of food likewise drove tens of thousands of women, who were both workers and the caretakers of home life, into the streets crying, "We're hungry!" With Soviet support, the Communist Party imposed a military government and in the winter of 1981 outlawed Solidarity. Dissidents, using global communications, kept Solidarity alive as a force both inside and outside of Poland. Workers kept meeting and a new culture emerged, with poets reading verse to overflow crowds and university professors lecturing on such forbidden topics as Polish resistance in World War II. The stage was set for communism's downfall.

Revolutions of 1989

The disintegration of communist power in Europe was also inspired by Gorbachev's visit to China's capital, Beijing, in the spring of 1989. There, hundreds of thousands of students massed in the city's Tiananmen Square to demand democracy and greet Gorbachev as democracy's hero. They used telex machines and satellite television to rush their message of reform to the international community. China's communist leaders, while pushing economic modernization, refused to introduce democracy. Workers joined the mass of prodemocracy students: "They say and they do what I have only dared to think," one man commented after giving money to the cause.[15] As numbers swelled and the international press broadcast the events, government forces crushed the movement, killing untold numbers and later executing as many as a thousand rebels.

Solidarity An independent Polish trade union that confronted the communist government in the 1980s and eventually succeeded in ousting the party from the Polish government.

The televised protests in Tiananmen Square offered an inspirational model to opponents of communism in Europe. In June 1989, the Polish government, lacking Soviet support for further repression, held free parliamentary elections. Solidarity candidates overwhelmingly defeated the communists, and in early 1990, Walesa became president of Poland. In Hungary, where citizens had boycotted communist holidays and lobbied against ecologically unsound projects such as the construction of new dams, popular demand led the Parliament in the fall of 1989 to dismiss the Communist Party as the official ruling institution. Meanwhile, Gorbachev reversed the Brezhnev Doctrine, refusing to interfere in the politics of satellite nations.

East Germans had likewise long protested communism, holding peace vigils throughout the 1980s and ceaselessly attempting to cross the Berlin Wall. Satellite television brought them visions of postindustrial prosperity and of open public debate in West Germany. In the summer of 1989, crowds of East Germans flooded the borders of the crumbling Soviet bloc, and hundreds of thousands of protesters rallied against the regime throughout the fall. On November 9, East Berliners crossed the wall unopposed and protest turned to festive holiday. Soon thereafter, citizens—East and West—released years of frustration by assaulting the Berlin Wall with sledgehammers and then celebrated the reunification of the two Germanys in 1990.

Protesters in Tiananmen Square, 1989

Student activists for democracy mounted a massive and prolonged demonstration for democracy in the spring of 1989. The protests in Tiananmen Square, where Mao Zedong had often addressed mass rallies, captured the imagination of the world and showed the protesters' own global imagination. Students displayed images of the Statue of Liberty and carried signs in English, playing to a worldwide audience. As workers joined the movement, Chinese authorities struck back, dispersing the crowds and executing many participants. (Jacques Langevin/Sygma/Corbis.)

The fall of communism in Czechoslovakia and Romania formed two extremes. In November 1989 Alexander Dubçek, leader of the Prague Spring of 1968, addressed the crowds in Prague's Wenceslas Square after police had beaten students who had called for the ouster of Stalinists from the government. Almost immediately, the communist leadership resigned, in a bloodless or "velvet" revolution. By contrast, Romanian president Nicolae Ceauşescu (nee-koh-LIE chow-SHES-koo), who had ruled as the harshest dictator in communist Europe since Stalin, met a far different end. Workers and much of the army rose up and crushed the forces loyal to Ceauşescu. On Christmas Day 1989, viewers watched on television as the dictator and his wife were executed. For many, the death of Ceauşescu meant that the very worst of communism was over.

The revolutions of 1989 accelerated the breakup of Yugoslavia into multiple states (see Map 30.4). Yugoslavia had the most ethnically diverse population in eastern Europe, and when Serbian president Slobodan Milosevic attempted in 1991 to seize territory and unite all Serbs (and in effect much of the former Yugoslavia) into a "greater Serbia," a tragic civil war broke out. Throughout the 1990s, the peoples of the former Yugoslavia fought one another, murdering neighbors of different ethnicities.

Meanwhile, amid deteriorating conditions and the threat of violence, the Soviet Union itself collapsed. Perestroika had failed to revitalize the Soviet economy, and by 1990 people faced unemployment and an even greater scarcity of goods than before. In 1991 a group of eight antireform top officials, including the powerful head of the Soviet secret police (the KGB), attempted a coup,

MAP 30.4

Post–Cold War Eastern Europe and Central Asia, c. 1990

The sudden collapse of the Soviet Empire in 1989 and the subsequent end of the USSR itself by January 1992 brought an end to the Cold War. More important to those in the region, it meant social, economic, and political change. New administrations were created; former nations fragmented as regions became independent states; many jobs disappeared; and the postcommunist-dominated social order appeared unpredictable well into the twenty-first century. The new Russian nation, however, remained influential as it began drawing on and marketing its natural resources more effectively.

holding Gorbachev under house arrest. Hundreds of thousands of residents of Moscow and Leningrad filled the streets, and units of the army defected to protect the headquarters of Boris Yeltsin, the reform-minded president of the Russian Parliament. People used fax machines and computers to coordinate internal resistance and send messages to the rest of the world. As the coup failed, the Soviet Union disintegrated and officially dissolved by January 1, 1992.

The USSR Dissolves

COUNTERPOINT

Agrarian Peoples in a Technological Age

FOCUS

How did some agrarian peoples resist the scientific and technological developments that threatened their ways of life?

As high-tech society expanded, millions of people in the world's rural areas felt themselves more hurt than helped. Even as breakthroughs in science and technology led to improved health and a higher standard of living for the majority, there were many others whom scientific advances harmed. Some farmers found that the application of scientific techniques damaged both their livelihoods and the environment. They objected especially to the genetic modification of plants and animals made possible by the discovery of DNA.

Contesting the Results of Technological Advance

As societies around the world developed technologically and economically, some of the results were shocking. Cubotão, a city in southeastern Brazil, is home to some two dozen steel, petrochemical, and other industries, which daily send about 875 tons of toxic gasses, 473 tons of carbon monoxide, and 182 tons of sulfuric oxide into the atmosphere. Residents call the area the "Valley of Death" because of the extreme air and water pollution and have lobbied successfully to curtail the most damaging dumping of toxic waste. This photograph shows a cement-producing section of the complex. (Miguel Rio Branco/Magnum Photos.)

Local Farmers Against Multinational Corporations

Farmers were especially angry about the ways in which companies took seeds from them and then patented them so that those same farmers could be sued for harvesting and using their own seeds. They also objected to the multinationals' practice of sterilizing seeds so that the resulting plants would not produce sowable seeds that farmers could harvest and plant the next year. In Africa, Asia, and Latin America, grassroots movements developed to stop the use of chemical fertilizers, the patenting of medicinal plants and seeds by multinational chemical companies, and the genetic modification of seeds, insects, fish, and other living organisms.

The immediate, practical problem of the failure of seeds to germinate and the erosion of soil caused by large-scale planting of a single crop led to the creation in the 1980s of the Institute for Production and Research in Tropical Agriculture in Venezuela. Officials from the Institute argued that the directives imposed by specialists and chemical companies from the North harmed Latin American farmers engaged in tropical agriculture. Whereas the many microclimates and diverse conditions found in Latin America should have led to the cultivation of many different crops, the Green Revolution of the 1950s and 1960s began directing farmers toward growing one crop and insisting that they use chemical pesticides. Top-down direction had depleted the soil and brought increasing poverty to many farmers. To correct this situation, the Institute collected the know-how of small and medium-sized rural producers. "We get knowledge from farmers," one worker for the Institute claimed. "We evaluate knowledge from farmers."[16]

Grassroots activists in other areas—India, for example—worked to protect local agricultural knowledge from being abused by the new postindustrial economy. Activists labeled the phenomenon of patenting plants and then suing farmers who continued to grow crops like rice in their own way as "biopiracy." "Patents are a replay of colonization as it took place five hundred years ago in a number of ways," farmers' rights activist Vandana Shiva maintained.[17] "The Basmati seed, the aromatic rice from India, which we have grown for centuries, right in my valley is being claimed as a novel invention by RiceTec." Biopiracy by the multinational corporations, activists charged, contributed to the impoverishment of Third World peoples: "Neem, which we have used for millennia for pest control, for medicine, . . . which my grandmother and mother have used for everyday functions in the home, for protecting grain, for protecting silks and woolens, for pest control, is treated as an invention held by Grace, the chemical company."[18] Entrepreneurs, while harming farmers, were seizing control of and profiting from their knowledge.

Government Measures to Protect Farmers

Moved by citizens' activism, governments in developing economies began taking steps to stop the piracy by multinational businesses. India, for example, began creating a database of its medicinal plants, teas, and yoga positions. The idea was to patent these as Indian property so that enterprises in other countries could not simply steal and market them as their own. The Indian government claimed to be doing just what industrialized nations had been doing for years: France, for example, sued any foreign firm that used the name *champagne* for sparkling wine. "Champagne" had been registered as a trademark branding wines from the Champagne region of France, one protected by law just as Toyota and Heinz were trademarks with full legal protection from theft by another company. These actions provided a strong counterpoint to postindustrial society's drift toward multinational markets seizing knowledge-based products and using them against the traditional livelihoods of tens of millions of agricultural workers around the world.

Conclusion

The last half of the twentieth century witnessed a surge in technological and scientific discovery with vast potential for improving people's lives and connecting them to one another. Asian Pacific nations advanced by adopting new technology and transforming their economies. Work changed, as societies across the globe expanded the service sector of their economies and entered a new, postindustrial stage. New patterns of family life, new relationships among the generations, and revised standards for sexual behavior also characterized these years. Youth culture spread globally, touching teens around the world like Raj and Bobby in India. A high-tech society demanded levels of innovation, efficiency, and coordination that spread unevenly and was especially lacking in the Soviet bloc. Despite improved postindustrial conditions, brutal coercion continued to plague workers in rapidly industrializing economies such as that of South Korea.

Inequalities in the distribution of goods and the persistent support of military dictators by the superpowers frustrated citizens worldwide, and especially pushed youths like Raj and Bobby to rebellion. From the 1960s, youth joined ethnic and racial minorities and women in condemning existing conditions, including the threat posed by the Cold War. By the early 1980s, wars in Vietnam and Afghanistan, protests against privations in the Soviet bloc, the power of oil-producing states, and the growing political force of Islam had weakened superpower pre-eminence. In the Soviet Union Mikhail Gorbachev attempted to bring about technological efficiencies and cultural reform, but he released dissent and exposed the flaws of communism. By 1992, the failure of the brutal experiment with communism had brought about both the dissolution of the Soviet Union and the end of the Cold War order. Although the former Soviet Empire faced painful adjustments, this development opened the world as a whole to the further spread of technology and the complex processes of globalization.

NOTES

1. Quoted in Ray Brown, "Children and Television," *Social Science* (1978): 7.
2. W. O. Baker, "Computers as Information-Processing Machines in Modern Science," *Daedalus* 99, no. 4 (Fall 1970).
3. Norman Borlaug, Nobel Prize Acceptance Speech, 1970, http://www.nobel.se.
4. Quoted in Sam Fiorani, "Soichiro Honda," *Automotive History Online*, http://www.autohistory.org/feature_7.html.
5. Quoted in Pun Ngai, *Made in China: Women Factory Workers in a Global Workplace* (Durham, NC: Duke University Press, 2005), 83.
6. Quoted in Peter Winn, *Americas: The Changing Face of Latin America and the Caribbean* (Berkeley: University of California Press, 2006), 447.
7. Ramachandra Guha, *India After Gandhi: The History of the World's Largest Democracy* (New York: HarperCollins, 2008), 710.
8. Quoted in Temma Kaplan, *Taking Back the Streets: Women, Youth, and Direct Democracy* (Berkeley: University of California Press, 2004), 113.
9. Quoted in Thomas E. Skidmore and Peter H. Smith, *Modern Latin America*, 3d ed. (New York: Oxford University Press, 2002), 111.
10. Quoted in Kaplan, *Taking Back the Streets*, 38.

11. Quoted in *Korea Observer* 32 (2001): 264.
12. Quoted in Paula Giddings, *Where and When I Enter: The Impact of Black Women on Race and Sex in America* (New York: William Morrow, 1984), 316.
13. Quoted in David Caute, *Sixty-Eight: Year of the Barricades* (London: Hamish Hamilton, 1988), 165.
14. Russian citizen's interview with author, July 1994.
15. Quoted in Orville Schell, "China's Spring," in *The China Reader: The Reform Era*, ed. Orville Schell and David Shambaugh (New York: Vintage, 1999), 194.
16. Quoted in *In-Motion Magazine*, http://www.inmotionmagazine.com/global/man_int.html#AnchorKnowledge-49575.
17. Quoted in *In-Motion Magazine*, 2003, http://www.inmotionmagazine.com/shiva.html.
18. Ibid.

RESOURCES FOR RESEARCH

Advances in Technology and Science

Although the powers that waged World War II led the way in converting wartime technology to peacetime uses, the impact of scientific advances was felt around the world. Marks's book on reproductive technology provides a look at science's global reach.

Borlaug, Norman. "The Green Revolution, Peace, and Humanity," Nobel Lecture, 1970. http://www.nobel.se.

Dickson, Paul. *Sputnik: The Shock of the Century*. 2001.

Marks, Lara V. *Sexual Chemistry: A History of the Contraceptive Pill*. 2004.

O'Mara, Margaret Pugh. *Cities of Knowledge: Cold War Science and the Search for the Next Silicon Valley*. 2005.

Schefter, James L. *The Race: The Uncensored Story of How America Beat Russia to the Moon*. 1999.

Changes in the World Economy

As technology swept the globe, manufacturing power began to move from the West to the rest of the world. Chu et al., Kynge, and Mazlish describe these developments.

Chu, Yun-Peng, and Hal Hill, eds. *The East Asian High-Tech Drive*. 2006.

Davis, Deborah, ed. *The Consumer Revolution in Urban China*. 2000.

Kynge, James. *China Shakes the World: A Titan's Rise and Troubled Future and the Challenge for America*. 2006.

Mazlish, Bruce. *Leviathans: Multinational Corporations and the New Global History*. 2005.

Sony history. http://www.sony.net/SonyInfo/CorporateInfo/History/SonyHistory/.

Politics and Protest in an Age of Cold War

As the Cold War advanced, citizens rose to fight off dictators and to protest superpower dominance. Suri's book shows the worldwide maneuverings that accompanied domestic instability, while Kaplan's work gives accounts of resistance to Latin American dictators.

Kaplan, Temma. *Taking Back the Streets: Women, Youth, and Direct Democracy*. 2004.

Lam, Andrew. *Perfume Dreams: Reflections on the Vietnamese Diaspora*. 2005.

Lesch, David. *1979: The Year That Shaped the Modern Middle East*. 2001.

Ngai, Pun. *Made in China: Women Factory Workers in a Global Workplace*. 2005.

Suri, Jeremy. *Power and Protest: Global Revolution and the Rise of Détente*. 2003.

The End of the Cold War Order

The year 1989 saw a series of threats to communist nations. These works describe the events in both Europe and China from a variety of perspectives.

Human Rights in China, ed. *Children of the Dragon: The Story of Tiananmen Square*. 1990.

Kenney, Padraic. *Carnival of Revolution: Central Europe, 1989*. 2002.

Kotkin, Stephen. *Escaping Armageddon: The Soviet Collapse, 1970–2000*. 2001.

Ost, David. *The Defeat of Solidarity: Anger and Politics in Postcommunist Europe*. 2005.

Thomas, Daniel C. *The Helsinki Effect: International Norms, Human Rights, and the Demise of Communism*. 2001.

Tolstoya, Tatyana. *Pushkin's Children: Writings on Russia and Russians*. 2003.

COUNTERPOINT: Agrarian Peoples in a Technological Age

The Green Revolution in agriculture provoked opposition, sometimes passionate, from many ranks of global society, as these books reveal.

Rosegrant, M., and P. Hazell. *Transforming the Rural Asian Economy: The Unfinished Revolution*. 2000.

Shiva, Vandana. *Biopiracy: The Plunder of Nature and Knowledge*. 1997.

▶ **For additional primary sources from this period**, see *Sources of Crossroads and Cultures*.

▶ **For Web sites, images, and documents related to topics in this chapter**, see Make History at bedfordstmartins.com/smith.

REVIEW

Online Study Guide
bedfordstmartins.com/smith

The major global development in this chapter ▶ The technological revolution of the late twentieth century and its impact on societies and political developments around the world.

IMPORTANT EVENTS

1957	USSR launches *Sputnik*
1963	Betty Friedan, *The Feminine Mystique*
1967	Arab-Israeli Six-Day War
1968	"Prague Spring" in Czechoslovakia
1969	U.S. astronauts land on moon
1972	U.S. president Richard Nixon visits China; SALT I agreement
1973	Arab-Israeli Yom Kippur War; OPEC raises oil prices and imposes embargo
1973–1976	Aleksandr Solzhenitsyn, *Gulag Archipelago*
1975	Vietnam War ends; Vietnam reunited
1978	World's first test-tube baby born
1978–1979	Islamic revolution in Iran
1979–1989	Soviet War in Afghanistan
1980	Solidarity labor union organizes resistance to communism in Poland; Prime Minister Margaret Thatcher introduces neoliberal program in Britain
1985	Mikhail Gorbachev becomes Soviet leader, introduces new policies of perestroika and glasnost
1989	Chinese students demonstrate at Tiananmen Square; communist regimes in eastern Europe fall
1992	Soviet Union no longer exists

KEY TERMS

glasnost (p. 1014)
Green Revolution (p. 996)
multinational corporation (p. 998)
neoliberalism (p. 1014)
OPEC (p. 1013)
Pacific tiger (p. 997)
perestroika (p. 1014)
postindustrial (p. 991)
Solidarity (p. 1015)
stagflation (p. 1014)

CHAPTER OVERVIEW QUESTIONS

1. How did the technological developments of these decades transform social and economic conditions?
2. What were the attitudes of young people toward technology and social change during these years, and how did they reflect the Cold War climate in which these changes occurred?
3. How did the technological developments influence the fall of communist regimes in Europe and the dissolution of the Soviet Union?
4. How did the scientific and technological developments of the second half of the twentieth century affect the waging—and the end—of the Cold War?

SECTION FOCUS QUESTIONS

1. What were the major postwar advances in technology and science, and why were they important?
2. How did changes in the global economy affect livelihoods and family life?
3. What developments challenged the superpowers' dominance of world politics, and how did the superpowers attempt to address those challenges?
4. Why did the Cold War order come to an end?
5. How did some agrarian peoples resist the scientific and technological developments that threatened their ways of life?

MAKING CONNECTIONS

1. Why is late-twentieth-century society in many parts of the world described as postindustrial?
2. How did technological development and the social changes it produced affect national and world politics?
3. Why did the economic, scientific, and political developments of the late twentieth century spark so many grassroots protests, and what did those protests achieve?

31

AT A CROSSROADS ▶

The Burj al Arab (Tower of the Arabs) makes a statement about its home—Dubai, the United Arab Emirates—as a global crossroads. Its name signals a regional pride, while the tower itself is a hotel that welcomes visitors from around the world. With vast international experience, Tom Wright from England and Kunan Chew from Singapore designed the exterior and the interior, respectively. Like the designers and visitors, many of the men and women who built the tower come from beyond Dubai's borders. (akg-images/Bildarchiv Monheim.)

A New Global Age

1989 to the Present

On February 11, 1990, South Africans celebrated the news that Nelson Mandela, deputy head of the African National Congress (ANC), had been freed after three decades in prison. Later that day Mandela stood before some fifty thousand cheering supporters in Cape Town, announcing his determination to end apartheid, the brutal South African system of racial discrimination. "Our path to freedom is irreversible," he stated. "Now is the time to intensify the struggle on all fronts." These were brave words in a society where the minority white population controlled the military and for decades had not hesitated to murder anyone who criticized white racist rule. But by 1990 black youth had taken up arms, protesting repression and unemployment. Their elders backed them with protests of their own, as the crowded South African ghettos became more miserable and more dangerous. Many whites hoped that Mandela's release would appease the protesters, but it became clear that white rule would not hold, and in April 1994 nearly 90 percent of South Africans went to the polls, many of them standing for hours in mile-long lines to vote in a free and fair election. One voter summed up his feelings at participating in democracy: "Now I am a human being." The ANC won 62 percent of the vote, and on May 10 that same year Nelson Mandela became president of South Africa.

Nelson Mandela's release from prison was noted not only by South Africans but by people around the world. Multinational companies had come to insist on racial equality in hiring at their South African plants, but as the apartheid government continued to torture and kill blacks, Coca-Cola, IBM, and others closed down their factories. The U.S. Congress

The Impact of Global Events on Regions and Nations

FOCUS How has globalization affected the distribution of power and wealth throughout the world in the early twenty-first century?

Global Livelihoods and Institutions

FOCUS How has globalization reshaped national economies and political institutions?

The Promises and Perils of Globalization

FOCUS What major benefits and dangers has globalization brought to the world's peoples?

Cultures Without Borders

FOCUS What trends suggest that globalization has led to a new mixing of cultures?

COUNTERPOINT: Who Am I? Local Identity in a Globalizing World

FOCUS How have peoples sought to establish and maintain distinctive local personal identities in today's global age?

BACKSTORY

As we saw in Chapter 30, a burst of technological innovation from the 1960s on changed the way many people lived and worked. In much of the West, the service sector surpassed industry and manufacturing as the most important components of the economy, with knowledge-based jobs leading the way. At the same time, industrial jobs were shipped overseas, and countries such as Korea and China joined the United States and Germany as centers of global manufacturing. As the economic balance of power began to shift, the United States and the Soviet Union found it more and more difficult to shape and control events around the world. In 1989, internal tensions led to the collapse of the Soviet Union, bringing the Cold War to a close and opening the way for still more dramatic change in the global economic and political order. With the Cold War over, technology flowed more freely across borders, and the increased pace of globalization created new connections among the peoples of the world. International tensions remained, however, and the new global landscape raised hopes around the world even as dangers persisted.

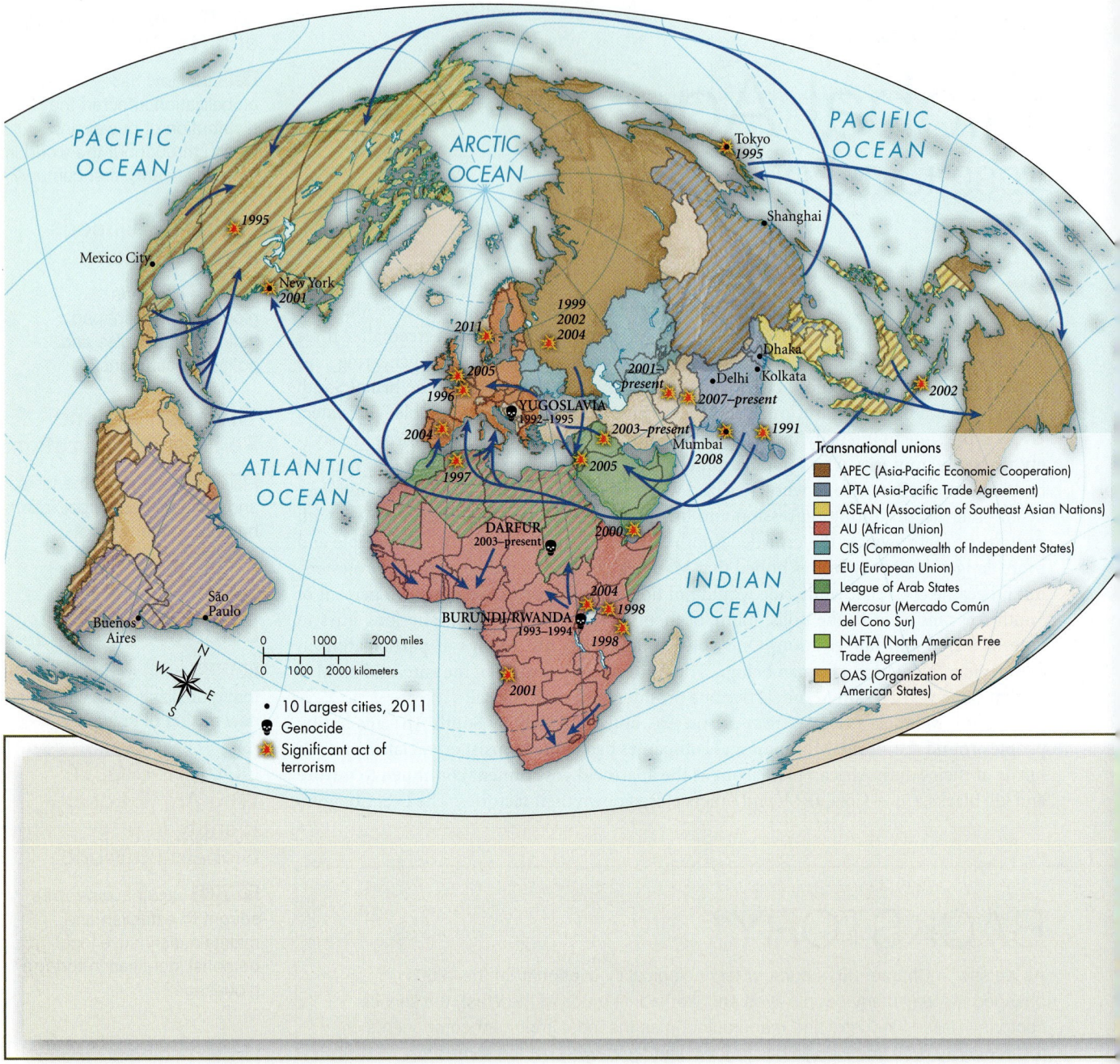

▪ **1986** Nuclear accident at Chernobyl power plant in Soviet Union

1990s New European nations emerge in wake of USSR collapse

Nelson Mandela elected president of South Africa; European Union officially formed; North American Free Trade Agreement implemented **1994** ▪

1985 | 1990 | 1995 | 2000

▪ **1989** Iranian leader Ayatollah Khomeini issues fatwa against Salman Rushdie

UN Fourth World Conference on Women held in Beijing **1995** ▪

▪ **1991** Mercosur establishes a free-trade zone among southern South American nations

Terrorists attack United States; United States declares "war on terrorism" **2001**

▪ **1997** Kyoto Protocol drafted

European Union adopts the euro as its new money **1999** ▪

banned the sale of South African gold coins, or Krugerrands, and legislated a boycott of South African products. Other countries took similar measures. The collective effect was devastating to the South African economy, whose leaders came to understand, as so many did from the 1970s on, that they were living in a world far more tightly connected than ever before. As satellite television and human rights groups brought the brutality of apartheid to the attention of the world, freedom in South Africa—like many other issues—became a concern of people everywhere. Nelson Mandela's release from prison and his election as president of South Africa symbolized a new and more intensely global stage in human history.

The end of the Cold War accelerated the continuing process of **globalization**—that is, the economic, political, social, and cultural interconnectedness of the world's regions. Now, instead of being forced to choose between two powerful and dangerous adversaries, people around the world could envision working and living together as global citizens and enjoying all aspects of one another's culture, including food, music, films, and books. Global organizations, regional trade alliances, and international businesses multiplied and drew more people into their tightening networks. Migration increased, with many migrants moving in search of opportunity. Others, however, sought to escape the dangers that cropped up after the Cold War as bitter conflicts among competing political and ethnic groups in Africa, the former Soviet Empire, India, and elsewhere brought horrific suffering. Radicals around the world publicized their aims with acts of terrorism. While improvements in medicine benefited much of the world, globalization facilitated the spread of infectious diseases, threatening people everywhere. Many soon realized that the same interconnectedness that fueled the economic boom of the late twentieth century also increased the potential for worldwide economic and environmental disasters.

Although the process of globalization drew people ever closer together, it also produced a backlash. Rejecting anything beyond the local community where they conducted their livelihoods, groups and individuals sought to retain their distinctive personal identities built on family ties and local traditions. In some cases, resistance to globalization took

globalization The economic, cultural, political, and social interactions and integration of the world's peoples.

MAPPING THE WORLD

A New Global Age

By the start of the twenty-first century, the world's peoples were bound together more significantly than ever. Migration brought unprecedented ethnic and cultural diversity to entire regions. At the same time, large regional alliances brought military, economic, and even political unity—at least superficially. No less real in their impact on everyday life were the mixing of cultures and the shared experience of terrorism and disease. Finally, the earth, humanity's common habitat, felt the effects of technological change, advancing industry, and growing population.

ROUTES ▼

→ Global migration, 1970s to present

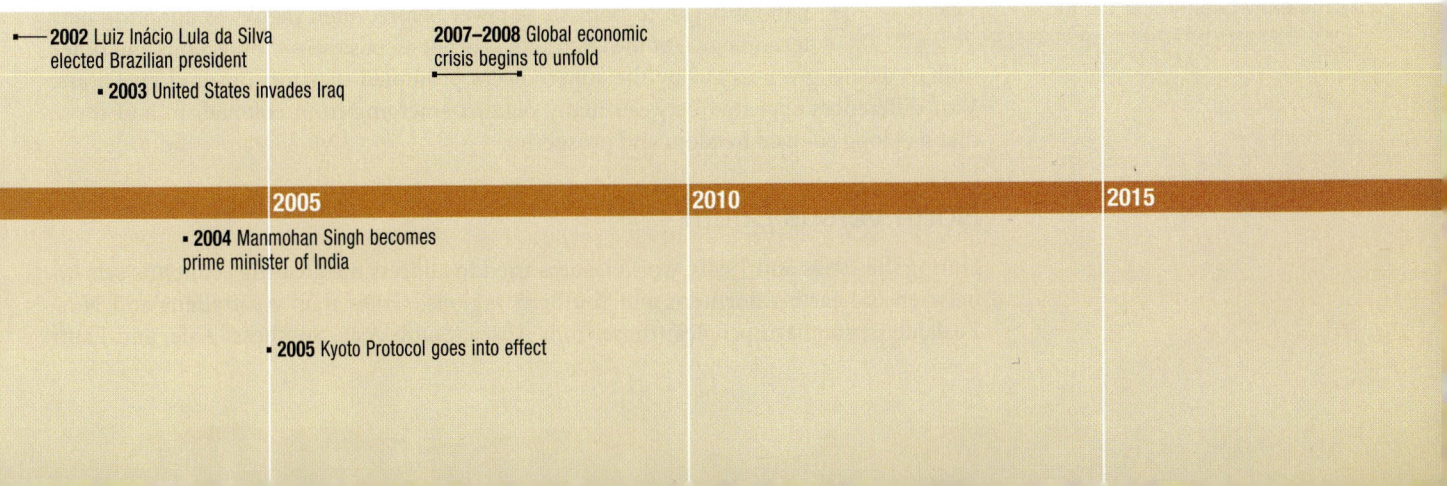

violent forms, including terrorist attacks on those seen as responsible for the erosion of traditional values and beliefs. Despite these efforts, the interdependence of the world's peoples, the connectedness of nations, and the sharing of culture that globalization had brought were nearly inescapable. In 1994 the European Economic Community (or Common Market) transformed itself from a mainly economic alliance into the European Union, which looked as if it might become a United States of Europe. When Barack Obama was elected the first African American president of the United States in 2008, it was a moment shared by the world, just as the release of Nelson Mandela had been less than two decades earlier.

As historians, the authors of this book have no firm idea how these recent events will appear a century from now, but in this chapter we follow trends that have evolved over decades and even centuries. In choosing events to recount in this analysis of the very near past we have also used generally accepted criteria for spotting historical significance. We hope—and you can be the judge several decades from now—that this account of our own global age stands the test of time and of history.

OVERVIEW QUESTIONS

The major global development in this chapter: The causes and consequences of intensified globalization.

As you read, consider:

1. What were the elements of globalization at the beginning of the twenty-first century?
2. How did globalization affect lives and livelihoods throughout the world?
3. How did globalization affect local cultures?
4. What people do you know whose roots and livelihoods are global?

The Impact of Global Events on Regions and Nations

FOCUS

How has globalization affected the distribution of power and wealth throughout the world in the early twenty-first century?

The end of the Cold War brought many advantages in terms of free speech, human rights, and economic opportunity. Peoples around the world no longer had to toe the line set by the superpowers, and some nations began to flourish as never before, often thanks to adopting new technology. Yet the aftermath was not all positive—the weapons and other military goods given as aid by the superpowers promoted dictatorships and civil wars. Vast differences appeared between many regions emerging from colonialism and those that had long enjoyed freedom and prosperity.

North Versus South

During the 1980s and 1990s, world leaders tried to address the growing economic schism between the earth's northern and southern regions. Other than Australians and New Zealanders, southern peoples (those from Africa, South Asia, Southeast Asia, and Latin

America) generally had lower standards of living than northerners. Long ruled as colonies or exploited economically by northerners, citizens in the southern regions could not yet count on their new governments to provide welfare services or education. International organizations such as the World Bank and the International Monetary Fund provided loans for economic development, but the conditions tied to them, such as cutting government spending for social programs, led to criticism that there was no real benefit if education and health care were sacrificed in the name of balancing national budgets. Disease soared and the pace of literacy and capacity-building slowed.

Obstacles to Development

Although the Southern Hemisphere had highly productive agriculture and abundant natural resources, southern peoples often found it difficult to export their products to developed countries. Both the United States and the European Union advocated free trade but nevertheless imposed tariffs on imported agricultural products and subsidized their own farmers, raising prices for imported products and lowering them for domestic ones in the process. As Amadou Toumani Touré, president of Mali, complained in 2002, "the North cannot massively subsidize its farm exports and at the same time try and give lessons in competitiveness to the South."[1] Tariffs and financial aid to wealthy farmers in the north diverted an estimated $100 billion worth of business away from poorer nations. "We cannot compete against this monster, the United States," one Mexican farmer claimed in 2008. "It's not worth the trouble to plant. We don't have the subsidies."[2] Understanding the situation but unwilling to challenge domestic agribusinesses, leaders from wealthy nations met in 2004 to draft plans to alleviate the debt of southern countries and to sponsor health-care and education initiatives as an alternative to lifting subsidies. It remained to be seen whether these programs would materialize and whether poverty, disease and death would decline as a result.

Southern regions experienced a number of internal barriers to peaceful development. Latin American nations grappled with government corruption, multibillion-dollar debt owed to international banks, widespread crime, and grinding poverty. The situation was not, however, universally grim. Some countries—Mexico and Brazil, for example—began to strengthen their economies by marketing their oil and other natural resources effectively on the global market.

Sub-Saharan Africa suffered from drought, famine, and civil war. In the African nations of Rwanda, Burundi, and Sudan, a lethal mixture of military rule, ideological factionalism, and the ethnic antagonism that had been encouraged under imperialism resulted in conflict and genocide in the 1990s. Millions perished; others were left starving and homeless while leaders drained national resources to build up their militaries and enrich themselves. Arms dealers and aid workers poured into these regions, both groups bringing resources that governments often used against their own people. In Sudan, children were among the first victims of starvation, disease, and outright murder in the half-century-long civil war between the north and south of the country. Those in southern Sudan opposed the north's creation of an Islamic republic and its control of the country's oil and agricultural wealth. As the dispute intensified and spread to central and western Sudan (Darfur) between 1985 and 2005, an estimated 2 million people were killed and some 4 million left homeless. Common to Africa and other embattled regions was the recruitment of children into armies, a practice that contributed to the long-term militarization of affected societies. Although negotiators achieved truces, political uncertainty and the lack of stable economic institutions continued to plague many southern regions.

Conflict and Genocide in Sub-Saharan Africa

Advancing Nations in the Global Age

Despite the challenges, the developing world was also the site of dramatic successes. After decades of strife and economic underperformance, officials, business people, farmers, and artisans rebuilt prosperity in India, Brazil, South Africa, and China as they took advantage of global technology and markets. The same groups also helped democracy materialize in Brazil and South Africa and mature in India. Politicians worked to accommodate opposition parties instead of stifling their critics, and they pulled supporters and rivals alike into the common cause of advancing representative government.

India

By the twenty-first century, democratic India had become an economic powerhouse, possessing robust industrial and service sectors connected to markets around the world. India's path to prosperity was hardly smooth, however. Its leaders had to overcome ethnic, religious, class, and caste conflict as they tried to integrate India's diverse peoples. The Congress Party, founded in 1885 to combat British domination, remained powerful, but Nehru's daughter and grandson, who followed him as prime ministers, were assassinated by offended members of religious and ethnic minorities, leaving Gandhi's and Nehru's goals of integration unfulfilled. Nonetheless, India remained the world's largest democracy.

For a brief period the Bharatiya Janata Party (BJP), which advocated a Hindu nationalist program aimed in part at halting the technological development behind India's growing wealth and secularization, attracted voters struggling with rapid economic change. In 2004, however, Indian voters soundly defeated the BJP, rejecting Hindu nationalism in favor of the economic fairness promised by an alliance of the Congress Party and smaller parties, including the communists. New prime minister and the first Sikh to hold that position, Manmohan Singh, was an economist with international experience, having served as a director of the International Monetary Fund and other global organizations. Known as "the cleanest politician in India,"[3] Singh supported a mixed economy—that is, one with both privately and publicly owned enterprises. Even as its economy soared under Singh, however, India continued to face problems that were part of the legacy of colonialism: lack of modern infrastructure and education for all, the poverty of several hundred million citizens, and persistent ethnic and religious terrorism. Amid both turmoil and prosperity, India's cities grew and its middle class expanded, in large part thanks to the global economic activities of its innovative business people. India's internal integration and development were also importantly linked to its continued connections with peoples and markets around the world.

Globalized Agriculture in India

This up-to-date Indian farmer harvests a bumper crop of wheat using machinery from the U.S.-based John Deere corporation. Not only did this harvester have parts made in other countries, but the seeds he used were probably developed in Mexico-based scientific laboratories. These laboratories produced seeds suitable for different agricultural conditions, such as varying climate and soil composition. The result was the "Green Revolution" that began in the 1960s. (akg-images/Yvan Travert.)

Brazil

Like other Latin Americans in the 1960s and 1970s, Brazilians had endured military dictatorship, soaring inflation, rising poverty, and a grossly inadequate system of education and social services. In 1985 Brazilian voters, tired of government brutality and human rights abuses, ousted the military dictatorship and installed an elected government. Civilian rule brought with it an emphasis on human rights and economic expansion, especially in the 1990s and thereafter. By the 1990s, government leaders had adopted a tight monetary policy and a commitment to pay down debts. In 2004 Brazil's economy expanded at a rate of 5.2 percent, despite the persistence of serious social problems, including crime and poverty.

There were several forces behind these developments. In the slums or *favelas* of the country's major cities, Rio de Janeiro and São Paulo, where the dictatorship provided no sanitary, educational, or other services, poverty-stricken residents organized themselves in the spirit of change, holding self-education meetings, teaching one another to read, and taking turns collecting and disposing of garbage. "I go to meetings every week now," one woman reported of her growing activism. "I think we women should participate in political parties."[4] Unions also played an important role. Luiz Inácio Lula da Silva, born in poverty in the countryside, had become a metalworker and then boosted his leftist union's membership to more than one hundred thousand. In the 1980s he brought together a broad coalition to found the Workers Party. On his fourth try for office in 2002, Lula da Silva was elected president—an incredible journey for a poor child who only learned to read when he was ten.

Global journalists described Lula da Silva as another Stalin or Mao. Yet Lula da Silva adopted an effective, pragmatic style: as president he promised that increased tax revenues on the wealthy would be used to pay off the dictatorship's foreign loans and thus free Brazil from indebtedness to the West. Alongside indebtedness, the populace was outraged at the brutal murders of reformers who wanted to stop the destruction of Brazil's rain forests by both global and local developers. The issue was one not only of murder, but of whether local peoples could keep their land in the forests or whether the government would let loggers strip the forests and murder opponents in the name of economic development. Although Lula negotiated a path between antiglobalizers and globalizers, some of the worst poverty was alleviated and the Brazilian economy surged, becoming a rising economic star in the Southern Hemisphere and indeed in the world as a whole.

South Africa

As president of South Africa, Nelson Mandela faced numerous pressing issues. Foremost among them were calming interethnic tensions, ending political violence, and unifying the nation around consensus-building rather than violence. Violence against blacks and white critics had been the main political strategy of the **apartheid** government; it included taking blacks' homes and land and herding them by force into small "townships." In 1976 government troops killed and wounded some three thousand youth and children at Soweto as they protested the lack of educational opportunities. "We want equal education, not slave education," they had chanted while being mowed down. The white apartheid government also pursued a divide-and-conquer strategy, doing what it could to encourage conflict between the Zulu Inkatha Freedom Party and Mandela's African National Congress. In the 1980s, violence from many sides kept the country in turmoil. After Mandela took control, the government set up in 1995 a Truth and Reconciliation Commission to hear testimony about the violence. The Commission allowed those whom the apartheid government had persecuted to talk about their experiences in public; then it allowed those who had participated in the persecutions to confess to what they had done and request amnesty. The aim was to provide some relief to victims and to construct a new model for nation building (see Reading the Past: Testimony to South Africa's Truth and Reconciliation Commission).

apartheid The South African system of laws and behaviors that enforced segregation of the black from the white population, with the intention of creating a society dominated by whites; apartheid laws were repealed in 1991.

While the Commission did its work, Mandela's presidency opened world markets to South African products, increased the flow of technology to the country, and created policies based on fairness to all social groups. For example, South African women had played a leadership role in opposing apartheid, and they received a quota of seats in the new government. Health care was declared a constitutional right of all citizens. The government's

READING THE PAST

Testimony to South Africa's Truth and Reconciliation Commission

In 1995 the South African government established the Truth and Reconciliation Commission to hear testimony from accusers and perpetrators alike about violence and human rights abuses during the apartheid regime. Usually the commission imposed fines, but in the aftermath of the hearings victims were often angrier than before. They saw the punishment as inadequate and complained that the fines were ridiculously low or never paid. Despite the drawbacks and objections, many around the world hailed the Truth and Reconciliation model as one with great potential.

Accounts by perpetrators of the violence make for especially horrific reading. In this excerpt, researchers followed up with one member of the government security forces to hear in more depth how he pursued his grim job in the 1970s and 1980s, getting paid by the head for black resisters captured and for black resisters killed.

> We would volunteer for a three-month stint on the border for the Security Branch up there. . . . It sounded like a bit of an adventure and [a] nice getting away kind of ploy, because my girlfriend and I were having hassles, probably because we were staying at my parents' place. I'd always been interested in doing something unconventional anyway, and I thought, well, this is it. This is my chance. . . .
>
> The amount of adrenaline that we were producing on a daily level, constantly aware that we could die or be wounded at any moment. . . . Having that adrenaline pumping, we became adrenaline junkies. . . . It became like a drug to me, to go out there and follow up on those tracks. . . . [It is] almost a sexual kind of stimulation. Not physical sexual, but mental sexual. . . .
>
> [On one particular captive] I knew that he was a veteran and that he would have been an excellent source of info. Sean, the Army medic, started patching him up while I was busy interrogating him. . . . Even at that stage he was denying everything and I just started to go into this uncontrollable [expletive deleted] rage and I remember thinking, "How dare you?" And then—this is what I was told afterwards—I started ripping. I ripped all the bandages, the drip that Sean had put into this guy . . . pulled out my 9 mm, put the barrel between his eyes and . . . I executed him.

Source: Don Foster et al., *The Theatre of Violence: Narratives of Protagonists in the South African Conflict* (Oxford, U.K.: James Currey, 2005), 130, 137, 140.

EXAMINING THE EVIDENCE

1. **What values appear to have motivated this member of the security forces as he pursued his livelihood?**
2. **Do you detect a change over time in his conduct, and if so, how do you explain it?**
3. **Why do you think the Truth and Reconciliation Commission came to be viewed as a powerful model in nation building?**

approach to land reform reflected its commitment to national integration and consensus-building. Instead of simply seizing land held by whites and giving it to blacks, the government set up a process by which the claims of dispossessed whites and blacks alike could be resolved. Nonetheless, South African blacks still remained an underclass, and migrants from neighboring Zimbabwe, Mozambique, and other hard-pressed African regions competed with them for jobs (see Map 31.1). Business people and farmers often fired their former employees and hired the migrants at rock-bottom wages.

At the same time, the rapid spread of HIV/AIDS (discussed later in the chapter) engulfed the nation in a horrific health crisis. South Africans themselves contracted the disease, and because of South Africa's growing prosperity, tens of thousands of other afflicted Africans came there to receive treatment. Twenty-four percent of all inhabitants of South Africa were HIV-positive in 2007. This trend, combined with ethnic tensions, economic inequalities, and the rise of new political factions, challenged the gains made after South Africa's hard-won victory over apartheid.

China

Of all the developing nations, China's was the most striking success story. Deng Xiaoping came out on top in the power struggle that followed Mao's death in 1976. Under his leadership, China began its drive to become an economic titan, at once producing an array of inexpensive products for the global marketplace and providing its citizens with jobs that raised their standard of living. As people from the countryside flocked to cities to find jobs in China's global workplace, skyscrapers sprouted like mushrooms, transforming China's urban landscape. One- and two-story buildings were demolished in a flash: "Buildings are being knocked down at such a rate that one doesn't even have time to film them anymore," said one Beijing resident.[5] With rising prosperity, consumers sought out luxury goods that would have been unimaginable just two decades earlier. Even relatively poor workers could afford pirated DVDs, and thousands supported themselves by counterfeiting imported goods in much the same way that U.S. hustlers more than a century earlier had helped build American prosperity through counterfeiting products.

Economic development was not, however, accompanied by democratization. The Communist Party kept its grip on government, clamping down hard on free speech, even on the Internet, and meting out harsh punishments to political and religious dissidents. While maintaining control at home, China sought business partners around the world, making deals for raw materials and even for used factories, which it dismantled piece by piece and then reconstructed in new Chinese industrial parks. It also used its trade surpluses to buy vast quantities of debt, especially from the United States, making this communist country the bankroller of capitalist economies and thus an increasingly powerful player on the global stage. The flow of wealth and productive energy appeared to have changed direction away from the Atlantic and toward the Pacific.

MAP 31.1 South Africa After Apartheid

Before the end of apartheid, legal migration into South Africa was restricted to whites and to African contract laborers who worked in the mines. After 1994, refugees seeking opportunity from the region around South Africa entered the country. The new South Africa also deported many illegal immigrants, and South Africans themselves migrated, creating a "brain drain" from the country, including people in the professions and those with technical skills.

Global Livelihoods and Institutions

FOCUS

How has globalization reshaped national economies and political institutions?

The same forces that created a global market for products and services created a global market for labor. Increasingly, companies took their operations to wherever labor was cheapest. As a result, workers around the world found themselves in competition for employment. At the same time, workers found it easier to move to where the jobs were. Better transportation and communication led people to travel thousands of miles to work: Indonesian village women, for instance, left their families to work as domestic servants in the Middle East; nurses from the Philippines went to Japan and other countries as health-care providers in a better-paying environment. Migration, innovations in communication technology, and the globalization of business combined to create global cities. London, Tokyo, and New York became crossroads for global finance, engineering, and legal decision-making. Finally, global financial, political, and activist institutions such as the World Trade Organization, the United Nations, and Doctors Without Borders operated worldwide, transcending the borders of the nation-state and even throwing the nation-state itself into question.

Doctors Without Borders
This doctor from the global nongovernmental organization Doctors Without Borders distributes plastic sheeting to construct refugee shelters during the 1994 civil war and genocide in Rwanda. In an age of ethnic conflict and civil war, refugees were an all-too-common type of global citizen, whose displacement was traumatic and whose needs were immense. The French founders of Doctors Without Borders aimed for this NGO to provide one of the most basic human rights—adequate health care—for the world's neediest peoples. (Louise Gubb/The Image Works.)

Global Networks and Changing Jobs

The Internet and Service Work

The Internet in particular advanced the globalization that multinational corporations and satellite communications had fostered in the first decades after World War II. By the early twenty-first century, as skills spread around the world, the Internet brought service jobs to a number of previously impoverished countries. One of the first to recognize the possibilities of computing and call desk services was Ireland, which attracted global business by stressing computer literacy. From the 1990s on, the people of this traditionally poor country began to prosper as the Internet allowed them to perform service jobs for clients throughout the world. The trend reached other nations as well. Moroccans could do help-desk work for French or Spanish speakers, and Nigerians could tend to U.S. telephone and credit card bills. India and China, both of which had good if unequally distributed systems of education, and eastern Europe with its well-educated workforce profited from the Internet revolution. Three percent of Indian domestic product came from the outsourcing work it did in payroll and other services for Europe, the United States, and Austronesia, but jobs flowed in multiple directions: jobs outsourced to the United States rose from 4.9 million in 1991 to 6.4 million in 2001 and continued to grow.

Global Consumerism

Those who worked in outsourced jobs were more likely to participate in the global consumer economy. Thus, consumption soared in India, China, Brazil, and other emerging markets. Service workers in these areas received intense language training to sound like American, Spanish, or British consumers, and global advertising introduced them to products from around the world. A twenty-one-year-old Indian woman, working for a service provider in Bangalore under the English name "Sharon," was able to buy a cellphone from the Finnish company Nokia with her salary. "As a teenager I wished for so many things," she said. "Now I'm my own Santa Claus."[6] North Africans, Indians, Chinese, and eastern Europeans had access to automobiles, CD players, and personal computers that would have been far beyond their means before the 1990s. Critics called the phenomenon "Consumania."[7]

Consumerism developed unevenly, however: 30 to 40 percent of the people in eastern Europe and even larger percentages in China and Indonesia could not participate fully in the consumer economy because they lacked the means for even basic purchases. The lion's share of global consumer benefits went to urban rather than rural workers. Urban workers in the global service economy also used their rising incomes to educate their families and themselves, hoping to advance even further.

Competition for Jobs

Globalization produced acute competition among lower-level workers in industrial countries for good jobs. "How can I prepare my children for a knowledge-based society when I can't even put food on the table," one French mother complained.[8] Minimum-wage workers in the urbanized countries of the north competed for jobs with people around the world. Much as rural people in the late nineteenth and early twentieth century had faced a drop in prices for their produce and a deterioration in their way of life with the development of global markets in grain and other agricultural products, now lower-level industrial and service workers faced lower wages because they competed with workers worldwide. In contrast, those with advanced managerial, technological, and other skills derived from university education fared better, showing the increasing importance of education to prosperity.

Neoliberalism and the Global Economy

In the 1990s neoliberalism as pioneered by Margaret Thatcher and Ronald Reagan (see Chapter 30) became a central economic model for promoting growth. Reducing social programs such as health care and education for ordinary people would lower costs to employers and boost profits and investment. Neoliberal policy encouraged business mergers, the elimination of rules for the industries and banks, and the free flow of capital across national borders. German companies, like U.S. firms, increased investments abroad in the early 1990s and thereafter; Germans set up companies in the United States where benefits to the workforce were low, and U.S. firms headed to places where benefits and taxes were even lower. An important tenet of neoliberalism was that profit and investment increase through downsizing—that is, reducing the number of jobs and enhancing the productivity of any individual worker. The resulting growth would eventually produce more jobs, thus creating new opportunities for those who were put out of work.

Neoliberalism and the Welfare State

The neoliberal model continued to challenge that of the postwar welfare state in which the government tried to create a minimum level of well-being for society as a whole. Although Europeans still believed government should provide social services and education for all, the tightening of budgetary rules in the European Union meant that these services had to constitute a smaller part of the budget. Some labor unions protested that neoliberals wanted to keep workers at bare subsistence levels. The Swedish government drastically cut pensions, leading one union member to complain: "It means that we have to work our entire life."[9] Because employers (like workers) paid taxes for social service programs, any reduction in benefits or education costs meant smaller employer contributions. Reductions in employer contributions freed up money for investment, thus advancing neoliberalism. Despite neoliberal convictions, some nations believed that certain services were too important to be left to those whose main concern was profit rather than the public good; for that reason these governments continued to run high-quality transportation systems and pave roads, for example.

Beyond the Nation-State

Supranational organizations fostered globalization by creating worldwide networks to improve and regulate societies, economies, and politics. In the 1990s Europeans made immense strides in moving their governmental institutions beyond those of the traditional nation-state, while countries of the "southern cone" of South America joined the effort to speed up economic and social progress. People from around the world packed into cities such as Tokyo, New York, and London, bringing new ideas and new customs.

Supranational Organizations

The International Monetary Fund (IMF) and the World Bank had been in existence for decades, but with globalization these supranational organizations gained in power and importance. Raising money from individual governments, the IMF made loans to developing countries to support modernizing projects or to pay off debts. Such assistance, however, came on the condition that the recipient countries restructure their economies according to neoliberal principles. Other supranational organizations not connected to governments and therefore called **nongovernmental organizations** (NGOs) were charitable or policy-oriented foundations. Because they controlled so much money, these NGOs often shaped national policies. After the fall of the Soviet bloc, NGOs used their resources to bring about political reform. Some NGOs, such as the France-based Doctors Without Borders, used global contributions to provide medical aid in such places as the former Yugoslavia, where people at war lacked any medical help except what outsiders could provide.

Activists Against Globalization

Globalization entailed the rise of global activism, even against globalization itself. For example, the Association for Taxation of Financial Transactions (known as ATTAC), founded in 1998, had adherents in forty countries who opposed the control of globalization by the forces of high finance. ATTAC's major policy goal was to tax financial transactions (just as purchases of household necessities were taxed) and use the money raised to create a fund for people in underdeveloped countries. By 2011, the European Union indeed proposed such a tax, although it was to support poorer countries in the EU itself. ATTAC held a conference at Porto Alegre, Brazil, in 2002 to develop policy alternatives that would protect ordinary people from the worst effects of globalization; political leaders flocked to "alternative" Porto Alegre just as they attended the more traditionally global Davos forum held annually in Switzerland for the world's leading executives.[10]

Women Activists and Globalization

Women activists also held global meetings. Feminists gathered in Beijing, China, in 1995 to discuss common issues and agree on a common platform that could serve as the basis for political action in individual countries. The event was eye-opening for many participants, especially those from industrialized countries who had thought themselves more advanced and active than women from Africa and South America. The reverse proved to be true. Sharp differences in agendas and priorities emerged, as well as dissent in shaping the final report, especially on matters of birth control and abortion. In the end, the activists created a declaration of principles and a set of specific actions designed, in the words of the Declaration, "to advance the goals of equality, development, and peace for all women everywhere in the interest of all humanity"[11] (see Reading the Past: Assessing Livelihoods for Women in a Global Economy). In the early twenty-first century, women became heads of state in Germany, Liberia, Chile, Argentina, and Brazil, a sign of women's increasing influence in politics and business.

The European Union

In 1992, the twelve countries of the European Economic Community (or Common Market) ended national distinctions in the spheres of business activity, border controls, and transportation. Citizens of member countries carried a common burgundy-colored passport, and governments, whether municipal or national, had to treat all member nations' firms the same. In 1994 by the terms of the Maastricht Treaty, the European Economic Community became the **European Union** (EU) (see again Mapping the World, page 1025), and in 1999 a common currency, the European Currency Unit—the ECU, or euro—was established. Common policies governed everything from the number of American soap operas aired on television to pollution controls on automobiles to standardized health warnings on cigarette packages. The EU parliament convened regularly in Strasbourg, France, and with the adoption of a common currency by most members, the EU's central bank gained more control over regionwide economic policy.

Between 2004 and 2007 the EU admitted ten new members, mostly from central and eastern Europe: Estonia, Latvia, Lithuania, Poland, the Czech Republic, Slovakia, Hungary, Malta, Cyprus, Slovenia, Bulgaria, and Romania. All new members hoped to

nongovernmental organization A group devoted to activism outside the normal channels of government, such as Doctors Without Borders.

European Union An expanded version of the European Economic Community, established in 1994 to increase political and economic cooperation among European nations.

READING THE PAST

Assessing Livelihoods for Women in a Global Economy

In 1995 delegates from around the world met in Beijing, China, for the Fourth World Conference on Women sponsored by the United Nations. The delegates listened, debated, and negotiated to come up with a platform for action addressing women's health, education, role in politics, safety, and—in this excerpt—their situation in the increasingly globalized economy of the 1990s.

> Although some new employment opportunities have been created for women as a result of the globalization of the economy, there are also trends that have exacerbated inequalities between women and men. . . .
>
> These trends have been characterized by low wages, little or no labor standards protection, poor working conditions, particularly with regard to women's occupational health and safety, low skill levels, and a lack of job security and social security, in both the formal and informal sectors. Women's unemployment is a serious and increasing problem in many countries and sectors. Young workers in the informal and rural sectors and migrant female workers remain the least protected by labor and immigration laws. Women, particularly those who are heads of households with young children, are limited in their employment opportunities for reasons that include inflexible working conditions and inadequate sharing, by men and by society, of family responsibilities.
>
> In countries that are undergoing fundamental political, economic, and social transformation, the skills of women, if better utilized, could constitute a major contribution to the economic life of their respective countries. Their input should continue to be developed and supported and their potential further realized.
>
> For those women in paid work, many experience obstacles that prevent them from achieving their potential. While some are increasingly found in lower levels of management, attitudinal discrimination often prevents them from being promoted further. The experience of sexual harassment is an affront to a worker's dignity and prevents women from making a contribution commensurate with their abilities. The lack of a family-friendly work environment, including a lack of appropriate and affordable child care, and inflexible working hours, further prevents women from achieving their full potential.
>
> In the private sector, including transnational and national enterprises, women are largely absent from management and policy levels, denoting discriminatory hiring and promotion policies and practices. The unfavorable work environment as well as the limited number of employment opportunities available have led many women to seek alternatives. Women have increasingly become self-employed and owners and managers of micro, small, and medium-scale enterprises.

Source: The United Nations Fourth World Conference on Women, "Action for Equality, Development and Peace," Beijing, China, September 1995, http://www.un.org/womenwatch/daw/beijing/platform/.

EXAMINING THE EVIDENCE

1. **According to this statement, what are the effects of globalization on women's place in the economy?**
2. **What other issues besides economic ones affect women's ability to pursue productive and fulfilling livelihoods?**
3. **Judging from this statement, what relationship do you see between women's economic participation and the well-being of nations?**

emulate the case of Greece, which had long been considered the poor relative of other EU countries. Greece had joined the European Common Market in 1981; in 1990 its per capita gross income was 58.5 percent of the European average. By the early twenty-first century, thanks to advice from the EU and an infusion of funds, the country reached 80 percent of the EU per capita gross domestic product. Candidates in 2010 for membership included Turkey, Croatia, and Macedonia.

Other Transnational Unions

The economic and political successes of the EU prompted the creation of other cooperative zones that imitated the early Common Market (see again Mapping the World,

Mercosur, 2011

page 1024). In 1967 five countries—Indonesia, Malaysia, the Philippines, Singapore, and Thailand—formed the **Association of Southeast Asian Nations** (ASEAN), later expanded to include Brunei Darussalam (1984), Vietnam (1995), Laos and Myanmar (1997), and Cambodia (1999). ASEAN members engaged in a range of cooperative ventures, but they particularly set their sights on rapid economic cooperation and expansion. The **North American Free Trade Agreement** (NAFTA), implemented in 1994, eliminated nearly all tariffs on goods traded between Canada, the United States, and Mexico. **Mercosur**, formed in 1991, established a free trade zone among South America's "southern cone" countries: Argentina, Brazil, Uruguay, and Paraguay, all of which were full members, and Chile and Bolivia as associates. These transnational organizations hardly matched the integration of the EU, and NAFTA explicitly rejected the kind of borderless opportunities for workers that the EU allowed. Workers in the United States watched in dismay as many jobs moved to Mexico, but as trade blossomed among the partners, the country's industrialists, financiers, and traders came to regard NAFTA and Mercosur as successes.

Global Cities

The changing function of cities in a global world reshaped livelihoods and identities. Cities had always served as regional crossroads, acting as centers of economic, political, and cultural activity. Now, as the twentieth century came to a close, some old urban areas, including Hong Kong, Paris, Tokyo, London, and New York, became global crossroads. Taking advantage of innovations in transportation and communication, they claimed critical roles in the global economy and became magnets for migrants from all over the world. Residents of other cities who took pride in maintaining their distinctive national culture or local way of life denounced global cities, often portraying them as corrupt and cold. Global cities, many of which were in the north, also drew criticism for their concentrated wealth, as their rise to global power and influence was seen by some to come at the expense of poorer people in rural areas or southern nations.

Life in Global Cities

A global city's institutions—its stock markets, legal firms, insurance companies, and financial service organizations—operated across national borders and were linked to similar enterprises in other global cities. Within these cities, high-level decision-makers interacted with one another to set global economic policy and to transact business worldwide. Their high pay drove up living costs and sent middle managers and engineers to live in lower-priced suburbs that nonetheless provided good schools and other amenities for these well-educated white-collar workers. Living in squalid conditions in the run-down neighborhoods of global cities were the lowest of service providers—the maintenance, domestic, and other workers who needed to be at the beck and call of global enterprise. According to one commentator, those at the top envisioned these people—many of them immigrants—as "lumpentrash." Thus, suburbanization and ghettoization alike flourished as part of globalization.

Huge numbers of willing migrants flocked to leading global cities. In the mid-1990s, for example, an estimated ninety thousand Japanese lived in England staffing Japan's global enterprises located there. Sometimes said to be "invisible migrants," they did not aim to become citizens, nor did they make any economic or political claims on the adopted country. The presence of massive numbers of like-minded wanderers and a rich array of cultures and peoples in their communities often kept these global citizens from suffering the trauma of exile from their native country. Global cities were sometimes criticized for producing a "de-territorialization of identities"—meaning that residents of these areas lacked both a national and a local sense of themselves, so much so that they were at home anywhere in the world (see Seeing the Past: The Globalization of Urban Space).

Association of Southeast Asian Nations A transnational organization formed in 1967 to facilitate economic cooperation among Southeast Asian countries.

North American Free Trade Agreement An agreement among Canada, Mexico, and the United States established in 1994 that eliminated most tariffs on goods traded among the signatories.

Mercosur The establishment in 1991 of a free trade zone among nations of South America's "southern cone."

SEEING THE PAST

The Globalization of Urban Space

The New Louvre, Paris, France (The Art Archive/Richard Nowitz/NGS Image Collection.)

One everyday sign of globalization is the homogenization of urban architecture. Travelers to urban capitals may see carefully preserved and distinctive buildings from centuries past that differ from one continent to another. Alongside these ancient buildings are recent ones, similar in style whether they are in Dubai, Malaysia, Japan, Brazil, or the United States. The similarity arises not only from the globalization of style but from the globalization of architects themselves, who bid on and construct buildings far beyond their home countries, often in collaboration with architects from other parts of the world.

The Louvre was once a royal palace. It evolved from a twelfth-century fortified residence of kings to a museum not only for the French but for millions of tourists from around the world. In the 1980s the French government undertook a major renovation of the central entrance to the Louvre, which was no longer adequate to deal with the throngs of visitors. The architect I. M. Pei, who designed buildings around the world, produced this entryway through a glass pyramid.

EXAMINING THE EVIDENCE

1. Why might so ancient a structure as a pyramid have been chosen to be placed in front of the Louvre?
2. Why might glass have been used instead of the stone from which the Egyptian pyramids were constructed?
3. What message does this update of the entrance to the Louvre convey?

The Promises and Perils of Globalization

FOCUS

What major benefits and dangers has globalization brought to the world's peoples?

Despite growing prosperity for many, the global age was filled with challenges. First, the health of the world's peoples and their environments came under a multipronged attack from industrial disasters, acid rain, epidemics, and global warming. Second, a surging population, especially in southern regions, although fueling economic growth in many places, increased demands on resources and often fed strife. Migration from imperiled areas mushroomed, and transnational religious and ethnic movements also competed for power around the world, sometimes through the use of terrorism. Growing prosperity in regions outside the West boosted confidence that the time had come for the redistribution of global power, especially as the West was hit with a devastating economic crisis.

Environmental Challenges

In the late twentieth century people became concerned that technological development threatened the environment and human well-being on a disastrous scale. In 1984 poisonous gas leaking from a Union Carbide plant in Bhopal, India, killed an estimated ten to fifteen thousand people, with many tens of thousands more permanently harmed and the region completely contaminated by chemicals. This was followed by the 1986 explosion at the Chernobyl nuclear power plant in present-day Ukraine, which killed thirty people instantly and left many more dying slowly from the effects of radiation. Levels of radioactivity rose for hundreds of miles in all directions, and by the 1990s cancer rates in the region were soaring, particularly among children. Fossil-fuel pollutants such as those from natural gas, coal, and oil mixed with atmospheric moisture to produce acid rain, a poisonous brew that destroyed forests and inflicted ailments such as chronic bronchial disease on children. In less populated areas, clearing the world's rain forests depleted the global oxygen supply and threatened the biological diversity of the entire planet.

Climate Change

By the late 1980s, scientists determined that the use of chlorofluorocarbons (CFCs), chemicals found in aerosol and refrigeration products, had blown a hole in the earth's ozone layer, the part of the blanket of atmospheric gases that prevents harmful ultraviolet rays from reaching the planet. Simultaneously, automobile and industrial emissions, especially of carbon dioxide produced by the burning of fossil fuels, were adding to that thermal blanket. The buildup of CFCs, carbon dioxide, and other atmospheric pollutants produced a "greenhouse effect" that resulted in **global warming**, an increase in the temperature of the earth's lower atmosphere. Changes in temperature and dramatic weather cycles of drought or drenching rain indicated that a greenhouse effect might be permanently warming the earth and thus causing climate change. Already in the 1990s, the Arctic ice pack was breaking up, and scientists predicted dire consequences: the rate of global ice melting, which had more than doubled since 1988, would raise sea levels 27 centimeters by 2100, flooding coastal areas, disturbing fragile ecosystems, and harming the fresh water supply (see Map 31.2).

Environmental Activism

Activism against unbridled industrial growth took decades to develop as an effective political force. American biologist and author Rachel Carson wrote a powerful critique, *Silent Spring* (1962), which advocated the immediate rescue of rivers, forests, and the soil from the ravages of factories and chemical farming. In 1979, the Green Party was founded in West Germany, and across Europe Green Party candidates came to force other politicians to voice their concern for the environment.

Competing voices and the demands of nation building, however, led politicians to push massive and questionable projects such as superhighways and dams. Egypt's Aswan Dam, built in the 1960s, and China's Three Gorges Dam, on which construction began in the 1990s, destroyed miles of villages and farmland and cost thousands of lives even as they produced much-needed hydroelectric power. Chinese Nobel Laureate Gao Xingjian explored questions of ecological disaster, as he described peasant reactions to the destruction and invoked the responsibilities of the human community for the earth's well-being in his novel *Soul Mountain* (2000). Gao had been punished more than once during times of political extremism in China, the final time leading to his self-imposed exile, during which he gathered thoughts, stories, and impressions for his novel. Modernizers around the world denounced Gao's work and that of other environmental critics, and there were many attempts to silence protesting voices. In 2007, former U.S. vice president Al Gore

global warming An increase in the temperature of the earth's lower atmosphere, resulting in dramatic weather cycles and melting of glaciers.

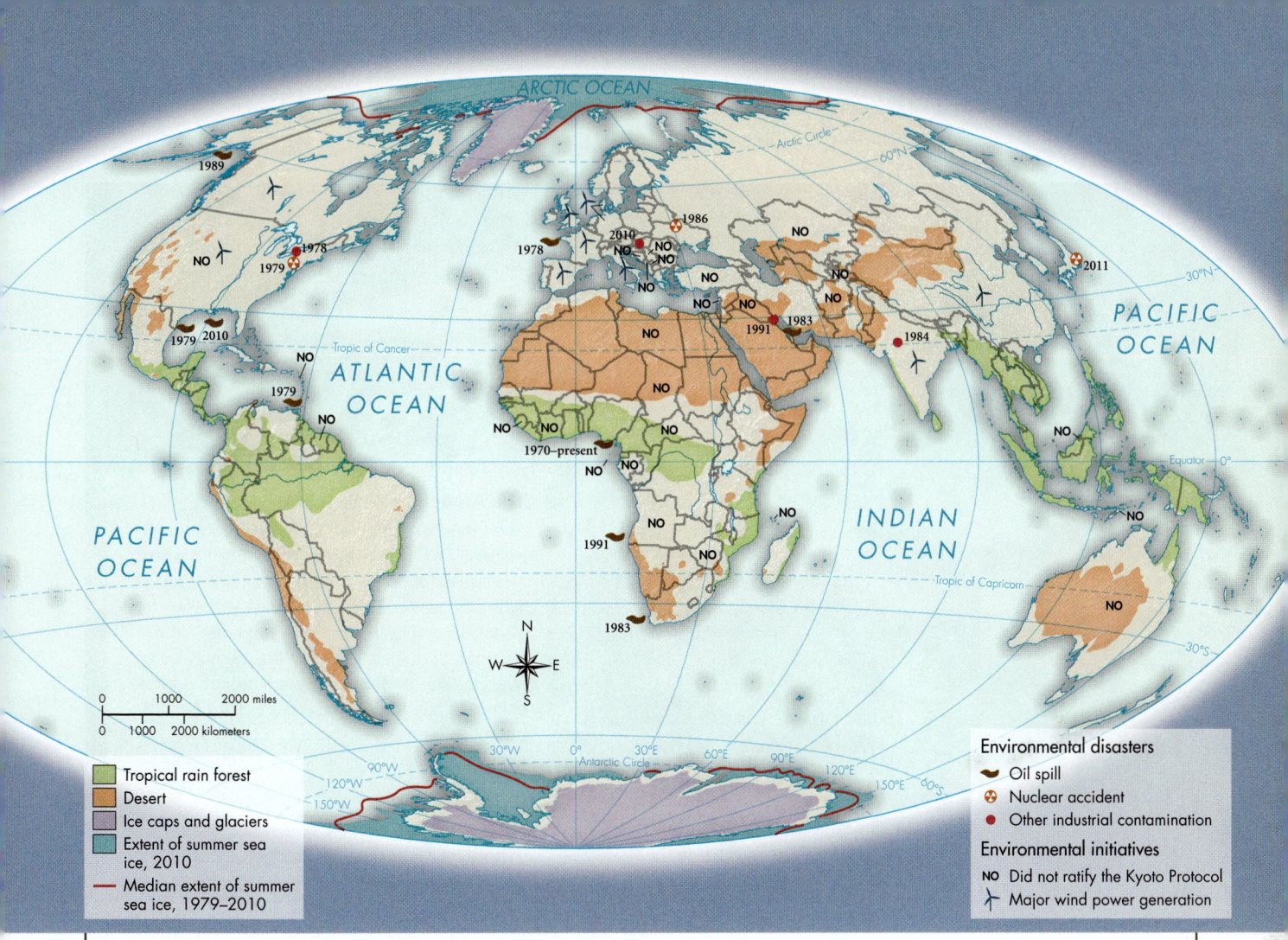

MAP 31.2

The Global Environment of the Early Twenty-First Century

As industry advanced and population grew, the earth itself came under assault. Degradation of the environment— including desertification (the transformation of formerly agrarian land into desert), depletion of rain forests, climate extremes, industrial catastrophes, and other changes caused by humans—threatened the sustainability of life.

won the Nobel Peace Prize for his fight to relieve the environmental crisis—"a moral and spiritual challenge to all of humanity," he called it.

People attacked environmental problems on both the local and global levels. Beginning in 1977, Wangari Maathai (wan-GAH-ree mah-DHEYE) enlisted women to plant trees to create green belts around Kenya's capital city of Nairobi. Born in Kenya, Maathai had studied botany in the United States and then returned to Africa to receive her doctorate in veterinary medicine. Local deforestation led her to take action and create a citizens' movement. "It's important for people to see that they are part of the environment and that they take responsibility for it," she explained. Maathai's project went against the wishes of powerful politicians and business people, who had her beaten up and run out of the country. Maathai returned, more powerful than ever, and in 2004 won the Nobel Peace Prize for her efforts to improve the environment and livelihoods of Africans.[12]

Frankfurt, Germany, and other European cities developed car-free zones. In Paris, when pollution reached dangerous levels, cars were banned. The Smart, a very small car using reduced amounts of fuel, became a popular way for Europeans to cut their use of fossil fuels. Cities also developed bicycle lanes on major city streets. Germany, Spain, the

The Arctic Ice Pack
The extent of Arctic sea ice was more than 25 percent smaller in the summer of 2011 than its average extent during the period 1979–2000. Whereas the Arctic ice pack once virtually closed shipping except for a brief time in the summer, by the early twenty-first century some ships could navigate the waters around it for an extended period. Scientists were alarmed at the potential to raise sea levels to a point that coastal cities around the world would disappear in the rising waters. They also saw rising ocean temperatures as a threat to marine life. (NASA/Goddard Space Flight Center/Science Source/Photo Researchers, Inc.)

United States, Denmark, and China had some 80 percent of the world's wind installations to generate electricity in 2005, and in 2007 China and the United States led in the creation of new capacity. By 2007 some one hundred ninety countries had signed and ratified the **Kyoto Protocol**, an international treaty fashioned in 1997 to reduce the level of emissions of greenhouse gases and other pollutants around the world. Even though the United States refused to ratify the agreement, much of the rest of the world began working to preserve the environment (see again Map 31.2).

Population Pressures and Public Health

Nations with less-developed economies struggled with the pressing problem of rapidly rising population. The causes of the population surge were complex. By 1995 Europe was actually experiencing negative growth (that is, more deaths than births), but less industrially developed countries accounted for 98 percent of worldwide population growth, in part because the spread of medicine enabled people there to live much longer than before. By late 2011, the earth's population had reached 7 billion and by 2050 was projected to reach 8 to 10 billion (see Map 31.3).

Life Expectancy and Birthrates

Life expectancy globally rose by an average of sixteen years between 1950 and 1980. The world's sole remaining superpower did not fare particularly well by this measure of social health: by 2009, the United States had fallen to fiftieth place in average life expectancy, below Albania and Puerto Rico. However, life expectancy in Russia and its former satellites was catastrophic, falling from a peak of seventy years for Russian men in the mid-1970s to fifty-three in 1995 and to fifty-one at the beginning of the twenty-first century. Although birthrates in nonindustrial countries were much higher than in industrialized ones, overall birthrates were rapidly declining, leading to great uncertainty in forecasting population growth. These rates had been dropping in the West for decades, and by 1995

Kyoto Protocol An international treaty fashioned in 1997 to reduce emissions of pollutants around the world.

they had also begun to fall in the less economically developed world, where an estimated 58 percent of couples used birth control.

Population Control

Non-Western governments were alarmed at their nation's rising population and took action. In 1979 Deng introduced the idea of a one-child policy for urban Chinese families, with a considerable number of exceptions. Chinese families had their own methods of population control, mostly focused on female infanticide. Finding that its population was growing rapidly, the Iranian government under Ayatollah Khomeini at first welcomed robust growth as strengthening Islam, but by the 1990s the government was urging families to space their children: the birthrate fell from 6.5 live births per Iranian woman in the 1970s to below 2 in 2010. For a time in the 1970s, the Indian government used a policy of forced sterilization; its recent stress on voluntary family planning has kept population growth at a high level. Yet family planning appeared in unexpected places: mullahs in Afghanistan studied the problems of population. "If you have too many children and you can't control them," one reported after a class on birth control, "that's bad for Islam."[13]

Medical Treatment

Vaccines and drugs for diseases such as malaria and smallpox helped improve health in developing nations. However, half of all Africans lacked access to basic public health facilities such as safe drinking water. Drought and poverty, along with political machinations in some cases, spread famine in Sudan, Somalia, Ethiopia, and elsewhere. In the West, specialists performed heart bypass surgery, transplanted organs, and treated cancer with radiation and chemotherapy, while preventive care for the masses received less attention. Wealthy people traveled the globe to find the best medical treatment, but although the poor and unemployed suffered more chronic illnesses than those who were better off, they received less care. The distribution of health services was a hotly debated issue.

HIV/AIDS

In the early 1980s, technological expertise was challenged by the spread of a global epidemic disease: acquired immunodeficiency syndrome (AIDS), caused by human immune deficiency virus (HIV). A deadly disease that shuts down the body's entire immune system, AIDS is transmitted through contact with bodily fluid (blood or semen) of an infected person. The disease initially afflicted heterosexuals in central Africa; later it turned up in Haitian immigrants to the United States and in homosexual men worldwide. The disease spread quickly among the heterosexual populations of Africa and Asia. Action against AIDS was often sporadic, targeting the wrong audiences, and in some cases the disease was even dismissed as nonexistent. The government of Vietnam launched a dramatic campaign, with

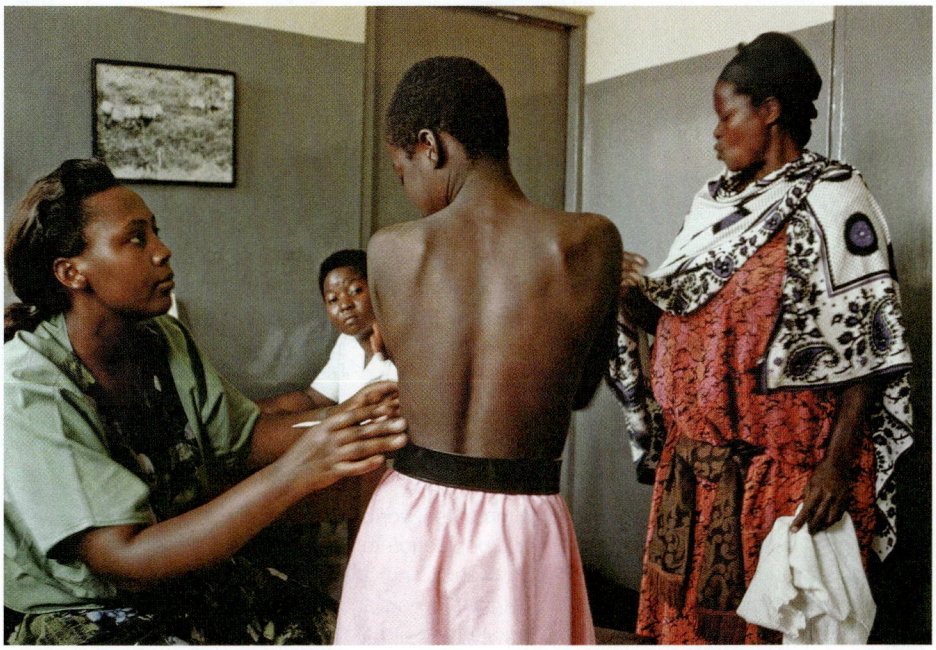

Treatment of AIDS in Uganda

Even as many Africans gained professional and technological expertise and as the continent's nations participated in the global economy, health remained a burning issue in the twenty-first century. Many diseases that had been eradicated elsewhere in the world still threatened the continent's population. Alongside the ravages of civil wars and genocide and the migration that followed, Africans also attempted to address the AIDS pandemic, often through the mobilization of local unions, doctors and nurses, and activists. (Véronique Burger/Photo Researchers, Inc.)

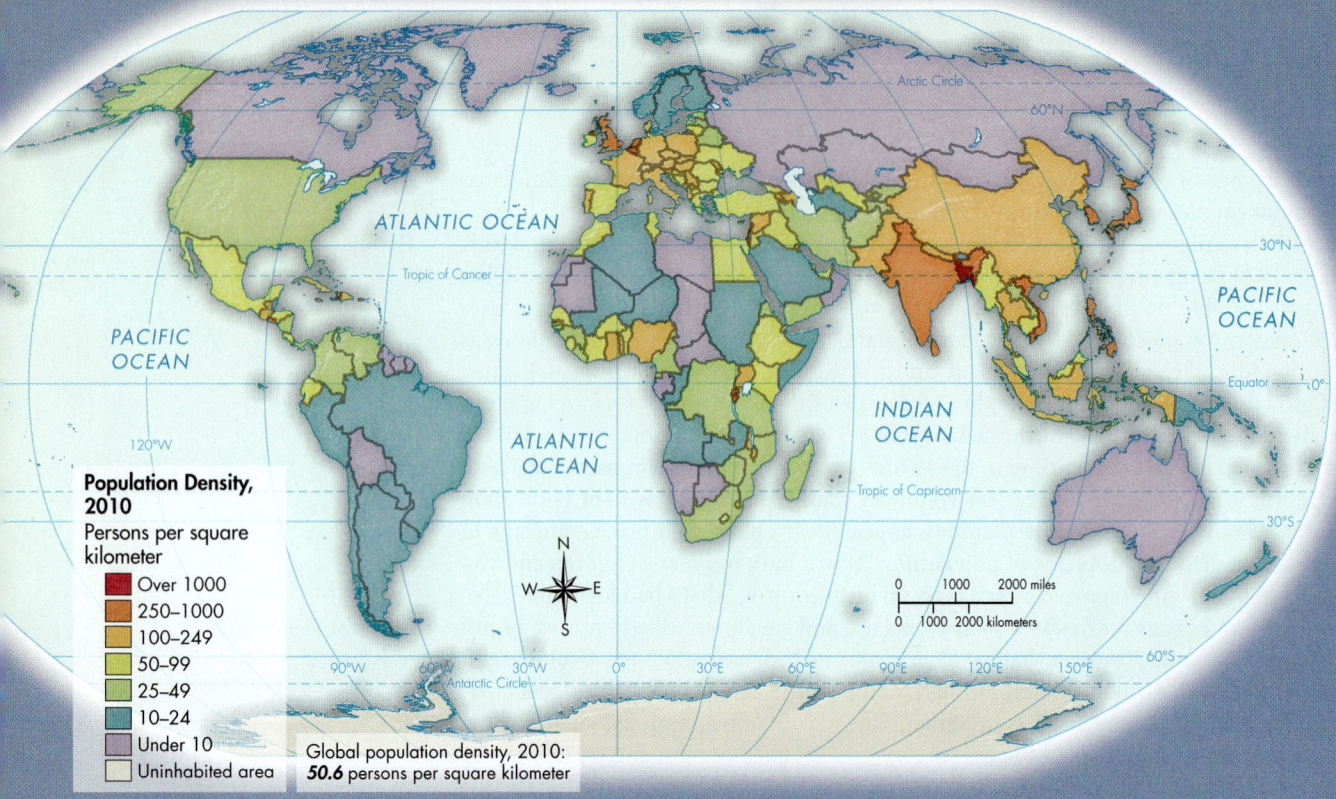

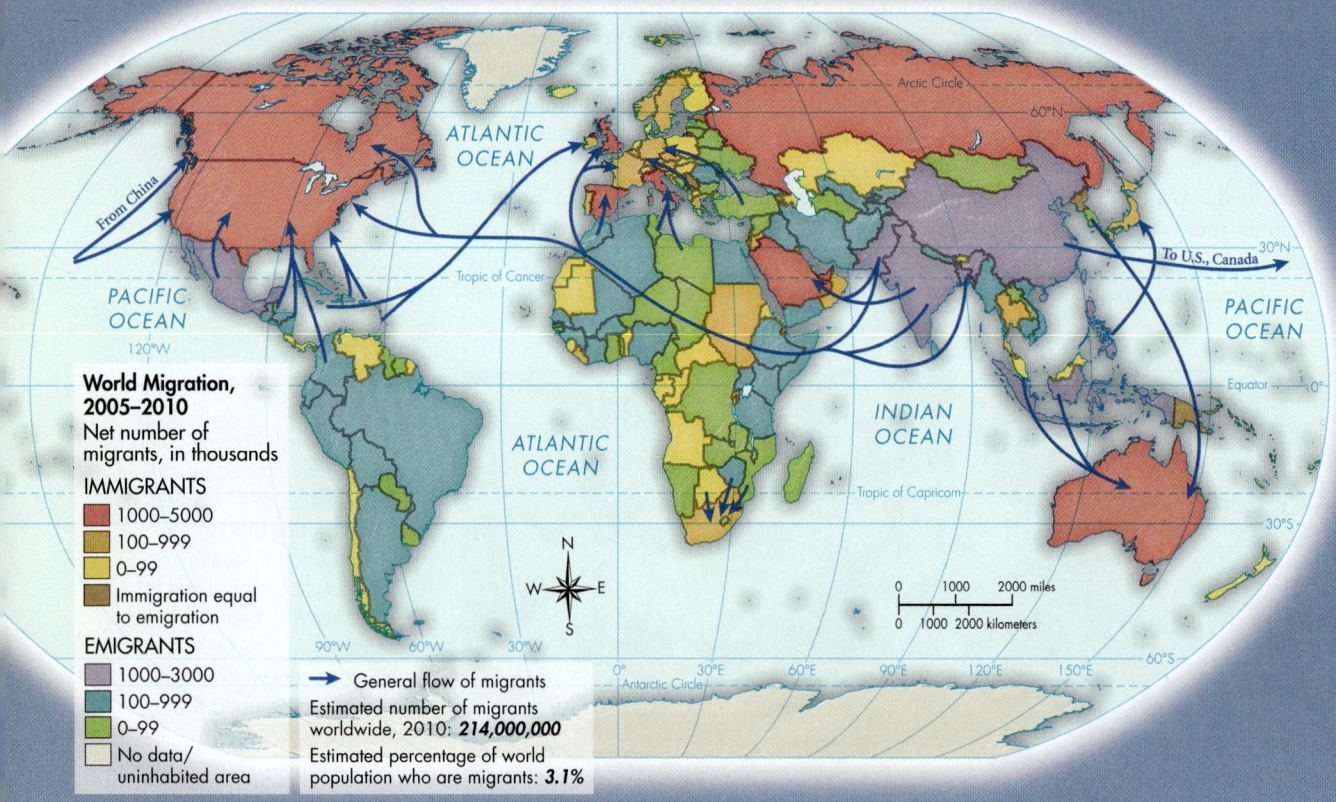

MAP 31.3 The World's Peoples, c. 2010

Migration, disease, and global religions contributed to the integration of the world's peoples in the early twenty-first century. Rising life expectancy caused the world's population to surge to 7 billion in late 2011, which led many people to migrate in search of opportunity and living space. Most of these migrants brought with them their ideas and traditions, including religious beliefs and practices, making their new homelands more culturally rich and diverse. A frightening and often tragic result of globalization and the interconnectedness of the world's peoples was the global spread of disease.

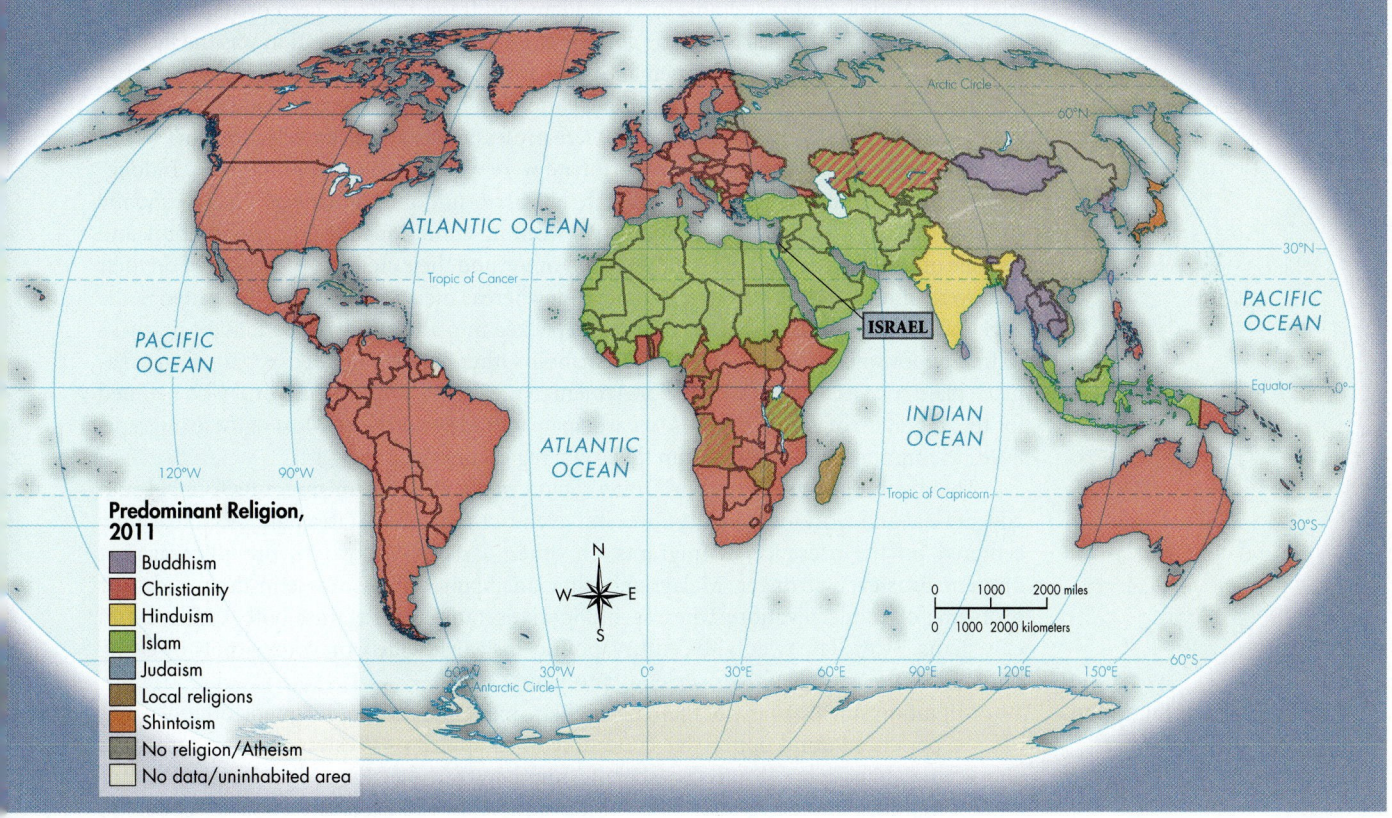

posters blanketing public space that blared "Do not use or accept harmful cultural products. Do not become addicted to smoking or injecting drugs." In fact, the major culprits for the spread of AIDS in Vietnam were privileged and sexually adventurous public officials.

By 2010, no cure had yet been discovered, though strong drugs that alleviated the symptoms had been developed (see again Map 31.3). Activists in Africa and Asia raised their voices louder still, protesting that these costly drugs existed but only the lives of white victims were being saved. The mounting death toll caused some to call AIDS the twentieth-century version of the Black Death, the bubonic plague that ravaged Eurasia during the fourteenth century. In 2005 Nelson Mandela announced the death of his grown son from AIDS in hope that such publicity would help advance prevention and encourage medical attention. AIDS was not the only epidemic disease ravaging the world's population. The deadly Ebola virus, bird flu, swine flu, and dozens of other viruses harbored the potential for global pandemics. Interconnectedness via disease was all too real, showing both the promises and perils of globalization.

Worldwide Migration

Motives for Migration

The early twenty-first century witnessed migration worldwide, building on the migration that followed decolonization and adding to the diversity of many regions of the world. Often economics was the motivation for migration. An estimated 190 million rural Chinese traveled to China's industrial cities to find work in 2004, while millions more went to Malaysia, Indonesia, and other regions in Southeast Asia to get jobs. About 5 percent of the U.S. population was foreign born in the early twenty-first century, including some 11 million undocumented workers. Sometimes danger prompted migration. Africans fled civil wars in Rwanda, Congo, and Sudan, often heading for Europe, Canada, and the United States, while an easier path to safety led people in the more southerly regions of the continent to migrate to South Africa. Civil wars and ethnic oppression drove civilians from states of the former Soviet Union and its satellites to Germany, Scandinavia, Austria, France, and England. Jordan and other countries of the Middle East were home to Palestinians and Iraqis who had been driven from their homelands by violence. A particularly abhorrent form of coerced migration was the increasing trafficking in children and women for sexual and other kinds of forced labor.

Conditions of Migration

The conditions of migration varied depending on one's class, gender, and regional origin. Among the most fortunate migrants were professionals and talented innovators in science and technology. Among the less fortunate were women from the Philippines, Indonesia, and other southern regions who migrated to perform domestic service. They frequently suffered rape by their employers, oppressive working conditions including long hours and no time off, and confiscation of their wages. Women and their children who escaped on their own were often unprotected from exploitation, whereas men and women alike waited at the edges of deserts such as the Sahara or traveled packed into airless storage containers in trucks to find opportunity or to escape political turmoil. Other people migrated as part of an organized plan, such as those of Chinese or Armenian merchants around the world who planned for the migration of young relatives to participate in trade or services. Most of these migrants lived in communities of people from their own region or ethnicity.

The diverse population of the United States made it easier for migrants to meld into educational and workforce institutions, but even in the United States politics increasingly centered on the presence of migrants. In other parts of the world, prejudice against migrants was even stronger. Malaysian politicians blamed the Chinese in their midst for problems of modernization, whereas Indonesians rampaged against both Chinese and Christians. By the late twentieth century, politicians worldwide won votes simply by citing migrants as the source of their societies' problems.

The Literature of Migration

Migration stories, many of them best sellers, related dreams of magnetic other worlds, often experienced amid oppressive conditions. The appeal of Western culture, consumer goods, and democracy inspired a striking number of these. Expatriate Russian author Andrei Makine, who emigrated to France, produced lyrical accounts of Soviet people in Siberia and their powerful imaginings of a better world. *Once Upon the River Love* (1998) recounts the fantasies of a group of Siberian teens who see a French adventure film and begin to dream of Western women and life in western Europe. In this tale, the teenagers' later lives outside of the USSR are bleak and even bitterly disillusioning. *Reading Lolita in Tehran* (2003), a memoir by Iranian author Azar Nafisi, who published her book after emigrating to the United States, and *Balzac and the Little Chinese Seamstress* (2003) by Dai

Sijie, a Chinese refugee in Europe, detail the powerful influence of Western literature under conditions of oppression. Nafisi, who left her post at a Tehran university during the Iranian theocracy, writes of bringing a group of young women to her home to read forbidden literature. As they read, both teacher and students discover that forbidden works contain beauty, values, and examples of personal courage. The two young men in Sijie's novel are banished to the countryside during China's Cultural Revolution and discover there a supply of nineteenth-century Western classics.

Terrorism Confronts the World

Even as insightful literature served as a force for global understanding, the world's people also experienced their interconnectedness in terrifying ways as radicals began to use violence rather than peaceful protests or regular politics to accomplish their goals. Many such radicals came from countries with dictatorships or dysfunctional democracies, but others simply saw violent tactics as a more effective means to publicize their cause. In the 1970s, terrorist bands in Europe, such as Italy's Red Brigades, responded to the restoration of political order after 1968 with kidnappings, bank robberies, bombings, and assassinations. In 1972, Palestinian terrorists kidnapped and murdered eleven Israeli athletes at the Olympic Games in Munich. The terrorists demanded the release of Palestinian prisoners held in Israeli jails. After Bloody Sunday (January 30, 1972) in Northern Ireland, when British troops fired on unarmed civil rights demonstrators, a cycle of violence ensued that left thousands dead. Protestants, fearful of losing their dominant position, battled a reinvigorated Irish Republican Army, which carried out bombings and assassinations to end the oppression of the Catholic minority in Northern Ireland and reunite Northern Ireland with the Republic of Ireland.

Terrorists aimed at the highest levels of government and at ordinary people alike. Prime Minister Indira Gandhi was assassinated by her Sikh security guards in 1984 after the Indian government attacked a Sikh temple; Tamil separatists from Sri Lanka assassinated Indira Gandhi's son Rajiv for his lack of support for their independence in 1991; antigovernment U.S. terrorists blew up a government building in Oklahoma City in 1995; in the same year Japanese religious radicals released deadly poisonous gas in the Tokyo subway system to promote their beliefs; in 2011 a Norwegian fundamentalist Christian and anti-Muslim extremist massacred close to eighty young political activists and wounded hundreds more.

Terrorism and the Middle East

Terrorism began to play an ever-larger role in world politics. Although it appeared that growing belief in religion, nationalism, and the power of oil would naturally make the Middle East a leader in the preservation of international order, the charismatic leaders of the 1980s and 1990s—Iran's Ayatollah Ruhollah Khomeini, Libya's Muammar Qaddafi, Iraq's Saddam Hussein, and Osama bin Laden, leader of the Al Qaeda transnational terrorist organization—all used violence to gain leverage. Throughout the 1980s and 1990s, terrorists from the Middle East and North Africa planted bombs in many European cities, blew up European airplanes, and bombed the Paris subway system—among other acts. Some attacks were said to be punishment for the West's support for both Israel and repressive regimes in the Middle East.

September 11, 2001

On September 11, 2001, Middle Eastern militants hijacked four planes in the United States and flew two of them into the World Trade Center in New York and one into the Pentagon in Virginia. The fourth plane crashed in Pennsylvania. The hijackers, most of whom were from Saudi Arabia, were inspired by Osama bin Laden, who was supported by the United States during the Cold War but now wanted U.S. military forces removed from Saudi Arabia. The loss of some three thousand lives led the United States to declare a "war against terrorism."

U.S. Invasion of Iraq

Global cooperation followed the September 11 attacks and the continuing lethal bombings around the world. European countries rounded up terrorists and conducted the first successful trials of them in the spring of 2003. Ultimately, Western cooperation fragmented when the United States invaded Iraq in March 2003, claiming falsely that Iraq's Saddam Hussein had weapons of mass destruction and suggesting ties between Saddam Hussein and Al Qaeda, bin Laden's terrorist group (see Map 31.4). Great Britain, Spain, and Poland were among those who joined the U.S. invasion, but Germany, Russia, and

MAP 31.4

Wars in Afghanistan and Iraq, 2001–2011

In the aftermath of the terrorist attack on the United States on September 11, 2001, the U.S. government, with the help of Western allies and the Northern Alliance of Afghani groups, launched an attack on the Taliban. This group had taken control of Afghanistan in the wake of the Soviet withdrawal and supported the Al Qaeda terrorist group behind "9/11." In 2003, the United States and its allies invaded Iraq on the grounds that it had weapons of mass destruction—which was not true. Both wars caused tens of thousands of deaths and produced millions of refugees.

France refused. The public in much of the world accused the United States of becoming a world military dictatorship to preserve its only value—wasteful consumerism. Supporters of the invasion countercharged that Europeans were too selfish in their enjoyment of democracy and creature comforts to protect freedom under attack. The Spanish withdrew from the U.S. occupation of Iraq after Al Qaeda–linked terrorists bombed four commuter trains in Spain on March 11, 2004. The British reeled too, when terrorists left bombs in three subway cars and a bus in July 2005. In 2011 American forces scored a symbolic victory in the "war against terror" through the capture and execution of Osama bin Laden. Nonetheless, as the wars in Iraq and Afghanistan continued into the second decade of the twenty-first century, terrorism became an additional ingredient in the globalization of warfare.

Terrorism in the twenty-first century knew no bounds. Chechens protested the Russian destruction of their country by bombing Moscow apartment buildings, blowing up packed buses and airplanes, and taking hundreds of hostages, including schoolchildren. In Bali, terrorists blew up nightclubs and resorts, while in Jordan Al Qaeda suicide bombers slaughtered wedding guests. Alongside the many promises of globalization—including the rich mixture of peoples and cultures and the victory for democracy wrought by people like Nelson Mandela—was the incredible toll in lives taken by terrorism, civil wars and genocide, disease, and other instruments of death around the globe.

The Promise of Arab Spring

Even as terrorism continued, a new manifestation of antigovernment sentiment appeared that brought hope and promise throughout the Middle East. In late 2010, an "Arab Spring" began in a series of popular uprisings, some of which forced dictators in North Africa and the Middle East to step down in favor of democracies and representative government. Uprisings in Tunisia, Egypt, and Libya succeeded, even in the face of brutal repression. In Egypt, long-time dictator Hosni Mubarak was forced from power and put on trial for the murder of many protesters. Hard on the heels of the Egyptian success, protest mounted against dictators in Libya and Syria, with NATO planes helping the Libyan rebels defeat Muammar Qaddafi.

Arab Spring in Egypt

At the end of 2010, protests erupted in Tunisia over the corruption of longtime dictator Zine El Abidine Ben Ali and his family. The overthrow of Ben Ali inspired others across the Arab world to call for change, and although some were crushed, dictators in Egypt and Libya were driven out. The Egyptians pictured here celebrate the fall of Hosni Mubarak in February 2011, a result of protests often organized via social media. The end of Muammar Qaddafi's reign in Libya later that year was only achieved through military means and proved more costly in terms of lives and the destruction of homes and infrastructure. (Ron Haviv/VII/Corbis.)

Hopes for a speedy transition to a full-blown democracy in liberated countries were not high. Working against representative institutions and civil rights were two facts: dictators had prevented the institutions of civil society, including open debate, from developing; in their place tribal organizations often controlled decision-making. However, others who saw a more hopeful future in the near-term pointed to the sophisticated means by which protesters had mobilized: they used features of the World Wide Web such as e-mail and social networking to create meeting points and devise strategies. The protesters were relatively peaceful, unless governments fought back, forcing protesters to defend themselves. Even as the situation often appeared chaotic and uncontrolled in the face of government repression, in fact, the promise of the Arab Spring was not just in its accomplishments but in the "virtual" societies young and older citizens had constructed through technology. The Arab Spring may have looked rough and ragged, but it showed the ever-changing capacities that can be brought to bear on human problems.

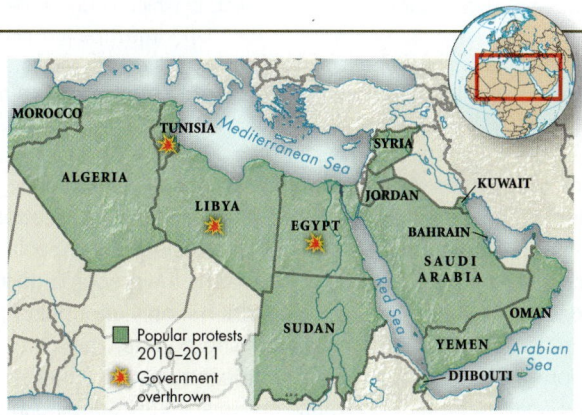

Arab Spring

Global Economic Crisis

Globalization meant tighter financial connections and a faster pace of doing business. As the twenty-first century opened, the global economy suffered a series of shocks, followed by the bursting in 2008 of a real estate bubble in the United States. Housing prices had escalated because of mortgage financing available on easy or even dishonest terms. Then, financiers distributed this often fraudulent debt around the world to those who hoped to make handsome profits because adjustable mortgage rates were set to rise dramatically. When people became unable to repay their rising debt, including credit card debt, credit became unavailable both to ordinary people and to banks and industry. A credit collapse followed, just as it had in the stock market collapse of 1929 (see Chapter 28). Banks and industries became insolvent, and governments around the world tried to prop them up with the infusion of billions of dollars. Unemployment rose as businesses and consumers alike stopped purchasing goods. Although by late 2009 Pacific economies had returned to growth, in 2011 European governments including Greece, Italy, and Spain faced possible bankruptcy. The globalization of economic crises remained yet another peril faced by the world's population.

Readers of the Qur'an

Readers of the Qur'an in Kazan, Russia

Despite the Soviet Union's official policy of atheism, Kazan has remained a center of Islamic culture and practice. It is the site of magnificent mosques and hosts expert readings of the Qur'an. In this 2008 photograph, a reader participates in a Qur'an reading contest, in which young experts from across Russia vie with one another for the best and truest performance. Although this contest is a national one, echoing secular contests in music, beauty, and even game shows, Islam remains a powerful global religion with a rising number of believers. (RIA Novosti/The Image Works.)

Among the most popular and prestigious stars in the global media are those who chant the Qur'an on cassettes, CDs, and radio. Specially trained and tested Qur'an reciters—literally thousands of them—make their recordings in dozens of cities in the Islamic world, but only after being certified to do so by official examining boards. The apprenticeship is arduous, for readers must know the Qur'an to perfection, because errors such as stopping in the middle of a word would mar recipients' understanding of the holy words of Allah as handed down through the Prophet Muhammad. Cassettes allow the Qur'an to inspire Muslims at home or work; for example, a carpenter in Cairo keeps his tape playing during the day. "I have two ears," the carpenter reports, "one for work, and one for listening to the Qur'an." Readings of the Qur'an can make up a third of sales by record companies, and cell phones now deliver Qur'an readings.

Although most reciters of the Qur'an are men, one of the best known is Maria Ulfah, a reciter from Indonesia. Taught as a child that men and women are equal, she has traveled to many parts of the world to read. Like Ulfah, well-loved readers of the Qur'an become celebrities. In Egypt Sheik Mohammed Gebriel is the most appreciated; listeners immediately recognize his voice. He is known to bring in crowds of over half a million when reading in public. "When I hear Sheik Gebriel, I feel that the angels are reading with him," a retired army officer said.

Despite the standardization involved in procedures for certification, the reading of the Qur'an and the issuing of calls to prayer five times a day have their variations according to region and language. Muslims in Kenya, for example, prefer the sounds of the call to prayer by their country's readers to those recorded in Egypt. Saudis object to musical recitations of the Qur'an, preferring those that are direct and plain-spoken. Recordings by the thousands of reciters show, in fact, differences and nuances by region that are welcome to local worshipers, again proving that even in the face of standardization and globalization at the highest levels of religion and faith, local identities remain both powerful and important to carrying out one's daily life. "You can get bored by a song in a few days," a record store owner said in analyzing the popularity of cassettes of the Qur'an, "but no one gets bored listening to the Qur'an."

QUESTIONS TO CONSIDER

1. **In the case of the Qur'an in people's lives, what has been the effect of modern communications technology?**
2. **How would you describe the role of the reciter of the Qur'an in modern society? Is he or she a religious leader, service worker, or media personality?**
3. **Over time, what has been the effect of books, television, CDs, and other media on religion generally?**

For Further Information:

Douglas Jehl, "Above the City's Din, Always the Voice of Allah," *New York Times International*, March 6, 1996.
Ali Asani lecture, November 2005.
Qur'an Explorer (recordings of recitations of the Qur'an in several languages, including Arabic, Urdu, and English). http://www.quranexplorer.com/.
Qur'an Reciters, including images of especially important reciters of the past. http://www.quranreciters.com/wp/.

Cultures Without Borders

FOCUS
What trends suggest that globalization has led to a new mixing of cultures?

In the global age, positive cultural values such as the quest for human rights began to mature. Communication and more extensive contact allowed widespread sharing and enjoyment of the world's cultural accomplishments in literature, art, and music. The global age, for all its deadly flaws, was rich in possibilities for improving human life and connecting people around the world.

The Quest for Human Rights

Human Rights as a Global Value

At the end of the twentieth century, human rights constituted a newly invigorated global value supported by people from many countries and traditions. Notions of human rights as transnational guarantees of just treatment for all people had grown up gradually over the course of the twentieth century. The idea of human rights as transcending any individual government's policies—that is, as being universal and not limited to citizens of a particular nation-state—emerged powerfully with the creation of supranational bodies such as the United Nations. In 1948 the General Assembly of the United Nations adopted a Declaration of Human Rights, which proclaimed the inalienable rights and fundamental freedoms of all people, including the rights to life, liberty, security, and equal protection of the law. In 1975 the Helsinki Accords, part of a series of agreements between the two sides in the Cold War, acknowledged Soviet gains in World War II in exchange for Soviet endorsement of human rights. This commitment to human rights, at first a pro forma statement, became central to dissidents within the Soviet bloc, and with globalization, it became a lynchpin of international activism. Some critics denounced the accords as simply another ploy for powers in the north to interfere in the political affairs of people from the south—a powerful critique once the United States began using torture during its war on terrorism.

Targeting Human Rights Abuses

Human rights activists found much to correct in the world around them, and after the 1970s they were better organized globally to take action. Human rights activists spoke out against the genocide in Rwanda and the former Yugoslavia in the 1990s, and the international community joined them in backing prosecution for these crimes in the International Tribunal at The Hague. Human rights activists investigated other abuses, such as violations of political freedoms, immunity from violence and torture, and the guarantee of food, clothing, and shelter. Activists protested the torture of prisoners in Turkey and the trial of Turkish novelist Orhan Pamuk for asserting Turkey's role in the Armenian genocide of 1915–1917. Latin American governments and China also wracked up long lists of abuses, which human rights activists publicized, often at their own peril. They targeted powerful leaders such as Russian president Vladimir Putin, who closed down independent television stations and imprisoned critics. Human rights activists were suppressed and sometimes murdered for speaking out. Shirin Ebadi, an Iranian lawyer who won the Nobel Peace Prize in 2005 for her human rights activism, was constantly attacked by the government; her offices were raided in December 2008 for tax fraud, even though she did not charge those she defended. Political opponents of Belarus's president Aleksandr Lukashenko, including young demonstrators on behalf of human rights, were murdered or beaten.

Religion Worldwide

Growth of World Religions

Many religions surrendered any national identity and sought out the faithful globally. Roman Catholicism had more adherents in Latin America and Africa than in its western European heartland, where many had embraced secularism. Beginning in the 1970s, Roman Catholic popes—most notably John Paul II—traveled widely to almost every corner of the world. Although some believers found the church's message against homosexuals, birth control, and abortion distasteful, Catholic clergy, such as the nuns assassinated in Brazil or Rwanda, gained a strong record as advocates for the poor around the world. They were said to practice "liberation theology," which stressed bringing Christian compassion to those suffering—wherever they lived. The Buddhist sect Soka Gakkai, once identified with its Japanese origins, also had a far-flung global membership, with more than a million adherents each in Brazil and South Korea and major followings in New York, Los Angeles, Sydney, and many other parts of the world. Soka Gakkai precepts include chanting for specific goals, most important among them world peace, compassion for others, and respect for all human life. The sect sponsored cultural events, hosted conferences for women, and supported environmental protection movements, thereby, like the Catholic Church, promoting transnational values and good works.

Spread of Islam

Islam also expanded worldwide, becoming the world's second-largest faith after Christianity (see again Map 31.3). Although Muslims held Mecca and Medina in Saudi Arabia in special regard as the birthplace of their faith, the population center of Islam by the late twentieth century lay in a more easterly direction, falling on a line from eastern Pakistan through western India. As many Muslims lived east of that line, in centers such as Jakarta and Kuala Lumpur, as lived west of it in Cairo and Istanbul. While practicing the Five Pillars of their faith, including charitable giving, Muslims embraced a wide variety of interpretations of Islam. In the 1990s, young Turkish people, raised with the nation's republican and secular beliefs, began to follow "green pop" stars and to read "green romances"—green being the color of paradise in the Muslim faith. While enjoying gossip, jokes, and the company of their best friends, young women decided to wear headscarves and follow the call to prayer, maintaining "we pray like you have fun."[14] Islam spread to the New World, and places where it had mostly been rejected, such as Europe, included centers of Islamic faith. Muslims also recruited members globally, often using sophisticated techniques based on marketing and demographic knowledge (see Lives and Livelihoods: Readers of the Qur'an).

Global Literature and Music

The Boom in Latin American Literature

A crucial ingredient of globalization was the deepening relationship among cultures as books and music from many different national traditions gained a worldwide audience. Latin American authors, for example, developed a style known as magical realism, which melded everyday events with elements of Latin American history, myth, magic, and religion. The novels of Colombian-born Nobel Prize winner Gabriel García Márquez were translated into dozens of languages. His lush fantasies, including *One Hundred Years of Solitude* (1967), *Love in the Time of Cholera* (1988), and many later works, portray people of titanic ambitions and passions who endure war and all manner of personal trials. García Márquez described the tradition of dictators in Latin America, but he also emphasized the legacy of business imperialism. *One Hundred Years of Solitude*, for example, closes with the machine-gunning in 1928 of thousands of workers at the request of the U.S. United Fruit firm because they asked for a single day off per week and breaks to use the toilet. Five years of rain flood the region, erasing all trace of the slaughter, even from local memory. Wherever they lived, readers snapped up the book, which sold 30 million copies worldwide. A host of other outstanding novels in the magical realism tradition followed, including Laura Esquivel's *Like Water for Chocolate* (1989). In the 1990s the work was translated into two dozen languages and became a hit film. Set in a Mexican kitchen during the revolution of 1910, it intertwines such themes as cooking, sexuality, and brutality.

The Latin American "boom," as it was called, continued into the early twenty-first century, with innumerable authors writing in the style of Márquez and his predecessor, Jorge Luis Borges (see Chapter 29). While acknowledging these geniuses, younger novelists such as Chilean-born Roberto Bolaño questioned the right of literary-minded people to focus on aesthetics amid the brutal dictatorships, torture, and poverty that were so powerful a part of Latin American reality.

Cultural Challenges to Traditional Values

In a global age, the power of literature seemed magnified because it challenged deeply held local beliefs and widespread values. Some writers faced real danger for producing controversial works: García Márquez went into hiding from time to time and rode in a bullet- and bomb-proof car. Feminist authors were menaced and even exiled from Pakistan and other countries that felt threatened by works describing women's oppression and calling for women's equality. Egyptian feminist, medical doctor, and writer Nawal El Saadawi was criticized for producing accounts of women's plight in the region. Her opponents charged her with trying to appeal to Westerners with chilling stories of abuse and backwards customs. Indian-born Salman Rushdie, who had settled in Great Britain, produced *Midnight's Children* (1981), a novel whose fantastic characters formed part of Rushdie's fictional depiction of India's history and whose style was influenced by the magical realism of Latin American authors. Rushdie's novel *The Satanic Verses* (1988) ignited outrage among Muslims around the world because it appeared to blaspheme the Prophet Muhammad. Banned in South Africa and India, the book led to riots worldwide. In 1989 Iran's Ayatollah Khomeini issued a fatwa, or edict, promising both a monetary reward and salvation in the afterlife to anyone who would assassinate the writer. In the 1990s Rushdie went into hiding, but assassins succeeded in murdering his Japanese and Italian translators. The conflict over *The Satanic Verses* reflected a "clash of civilizations," pitting the right to free speech against the right not to have one's religion slandered.

Popular music also flourished in the global marketplace. Pop musicians mixed styles from all over the world, and people brought their music with them as they migrated. Hip-hop, rap, and salsa music, for example, combined African, Latin American, and African American traditions into new musical genres. African hip-hop artists claimed hip-hop and rap as part of an African heritage based on the poet singers, or griots, who for centuries had lyrically recited history and legends. In 1988 the South African group Black Noise produced the region's modern version of rap, and they participated in the antiapartheid movement. Other groups from East Africa rapped about the problems of HIV/AIDS and the urban crime that ruined many of their neighbors' lives. Hip-hop and rap music circled the world, soaking up influences from various cultures. Salsa music did likewise, flourishing not just in Latin America and the Caribbean, but also in the United States as more Hispanics migrated there. African influences shaped salsa too via the slave heritage of the Western Hemisphere. Countries made their own adaptations of musical styles, but the mixing of global styles remained constant, especially as promoters sought new products and novel sounds to sell globally.

Contemporary popular music was the music of diasporas as the world's peoples migrated and interacted with others. Raï, the popular music of North African cities, echoed in the Algerian suburbs of Paris, and performances by raï stars attracted tens of thousands of fans. Dangdut, a form of popular music in Indonesia, used tunes from Bollywood film while its lyrics expressed Islamic values—the combination appealing to diasporas in the world's largest Islamic state. "Chutney" generally described the fusion music of the Caribbean, but particularly the influence of the many South Asian indentured workers who settled there in the nineteenth and early twentieth centuries. As with political and economic institutions, the globalization of people's lives made literary and musical culture a dense crossroad of influences.

Global Pop Culture

Inul Daratista, a sensation in Indonesia and beyond for her singing and dancing performances, blends Indian, Middle Eastern, Malay, and Portuguese styles into unique rock routines. Inul's body moves sensuously and rapidly, and Muslim clergy object to her lack of modesty. The controversy is reminiscent of Elvis Presley's notoriety back in the 1950s in the West, but some see her moves as looking simply like sped-up aerobics, albeit with many Indian and Indonesian gestures. Although Inul Daratista's "dangdut" music originates in folk performances, she has made it not just a local but a global phenomenon. (BAZUKI MUHAMMAD/Reuters/Corbis.)

COUNTERPOINT

Who Am I? Local Identity in a Globalizing World

FOCUS

How have peoples sought to establish and maintain distinctive local personal identities in today's global age?

As globalization linked the world's people in multiple ways, individuals also claimed local, personal identities as a counterpoint to the globalizing trend. Traditionally, individuals took their identities from families, villages, and eventually nation-states. The advance of globalization produced both a sense of loss and a feeling that something other than global forces and even nation-states was needed to provide values. People sought various ways to proclaim their personal identities: through local religious customs or by emphasizing age-old local traditions of dress, food, and celebration. Personal identity also developed through showing loyalty to local sports teams, despite the fact that many such teams were allied with global business, including television networks and marketers of consumer goods.

Ethnic Strife and New Nations

One countermovement to globalization aimed at empowering smaller units of political alliance. Such groups as the Tamils in Sri Lanka and Sikhs in India struggled for autonomy for their people, threatening nation-states with fragmentation. These groups did not achieve their aims. However, by 2000 there were more nations than there were at the end of World War II in 1945. This was not only because of decolonization but because the rising tide of ethnic distinctiveness divided some countries. Since 1990, twenty-nine new nations have been born, including South Sudan in 2011. Yugoslavia splintered into several states in bloody civil wars among ethnic groups, including Serbs, Bosnians, Croatians, and Slovenians. New Asian states such as Kazakhstan and Uzbekistan came into being when they separated from Russia.

Activists also worked to assert regional autonomy, fostering movements for the independence of Quebec from Canada. Basques assassinated tourists, police, and other public servants in their quest for independence from Spain. Many a politician found campaigning for ethnic secession to be the path to public office.

Movements to Protect Tradition

The desire to maintain a local identity also encompassed the movement to preserve local customs and practices, including some of the world's thousands of languages, which were under threat of being swallowed up by Chinese, Hindi, Spanish, and English. In January 2005 Guatemalan forces killed a Maya-Kakchiquel man who sought to block a global mining firm's inroads into his community. At issue in hundreds of other similar protests across Central America was the preservation of local customs and traditional rights, including age-old rights to specific plots of land and sources of water. In late 1993 a group of activists in the Chiapas state of Mexico declared themselves a local liberation army devoted to stanching the "bleeding" of their locality by stopping the flow of oil, coffee, bananas, and other resources out of the area, leaving the local people destitute. These activists, known as the Zapatistas (recalling the name of the hero of the 1910 revolution), also decried the decline in the use of their language and the national and international ridicule heaped on their way of life. Many of these Mexicans still worshiped at ancient Maya shrines, just as locally oriented people around the world focused on their own ancient altars. In seeking to preserve their local identity, the activists were similar to the pilgrims in Vietnam, who brought fruit to special shrines around Hanoi so that it could be blessed by local gods. Native Americans in the United States worked to preserve their ancestral burial sites against industrial and agricultural development. The rap group

Local Customs in a Global Age: Mexico

This image from 2004 shows a Mexican father carrying a bouquet to the Holy Death temple in Mexico City as he presents his infant to Mictlantecuhtli and Mictecacihuatl, the "Señor and the Señora" of Mictlan—that is, the region of the dead people. In so doing, he keeps alive an Aztec custom from the fifteenth century, some six hundred years later in a much changed, cosmopolitan world. (AFP/Getty Images.)

Xplastaz in Tanzania promoted the wearing of traditional garb to fight the globalization of clothing that threatened to erase their local culture.

Although the global media have worked to make family life more standardized, individuals continued to take their identities from their families and to promote distinctiveness. They spent more effort to trace their genealogies. Despite high divorce rates, in fact there are more marriages in the twenty-first century than ever before in human history. National politicians often invoke "family values" to get people to vote for them, and in fact daily family life remains for many a shelter for individual identity, just as local activism is a bulwark against global national forces.

Conclusion

"Sometimes I tell myself, I may only be planting a tree here, but just imagine what's happening if there are billions of people out there doing something. Just imagine the power of what we can do." Wangari Maathai's motivation reflected a belief that billions of citizens, acting as individuals, can effect change on a global scale. Innovations in global communications, transportation, migration, and the development of strong transnational organizations have accelerated the pace of globalization in the past four decades. Globalization is evident everywhere: in the worldwide spread of disease and the worldwide consequences of industrialization. It is seen in the spread of campaigns like Nelson Mandela's on behalf of human rights and in dastardly acts of global terrorism.

As the world's peoples come to work on common projects and share elements of one another's cultures, their mental outlook has become more global, more cosmopolitan. The Chinese painter Wu Guanzhong, even after years of repression for his cosmopolitan style, combined elements from around the world in his work. "In my art," Wu said, "I really belonged to a hybridized breed."[15] Many rightly protest that much of value can be lost at the hands of global forces at work in the world today; others foresee some great irreconcilable clash among civilizations. The question remains whether, given the meeting of humans on the world's crossroads, we are not all hybrids—that is, mixtures of one another's thoughts, traditions, cultures, and livelihoods. Isn't this mixture of peoples and cultures what has given texture to the recent history of the world?

NOTES

1. Quoted in *Guardian Weekly*, September 19–25, 2002.
2. Quoted in James C. McKinley, Jr., "Mexican Farmers Protest End of Corn-Import Taxes," *New York Times*, February 1, 2008.
3. Soutik Biswas, "India's Architect of Reforms," *BBC News*, May 22, 2004.
4. Quoted in Yvonne Corcoran-Nantes, "Female Consciousness or Feminist Consciousness: Women's Consciousness-Raising in Community-Based Struggles in Brazil," in *Global Feminisms Since 1945*, ed. Bonnie G. Smith (London: Routledge, 2000), 89.
5. Quoted in Michael Dutton, et al., *Beijing Time* (Cambridge, MA: Harvard University Press, 2008), 10.
6. Saranya Sukumaran, quoted in Saritha Rai, "India Is Regaining Contracts with the U.S.," *New York Times*, December 25, 2002, W7.
7. Georges Quioc, "La 'consomania' de l'Europe de l'Est électrise les distributeurs de l'Ouest," *Le Figaro économie*, January 13, 2003.
8. Quoted in *Le Monde*, June 2, 2002.
9. Quoted in *Le Monde*, January 17, 2003.
10. Quoted in *Libération*, January 20 and 21, 2002.
11. Fourth World Conference on Women Beijing Declaration, 1995. http://www.un.org/womenwatch/daw/beijing/platform/declar.htm.
12. Quoted in "Nobel Peace Prize for Woman of 30m Trees," *The Guardian*, October 9, 2004.
13. Quoted in "At Birth Control Class, Mullahs Face New Reality," *International Herald Tribune*, November 12, 2009.
14. Quoted in Ayse Saktanber, "'We Pray Like You Have Fun': New Islamic Youth in Turkey Between Intellectualism and Popular Culture," in *Fragments of Culture: The Everyday of Modern Turkey* (London: I. B. Tauber, 2006), 254.
15. Wu Guanzhong, "Preface by the Artist," in Anne Farrer, *Wu Guanzhong: A Twentieth-Century Chinese Painter* (London: British Museum, 1991), 9.

RESOURCES FOR RESEARCH

The Impact of Global Events on Regions and Nations

The decades around the turn of the twenty-first century were full of events that shifted balances of economic and political power. The South African Web site provides a look at the innovative postapartheid constitution, which ensures an array of human rights.

Bayly, Susan. *Asian Voices in a Post-Colonial Age: Vietnam, India and Beyond*. 2007.

Kynge, James. *China Shakes the World: A Titan's Rise and Troubled Future and the Challenge for America*. 2006.

Prunier, Gérard. *Darfur: The Ambiguous Genocide*. 2005.

Rosefielde, Steven. *Russia in the 21st Century: The Prodigal Superpower*. 2006.

South Africa. http://www.info.gov.za/documents/constitution/1996/96cons2.htm.

Taylor, Lance, ed. *External Liberalization in Asia, Post-Socialist Europe, and Brazil*. 2006.

van Kessel, Ineke. *Beyond Our Wildest Dreams: The United Democratic Front and the Transformation of South Africa*. 2000.

Global Livelihoods and Institutions

The spread of global communication brought on by the Internet dramatically affected livelihoods and institutions. Greenspan and Rowen chart developments in information technology.

Greenspan, Anna. *India and the IT Revolution: Networks of Global Culture*. 2004.

Rowen, Henry S., Marguerite Gong Hancock, and William F. Miller. *Making IT: The Rise of Asia in High Tech*. 2007.

Sassen, Saskia. *Cities in a World Economy*. 2006

United Nations. http://www.un.org/womenwatch/. Provides ample information on women around the world and also on the UN's programs for women.

Wasserstrom, Jeffrey N. *China's Brave New World—and Other Tales for Global Times*. 2007.

The Promises and Perils of Globalization

Globalization is hotly debated, and this selection of works shows why. AIDS, terrorism, and environmental decline increased as the world's peoples became more tightly linked. Louie and Smith and Siplon, however, discuss activism and spirited movements for change.

Baldwin, Peter. *Disease and Democracy: The Industrialized World Faces AIDS*. 2005.

Hefner, Robert W. *Civil Islam: Muslims and Democratization in Indonesia*. 2000.

Khalid, Adeeb. *Islam After Communism: Religion and Politics in Central Asia*. 2007.

Louie, Miriam Ching Yoon. *Sweatshop Warriors: Immigrant Women Workers Take on the Global Factory*. 2001.

McNeill, J. R. *Something New Under the Sun: An Environmental History of the Twentieth Century*. 2000.

Smith, Raymond A., and Patricia Siplon. *Drugs into Bodies: Global AIDS Treatment Activism*. 2006.

Cultures Without Borders

As the media became a global force, culture knew even fewer boundaries than it had in the past. These works chart a variety of trends and global mixing of cultures.

Allison, Anne. *Millennial Monsters: Japanese Toys and the Global Imagination*. 2002.

Iwabuchi, Koichi. *Recentering Globalization: Popular Culture and Japanese Transnationalism*. 2002.

Kato, M. T. *From Kung Fu to Hip Hop: Globalization, Revolution, and Popular Culture*. 2007.

Lopez, A. M. *To Be Continued . . . Soap Operas Around the World*. 1995.

Osumare, Halifu. *The Africanist Aesthetic in Global Hip-Hop: Power Moves*. 2007.

Seager, Richard. *Encountering the Dharma*. 2006.

COUNTERPOINT: Who Am I? Local Identity in a Globalizing World

Whether praying or shopping, people around the world maintain local customs and practices. Even a global chain such as McDonald's needs to adjust to local preferences, as Watson's work shows.

Benjamin, Thomas. "A Time of Reconquest: History, the Maya Revival, and the Zapatista Rebellion." *The American Historical Review*. 2000.

Malarney, Shaun Kingsley. *Culture, Ritual and Revolution in Vietnam*. 2002.

Parkin, David, and Stephen C. Headley, eds. *Islam: Prayer Across the Indian Ocean and Outside the Mosque*. 2000.

Saxenian, Anna Lee. *The New Argonauts: Regional Advantage in a Global Economy*. 2006.

Watson, James L., ed. *Golden Arches East: McDonald's in East Asia*, 2d ed. 2006.

▶ **For additional primary sources from this period**, see *Sources of Crossroads and Cultures*.

▶ **For Web sites, images, and documents related to topics in this chapter**, see Make History at bedfordstmartins.com/smith.

REVIEW

Online Study Guide
bedfordstmartins.com/smith

The major global development in this chapter ▶ The causes and consequences of intensified globalization.

IMPORTANT EVENTS

1986	Nuclear accident at Chernobyl power plant in Soviet Union
1989	Iranian leader Ayatollah Khomeini issues fatwa against Salman Rushdie
1990s	New European nations emerge in wake of USSR collapse
1991	Mercosur establishes a free-trade zone among southern South American nations
1994	Nelson Mandela elected president of South Africa; European Union officially formed; North American Free Trade Agreement implemented
1995	United Nations Fourth World Conference on Women held in Beijing
1997	Kyoto Protocol drafted
1999	European Union adopts the euro as its new money
2001	Terrorists attack United States; United States declares "war on terrorism"
2002	Luiz Inácio Lula da Silva elected Brazilian president
2003	United States invades Iraq
2004	Manmohan Singh becomes prime minister of India
2005	Kyoto Protocol goes into effect
2007–2008	Global economic crisis begins to unfold

KEY TERMS

apartheid (p. 1029)
Association of Southeast Asian Nations (p. 1036)
European Union (p. 1034)
globalization (p. 1025)
global warming (p. 1038)
Kyoto Protocol (p. 1040)
Mercosur (p. 1036)
nongovernmental organization (p. 1034)
North American Free Trade Agreement (p. 1036)

CHAPTER OVERVIEW QUESTIONS

1. What were the elements of globalization at the beginning of the twenty-first century?
2. How did globalization affect lives and livelihoods throughout the world?
3. How did globalization affect local cultures?
4. What people do you know whose roots and livelihoods are global?

SECTION FOCUS QUESTIONS

1. How has globalization affected the distribution of power and wealth throughout the world in the early twenty-first century?
2. How has globalization reshaped national economies and political institutions?
3. What major benefits and dangers has globalization brought to the world's peoples?
4. What trends suggest that globalization has led to a new mixing of cultures?
5. How have peoples sought to establish and maintain distinctive local identities in today's global age?

MAKING CONNECTIONS

1. What have been the most important features of globalization—good and bad—in the past thirty years, and why are they so significant?
2. Consider Chapter 24. How have livelihoods changed since the era of industrialization, and what factors have caused these changes?
3. Do you consider local or global issues more important to people's lives? Explain your choice.
4. How do you describe your identity—as global, national, local, familial, religious—and why?

ADDITIONAL CREDITS

Text Credits

Chapter 23

Paul Dukes. *Russia Under Catherine the Great: Select Documents on Government and Society*, edited and translated by Paul Dukes, Oriental Research Partners, 1978. Reprinted by permission of the publisher.

Chapter 24

J. N. Westwood. *A History of the Russian Railways*, George Allen and Unwin, 1964. Used by permission of the author.

Chapter 25

Alexander Nikitenko. *Up from Serfdom: My Childhood and Youth in Russia 1804–1824*, translated by Helen Saltz Jacobson. Copyright © 2001 Yale University Press. Used by permission of Yale University Press.

Anne Walthall. *The Weak Body of a Useless Woman: Matsuo Taseko and the Meiji Restoration.* © 1998 by The University of Chicago. Used by permission of the University of Chicago Press.

William R. Braisted. From *Meiroku Zasshi: Journal of the Japanese Enlightenment* by William R. Braisted, pp. 401–403, Cambridge, Mass.: Harvard University Press, Copyright © 1976 by the University of Tokyo Press.

Chapter 26

Wang Gungwu. *Community and Nation* by Wang Gungwu (2000), published by Allen & Unwin, Sydney (www.allenandunwin.com).

Chapter 27

Patricia Buckley Ebrey. Adapted with permission of Free Press, a division of Simon & Schuster, Inc., from *Chinese Civilization and Society: A Sourcebook* by Patricia Buckley Ebrey. Copyright © 1981 by The Free Press. All rights reserved.

Léopold Sédar Senghor. *The Collected Poetry*, pp. 47–48. Translated by Melvin Dixon. © 1991 by the Rector and Visitors of the University of Virginia. Reprinted by permission of the University of Virginia Press.

Chapter 28

Keith Howard. "Comfort Women" from *True Stories of the Korean Comfort Women*, edited by Keith Howard. Continuum Books, 1995. By the kind permission of Continuum International Publishing Group.

Chapter 29

Isidore Ndaywel è Nziem. *Histoire générale du Congo: De l'héritage ancien à la République Démocratique,* De Boeck & Larcier, 1998. Used by permission of Edition le Cri. [English translation by Bonnie G. Smith.]

Khang Zhengguo. From *Confessions: An Innocent Life in Communist China* by Khang Zhengguo, translated by Susan Wilf. Copyright © 2005, 2004 by Khang Zhengguo, translation copyright © 2007 by Susan Wilf. Used by permission of W.W. Norton & Company, Inc.

Chapter 30

Jennifer Schirmer. "The Seeking of Truth and the Gendering of Consciousness: The CoMadres of El Salvador and the CONAVIGUA Widows of Guatemala," in Sarah A. Radcliffe and Sallie Westwood, editors, *"VIVA": Women and Popular Protest in Latin America* (London: Routledge, 1993). Used by permission of Taylor & Francis Group.

Art Credits

Opener to Part 4

Chapter 23: The Art Archive/Museo Historico Nacional Buenos Aires/Gianni Dagli Orti; Chapter 24: Cotehele House, Cornwall, UK/Bridgeman Art Library; Chapter 25: Tetra Images/Corbis; Chapter 26: The Art Archive/Museo Civico Revoltella Trieste/Collection Dagli Orti; Chapter 27: The Granger Collection, New York; Chapter 28: Bettmann/Corbis; Chapter 29: Universal Images Group/SuperStock; Chapter 30: Jacques Langevin/Sygma/Corbis; Chapter 31: akg-images/Bildarchiv Monheim

INDEX

A note about the index:

Letters in parentheses following pages refer to:
(*b*) boxed features
(*i*) illustrations, including photographs and artifacts
(*m*) maps

Abd al-Wahhabi, Muhammad ibn (Islamic reformer), 785, 786
Abdul Hamid II (Ottoman sultan), 884
Abolition and abolitionism
  in Denmark, 810
  in England, 810
  religion and, 785
Abortion and abortion rights, 934, 938, 996, 1011
Abstract expressionism, 983
Accommodation, of imperialism, 872
Acid rain, 1038
Activism
  Bandung Conference and, 983–984
  by farmers, 1018–1019
  feminist, 1009–1010
  global, 1034
  for human rights, 1049
  protests by, 1009–1012
  in Soviet bloc, 1011–1012
  in United States, 1012
  of women, 851–852
  after World War II, 961–962
  youth, 1009
Adams, John, Enlightenment and, 764
Addis Ababa, 940
Administration. *See* Government
Advertising, middle-class "look" promoted by, 914
Afghanistan
  British in, 863
  population growth in, 1041
  Soviet Union and, 1008, 1015
  wars in (2001–2011), 1046, 1046(*m*)
Africa. *See also* North Africa; specific locations
  Europeans in, 864–868
  famine in, 868
  during Great Depression, 931
  HIV/AIDS in, 1030
  indentured servants in, 876(*i*)
  industrialization and, 810–812
  mandate system in, 907(*m*)
  migration from, 1044
  migration in, 858(*m*), 874–875
  missionaries in, 871
  new nations in, 973–975, 974(*m*)
  resistance to imperialism in, 872
  1750–1880, 811(*m*)
  textiles and independence in, 975(*b*), 975(*i*)
  troops in World War I, 904
  underdevelopment of, 812
  women farmers in, 818–820, 819(*i*)
  World War I soldiers from, 897
African Americans, 840, 850
  in armed forces, 947(*b*)
  civil rights and, 851, 981–982, 1009
  music of, 848
  sailors in World War II, 946(*i*)
  as U.S. president, 1026
African National Congress (ANC), 1023, 1029
Agrarianism
  literacy and, 847
  in technological age, 1017–1019
Agriculture. *See also* Farms and farming
  in Africa, 870
  in eastern Europe, 964
  in Great Depression, 929
  in India, 1028(*i*)
  scientific help for, 996
  seed sterilization and, 1018
  slave workers in, 797
  women and slave agriculture, 818–820, 819(*i*)
AIDS. *See also* HIV
  epidemic of, 1041–1044
  in South Africa, 1030
  treatment in Uganda, 1041(*i*)
Ainu people (Japan), 849
Airplanes, in World War II, 942
Akhmatova, Anna, 934
Alaska, U.S. purchase of, 881
Albania
  First Balkan War and, 896
  Ottoman Balkans as, 776
Alcohol, in industrial society, 815
Aldrin, Edwin ("Buzz") (U.S. astronaut), 994
Alexander II (Russia), 833, 835, 836
Algeria
  France and, 865, 974–975
  independence for, 975
  World War II in, 951
Ali, Muhammad (Egypt), 761, 776, 809, 864
Ali, Sharif Husayn ibn (Syria), 908
Allende, Isabel, 920
Allende, Salvador, 1005
Alliances. *See also* specific alliances
  in Cold War, 966–969
  Egyptian-European, 864–865
  regional, 968–969, 968(*m*)
  before World War I, 896
  in World War I, 896
Allies (World War I), 896
  in Ottoman Empire, 908
  at Paris Peace Conference, 905
  Russian civil war and, 904
  treaties of, 906–907
  victory of, 904
Allies (World War II), 943(*m*), 944(*m*), 945, 948, 951
  division of Germany and Berlin by, 964
Al Qaeda, 1045, 1046(*m*)
Alsace, 897
  after World War I, 906
America(s). *See* Latin America; Native Americans; North America; Spanish America; specific locations
American Federation of Labor (AFL), 932
American Revolution (1775–1789), 768–771, 769(*m*)
Amin, Idi, 1007, 1007(*i*)
Amritsar, protests at, 911
Anatolia (Turkey). *See also* Turkey
  Ottomans in, 908
Anglo-Zulu War (1879), 867
Animals, genetic modification of, 1017, 1018
Ankara, as Turkish capital, 908
Annexation, of South Africa, 881
Anthony, Susan B., 852
Anticolonialism, 918(*i*)
  Bandung Conference and, 983
Anticommunism, after World War II, 963
Antiforeign uprisings, in China, 857, 860
Anti-Semitism. *See also* Jews and Judaism
  in Argentina, 919
  of Hitler, 936–937
  migration due to, 875
  in Nazi Germany, 937–938
  in United States, 953
Apache Indians, 840–841
Apartheid
  in South Africa, 1023–1024, 1029
  South Africa after, 1031(*m*)
Appeasement, of Hitler, 940
Appliances, family life and, 1002
Arabia, in 1802–1807, 786(*m*)
Arabian peninsula, al-Wahhabi and, 785, 786
Arabs and Arab world. *See also* Middle East
  decolonization and, 969
  Israeli wars with, 1013
  as Muslims, 786
  Palestinians and, 972
  tensions in (1967–1990), 1013(*m*)
Arab Spring (independence movements), 1046–1047, 1047(*m*), 1047(*i*)
Archaeology. *See* Culture(s)
Architecture. *See also* Housing
  in China, 1031
  of cities, 913
  globalization of, 1037
Arctic pack ice, melting of, 1038, 1040(*i*)
Argentina, 919(*m*)
  culture of, 920
  "dirty war" in, 1005
  economy of, 919
  golden age of, 919–920
  human rights in, 1005
  industrialization in, 802
  in Mercosur, 1036
  Perón in, 977–978

Argentina (*continued*)
San Martin in, 781
society in, 919
Aristocracy. *See* Nobility
Arkwright, Richard (English inventor), 798, 805
Armed forces. *See also* Military; specific battles and wars
of Bolsheviks in civil war, 904
French in North Africa, 865
in Japan, 842
Armenia
attack on Turkey, 909(*m*)
genocide in (1915–1917), 1049
Armenians, Ottoman deportations of, 908
Armistice, ending World War I, 904
Arms manufacturers, militarization during Great Depression and, 931
Arms race, Kennedy, John F., and, 969
Armstrong, Neil (U.S. astronaut), 994
Art(s). *See also* specific arts and artists
imperialism and, 879–880
in industrial society, 815–816, 817
in Japan, 790(*i*), 803(*b*), 803(*i*)
modernism in, 878
non-Western impact on Western, 885–886
socialist realism in, 934, 934(*i*)
after World War II, 983
Articles of Confederation (U.S.), 769–770
Artigas, José Gervasio, 780–781
Artisans
in industrial age, 814
in Industrial Revolution, 796
Art of War, The (Sun Tzu), 887
Aryans, in Nazi Germany, 937
ASEAN. *See* Association of Southeast Asian Nations
Asia. *See also* specific locations
in Cold War, 966–967
economy in, 913, 997
end of empires in, 970–972
famine in, 868
imperialism in, 861–864, 862(*m*)
missionaries in, 871
Russia and, 868
World War II in, 940–941, 944–945, 944(*m*)
Asian-African Conference. *See* Bandung Conference
Assassinations, of Mexican leaders, 895
Association for Taxation of Financial Transactions (ATTAC), 1034
Association of Southeast Asian Nations (ASEAN), 1036
Astronomy, big bang theory of universe and, 995
Aswan Dam, 973, 1038
Atatürk. *See* Kemal, Mustafa
Atlantic Ocean region
revolutions in, 759–762
trading network in, 767–768
wars and revolutions in (1750–1830), 760(*m*)
Atomic bomb
Soviet, 963
in World War II, 951, 952(*b*), 952(*i*)
Atomic power, after World War II, 977
ATTAC. *See* Association for Taxation of Financial Transactions
Auschwitz-Birkenau, 925, 945
Australia
native children in, 849
World War I and, 897, 898–899
Austria
French Revolution and, 773
German war with, 838
Italy and, 837
Nazi annexation of, 940
Peace of Paris treaties and, 906
Piedmont and, 837
war against France and, 773
Austro-Hungarian Empire. *See also* World War I
Balkans and, 893, 896
in Triple Alliance, 896
World War I and, 896, 897
Austronesia, Indian outsourcing for, 1032
Authoritarianism, control of information and culture in, 915
Autocracy. *See also* Dictators and dictatorships
collapse of, 913
Russia as, 852
Automation, industrial, 998–999
Automobiles and automobile industry, 799–800, 913
Awadh, India, 863
Axis powers (World War II), 943(*m*), 944(*m*), 945, 947–948
postwar trials of leaders, 980

"Back to Africa" movement (Garvey), 981
Baghdad, in World War I, 904
Bahrain, 1046
Balance of power
Crimean War and, 833
economic, 1023
after Napoleonic wars, 774
shifts in, 912–913, 1012–1017
Balance of trade. *See* Trade
Balkan region
Ottomans and, 894
wars in, 892(*m*), 893, 894, 896
Baltic region
Soviet Union and, 963
World War II in, 942
Balzac and the Little Chinese Seamstress (Sijie), 1044–1045
Bandung Conference (Indonesia, 1955), 971(*m*), 983–985, 984(*i*)
Bangalore, India, global service work in, 988(*i*)
Bangladesh, women in, 851(*i*)
Banking, in Gold Coast, 930(*b*)
al-Banna, Sheikh Hassan (founder of Muslim Brotherhood), 918(*i*)
Barbed wire, 801
Barnard, Christiaan, 995
Barriers to development, in global South, 1027
Barton, Clara, 850
Basmati seed, 1018
Basques, independence and, 1052
Bastille (Paris), storming of, 771
Battle of Britain, 942, 943(*m*), 945
Battle of the Somme, The (film), 901(*b*)
Battles. *See* Wars and warfare; specific battles and wars
Bay of Pigs, invasion of, 969
Beauvoir, Simone de, 981
Beijing, China
feminist gathering in, 1034
Gorbachev in, 1015
Tiananmen Square riots in (1989), 1015–1016, 1016(*i*)
Belarus, human rights and, 1049
Belgian Congo, 870
poll (head) tax in, 929
Belgium
Africa and, 865
World War I and, 897
World War II and, 942
Belief systems. *See also* Christianity; Hindus and Hinduism; Ideologies; Islam; Jews and Judaism; Muslims; Philosophy; Religion(s)
in China, 895
in Enlightenment, 762–765
in Mexico, 890(*i*)
non-Western impact on Western, 885–887, 886(*i*)
uniformity of, 847–848
in warfare, 947(*b*)
Bengal, famine in, 949
Benz, Karl (German car designer), 799
Berlin, postwar zones in, 964–965, 965(*m*)
Berlin airlift, 965
Berlin Conference, 867
Berlin Wall, 965
fall of, 1016
Bharatiya Janata Party (BJP, India), 1028
Bhopal, India, Union Carbide gas leak in, 1038
Bicycles, in cities, 1039
Big bang theory, of universe, 995
Big business, labor unions and, 932
Big Three (Roosevelt, Churchill, Stalin), 952
Bill of Rights (U.S.), 773
Bin Laden, Osama, 1045, 1046
Biology, molecular, 995
Biopiracy, 1018
Bird flu, 1044
Birth control, 995
Gandhi and, 917
in Nazi Germany, 938
population and, 1041
in Soviet Union, 918, 934
Birthrate
in Iran, 1041
in Soviet Union (1930s), 934
in Sweden, 939
Bismarck, Otto von (Prussia), 836, 837–838
Cameroon and, 866
Triple Alliance of, 896
Black market, in World War I, 902
Black Noise (musical group), 1051
Black power, 982, 1009
Blacks. *See also* African Americans
whites compared with, 766–767
Blacks and Tans, in Ireland, 910
Black Shirts (Italy), 918
Black Skin, White Masks (Fanon), 981
Blanc, Honoré (French inventor), 798
Blincoe, Robert (English author and former child laborer), 791–793, 813, 817

Blitz (Battle of Britain), 942, 943(*m*), 945
Blitzkrieg (lightning war), 941–942
Blockades, in World War I, 897, 908
Blood of the Revolutionary Martyrs Fertilizing the Earth (Rivera mural), 890(*i*)
Bloody Sunday (January 30, 1972), in Northern Ireland, 1045
Blue-collar workers, decline in, 999
Blues music, 848
Blum, Léon (French Socialist Party leader), 939
Bobby (film), 989, 991, 1002(*i*), 1003
Boers, 867, 881
Boer War, 881
Bogotá, 781
Bolaño, Roberto (Chilean writer and poet), 1050
Bolivar, Simon, 758(*i*), 759, 781, 783
Bolivia, 946(*b*)
  Bolivar in, 781
  in Mercosur, 1036
Bollywood, 989–991
Bolshevik Revolution (1917), 963
Bolsheviks
  civil war and, 903–904
  as Communists, 903
  takeover by, 903
Bombs and bombings. *See also* Nuclear weapons
  in England (2005), 1046
  in World War II, 945, 951
Bonafini, Hebe de (Argentinean activist), 1005
Bonaparte family. *See* Napoleon I
Bond, James (book and film character), 982
Book-burnings, in Nazi Germany, 937
Books. *See* Literature; specific works
Borges, Jorge Luis (Argentinean writer and poet), 920, 1050
Boriquen. *See* Puerto Rico
Borlaug, Norman (U.S. founder of Green Revolution), 996
Bose, Subhas (member of Indian Congress party), 949
Boston Tea Party (1773), 768
Botchan (Soseki), 879–880
Bourbon Reforms, 767
  in Spain, 765–766
Bourgeoisie, 812
  Marx on, 817
Boxer Rebellion (China, 1899–1900), 857, 860, 884, 895
Brain drain, 1001
  from South Africa, 1031(*m*)
Braun, Eva, 951
Brazil, 1029
  dictatorship in, 1005
  economy in, 998, 1029
  ethnic and racial exploitation in, 849
  independence of, 781–783
  industrialization in, 802
  in Mercosur, 1036
  modernization of, 829–831
  multinational corporations in, 1004(*m*)
  plantation workers in, 831(*i*)
  pollution of Cubotao in, 1018(*i*)
  Rio de Janeiro and, 977(*i*)
  slavery and, 830
  space program in, 967(*i*)
  television in, 993
  women in, 781(*i*)
Brest-Litovsk, Treaty of (1918), 903
Brezhnev, Leonid, 1011–1012
Brezhnev Doctrine, 1011–1012, 1016
Britain. *See also* England (Britain)
  Battle of, 942, 943(*m*), 945
British Commonwealth, World War I and, 897
British Empire. *See also* England (Britain)
  colonial crisis in (1764–1775), 768
  independence in, 970
Brotherhood, Muslim, 916, 917
Brown, Louise (first person successfully conceived through in vitro fertilization), 996
Brown v. Board of Education (1954), 981–982
Brunei Darussalam, in ASEAN, 1036
Buddha and Buddhism
  in Japan, 980
  Soka Gakkai, 1050
  Western study of, 886
Budget(s)
  deficit in United States, 1014
  reduction in government, during Great Depression, 929
Buenos Aires, 781, 919
  department stores in, 805
Buffer zone, Stalin and, 952
Bulgaria
  as autonomous state, 896, 898(*m*)
  in World War II, 942, 951
Bulgarians, nationalism of, 884
Burial(s), ancestral Native American, 1052
Burj al Arab (Dubai tower), 1022(*i*)
Burke, Edmund, 783
Burma (Myanmar), 944
  British in, 863
  ecological destruction in, 864
Business. *See also* Commerce; Corporations
  Chinese, 1031
  in Egypt, 865
  in Great Depression, 930(*b*)
  in Japan, 999(*b*)
  mergers of, 1033
  worldwide transactions of, 1036
Business imperialism, defined, 861. *See also* Imperialism
Byron, Lord, 761

Cairo, Egypt
  Kulthum, Umm, in, 959
  modernization of, 864
Calcutta, 929
Calendar, in France, 773
Call desk services, in Ireland, 1032
Cambodia, 1008
  genocide in, 971(*m*)
  U.S. invasion of, 1008
Cameroon, Germany and, 866
Camus, Albert (French writer and philosopher), 981
Canada
  British in, 768
  in NAFTA, 1036
  native children in, 849
  World War I and, 897
Candide (Voltaire), 763
Canisius, Edgar, in Congo Free State, 871(*b*)
Cape Colony, 867
  South African War and, 881
Capital (financial). *See also* Capitalism
  international flows of, 1033
Capitalism
  consumer, 805
  Marx on, 817
Caracas, 781
  Bolivar in, 759
Carbon dioxide, from fossil fuels, 1038
Car-free zones, 1039
Caribbean region, 912. *See also* specific locations
  migrants to, 814
  revolts in 18th century, 767
  slavery in, 777–778
Carnegie, Andrew, 802
Carson, Rachel, 1038
Cartels, 805
Casino Royale (Fleming), 982
Cassatt, Mary, 885
Castes and caste system. *See also* Class(es)
  cinematic portrayals and, 915
  Gandhi and, 917
  in India, 813
  of Spanish Empire and Brazil, 849
Castro, Fidel, 968–969, 993
Catherine the Great (Russia), 765, 766–767(*b*)
Catholic Church. *See* Roman Catholic Church
Cattle, raising of, 801
Caudillos (strongmen), in South America, 780–781, 831–832
Cavour, Camillo di (Italy), 827(*m*), 836–837
Ceauşescu, Nicolae (Romania), 1016
Censorship
  of films, 917(*b*)
  in Nazi Germany, 937
Central America. *See also* Latin America; specific locations
  1960–1992, 1004(*m*)
  protests for traditional rights, 1052
Central Asia
  British in, 863
  after Cold War (c. 1990), 1017(*m*)
  imperialism in, 861–862
  Russia in, 863
Central economic planning, in Soviet Union, 933
Central Europe, Peace of Paris in (1920), 906(*m*)
Central Intelligence Agency. *See* CIA (U.S.)
Centralization, political, 891
Central Powers (World War I), 896, 904
Ceramics, English, 796
Ceylon. *See* Sri Lanka
Chaco War (1932–1935), 946(*b*)
Chamberlain, Neville, 940
Chamber of Deputies (France), 939
Chaplin, Charlie, 915, 939
Charter Oath (Japan), 824(*i*)
Chavez, César, 1009
Chechens, terrorism by, 1046
Cheka (secret police), in Russia, 904

Chemicals
fertilizers and, 1018
industrial, 801
as pesticides, 1018
Chernobyl nuclear power plant, explosion at, 1038
Cherokee Indians, 840
Chew, Kunan (designer), 1022
Chiapas, Mexico, local liberation army in, 1052
Childbirth, scientific transformation of, 996
Child care, in Sweden, 939
Child labor, 813
in England, 814(*i*)
Children
during Great Depression, 931
in postindustrial families, 1002–1003
in Sudan, 1027
trafficking in, 1044
Chile
democracy in, 1005
industrialization in, 802
in Mercosur, 1036
San Martin in, 781
U.S. and, 1003–1004
women in, 1011
China
Communists in, 910, 911(*b*), 936, 965–966, 1031
conditions in (1900), 856(*i*)
consumerism in, 1032
Cultural Revolution in, 962, 979–980, 1002
disintegration of Qing, 807–809
economy in, 794, 997, 1030–1031
Enlightenment and, 764
famine in, 857
film industry in, 916(*i*), 917(*b*)
foreign trade in, 807
Great Leap Forward in, 978(*b*), 979
Guomindang in, 895
imperial conditions in (1850–1914), 857–860
Japan and, 868, 868(*m*), 910(*m*), 940–941
Manchurian Incident and, 935
Marx and, 817
May 4th Movement in, 910
migration and, 814, 858(*m*), 877, 1044
Nationalists in, 910
New Life Movement in, 935–936
opium and, 807
People's Republic of (1949), 965
population of, 1041
republic in, 895
resistance to imperialism in, 883–884
revolution in (1911–1912), 891–893, 895–896
Russia and, 863
silver in, 794
strikes in, 914
tea from, 807
Three Gorges Dam in, 1038
Tiananmen Square riots in (1989), 1015–1016, 1016(*i*)
U.S. and, 1002
women in, 851, 914, 965
Chinaware, Wedgwood pottery as, 796, 796(*i*)
Chinese Communist Party, 910, 1031
Chlorofluorocarbons (CFCs), 1038
Chon T'ae-il, 1008
Christianity
Hong Xiuquan and, 807
as world's largest faith, 1050
Church(es), in French Revolution, 784–785
Churchill, Winston, 942, 953
"Chutney" music, 1051
CIA (U.S.)
Allende (Chile) and, 1005
Castro and, 969
Cinema houses, 917(*b*)
Cities and towns. *See also* Urban areas
in Africa, 973
bombings of (World War II), 945, 951
car-free and bicycle zones in, 1039
global, 1031, 1036–1037
growth of, 913
in India, 1028
in Italy, 919
modernization of, 846
railroads in, 799
Citizens and citizenship
equality for women and, 770(*i*)
literacy and, 847
struggles for rights of, 851–852
women and, 850
Civil disobedience, 953–954
by Gandhi, 954–955
Civilians
in World War I, 900–902
in World War II, 945–950
Civil rights. *See also* Rights
for African Americans, 981–982
in Nazi Germany, 937
in United States, 849–852, 850(*i*)
Civil rights movement (U.S.), 954, 1009
Civil war(s)
in former Yugoslavia, 1016
in Russia, 903–904
in Sudan, 1027
in United States, 839(*m*), 840
Cixi (Chinese empress), 884
Class(es). *See also* Castes and caste system; specific groups
cinematic portrayals and, 915
in cities, 913
industrialization and, 914
Marx on, 816–817
after World War I, 914
Class conflict, in World War I, 902
Climate, greenhouse effect and, 1038
Cloning, 995
Cloth and clothing. *See also* Textiles and textile industry
migration of, 879
non-Western impact on Western, 886
Western dress in Turkey, 908–909
Clubs, political, 832
Coal and coal industry
cartel in Germany, 805
coke (refined coal), 832
decline of, 998–999
Coalitions
Napoleonic wars and, 774
in World War II, 928
Cochin China. *See also* Vietnam
France in, 864
Cocoa growers cooperative, 930(*b*)
Code Napoleon, 774, 783
Codes of law. *See also* Law(s)
of Napoleon, 774, 783
Coerced labor
of colonized peoples in World War II, 949, 949(*i*)
Jews in, 938
of Nazis, 945–946
World War I and, 905
Coerced migration, trafficking in children and women as, 1044
Cold War (1945–1989), 928, 959, 961, 963–965
alliances in, 965–969
beginning of, 952–953
culture of, 982–983
eastern Europe and central Asia after (c. 1990), 1017(*m*)
end of, 989–991, 1012–1017, 1023
nonalignment in, 984(*i*)
protests against, 1009
Southeast Asian nations and, 971(*m*)
Soviet Union and, 978–979
Vietnam War and, 1008
weapons production in, 976
world politics and, 962–969
Collaboration
on communications satellites, 994–995
in World War II, 949
Collective farms, in Soviet Union, 933–934
Collective security, 907
Collectivization
in China, 965
in eastern Europe, 964
Collectivized agriculture, in Soviet Union, 964
Colonialism. *See* Colonies and colonization
Colonies and colonization
American Revolution and, 768–771, 769(*m*)
British India as, 863
collaboration with Axis conquerors in, 949
decolonization and, 969–975
end of system, 961
Enlightenment and U.S. government, 764
exploitation in, 870
Great Depression in, 929
imperial culture and values in, 872(*b*), 872(*i*)
imperialism and, 861
independence revolts in, 910–911
Japanese, 883
mandate system and, 907–908, 907(*m*)
as markets, 869
medicine in, 872–873
in North America (1754–1789), 769(*m*)
protests during Depression in, 932
after World War I, 925
World War I and, 896, 897, 899–900, 904, 912(*b*)
World War II and, 944–945, 949, 949(*i*), 950(*i*)
CoMadres (El Salvador), 1006
Comintern (Communist International), 904
Commerce. *See also* Business; Trade
in Atlantic region, 767–768
in Japan, 802

Committee of Public Safety (France), 773
Common Market. *See* European Economic Community; European Union
Communication(s)
in Crimean War, 833
devices for, 988(*i*)
in industrial society, 815–816
technologies for, 893–894
Communications satellites, 993, 994–995
Communism. *See also* Communists
in China, 910, 911(*b*)
in eastern Europe, 962, 964
fall in eastern Europe, 1014–1017
fears of spread, 963–964
in Nazi Germany, 937
in Soviet Union, 978–979
Communist Manifesto, The (Marx and Engels), 816, 817
Communist parties
in China, 910, 1031
during Great Depression, 931
Indochinese, 932
Communists. *See also* Communism
Bolsheviks as, 903
in China, 965
McCarthy witch-hunt for, 983
Rivera, Diego, as, 890(*i*)
in Vietnam, 1008
Competition
for empire, 891
of global workers, 1033
of imperial powers, 880, 881–882
in Japan, 804
Computers, 993
Irish economy and, 1032
programmers for (1940s), 994(*i*)
Concentration camps
for Japanese Americans, 948–949
Nazi, 937, 945(*m*)
Conception, scientific transformation of, 996
Concord, Battle of, American Revolution and, 768, 769
Condition of the Working Class in England, The (Engels), 817
Confederate States of America, 840
Conflict. *See also* Revolts and rebellions; Violence; Wars and warfare
over African independence, 973–975
class, 902
global, 1025
in South Africa, 1029
in sub-Saharan Africa, 1027, 1027(*m*)
Conglomerates, 913
Congo
Belgium and, 865–866, 870
rubber workers in, 871(*b*)
Congress of Vienna (1814–1815), 774
Congress Party (India). *See* Indian Congress Party
Conscription. *See* Draft (military)
Consensus politics, in U.S. Constitution, 771
Conservatism, 783
in Japan, 826, 827
Constantinople. *See also* Istanbul
as Istanbul, 908
Constitution
Mexican (1917), 895
U.S., 770, 773
Constitutional Convention (U.S., 1787), 769–770
Constitutional monarchy, in Spain, 1007
Consumer capitalism, 805
Consumer prices, during Great Depression, 931
Consumers and consumerism, 915(*i*)
in China, 1031
global jobs and, 1032–1033
in United States, 982
Containment policy, 964, 967
Continental Congress, 768
Contraceptives. *See also* Birth control
oral, 995
Contract government, 763
Cook, Thomas (English entrepeneur), 1000–1001, 1001(*b*)
Cook's Tours, 1001(*b*)
Cooper, Maria (U.S. feminist activist), 852
Cooperative zones, 1035–1036
Corporations
conglomerates, 913
limited-liability, 805
multinational, 913, 998
Cosmetics industry, 915–916
Cosmonauts, 966–967(*b*), 966(*i*)
Cosmopolitanism, 879–880
Countryside. *See* Rural areas
Coups, in Soviet Union, 1016–1017
Covenant, of League of Nations, 907
Cowboys
gauchos as, 782(*b*), 782(*i*)
llaneros as, 781, 782(*b*)
vaqueros as, 782(*b*)
Craftworkers, Industrial Revolution and, 809
Credit, collapse of, 1047
Creoles
independence for, 779
in Latin America, 767, 780–781
Crick, Francis, 995
Crimean War (1853–1856), 833, 833(*m*)
Crimes against humanity, 980
Croatia, as EU membership candidate, 1035
Crops. *See also* Agriculture
in Egypt, 865
globalization of, 794
Cross-cultural exchange. *See also* Trade
Crystal Palace Exhibition (London, 1851), 1001(*b*)
Cuba, 968–969
during Great Depression, 931
nation building in, 832
Soviet aid to, 1003
Spanish-American War and, 881
sugar exports from, 975–976
television and, 993
Cuban missile crisis (1962), 961, 969
Cult of domesticity, 812
"Cult of personality," in Soviet Union, 979
"Cult of the offensive," 897
Cultural Revolution (China), 962, 979–980, 1002
Culture(s)
of Argentina, 920, 920(*i*)
during Chinese Revolution (1911–1912), 896
in Cold War, 980–983
communist, 918, 983
cosmopolitan, global, 915
democratic, 939
global, 879
in imperial age, 878–880
imperial impact on, 872(*b*), 872(*i*)
of industry, 815–817
Japanese, 935, 936
of liberation, 981–982
mass, 893–894, 914–916
mass proletarian, 918
Mexican Revolution's impact on, 895
national, 843–849
and political styles, 890(*i*)
uniformity of, 847–848
urban, 913
Westernization of Turkish, 908–909
Czechoslovakia
fall of communism in, 1016
Nazi invasion of, 940
Prague Spring in, 1011
Soviet Union and, 964
after World War I, 906, 906(*m*)

Daboya (king of Ghana), England and, 866
Dachau concentration camp, 937
Daimyo (local lord, Japan), 802
Dairy farming, 801
Daladier, Édouard (French premier), 940
Dams, environment and, 1038
Dance
Indian woman and, 879(*i*)
non-Western impact on Western, 886
tango, 920, 920(*i*)
Dangdut (Indonesian music), 1051, 1051(*i*)
Daratista, Inul (dangdut performer), 1051(*i*)
Dardanelles Strait, World War I and, 898
Darfur, 1027
Darwin, Charles, 845, 861
Das Kapital (Marx), 816
Davis, Angela, 1011
Davos forum, 1034
D-Day invasion, 951
Death. *See* Burial(s); Mortality
Death camps. *See also* Concentration camps
memoirs of, 980
Debt
in Brazil, 1029
fraudulent, 1047
Debussy, Claude, 886
Declaration of Human Rights (UN), 1049
Declaration of Independence (U.S.), 768
"Declaration of the Rights of Man and Citizen" (France), 772, 773
"Declaration of the Rights of Woman and the Female Citizen," 772
Decolonization, 958(*i*), 959–961, 969–975
Decorative objects. *See* Art(s)
De Gaulle, Charles, Free French and, 949–950, 975
De Kooning, Willem, 983
Delhi, British in, 863

Democracy
during Great Depression, 927–928
in India, 1028
in Latin America, 1003–1006
in Middle East, 1047
Demography. *See also* Population
population and, 1040–1041
Demonstrations. *See also* Protest(s); Resistance; Revolts and rebellions
in Egypt, 972
in South Korea, 1007
Deng Xiaoping (China), 1030, 1041
Denmark
German war with, 838
slave trade and, 810
World War II in, 942
Department stores, 805–806, 806(*i*)
Depressions (economic). *See also* Great Depression
in China, 807
Detention camps, of Cheka, 904
Developed nations, research in, 1001
Developing nations
economic inequities in, 984–985
research in, 1001
Diary of a Young Girl (Frank), 980
Diaspora, 877
contemporary popular music and, 1051
migration and, 874–878
Diaz, Porfirio, 891, 894, 895
Dickens, Charles, 817
Dictators and dictatorships
in Brazil, 1029
in Korea, 1007
in Latin America, 1003–1006
in Uganda, 1007, 1007(*i*)
Diderot, Denis, 764
Dien Bien Phu, Battle of (1954), 972
Diplomacy, U.S.-China, 1002
Disabled people, in Nazi Germany, 938
Discrimination
racial, in U.S., 938
in South Africa, 1023
Diseases, 1027. *See also* AIDS
in colonies, 873
global spread of, 1042(*m*)
influenza epidemic (1918–1919), 904–905
research after World War II, 995
vaccines and drugs for, 1041
of workers, 813–814
Dissent. *See also* Protest(s); Revolts and rebellions
in Soviet Union, 983
Diversity. *See also* Ethnic groups
in Balkan region, 896
global migration and, 1024(*m*)
Division of labor, sexual, 815
DNA, 995
Doctors Without Borders, 1031, 1032(*i*), 1034
Doctor Zhivago (Pasternak), 983
Doll's House, A (Ibsen), 880
Domesticity, after World War II, 982(*i*)
Dominican Republic, 777
Domino effect, in Asia, 967–968
Dostoevsky, Fyodor, 845
Douglass, Frederick, 850(*i*), 851
Draft (military)
of colonized peoples, 949
in Japan, 842
Draft-dodging, 947(*b*)
Drama, non-Western impact on Western, 885–886
Dresden, firebombing of, 945
Drought, 1041
in colonies, 873
Dual monarchy, in Austria-Hungary, 896
Dubai, Burj al Arab in, 1022(*i*)
Dubçek, Alexander (Czechoslovakia), 1011, 1016
Du Bois, W. E. B., 908
Duma (Russian parliament), 883, 902
Dutch. *See also* Boers; Netherlands
colonial protests and, 911
Indonesian independence and, 971
Japan and, 802
"Dutch Studies," in Japan, 764
Duties. *See* Taxation

Earth. *See* Astronomy; Environment
Earthquakes, in Japan, 935
East Africa. *See also* Africa
Germany and, 866, 885
resistance to imperialism in, 872
violence in, 973
World War I in, 902, 904
East Asia. *See* Asia; specific locations
East Berlin, Berlin Wall and, 1016
Eastern Europe. *See also* specific locations
after Cold War (c. 1990), 1017(*m*)
consumerism in, 1032
fall of communism in, 1014–1017
Peace of Paris in (1920), 906(*m*)
as Soviet buffer zone, 964
Eastern front, in World War I, 897
Easter rebellion (Ireland, 1916), 910
East Germany, 964(*m*), 965
Berlin Wall and, 1016
East Prussia, World War I in, 897
Ebadi, Shirin (Iran), 1049
Ebola virus, 1044
Ecology. *See also* Environment
of Africa, 868–869
changes in human community and, 1038
Economic classes. *See* Class(es)
Economic depressions. *See* Depressions; Great Depression
Economy and economic systems. *See also* Great Depression; Industrial Revolution; Industry; Livelihood(s); Trade
abolition of slavery and, 810
in Argentina, 919
balance of power in, 1023
in Brazil, 1029
in China, 794, 997, 1030–1031
consumer, 1032–1033
crises and solutions in 19th century, 804–806
in developing countries, 984
in Egypt, 864, 865
expansion of prosperity, 976–978
global, 996–1003, 1027, 1047
global North vs. South and, 1026–1027
growth after World War II, 975–978
in India, 794, 976, 1028
in Industrial Revolution, 794
in Ireland, 1032
in Japan, 935, 996–997
in Korea, 1007
Marxian socialism and, 816–817
in Mexico, 893
modernization of, 913
as motive for migration, 1044
in Nazi Germany, 937
neoliberalism and, 1033
in 1970s, 1014
in North Africa, 865
postindustrial, 991
in Russia, 834
Smith, Adam, on, 763–764
in South Korea, 996–997
Soviet, 918, 933–934, 963
in Sweden, 938
in United States, 963
in the West, 1014
Ecosystems. *See also* Environment
global warming and, 1038
Education
family life and, 1002–1003
reforms of, 846–847
of Russian serfs, 834
Edward VII (England), celebration for, 880(*i*)
EEC. *See* European Economic Community
Egypt. *See also* Cairo
Ali, Muhammad, in, 761, 776, 809
Arab spring in, 1047(*i*)
Aswan Dam in, 1038
economy in, 864, 865
modernization of, 864, 864(*m*)
Muslim Brotherhood in, 916, 917
Napoleon and, 760, 774, 776, 776(*i*)
Nasser and, 972–973
nationalism in, 959
revolt in, 911
in Six-Day War, 1013
Suez Canal and, 864
uprising in, 1046
in Yom Kippur War, 1013
Eiffel Tower, 800
Einstein, Albert, 952(*b*)
Eisenhower, Dwight, 967
Electricity, 800, 815–816
Electronic circuits, 993
Electronic networks, for protests, 1047
Elites. *See also* Class(es)
in Africa, 810
in Argentina, 919
in Egypt, 775–776
imperialism and, 869–870
in military, 947(*b*)
in Soviet Union, 933
El Niño
famine from, 869
taxation during, 873
El Saadawi, Nawal (Egyptian feminist and writer), 1051
El Salvador, terror and resistance in, 1006(*b*)
Emancipation, of Russian serfs, 834–836, 834(*i*)

Emigration. *See also* Immigrants and immigration; Migration
of Jews from Nazi Germany, 938
Emile (Rousseau), 763
Emissions, environmental damage from, 1038
Emperors. *See also* Empires; specific empires and rulers
in Japan, 825, 841–842
Empires. *See also* Imperialism; specific empires and rulers
arts and, 879–880
in Asia, 970–972
German, 838
race for, 891
World War I and, 893
Empire State Building, 913
Employment. *See also* Livelihood(s); Work
in global manufacturing, 1023
global networks and, 1032–1033
during Great Depression, 931
as managers, 805
of samurai, 802–803
of women, 815
Enabling Act (1933), 937
Encouragement of Learning (Fukuzawa Yukichi), 845
Encyclopedia (Diderot), 764
Energy crisis, oil embargo and, 1013–1014
Enfield rifles, 863
Engels, Friedrich, 817
Engineering
German, 802
industrial, 799–800
England (Britain). *See also* Britain; World War I; World War II
abolition of slave trade in, 810
Africa and, 866
American Revolution and, 768–769
at Battle of Omdurman, 868
Bengali famine and, 949
Blitz in, 942, 943(*m*), 945
child labor in, 814(*i*)
colonial protests and, 911
colonial taxation by, 768
contract government in, 763
Egypt and, 865
18th century drawing room in, 765(*i*)
expansion of, 863–864
Germany after World War II and, 964–965, 965(*m*)
Great Awakening in, 785
during Great Depression, 929
imperialism by, 912
India and, 813(*i*), 916–917, 929, 932
Industrial Revolution in, 794, 795–796
industry in, 797(*b*)
innovation in, 796
Ireland and, 910
labor unions and, 914
Luddites in, 814
Napoleon and, 776
opium trade and, 807
Palestine and, 972
at Paris Peace Conference, 905
revolt by Nigerian women against, 953
as secular state, 784–785
after Seven Years' War, 768
South Africa and, 867–868, 867(*i*)
South African War and, 881
Suez crisis and, 973
Thatcher in, 1014
tourism in, 1001
in Triple Entente, 896
women in, 773
World War I and, 897
English East India Company (EIC), 810, 862–863
Enlightenment, 761, 762–771
in American colonies, 769
French Revolution and, 772
ideas in, 762–765
Old Order and, 765–767
revolts in, 767
spread of, 764
Entertainment, after World War II, 993
Entrepreneurs, industrial, 798–799
Environment. *See also* Ecosystems
of Africa, 866
consequences of British in Burma, 864
global, 1039(*m*)
as global issue, 1038–1040
imperialism and, 868–869, 871–872
Epidemic disease. *See also* Diseases
influenza as, 904–905
Equal Employment Opportunity Commission (U.S.), 1009
Equality
for African Americans, 1009
racial and gender, 852
for women, 1010
Española. *See* Hispaniola
Espionage. *See* Spies and spying
Esquivel, Laura, 1050
Estates General (France), 771
Estonia, 942
Ethiopia
famine in, 1041
Mussolini's invasion of, 940, 940(*m*)
Ethnic groups and ethnicity
in Africa, 868
in Balkans, 896
diasporas of, 877
as global issue, 1038
as outsiders, 849
strife among, 1052
in Yugoslavia, 1016
Eurasia. *See* Asia; Europe and Europeans; specific locations
Euro (European Currency Unit), 1034
Europe and Europeans. *See also* specific locations and groups
in Africa, 865–868
China and, 857
economy and, 913
Enlightenment and, 762–767
Indian outsourcing for, 1032
industrialization in (c. 1900), 795–796
Japanese expansion and, 868
Napoleonic (1796–1815), 775(*m*)
postwar prosperity and, 976
production and, 794–795
U.S. Great Plains and, 840–841
U.S. aid to, 964
European Economic Community (Common Market), 976, 1026, 1034
European Recovery Program. *See* Marshall Plan
European Union (EU), 1026, 1034
membership of (to 2010), 1034–1035
Europe first strategy (World War II), 944(*m*), 951
Evangelicalism, in Great Awakening, 785
Evil empire, communist world as, 1014
Exchange. *See also* Trade
expansion and, 891
Exercise, non-Western impact on Western, 886
Existentialism, 980–981
Expansion. *See also* Imperialism
by Germany, 926(*m*)
by Italy, 926(*m*)
by Japan, 926(*m*), 935–936, 935(*m*)
migration and, 874–875
Nazi, 940, 941(*m*)
in 19th century, 857
overseas, by Western powers, 891
postwar imperial, 912–913
Russian, 832–833
of United States, 838–841
Exploration. *See* Space exploration
Exports, of Russian grain, 836
Extermination camps, 945, 945(*m*)

Factories. *See also* Industrialization; Industry
in India, 810
in Japan, 803
Luddites and, 814
Faisal (Syria), 908
Families
in China, 1041
female support of, 815
during Great Depression, 931
postindustrial, 1002–1003
standardization of, 1053
in Sweden, 939
Family (Pa Chin), 939
Family planning, 1041
centers for, 931
Famine, 1041. *See also* Starvation
in Africa, 868
in Asia, 868
in China, 857
in colonies, 873
in India, 949
Fanon, Frantz, 981, 981(*i*), 982
Farms and farming. *See also* Agriculture; Crops
collective farms, 933–934
dairy farming, 801
government protection of, 1018–1019
during Great Depression, 929, 931
in Mexico, 891
multinational corporations and, 1018
scientific techniques for, 1017
women in Africa and, 818–819
Fascism. *See also* Italy; Nazi Germany; Spain
in France, 939
of Mussolini, 918–919

Federalism, in Latin America, 831
Federation, in United States, 769
Female infanticide, in China, 1041
Females. *See* Women
Feminine Mystique, The (Friedan), 1010
Femininity, during World War I, 900–902
Feminists
  activism by, 1009–1010
  as authors, 1050–1051
  Brezhnev and, 1012
  global meetings by, 1034
  nationalism and, 884–885
  pacifism and, 954
  World War I and, 900
Fertilizers, 801
  chemicals and, 1018
Fiji, 877
Filipino people, U.S. and, 881–882
Films, 893, 914
  in Bollywood, 989
  star system in, 917(*b*)
  about warfare, 980
  after World War I, 915, 916–917(*b*)
  World War I propaganda in, 901(*b*)
  in World War II, 948
"Final Solution," Holocaust as, 945
Firearms. *See* Weapons
First Balkan War (1912), 892(*m*), 896
First World War. *See* World War I
Fitness, non-Western impact on Western, 886
Five Pillars of Islam, 1050
Five-year plans (Soviet Union), 933
Flags, as national symbols, 844(*b*), 844(*i*)
Flappers, 914, 915
Fleming, Ian, 982
FLN. *See* Front for National Liberation
Florida, British in, 768
Flowering Plum Tree (Van Gogh), 886(*i*)
Flying shuttle, 798
Foods. *See* Agriculture; Crops; Farms and farming; specific foods
Foot-binding, in China, 851
Ford, Henry, violence against unemployed workers and, 932
Foreign aid
  to defeated enemies, 964(*i*)
  to Europe, 963–964
  to Japan, 964, 964(*i*)
  to Latin America, 1003–1004
Foreign-born population, of United States, 1044
Foreigners, in Japan, 803–804, 825
Formosa, Japanese invasion of, 868
Fossil fuels, gases from burning, 1038
Fourteen Points, 905
France. *See also* French Revolution; World War I
  Algeria and, 974–975
  Alsace and Lorraine and, 802
  colonial uprisings and, 911, 932
  colonies of, 869
  education in, 847
  Egypt and, 864, 865
  expansion of, 863, 864
  Germany after World War II and, 964–965, 965(*m*)
  Haiti and, 777–778
  imperialism by, 912
  independence of African nations and, 974
  Indochina and, 864, 885
  Italian unification and, 837
  July 14 as national holiday, 771
  in North Africa, 865
  at Paris Peace Conference, 905
  Popular Front in, 939
  republicanism in, 773–774
  response to Great Depression, 939
  Saint-Domingue and, 777
  as secular state, 784–785
  in Southeast Asia, 864
  strike in, 1010
  Suez crisis and, 973
  in Triple Entente, 896
  U.S. consumerism and, 982
  women in, 773, 774
  World War I and, 897, 905
  World War II in, 942
Franco, Francisco, Spain after, 1006–1007
Franco-Prussian War (1870–1871), 838, 897
Frank, Anne, 980
Franklin, Benjamin, Enlightenment and, 764
Franz Ferdinand (Austria-Hungary), 896
Frederick the Great (Prussia), 765
Free blacks, in Haiti, 777
Freedom(s). *See also* Rights
  economic, 763–764
Free France, 949–950
  de Gaulle and, 975
Free labor. *See also* Labor; Slaves and slavery
  costs of production and, 797
Free soil, in United States, 840
Freetown, Sierra Leone, 872
Free trade, 1027
  zones, 1034–1036
French Indochina. *See also* Indochina
  World War II in, 944
French Revolution (1789–1799), 771–774
  European war against, 773
  Napoleon and, 774
French West Africa, independence in, 974
Freud, Sigmund, 886
Friedan, Betty, 1010
Front for National Liberation (FLN, Algeria), 974, 975
Fundamentalist Muslims, Taliban as, 1008

Gagarin, Yuri (Soviet cosmonaut), 966, 966–967(*b*), 966(*i*)
Galicia, World War I in, 897
Gallipoli, Battle of, 898–899
Gandhi, Indira, assassination of, 1045
Gandhi, Mohandas (Mahatma), 958(*i*)
  activism by, 916–917
  assassination of, 970
  civil disobedience by, 954–955
  jailing of, 932
  Satyagraha strategy of, 954, 954(*i*)
Gandhi, Rajiv, assassination of, 1045
Gao Xingjian (China), 1038
García Márquez, Gabriel, 920, 1050
Garibaldi, Giuseppe (Italy), 837
Garvey, Marcus, 981
Gasoline engine, 799–800
Gath y Chaves (department store), 805, 806(*i*)
Gays. *See also* Homosexuality
  equal rights for, 1011
Gaza, 1013
Gebriel, Mohammed (Sheik), 1048
Gender and gender issues
  cultural change and, 878
  during Great Depression, 931
  in Nazi Germany, 937
  World War I and, 900–902
  youth culture and, 1003
General will, in France, 773
Genetics, 995
  modification of plants and animals, 1017, 1018
Geneva Conference (1954), 972
Genocide
  in Armenia (1915–1917), 1049
  in Cambodia, 971(*m*)
  Holocaust as, 925
  in Rwanda, 1049
George V (England), 899
German East Africa, 866, 872, 885
German Empire, 838
Germany. *See also* Nazi Germany; World War I; World War II
  Africa and, 865
  Alsace and Lorraine and, 802
  coal cartel in, 805
  East Africa and, 866
  historiography in, 846(*b*), 846(*i*)
  industrialization of, 802
  international capital flows and, 1033
  League of Nations and, 907
  mutinies and rebellions in, 904
  Napoleon and, 774
  nation building in, 837–838
  postwar division of, 964–965, 965(*m*)
  reparations and, 906
  reunification of (1990), 1016
  Schlieffen Plan of, 897
  Treaty of Versailles and, 906–907
  in Triple Alliance, 896
  unification of (1871), 837–838, 838(*m*)
  war guilt and, 907
  World War I and, 896, 897
  World War I homefront in, 900
Gestapo, 937
Ghana
  cocoa protest in, 932
  England and, 866
  independence of, 958(*i*), 973
Glasnost (openness), 1015
Glenn, John, 967(*b*)
Global economy, 996–1003. *See also* Economy and economic systems
  neoliberalism and, 1033
  networks and job changes in, 1032–1033
  trade in, 794–795
  United States in, 770–771
Global issues, 1037–1047
  economic crisis as, 1047
  migration as, 1044–1045
  terrorism as, 1045–1047

Globalization, 860–861, 1024(*m*), 1025. *See also* Global issues
of cities, 1036–1037
of communications linkages, 995
culture and, 878–879
environment and, 1039(*m*)
ethnic strife and, 1052
global activism and, 1034
impact of events on regions and nations, 1026–1031
of literature and music, 1050–1051
livelihood and, 1031–1037
migration and, 1024(*m*)
protecting tradition and, 1052–1053, 1052(*i*)
resistance to, 1025–1026
of technology, 988(*i*)
of trade and finance, 859–860
worker competition and, 1033
Global networks, 1032–1033
Global politics, terrorism in, 1045
Global recovery, in 1950s and 1960s, 975–980
Global structures and organizations. *See also* Globalization
Cold War alliances and, 967–969
economic development and, 1027
supranational, 1033–1036
Global trade, 796–798
Global war, World War I as, 893, 896
Global warming, 1038
Gold Coast
British in, 870
cocoa growers cooperative in, 930(*b*)
Nkrumah in, 973
Gold standard, England and, 929
"Good wives, wise mothers," in Japan, 848(*b*)
Gorbachev, Mikhail (Soviet Union), 991–992, 1002
KGB coup against, 1016–1017
reforms of, 1014–1015
Gouges, Olympe de, 764, 766, 772, 773
Governance. *See* Government
Government
of Brazil, 1029
changes in nature of, 925
contract, 763
economies and, 805
of Egypt, 775
farm protection by, 1018–1019
imperial, 870
intellectual thought on, 763, 764
in Latin America, 1003–1006
of Meiji Japan, 842
Nazi, 937
religion and, 785
responses to Great Depression, 929, 932
of South Africa, 1029–1030
standard of living and, 977
TV programming and, 993
of United States, 769–771
during World War I, 900, 901(*b*)
Grain
Russian exports of, 836
science and, 996
Gran Colombia, 781
Grand Alliance (World War II), 945
Grand Army (France), 775(*m*)
Grass-roots activism, in farming, 1018
Great Awakening, 785
Great Britain. *See* England (Britain)
Great Depression (1929–1941), 919, 926(*m*), 927
business in, 930(*b*)
commodity prices in, 929
communism and socialism ideologies during, 932(*i*)
democracies responses to, 938–939
gender relations during, 931
government response to, 929
protests during, 931–932
social effects of, 930–931
U.S. stock market crash and, 927, 928–929
Greater East Asia Co-Prosperity Sphere, 941
"Greater Serbia," 1016
Great Game, imperialism in Asia as, 862
Great Leap Forward (China), 978(*b*), 979
Great Plains (North America), Native Americans in, 840
Greece
as autonomous state, 896, 898(*m*)
communists in, 963
EU and, 1035
invasion of Turkey, 909(*m*)
U.S. aid to, 964
Green, William (head of American Federation of Labor), 932
Greenhouse effect, 1038
Green movement. *See* Green Party; Green Revolution
Green Party, 1038
Green Revolution, 996
in India, 1028(*i*)
Griot (oral poet), 848
Guadalcanal, Battle of, 944(*m*), 951
Guam, 944
U.S. annexation of, 881
Guatemala
tradition in, 1052
U.S. and, 1003–1004
Guerilla warfare, in Indonesia, 971
Guerrero, Vicente, 779–780
Guest workers, 976
Guevara, Che, 981, 1011(*i*)
Guillotine, in France, 773
Gulag Archipelago (Solzhenitsyn), 1012
Gulags, in Soviet Union, 934
Guomindang (China), 895, 910, 935–936

Habsburg dynasty
Balkan wars and, 896
Peace of Paris treaties and, 906
Hague, The
International Tribunal on human rights abuses and, 1049
peace meeting in, 900
Hai-Feng Peasant Union, 911(*b*)
Haiku poetry, 885
Haiti, revolution in, 777–778, 778(*m*), 779(*i*)
Hamilton, Alexander, 769, 770
Hargreaves, James, 798
Hawaii
U.S. annexation of, 881
U.S. overthrow of queen in, 882(*b*)
Head, Bessie (South African writer), 981
Health. *See also* Diseases; Medicine
in colonies, 872–873
as global issue, 1037, 1041–1044
HIV/AIDS crisis and, 1030
vaccines and, 1041
of workers, 813–814
after World War II, 977
Health care. *See also* Health; Medicine
in South Africa, 1029
Heart transplant, 995
Helsinki Accords (1975), 1049
Heresy. *See* Christianity
Herzl, Theodor (founder of Zionism), 851
Hidalgo, Miguel (Mexican rebel leader), 779, 780
Higher education, for postindustrial economy, 991
High-tech industries, 993–994, 997–998
High-tech society, agrarian peoples and, 1017–1019, 1018(*i*)
Hijackings, on September 11, 2001, 1045
Hind Swaraj (Indian Home Rule), 917
Hindus and Hinduism
nationalism of, 885
Partition of India and, 970
Western study of, 886
Hip-hop music, 1051
Hirohito (Japan), 935, 945
Hiroshige, Ando, 803(*i*), 817
Hiroshima, atomic bombing of, 951, 952(*b*), 952(*i*)
Hispaniola, 777
History and historiography
nationalism and, 844–845
on nation-states, 829, 846(*b*)
Hitler, Adolf, 927, 933, 945. *See also* Nazi Germany
expansionism of, 940
Lebensraum and, 940
masses and, 924(*i*)
propaganda use by, 937
rise to power of, 936–938
suicide of, 951
World War II and, 947–948
young people and, 924(*i*), 937
HIV. *See also* AIDS
in 2009, 1042(*m*)
Ho Chi Minh (Vietnam), 932, 960(*m*), 971, 971(*m*), 983
Holidays, in France, 773
Holland. *See* Dutch; Netherlands
Holocaust, 925, 945–947, 945(*m*)
Israel and, 972
Home front, in World War I, 900–902
Home rule, for India, 917
Homosexuality
criminalization in Soviet Union, 934
gay rights and, 1011
Nazis and, 947
Honda, Soichiro, 998
Hong Kong, 970, 997, 1036
British in, 914, 970
Hong Xiuquan (China), 807
Horses, Latin American cowboys and, 782(*b*), 782(*i*)

Horticulture. *See* Ecosystems
Hostage crisis, in Iran (1979), 1009, 1010(*b*), 1010(*i*)
Hotel industry, 1001(*b*)
Housing, non-Western impact on Western, 886
Hu, Butterfly (Chinese film star), 916(*i*), 917(*b*)
Huerta, Dolores (U.S. civil rights activist), 1009
Human rights
activism for, 1049
Bandung Conference and, 984
as global value, 1049
in Soviet Union, 1012
Hungary
Peace of Paris treaties and, 906
rebellion in (1956), 979
Soviet Union and, 964
in World War II, 942, 951
Hunger, scientific advances against, 996
Hunter's Sketches, A (Turgenev), 834
Hydroelectric power, from dams, 1038
Hydrogen bomb, 963
Hygiene, promotion of, 915–916

IBM, 998
Ibo women's tax protest, 911
Ibsen, Henrik, 880
Ice, global melting of, 1038, 1040(*i*)
Ideas
in Enlightenment, 762–765
non-Western impact on Western, 886
Identity
in globalizing world, 1052–1053, 1053(*i*)
local, 827
national, 827–828
resistance to globalization and, 1025–1026
Ideologies
communication technology and political, 893–894
communism in Depression and, 932(*i*)
conservatism as, 783
Japanese military, 944–945
liberalism as, 763, 783
nationalism as, 783
revolutionary Marxism as, 903, 904
romanticism as, 783
socialism in Depression and, 932(*i*)
Immigrants and immigration. *See also* Migration
to Argentina, 919
in global cities, 1036
to United States, 769
Imperialism. *See also* Empires
arts and, 879–880
business, 861, 998
competition among powers and, 881–882
contests over, 880–885
culture and, 878–880
decolonization and, 969
defined, 860–861
1850–1914, 858(*m*)
environment and, 868–869, 871–872
European cooperation with, 869–870
global (1930s), 940
governments under, 870
by Japan, 868
migration and, 874–875
motivations for, 861
nationalism and, 959
new, 925
post–World War I expansion, 912–913
resistance to, 883–885
scramble for Africa and, 867–868
social disorder under, 870–871
society under, 869–878, 872(*b*), 872(*i*)
technology and, 868–869
tensions from, 894
by United States, 881–882
World War I and, 893, 897
Impressionism, 817
Inca people, revolt in 18th century by, 767
Income tax, cuts for wealthy, 1014
Indenture and indentured labor, 876–877(*b*), 876(*i*)
Independence
in Africa, 975
African textile for, 975(*b*), 975(*i*)
for Algeria, 975
decolonization and, 969–975
in Haiti, 778, 778(*m*)
in Latin America, 759–761, 778–783, 832
in Middle East, 972–973
movements for, 932, 960(*m*)
nation builders after, 847–848
in sub-Saharan Africa, 958(*i*)
after World War I, 908–911
India. *See also* Pakistan
Amritsar massacre in, 911
anti-British nonviolent mass movement in, 916–917
Awadh takeover and, 863
Basmati rice from, 1018
Britain and, 813(*i*), 861, 862–863
castes in, 914
celebration for Edward VII in, 880(*i*)
classes, castes, and religious divisions in, 914
consumerism in, 1032
economy in, 794, 976, 1028
Gandhi, Indira, and, 1045
Gandhi, Mohandas, in, 916–917
general strike in, 932
imperial government in, 870
indentured workers in, 877
independence for, 970
industrialization in, 810, 810(*m*)
literature in, 879
middle-class family in, 813(*i*)
movies in, 915
nationalism in, 885, 958(*i*)
opium in, 809(*i*)
outsourcing in, 1032
partition of (1947), 970(*m*)
population control in, 1041
protection of farmers in, 1018–1019
railroads in, 810
resistance to imperialism in, 872
Russia and, 863
sepoys in, 863
strikes in, 914
taxation of, 929
tea from, 807
textiles from, 810
Untouchables in, 813
World War I soldiers from, 897
World War II in, 949
Indian Congress Party, 949, 1028
Indian National Congress, 863, 885
Indians. *See* Native Americans; specific groups
Indian Uprising (1857), 863
Indigenous peoples. *See also* Native Americans
as outsiders, 849–850
Indochina. *See also* Cambodia; Laos; Vietnam
France and, 864, 885
nationalists in, 911, 971
Indochinese Communist Party, 932
Indonesia, 911, 944
in ASEAN, 1036
independence for, 970
Industrialization. *See also* Industrial Revolution; Industry
in Africa, 810–812
in China, 978(*b*)
in colonies, 873
costs of, 804
after 1830, 798–806
in Europe (c. 1900), 795–796
European expansion and, 891
global roots of, 794–795
in India, 810, 810(*m*)
innovation and, 796, 799–802
interchangeability of parts and, 798
in Japan, 802–804, 804(*m*), 935(*m*)
middle class and, 812–813
migration and, 874–875
non-European, 802–804
railroads and, 790(*i*)
in Soviet Union, 933, 963
spread of, 792(*m*)
in United States, 802
workers and, 791–793, 813–815
Industrial Revolution, 791–793
Crimean War and, 833
in England, 794, 795–796
middle class and, 812–813
periods of, 800–801
in western Europe, 794
world and, 806–812
Industry
arts and, 817
culture of, 815–817
in Depression, 929
environmental damage from, 1038
everyday life and (1750–1900), 791–793
globalization of, 794
resources for, 797
in rural England, 797(*b*)
slavery and, 797
society and, 812–815
technology of, 798
women and children in, 813
after World War I, 913
Influenza, epidemic of (1918–1919), 904–905
Information evolution, 993–994
Infrastructure
colonial taxation and, 873
in Latin America, 832

Innovation. *See also* Inventions; Technology
industrial, 796, 799–802
in Japan, 802–803
Institute for Production and Research in Tropical Agriculture (Venezuela), 1018
Institutions
global, 1031–1037
national, 846–849
Intellectual thought
in Enlightenment, 763–765
industrial knowledge and, 812–813
non-Western impact on Western, 886
after World War II, 980–981
Intelsat I and *III*, 994
Interchangeability of parts, 798
Interest rates, in mid-1970s, 1014
International Exhibit (Paris, 1889), 800
International Monetary Fund, 1027
International order, changes in, 1006–1009
International organizations. *See also* specific organizations
Cold War alliances and, 967
economic development and, 1027
International trade. *See* Trade
International Tribunal (The Hague), human rights abuses and, 1049
International Women's Day, in Russia, 902
International women's movement, 900
Internet, global employment and, 1032
Interpretation of Dreams, The (Freud), 886
Interstate relations. *See* Commerce; Diplomacy; Wars and warfare
Intervention, in society, 977
Invasions, of Iraq by U.S., 1045–1046
Inventions. *See also* Innovation; specific inventions
in Japan, 804
In vitro fertilization, 996
iPhone, 988(*i*)
Iran. *See also* Persia
hostage crisis in (1979), 1009, 1010(*b*), 1010(*i*)
population growth in, 1041
religious uprising in, 1008–1009
revolt in, 911
Iraq
independence for, 973
U.S. invasion of (2003), 1045
wars in (2001–2011), 1046(*m*)
Ireland. *See also* Northern Ireland
Easter rebellion in, 910
economy of, 1032
in 1921, 910(*m*)
Irish Free State, 910
Irish Republican Army, 1045
Iron curtain, 953
Irrigation, in colonies, 873
Islam. *See also* Muslims
expansion of, 1050
in Kazan, 1048
Muslim Brotherhood and, 918
nationalism in Ottoman Empire and, 884
in Sudan, 1027
Wahhabism in, 785–786, 785(*i*)
Israel. *See also* Jews and Judaism
Arab wars with, 1013
Palestine and (1949), 972(*m*)
in Six-Day War, 1013
Suez crisis and, 973
Istanbul. *See also* Constantinople
British in, 908
Italy
in Africa, 865
Cavour and, 836
Ethiopia and, 940, 940(*m*)
expansion by, 926(*m*)
fascism in, 918–919
Mussolini in, 916, 918–919
Napoleon and, 774
paramilitary groups in, 946(*b*)
Red Brigades in, 1045
Treaty of London and, 897
in Triple Alliance and Entente, 896
unification of, 836–837, 837(*m*)
World War II in, 951
Iturbide, Augustin de, 779–780

Jacobin club, 773
Jainism, nonviolence and, 953
Janissaries (Ottoman Empire), 775
Japan
Ainu in, 849
Asian imperialism by, 862(*m*)
atomic bombing of, 963
business practices in, 999(*b*)
China and, 868, 868(*m*), 884, 904, 910, 910(*m*), 935–936
colonization by, 883
earthquake in, 935
economy in, 976, 996–997
c. 1860–1889, 842
Enlightenment and, 764
expansion by, 926(*m*), 935–936, 935(*m*), 940–941
films in, 917(*b*)
foreigners in, 803–804
Great Depression in, 931, 935
Greater East Asia Co-Prosperity Sphere of, 941
high-tech industries in, 997–998
imperialism by, 868
Indonesian independence and, 970
industrialization in, 802–804, 803(*i*), 804(*m*)
industrial museum in, 812–813
Korea and, 868, 883
literature in, 879
Meiji Restoration in, 824(*i*)
merchants in, 803
militaristic imperial system in, 935
militarization in, 932
modernization of, 841–843
at Paris Peace Conference, 905
research and development in, 1001(*b*)
Russia and, 868
Russo-Japanese War and, 882–883
Siberia and, 904
tourism workers in, 1000–1001(*b*), 1000(*i*)
trade and, 798, 803–804
U.S. aid to, 964, 964(*i*)
Western arts and, 885
Westernization of, 845
women in, 848(*b*)
woodblocks in, 817
workday in, 813
after World War I, 912–913
in World War I, 896
in World War II, 940–941
Japanese Americans, relocation of, 948–949
Japan in the National Emergency (film), 936
Jazz, 848
Jefferson, Thomas
Continental Congress and, 768
Enlightenment and, 764
Jennings, Samuel (U.S. painter), 770(*i*)
Jesuits, in Spanish America, 766
Jews and Judaism
in Argentina, 919
Holocaust against, 925, 945–947, 945(*m*)
homeland for, 972
migrations in 19th century, 858(*m*)
in Nazi Germany, 937, 938
pogroms against, 875
U.S. anti-Semitism and, 953
in Warsaw Ghetto (1943), 948(*i*)
Zionism and, 851
Jiang Jieshi (Chiang Kai-Shek, China), 910, 935–936, 936(*i*), 947(*b*), 965
Jim Crow, in United States, 850
Job discrimination, outlawing of, 1009
Jobs. *See also* Employment; Livelihood(s); Work
global networks and, 1032–1033
Johannesburg, 881
John Paul II (pope), 1015, 1049
Johnson, Lyndon B., civil rights legislation and, 1009
Johnson, Samuel, 796
Jordan
Al Qaeda suicide bombers in, 1046
independence for, 973
in Six-Day War, 1013
Joseph the Provider (Mann), 939
Juan Carlos (Spain), 1007
Judaism. *See* Jews and Judaism
Junichiro Tanizaki (Japanese author), 935
Juntas, 778
in South Korea, 1007

Kabul, British in, 863
Kaiser (Germany), 838
Kamikaze attacks, 947, 951
Kang Zhengguo (China), on Great Leap Forward, 978
Kantorowsky, Eva (Holocaust survivor), 925, 928, 953
Kantorowsky, Hans (brother of Eva), 925, 945
Kashmir, 970
Kazan, Russia, Qur'an in, 1048(*b*)
Keep Smiling (film), 939
Kemal, Mustafa, Turkey under, 908–909, 909(*m*)
Kennedy, John F.
civil rights movement and, 1009
Cuba and, 969
Kenya, independence of, 974
KGB (Soviet secret police), 1016–1017

Khaw Soo Cheang, 869–870
travels of, 858(*m*)
Khmer Rouge (Cambodia), 1008
Khomeini, Ayatollah Ruhollah, 1008–1009, 1010(*b*), 1010(*i*), 1041, 1045
Khrushchev, Nikita (Soviet Union), 979
Cuban missile crisis and, 969
Soviet culture and, 983
Kikuyu people, 973–974
King, Martin Luther, Jr., 982, 1009
Kingdom of the Serbs, Croats, and Slovenes. *See* Yugoslavia
Kings and kingdoms. *See also* specific rulers and locations
nation-states and, 826(*m*)
Kipling, Rudyard, 881
Kissinger, Henry, 1002
Kiyochika Kobayashi, 790(*i*)
Knowledge. *See* Intellectual thought
Knowledge-based society, 1033
Kobe, Japan, workers' demonstration in, 932
Kollwitz, Käthe (German artist), 817, 818(*i*)
Komei (Japan), 837, 841, 842
Korea, 935(*m*)
"comfort women" and, 942(*b*)
flag of, 844(*b*), 844(*i*)
Japan and, 868, 883
Korean War (1950–1953), 967
economy after, 976
Korematsu, Fred (Japanese American civil rights activist), 948–949
Kristallnacht (Night of Broken Glass), 938
Ku Klux Klan, 850
Kulaks, 933
Kulthum, Umm (Arab singer), 959, 961, 961(*m*), 962
Kulturkampf (Bismarck), 848
Kyoto Protocol, 1040

Labor. *See also* Serfs and serfdom; Slaves and slavery; Workers; Working class
abolition of slavery and, 810
child, 813
in colonies, 873
free vs. slave, 797
global market and, 1031–1032
in imperial societies, 872
indentured, 876–877(*b*), 876(*i*)
migrations of, 976
sexual division of, 815
women's agricultural, 818–820
Laborsaving machines, 814
Labor unions. *See also* Strikes
in Brazil, 1029
in Great Depression, 931–932
growth of, 914
in Italy, 919
Japanese, 936
Nazis and, 937
neoliberalism and, 1033
Lafayette, Marquis de, American Revolution and, 769
Lagos, 973
Laissez faire, 763–764
Lakshmibai (Jhansi, India, queen), 863
Land
in Brazil, 1029
in colonies, 870
confiscation in Soviet Union, 933–934
in eastern Europe, 964
to former Russian serfs, 835–836
in Mexico, 891, 894–895
in South Africa, 1030
Land and Freedom Army, of Kikuyu, 973, 974
Landowners
eviction of tenants in Depression, 931
in Mexico, 894–895
Languages, disappearance of, 1052
Laos, in ASEAN, 1036
La Paz, rebels in, 778
Latin alphabet, in Turkey, 909
Latin America, 912. *See also* Spanish America; specific locations
Carnival in, 848
democracy in, 1003–1006
dictatorships in, 1005–1006
economy in, 975–976
federalism in, 831
feminist activists in, 852
during Great Depression, 929
independent states in, 759–761
literature in, 1050–1051
nationalism and, 783
nation building in, 829–832
in c. 1900, 830
Organization of American States and, 968
population growth in, 976
problems in, 1027
rebellions in 18th century, 767
revolutions in (1810–1830), 778–784, 780(*m*)
tariffs in, 805
women's rights in, 1011
Latvia, 942
Law(s). *See also* Codes of law; specific laws
nationalism and, 783
reforms in, 791
Law codes. *See* Codes of law
League of Nations
covenant (charter) of, 907, 908
creation of, 907
Japan and, 913, 935
mandate system of, 907–908, 907(*m*)
Learning. *See* Education; Intellectual thought
Leaves of Grass (Whitman), 848
Lebanon
diaspora from, 877
migrations in 19th century, 858(*m*)
Lebensraum (living space), 940
Legal systems. *See* Law(s)
Legislation. *See also* Law(s); specific laws
U.S. segregation forbidden by, 1009
Lenin, V. I., 903(*i*)
New Economic Policy of, 918, 933
Russian Revolution and, 903
Leningrad, starvation in, 949
Leopold II (Belgium), Africa and, 865–868, 870, 871(*b*)
Lesbians. *See* Gays
Less developed economies, population control and, 1040–1041
Levi, Primo, 946
Lexington, Battle of, American Revolution and, 768, 769(*m*)
Liberalism, 783
economic, 763
Liberation, culture of, 981–982
Liberation army, in Chiapas, Mexico, 1052
Liberation theology, of Catholic Church, 1049–1050
Liberty Displaying the Arts and Sciences (Jennings), 770(*i*)
Libya
in 2011, 1047(i)
uprising in, 1047
Life expectancy
increasing, 1040
world population and, 1042
Lifestyle. *See also* Livelihood(s); Standard of living
in Cold War, 982–983
in colonies, 873
in 18th century England, 765(*i*)
imperialism and, 869–872
industrial, 791–793
of migrants, 876–877
non-Western impact on Western, 886–887
of postindustrial families, 1002–1003
of soldiers, 947(*b*)
in Soviet Union, 1014–1015
Like Water for Chocolate (Esquivel), 1050
Liliuokalani (Hawaiian queen), 882(*b*)
Lima, Peru, Bolívar in, 781
Limited liability, 805
Lincoln, Abraham, 840(*i*)
Civil War and, 840
Literacy, 1027
in agrarian societies, 847
in Europe, 762
in North American colonies, 768
in Soviet Union, 918
after World War I, 914–915
Literature. *See also* Poets and poetry; specific works and writers
in Argentina, 920
in Brazil, 830
in China, 896
global, 1050–1051
in Japan, 935
Mexican Revolution and, 895
in 1930s, 939
non-Western impact on Western, 885
Western, 880
Lithuania, 942
"Little Red Book" (Mao Zedong), 981
Little Tramp (film), 915
Livelihood(s). *See also* Economy and economic systems; Employment; Labor; Work
global, 1031–1037
industrialization and, 814–815
migrations for improved, 859–860
in Soviet Union, 964
Llaneros (cowboys), 781, 782(*b*)
Locke, John, contract government and, 763
Locomotives, 798
Lodz, 814

Lombardy, 837
London, England, 1031, 1036
  Treaty of (1915), 897, 905
Lords. *See also* Nobility
  in Japan, 802
Lorraine, 897
  after World War I, 906
Louis XVI (France), French Revolution and, 771, 773
Louvre (Paris), 1037(*b*), 1037(*i*)
Love in the Time of Cholera (García Márquez), 1050
Ludd, Ned, 814
Luddites, 814
Lukashenko, Aleksandr (president of Belarus), 1049
Lula da Silva, Luiz Inácio (president of Brazil), 1029
Lunar landings, 995, 996
Luxembourg, 897
Lu Xun (China), 896
Luxury goods, 805
Lytton, Lord (viceroy of India), 873

Maastricht Treaty (1994), 1034
Maathi, Wangari, 1039, 1053
Macedonia
  as EU membership candidate, 1035
  First Balkan War and, 896
Macedonians, nationalism of, 884
Machado de Assis, Joachim, 830
Machiavelli, 776
Machine guns, 868
  in World War I, 904
Machinery. *See also* Industrialization
  laborsaving, 814
Made in Japan (Morita), 999(*b*)
Madero, Francisco (president of Mexico), 894, 895
Magazines, 915
Magical realism, in Latin American literature, 1050
Mahabharata epic, movies retelling, 915
Mai-ling Soong, 936(*i*)
Makioka Sisters, The (Junichiro Tanizaki), 935
Malaria, 868, 1041
Malaya, 944
  in ASEAN, 1036
Malay peninsula, British in, 863
Mali, 1027
Mamluk Sultanate (Egypt), 775, 776
Management, 805
Man at the Crossroads (Rivera mural), 932(*i*)
Manchuria
  Russia and, 868
  Russo-Japanese War and, 882–883
Manchurian Incident (1931), 935
Manchus (China), 895
Mandate system (League of Nations), 907–908, 907(*m*)
Mandatory education, Great Depression and, 931
Mandela, Nelson, 1023–1024
  on AIDS, 1044
  as South African president, 1029–1030
Manifest Destiny, in United States, 839
Mann, Thomas, 939
Manufacturing
  global, 1023
  underconsumption of, 804
Mao Zedong (China), 946(*b*), 962, 966–967
  Cultural Revolution and, 1002
  Great Leap Forward and, 978(*b*)
  "Little Red Book" of, 981
  modernization by, 978, 979–980
Maracaña (Rio de Janeiro), 977(*i*)
Marconi, Guglielmo, 915
Marie Antoinette (France), 773
Market(s)
  colonies as, 869
  laissez faire and liberalism on, 763–764
  South African, 1029
  youth, 1003
Marketing, mass, 915–916
Marriage, in Nazi Germany, 937
Married women. *See* Gender; Women
Marshall, George C., 964
Marshall Plan (1947), 964
Marta, Rilda, 915–916
Martyrdom, Mexican belief about, 890(*i*)
Maru (Head), 981
Marx, Karl, 816–817
Marxian socialism, vs. Sun Yatsen's socialism, 895
Marxism, 816–817
  revolutionary, in Russia, 903, 904
  worldwide revolutionary, 904
Masculinity. *See also* Gender and gender issues; Men
  cowboy way of life and, 782(*b*)
Mass culture, 893–894
Masses
  age of, 913–919
  culture for, 914–916
  Hitler and, 924(*i*), 937
  militarization of, 934
  mobilization of, 916–919, 932–939
Mass marketing, 915–916
Mass media
  development of, 878–879
  dictators and, 915, 925
  in Japan, 936
  Roosevelt, Franklin D., use of, 938
  uniform culture and, 925
  after World War I, 914–915
Mass politics, 893–894
Mass production, 913
  in Germany, 802
  industrial, 802
Mass proletarian culture, 918
Mass society, 893, 913–914
Mass unionization, 913
Master race, 945
Materialism, Marx on, 816–817
Mau Mau, 973–974
May 4th movement (China), 910, 914
Maya-Kakchiquel people, 1052
May Day rally (Czechoslovakia,1967), 1011
McCarthy, Joseph, witch-hunt for communists by, 983
Mecca
  pilgrimages to, 785
  Sa'uds in, 786
  Wahhabism in, 785(*i*)
Mechanization, of textile industry, 798
Medellin, Columbia, protest by women textile workers in, 932
Media. *See also* Mass media
  Gandhi's use of, 917
  sexuality in, 1003
Media experts, 993
Medicine. *See also* Health; Health care
  in colonies, 872–873
  growth of, 977
  population growth and, 1040
  after World War II, 995
Medina, 786
Meiji Restoration (Japan), 804, 824(*i*), 842, 935(*m*)
Mein Kampf (Hitler), 936
Men. *See also* Gender; Women
  during Great Depression, 931
  imperialism and, 870–871
  sexual division of labor and, 815
Ménétra, Jacques, 764–765
Mercantilism, 763
Merchants
  in Japan, 803
  migration by, 1044
Mercosur, 1036
Mergers, business, 1033
Mesopotamia, in World War I, 904
Metals and metalwork. *See also* Gold; Silver
  industrial, 800
Methodism, 785
Mexican Americans, protests by, 1009
Mexican-American War (1846–1848), 831–832, 839
Mexican Revolution (1910–1920), 891, 892(*m*), 894–895, 895(*m*)
  factions in, 895
  Rivera mural of, 890(*i*)
Mexico
  economy and, 1027
  Hidalgo in, 779
  Independence Day in, 780
  industrialization in, 802
  influenza epidemic in, 904–905
  land grants to U.S. companies in, 895
  land reform in, 895
  multinational corporations in, 1004(*m*)
  in NAFTA, 1036
  revolt in, 779–780
  Santa Anna in, 831–832
  television and, 993
  U.S. war with, 839
  U.S. intervention in, 893
Mexico City, 1011(*i*)
Middle class
  growth of, 914
  in India, 813(*i*), 1028
  industrial revolution and, 812–813
Middle East. *See also* Arabs and Arab world; specific locations
  independence struggle in, 972–973

Middle East (*continued*)
mandate system in, 907(*m*)
1967–1990, 1013(*m*)
oil in, 972, 1013
at Paris Peace Conference, 905, 905(*i*)
rebellions in after World War I, 908
Six-Day War in (1967), 1013
terrorism and, 1045
World War I in, 898(*m*)
Midnight's Children (Rushdie), 1051
Midway Island, Battle of, 944(*m*), 951
Migrant workers, industrialization and, 814
Migration, 1042–1043(*m*)
in Africa, 973
culture and, 878
diasporas and, 874–878
1850–1910, 858(*m*)
family life and, 1002
global, 875(*m*), 928, 990(*m*), 1024(*m*), 1042–1043(*m*), 1044–1045
to global cities, 1036
as global issue, 1038
of labor, 976, 1031
of Lebanese, 877
lifestyle and, 876–877
in 19th century, 859
on Trail of Tears, 840
Militarism
Great Depression and, 927
revival of, 939
Militaristic authoritarian regimes, Great Depression and, 927
Militarization
during Great Depression, 931, 932–933
in Japan, 935, 936
in 1930s, 934
Military. *See also* Armed forces; specific battles and wars
in Argentina, 978
elites in, 947(*b*)
German, 802
in South Korea, 1007
Military occupation, by Soviets of eastern Europe, 964
Military spending
in Cold War, 968(*m*), 976
Soviet, 1015
Mill, John Stuart, 845
Mills. *See also* Textiles and textile industry
in England, 798
workers in, 791–793
Milosevic, Slobodan (Serbia), 1016
Minerals. *See also* Mines and mining
industry and, 802
from Mexico, 894
Mines and mining
for industry, 800
in Mexico, 894
Minimum wage, workers and, 1033
Ministry of Trade and Industry (Japan), 996
Minorities. *See also* specific groups
activism by, 1009
rights of, 851
Mir (peasant communities), 835–836
Missiles, in Cuba, 969
Missions and missionaries
in China, 857
in imperial Africa and Asia, 871
Mixed economy, in India, 1028
Mobility. *See* Migration
Mobilization
of democracies, 938–939
of masses in Japan, 936
for World War I, 897
Modernism, cultural change and, 878
Modernization
of Brazil, 829–831
of China, 895, 896, 979–980
of cities, 846
ecological destruction and, 1038
of Egypt, 776, 864, 864(*m*)
during Great Depression, 930
of Japan, 841–843
national, 828–838
of Russia, 834–836
in Soviet bloc, 964
of Soviet Union, 978–979
in Turkey, 908–909, 909(*i*)
women and, 847
Modernizers, in Mexico, 894
Modern Times (film), 939
Molecular biology, 995
Monarchs and monarchies. *See* Kings and kingdoms; specific rulers and locations
Monet, Claude, 817
Monetarism, 1014
Moneylenders, in Depression, 931
Mono no aware concept (serenity), 885
Monroe Doctrine (1823), 881
Montano, Otilio, 890(*i*)
Montenegro, as autonomous state, 896, 898(*m*)
Montesquieu, Louis (Baron), 763
Monuments, national, 844–845
Moon landing, 994
Morelos, José Maria, 779
Morita, Akio, 999(*b*)
Morocco
France and, 974
help desk services in, 1032
World War II in, 951
Mortality
in colonies, 873
in West, 1040–1041
Mortgages, economic crisis and, 1047
Moscow, Chechen bombings in, 1046
Mothers, in El Salvador, 1006
Mothers for Life (Chile), 1005–1006
Movement of peoples. *See* Immigrants and immigration; Migration
Movies. *See* Films
Mozambique, 1030
Mubarak, Hosni (Egypt), 1046, 1047(*i*)
Mughal Empire (India), English East India Company and, 862–863
Multiethnic empires, Ottoman Empire as, 884
Multinational corporations, 913, 998
farmer protests against, 1018
in Latin America, 1004(*m*)
South African apartheid and, 1023–1024
Munich, terrorism at Olympic Games in (1972), 1045
Murals, by Rivera, Diego, 890(*i*), 895, 931, 932(*i*)
Music. *See also* Dance
culture and, 848
global, 1051
Industrial Revolution and, 817
national Mexican, 845–846
non-Western impact on Western, 886
youth, 1003
Muslim Brotherhood, 916, 917
Muslim League, 885
Muslims. *See also* Arabs and Arab world; Islam
Ottomans as, 775
Partition of India and, 970
range of interpretations of, 1050
Taliban and, 1008
USSR and, 948
women and, 914
Mussolini, Benito, 916, 918–919, 932, 933, 940
Myanmar, in ASEAN, 1036
Myrdal, Alva, 938–939

NAACP. *See* National Association for the Advancement of Colored People
Nafisi, Azar, 1044, 1045
NAFTA. *See* North American Free Trade Agreement
Nagasaki, Japan
atomic bombing of, 951
port of, 802
Nain Singh (Indian explorer), 858(*m*), 869, 870(*i*)
Nairobi, 973
Nanjing, China
Japanese massacre in, 941
Nationalists in, 910
Treaty of (China, 1842), 807
Naomi (Junichiro Tanizaki), 935
Napoleon I (Bonaparte, France), 761, 774
education and, 847
Egypt and, 776(*i*)
French Revolution and, 771
Muhammad's birthday and, 776(*i*)
Napoleonic Code. *See* Code Napoleon
Napoleonic Europe (1796–1815), 775(*m*)
Napoleonic Wars, 774–775, 779
Napoleon III (France), 864
NASA (National Aeronautics and Space Administration), 967(*b*)
Nasser, Gamal Abdel (Egypt), 972–973, 983
Natal, 867
Nation(s). *See also* Nation building; Nation-state
in Africa, 973–975, 974(*m*)
in Brazil, 829–831
creation of, 969–975
culture of, 843–849
defined, 829
in global age, 1027–1031
independent, 960(*m*)
institutions in, 846–849
modernization of, 828–838
National Assembly (France), 771, 772, 783
National Association for the Advancement of Colored People (NAACP), 981–982

Nationalism, 783
in Balkans, 896
at Bandung Conference, 985
decolonization and, 959
in Egypt, 959
feminists and, 884–885
Hindu, 1028
history writing and teaching and, 844–845
in India, 885
in Indochina, 971
in Italy, 837
in Japan, 843, 912
migration and, 876
nation-states and, 827–828
in Ottoman Empire, 884–885
romantic, 783
of Slavic Serbs, 896
in World War I, 900
Nationalist China, 965
Nationalist Party (China). *See* Guomindang (China)
Nationalization, of Suez Canal, 973
National Organization for Women (NOW), 1010–1011
National Tobacco Company, 802
Nation building, 828, 829. *See also* State-building
in Brazil, 830–832, 831(*i*)
ethnic and racial thinking in, 849
in Germany, 837–838
after imperialism, 961
in Italy, 836–837
in Latin America, 829–832
national culture and, 843–849
Native Americans and, 840–841, 841(*i*)
in Russia, 832–836
in United States, 838–841
Westernization and, 845–846
after World War II, 962
Nation-state
citizens' rights in, 851–852
c. 1850, 826(*m*)
historians of, 846(*b*), 846(*i*)
literacy in, 847
nation and, 829
outsiders in, 849–852
rise of, 827–828
supranational organizations and, 1033–1036
Native Americans
ancestral burial sites of, 1052
forced migrations of, 827(*m*)
Manifest Destiny and, 840
in Mexico, 890(*i*)
Native peoples. *See also* Native Americans
in Algeria, 865
lands seized from, 827(*m*)
missionaries and, 871
as outsiders, 849–850
NATO (North Atlantic Treaty Organization), 967
Natural resources
decline in, 998
industrialization and, 795–796, 797
in United States, 802
Navy
in World War I, 897–898
in World War II, 951
Nayemwezi women, sorghum and, 819(*i*)
Nazi Germany. *See also* Germany
annexation of Austria, 940
civilians in conquered regions and, 945
expansion by, 926(*m*)
Frank, Anne, and, 980
Holocaust of, 945–947, 945(*m*)
Jews in, 937–938
Nuremberg rally in, 924(*i*)
paramilitary groups in, 946(*b*)
propaganda in, 937
racism of, 937–938
repression in, 937
women in, 937, 938
Nazi Party (National Socialist German Workers' Party), 936–937
Nazi-Soviet Pact (1939), 941, 942, 963
Nehru, Jawaharlal, 976, 983, 984, 1028
Neoliberalism, 1014, 1033
Nestlé, 913
Netherlands, World War II in, 942
Networks, global, 1032–1033
Neutrality, U.S., in World War I, 897
Neutron bomb, 963
New Economic Policy, 918, 933
New imperialism, 860. *See also* Imperialism
expansion of, 925
New Left, 1010
New Life Movement (China), 935–936
"New look," for women after World War II, 982(*i*)
Newly independent countries, Bandung Conference and, 983–984
New Order, in Asia, 941
Newspapers, 878, 915
New Woman (film), 915
New woman, World War I and, 902, 914
New York, 1031, 1036
New Zealand, World War I and, 897, 898–899
NGOs. *See* Nongovernmental organizations
Nicaragua, U.S. and, 1003–1004
Nicholas I (Russia), 832–833
Nicholas II (Russia), 902
Nigeria
help desk services in, 1032
independence in, 975
revolt by women in, 953
Nightingale, Florence
in Crimean War, 833
travels of, 826(*m*)
Nihilists, in Russia, 836
Nihon-bashi (*Fifty-three Stations on the Tokaido*) (Hiroshige), 803(*i*)
Nikitenko, Alexander (Russia), 834, 835(*b*)
Nixon, Richard
in China, 1002
Vietnam and, 1008
Nkrumah, Kwame, 958(*i*), 961(*m*), 973, 983
Nobility. *See also* Lords
in Russia, 836
Noble savages, slaves and, 766
Noh theater (Japan), 885–886
Nonalignment, in Cold War, 984(*i*)
Nondiscrimination clause, League of Nations charter and, 913
Nongovernmental organizations (NGOs), 1032(*i*), 1034
Nonindustrial nations. *See also* Industrialization; Industrial Revolution
economic inequities in, 984–985
research in, 1001
underdevelopment of Africa and, 812
Nonviolent resistance
Gandhi and, 916, 917, 954(*i*)
by Mexican Americans, 1009
by Nigerian women, 953
in 20th century, 953–954
Normandy, D-Day invasion in, 951
North (U.S.), 840
North (global), vs. South (global), 985, 1026–1027
North Africa
consumerism in, 1032
Europeans in, 865
France in, 865
World War II in, 943(*m*), 951
North America
colonial crisis and revolution in, 769(*m*)
revolution in, 767–771
North American Free Trade Agreement (NAFTA), 1036
North Atlantic Treaty Organization. *See* NATO (North Atlantic Treaty Organization)
Northern Ireland, 910
Bloody Sunday in (January 30, 1972), 1045
North German Confederation, 838
North Korea, 967
North-South divide (global), Bandung Conference and, 985
North Vietnam, 972, 1008. *See also* Vietnam War
Norway
massacre of political activists in (2011), 1045
World War II in, 942
Novels, 893. *See also* Literature
in 1930s, 939
Nuclear war, Cuban missile crisis and, 969
Nuclear weapons, 963
Nuremberg, Germany
Nazi rally in, 924(*i*)
trials in, 980
Nuremberg Laws (1935), 938
Nursing
in Crimean War, 833
women in, 900–902

Obama, Barack, 1026
Occupation (military). *See* Military occupation
Occupations (labor). *See* Livelihood(s)
Off-shore manufacturing, 998
Oh Omok, as comfort woman, 942(*b*)
Oil and oil industry
imperialism and, 912
in mandates, 907(*m*)
in Middle East, 972
trade routes in (c. 1975), 990(*m*)
uses of, 998
Oil embargo, 1013–1014
Oklahoma, Native Americans in, 840
Oklahoma City government building, destruction of (1995), 1045

Old Order, Enlightenment and, 765–767
Oliver Twist (Dickens), 817
Olympic Games
in Mexico City (1968), 1011(*i*)
terrorism at Munich games (1972), 1045
Omdurman, Battle of (Sudan), 868
Once Upon the River Love, 1044
One-child policy (China), 1041
One Hundred Years of Solitude (García Márquez), 1050
On the Wealth of Nations (Smith), 763–764
OPEC (Organization of Petroleum Exporting Countries), 990(*m*), 1013
Opera, in Mexico, 845
"Operation Vittles," 965
Opium, 807
China and, 807
India and, 809(*i*)
Opium War (1839–1842), 807
taxation and, 873
Orange Free State, 867, 881
Organization of American States (OAS), 968
Organization of Petroleum Exporting Countries. *See* OPEC
Organizations. *See* Global structures and organizations
Orphans, as industrial labor, 791
Orwell, George, on pacifists, 954
Ottoman Balkans (Albania), 776
Ottoman Empire (1453–1750)
Armenian deportations by, 908
Balkans and, 893, 894, 896
Crimean War and, 833, 833(*m*)
dissolution of, 909(*m*)
industrialization and, 809
Mecca, Medina, and, 786
Napoleon and, 775, 776
nationalism in, 884–885
Nicholas I and, 832–833
Peace of Paris treaties and, 906
Russia and, 863
World War I and, 896, 898(*m*), 904, 908
Young Turks and, 884–885, 884(*i*)
Outsiders, in nation-states, 849–852
Outsourcing, to India, 1032
Outwork, 801
Oxygen, depletion of, 1038
Ozone layer, hole in, 1038

Pa Chin, 939
Pacific Ocean region
economies in, 1047
wealth and production in, 1031
World War II in, 944–945, 944(*m*), 951
Pacific tigers, 990(*m*), 997(*m*)
Pacifism
Asian religions and, 953
in 20th century, 953–954
after World War I and World War II, 954
Pahlavi, Mohammed Reza (Shah of Iran), 1008
Painting
impressionism in, 817
after World War II, 983
Pakistan, 970, 985. *See also* India
in SEATO, 968
Palestine and Palestinians, 1013(*m*)
Israel and (1949), 972(*m*)
Jewish homeland and, 972
migration of Jews to, 940
strike in, 932
terrorists at Munich Olympic Games, 1045
in World War I, 904
Pamuk, Orhan, 1049
Pan-Africanism, 851, 908, 958(*i*)
Pandemics. *See also* Disease
AIDS, 1041(*i*)
Pankhurst, Emmeline, 900
Papacy. *See* Roman Catholic Church; specific popes
Paraguay, 946(*b*)
in Mercosur, 1036
Paramilitary groups, 946(*b*)
Paris, 1036
battle in (1814), 774
Paris Peace Conference (1919–1920), 905–908, 905(*i*)
Park Chung Hee, 1007
Parliaments, European assemblies as, in Russia (1905), 883
Partisans, in World War II, 950
Partition, of India, 970, 970(*m*)
Pasternak, Boris, 983
Patents, 805
agricultural, 1018–1019
as colonization, 1018
Patriarchal authority, Great Depression and, 931
Patriotism, in World War I, 900
Paz Soldán, José Gregorio, 832
Peace movements, during World War I, 900
Peace of Paris treaties, 906–907
Pearl Harbor, Japanese bombing of, 927, 944
Peasants. *See also* Serfs and serfdom
in China, 911(*b*), 965
in eastern Europe, 964
in French Revolution, 772
in Italy, 918–919
Mexican Revolution and, 895
in Russia, 834(*i*), 835–836, 902
Pedro I (Brazil), in Rio de Janeiro, 781
Pedro II (Brazil), 829–831, 830(*i*), 847
Pei, I. M., 1037
P'eng P'ai, 911(*b*)
Pennsylvania, September 11, 2001, terrorist attack and, 1045
Pensions, cuts in, 1033
Pentagon, terrorist attack on, 1045
People of color, as outsiders, 849–850
People's patriotism (Japan), 936
People's Republic of China, 965. *See also* China
"People's Rights," in Japan, 842–843
Peralta, Angela (Mexican opera singer), 845–846, 847
travels of, 827(*m*)
Perestroika (restructuring), 1015
Perón, Eva, 977
Perón, Juan, 977–978, 1005
Perry, George, English industrialization and, 797(*b*)
Persia. *See also* Iran
Russia and, 863
Persian Letters, The (Montesquieu), 763
Peru
Indians taxed in, 849
nation building in, 832
revolt in, 767
San Martin in, 781
Pesticides, chemical, 1018
Pétain, Philippe, 949
Peter III (Russia), Pugachev as, 767
Petrograd, St. Petersburg as, 902
Peugeot, Armand, 800
Philippines, 944
in ASEAN, 1036
U.S. control of, 881–882
Philosophy as Matonetics (Tanabe), 980
Phonographs, 914
Photography, 878–879
Piedmont, 837
Piedmont-Sardinia, 836
"Pill, the" (oral contraceptive), 995
Pinochet, Augusto, 1005–1006
Pirates and piracy, bio-, 1018
Plantations
in Brazil, 831(*i*)
in Haiti, 777–778
Plants, genetic modification of, 1017, 1018
Pluralism, in national tradition, 849
Pneumonia, 814
Poets and poetry, non-Western impact on Western, 885
Pogroms, anti-Semitic, 875
Poland
industry in, 814
rebellion (1956), 979
Russia and, 897
Solidarity movement in, 1015
Soviet Union and, 963, 964
after World War I, 906, 906(*m*)
World War II in, 927, 941–942, 951
Political clubs, in Latin America, 832
Political heroes, in United States, 840(*i*)
Political parties. *See also* specific parties
in Chile, 1005
Green Party and, 1038
World War I and, 900
Political power
in Africa, 810
as global issue, 1038
in Japan, 841–843
Political structures. *See* Economy and economic systems; Political power
Political styles, culture and, 890(*i*)
Political thought, socialism, Marxism, and, 816–817
Politics. *See also* Political power
Cold War and, 962–969, 1003–1012
global, 893
labor unions in, 914
mass, 893–894
mobilization of masses and, 916–919
post–World War I, 905–913
radio use and, 915
rights in United States, 770–771
television and, 993
World War I and, 900

Pollock, Jackson, 983
Poll (head) tax, 929
Pollution
  global warming from, 1038
  technology and, 1018(*i*)
Pol Pot (Cambodia), 1008
Polygamy, abolished in Turkey, 909
Polynesia. *See* Pacific Ocean region; specific locations
Poor people, uprisings by, 767
Popes. *See* Christianity; specific popes
Popp, Adelheid (Austrian feminist), 815
Popular Front (France), 939
Population
  of Algeria, 865
  characteristics of worldwide, 1042–1043(*m*)
  in colonial cities, 929
  global (1920), 913
  as global issue, 1037–1038, 1040–1041
  in Iran, 1041
  of Latin America, 976
  migrants in U.S. and, 1044
Porcelain
  efforts to copy Chinese, 796
  Wedgwood pottery as, 796
Pornography, transmission of, 994
Port Arthur, 882
Porto Alegre, Brazil, 1034
Portugal
  Africa and, 865
  Brazil and, 781–783
  imperialism of, 861
Posters, propaganda, 901(*b*), 901(*i*)
Postindustrial course, 996
Postindustrial economies, 991
  family life in, 1002–1003
Postsecondary education, in France, 847
Potemkin (film), 915
Pottery. *See* Porcelain
Poverty, 1041
  in Brazil, 1029
  rural, 996
Power (political). *See* Political power
Power (energy), steam engine and, 798
Prague Spring, 1011
Prices
  of commodities, 929
  declines in, 804
Prince, The (Machiavelli), 776
Print making. *See also* Woodblock printing
  in Japan, 803(*b*)
Print media
  advertising in, 915
  newspapers as, 878, 915
  after World War I, 914–915
Prison camps, Gulags in Soviet Union, 934
Privacy rights, 994
Production
  European, 794–795
  industrial, 794–795
  mass, 913
  in Soviet Union, 964
Productivity
  growth in, 893
  price declines and, 804
Proletariat, Marx on, 817
Propaganda
  Bolshevik, 916
  Hitler's use of, 937
  Japanese, 936
  in World War I, 900, 901(*b*), 901(*i*)
  in World War II, 948
Property rights, 994
Prosperity
  expansion of, 976–978
  in middle class, 812–813
  in 19th century, 804
  after World War II, 975–976
Prostitution
  during Great Depression, 931
  industrialization and, 814
Protest(s). *See also* Revolts and rebellions
  against globalization, 1052–1053
  during Great Depression, 931–932
  against Japan in China, 910
  in Latin America, 1005
  in Middle East, 1046–1047
  by young people, 1009–1010
Protestants and Protestantism
  Great Awakening and, 785
  in Northern Ireland, 1045
  in World War II, 950
Provisional Government (Russia), 902, 903
Proxy war, 962
Prussia
  Bismarck and, 836
  Danish war with, 838
  Enlightenment and, 765
  king as German kaiser, 838
  war against France and, 773
Psychoanalysis, 886
Public, the, 828
Public affairs, in Latin America, 832
Public health, in colonies, 873
Public sphere, 764–765
Publishing, in Japan, 980
Puerto Rico, U.S. annexation of, 881
Pump priming
  by Nazis, 937
  in Sweden, 938
Purges, by Stalin, 934
Putin, Vladimir, 1049

Qaddafi, Muammar, 1045, 1047, 1047(i)
Qing (Manchu) Empire (China), 808(*m*), 893, 894, 910
  disintegration of, 807–809
  downfall of, 884
  infrastructure in, 873
  reform and, 895
Quebec, independence and, 1052
Quinine, malaria and, 868
Quisling, Vidkun (president of Norway), 949
Quito, Ecuador, 781
Qur'an
  in Kazan, Russia, 1048(*b*)
  readers of, 1048(*b*), 1048(*i*)

Race and racism
  African Americans and, 981–982
  Enlightenment thinkers on, 764
  of Hitler, 936–937
  inferiority of blacks as, 767
  Japanese militarism and, 935
  mobilization of masses and, 933
  outsiders and, 849
  scientific, 861
  in South Africa, 1023
  in United States, 850, 1009
  youth protests against, 1009
Radar, 942
Radical Civil Union (Argentina), 919
Radicals and radicalism, terrorism and, 1025
Radio, 893, 914, 915
  Cold War culture and, 982–983
  Nazi use of, 937
  politicians use of, 915
  in World War II, 948
Radiotelescope, 995
Railroads, 790(*i*), 798, 816, 818(*i*)
  in Africa, 868
  in Egypt, 864
  in India, 810, 863
  in Italy, 837
  in Mexico, 894
  in c. 1914, 792(*m*)
  in North Africa, 865
  refrigerated cars for, 801–802
  spread of (c.1900), 799(*m*)
  trans-Siberian, 799–802, 800(*b*), 800(*i*)
Rain forests
  in Brazil, 1029
  clearing of, 1038
Ramayana, 877
Ranke, Leopold von (German historian), 846(*i*)
Rape of Nanjing, 941, 945
Rap music, 1051
Rationing, in World War I, 902
Raw materials. *See* Natural resources
Reading Lolita in Teheran (Nafisi), 1044
Reagan, Ronald, 1033
  economy and, 1014
  Iran hostage crisis and, 1009
Reaganomics, 1014
Realpolitik, in Germany, 838
Rebellions. *See* Revolts and rebellions
Recessions, in 19th century, 804
Reconstruction (U.S.), 840
Red Army (China), 904, 946(*b*)
Red Brigades (Italy), 1045
Reds, in Russian civil war, 903–904
Reform(s), 846–849
  in China, 895
  in Czechoslovakia, 1011
  of education, 846–847
  in Egypt, 776
  emancipation of Russian serfs and, 834–836
  in Latin America, 778
  legal, 791
  Meiji Restoration as, 826–827
  in Mexico, 894, 895
  after Napoleonic wars, 774–775
  NGOs and, 1034
  political, in Mexico, 894, 895
  Soviet Union and, 1011–1012

Reform(s) (*continued*)
Western ideas and, 845
after World War I, 908–911
Refrigerated railroad cars, 801–802
Refugees
blocking of Jewish, 953
in World War II, 925, 928
Regional alliances, 968–969, 968(*m*)
Regionalism, migration and, 874–875
Reich (empire), in Germany, 838
Reincarnation, South Asian ideas of, 886
Religion(s). *See also* Buddha and Buddhism; Christianity; Hindus and Hinduism; Islam; Jews and Judaism; specific groups
in Germany, 848
as global issue, 1038
government and, 785
in Indonesia, 971
revival in secular age, 784–787
in Spanish and Portuguese colonies, 861
Western study of non-Western, 886
worldwide, 1043(*m*), 1049–1050
Religious revivalism, 785–787
Renan, Ernest (French philosopher and writer), 829
Reparations, German (World War I), 906
Republic, in United States, 771
Republicanism, in France, 773–774
Research and development
military, 976
in science and technology, 1001
Reservations, for Native Americans, 840
Resistance. *See also* Revolts and rebellions
in El Salvador, 1006(*b*)
to foreign domination, 883–885
to globalization and, 1025–1026
to imperialism, 872, 891
in Soviet Union, 934
in World War II, 949–950
Resources. *See* Natural resources
Restaurants, 1001(*b*)
Retailing, 805
Reunification, of Germany (1990), 1016
Revivals and revivalism, Great Awakening as, 785
Revolts and rebellions
Boxer Rebellion (China), 857
in colonies, 880
in Enlightenment, 767
in Hungary, 979
in India (1857), 863
in Iran, 1008
in Mexico (1810), 779
between 1945 and 1990, 991
in Poland, 979
by proletariat, 817
in Soviet Union (1920s), 918
Taiping (China), 808–809
after World War I, 910–911
Revolution(s). *See also* Scientific revolution
in Atlantic Ocean region, 760(*m*)
in Balkan region, 893
in China (1911–1912), 891–893, 895–896
domestic, 1006–1009
economic constraints and, 791
Enlightenment and, 761
in Haiti, 777–778, 779(*i*)
in Latin America (1810–1830), 778–784, 780(*m*)
in Mexico, 890(*i*), 891
from 1910–1929, 892(*m*)
of 1989, 1016–1017
in North America, 767–771
in Poland, 1015
in Russia (1905), 883
in Russia (1917), 893
Rhee, Syngman, 1007
Rhodes, Cecil, 867, 881
Rhodesia, 867
Rieger, Albert (Austrian painter), 865(*i*)
Rights
of citizens, 851–852
in Declaration of Independence, 768
exclusion of Americans from, 850
in French Revolution, 772–773
in United States, 840
of women, 850
Rio de Janeiro, 781, 1029
schools in, 847
after World War II, 977(*i*)
Risorgimento (rebirth, Italy), 847
Rivera, Diego, 890(*i*), 895, 931, 932(*i*)
"Roaring Twenties," 893
Robespierre, Maximilian, 773
Rockefeller, John D., 802
Rockefeller Center, 932(*i*)
Roma (gypsies), Nazis and, 925, 947
Roman Catholic Church, 1049–1050. *See also* Christianity
in Ireland, 1045
Napoleon and, 774
in Spanish and Portuguese colonization, 861
in World War II, 950
Romania
as autonomous state, 896, 898(*m*)
fall of communism in, 1016
in World War II, 942, 951
Romanov dynasty (Russia), end of, 902
Romanticism, 783
Rommel, Erwin, 951
Roosevelt, Eleanor, 938
Roosevelt, Franklin Delano, 944, 952
fireside chats of, 938
response to Great Depression, 938
Roosevelt, Theodore, Spanish-American War and, 881–882
Rosas, Juan Manuel (Argentinian dictator), 851
Rousseau, Jean-Jacques, 763, 765, 773
Royal Dutch Shell, 913
Royalty. *See* Kings and kingdoms; specific rulers and locations
Rubber industry, in Congo, 871(*b*)
Rulers. *See* Kings and kingdoms; specific rulers and locations
Rural areas
British industry in, 797(*b*)
Great Depression and, 931
Green Revolution and, 996
Rushdie, Salman, 1051
Russia. *See also* Russian Revolution; Soviet Union; World War I
Bolshevik takeover in, 903
Catherine the Great in, 765, 766–767(*b*)
Chechnya and, 1046
civil war in, 903–904
Crimean War and, 833, 833(*m*)
emancipation of serfs in, 834–836, 834(*i*)
Enlightenment in, 765
Japan and, 868
League of Nations and, 907
life expectancy in, 1040
Napoleon and, 761, 774
peasants in, 834(*i*)
peoples moved within, 850
pogroms in, 875
Poland and, 814
Provisional Government in, 902
Pugachev's revolt in, 767, 767(*m*)
serfdom in, 834, 835(*b*)
trans-Siberian railroad in, 800(*b*), 800(*i*)
in Triple Entente, 896
women in, 836
World War I and, 897, 903
Russian Empire
German occupation of, 903
nation building and, 832–836
Russian Revolution
of 1905, 883
of 1917, 817, 893, 902–904, 963
Russification, 847
Russo-Japanese War (1904–1905), 882–883
Rwanda, 1027
Doctors Without Borders and, 1032(*i*)
genocide in, 1049

Saddam Hussein, 1045
Sáenz Peña, Roque (president of Argentina), 919
Saigon, 929
colonialism in, 872(*b*)
France and, 864
Sailing. *See* Ships and shipping
Sailors, African American in World War II, 946(*i*)
Saint-Domingue, 777. *See also* Haiti revolt in, 759–760
Salsa music, 1051
SALT I. *See* Strategic Arms Limitation Treaty (SALT I)
Samurai (Japanese warriors), 842
Japanese industrialization and, 802–803
Sanitation, in Crimean War, 833
San Martin, José de (Argentinean independence fighter), 781
Santa Anna, Antonio Lopez de, 831–832
São Paulo, 1029
Sarajevo, Franz Ferdinand assassinated in, 896
Sari, in India, 813(*i*)
Sartre, Jean-Paul, 981
Satanic Verses, The (Rushdie), 1051
Satellites (artificial)
communications, 988(*i*), 993, 994–995
Sputnik as, 966
technology for, 994
Sati (widow suicide, India), 870
Satyagraha strategy (Gandhi), 954, 954(*i*)
Sa'ud, house of, 786

Sa'ud, Muhammad ibn, 785
Scholarship. *See* Intellectual thought; specific scholars
School and schooling. *See* Education
Science, astronomy and, 995
Scientific management, 913
Scientific racism, 861
Scientific revolution, after World War II, 995–996
Scientific socialism, 816
SEATO. *See* Southeast Asia Treaty Organization
Secondary education, in Europe, 847
Second Balkan War (1913), 892(*m*), 896
Second Great Awakening, 785
Second Sex, The (Beauvoir), 981
Second World War. *See* World War II
Secret Speech (Soviet Union), 979
Secularism, religion and, 784–787, 1049–1050
Security, collective, 907
Security Council (UN), Korean War and, 967
Segregationism, in U.S., 1009
Self-determination, 905
Senate (U.S.)
  League of Nations and, 907
  World War I peace settlement and, 907
Senegalese soldiers, 912(*b*)
Senghor, Léopold Sédar, 912(*b*)
Sepoys, 863
September 11, 2001, terrorism, 1045
Serbia
  as autonomous state, 896, 898(*m*)
  World War I and, 896
Serbs
  Balkan wars and, 896
  Milosevic and, 1016
  nationalism of, 884
Serfs and serfdom. *See also* Peasants
  protests against, 767
  in Russia, 833–834, 834(*i*), 835(*b*)
Servants. *See also* Slaves and slavery
  indentured, 876–877(*b*), 876(*i*)
Services, social, 1033
Service sector, 805, 1023
  global, 991
  growth of, 999
  technological, 988(*i*)
Sevastopol, 833
Seven Years' War, 768
Sex and sexuality
  birth control and, 995–996
  comfort women, 942(*b*)
  South Asian ideas and, 886
  youth culture and, 1003
Sex slaves, in World War II, 942(*b*), 949(*i*)
Sex tourism, 1001(*b*)
Sexual division of labor, 815
Shanghai, China
  film industry in, 916(*b*)
  Nationalists in, 910
  refugees in, 925
Shelter. *See also* Housing
Ships and shipping
  global, 796–797
  in Japan, 803–804, 913
  in World War I, 897–898
Shoguns and shogunate (Japan), 825
Show trials, Soviet, 934
Siam. *See* Thailand
Siberia
  Japanese withdrawal from, 904
  in Russian Empire, 863
Sicily, Garibaldi in, 837
"Sick man of Europe," Ottoman Empire as, 832–833
Sieyès, Abbé, 771
Sijie, Dai (Chinese writer), 1044–1045
Sikhs, 1052
  in India, 1028, 1045
Silent Spring (Carson), 1038
Silicon chips, 993
Silk and silk industry, in Japan, 802
Silk Road, Russia and British destruction of, 863
Silver, in China, 794
Simyonov, Yulian (Russian novelist), 982
Sinai peninsula, 1013
Singapore, 944
  in ASEAN, 1036
  Chinese traders in, 877
Singh, Manmohan (prime minister of India), 1028
Sino-Japanese War (1894), 868, 868(*m*), 895
Sioux Indians, 841(*i*)
Six-Day War (1967), 1013
Skin color, Enlightenment thinkers on, 764
Slave labor, Jews as, 938
Slaves and slavery
  abolition and, 810
  in Brazil, 830
  in Caribbean region, 777–778
  Enlightenment ideas and, 766–767
  indentured servitude as, 877
  industry and, 797
  in Saint-Domingue, 759–761
  Smith, Adam, on, 764
  Uncle Tom's Cabin and, 817
  U.S. Constitution and, 770
  in United States, 840
  Wheatley as, 786(*b*)
  women and agriculture in, 818–820
Slave trade
  abolition of, 810
  to 1860, 792(*m*)
Slavs, Nazis and, 925, 947
Smallpox, 1041
Smith, Adam, 763–764
Soccer, in Rio de Janeiro, 977(*i*)
Social classes. *See* Class(es)
Social Contract, The (Rousseau), 763
Social Darwinism, 861
Social health, in United States, 1040
Socialism, 816–817
  in Czechoslovakia, 1011
  of Sun Yatsen, 895
  World War I and, 900
Socialist realism, in Soviet art, 934, 934(*i*)
Social Security Act (U.S., 1935), 938
Social services, taxes for, 1033
Society
  in Argentina, 919, 977–978
  in Brazil, 1029
  in China, 965
  complexity of, 914
  disorder under imperialism, 870–872
  Enlightenment thinkers on, 763
  Great Depression and, 930–931
  imperial, 869–878
  industry and, 812–815
  in Japan, 842
  mass, 893, 913–914
  in Nazi Germany, 937–938
  public sphere and, 764–765
  in Russia, 836
  Soviet, 978
  in World War II, 947–948
Society for Friends of the Blacks (1788), 777
Society of Jesus. *See* Jesuits
Society of the Righteous and Harmonious Fists (Boxers, China), 884
Soil, depletion of, 1018
Soka Gakkai (Buddhist sect), 1050
Soldiers. *See also* Armed forces; Military; specific battles and wars
  colonial, in World War I, 897, 898, 899–900, 899(*i*), 904, 912(*b*)
  in Vietnam, 1008
  in World War II, 946–947(*b*), 949, 950(*i*)
Solidarity movement (Poland), 1015, 1016
Solzhenitsyn, Aleksandr, 990(*m*), 1012
Somalia, famine in, 1041
"Song of Revolution" (Chinese diaspora), 878
Sony, 999(*b*)
Sophie (Austria-Hungary), 896
Soseki Natsumi (Meiji writer), 879–880
Soul Mountain (Gao Xingjian), 1038
South (U.S.)
  Civil War and, 840
  women farmers in, 819–820
South (global), vs. North (global), 985, 1026–1027
South Africa, 1029–1030. *See also* Africa
  after apartheid, 1031(*m*)
  Boers in, 881
  British annexation of, 881
  HIV/AIDS in, 1030
  Mandela and, 1023–1024
  resistance to Britain in, 867–868, 867(*i*)
South African (Boer) War, 881
South America. *See also* specific locations
  Bolivar and, 758(*i*)
  caudillos in, 780–781
  economic and social progress in, 1033
  Mercosur free trade zone in, 1036
  1960–1992, 1004(*m*)
South Asia. *See also* India
  migrations in, 990(*m*)
  Western ideas and, 886
Southeast Asia. *See also* specific locations
  France in, 864
  imperialism in, 862
  migrations in, 990(*m*), 1044
  new states of (1945–1999), 971(*m*)
  Vietnam War and, 1008
Southeast Asia Treaty Organization (SEATO), 968
Southern cone (South America), 1033, 1036

Southern Hemisphere, trade and, 1027
South Korea, 967
demonstrations in, 1007
economy in, 996–997, 998
South Vietnam, 972, 1008. *See also* Vietnam War
Southwest Asia. *See also* Mesopotamia
Soviet bloc, 964–965
activism in, 1009
collapse of, 991–992, 1014–1017
protests in 1967, 1011
science and technology applications in, 1001
Soviets, 903
defined, 902
Soviet Union, 904. *See also* Cold War; Russia; Soviet bloc; World War II
Afghanistan and, 1008
communism and, 963–964, 978–979
cosmonauts in, 966–967(*b*), 966(*i*)
Cuba and, 969
dissolution of (1992), 1017
eastern Europe and, 964
economy in, 963
end of, 991–992, 1012, 1014–1017
film industry in, 915
five-year plans in, 933
Germany after World War II and, 964–965, 965(*m*)
in Grand Alliance, 945
human rights and, 1049
modernization of, 978–979
Nazi invasion of, 942–943
New Economic Policy in, 918, 933
nonaggression pact with Nazis, 941
postwar radio in, 982
Prague Spring and, 1011
propaganda by, 916
secret policy (KGB) in, 1017
socialist realism in, 934, 934(*i*)
space exploration by, 966–967(*b*), 966(*i*)
as superpower, 962
Warsaw Pact and, 967
after World War II, 962–970
in World War II, 942, 943(*m*), 948, 950–951
Soviet Union (former), migration from, 1044
Space Age, 994–995
Space exploration, 994–995
countries with programs, 967(*b*)
Soviet and U.S., 966–967(*b*), 966(*i*)
Space race, 966–967(*b*), 966(*i*)
Cold War and, 994
Spain. *See also* Latin America; Peru; Spanish Empire
Enlightenment and, 765–766
after Franco, 1006–1007
imperialism of, 861
Latin American rebellions against, 778–781
Napoleon and, 774
revolutions in Latin American empire of, 778–784
Spanish-American War and, 881–882
Spanish America. *See also* Latin America
Jesuits in, 766
Spanish American War (1898), 881–882, 881(*m*)
Spanish Empire, ethnic and racial exploitation in, 849
Spheres of influence, in China, 910
Spies and spying
satellites for, 995
in World War II, 949
Spinning jenny, 799
Spinning machines, 798
Sputnik, 966, 994
Sri Lanka (Ceylon), Tamil separatists in, 1045
SS (Schutzstaffel), 937
Stagflation, 1014
Stalin, Joseph
central economic planning and, 933
death of (1953), 978
industrialization and, 927
kulaks and, 933–934
modernization and, 978
purges by, 934
Soviet security and, 952
after World War II, 963
Stalingrad, Battle of, 950–951
Stalinism, 933–934
Stamp Act (1765), 768, 769(*m*)
Standard of living. *See also* Lifestyle
in global North and South, 1027
in Soviet Union, 1014–1015
after World War II, 977
Stanton, Elizabeth Cady, 852
Starvation. *See also* Famine
in Soviet Union, 934
World War I blockades and, 908
in World War II, 949
State (nation). *See* Nation-state; specific locations
State-building. *See also* Nation building; Nation-state
in Central and Eastern Europe (1920), 906(*m*)
in China, 910
in 1910, 894
Peace of Paris treaties and, 906
in Turkey, 908–909, 909(*i*)
State Department (U.S.), 952
States (U.S.), 769
Steam engine, 798
Stephenson, George (inventor), 798
Sterilization
forced, in India, 1041
voluntary, 996
Stock market, 805
crash of (1929), 927, 928–929
Storm troopers (Nazi Germany), 937
Stowe, Harriet Beecher, 817
Strategic Arms Limitation Treaty (SALT I), 1012
Strikes (labor)
in Argentina, 919
in China, 910
in colonies, 932
in France, 1010
in postwar period (World War I), 914
during World War I, 902
Submarines, in World War I, 897, 902
Sub-Saharan Africa
conflict in, 1027, 1027(*m*)
problems in, 1027
in World War I, 904
Subsistence agriculture, in Africa, 870
Sudan, 1027
Battle of Omdurman in, 868
famine in, 1041
Sudetenland, Hitler and, 940
Suez Canal, 864, 972–973
England and, 972
nationalization of, 973
Suez Canal (Rieger), 865(*i*)
Suffragists, 852
Sugar Act (England 1764), 768
Sugar and sugar industry, Cuban exports and, 975–976
Sukarno, Achmed (Indonesia), 970, 971
Bandung Conference and, 983
Sultans. *See* Mamluk Sultanate
Sun Tzu (Chinese military strategist), 887
Sun Yatsen (China), 895, 910
Superpowers
activist challenges to, 1009–1012
Cold War alliances and, 966–969
end of Cold War and, 989
after World War II, 928, 962–963
Supply-side economics, 1014
Supranational organizations, 1033–1036
NGOs as, 1034
Supreme Court (U.S.), *Brown v. Board of Education* (1954) and, 981–982
Sweden
cream separator in, 801
pension cuts in, 1033
response to Great Depression, 938–939
Swine flu, 1044
Synthetic goods, 976
Syria, 908
uprising in, 1047
in World War I, 904

Tagore, Dwarkanath (India), 810, 812
Tagore, Rabindranath, 879
Taiping Rebellion (China), 808–809
Taiping Tianguo, 807–809
Taiwan, 935(*m*), 997
Taliban, 1008, 1046(*m*)
"Talkies," 917(*b*)
Tamil people, 1052
as separatists, 1045
Tanabe Hajime (Japanese philosopher), 980
Tango, 920, 920(*i*)
Tanks
in World War I, 904
in World War II, 951
Tanzania, Germany and, 866
Tariffs
in Depression, 931
in EEC, 976
free trade and, 1027
in Latin America, 805
Taseko, Matsuo (Japanese activist), 825, 826, 828, 841, 842, 843–844
Tata family (India), 913
Jamsetji, 810, 813
Taxation
of American colonies, 768, 769
ATTAC and, 1034
of colonies, 929

imperialism and, 869
in India, 810, 872
for Seven Years' War, 768
in Spanish Bourbon Reforms, 765–766
Tea
in England, 765(*i*)
trade in, 807
Technology, 992. *See also* Industrialization
agrarian peoples in age of, 1017–1019
AIDS and, 1041–1042
in Crimean War, 833
environmental damage from, 1038
global, 988(*i*)
imperialism and, 868–869
industry and, 798, 799–802
information revolution and, 992–994
pollution from, 1018(*i*)
postwar, 893
service sector and, 1023
sexuality, procreation, and, 995–996
transformation of, 989–992
warfare and, 891, 952(*b*)
World War I weapons, 897
Tehran, Iran, hostage crisis in (1979), 1009
Television, 993
in 1960s, 976
state-sponsored, 993
Ten Days That Shook the World (film), 915
Tereshkova, Valentina (Soviet cosmonaut), 966(*i*)
Terror, the (France), 773
Terrorism
in El Salvador, 1006(*i*)
in England, 1046
global, 1025, 1038, 1045–1047
in India, 1028
in Ireland, 910
on September 11, 2001, 1045
"Test-tube babies," 996
Tete-Ansa, Winifred (African businessman), 930(*b*)
Textiles and textile industry. *See also* Cloth and clothing
African liberation and, 975(*b*), 975(*i*)
in India, 810
industrial, 793
mechanization of, 798
slaves and, 812
workers in, 813
T4 project, 938
Thailand, in ASEAN, 1036
Thatcher, Margaret (England), 1012, 1014, 1033
Theater. *See* Drama
Third Balkan War, 894, 896. *See also* World War I
Third World, biopiracy in, 1018
Three Gorges Dam (China), 1038
Three Guineas (Woolf), 939
Three Modern Women (film), 915
Tiananmen Square, Beijing, riots in (1989), 1015–1016, 1016(*i*)
Tibet, 869
Tigers. *See* Pacific tigers
Tilak, B. G. (Indian Hindu leader), 885
Tobacco, industrialization of, 802
Tokugawa Shogunate (Japan, 1603–1868), 841
Tokyo, Japan, 1031, 1036
attack on subway system, 1045
earthquake in, 935
firebombing of, 945, 951
postwar trials in, 980
U.S. aid to, 964(*i*)
Torres, Marcela de, 815
Torture, human rights and, 1049
Totalitarianism, 932, 933
Total war
World War I as, 900
World War II as, 945
"To the Senegalese Soldiers Who Died for France" (Senghor), 912(*b*)
Touré, Amadou Toumani (Mali), 1027
Tourism
Cook, Thomas, and, 1000–1001(*b*)
in Japan, 1000–1001(*b*), 1000(*i*)
Toussaint Louverture, Pierre-Dominique, 777–778, 779(*i*)
Towns. *See* Cities and towns
Townshend Acts (1767), 768
Toxic wastes, 1018(*i*)
Trade, 1027. *See also* Commerce
in Atlantic region, 767–768
domestic, in Great Depression, 931
global, 794–795, 796–798
Japanese, 802
laissez faire and, 764
opium, 807
tea, 807
world economy and, 997
worldwide, 806–807
Trademark branding, 1018–1019
Trade routes, by sea (c. 1775), 792(*m*)
Tradition
culture of, 843–845
protecting, 1052–1053, 1053(*i*)
Trail of Tears, Cherokee Indians and, 840
Transplants, 995
Transportation. *See also* Automobiles; Railroads
in cities, 913
Transregional structures. *See also* Global structures and organizations; United Nations
Mercosur as, 1036
NAFTA as, 1036
NATO as, 968
SEATO as, 968
Trans-Siberian railroad, 800(*b*), 800(*i*), 863, 868
Transvaal, 867, 881
Treaties
Chinese ports and, 807
ending World War I, 906–907
after Second Balkan War, 896
Trench warfare, in World War I, 897, 899
Trickle-down economy, 1014
Triple Alliance, 896
Triple Entente, 896
Trotsky, Leon, 904
True Story of Ah Q, The (Lu Xun), 896
Truman, Harry, 963–964
Truman Doctrine (1947), 963–964
Truth, Sojourner, 852
Truth and Reconciliation Commission (South Africa), 1029, 1030(*b*)
Tsushima Strait, Battle of (1905), 882
Tuberculosis, 814
Tunisia
France and, 865, 974
protests in (2010), 1047(*i*)
uprising in, 1046
Tupac Amaru II (Inca), 767
Turgenev, Ivan, 834
Turkestan, Russia and, 863
Turkey. *See also* Anatolia; Ottoman Empire
as EU membership candidate, 1035
under Kemal, Mustafa, 908–909, 909(*m*)
Young Turks and, 884–885
Turks. *See* Ottoman Empire; Turkey
Tuscany, 837
Twin Sisters (film), 916(*i*)

U-boats. *See* Submarines
Uganda, 1027
AIDS in, 1041(*i*)
dictatorship in, 1007(*i*)
Ukraine, Chernobyl power plant in, 1038
Ulamas (Muslim authorities), in Egypt, 775
Ulfah, Maria, 1048
Ultra (code-detecting group), 942
Uncle Tom's Cabin (Stowe), 817
Underconsumption, of manufactured goods, 804
Undocumented workers, 1044
Unemployment
from Arab oil embargo, 1013
during Great Depression, 929
Unification
of Germany, 837–838, 838(*m*)
of Italy, 836–837, 837(*m*)
Union Carbide, gas leak from, 1038
Union of Soviet Socialist Republics (USSR). *See* Soviet Union
United Nations (UN), 1031
Declaration of Human Rights, 1049
founding of, 952
Israeli independence and, 972
Korean War and, 967
Nehru and, 984
United States. *See also* Cold War
African Americans in, 850
civil rights movement in, 954
as economic leader, 913
economy in, 963
expansion and consolidation of, 838–841
foreign policy in, 1002
Germany after World War II and, 964–965, 965(*m*)
government of, 769–771
in Grand Alliance, 945
Great Awakening in, 785
Great Depression and, 931, 938
immigration to, 769
imperialism by, 881–882
Indian outsourcing for, 1032
industrialization in, 799, 802
international capital flows and, 1033
League of Nations and, 907
life expectancy in, 1040
Mexican-American War and, 831–832
migrants in, 1044

United States (*continued*)
music in, 848
in NAFTA, 1036
nationalism and, 783
neutrality policy of, 897
outsourcing of jobs and, 1032
overthrow of Hawaiian queen by, 882(*b*)
at Paris Peace Conference, 905
Pearl Harbor bombing and, 927, 944
relocation of Japanese Americans by, 948–949
South Korea and, 1007
space exploration by, 966–967(*b*)
Spanish-American War and, 881–882
stock market crash in (1929), 927, 928–929
Suez Canal and, 973
as superpower, 962
television in, 993
Versailles Treaty and, 907
Vietnam War and, 1008(*m*)
in World War I, 896, 902
after World War II, 962–970
in World War II, 944, 945
Universe. *See also* Astronomy
big bang theory of, 995
Universities and colleges. *See* Higher education
Unrestricted submarine warfare, 897
Untouchables, in India, 813
Upper classes. *See also* Elites; Nobility
in France, 939
during Great Depression, 930–931
Urban areas. *See also* Cities and towns
family life in, 1002
Urbanization, 893
culture and, 878–879
after World War I, 913
Uruguay
in Mercosur, 1036
revolt in, 780–781
USSR (Union of Soviet Socialist Republics). *See* Soviet Union
Utopian socialism, 816

Vaccines, 977, 1041
Van Gogh, Vincent, 885, 886(*i*)
Vaqueros (cowboys), 782(*b*)
"Velvet" revolution (Czechoslovakia), 1016
Venereal disease, 814
Venetia, 837
Venezuela
agricultural modifications in, 1018
independence fight in, 781
Verdun, battle at, 899
Versailles, Treaty of, 906–907
Hitler and, 940
Versailles palace, women's march to (1789), 772, 772(*i*)
Victoria (England), 860
Video recorders, 993
Vietcong, 1008
Viet Minh, 971, 972
Vietnam
AIDS in, 1041–1042
in ASEAN, 1036
division of, 972
forced labor in, 949(*i*)
France and, 864, 872(*b*), 872(*i*)
Ho Chi Minh in, 971(*m*)
pilgrims in, 1052
Vietnam War (1968–1975), 1008, 1008(*m*)
protests against, 1009–1010
Villa, Pancho (Mexico), 905
Vindication of the Rights of Man, A (Wollstonecraft), 773
Vindication of the Rights of Women, A (Wollstonecraft), 773
Violence. *See also* Conflict; Wars and warfare
civil rights, 1009
in colonies, 885
in East Africa, 973
in Middle East, 1045
political, 933
in South Africa, 1029
Viruses, 1044
Voice of America, 982–983
Voltaire (French writer), 763
Vostok I (spacecraft), 966(*b*)
Voting and voting rights
in Argentina, 919
in Japan, 935
in United States, 770–771
for women, 852, 1011

Wages
for women, 914
workers and, 1033
Wahhabism, 785(*i*), 786
Walentynowicz, Anna (Polish activist), 1015
Walesa, Lech (Polish activist), 1015, 1016
War against terrorism, 1045
War crimes. *See also* Human rights
in World War II, 980
War guilt, Germany and, 907
Wars and warfare. *See also* specific battles and wars
in Atlantic Ocean region, 760(*m*)
in Crimean War, 833
against France, 773
guerilla warfare, 971
industrial technology applied to, 891
Napoleonic, 774–775, 779
from 1910–1929, 892(*m*)
political beliefs in, 947(*b*)
submarine, 897
technological, 952(*b*)
trench, 897
by United States, 838
Warsaw Ghetto (1943), 948(*i*)
Warsaw Pact, 967
Washington, George, 768, 769
on Constitution (U.S.), 771
Water, for drinking, 1041
Water frame, 798, 799
Waterloo, battle at (1815), 774
Water power, in textile industry, 798
Watson, James, 995
Watt, James, 798
Wealth. *See also* Gold; Silver
in Mexico, 894
in new imperialism, 860
in suburbs, 913
tax cuts and, 1014
in World War I, 902
Weapons. *See also* Missiles
atomic, 951, 952(*b*)
Cold War production of, 976
in Crimean War, 833
imperialism and, 868
in India, 863
interchangeability of parts and, 798
nuclear, 963
in World War I, 897, 904
in World War II, 942
Weapons of mass destruction, 1045
Weather. *See also* Climate
global warming and, 1038
greenhouse effect and, 1038
Weaving, 793. *See also* Textiles and textile industry
improvements in, 798
industrialization and, 798
Wedgwood, Josiah, 796, 796(*i*)
Weimar Republic (Germany), labor unions and, 914
Welfare benefits, in United States, 1014
Welfare state, 977
in Sweden, 938–939
Wells, Ida B., 851
Wesley, John, 785
West, in United States, 839–841, 839(*m*)
West Africa
nations in, 973
power in, 810
slave trade and, 812
West Asia, Russia and, 863
Western Africa. *See* West Africa; specific locations
Western Europe, Industrial Revolution in, 794
Western front, in World War I, 897
Western Hemisphere
Haitian revolution in (1791–1804), 777–778
U.S. influence in, 881
Westernization, 845–846
of China, 808–809, 910
in French Indochina, 864
of Turkey, 908–909
Western powers
competition between, 891
after World War I, 925
Western world
economic change in, 998–999
economics in, 1014
global commerce and, 825
imperialism in Asia by, 862(*m*)
Japan and, 842
literature from, 880
medicine in, 1041
non-Western industrialization and, 806–812
non-Western religion, art, literature, and, 885–887
West Germany, 965, 965(*m*)
Berlin Wall and, 1016
Green Party in, 1038
Westward expansion, of United States, 839–841, 839(*m*)

Wheat, production of, 929
Wheatley, Phillis, 786(*b*)
White-collar service sector, 805
White-collar workers, 815, 914
Whitefield, George, 785
"White man's burden" (Kipling), 881
Whites
  African slaves compared with, 766–767
  Darwinism and, 861
  Native Americans and, 840–841
  in South Africa, 1023, 1029
Whites, in Russian civil war, 904
White supremacy, decolonization and, 969
Whitman, Walt, 848
William II (Germany), 900
  World War I and, 899
Wilson, Woodrow
  Fourteen Points of, 905
  League of Nations and, 907
Wind power, 1040
Wire fencing, 801
Witch-hunt, by McCarthy, 983
Wollstonecraft, Mary, 773
Women. *See also* Feminists; Gender and gender issues; Men
  as African farm labor, 818–820, 819(*i*)
  in American Revolution, 769
  Beauvoir on, 981
  in Brazil, 781(*i*)
  in Chile, 1005–1006
  in China, 965
  as citizens, 829
  "comfort women," 942(*b*)
  cult of domesticity and, 812
  in England, 773
  environment and, 1039
  family life and, 1002
  feminist activism by, 1009–1010
  films for, 915
  in France, 773, 774
  as global activists, 1034
  during Great Depression, 931, 932
  imperialism and, 870
  in Italy, 918–919
  labor unions and, 914
  Latin America dictatorships and, 1005
  march to Versailles by (1789), 772, 772(*i*)
  modernization and, 847
  in Nazi Germany, 937, 938
  "new look" after World War II, 982(*i*)
  new woman and, 902, 914, 915(*i*)
  rights and status of, 850–852
  in Russia, 836
  sexual division of labor and, 815
  in South Africa, 1029
  in Soviet Union, 963
  trafficking in, 1044
  in Turkey, 909, 909(*i*)
  in United States, 770(*i*)
  voting rights for, 1011
  wages for, 914
  in working class, 813
  during World War I, 900–902
  in World War II, 946(*b*), 948, 949(*i*)
Women's International League for Peace and Freedom, 954
Women's Social and Political Union, 852
Woodblock printing, Japanese, 790(*i*), 817
Woolf, Virginia, 939
Wordsworth, William, 773
Work. *See also* Labor; Livelihood(s); Workers
  computers and, 993–994
  global changes in, 998–999
  outwork as, 801
  sexual division of labor and, 815
Workday, 813, 814–815
Workers. *See also* Labor
  in Brazil, 831(*i*)
  in China, 807
  competition for jobs among, 1033
  efficiency and, 913
  industrial, 793
  Industrial Revolution and, 809
  Marx on, 816–817
  in Mexico, 890(*i*)
  Ottoman, 809
  in Soviet German zone, 965
  in Soviet Union, 918, 933
  on trans-Siberian railroad, 800(*b*), 800(*i*)
  undocumented, 1044
Workers Going Home at the Lebrter Railroad Station, 1897 (Kollwitz), 818(*i*)
Workers Party (Brazil), 1029
Workforce, women and, 900
Working class
  in Argentina, 920
  industrial, 813–815
Workplace, global, 998
World Bank, 1027
World Tourism Organization (UN), 1001(*b*)
World Trade Center, September 11, 2001, terrorist attack on, 1045
World Trade Organization, 1031
World War I (1914–1918)
  casualties in, 898, 899, 899(*i*), 904
  eastern front in, 897
  end of, 904–905
  in Europe and Middle East (1914–1918), 898(*m*)
  events leading to, 893
  as global war, 893, 896
  home front during, 900–902
  imperialism and, 897
  outbreak of, 896
  Paris Peace Conference after, 905–908
  Russian withdrawal from, 903
  soldiers in, 898, 899–900, 899(*i*)
  strategies, 897, 899
  as total war, 900
  United States in, 896, 902
  war at sea, 897–898, 902
  weapons in, 897
  western front in, 897, 899
  women during, 900–902
World War II (1937–1945), 926(*m*)
  atomic bombings in, 951, 952(*b*), 952(*i*)
  Axis and Allies advantages/disadvantages in, 947–948
  Axis defeat in, 950–951
  casualties in, 925–927, 945, 951
  civilians in, 945–950
  collaboration in, 949
  "comfort women" in, 942(*b*)
  economic growth after, 975–978
  in Europe, 941–944, 943(*m*)
  events leading to, 939–940
  Germany divided after, 964
  Holocaust in, 925, 945–947, 945(*m*)
  India and, 970
  Japanese invasion of China, 940–941
  Jewish homeland after, 972
  from 1937–1943, 940–945
  in North Africa, 943(*m*), 951
  in Pacific, 944–945, 944(*m*), 951
  Pearl Harbor bombing and, 927
  programs exalting losers of, 980
  resistance in, 949–950
  soldiers in, 946–947(*b*)
  in Soviet Union, 942–943, 943(*m*)
  weapons in, 942
  women in, 948
Wretched of the Earth, The (Fanon), 981
Wright, Richard, 984
Wright, Tom (architect), 1022(*i*)
Wu Guanzhong (China), 960(*m*), 979–980, 1054

Xhosa people, 867
Xplastaz rap group (Tanzania), 1053

Yalta Conference (1945), 964
Yeats, William Butler, 885–886
"Yellow peril," China and, 884
Yeltsin, Boris, 1017
Yokohama, earthquake in, 935
Yom Kippur War (1973), 1013
Yorktown, Battle of, 769
Young people. *See also* Youth culture
  in Nazi Germany, 924(*i*), 937
  protests by, 1009–1010
Young Turks, 884–885, 884(*i*)
Youth culture, 1002(*i*), 1003
Yrigoyen, Hipólito (president of Argentina), 919
Yuan Shikai (Chinese leader), 895
Yugoslavia
  breakup of, 1016
  former, 1049
  after World War I, 906, 906(*m*)
Yukichi, Fukuzawa (Japanese author and educator), 848

Zadig (Voltaire), 763
Zaire. *See* Congo
Zapata, Emiliano, 890(*i*), 891, 893, 894, 895
Zapatistas, 1052
Zemstvos (regional councils), 836
Zeng Guofan (Chinese official), 808
Zhou Enlai (Chinese leader), 983
Zhu Su'e (New Woman, China), 914
Zimbabwe, 1030
Zionism, 851
Zones, in Berlin and Germany, 964–965, 965(*m*)
Zulu Inkatha Freedom Party, 1029
Zulu people, Anglo war with, 867(*i*)

160°W
140°W
120°W
100°W
80°W
60°W
40°W
20°W
Arctic Circle
NORTH AMERICA
ROCKY MTS.
APPALACHIAN MTS.
Mississippi R.
ATLANTIC OCEAN
Gulf of Mexico
Tropic of Cancer
Caribbean Sea
PACIFIC OCEAN
Equator
Amazon R.
SOUTH AMERICA
ANDES MTS.
Tropic of Capricorn
ATLANTIC OCEAN
0 1000 2000 3000 miles
0 1000 2000 3000 kilometers
N
W
E
S
Antarctic Circle

20°E
40°E
60°E
80°E
100°E
120°E
140°E
160°E
80°N
Arctic Circle
60°N
40°N
Tropic of Cancer
20°N
Equator
0°
20°S
Tropic of Capricorn
40°S
60°S
Antarctic Circle
80°S
URAL MTS.
Volga R.
Ob R.
EURASIA
PS
GOBI
Yellow R.
ASIA
Mediterranean Sea
SYRIAN DESERT
HIMALAYA MTS.
Ganges R.
Yangzi R.
Nile R.
FRICA
Arabian Sea
Bay of Bengal
South China Sea
PACIFIC OCEAN
Congo R.
INDIAN OCEAN
Zambezi R.
KALAHARI DESERT
AUSTRALIA
Vegetation zones
Tundra
Northern forest
Temperate forest
Temperate grassland
Desert and dry shrub
Temperate shrub
Mountain grassland
Tropical grassland and savanna
Tropical forest
Permanent ice cover

THE CONTEMPORARY WORLD
CANADA
UNITED STATES
Alaska (U.S.)
Greenland (Den.)
ICELAND
MEXICO
Hawaii (U.S.)
BAHAMAS
Bermuda (U.K.)
CUBA
HAITI
DOMINICAN REPUBLIC
Puerto Rico (U.S.)
JAMAICA
BELIZE
HONDURAS
GUATEMALA
NICARAGUA
EL SALVADOR
COSTA RICA
PANAMA
Guadeloupe (Fr.)
Martinique (Fr.)
ST. KITTS AND NEVIS
ANTIGUA AND BARBUDA
DOMINICA
ST. VINCENT AND THE GRENADINES
ST. LUCIA
BARBADOS
GRENADA
TRINIDAD AND TOBAGO
GUYANA
SURINAME
French Guiana (Fr.)
VENEZUELA
COLOMBIA
ECUADOR
Galápagos Is. (Ec.)
PERU
BRAZIL
BOLIVIA
PARAGUAY
CHILE
URUGUAY
ARGENTINA
Falkland Is. (U.K.)
Easter I. (Chile)
SAMOA
TONGA
PACIFIC OCEAN
ATLANTIC OCEAN
ATLANTIC OCEAN
Azores (Port.)
Madeira Is. (Port.)
Canary Is. (Sp.)
Western Sahara (Mor.)
CAPE VERDE
SENEGAL
GAMBIA
GUINEA-BISSAU
GUINEA
SIERRA LEONE
LIBERIA
IVORY CO.
BURKINA F.
GH.
MAURITAN
MORO
PORTU
SPAIN
FRAN
IRE
UNI KINGL
Equator
80°N
60°N
40°N
20°N
0°
20°S
40°S
60°S
80°S
160°W
140°W
120°W
100°W
80°W
60°W
40°W
20°W
0 1000 2000 3000 miles
0 1000 2000 3000 kilometers
N
W
E
S

ABBREVIATIONS

ALB.	ALBANIA
AUS.	AUSTRIA
BEL.	BELGIUM
B.H.	BOSNIA AND HERZEGOVINA
CR.	CROATIA
CZ.	CZECH REPUBLIC
DEN.	DENMARK
HUNG.	HUNGARY
KO.	KOSOVO
LUX.	LUXEMBOURG
MAC.	MACEDONIA
MO.	MONTENEGRO
NETH.	NETHERLANDS
SE.	SERBIA
SLK.	SLOVAKIA
SLN.	SLOVENIA
SWITZ.	SWITZERLAND

About the authors

Bonnie G. Smith (Ph.D., University of Rochester) is Board of Governors Professor of History at Rutgers University. She has written numerous works in European and global history, including *Ladies of the Leisure Class*; *Changing Lives: Women in European History since 1700*; and *Imperialism*. She is editor of *Global Feminisms since 1945* and *Women's History in Global Perspective*; coeditor of the New Oxford World History series; and general editor of *The Oxford Encyclopedia of Women in World History*. Currently she is studying the globalization of European culture and society since the seventeenth century. **Bonnie treats the period 1750 to the present (Part 4) in *Crossroads and Cultures*.**

Marc Van De Mieroop (Ph.D., Yale University) is Professor of History at Columbia University. His research focuses on the ancient history of the Near East from a long-term perspective and extends across traditionally established disciplinary boundaries. Among his many works are *The Ancient Mesopotamian City*; *Cuneiform Texts and the Writing of History*; *A History of the Ancient Near East*; *The Eastern Mediterranean in the Age of Ramesses II*; and *A History of Ancient Egypt*. **Marc covers the period from human origins to 500 C.E. (Part 1) in *Crossroads and Cultures*.**

Richard von Glahn (Ph.D., Yale University) is Professor of History at the University of California, Los Angeles. A specialist in Chinese economic history, Richard is the author of *The Country of Streams and Grottoes: Expansion, Settlement, and the Civilizing of the Sichuan Frontier in Song Times*; *Fountain of Fortune: Money and Monetary Policy in China, 1000–1700*; and *The Sinister Way: The Divine and the Demonic in Chinese Religious Culture*. He is also coeditor of *The Song-Yuan-Ming Transition in Chinese History* and *Global Connections and Monetary History, 1470–1800*. His current research focuses on monetary history on a global scale, from ancient times to the recent past. **Richard treats the period 500 to 1450 (Part 2) in *Crossroads and Cultures*.**

Kris Lane (Ph.D., University of Minnesota) is the France V. Scholes Chair in Colonial Latin American History at Tulane University. Kris specializes in colonial Latin American history and the Atlantic world, and his great hope is to globalize the teaching and study of the early Americas. His publications include *Pillaging the Empire: Piracy in the Americas, 1500–1750*; *Quito 1599: City and Colony in Transition*; and *Colour of Paradise: The Emerald in the Age of Gunpowder Empires*. He also edited Bernardo de Vargas Machuca's *The Indian Militia and Description of the Indies* and *Defense and Discourse of the Western Conquest*. **Kris treats the period 1450 to 1750 (Part 3) in *Crossroads and Cultures*.**

About the cover image

Beijing, China

China's emergence as the world's fastest growing major economy has transformed the landscape of the ancient capital of Beijing. The Sihui Bridge overpass connects two expressways at the edge of the Central Business District, designated by the Chinese government in 2008 as Beijing's new center for international business and finance. Modernizing roads and railways to meet escalating transportation needs is one of the major challenges facing China's leaders today.